A Companion to
the American Short Story

Blackwell Companions to Literature and Culture

This series offers comprehensive, newly written surveys of key periods and movements and certain major authors, in English literary culture and history. Extensive volumes provide new perspectives and positions on contexts and on canonical and post-canonical texts, orientating the beginning student in new fields of study and providing the experienced undergraduate and new graduate with current and new directions, as pioneered and developed by leading scholars in the field.

Published Recently

A COMPANION TO

THE AMERICAN SHORT STORY

EDITED BY

ALFRED BENDIXEN AND JAMES NAGEL

WILEY-BLACKWELL
A John Wiley & Sons, Ltd., Publication

This edition first published 2010

© 2010 Blackwell Publishing Ltd except for editorial material and organization

© 2010 Alfred Bendixen and James Nagel

Blackwell Publishing was acquired by John Wiley & Sons in February 2007. Blackwell's publishing program has been merged with Wiley's global Scientific, Technical, and Medical business to form Wiley-Blackwell.

Registered Office

John Wiley & Sons Ltd, The Atrium, Southern Gate, Chichester, West Sussex, PO19 8SQ, United Kingdom

Editorial Offices

350 Main Street, Malden, MA 02148-5020, USA

9600 Garsington Road, Oxford, OX4 2DQ, UK

The Atrium, Southern Gate, Chichester, West Sussex, PO19 8SQ, UK

For details of our global editorial offices, for customer services, and for information about how to apply for permission to reuse the copyright material in this book please see our website at www.wiley.com/wiley-blackwell.

The right of Alfred Bendixen and James Nagel to be identified as the authors of the editorial material in this work has been asserted in accordance with the UK Copyright, Designs and Patents Act 1988.

Wiley also publishes its books in a variety of electronic formats. Some content that appears in print may not be available in electronic books.

Designations used by companies to distinguish their products are often claimed as trademarks. All brand names and product names used in this book are trade names, service marks, trademarks or registered trademarks of their respective owners. The publisher is not associated with any product or vendor mentioned in this book. This publication is designed to provide accurate and authoritative information in regard to the subject matter covered. It is sold on the understanding that the publisher is not engaged in rendering professional services. If professional advice or other expert assistance is required, the services of a competent professional should be sought.

Library of Congress Cataloging-in-Publication Data

A companion to the American short story / edited by Alfred Bendixen and James Nagel.

    p. cm. – (Blackwell companions to literature and culture)

Includes bibliographical references and index.

ISBN 978-1-4051-1543-8 (alk. paper)

1. Short stories, American–History and criticism.   I. Bendixen, Alfred.   II. Nagel, James.

PS374.S5C58 2010

813'.0103–dc22

2009035861

A catalogue record for this book is available from the British Library.

Set in 11 on 13 pt Garamond 3 by Toppan Best-set Premedia Limited

Printed and bound in Singapore by Fabulous Printers Pte Ltd

1   2010

Contents

Notes on Contributors

Ruth M. Alvarez is the Curator of Literary Manuscripts at the University of Maryland Libraries. She has responsibility for the Papers of Katherine Anne Porter as well as nearly twenty related collections of primary materials that support the study of Katherine Anne Porter. With Thomas F. Walsh, she edited *Uncollected Early Prose of Katherine Anne Porter* and, with Kathryn Hilt, *Katherine Anne Porter: An Annotated Bibliography*. For Mexico's Consejo Nacional para la Cultura y las Artes, she edited *Un país familiar: Escritos sobre México* ["My Familiar Country": Katherine Anne Porter's Writings on Mexico].

Alfred Bendixen is Professor of English at Texas A&M University. He is the founder of the American Literature Association, which he currently serves as Executive Director. His books include *Haunted Women* (1985), an edition of the composite novel *The Whole Family* (1986), *"The Amber Gods" and Other Stories* by Harriet Prescott Spofford, (1989), and *Edith Wharton: New Critical Essays* (1992). He is the associate editor of the *Continuum Encyclopedia of American Literature* (1999), the co-editor of the recently published *Cambridge Companion to American Travel Writing* (2009), and the editor of the forthcoming *Blackwell Companion to the American Novel*.

Jeff Birkenstein has strong interests in the short story and the story sequence as well as in food and cultural criticism. His co-edited collection of essays entitled *Reframing 9/11: Film, Popular Culture and the "War on Terror"* (with Anna Froula of East Carolina University and Karen Randell of Southampton Solent University) is due out in the Spring of 2010. He is working currently on *Cultural Representation in the International Short Story Sequence*, co-edited with Robert M. Luscher. He is an Associate Professor of English at Saint Martin's University.

Donna Campbell is Associate Professor of English at Washington State University. She is the author of *Resisting Regionalism: Gender and Naturalism in American Fiction, 1885–1915* (1997), and her work has appeared in *Legacy, Studies in American Fiction, American Literary Realism*, and *Studies in American Naturalism*, among other journals.

Recent publications include essays on Kate Chopin's *At Fault* in *The Cambridge Companion to Kate Chopin* and on Naturalism in the forthcoming *Cambridge History of the American Novel*. Her work on Edith Wharton includes a critical introduction to Edith Wharton's *The Fruit of the Tree* (2000) and essays in the *Edith Wharton Review*, *Jack London: One Hundred Years a Writer*, and *Twisted from the Ordinary: Essays on American Literary Naturalism*. Her current project is a book on American women writers of Naturalism.

Gloria L. Cronin is College of Humanities Professor and Professor of English at Brigham Young University. She is the editor of the *The Saul Bellow Journal*, an executive coordinator of the American Literature Association, recipient of the Pozner Bibliography Prize awarded by the Jewish Library Association, director of the Jewish American and Holocaust Literature Annual Symposium, and board member of the African American Literature and Culture Association. She has published extensively in Saul Bellow studies and in the fields of Jewish American and African American literatures. She recently edited, with Alan L. Berger, the *Jewish American Literature Encyclopedia*.

Kirk Curnutt is Professor and Chair of English at Troy University Montgomery. He is the author of two novels, *Breathing Out the Ghost* and *Dixie Noir*, as well as several other books, including *The Cambridge Introduction to F. Scott Fitzgerald* and *Coffee with Hemingway*.

Martha J. Cutter is an Associate Professor of English and African American Studies at the University of Connecticut and the editor of *MELUS: Multi-Ethnic Literature of the United States*. Her first book, *Unruly Tongue: Identity and Voice in American Women's Writing 1850–1930*, won the 2001 Nancy Dasher Award from the College English Association. Her second book, *Lost and Found in Translation: Contemporary Ethnic American Writing and the Politics of Language Diversity*, was published in 2005. Her articles have appeared in *American Literature*, *African American Literature*, *Callaloo*, *Women's Studies*, *Arizona Quarterly*, *MELUS*, *Legacy*, *Criticism*, and in the collections *Mixed Race Literature* and *Passing and the Fictions of Identity*.

Josephine Donovan has written or edited eleven books in literary criticism, feminist theory, and animal ethics, including *New England Local Color Literature*; *Sarah Orne Jewett*; *After the Fall: The Demeter-Persephone Myth in Wharton, Cather, and Glasgow*; *Feminist Theory: The Intellectual Traditions*; *"Uncle Tom's Cabin": Evil, Affliction and Redemptive Love*; and *Gnosticism in Modern Literature*. Most recently, she co-edited (with Carol J. Adams) *The Feminist Care Tradition in Animal Ethics*. She is Professor Emerita of English at the University of Maine.

Charles Duncan is Professor of English, Head of the English Department, and Moderator of the Faculty at Peace College, where he teaches American and African American Literature. He has published two books, *The Absent Man: The Narrative Craft of Charles W. Chesnutt* and *The Northern Stories of Charles W. Chesnutt*, as well as several articles on Chesnutt, the first African American fiction writer to earn a national reputation. In addition, he has written essays on figures including James Baldwin, Frank Norris, Mary Wilkins Freeman, Kate Chopin, Herman Melville, Nathaniel Hawthorne, and Timothy Flint.

Benjamin F. Fisher, Professor of English, University of Mississippi, has many publications focusing upon or related to Poe and his writings. He is a past president of the Poe Studies Association. Fisher is a member of editorial boards for the *Edgar Allan Poe Review, Poe Studies/Dark Romanticism*, Gothic Studies, Victorian Poetry, and several other journals. He has recently published *The Cambridge Introduction to Edgar Allan Poe* (2008), has forthcoming from University of Iowa Press, *Edgar Allan Poe in His Own Times*, and another book about Poe (The Contemporary Reviews) with Cambridge University Press. In 1988 Fisher was awarded a Governor's Citation, State of Maryland, for his outstanding contributions to Poe studies.

Andrew J. Furer has taught at the University of Connecticut, Harvard University, Emerson College, and Fordham University. He is the author of essays on such writers as Jack London, Stephen Crane, and James Weldon Johnson, including the first major article-length overview of London's racial views, as well as a similar essay on London's ideal of "the new womanhood." Furer is the editor of a forthcoming volume, *The Genders of Naturalism*, and is currently working on a book-length study of London's radicalism. His other research interests include Zitkala-Sa, Paul Robeson, Richard Wright, Bernarr Macfadden, and Jazz and Literature.

Andrew Furman is Professor and Director of Graduate Studies in the Department of English at Florida Atlantic University. His essays and articles on American literature and other topics have appeared in a variety of publications, including *Contemporary Literature, MELUS, Poets & Writers, The Chronicle of Higher Education, JBooks*, and *Zeek*. He is also a regular fiction reviewer for the *Miami Herald*. His most recent book is the novel *Alligators May Be Present* with Syracuse Press. His non-fiction book on the effort to desegregate the Los Angeles Unified School District will be published in 2010.

Leah B. Glasser teaches American literature and Creative Writing at Mount Holyoke College in South Hadley, Massachusetts, where she is also the Dean of First-Year Studies. Her publications include essays in numerous literary journals and, more recently, in the *Chronicle of Higher Education*. Her focus is on nineteenth- and early twentieth-century American women writers. Glasser is the author of the literary biography *In a Closet Hidden: The Life and Work of Mary E. Wilkins Freeman*. She is currently working on a new book tentatively titled *A Landscape of One's Own: Nature-Writing and Women's Autobiography*.

Sandra Lee Kleppe is Associate Professor of English/American Studies at Hedmark University College, Norway. She is the director of the International Raymond Carver Society and the co-editor of *New Paths to Raymond Carver: Critical Essays on His Life, Fiction, and Poetry*. Her articles on Carver have appeared in *Classical and Modern Literature, Journal of Medical Humanities*, and *Journal of the Short Story in English*.

Robert M. Luscher, Professor of English at the University of Nebraska at Kearney, is the author of *John Updike: A Study of the Short Fiction*, as well as critical essays on the short fiction of Updike, Robert Olen Butler, Clark Blaise, Ernest Gaines, Mary Wilkins Freeman, and J. D. Salinger. His essay "The Short Story Sequence: An Open Book," appeared in *Short Story Theory at a Crossroads*, and he has published pieces in a number of reference works on the short story sequence and the short fiction of William Faulkner, Fred Chappell, Susan Minot, and John Updike. He is currently co-editing a collection of essays with Jeff Birkenstein, *Cultural Representation in the International Short Story Sequence*, to which he is contributing an essay on Butler.

George Monteiro, who has spent his teaching career at Brown University, is the author or editor of books such as *Robert Frost and the New England Renaissance*, *The Correspondence of Henry James and Henry Adams*, *Stephen Crane's Blue Badge of Courage*, *The Presence of Pessoa*, *Conversations with Elizabeth Bishop*, and, most recently, *Stephen Crane: The Contemporary Reviews*. His work on Ernest Hemingway includes essays on the short stories in *Prairie Schooner*, *Journal of Modern Literature*, *Criticism*, *Georgia Review*, *Journal of American Studies*, and *Journal of Medical Humanities and Bioethics*. "The Jungle Out There: Nick Adams Takes to the Road" will appear in the Fall 2009 issue of the *Hemingway Review*.

James Nagel is the Eidson Distinguished Professor of American Literature at the University of Georgia. Early in his career he founded the scholarly journal *Studies in American Fiction* and the widely influential series *Critical Essays on American Literature*, which published 156 volumes of scholarship. Among his twenty-two books are *Stephen Crane and Literary Impressionism*, *Hemingway in Love and War* (which was made into a Hollywood film directed by Lord Richard Attenborough), *The Contemporary American Short-Story Cycle*, and *Anthology of the American Short Story*. He has been a Fulbright Professor as well as a Rockefeller Fellow. He has published some eighty articles in the field and lectured on American literature in fifteen countries.

Catherine Ross Nickerson is Associate Professor of American Studies at Emory University. She is the author of *The Web of Iniquity: Early Detective Fiction by American Women* and the editor of *The Dead Letter and the Figure Eight* by Metta Victor and *That Affair Next Door and Lost Man's Lane* by Anna Katharine Green. She is editor of the forthcoming *Cambridge Companion to American Crime Fiction*.

Jeanne Campbell Reesman is Professor of English at the University of Texas at San Antonio, where she has also served as Graduate Dean and Director of English, Classics, Philosophy and Communication. She has taught at the University of Pennsylvania, Baylor University, and at the University of Hawaii. She has published over 40 monographs, collections, textbooks, and editions. Reesman has received awards from the US Fulbright Commission, the National Endowment for the Humanities, the Huntington Library, the American Philosophical Society, and the National Science Foundation. Her critical biography, *Jack London's Racial Lives*, was published in 2009, the first full study of the role of race in his life and writings. Additional Jack London titles include *Jack London: One Hundred Years a Writer* (with Sara S. Hodson), *No Mentor but Myself: Jack London on Writing and Writers* (with Dale Walker), *Jack London: A Study of the Short Fiction*, *Rereading Jack London*, and *Jack London, Revised Edition* (with Earle Labor).

Charlotte Rich is an Associate Professor of English at Eastern Kentucky University. Her book *Transcending the New Woman: Multiethnic Narratives in the Progressive Era* was published in 2009. She has published an edition of Charlotte Perkins Gilman's novel *What Diantha Did* and essays in *The Edith Wharton Review*, *Legacy*, *MELUS*, and *The Southern Quarterly*. She also contributed an essay to *Charlotte Perkins Gilman among Her Contemporaries*. She has served as newsletter editor for the Charlotte Perkins Gilman Society and has coordinated national conference panels for the Wharton Society and the Gilman Society.

Hugh Ruppersburg is Senior Associate Dean of Arts and Sciences and Professor of English at the University of Georgia. He has written books on Faulkner and Robert Penn Warren and edited four anthologies of Georgia writing as well as a collection of essays about Don DeLillo. He recently received the Governor's Award in the Humanities in Georgia. He is writing a book on films about the American South.

Steven T. Ryan has taught American literature at Austin Peay State University since 1977. He has co-edited special issues for the *Southern Quarterly* on Evelyn Scott, Caroline Gordon, and Robert Penn Warren. In addition to publishing extensively on these authors, he has published articles on Herman Melville, William Faulkner, Flannery O'Connor, Ernest Hemingway, Allen Tate, and Kate Chopin. He has also written a performed dramatic adaptation of Gordon's *The Strange Children*.

David E. E. Sloane is Professor of English and Education at the University of New Haven and is past president of the American Humor Studies Association and the Mark Twain Circle. He was named Carnegie-Mellon College Teacher of the Year for Connecticut in 2001. His books include *Mark Twain as a Literary Comedian*, *The Literary Humor of the Urban Northeast, 1830–1890*, *American Humor Magazines and Comic Periodicals*, *Adventures of Huckleberry Finn: American Comic Vision*, and *A Student Companion to Mark Twain*, among others. In recognition of ten years of outstanding contributions to humor studies from 1976 to 1986, he was named the first Henry Nash Smith Fellow of the Center for Mark Twain Studies at Elmira College.

Paul Sorrentino is Professor of English at Virginia Tech, and the founder of the Stephen Crane Society and editor of its journal, *Stephen Crane Studies*. His most recent book is an edition of *The Red Badge of Courage*.

Mikko Tuhkanen is Assistant Professor of English and Africana Studies at Texas A&M University. His teaching and research interests include African American literature and culture, especially in their diasporic contexts, LGBT studies, queer theory, critical theory, and critical race theory. He has published essays in these fields in *American Literature*, *diacritics*, *Modern Fiction Studies*, *GLQ*, *Cultural Critique*, and elsewhere. He is also the author of *The American Optic: Psychoanalysis, Critical Race Theory, and Richard Wright* and the editor of "Sameness," a special queer theory issue of *Umbr(a): A Journal of the Unconscious*.

Karen Weekes is an Associate Professor of English and Division Head of Arts and Humanities at Pennsylvania State University. She has published criticism on American writers Lorrie Moore, Audre Lorde, Don DeLillo, and Edgar Allan Poe, among others. She is the editor of *Privilege and Prejudice* (Cambridge Scholars Press, 2009) and *Women Know Everything!* (Quirk, 2007). Her current project is a book manuscript on women's automythographical life-writing.

Jeffrey Andrew Weinstock is Professor of American Literature and Culture at Central Michigan University. He is the author of *Scare Tactics: Supernatural Fiction by American Women*, *The Rocky Horror Picture Show*, and *Vampires: Undead Cinema*. He has edited or co-edited six academic collections on topics ranging from Poe to South Park. In addition to editing four volumes of the fiction of H. P. Lovecraft, he is at work on a monograph on American Gothicist Charles Brockden Brown.

Ruth D. Weston has taught at Tulsa Community College, the University of Tulsa, the US Military Academy at West Point, and Oral Roberts University, where she retired as Professor of English in 1998. She was twice named Outstanding Scholar at Oral Roberts; at West Point she received the US Army's Outstanding Civilian Service Medal in 1993. Weston has published extensively on the literature of the American South, including books on Eudora Welty and on Barry Hannah. Focusing often on narrative technique and on the short story, she has contributed articles on lyric technique in the journal *Short Story* and on surfiction in the essay collection *Creative and Critical Approaches to the Short Story*. She is past president of the Eudora Welty Society and is the recipient of the Society's *Phoenix* award for Distinguished Achievement in Welty Studies. In 2009, she came out of retirement to be Adjunct Professor of English at the University of Tulsa.

Molly Crumpton Winter is Associate Professor of English at the California State University at Stanislaus. Her book, *American Narratives: Multiethnic Writing in the Age of Realism*, examines how multicultural writers represented ideas of assimilation and exclusion at the turn into the twentieth century. Her work on multicultural topics has also appeared in *Western American Literature*, *Meridians: Feminism, Race, Transnationalism*, *Humanities in the South*, and in the collection *Post-Bellum, Pre-Harlem: Rethinking African American Literature and Culture, 1880–1914*. Her current project is a study of multiethnic California writing.

Wenying Xu is Professor and Chair of English at Florida Atlantic University. She is the author of *Eating Identities: Reading Food in Asian American Literature*, *Ethics, Aesthetics of Freedom in American and Chinese Realism*, and numerous articles on Asian American stories in *Cultural Critique, boundary 2, MELUS*, and *LIT*.

Acknowledgments

Both editors want to thank all of the scholars who contributed essays to this volume and responded professionally, cheerfully, and promptly to requests for revisions. Emma Bennett at Wiley-Blackwell invited us to undertake this project and provided generous encouragement at every step, and we appreciate her confidence and support. We are also grateful for the skilled work of the editorial team at Wiley-Blackwell, particularly Caroline Clamp, Isobel Bainton, and Pandora Kerr Frost.

Alfred Bendixen also wishes to express his appreciation to his colleagues in the English Department at Texas A&M University, who provided valuable advice on various essays, particularly Dennis Berthold, M. Jimmie Killingsworth, Jerome Loving, David McWhirter, and Larry Reynolds. He also wishes to thank the Department and Texas A&M University for providing funds to cover part of the costs of preparing the index. His greatest expression of appreciation is reserved for his wife and partner, Judith Hamera, who makes every scholarly act a pleasure.

James Nagel wishes to express his gratitude to the University of Georgia Foundation for the support of his position as J. O. Eidson Distinguished Professor of American Literature. His research assistant, Katherine Barrow, provided professional support with every phase of the project, and he is appreciative of her dedication and attention to detail. Many scholars within the field of American literature contributed wise counsel for the development of the volume, and together we share the mutual stimulation and warm colleagueship afforded by the American Literature Association.

Part I
The Nineteenth Century

1

The Emergence and Development of the American Short Story

Alfred Bendixen

The short story is an American invention, and arguably the most important literary genre to have emerged in the United States. Before Washington Irving created the two masterpieces that may be said to have inaugurated this new literary form, "Rip Van Winkle" and "The Legend of Sleepy Hollow," there certainly were an abundance of prose forms that contained some of the elements that characterize the short story. Storytelling is, after all, one of the oldest human activities, and oral narratives, especially fairy tales and folk tales, have played a significant role in most cultures. Various other kinds of narratives also contributed to the nation's political and domestic life. For instance, the histories written during the early national period often provided strong character sketches as well as imaginative episodes designed to illuminate some moral virtue or quality. Some of these, perhaps most notably Parson Weems's famous story of the young George Washington admitting to chopping down his father's cherry tree, became enshrined in the cultural mythology of the United States. Fictional elements can also be found in the illustrative episodes and anecdotes of eighteenth-century sermons and in some of the moral and satiric essays that were popular during the Enlightenment, particularly the *bagatelles* of Ben Franklin. Indeed, it is tempting to see the best of Franklin's comic pieces, such as "The Speech of Miss Polly Baker," as proto–short stories. All of these works probably deserve some credit for contributing to the development of the short story, but they, like the self-contained episodes one sometimes finds in eighteenth-century novels, lack the development of theme and technique that we now think of as distinguishing this genre as a literary form. In these works, setting is rarely more than the listing of a place or type of scene; characterization consists largely of ascribing a few virtues or vices and perhaps a couple of physical details to the primary figures; plot development is generally either very straightforward or very clumsy, culminating in a conclusion that is usually either overtly moral or sentimental but occasionally comic. Almost no thought is given to the possibilities implicit in narrative point of view, and the style of most of the works that prefigure the true short story can be charitably described as artificial, wordy, and awkward.

Washington Irving changed all of that. The short story as Irving shaped it in the installments of *The Sketch Book* was a work rich in description of scenery and locale, with memorable characters and vivid situations rendered through a highly polished style that shifted easily through a variety of moods but seemed especially successful in its mastery of a new kind of comedy. *The Sketch Book* also gave American culture its first literary best-seller, a critical and commercial success so great that the new democracy finally had an answer to those critics who had emphasized its paucity of cultural achievement. In the January 1820 *Edinburgh Review*, critic Sydney Smith had been able to begin a list of insulting questions about the United States with the phrase, "who reads an American book?" Because of Irving's success, the answer soon became "almost everybody." Nevertheless, current scholarship fails to emphasize how original Washington Irving was in his invention of a new genre. Even in his own time, he was unfairly labeled as a mere imitator of Goldsmith and Addison, two writers whose graceful style certainly influenced him, or criticized for lifting his plots from German folk stories. Such criticism, however, fails to recognize the amount of inventiveness demonstrated in the masterpieces, "Rip Van Winkle" and "The Legend of Sleepy Hollow." Although European folk stories may have provided him with some elements of plot, Irving was the first to bring the American landscape to life in works of fiction, giving the short story a specificity and definiteness of locale and ultimately making it the dominant form for expressions of literary regionalism in the United States. Since Irving, the short story has been the primary mode by which American authors define and express the values of a particular culture in a specific time and place. In their fidelity to the qualities of a certain place and their expressions of nostalgia for a simpler and easier past, these two great Knickerbocker tales created the literary mode that came to be called "local color" and dominated American short fiction for most of the nineteenth century.

Irving's achievement in giving a fictional reality to the American landscape is all the more remarkable considering that the bulk of *The Sketch Book* consists of travel writing about England, not the United States. The idea of representing place with meticulous care and sometimes even loving devotion marks both Irving's travel writing and his best short fiction. In his time, travel writers often explicitly expressed their belief in the theory of association, which proclaimed that natural scenes were inherently without meaning, and that only associations with historical or literary connections could provide real significance to the landscape. Irving's emphasis on setting was thus part of a conscious and largely successful effort to endow a portion of his native terrain, the Catskill Mountains, with the kind of value that association with powerful works of literature can provide (Bendixen 108–9). In the process, Irving certainly did a service to the tourist industry, which would use his fiction to market the region, but his placement of these vivid American stories in a book about England served other, less commercial purposes. The vitality of these American scenes provides an important counterpoint to the quieter, duller, more peaceful scenes of rural England that Irving likes to emphasize. Although he is often accused of being an anglophile, his Knickerbocker stories both claim a space for American scenes on the map of serious literature and also emphasize the exceptional vigor and energy that mark democratic life. Indeed, his best fiction relies on a discovery and exploration of the special qualities that distinguish American life, demonstrating the capacity of the short story to move beyond the narrow moralizing that had characterized earlier attempts at prose fiction into a new kind of national myth making.

Irving freed American prose fiction from the didactic, from the need to preach a pointed moral, and endowed it with a rich playfulness that suggested new ways of achieving the kind of literary nationalism that Americans had been calling for since their revolution. Rip Van Winkle, Ichabod Crane, and Brom Bones are the first memorable characters in American fiction, and their adventures engage them directly, if comically, in a confrontation with fundamental questions about the meaning of identity in this new world. In the act of fleeing his nagging wife, Rip retreats into the countryside, into the bounties of nature where he can avoid the demands of women, work, and civilization, thus establishing the pattern that marks many important male characters in American fiction, and foreshadowing a range of figures that includes Huck Finn's lighting out for the territory and Hemingway's Nick Adams's complex engagement with the Big Two-Hearted River. During his famous nap of twenty years, Rip winds up sleeping through the entire American Revolution, and returns home to a town that has been transformed from a sleepy Dutch village into a busier, more active community engaged in arguments about a local election. Feeling out of place in this new democracy, Rip momentarily loses his sense of identity, but ultimately recovers it, or perhaps more accurately, recreates it by finding a role in this strange new world as a storyteller. Thus, Irving demonstrates how a new kind of highly developed short fiction can probe the complexities, both comic and tragic, entailed in citizenship in a new democratic society.

His engagement with issues of national identity, with the changing demands of a democratic society, with the possibilities entailed in a society marked by multiplicity and fluidity, and with the conflicting demands of agrarian versus commercial values also forms the foundation of "The Legend of Sleepy Hollow." As the sturdy Brom Bones competes with the ambitious schoolteacher, Ichabod Crane, for the love of Katrina Van Tassel, Irving emphasizes two underlying sets of values that are inherently in conflict. Brom Bones and the Van Tassels stand for an easy contentment based on a settled agricultural existence rooted in general prosperity and life in nature. Crane represents a set of values that are more abstract, more commercial, more ambitious, and ultimately more unnatural. Just as the virtues of the Van Tassels' agrarian way of life are summed up in the lengthy and lush description of their farm, the limitations of Crane are defined for us initially by the depiction of his small and shabby schoolhouse, which is shown clearly as a place to imprison young spirits rather than develop the intellect. The contrast between easy Dutch contentment and bustling New England ambition seems to reflect regional differences, but Irving's depiction of Crane's gluttonous lust for Katrina and the family land reveal broader concerns. Crane may be a schoolteacher from New England, but he fantasizes about becoming a land speculator who will convert the Van Tassel estate into cash to buy up the western wilderness, which he then plans to transform through endless real estate schemes, and he will end up becoming the most dreaded of American creatures, a politician. In tracing the career of Ichabod Crane, Irving shows us a fluid society in which identity may be based more on aspiration and ambition (for good or bad) than on accidents of birth, and in which the development of a meaningful national identity will be based on the ways in which competing values are resolved. What is at stake in "The Legend of Sleepy Hollow" and the best of Irving's stories is the future of America.

Irving employed a graceful style that seemed to refuse to take itself or anything too seriously while raising fundamental questions about the meaning of American democracy. His artistry rests on his understanding of the importance of narrative point of view and the value of adopting a specific narrative *persona*, whether that be Geoffrey Crayon, Gentleman, or Dietrich Knickerbocker, the sly chronicler of Dutch New York. He is almost certainly the first writer of short fiction to understand and to articulate the degree to which the manner of telling would always have to be at least as important as the subject matter of the story. In fact, one of his letters indicates that he was clearly a conscious artist who was able to articulate his achievement with rare precision:

> I fancy much of what I value myself upon in writing escapes the observation of the great mass of my readers, who are intent more upon the story than the way it is told. For my part, I consider a story merely as a frame on which to stretch my materials. It is the play of thought, and sentiment, and language; the weaving in character, lightly, yet expressively delineated; the familiar and faithful exhibition of scenes of common life; and the half-concealed vein of humour that is often playing through the whole – these are among what I aim at, and upon which I felicitate myself in proportion as I think I succeed. (*Letters to Brevoort* II. 185–6)

In the same letter, he goes on to argue that the long tale can get away with much dull writing because the author can count on plot and character to keep the reader turning the pages, but short fiction requires a continued commitment to artistry:

> The author must be continually piquant; woe to him if he makes an awkward sentence or writes a stupid page; the critics are sure to pounce upon it. Yet if he succeed, the very variety and piquancy of his writings – nay, their very brevity, make them frequently recurred to, and when the mere interest of the story is exhausted, he begins to get credit for his touches of pathos or humor; his points of wit or turns of language." (*Letters to Brevoort*. II. 187)

The short story as Irving fashioned it was clearly a work of conscious literary artistry with vivid characters, a carefully delineated setting, and a mastery of stylistic nuance, and it was also a form ideally suited for the exploration of the meaning of democratic life in the newly formed United States. Nevertheless, Irving's short stories certainly did not represent the final word in this new genre. In what remains one of the most perceptive studies of his contribution to the development of American writing, Fred

Lewis Pattee chastises Irving for a lack of masculine vigor and notes that the American short story would come to rely less on the detailed descriptive writing that Irving relished and more on dialogue and the dramatic presentation of incident.

The development of the short story was limited by one major fact: there really was almost no market for it that would enable a writer to win both a critical reputation and a significant livelihood, a fact that clearly struck the writers who tried to follow the path that Irving had opened. Irving's short stories were really not designed to stand alone as separate literary artifacts with an audience and market of their own; they were meant to be appreciated aesthetically and marketed financially as components of a larger work. Irving's strategy for *The Sketch Book* involved issuing a series of parts, each of which would offer a blend of fiction and familiar essays, balancing sentiment and comedy. The comedy of the two Knickerbocker tales serves to balance and play off the sentiment of the other selections, sometimes in intriguing ways. Thus, the comic story of a man fleeing his nagging wife, "Rip Van Winkle," is placed directly next to a sentimental piece, "The Wife," which assures the reader that a loyal and loving wife is the most precious thing any man can possess. These stories were meant to exist within a larger context established by other works, not as stand-alone pieces, and to be marketed as contributions to a work that relied on a variety of forms and moods. Irving attempted to bring out a collection of short stories without any of the supporting apparatus provided by familiar essays and travel writing with *Tales of a Traveler* (1824), which contains two of his most important stories, "The Adventure of the German Student" and "The Devil and Tom Walker," but critics responded harshly. After the critical failure of that book, most of Irving's literary energy went to the production of works of creative non-fiction, including travel books, histories, and immensely popular biographies of Christopher Columbus and George Washington. Although almost completely neglected by critics and scholars, *The Alhambra* (1832), which is generally described as a Spanish Sketch Book, contains some of his finest writing.

Irving's success certainly encouraged other Americans to explore the possibilities of short fiction, and some of these works from the 1820s and 1830s probably merit more consideration from scholars. Perhaps the most notable attempt to build on Irving's skillful use of the supernatural for national myth making may be found in the three stories William Austin wrote about "Peter Rugg, the Missing Man" (1824–6). Austin places the old Flying Dutchman story into a new American context which vividly portrays the American landscape as a place in which one can become irretrievably lost. James Kirke Paulding, with whom Irving had collaborated on the *Salmagundi* papers (1807–8), attempted to work in virtually every genre available and managed to produce some significant pieces of short fiction, particularly his attempt to create a specifically American mythology in *The Book of St. Nicholas* (1836) and his remarkable collection of democratic fairy tales for children, *A Gift from Fairy Land* (1837). Many of his most interesting stories remained uncollected during his lifetime and were not brought together into book form until his son, William I. Paulding, edited *A Book of Vagaries* (1867). Some of William Cullen Bryant's short stories also deserve attention, especially his comic treatment of an encounter with the wilderness and Native Americans in "The Indian Spring" (1828). Several women writers also produced intriguing short stories that deal specifically with the position of women in a democratic society, perhaps most notably Catherine Sedgwick's "Cacoethes Scribendi" (1830), Eliza Leslie's "Mrs. Washington Potts" (1832), and the tales Lydia Maria Child eventually collected in her volume, *Fact and Fiction* (1846). Other important fiction by both men and women may still remain buried in the pages of early American periodicals.

These writers might have had more success with the short story if there had been a market that made such writing profitable. The lack of an international copyright agreement made it more profitable for American printers to pirate best-selling British writers than to take a chance on an unknown American author who expected to be paid for his or her work. The short story as a marketable commodity has always depended on the availability of both periodical and book publication, and it took the United States a long time to develop viable magazines with an interest in literature. The history of American publishing in the early nineteenth century is filled with failed attempts to establish significant literary magazines, and the relatively small number that survived for a time rarely paid very well. Furthermore, book publishers were generally reluctant to produce collections of stories, deeming them inherently unprofitable. Both Edgar Allan Poe and Nathaniel Hawthorne attempted to launch their literary careers with collections of short stories, but had great difficulty in finding publishers for their first projected books. The stories that were to comprise Poe's *Tales of the Folio Club* and Hawthorne's *Provincial Tales* and *The Story-Teller* were instead scattered in various publications and not collected until later and then in very different arrangements from the authors' original plans. Hawthorne's careful plans for his first volumes were discarded and the individual stories were simply lifted out of context and published in magazines or *The Token*, one of the gift-books that publishers discovered they could sell annually. The gift-books provided one of the few outlets available to writers of short stories, but they paid poorly and usually published anonymously, which meant that they also added little to a young writer's reputation. Moreover, these very pretty volumes appeared designed as decorative gifts that were suitable for gracing a parlor table; there was little in their appearance to suggest they contained literary works meant to be taken seriously. Nevertheless, these annuals published a number of writers whose importance is now firmly established, and *The Token* had the distinction of providing the first home for many of Hawthorne's most powerful stories.

If Irving merits credit as the inventor of the American story, then Hawthorne and Poe surely deserve praise for solidifying its status as a work of art. They grounded the short story more firmly in a clear commitment to narrative structure and plot, replacing Irving's genial rambling and lengthy descriptions with a firm sense of architectural form. Furthermore, they added a startling psychological depth to the development of character, employing a treatment of aberrational psychology in ways that transformed the Gothic mode into an enduring part of the American short story tradition.

They also expanded the range of subject matter available to short story treatment by introducing new forms and genres. As a short story writer, Hawthorne's current reputation rests almost entirely on the great historical tales of the New England Puritans that he produced in the 1830s at the start of his long literary career, but these represent only a relatively small part of his work in short fiction. The achievement of these historical tales is, of course, enormous. At a time when the literary treatment of American history was inclined largely to patriotic fervor, Hawthorne daringly introduced stories of guilt, repression, cruelty, and injustice and detailed the psychological turmoil that ensued. His most famous story, "Young Goodman Brown" (1835), begins with a young man leaving his wife to go into the forest – basically the same starting point as Irving's "Rip Van Winkle." Yet, by the time Brown wakes up from the nightmare he has experienced in the moral wilderness that he has entered, Hawthorne has taken us into a symbolic realm that challenges almost all the conventional boundaries: we have been moved from the world of historical fact into a psychological landscape filled with surrealistic imagery that compels us to question the most fundamental issues of both ontology and epistemology. The most powerful of the great historical tales – "Roger Malvin's Burial" (1832), "The Gentle Boy" (1832), "My Kinsman, Major Molineaux" (1832) – are deeply unsettling, because they insist on raising troubling questions about both the American past and the human psyche. Hawthorne's fascination with how individuals perceive a complex reality – with how perception can create reality – is also the focus of his short story masterpiece, "The Minister's Black Veil" (1836), and an important element in his finest novel, *The Scarlet Letter* (1850).

Yet, in his own time, Hawthorne was best known and most widely praised as the writer of genial sketches and gentle allegories. In fact, he was most often compared to the British essayist, Charles Lamb, and sometimes even called the American Elia. We have lost the taste for works like "Little Annie's Rambles" (1835), "A Rill from the Town-Pump" (1835), and "Sights from a Steeple" (1831), but the contemporary reviews suggest that these works defined Hawthorne for much of his own audience. In fact, he was a writer who experimented with a wide variety of forms and themes throughout his career. He always maintained an interest in the fictional possibilities of allegory and in the 1840s probably even considered creating a series of parables to be called "Allegories of the Heart." This allegorical impulse resulted in numerous works, including his brilliant satire of his own times, "The Celestial Rail-road" (1843). In the 1840s, Hawthorne also helped to create the genre now known as science fiction. He produced stories about the end of the world, such as "The New Adam and Eve" (1843) and "Earth's Holocaust" (1844), and a number of tales focusing on scientists who end up destroying those they love, most notably "The Birth-mark" (1843) and "Rappaccini's Daughter" (1844). These works reflect the author's distrust of disembodied thought and his rejection of the nineteenth century's commitment to technology and belief in unlimited progress. His tales of scientists are often linked to his study of artists, particularly in "The Artist of the Beautiful" (1844), but a focus on the power and limitations of the artist in a materialistic world shapes his entire career. Hawthorne was also one of the first major American authors to devote himself to the creation of stories expressly designed for children. The skillful refashioning of Greek myths for children in *A Wonder-Book for Girls and Boys* (1851) and *Tanglewood Tales* (1853) are significant achievements in this mode. In fact, Hawthorne's "The Golden Touch" was responsible for the version of the King Midas story in which Midas mistakenly turns his own daughter into gold; in earlier versions, the King's repentance stemmed solely from his inability to eat normal food. He also produced a series of historical stories for children, *The Whole History of Grandfather's Chair* (1820–41), that traced the key events of New England history up to the time of the American Revolution.

The only writer who did as much to make the American romantic tale into a significant literary achievement was Edgar Allan Poe, who began by writing satires and hoaxes and ended up transforming the tale of terror into a serious literary form and inventing the detective story. In his critical writings, Poe emphasized the importance of a single effect to which every element of the short story must contribute. He also continually affirmed the artistic superiority of works that were long enough for full development and short enough to be read in a single sitting, and was one of the very few critical voices in the nineteenth century to argue that the tale was therefore superior to the novel. Poe was the master of a wide range of fictional forms. Although his comic pieces rarely receive the same critical attention as his darker, more pessimistic works, there is no better way to discover the conventions of the nineteenth-century Gothic tale than his brilliant parody, "How to Write a Blackwood's Article" (1838) and its accompanying example, "A Predicament" (1838). He also created some of our earliest stories of science fiction with "The Balloon-Hoax" (1844) and "The Facts in the Case of M. Valdemar" (1845). The diversity of Poe's achievement is perhaps best represented by his ability to both invent the detective story, which depends upon a faith in analytic reasoning and the capacity of the rational mind to detect the perpetrators of crime and reestablish justice and order, and also become the great acknowledged master of the horror tale, which seems to rely on opposing values, on a fascination with the irrational and the aberrational, with cruelty and pain and suffering, and with bizarre acts of violent revenge. The best of the works that he called his "tales of ratiocination" – "The Murders in the Rue Morgue" (1841), "The Gold Bug" (1843), and "The Purloined Letter" (1845) – established most of the conventions on which detective fiction still rests, including the narrative strategies for presenting an extraordinarily penetrating mind which is able to perceive and finally explain the truth that lies hidden within a great mystery that puzzles everyone else.

If the detective stories seem to affirm the power of human reason and an underlying faith in justice, Poe's horror tales often seem founded on acts of senseless violence which almost always turn out to be self-destructive, and on a very different view of human nature. In "The Black Cat" (1843), the narrator blames his own actions on the "spirit of PERVERSENESS," which he insists is "one of the primitive impulses of the human heart" and describes as "an unfathomable longing of the soul to vex itself – to offer violence to its own nature – to do wrong for wrong's sake" (Poe, *Tales* 599). Of course, we must remember that axe murderers do not make reliable narrators. Poe's mad narrators never understand their own actions or the underlying causes of their strange compulsions, which usually include a need to verbally reenact their crimes by narrating them. Ultimately, the source of terror in Poe's greatest stories stems from the inability of their narrators to understand the worlds they inhabit and the reasons for their own actions. In these tales, it is the failure to understand the self that leads to acts of mutilation that divide the physical body and shatter the spiritual nature, or to characters being buried alive, which presents an almost perfect metaphor for the psychological idea of repression. In some of these tales, perhaps most notably "Ligeia" and "The Black Cat," the inability of the male narrator to accept the reality of sexuality and the female body seems to be the chief motivating factor. In almost all of Poe's major tales of horror, however, the single great metaphor is the divided self and the over-arching theme points to the inability of an individual to come to terms with a double or some figure that represents an aspect of the narrator's own personality. In "The Fall of the House of Usher" (1839), "The Tell-Tale Heart" (1843), and "The Cask of Amontillado" (1846), the chief source of terror is ultimately the inability of the self to understand itself.

Poe brought a level of craftsmanship and psychological insight to the horror tale that exceeded anything that had been done before and most of what has been done since. In addition to his frequent use of unreliable and sometimes mad narrators, he brought a unity of tone, mood, and atmosphere to the development of American fiction. Although his critical writings emphasize the single effect to which everything in a short work must lead, he also recognized that strong writing would have what he (and his times) called "suggestiveness," a broad term implying that great works of art carry with them multiple layers of meanings that invite thought and analysis. In short, his works lend themselves to symbolic interpretation on multiple levels. The romantic tale, particularly as mastered by Hawthorne and Poe, heavily favors the use of symbolic language, but has very little interest in the accurate rendition of normal human speech; there is an artificial and sometimes heavily Latinate quality to both the narrative language and the treatment of dialogue. At this point, it is important to distinguish between the romantic tale and the realistic short story. Although some writers and critics use the terms "tale" and "story" indiscriminately, those who distinguish between the two view the story as chiefly concerned with the presentation of character, usually within a realistic context that is established by a reasonably accurate portrayal of a recognizable place in either the present or the recent past. In contrast, the tale suggests a focus on action, adventure, and plot; a bold development of larger than life characters who move through unusual or exotic landscapes that often seem to be symbolic projections of some psychological state; and a setting that usually shuns the here and now in favor of the distant past, foreign realms, natural scenes of awe-inspiring danger, or some world outside of normal time and space. Suggestions of the supernatural are often deeply interwoven into the basic texture of the romantic tale. These points of shared values should not obscure the very real differences among authors of romantic fiction; for instance, Hawthorne often indulges in moralizing while Poe clearly rejects didacticism and Melville emphasizes a multiplicity of possible interpretation that seems to completely redefine the genre and expand the idea of moral interpretation.

Melville's experiments with short fiction did not attract much attention in his own time, but twentieth-century scholars established him as one of our finest, most subtle masters of short fiction. Of his short works, the most romantic in tone and texture is certainly the long story "Benito Cereno" (1856), with its portrayal of violent adventure and unending mystery, its heightened contrast of characters appearing to represent American innocence and European corruption, and its insistence on probing the issues of slavery and racism from multiple perspectives. On the other hand, Melville's most studied story, "Bartleby the Scrivener: A Story of Wall Street" (1853), appears to be moving towards a kind of realism in its critique of the deadening effects of meaningless labor in a commercial society, but this story demands to be read and reread on multiple levels. "Bartleby" focuses on both its purported subject, a copyist who engages in a passive-aggressive rejection of trivial and debasing work, and its very unreliable narrator, an apparently genial man in flight from any confrontation with the reality he has helped to create. Both narrator and protagonist are isolated individuals who are marked by a failure of vision in a narrative filled with symbolism emphasizing the blank walls, spiritual hunger, and fragmentation of this alienating world. Like the best of Melville's short fiction, the story is complex, subtle, and even devious – at times giving the impression that its author is engaged in constructing an elaborate joke on a reading public incapable of appreciating real artistry. This devious complexity is clearest in the stunning sexual comedy that underlies some of Melville's other short stories, perhaps most notably "Cock a Doodle Doo!" (1853), "I and my Chimney" (1856), and "The Apple-Tree Table" (1856). In his best works, Melville insists on asking us to view the world on multiple levels, suggesting to us that the human experience is simultaneously a rich source of philosophical inquiry and a dirty joke.

The romantic tale continued to attract talented adherents even in the late 1850s, most notably Fitz-James O'Brien and Harriet Prescott Spofford. O'Brien's best tales remain surprisingly neglected by contemporary critics even though Jessica Amanda Salmonson provided important new revelations in her introduction to her 1988 edition of his stories, most notably the fact that he was gay. Read through the lens of queer theory, his finest stories take on new and intriguing dimensions. For example, his famous ghost story, "What Was It?" (1859), is about the threat posed by an invisible man in the bedroom. "The Diamond Lens" (1858), his best work of science fiction, focuses on a man unable to come to terms with sexuality, his own desires, and his own small perception of the world. His finest work of fiction, "The Lost Room" (1858), depicts a man who loses his place in the world, or more precisely, discovers that his room has disappeared after he has been told by a strange being that he lives in a "queer" house (Salmonson, I. 7). In short, O'Brien's best stories are built on anxieties and issues that would have a special resonance for homosexuals in a repressive society.

Harriet Prescott Spofford brought a feminine and sometime feminist dimension to the romantic tale with her best works of short fiction. She first gained attention with the publication of "In the Cellar" (1859), a lavishly detailed story of Parisian intrigue and one of our first important detective stories by an American woman. "Circumstance" (1860), her tale of a pioneer woman who keeps a menacing panther at bay by singing songs throughout a long night, drew immense attention and apparently even gave Emily Dickinson nightmares. Her long and difficult masterpiece, "The Amber Gods" (1860), offers one of the most remarkable and luxuriantly poetic monologues in American fiction and features a heroine whose self-indulgence seems to transcend even death. Her finest work of short fiction is probably "Her Story" (1872), which provides a treatment of madness and marriage that prefigures Gilman's "The Yellow Wallpaper" (1891). During a long and prolific writing career that lasted almost until her death in 1921, Spofford found herself forced to surrender to the demands of the marketplace and shifted to realistic fiction, where she occasionally produced able work but never matched the distinction of her best romantic tales. Her early work represents the final flourish of New England romanticism and provides the most significant and most daring treatment of the devices of the romantic tale by an American woman writer.

Important new markets for American short stories appeared in the middle of the nineteenth century, most notably the advent in 1857 of the *Atlantic Monthly*, which included three stories in each of its early issues, attracted significant talent, and paid well. *Harper's Magazine*, which had been established in 1850, abandoned its initial practice of publishing mostly reprints of British material and began soliciting American writers. Although *Putnam's* (1853–7) did not last very long, other magazines soon provided a meaningful market for short fiction, including *The Galaxy* (1866–78), *Lippincott's Magazine* (1868–1915), and *Scribner's Monthly* (1870–81) and its successor, *The Century Magazine* (1881–1930). Unfortunately, book publishers continued to believe that collections of short stories were unmarketable, and a writer needed to earn a substantial reputation before publishers would risk bringing out a volume of short fiction. That changed in the 1880s, when Scribner's discovered that it could successfully market collections of short stories if they were focused on life in a specific region of the United States. The result was the wave of regionalist fiction known as the local color movement. Although publishers tended to favor collections of short stories that shared a common setting and sometimes a recurring cast of characters, American writers of short fiction finally had access to both strong periodical and book markets by the end of the nineteenth century.

The major shift in the development of the American short story during the last half of the nineteenth century was the rise of realism, which dominated American fiction for most of the period following the Civil War. Although it is possible to find many antebellum precursors and sources for the emergence of realism, at least two deserve special emphasis in any treatment of the short story: the Southwestern humorists who brought a fresh vitality to the comic story and the group of New England women writers who established the basic traits of the realistic short story. There are multiple examples of pre-Civil War writers who fashioned short fiction out of regional material and the American frontier, including the western stories of James Hall, Timothy Flint, and William Joseph Snelling, but the Southwestern humorists had the most enduring impact. For most scholars, the classic example of the genre is Thomas Bangs Thorpe's "The Big Bear of Arkansas" (1841), but the works that established this important sub-genre of American fiction include Augustus Baldwin Longstreet's *Georgia Scenes* (1835), Johnson Jones Hooper's *Some Adventures of Captain Simon Suggs* (1845), Joseph Baldwin's *Flush Times of Alabama and Mississippi* (1853), and George Washington Harris's *Sut Lovingood's Yarns Spun by a "Nat'ral Born Durn'd Fool"* (1867). While mainstream authors tended to use a highly artificial and ornate literary language, these writers embraced the American vernacular and pioneered the development of American dialect in short fiction. They offered tall tales of tricksters and conmen, boastful frontiersmen and prodigious hunters, brave figures who define themselves and measure themselves against the vast and magnificent American wilderness. The worst of these tales – the anecdotes about Mike Fink, a brawling bully who appears in some of the stories about Davy Crockett – are marred by crude humor, physical cruelty, bad practical jokes, and blatant racism. The best of them offer brilliant accounts of class conflicts usually derived from the contrast between a highly educated and somewhat pompous narrator from the cities of the east and the more vibrant, more vivid speech of a figure who lives the most natural of lives on what was then the American frontier. Although these stories were largely considered sub-literary in their own time, scholars have recognized their influence on writers as important as Mark Twain and William Faulkner. In their insistence on honestly confronting the harsh realities of life and their affirmation of a narrative language that affirms the plain, honest, sometimes earthy speech of simple people, these works also opened paths that would be crucial to the development of realism.

In sharp contrast to the Southwestern humorists, whose works often rely on the portrayal of male violence, are the northeastern women writers who pioneered a different kind of realism in their stories. Although she is best known for her abolitionist novel, *Uncle Tom's Cabin* (1852), Harriet Beecher Stowe also deserves credit for developing the kind of realistic story of New England village life that we now know mostly through the works of Mary E. Wilkins Freeman and Sarah Orne Jewett. The best of Stowe's short works were collected in *The Mayflower* (1843, rev. 1855), *Oldtown Folks* (1869), and *Sam Lawson's Old Town Fireside Tales* (1871), and represent the beginnings of a tradition of realism which recognized the domestic life of ordinary citizens as worthy of literary treatment. Stowe emphasizes domestic spaces, kitchens and firesides, as sites for both storytelling and the dramas of daily life. She focuses primarily on the study of character and the exploration of the normal but sometimes complex relationships between men and women within a social community. Her writing clearly values the ordinary speech of average individuals and attempts to represent it with accuracy and precision as they struggle to express their aspirations and frustrations. As Rose Terry Cooke demonstrated in the more than 200 stories she wrote throughout her long career, this new realistic mode was equally effective in the comic deflation of pretense and the depiction of the quiet tragedies of repressed lives. In her stories about Polly Mariner, an independent single woman, Cooke helped make the "spinster" into one of the mainstays of the New England feminist tradition. Her bold treatment of bad marriages and her critique of the repression of women within the Calvinistic tradition of New England add force to many of her best works, particularly her grim masterpiece, "Too Late" (1875). Elizabeth Stuart Phelps Ward also helped to introduce a feminist literary tradition in some of her short fiction, the best of which appears in *Men, Women, and Ghosts* (1879) and *Sealed Orders* (1880), but her major contribution is the creation of a social fiction that seeks both compassion and justice for the working poor. The most powerful of the new realistic stories about poverty is almost certainly "Life in the Iron Mills" (1861) by Rebecca Harding Davis, who went on to produce other important pieces of realistic fiction, some of which were eventually collected in *Silhouettes of American Life* (1892).

Women writers played a decisive role in the establishment of realism after the Civil War and in making realism into the dominant literary mode for most (but certainly not all) major American women writers. This is partly because realism tends to be more interested in the dynamics of gender relationships and social relationships within specific kinds of communities than some forms of romantic fiction, which may focus on individuals confronting a symbolic landscape or deal with situations in which women play relatively minor roles, sometimes serving largely as moral touchstones by which one measures the virtues or failings of a central male figure. Women tend to play more substantial roles in realistic works of fiction, including those written by male writers. For instance, whenever Henry James attempted to define the special nature of American life, he almost always found himself writing explicitly about women protagonists and their relationships with men. A number of now neglected male writers also helped to institute realism as the dominant literary mode of the last four decades of the nineteenth century. Thomas Bailey Aldrich, who was one of the most admired writers of his time, made the surprise ending into an important device for short story writers with his epistolary masterpiece, "Marjorie Daw" (1873), and he produced other effective pieces, most of which appear in the collections *Marjorie Daw and Other People* (1873) and *Two Bites at a Cherry* (1894). Frank Stockton won fame with his puzzle story, "The Lady or the Tiger" (1882), a work that raises complex questions about both the reality and the perception of women; the comic fables that appeared in his *The Bee Man of Orn* (1887) also once attracted a great deal of attention. Of the early writers of realism, none attracted more initial acclaim than Bret Harte with his stories of life in the California mining towns. Although his works can now seem surprisingly sentimental and even conventional, his continuous satire of moral pretense and his apparent fascination with disreputable characters were once considered daring.

The major writers of American realism – William Dean Howells, Henry James, and Mark Twain – are best known for their novels, but all produced a significant number of short stories. Although contemporary polls often ranked him as the most important American writer of his time, Howells's great importance now appears to lie primarily in his work as an editor and as an advocate for realism. Of his many stories, the only one now anthologized is "Editha" (1907), which is both an anti-war story and an attack on the romantic imagination that glorifies warfare. Twain's best-known short works are really comic sketches that were heavily influenced by the Southwestern humorists, particularly the work that first gave him a national reputation, "The Celebrated Jumping Frog of Calaveras County" (1865). Although his imagination was at its very best when it had the space provided by the novel or the novella (which he called the "beautiful and blest nouvelle"), Henry James made several significant contributions to the American short story. He produced many thought provoking stories about artists and the creation of art, thus endowing short fiction with a new kind of critical self-consciousness, a new kind of self-referential capacity for aesthetic examination. James also revived the Gothic, transforming it into what Leon Edel has called the "ghostly tale," a work that relies less on the trappings of supernatural literature and more on a full exploitation of its psychological possibilities. Finally, in his last phase, he produced works like "The Beast in the Jungle" (1903), which transform realism into a densely psychological form of impressionism that ultimately led naturally to the stream of consciousness and stylistic experimentation central to high modernism. James was among the most influential writers of his time, not only on the modernists who followed him, but on a group of women writers who began their literary careers with stories highly imitative of his work, most notably Edith Wharton and Willa Cather.

A commitment to realism transformed the American short story, making its primary subject life in the here and now and casting away romanticism's reliance on a distant past and exotic setting. While a typical romantic story might involve a young man's adventure in the wilderness or immersion in some fundamentally symbolic landscape, realism was more concerned with the complex relationships of individuals with each other in a social setting. In most works of realism, the primary forms of violence described are more likely to be psychological than physical. While the romantic tale prefers to emphasize action and symbolism and shows little concern with the accurate rendition of speech, realism is not only suspicious of highly artificial forms of speech and inflated language, but it generally relies on a style that is relatively simple and clear, emphasizing the accurate portrayal of common speech in moments of dialogue and sometimes even insisting on the importance of capturing a specific dialect with meticulous care. This preference for the plain and simple may reflect a distrust of the abstract rhetoric that glorified the mass slaughter of the Civil War, but it also entails a new fascination with the ways in which human beings communicate or fail to communicate. Realism tends to rely less on the big symbols that often shape romantic fiction and more on the creation of complex characters who make difficult choices in complicated situations. In general, the depiction of setting either defines the choices a character has made or the limited choices available to that individual. The criticism of the time often cites the creation of memorable and vivid characters as the distinguishing quality of great literature; realism's great art form is a kind of portraiture that relies on complex methods of characterization that recognize the importance of both psychological and social realities.

Realism also values specificity and verisimilitude, particularly in its commitment to capturing the special qualities of particular places. Realists believe that who we are is shaped partly by where we come from, and that geography is thus intimately connected to the development of character. In some sense, this emphasis on regionalism is realism's response to the acute sense of fragmentation and dislocation that followed the Civil War.

By the end of the nineteenth century, the United States of America occupied a huge part of an entire continent, and its citizens had a natural curiosity about those who lived in other places, other regions. In showing readers how the inhabitants of the different parts of the country talked, dressed, and acted, realism performed important cultural work. While presenting the distinctive qualities of particular places and different cultures, realist writers usually affirmed the common humanity that united the citizens of the various regions of a vast nation. In this respect, realism was fundamentally optimistic in its belief that an honest confrontation with difference will usually lead towards greater understanding and tolerance.

It is possible to find realistic stories that deal with almost every part of the United States. New England was particularly well served by the women writers mentioned earlier who helped to create realism and later by Mary E. Wilkins Freeman and Sarah Orne Jewett. The West had Bret Harte and Mark Twain, and eventually Owen Wister. The Midwest was represented in literature by Edward Eggleston, E. W. Howe, and Hamlin Garland, all of whom fashioned a specific kind of literary landscape that would be reshaped into the modern fiction of Sherwood Anderson and Sinclair Lewis. The South had Mary Noailles Murfree, Thomas Nelson Page, James Lane Allan, Joel Chandler Harris, and Charles Chesnutt (whose short stories provided the most significant representation of African American experience of his time). Louisiana produced its own bounty of distinguished writing with masterful short stories by George Washington Cable, Grace King, Kate Chopin, and Alice Dunbar-Nelson. There were also writers who traveled to and wrote about a wide variety of regions and places, such as Constance Fenimore Woolson, who produced significant collections of stories about the Great Lakes region, the American South, and Italy.

As noted earlier, gender roles are often foregrounded as a specific subject of inquiry in works of realism. By the final decade of the nineteenth century, it is possible to see the emergence of literary feminism as one of the major achievements of this literary tradition. The aspirations of women received special attention in the stories of Sarah Orne Jewett, Mary E. Wilkins Freeman, Kate Chopin, Grace King, Charlotte Perkins Gilman, and numerous other writers of the time. Although these writers shared a concern with depicting the way women succeed or fail in a world that is largely controlled by men, it is important to recognize the variety of forms that this literary feminism can take. Jewett frequently focuses on the healing qualities that can be found in a community of women while Freeman's most famous stories usually deal with an unmarried woman who tries to stake out a meaningful independent existence on her own terms. Both Chopin and King write about Louisiana, but they have very different views of the role of female desire and the possibility for fulfillment that can be found in marriage. Gilman devoted herself to the production of clearly feminist fiction, but her most effective stories are probably her early tales of the supernatural, particularly "The Yellow Wallpaper" (1891). In demonstrating the multiple ways in which the realistic short story could explore the situation of women, these authors opened up a path that would be followed by Edith Wharton, Mary Austin, Anzia Yezierska, Willa Cather, Ellen Glasgow, Katherine Anne Porter, and others.

The final decade of the nineteenth century also saw the development of a new kind of fiction, which we now call naturalism. Some critics seem to portray naturalism as simply realism with a rougher view of the world, but this ignores the very real differences between the two literary movements. Naturalism is best understood as a literary response to the ideas of scientific determinism, to the belief that we are victims of forces, both external and internal, that we cannot control and perhaps cannot even understand. As such, it is fundamentally opposed to realism's focus on complex choices made by complex individuals. In fact, naturalism rarely views human beings as complex at all; instead, it sees and portrays people in fairly generic terms, usually as victims. The naturalist sometimes does not even provide a name for his main character, and often relies largely on animal and/or machine imagery to describe human behavior. Works of naturalistic fiction often devote more time and energy to the description of setting, which often embodies the forces operating on characters, than to characterization. These stories frequently plunge rather crude characters into violent situations, testing moments in which the human pretense to superiority over other creatures is exposed as a sham. For naturalists, the world is a violent and dangerous place and the best that a protagonist can achieve is a greater insight into his own limitations. Although naturalists tend to emphasize the importance of their own "honest" vision of the world over the niceties of literary style, naturalism produced a remarkable number of brilliant short stories, including Stephen Crane's "The Open Boat" (1897), Frank Norris's "A Deal in Wheat" (1902), and Jack London's "To Build a Fire" (1908). The influence of naturalism can also be seen in the harsh depictions of Midwestern life in the stories of Hamlin Garland and in the Civil War stories and horror stories of Ambrose Bierce. As a literary movement, naturalism produced a number of powerful works and raised a number of crucial questions: Are human beings more than animals or machines, and what do we have to do to remain or become complete human beings in a dehumanizing world? While naturalism as a literary movement flourished for a relatively short time, its influence on the writers of the twentieth century was enormous.

By the start of the twentieth century, the American short story was clearly established as a vital and vibrant genre with a wide readership. Strong periodical and book markets offered aspiring writers the prospect of both significant pay and critical recognition. In the early decades of the century, the short story would become an important form for the development of a significant multicultural literature and for a remarkably wide range of literary experiments. Thus, within a hundred years of its invention, the American short story had established itself as a highly flexible, diverse, and enduring form that could represent and explore the various phases of democratic life in the United States.

References and Further Reading

Bendixen, Alfred. "American Travel Books about Europe before the Civil War." *The Cambridge Companion to American Travel Writing*. Eds. Alfred Bendixen and Judith Hamera. Cambridge: Cambridge University Press, 2009. 103–26.

Blair, Walter. *Native American Humor*. San Francisco: American Book Co., 1937.

Colacurcio, Michael J. *The Province of Piety: Moral History in Hawthorne's Early Tales*. Cambridge, MA: Harvard University Press, 1984.

Current-Garcia, Eugene. *The American Short Story Before 1850: A Critical History*. Boston: Twayne, 1985.

Hedges, William. *Washington Irving: An American Study 1802–1831*. Baltimore: Johns Hopkins University Press, 1965.

Fetterley, Judith. *Provisions: A Reader from 19th-Century American Women*. Bloomington: Indiana University Press, 1985.

Fetterley, Judith, and Marjorie Pryse. *Writing Out of Place: Regionalism, Women, and American Literary Culture*. Urbana: University of Illinois Press, 2003.

Habegger, Alfred. *Gender, Fantasy and Realism in American Literature*. New York: Columbia University Press, 1982.

Irving, Washington. *The Letters of Washington Irving to Henry Brevoort*. 2 vols. Ed. George S. Hellman. New York: G. P. Putnam's Sons, 1915.

Levy, Andrew. *The Culture and Commerce of the American Short Story*. Cambridge: Cambridge University Press, 1993.

Lohafer, Susan, and Jo Ellen Clary, eds. *Short Story Theory at the Crossroads*. Baton Rouge: Louisiana State University Press, 1983.

Martin, Jay. *Harvests of Change*. Englewood Cliffs, NJ: Prentice-Hall, 1967.

Matthews, Brander. *The Philosophy of the Short Story*. 1901. Rpt. New York: Peter Smith, 1931.

May, Charles B., ed. *Short Story Theories*. Athens: Ohio University Press, 1976.

Mott, Frank Luther. *History of American Magazines*. 5 vols. Cambridge, MA: Harvard University Press, 1938.

Pattee, Fred Lewis. *The Development of the American Short Story*. New York: Harper, 1923.

Poe, Edgar Allan. *Essays and Reviews*. New York: Library of America, 1984.

———. *Poetry and Tales*. New York: Library of America, 1984.

Salmonson, Jessica Amanda, ed. *The Supernatural Tales of Fitz-James O'Brien*. 2 vols. Garden City, NY: Doubleday, 1988.

Scofield, Martin. *The Cambridge Introduction to the American Short Story*. Cambridge: Cambridge University Press, 2006.

Sloane, David E. E., ed. *The Literary Humor of the Urban Northeast, 1830–1890*. Baton Rouge: Louisiana State University Press, 1983.

Tallack, Douglas. *The Nineteenth-Century American Short Story: Language, Form, and Ideology*. London: Routledge, 1993.

Von Frank, Albert J., ed. *Critical Essays on Hawthorne's Short Stories*. Boston: G. K. Hall, 1991.

Werlock, Abby H. P., ed. *Facts on File Companion to the American Short Story*. New York: Facts on File, 2000.

2

Poe and the American Short Story

Benjamin F. Fisher

The American short story and Edgar Allan Poe have a natural, strong bond. He created some of the finest works in the English language in that genre and subsequently offered the first systematic critical principles for what constitutes true art in the short story – though he preferred the term "tale." Although American writers of short fiction have since moved into somewhat different pathways, Poe's critical opinions about the short story remain significant in terms of both literary history and aesthetics, just as his own short stories continue to receive accolades for their artistry. Thus on several levels, Poe's own fiction and his critical dicta concerning the short story are signal features on the profile of World literature. Clarence Gohdes repeatedly stated to his students that what the rest of the literate world in the nineteenth century perceived as American writers' chief contributions to literature were in genre, the short story, and in theme, humor. Poe's own body of short fiction reveals excellences both in form and in comic substance; therefore, the stories, as well as his pronouncements concerning the genre's ideal qualities, invite attentive consideration.

A point to keep firmly in mind: when Poe contemplated turning author he initially thought exclusively in terms of becoming a poet. Understandably, the antecedent British Romantic movement's focus on intense emotionalism customarily found expression in the lyric poem. At an early age, when he realized that he was temperamentally disinclined to take a place in the commercial business of his foster father, John Allan, Poe determined that he would engage poetry as his chosen literary form. For him, the most lyrical poetry in the English language was written by Shelley and Byron, and his own poems bear signs of admiration for their works. In contrast, Poe found that much verse published by Americans was not worthy to be called poetry because it was far more didactic, i.e., preachy and moralizing, than artistic. Consequently, his poetry seemed either too imitative or, given his own techniques, simply too weird to win popularity among American readers and critics.

Gaining neither monetary returns nor increasing recognition from his three slim volumes of poems, published respectively in 1827, 1829, and 1831, Poe turned to short fiction in hopes of realizing greater financial remuneration. When we remember that his total literary income for twenty-two years of creative writing and editorial work amounted to just over ten thousand dollars (poverty level earnings even at that time), we readily comprehend his frustration with what seemed to be minimal success in the literary profession. His fame has certainly burgeoned posthumously, and he has become a world renowned author. Ironically, Poe has not been nearly so well remembered as a poet compared with his high status as a writer of fiction – and, chiefly, of short stories, despite the serious attention that since the late 1950s has been given to his novel, *The Narrative of Arthur Gordon Pym*.

Several comments from respected specialists in American literature are noteworthy in regard to Poe's short fiction. In *Ideas in America*, Howard Mumford Jones stated: "The seventy-odd stories he wrote had been anticipated in almost all their aspects by British and American magazine fiction, and what Poe was principally trying to do … was to master a market" (Jones 41). Another eminent scholar claimed that: "Poe's tales are his chief contribution to the literature of the world" (Mabbott, "Introduction" xv). That statement, coming as it did from the late Thomas Ollive Mabbott, long recognized as one of the world's foremost authorities in Poe studies, stands as powerful testimony to Poe's significance in the history of the short story. Kindred thought comes from Robert E. Spiller, who thought that in American literary history (and today we might extend Spiller's remark to include the histories of much non-American writing), "Poe makes his very significant contribution … by bringing the Gothic element … to the level of aesthetic maturity" (Spiller 77). Taken collectively, these observations, from several founding fathers of American literature as a subject worthy of academic study, provide important testimony to Poe's high place as a creator of short stories. His critical ideas about the short story reinforce his position as a force to conjure with in any discussion of the form.

I

With the preceding general background in mind, we may turn to Poe's shift from poetry to experimentation with short stories. Once he left West Point in 1831 and traveled south to reside in Baltimore with his Grandmother Poe and her family, the young writer must have undertaken what in today's academic world would amount to an independent study course in the writing of short stories. The preceding comments by Spiller and Jones suggest that Poe looked to well-established models when he ventured to write short fiction. Like many other American writers in his day, Poe was an attentive reader of such great British literary periodicals as the *London Magazine*, *Fraser's*, the *Edinburgh Review*, the *Quarterly Review*, the *Metropolitan Magazine*, and the *New Monthly Magazine*. As regards fiction, however, he was even more attentive to *Blackwood's Edinburgh Magazine*, which featured tales of terror as a staple. Such fiction enjoyed longtime popularity in the Anglo-American literary world. Many of Poe's stories seem at their surface levels to advance little beyond what typified great numbers of Gothic predecessors. Consequently, despite the high quality in his short stories overall, many readers have presumed that Poe had no originality, and therefore that his fiction was never first rate.[1]

Divergent opinions are on record, to be sure, though many aficionados of Poe's fiction enjoy it mainly because of the obvious lurid sensationalism or ghost-story trappings. Ironically, too, many readers who would claim considerable knowledge of Poe and his writings are really unaware of all the stories in the Poe canon. Certainly "The Fall of the House of Usher," "Ligeia," "The Masque of the Red Death," "The Black Cat," "The Tell-Tale Heart," "The Cask of Amontillado," "The Murders in the Rue Morgue," "The Purloined Letter," and "The Gold-Bug" are well known. Conversely, "Silence – A Fable," "Shadow – a Parable," "The Conversation of Eiros and Charmion," "The Island of the Fay," "The Oblong Box," "The Business Man," "The Power of Words," "The System of Dr. Tarr and Professor Fether," or "Von Kempelen and His Discovery" are, for the average reader, far less familiar. In anthologies of American literature aimed at the college market, we tend to find the same half-dozen titles selected as representative of Poe's finest achievements in the short story, leaving others to the dustbins of oblivion – though such shadowiness should be resisted. There are, of course, many readers whose knowledge of and regard for Poe's short stories extend far beyond the few that often seem to represent his best (and, perhaps, his only works of short fiction).

When he turned to the short story, what Poe rapidly comprehended was that (a) not only could he write the tale of terror extremely well, but that (b) being so perceptive about what constituted a marketable piece of fiction, he could treat comically what he divined were its potential weaknesses. One may never be certain precisely when many of Poe's stories were composed, although he probably did not retain a manuscript for extended periods, wanting instead to secure acceptance, publication, and pay.[2] Five of his earliest tales were sent in late 1831 to a prize competition sponsored by a Philadelphia newspaper, the *Saturday Courier*. Poe won no prize; that went instead to a greatly inferior piece. Publishing conditions being as they were, however, with no systematic copyright laws governing the practice, the editor of the *Saturday Courier* published the five stories during 1832. All appeared anonymously, as was also customary in that era, and the question remains whether Poe himself knew that they had appeared.

The first of the five to see print,[3] "Metzengerstein," would no doubt have impressed most readers in that day as a specimen of typical "German" (what we today call "Gothic") fiction. The setting in a remote area of Hungary, the Metzengersteins longtime feud with the neighboring Berlifitzings, a family curse hovering over the Metzengersteins, a profligate heir succeeding to that family's estate and fortunes, the mysterious death of his aged opponent and a gigantic supernatural horse's appearing from the burning stables of the Berlifitzings, a seemingly haunted castle for young Baron Metzengerstein's abode, implications of violence, death, and murder involving the two families, a lurid conclusion to young Frederick Metzengerstein's life, assisted by the great horse who has come to overwhelm him (the animal is the reincarnation of old Berlifitzing): all these features would have found many readers easily satisfied with this seemingly straightforward Gothic story.

Poe's creative impulse gives greater artistic dimension to "Metzengerstein," once he revised it, however, than we find in the general run of magazine terror fiction in his era. The avenging spirit of old Berlifitzing, taking the form of a horse – rather than a robed, hooded ghost dogging the footsteps of its enemy to avenge wrongs perpetrated by the villainous protagonist – is made by Poe to symbolize the animal or non-rational impulses in young Baron Frederick Metzengerstein's nature. Just as artistic, a symbolic marriage takes place between Frederick and the horse. Indeed, they become inseparable; well before the end of the story Frederick is rendered subservient to his uncontrollable other, as the horse may reasonably be designated. In this tale Poe may have adapted the folk theme of Satan's appearing astride a great black horse to claim his victims. Poe also adapted the folk belief that unions between humans and non-humans culminated in tragedy. Fittingly, amidst the destruction of Castle Metzengerstein occasioned by a great storm and fire, Frederick is transported into the unknown by the horse. This bonding of human with animal, here representative of bestial impulses subsuming human(e) emotion, becomes a repeated theme in Poe's fiction (as well as in his renowned poem, "The Raven," composed years after he commenced experimenting with fiction).

For example, in "The Black Cat," the murderous protagonist seems to become less and less like a human and more and more like an animal, whose temperament shifts unexpectedly from docile and companionable to vicious and destructive. Meantime, the cat comes to the fore as motivated by human emotions, i.e., revealing the murder and its perpetrator. Poe's protagonists usually move relentlessly into emotional-intellectual isolation. "The System of Dr. Tarr and Professor Fether" and "Hop-Frog" are also stories in which human-animal characteristics are delightfully ambivalent. Poe's creative writings often leave readers thinking that they have confronted an enigma, so we may well wonder if, in considering another story, "The Murders in the Rue Morgue," we should think of the orangutan as merely an unusual type of murderer, or whether we witness a symbolic construct of human-animal-sexual impulses. Whether Poe's own readers would immediately discern such coalescences we may never know, though more recent academic audiences certainly have offered such hypotheses.[4]

Creating "The Murders in the Rue Morgue" as the first modern detective story, Poe was also in part perpetrating a literary hoax. That is, the story may be read as a subtle transition from antecedent Gothic thrillers to what in many cases still constitute the hallmarks of first-rate detective fiction, despite the narrator's disclaimers about writing a romance (another frequent early synonym, as was "tragedy," for what we now call Gothic fiction). Many recent chroniclers of detective fiction seem to forget its derivations from Gothicism, and so a corrective is in order.[5] We might also detect kindred hoax elements in "The Mystery of Marie Rogêt" and "The Purloined Letter." In the former Poe had apparently planned a conclusion based on what newspaper accounts of the murder in New York of Mary Rogers, on whom he based his character, might have suggested as the cause for her murder. So he had to mull and rewrite once newspapers reported causes different from what were originally presumed to bring about the murder of Mary. In "The Purloined Letter" Dupin, Poe's sleuth, effects a hoax upon the villainous Minister D – when he purloins the incriminating letter the Minister had pilfered from a noble lady for blackmail purposes.

Not only the characters but also the settings in Poe's stories function symbolically to enhance those trajectories. Poe discerned how to rework what by his time had become fairly shopworn types of settings into symbolic art. Although some readers might object to the recurrent macabre architecture and landscapes obviously indebted, in part, to the haunted castle that quickly became a(n overworked) hallmark in Gothic fiction, Poe transformed that trope into functional art representative of the housing for the human mind. Conversely, in some stories, for example, "MS. Found in a Bottle" or "A Descent into the Maelström," landscapes operate to rouse terror within the protagonist who is subsumed by them, just as the prison and its appointments nearly overcome the protagonist in "The Pit and the Pendulum." Poe's often extended descriptions of settings have led some readers to view them as excrescences in his work, though a counter-line of interpretation has likewise enjoyed great currency. The Signora Psyche Zenobia, in "How to Write a Blackwood Article," is advised: "Sensations are the great things after all" (*CW* 2. 340), and that precept serves as a succinct definition for Poe's method of literary symbolism.

Although "Metzengerstein" may seem to be little more than an assembly of trite Gothic elements, a somewhat different outreach characterizes the other four tales published in the *Saturday Courier*. "Loss of Breath," "Bon-Bon," and "The Duc De L'Omelette" contain features that could be commonplaces in terror tales of the day. Mr. Lackobreath, the protagonist in the first story, might be near literary kin to old Wilhelm von Berlifitzing in "Metzengerstein" because Lackobreath's soul moves through several transmigrations before his adventures conclude. This process, metem-psychosis, has origins in ancient classical thought, and several other writers who were contemporaries of Poe experimented with it, most notably Robert Montgomery Bird, whose novel, *Sheppard Lee* (1836) Poe reviewed, not wholly favorably, as if the critic's censure might have resulted from envy toward a rival creator of supernatural/comic fiction. From another perspective, "Loss of Breath" may depict male sexuality (more precisely temporary impotence) as a major theme. Thus notwithstanding the comic touches, as if the story were a parody of then current terror fiction, there may be a more sober undercurrent at work.[6]

"A Tale of Jerusalem" differs from the other four tales because it has no Gothic substance at all. Here Poe deftly satirized Horace Smith's popular novel, *Zillah: A Tale of the Holy City*, which had the running header "A Tale of Jerusalem" (1828). Poe's story features none of the supernaturalism that is uppermost in the other four. Roman conquerors slyly substitute a pig for a requested lamb to use in Jewish sacrifice; the Jews, who are confined within the city and want a suitable animal, are so surprised and upset when they discover the pig that they permit the basket containing the animal to drop outside the walls. Poe's lifting many phrases from Smith's novel and fashioning them for his own purposes suggest that his primary intent was to burlesque a best-selling novel and its author. With the passage of time, and the fading of Horace Smith's literary reputation, the parallels between Poe's tale and *Zillah* are no longer as evident to us as they would have been to Poe's readers.

II

Just what Poe's original intents as regards the five tales published in the *Saturday Courier* may have been remains unclear. Because he recognized in the Gothic tale and other popular fictional forms of his day ready targets for satire and parody, he undertook a project in which humor and horror often intertwined, a contemplated book to be called "Tales of the Folio Club." The Folio Club membership included caricatures of popular authors, mostly writers of fiction, who met one evening a month, beginning the event with ample (alcoholic) drink and much good food. Gluttony and intoxication often resulted, such that by the time each tale was read and debate over its merits and demerits ensued, the critical abilities of those assembled were muddled. Part of Poe's plan was to lampoon not just popular fiction and its authors, but also the state of literary criticism as it then existed. The reader of each tale doubled as the narrator-protagonist, each evincing takeoffs of the personal characteristics and literary methods of the actual writer being mimed. Differences in opinions concerning who was to have presented a particular tale continue to be debated by scholars.[7]

Had "Tales of the Folio Club" been published, Poe may well have been credited for creating a frame narrative book comparable with *Tales of a Traveller*, *The Country of the Pointed Firs*, *Winesburg, Ohio*, to name a few among many cycles/sequences of short fiction, or, for that matter, in verse, *Idylls of the King*, *Modern Love*, or the *Spoon River Anthology*. Poe's experimental book never saw print, however, because his subtle humor, evaluators reported, would baffle average readers, thereby putting sales at risk. Poe may have revised his earlier tales to fit within the Folio Club frame, to which he added others besides the *Saturday Courier* submissions. Another Folio Club tale, "MS. Found in a Bottle," won the prize for the best prose story in another contest, sponsored by the Baltimore *Saturday Visiter*. Poe actually submitted several stories, assembled into booklet form, so the judges had difficulties in choosing because all the tales seemed equally fine. "MS Found" may have had greater timely appeal because Baltimore at the time was a far more important port city than it is today.[8]

The bizarre situations, the overwrought characters, and the hyperbolic language in these early stories may have been perfect features in stories presumably read by authors who had eaten and imbibed too freely. Such an aura might also have made "Metzengerstein" appear in context as an altogether splendid accomplishment – its evident "German" features appealing to the befuddled audience listening to its author reading. Poe at one point stated that the critical debates concerning each tale were intended as a hit at the pretensions of contemporary literary criticism, and thus the typical Gothic qualities evident on the surfaces of the tale might have met with critical commendation. The overfed and intoxicated audience might, of course, have differed markedly in their evaluations of this and other equally fantastic stories. For example, "The Visionary" (the original title of the story more commonly known as "The Assignation"), might well have stirred controversy because of the mysterious Byronic lover. The varied biographical accounts of Lord Byron that had been appearing since his death not quite a decade before Poe's story was published, brought forth divergent opinions, and "The Assignation" presents an imaginative conclusion to the Byronic character's life that is far more sensational than Lord Byron's inglorious death. This story may also be read as a drunkard's narrative, where the suspenseful events, the strange actions of the characters, and the extravagant language may reasonably hint at an intoxicated narrator. A like technique enriches the characterization of Montresor in "The Cask of Amontillado." Fortunato may not be the sole drunkard in that story.

III

"Tales of the Folio Club" finding no publisher, Poe dismantled the book, circulated individual tales in literary periodicals and annuals, and thereby created puzzlement for many readers. Some sensed that there were comic aspects underlying certain stories, e.g., "Loss of Breath," "Bon-Bon"; others singled out the "German" elements for censure. Such divergences continue among Poe scholars even today. Nevertheless, Poe's literary hoaxes have gained widespread recognition of their superb artistry.[9] Just as significant, Poe divined that he could create stories in which the eerie situations, bizarre characters and hyperbolic language emanate from the most genuine source of terror, the human mind, instead of from drunken, gluttonous characters spouting what may seem to be nonsensical dialogue. Consequently, his later stories often evince a greater seriousness than many of the earlier stories do, albeit some of these later pieces are not without enhancing comic touches.

At the same time as Poe's stories began to shift from obvious comedy to greater psychological depth, Poe the critic began to offer principles for effective short fiction. Earlier, he stated that a long poem is a contradiction in terms. Subsequently, and in line with his emphasis on unified effect or impression's being essential to genuine literary art – what a reader can comprehend within a single sitting, to last no longer than an hour-and-a-half – he contended that the short story often allowed greater opportunities than a novel (or even a poem) allowed for creating great literature. Simply stated, engagement with a novel could not be completed within Poe's ideal time span, and the interruptions between readings negated unity of effect.

Poe's concept of the short story, or "tale," as he preferred (as superior to the novel), was early articulated in his review of Dickens's *Watkins Tottle and other Sketches* (*Southern Literary Messenger* June 1836, a volume of reprinted short pieces; *E&R* 205). In three reviews of Hawthorne's short fiction, respectively in *Graham's Magazine* (April 1842; *E&R* 568–9), *Graham's Magazine* (May 1842; *E&R*: 569–76) and *Godey's Lady's Book* (November 1847; *E&R* 577–88), Poe most succinctly set forth his commendation of the short story as a form which at times manifests "superiority over the poem" (*E&R* 568) – high praise indeed from Poe. So his theories of poetry and fiction were almost indistinguishable. He also commented that, implicitly, what distinguishes creative from informational writing are the undercurrents of suggestion or meaning (i.e., symbolic art) in the former. He deplored too obvious allegory in literature, however, and so his own stories, e.g., "The Fall of the House of Usher" or "The Masque of the Red Death," embody more subtle allegorical features. As for his tales of terror in general, he responded to critics who objected to this type of fiction in the "Preface" to *Tales of the Grotesque and Arabesque*: "If in many of my productions terror has been the thesis, I maintain that terror is not of Germany but of the soul, – that I have deduced this terror only from its legitimate sources, and urged it only to its legitimate results" (*CW* 2. 473).

One might understandably suspect that Poe's advocacy of the lyric poem and the short story as the greatest forms of literary art dovetailed naturally with the literary genres in which he excelled. Conversely, one may justly argue that Poe commanded a sound understanding of psychology, thus realizing the brevity or fragility in the average human attention span. So much, then, for Poe the hack writer that his detractors propose. We should also recall that although he championed brevity in creative writing, Poe could sensibly evaluate the merits and demerits in longer works, as his critiques of many novels attest. In most of these evaluations he does not bear down heavily on length qua length, for example, in his review of Dickens's *Barnaby Rudge* or in the critiques of novels by Edward Bulwer-Lytton. A notable exception, in which Poe's opinion of length is severe, appears in the review of Theodore Sedgwick Fay's tedious novel, *Norman Leslie* (1835). Poe's antipathy toward the repetitions in this book is evident, not to mention what could be considered Fay's own narrow vocabulary. Overall, Poe's concept of plot (i.e., unity) reveals Aristotelian influence (Jacobs 250–2).

IV

Although unity of effect is evident throughout Poe's seventy-plus stories, we might attend in greater detail to one that most emphatically displays his theories in practice, namely, "The Fall of the House of Usher." This story has long and deservedly been recognized as one of Poe's very greatest achievements in short-story writing, despite his own reiterated championing of "Ligeia" as his best fiction. At the level of surface plot, we encounter in "The Fall of the House of Usher" a story enlivened by Gothic tropes. A haunted house, a naïve narrator, a domineering villain who is also a relative of the person he wishes to destroy, mysterious occurrences that culminate in the return of a ghostly character and the collapse of the house, the harried narrator managing to escape so he can relate the frightening events to readers. If we recognize that surface characteristics and undercurrents of suggestion contribute strongly to a symbolic unity, then Poe's art in this story is unquestionable.

Here the narrator is the genuine central character, not Roderick Usher, as casual readers sometimes believe. Of course, since the narrator and Roderick have been longtime friends, and since Roderick and Madeline are closely bonded, what the narrator beholds in the others represents his own life/self. Poe deftly manipulates Gothic conventions to create a plausible psychological story in which the unified effect is that of unrest mounting inexorably to fear. The haunted house of Usher represents the warped mindset and likely the physical deterioration of the narrator. That he and Roderick have been close friends since childhood, and that he cannot choose but heed Usher's plea that they meet again, implies that whatever informs Usher and the house (literal and symbolic) likewise affects him. Thus his journey to the Usher mansion, through a "singularly dreary tract of country," which affects him with claustrophobia (*CW* 2. 397), represents a journey through his own depression toward its underlying causes.

Arriving at the Usher home, the narrator's depression becomes more uneasy when he looks up and sees the weird appearance of the mansion. The building resembles a debilitated human head, replete with windows that resemble ineffectual eyes (and vision otherwise), a crack coursing through the middle of the structure, fungi that overspread the stone walls, and that look like unkempt human hair. When his gaze descends to the inverted vision of the house in the tarn he becomes even more unsettled – because he also sees a mirror image of his own head, which, we comprehend, resembles the Usher "head" (the mansion and what it suggests) reflected in the tarn. That he does not forthrightly relate this correspondence further hints at his own reluctance to have us comprehend directly his own nature. The narrator's emotional deterioration (perhaps with accompanying physical degeneration), which resembles that of Roderick, is thus well established at the outset of the story, and his emotional downward spiral culminates in destruction brought about by fractures in the physical-emotional self. The men's psychosomatic disorders produce unpleasant consequences since Roderick and his friend are doubles of each other in this story of mirroring.

After giving us sufficient information to comprehend his fragile mental condition, the narrator's entry into the Usher mansion – through a portal that looks like a devouring human mouth – symbolizes his delving into the interior of his own being. Although he would have us believe that he is psychically and physically sound, as compared with Roderick, we soon divine that he is no more stable than his friend, or that if he is when he arrives at the House of Usher he quickly succumbs to torments akin to those bedeviling Roderick. The subsequent yielding to fear propels Roderick to literal death. Just so, the narrator's kindred downward spiral culminates in what could be organic and emotional death brought about by fractures in the physical-emotional self – not a pleasant destiny. "The Fall of the House of Usher" unfolds a classic case of emotional stress producing debilitating physical symptoms. Inside the House of Usher the narrator beholds a symbolic drama in which Roderick and Madeline's circumstances represent those in his own psycho-physical makeup.

The Ushers' names are richly symbolic of the narrator's plight. To readers in Poe's day a literary character named Roderick would immediately have recalled Roderick, the last great Spanish Visigoth king, a tragic figure whose overthrow, which may have involved his seduction of the daughter of Count Julian, who consequently became his enemy, furnished subject matter for the British Romantic poets, Robert Southey and Sir Walter Scott. Poe's Roderick is also presumably the leader of his domain, though the unsound domain-house of the Ushers verges on collapse. The collapse in Poe's tale is brought about because Roderick Usher attempts to overwhelm his twin (the feminine component in what should be an integrated, harmonious self), eschewing what she represents, to focus instead upon his artistic endeavors. The distortions evident in his music (dirges), painting (a tomb), and poetry (madness destroys a once lovely house and its inhabitants) indicate how skewed such a dislocation becomes. Clearly, Roderick has paved the way for his own illness and death. His perverse course has led also to Madeline's circumstances.

Poe carefully named the Usher twins, and just as Roderick's name indicates destruction, Madeline's resonates with related significances – their relationship is not so close-knit for nothing. The name "Madeline" derives from that of biblical Mary Magdalene; it may also mean "lady of the house" or "tower of strength."[10] Whatever her true nature may have been, Mary Magdalene became associated in folklore with sexual promiscuity. Some readers of Poe's story believe that the downfall of the Ushers results from brother–sister incest, though the text does not provide convincing evidence that incest occurred. Madeline is undeniably the lady of the House of Usher; therefore, the bizarre qualities she seems to possess are in perfect keeping with those in her surroundings. Her escape from her sealed coffin and imprisoning cellar necessitate immense strength, an oddity because of her thoroughly debilitated physical appearance.

In addition to implications in her name, Madeline's role is linked with Roderick's in another way, though Poe was not heavy-handed in establishing this connection. To palliate Roderick's paranoia, the narrator and he read from some of the hypochondriac's favorite books. Most are treatises on the interrelationships bonding animal and vegetable life (therefore recalling the combination of the Usher mansion resembling a human head overspread with hair-like fungi). Gresset's works, poems, treat in *Ververt* the comic adventures of a talking parrot, and *La Chartreuse* is another comic work, though some readers perceive mystical treatment of human frailty in this book (*CW* 2. 419 n.16). The humorous intent in Gresset's text should alert us that appearances may be deceptive in the House of Usher, as indeed they prove to be. The last title mentioned, as a particular favorite of Roderick's, the *Vigiliae* ..., was long thought to be bogus, but in the early 1960s copies of the actual book were discovered in European libraries. This mass for the dead from the second church in Mainz, Germany (1500), could be used to ward off vampires. Poe fashioned Madeline Usher as a vampire figure who was as terrifying as vampires in literary texts typically are, and who was also terrifying because of what her circumstances suggest in the psychological-physical-sexual theme in the story (Bailey, "What Happens"; Mabbott, "The Books" v).

The narrator and Roderick represent the masculine element in the self, Madeline the feminine. Very simply stated, Roderick and the narrator attempt to repress (bury)

what Madeline symbolizes. That is, they abrogate the earthy and also the creative
strengths in the self, preferring to repress or "bury" those qualities. Consequently,
lacking a dynamic creativity, Roderick can fashion in his artistic productions only
grotesque, frightening results, all suggestive of the imbalance and accompanying
decay in the house. Roderick and Madeline share a soul with their literal and figurative house, and that bonding extends to encompass the narrator, all rapidly degenerat-
ing because of repression. Madeline as vampire figure is equally appropriate in this
construct. According to longstanding folklore, vampires are possessed of great strength,
are also sexually rampant but cannot love, and seek their first victims from among
family members and loved ones. To some extent, Madeline partakes of these characteristics, albeit what had been great love for her brother ultimately transforms into a
(to him) horrifying rebounding force because of his attempts to repress what she could
contribute to maintain health in the self. Roderick's and the narrator's repression of
psycho-sexual impulses rebounds upon them, first, with depression. Depression in
turn blunts any normal attempt to regain dynamic life, so fears mount, eventually to
explosive levels. No wonder, then, that Madeline's horrifying return is depicted with
an aura of vampirism. The repressed will make itself known, but in overpowering
ways, and the realization of such overwhelming force occasioned by release from confinement makes the fear of the repressor(s) unbearable.

Roderick's recognition of these possibilities, combined with his great, if warped,
affection for his sister, motivate his attempted burial of Madeline in the sub-cellar
of the mansion. This act symbolizes his desire to bury, or repress (but not actually
kill), all that she represents, namely creativity in artistic and physical (reproductive)
ventures. By means of this fracturing of what otherwise might be a balance of the
psychical and physical in the self, in which masculine and feminine presences live
harmoniously to promote life, Roderick releases death-dealing forces. His reluctance
to bury Madeline in the distant family graveyard may be a wish to prevent the doctor
from exhuming her body and learning the true nature of her malady – a "malady" in
Roderick's estimation because of the evil or threat, to him, that she represents. The
family doctor, significantly, exits the mansion. Implicitly, his leaving signals a departure of the realism and objectivity commonly associated with science. Along with his
vanishing from the scene goes what in different situations would be healthy life. Of
course, the narrator's imputing negative characteristics to the doctor may result from
his own anxiety that the doctor, were he to revisit, could diagnose his, the narrator's,
own imperfect condition.

Other significant departures reflect the narrator's decaying stability and that of the
Ushers, who represent aspects of his being. The narrator's horse and all the commonplaces that it called up in nineteenth-century life – everyday transportation, great
intelligence, and strong sexual impulses (folk themes of widespread circulation) –
likewise fittingly disappear. So do the servants. Ultimately, everyday life no longer
obtains for the characters or the house that resembles them, and vice versa. No wonder,
then, that Roderick and the narrator both succumb to the fear of fear itself, which
Roderick thinks will lead to his death. Although the narrator suffers no literal death,

his sojourn in the "mansion of Gloom" so works upon him that, like Coleridge's ancient mariner, he ultimately cannot choose but to retell the story, employing Gothic tropes as outward manifestations of emotional turmoil. This narrator beholds what seems to be his own plight in terms of emotional, physical, and sexual health, and the vision is so bleak as to inspire terror and flight. The same sense of death that hovers about the Usher twins overtakes the narrator, who in chronicling the terrifying events in the House of Usher provides a warning against the dangers of repressing creative impulses – save, for him, that of storytelling.

At the same time that "The Fall of the House of Usher" was in process, Poe was preparing an edition of his stories for hardcover publication. In the preface to that collection, *Tales of the Grotesque and Arabesque*, published in late 1839 but dated 1840, Poe responded to those readers who deplored his "German" (Gothic) stories rife with atmospheres of terror: "I maintain that terror is not of Germany, but of the soul – that I have deduced this terror only from its legitimate sources, and urged it only to its legitimate results" (*CW* 2. 473). In "The Fall of the House of Usher" and Poe's other tales of genuine terror, this intent to treat genuine origins and results of terror, as tersely stated, is uppermost, no matter the varied implications readers discern. One should keep in mind that "soul" may be equated with "psyche." Both are everyday synonyms for the human mind, but in classical mythology Psyche was a winged female figure with a lamp, whose function as a nurturer of creativity is carried over into the symbolism of several of Poe's poems and stories. In "The Fall of the House of Usher" Madeline-as-Psyche is frustrated from nurturing her twin's artistic impulses, perhaps also fostering his sexuality though not engaging in actual sex with him.

Roderick's perverse interference with what should be natural impulses hinders him from creating artistic or other life, and so the Usher line must cease to be. Unity between masculinity and femininity, deriving for Poe perhaps from biblical and classical sources, is broken, thereby creating ennui and, later, terror within the narrator, whose own state of being is at one with that of the Usher siblings. In this respect "The Fall of the House of Usher" adumbrates much that we find in postmodern literature and culture, where fragmentation of the self is a paramount motif, one that carries along Poe's conception of terror of the soul producing overwhelming effects. Therefore, in all respects this story is undoubtedly one of Poe's greatest successes as a writer of short stories. The richly symbolic texture demonstrates his championed unity of effect. There is also well-wrought allegory in evidence, albeit the allegory is not so heavy-handed as to be readily perceived, in Poe's mind a great defect. Poe's handling of allegory is also consistent with his theories of the short story (*E&R* 582–834), just as it is with his concept of undercurrents of suggestion or meaning as features in a first-rate story (*E&R* 571).

Those undercurrents are unavoidable elements in "The Fall of the House of Usher," and they provide the literary art in that story. In this piece Poe manipulated conventions of literary Gothicism so as to create excellent psychological fiction. His probing of issues that continue to be important to us – interactions between the sexes, sexuality, the family, artistic creativity – reveal how fraught with ambiguities human nature may be. Poe's adapting of the haunted castle from antecedent Gothic fiction, as well as the stereotypical inhabitants of such a house, impart a new and energetic life to literary Gothicism. That dynamic is wholly consistent with Poe's own conception of the greatest in short-story art, albeit the traditional atmosphere of suspense and mounting fear, which bring about emotional and physical destruction, is ever-present. Although some of the features of the Gothic that I have listed above appear frequently throughout the canon of Poe's stories (as well as in his poetry and in his novel, *The Narrative of Arthur Gordon Pym*), they seem to be exceptionally abundant and artistically integrated in "The Fall of the House of Usher."[11] This story, then, may stand as a thoroughly representative short story by Poe, as well as a work of subtle symbolic achievement. This latter quality has continued to serve as the mainstay in many other American short stories and indeed in short stories in any national or ethnic literature.

NOTES

1 Contemporaneous responses to Poe's early stories, in which he was rebuked for too much that seemed "German," or horrible, may be found in Thomas and Jackson, *The Poe Log*, 140, 156, 182–3, 270, 272, 276. See also Fisher, *The Gothic's Gothic*, 345–56, concerning the pervasiveness of "German" substance in Anglo-American literary works during the first half of the nineteenth century. Continuing deprecation of Poe's Gothicism appears, for example, in Willard, "For Young Readers," 30; and in the "Introduction" to Bloom, *Edgar Allan Poe*, 1–14.

2 A contradictory, though conjectural, hypothesis by Richard P. Benton – that "Tarr and Fether" was composed far earlier than the mid-1840s, and then permitted to rest for some years before it was revised and published – has never been confirmed. See "Poe's 'The System of Dr. Tarr and Prof. Fether': Dickens or Willis?"

3 Mabbott, ed. *Collected Works of Edgar Allan Poe* 2. 83, suggests that "The Bargain Lost," which, revised, became the more familiar "Bon-Bon," may have been composed earlier than the other *Courier* stories. Hereinafter, the Mabbott edition will be cited parenthetically within my text as *CW*. All citations to/quotations from Poe's poems and short fiction are to this edition. For Poe's critical writings I cite Thompson, ed. *Edgar Allan Poe: Essays and Reviews*; hereinafter

cited parenthetically within my text as *E&R*.

4 Woolf, "Prostitutes, Paris and Poe."

5 See Fisher, "Blackwood Articles à la Poe." Notable exceptions to those who overlook Gothic antecedents for detective fiction are Murch, *The Development of the Detective Novel*, 27–36; and Greene, *John Dickson Carr*, 97–8, 109. Many of Carr's detective novels reveal links with earlier Gothic works, several specifically with Poe's stories.

6 Bonaparte, *The Life and Works of Edgar Allan Poe*, 373–410. Bonaparte also suggests that Poe himself may have been impotent, and that this story is autobiographical. See also Hoffman, *PoePoePoePoePoePoePoe*, 244–5.

7 Long ago, Mabbott stated that his own identifications were speculative – "On Poe's 'Tales of the Folio Club.'" Cf. Hammond, "A Reconstruction of Poe's 1833 *Tales of the Folio Club*"; "Further Notes on Poe's Folio Club Tales"; and "Edgar Allan Poe's *Tales of the Folio Club*: The Evolution of a Lost Book."

8 John H. B. Latrobe, one of the judges for the *Saturday Visiter* competition, recalled many years afterward, and probably inaccurately, that "A Descent into the Maelström" was among the submissions to the *Visiter* competition. See "Reminiscences of Poe," 59. See also Fisher, *The Very Spirit of Cordiality*, 3, 5–6, 19–22.

9 An early negative opinion of Poe's humor appears in Boyd, "Edgar Allan Poe." As late as 1969 Poe's comic tales were deemed "rather regrettable efforts," by Michael Allen in *Poe and the British Magazine Tradition*, 142. That Poe's humor serves more sophisticated artistic purposes is the argument in Benton, "Some Remarks on Poe and His Critics," ii, vi, x; Eddings, *The Naiad Voice*; Ljungquist, "Prospects for the Study of Edgar Allan Poe," 178, 180–2; and Lamb, "The Flight of the Raven."

10 Poe revised his original version of "Usher" so that Roderick and Madeline were no longer identical twins, such being a scientific impossibility (*CW* 2. 404). The significance of the Ushers' names is noted in Mabbott's "Poe's Vaults," 542–3.

11 This story may also admit of comic-ironic readings; see Thompson, *Poe's Fiction*, 87–97; and Fisher, "Playful Germanism in 'The Fall of the House of Usher.'"

REFERENCES AND FURTHER READING

Allen, Michael. *Poe and the British Magazine Tradition*. New York: Oxford University Press, 1969.

Bailey, J. O. "What Happens in 'The Fall of the House of Usher.'" *American Literature* 35 (January 1964): 445–66.

Benton, Richard P. "Poe's 'The System of Dr. Tarr and Prof. Fether': Dickens or Willis?" *Poe Newsletter* 1 (1968): 7–9.

———. "Some Remarks on Poe and His Critics." *University of Mississippi Studies in English* n.s. 3 (1982): i–xii.

Bloom, Harold, ed. *Edgar Allan Poe: Modern Critical Views*. New York: Chelsea House, 1984.

Bonaparte, Marie. *The Life and Works of Edgar Allan Poe: A Psycho-Analytic Interpretation*. Trans. John Rodker. London: Imago, 1949.

Boyd, A. K. H. "Edgar Allan Poe." *Fraser's Magazine* 55 (June 1857): 684–700.

Eddings, Dennis W., ed. *The Naiad Voice: Essays on Poe's Satiric Hoaxing*. Port Washington: Associate Faculty Press, 1983.

Fisher, Benjamin F. "Blackwood Articles à la Poe: How to Make a False Start Pay." *Revue des Langues Vivantes* 39 (1973): 418–32. Rev. rpt., *Perspectives on Poe*. Ed. D. Ramakrishna. New Delhi: ABC Publications, 1996. 63–82.

———. *The Gothic's Gothic: Study Aids to the Tradition of the Tale of Terror*. New York: Garland, 1988.

———. Playful Germanism in 'The Fall of the House of Usher': The Storyteller's Art." *Ruined Eden of the Present. Hawthorne, Melville, and Poe: Critical Essays in Honor of Darrel Abel*. Eds. G. R. Thompson and Virgil L. Lokke. West Lafayette, IN: Purdue University Press, 1981. 355–74.

———. *The Very Spirit of Cordiality: The Literary Uses of Alcohol and Alcoholism in the Tales of Edgar Allan Poe*. Baltimore: Enoch Pratt Free Library and the Edgar Allan Poe Society of Baltimore, 1978.

Greene, Douglas G. *John Dickson Carr: The Man Who Explained Miracles*. New York: Otto Penzler, 1995.

Hammond, Alexander. "Edgar Allan Poe's Tales of the Folio Club: The Evolution of a Lost Book." *Poe at Work: Seven Textual Studies*. Ed. Benjamin F. Fisher. Baltimore: Edgar Allan Poe Society, 1978. 13–43.

———. "Further Notes on Poe's Folio Club Tales." *Poe Studies* 8 (1975): 38–42.

———. "A Reconstruction of Poe's 1833 Tales of the Folio Club: Preliminary Notes." *Poe Studies* 5 (1972): 25–32.

Hoffman, Daniel. *PoePoePoePoePoePoePoe*. Garden City, NY: Doubleday, 1972.

Jacobs, Robert D. *Poe: Journalist and Critic*. Baton Rouge: Louisiana State University Press, 1969.

Jones, Howard Mumford. *Ideas in America*. Cambridge, MA: Harvard University Press, 1944.

Lamb, Robert Paul. "The Flight of the Raven: A Retrospective on the Scholarship of G. R. Thompson." *Poe Studies/Dark Romanticism* 39–40 (2006–7): 1–4.

Latrobe, John H. B. "Reminiscences of Poe." *Edgar Allan Poe: A Memorial Volume*. Ed. Sara Sigourney Rice. Baltimore: Turnbull Brothers, 1877.

Ljungquist, Kent P. "Prospects for the Study of Edgar Allan Poe." *Resources for American Literary Study* 21 (1995): 173–88.

Mabbott, Thomas Ollive, ed. *The Collected Works of Edgar Allan Poe*, vol. 2. Cambridge, MA: Belknap Press of Harvard University Press. 1978.

——. "Introduction." *The Collected Works of Edgar Allan Poe*, vol. 2. Ed. Thomas Ollive Mabbott, with the assistance of Eleanor D. Kewer and Maureen Cobb Mabbott. Cambridge, MA: Belknap Press of Harvard University Press. 1978.

——. "On Poe's 'Tales of the Folio Club.'" *Sewanee Review* 36 (1928): 171–6.

——. "Poe's Vaults." *Notes & Queries* 98 (December 1953): 542–3.

——. "The Books in the House of Usher." *Books at Iowa* 19 (November 1973): 3–7, 17.

Murch, Alma E. *The Development of the Detective Novel*. Rev. edn. London: Peter Owen, 1968.

Spiller, Robert E. "The Task of the Historian of American Literature." *Sewanee Review* 42 (1935): 70–7.

Thomas, Dwight, and David K. Jackson. *The Poe Log: A Documentary Life of Edgar Allan Poe 1809–1849*. Boston: G. K. Hall, 1987.

Thompson, G. R. *Poe's Fiction: Romantic Irony in the Gothic Tales*. Madison: University of Wisconsin Press, 1973.

Thompson, G. R., ed. *Edgar Allan Poe: Essays and Reviews*. New York: New American Library, 1984.

Willard, Nancy. "For Young Readers." *New York Times Book Review* (3 October 1976): 30.

Woolf, Paul. "Prostitutes, Paris and Poe: The Sexual Economy of Edgar Allan Poe's 'The Murders in the Rue Morgue.'" *Clues: A Journal of Detection* 25 (2006): 6–19.

3
A Guide to Melville's "Bartleby, the Scrivener"

Steven T. Ryan

Let's begin with possibly the best dash in American literature:

> I seldom lose my temper; much more seldom indulge in dangerous indignation at wrongs and outrages; but I must be permitted to be rash here and declare, that I consider the sudden and violent abrogation of the office of Master in Chancery, by the new Constitution, as a – premature act; inasmuch as I had counted upon a life-lease of the profits, whereas I only received those of a few short years. But this is by the way. (Melville, "Bartleby" 636)

This passage is best read aloud with crescendo until the abrupt cessation at the dash, breaking with the calm, modest suggestion of a "premature act." At this early moment in the story, Melville allows his lawyer-narrator to digress, but it certainly is no arbitrary digression by either Melville or his narrator. For the narrator, it is an irresistible digression, a side road he cannot avoid any time he ventures near the topic of the lost position. For Melville it is the early moment in which he reveals the internal battle that bubbles within this rather ordinary businessman. It is equally important that the narrator nearly loses his temper and that he does not do so. A man whose pride is based upon his "prudence" and "method" (636) cannot permit rage to take control. Yet from this moment we know his self-image is contradicted by a more complex and more conflicted personality than he is willing to accept. We also have our first clue as to what will propel him into a highly emotive state which he finds repugnant in himself and in others: he cannot tolerate losing something he "counted upon" (regularity) and hates to lose money (materialism). Throughout the story, these two factors are intertwined within the narrator's psyche. Both have to do with a sense of security based upon the object world but not upon object relationships, for the narrator is both a social man and a solitary man – social in the sense of his dependency upon a social system and wealth and solitary in the sense that he actually has no one and has nothing but the social construct of his office. He stands as Melville's accomplished man even if his accomplishments ring hollow.

Appreciation for Melville's "Bartleby, the Scrivener: A Story of Wall-Street" requires an appreciation for the narrator. This is the central reversal within the story. What is presented as a study of the title character is actually a study of the justifiably unnamed narrator. Assume for a moment that we are among the first readers of the story within the two 1853 installments of *Putnam's Monthly Magazine*, each appearing without authorial credit. The first installment in particular gives us the voice of an amiable gentleman commonly associated with the sketch writing of authors like Washington Irving and Nathaniel Hawthorne. R. Bruce Bickley, Jr., makes this association when he calls the narrator "a Crayonesque sketcher" (Bickley 29). The subtitle, "A Story of Wall-Street," does not necessarily shift our genre paradigm from sketch to story. The story opens as a leisurely invitation into the comfortable world of the narrator. As is common in sketch writing, the narrator is congenial and wants us to share his worldly experience. He suggests that he could entertain us with the accounts of any number of scriveners whom we would find "interesting and somewhat singular" but that instead he will opt to give us what he can of the "strangest" ("Bartleby" 635). When he then continues at a casual pace through the introduction of himself, his office, and his other employees, we, if among the original readers, would have to associate this leisurely pace more with the easy gait of sketch writing than the intensity of either sentimental or Gothic stories. The narrative voice of nineteenth-century sketch writing offers a sharp contrast to Poe's finest stories. Whimsy rules – we sense that the narrative sharing of life experiences may be enjoyed as long as we sit back and spend our time with a narrator who is refined, unpretentious, and worldly. In American literature the voice associates with Ben Franklin and Irving, but actually it dates back to the stylistic ease and syntactical purity of Addison and Steele. The narrator's introduction of himself constitutes an attempt to conform to the bemused persona of sketch writing. This is suggested by his self-portrait as an "unambitious lawyer," comfortable in "the cool tranquility of a snug retreat" (635).

Of course, the dash undermines his attempt to sell himself as the quintessence of ease and self-containment. He would like us to believe that we are sharing a highly civil and relaxed examination of a curiosity. This assumption is gradually subverted by our realization that the narrator is a haunted man. Just as he is compelled to fume over the lost Master of Chancery position, he also is compelled to recount the story of Bartleby, even if he has limited information and limited insight to help the reader plummet the depth of Bartleby's mystery. The narrator is in fact incapable of the wit commonly associated with the sketch writer. The wit of Melville passes through the narrator without the character's awareness. The importance of understanding the narrator cannot be overstressed. In the history of the short story, the characterization has more in common with Flaubert's later accomplishment with Félicité in "A Simple Heart" than with character portrayal within either the neoclassical or romantic conventions. Melville and Flaubert achieve their more complex characterizations similarly by teasing their readers with the potential of both satire and sentimentality but resisting the simplification inherent in either direction. On different occasions Melville's reader may laugh at the narrator's rationalization and smug self-assurance or may be touched by his fundamental humanity. The crucial check to the reader's sense of superiority is the aching realization that we would be unlikely to do any better in dealing with Bartleby.

The Lawyer-Narrator

Critical arguments are common in reactions to the narrator and typically hinge upon the extent to which we either detach from him or identify with his frustrations. A good reading of the story requires an appreciation of his central position but does not require agreement as to whether he is closer to a satiric or a sentimental portrait. Melville does undermine his authority, but also permits the narrator as much humanity as we are likely to find in an employer. Consider, for example, the narrator's name-dropping as he points out that he worked for John Jacob Astor, who complimented his "prudence" and "method." The narrator admits that he loves to repeat the name "for it hath a rounded and orbicular sound to it, and rings like unto bullion" (636). The simile is the narrator's momentary poetic flourish and works well to express a love of sound. Then we realize that the simile is also dependent upon the assumption that the ring of bullion is a good sound for reasons that go well beyond the pure love of sound (as is the love of the musical name "John Jacob Astor"). Thus Melville takes us into the narrator's values simply through the choice of vehicle. Like his struggle to contain his temper, the narrator tries to disguise his love of wealth beneath his "unambitious" demeanor. Again, this does not reflect hypocrisy but rather the more common contrast between self-definitions and a larger, more complex reality that lies beneath.

Two important characteristics of the narrator are: (1) his defense of his own domain, and (2) his desire to rely upon a simplistic materialism in interpreting reality. These two are closely aligned, for it is in defense of his domain that his simplistic materialism often appears. We must first note how the narrator couches his professional choices in language that never suggests that such things as timidity and greed play any role in addition to his lack of vanity and his equanimity. His slanting becomes more extreme when he dismisses the "landscape painters" who would find his office deficient in "life" (636) and brags of the wall within ten feet of his windows, "black by age and everlasting shade" as "requiring no spy-glass to bring out its lurking beauties" (wit credited to Melville, not the straight-shooting narrator).

His early description of Turkey and Nippers, as will be true of his central treatment of Bartleby, reveals as much about the narrator and his world as about his employees. For example, note the description of Turkey's disruptive behavior in the afternoon as he "made an unpleasant racket with his chair; spilled his sand-box; in mending his pens, impatiently split them all to pieces, and threw them on the floor in a sudden passion; stood up and leaned over his table, boxing his papers about in a most indecorous manner" (637). Now note the similarity to Nippers's disruptive behavior in the morning:

Nippers could never get his table to suit him. He put chips under it, blocks of various sorts, bits of pasteboard, and at last went so far as to attempt an exquisite adjustment by final pieces of folded plotting paper. But no invention would answer. If, for the sake of easing his back, he brought the table lid at a sharp angle well up towards his chin, and wrote there like a man using the steep roof of a Dutch house for his desk: – then he declared that it stopped the circulation in his arms. If now he lowered the table to his waistbands, and stooped over it in writing, then there was a sore aching in his back. In short, the truth of the matter was, Nippers knew not what he wanted. Or, if he wanted any thing, it was to be rid of a scrivener's table altogether. (639)

Rid of the scrivener's table indeed. The similar discomfort and irritation reflected in both descriptions would suggest that the behavior has *something* to do with the work itself. If Turkey could actually afford to become a half-time employee, the narrator's recommendation that he reduce to such employment would make good sense, but the lawyer drops several clues as to the low pay of the scriveners, like his reference to "so small an income" (640). The long hours are suggested by the long days of Bartleby's diligent performance: "He ran a day and night line, copying by sunlight and by candle-light" (642). One may safely conclude that Turkey and Nippers often find these long hours of tedious copying within this stark setting unbearable. It's not surprising that the body and mind rebel in either the morning or afternoon.

However, the analysis of the narrator avoids this obvious interpretation. He considers the age and drinking habits of Turkey, then goes into greater detail in analyzing the "ambition and indigestion" of Nippers (638). In each case we are encouraged to believe that the weakness lies within the man's constitution. This is preparation for the narrator's attempt to interpret the odd behavior of Bartleby. The most striking moment occurs after Bartleby tells the narrator that "he had decided upon doing no more writing" (656). At this moment Bartleby is again in his "dead-wall revery" (656). The narrator is shocked and asks for a reason, to which Bartleby responds, "Do you not see the reason for yourself?" (656). The narrator's reaction is to look "steadfastly" at Bartleby (656). It is at this point that the narrator judges that the eyes are "dull and glazed" and concludes that Bartleby's "unexampled diligence in copying by his window for the first few weeks" has "temporarily impaired his vision" (656). The narrator is "touched" and concludes that Bartleby *should* abstain from writing (656). The narrator's response is an excellent example of how Melville gives the man his due while more quietly suggesting an undeniable level of obtuseness. What the narrator observes and his response to it are logical and humane. He's an employer who can see his employee as more than a machine and can even appreciate the difficulty of the work and potential damage incurred. At the same time, how very strange that the narrator reacts to the question, "Do you not see the reason for yourself?" by looking at Bartleby rather than where Bartleby is looking. *If* he were to look at the wall, the next question would have to be, "What do you see in that wall, Bartleby?" The narrator will never ask such a question because he will never go so far in sharing Bartleby's vision. Whatever Bartleby sees is more metaphysical than physical, and despite the lawyer's convenient, momentary ruminations on Jonathan Edwards and Joseph

Priestley – on will and necessity – he senses at some level the metaphysical risk and prefers not to plummet. In addition, whatever Bartleby sees is clearly too close to home; it implicates the narrator's own world in ways that extend well beyond a temporary impairment of physical vision. After all, the narrator truly is "an eminently *safe* man" (635). When he examines the weaknesses of Turkey and Nippers, he is telling us with some accuracy what he can see. While Melville is not contradicting him, he is inviting us to consider how carefully the narrator avoids implicating his own world and his own life in a way that may go well beyond "temporarily impairing" our vision.

In 1953 Leo Marx published the first in-depth analysis of "Bartleby," and his article has remained one of the most respected and quoted essays on the story. He builds upon the autobiographical connection between author and text which had been suggested since the 1920s Melville revival, but he offers a more extensive and perceptive analysis. He also takes a position that establishes a central debate in regard to the portrayal of the narrator. In the conclusion of his essay, Marx argues that on the one hand the narrator "does not understand Bartleby then or at any point until their difficult relationship ends" (Marx 606), yet, in the end, Marx sees the blades of grass mysteriously located in the Tombs as affirmation associated with the narrator's "deeply felt and spontaneous sympathy" (626). While Marx is well aware of the limitations of the narrator, noting that "Wall Street was American" (618) and that "the difference between Wall Street and the Tombs was an illusion of the lawyer's, not Bartleby's" (618), his final movement is to shift responsibility toward Bartleby as writer, noting that "Melville does not exonerate the writer by placing all the onus upon society" (620). While "Bartleby's state of mind may be understood as a response to the hostile world of Wall Street" (619), Marx sees Bartleby as Melville's "compassionate rebuke to the self-absorption of the artist" who rejects the bonds of mankind (620) and errs in his interpretation of the social world as equivalent to the natural state: "In his disturbed mind metaphysical problems which seem to be timeless concomitants of the conditions of man and problems created by the social order are inextricably joined, joined in the symbol of the wall" (619). Marx's reading seems to associate Melville's position with Hawthorne's frequent rebuke of the intellectual/writer who becomes isolated within his/her ego and loses his/her awareness of communal love. Thus the narrator may represent the social order with all of its weaknesses, but his final sympathy is like the blades of grass and offers the affirmation of community bonding – the ultimate redemption to which Bartleby is blind. Marx's view is reminiscent of Cleanth Brooks's New Critical approach to Faulkner. Within this view, society's flaws are dissected but are secondary to the flawed vision of the outcast who divorces himself from society. Thus the narrator is too blind at the intellectual level to appreciate what Bartleby reacts to within his social world; however, Bartleby is too stunted emotionally to appreciate the sympathy the narrator experiences through the redemptive power of nature.

Curiously, this ironic defense of the narrator surfaces frequently within the fifty-plus years of "Bartleby" criticism. For example, Jeffrey Andrew Weinstock in 2003 offers a post-structural, linguistic-based analysis of "Bartleby" based upon Derrida's idea "that every letter is potentially a 'dead letter'" (Weinstock 23). According to Weinstock, "Bartleby's 'textualization,' that is, the identification of him with an unreadable letter, points to the ways in which all human subjects are 'texts,' are socially constructed and endowed with meaning by virtue of their places within language and culture" (27). To Weinstock, the mystery of "Bartleby" "foregrounds lack, which is the nature of haunting, and in haunting, intimates that to be human is precisely to be haunted" (23). Thus Bartleby and his story "are lost – and dramatize the loss at the heart of language and life" (30). Yet, like Marx, in Weinstock's final moment, he looks for redemption in the attempt of the hapless narrator's struggle for comprehension: "What Bartleby compels the narrator to do is to tell the story of why he cannot tell the story of Bartleby" (40), and in doing so the lawyer-narrator's "dead letter" becomes his "love letter," which permits him to mourn the loss.

Weinstock uses the narrator's entire narrative much as Marx fifty years earlier uses the narrator's attempt to arouse hope in Bartleby through the image of grass in the Tombs. In each case, the critic offers affirmation through love, which suggests a final reversal of the positions of Bartleby and the narrator. Whether based upon the blades of grass or the telling process, the core of the interpretation derives from the assumption that the narrator's final words "Ah Bartleby! Ah, humanity!" ("Bartleby" 672) constitute a true crescendo. Thus, regardless how blind the narrator is, he has progressed by the end of the story. Both interpretations posit love or the social bond as real despite the delusions of Wall Street and language. This does represent a viable but minority position within "Bartleby" criticism, as critical analysis is more likely to question the assumption that the story constitutes the narrator's building to a higher level of love and/or awareness. The most extreme defense of the narrator occurs in Dan McCall's "The Reliable Narrator" in his book, *The Silence of Bartleby*. McCall believes that twentieth-century critics often err in their analysis of supposedly unreliable narrators. Two major directions of twentieth-century interpretation, the existentialist and Marxist inspired, tend to see the wall as the central symbol in the story and doubt the narrator's ability to see beyond the hegemony of his socially constructed, self-imposed prison.

The Wall

At the core of the story's symbolism is the question, "What does Bartleby see in his dead-wall revery?" The importance of walls has frequently been analyzed, and justifiably so. The subtitle of the original publication is "A Story of Wall-Street." Beyond the key image of Bartleby staring at the wall three feet outside his window is the narrator's wall of windows that looks upon the "lofty brick wall, black by age and everlasting shade" (636), the "ground glass folding-doors" that separate the narrator from his employees, the "high green folding screen" that the narrator "procured" to "entirely isolate Bartleby" from his sight, and finally Bartleby's stay in the Tombs with frequent references to the walls: "his face toward a high wall" (669), "took up a position fronting the dead-wall" (670), "the surrounding walls, of amazing thickness, kept all sound behind them" (671), and "Strangely huddled at the base of the wall, … his head touching the cold stones" (671). Walls constitute a leitmotif, and how we see the story is inseparable from how we interpret the walls. An existential perspective builds upon Leo Marx's early analysis of "blankness" in relationship to the walls. More recent criticism has seen the wall images more as an expression of Wall Street, thus of capitalistic culture. Since the 1990s, much of the best criticism has focused on the historical context of walls/Wall Street, often with Marxist implications, offering sharp insights into the labor struggles in the middle of the nineteenth century.

Norman Springer's "Bartleby and the Terror of Limitation" (1965) and Kingsley Widmer's "Melville's Radical Resistance: The Method and Meaning of *Bartleby*" (1969) are excellent readings from an existential perspective. Springer's essay uses Leo Marx's equation of the wall and blankness but then departs from his position, arguing that "Blankness is the only truth" and that the narrator attempts to "make meaning where there is no meaning" (Springer 414). The nihilistic recognition associated with the blank wall negates any attempt on the narrator's part to appreciate Bartleby's condition. According to Springer, Bartleby "is a kind of wall without reason, incomprehensible and blank" (415). Springer does not deny that the narrator tries to penetrate this wall, but he argues that he backs off each time he comes close to seeing the wall for what it is (411). Rather than Leo Marx's contention that the narrator discovers the source of true affirmation ignored by Bartleby, Springer argues that the narrator is "limited, flawed, with a built-in protective device: his self-esteem" (413). Springer's view also contradicts Weinstock's argument that the lawyer's narrative constitutes an affirmative "love letter," for a human's "compassion can never be as large as the need for it" (415). Thus Springer substitutes, for the redemptive power of love, the recognition of nothingness. For Springer, the "dead-wall revery" is an apt representation for an existential moment – "a choosing of nothing" and the power of the story lies within "the fully-made paradox of a preference for no thing" (416). This existential perspective places primary emphasis on two factors: choice as reflected in Bartleby's life of preference and the realization of nothingness or blankness as associated with the wall image.

Kingsley Widmer continues this focus on an existential perspective and defines the existentialist's attraction to Melville's story as based upon Melville's awareness of the "solitude and absurdity and nothingness we must face if we are to achieve authentic awareness" (Widmer 458). For Widmer, the wall and the lawyer are both at the source of Bartleby's existential recognition as the "walled-in lawyer" cannot see himself as associated with "the walls of gloom" (449). While Bartleby represents people who see "the larger isolation of man and frequent futility of his endeavours" (448), to Widmer the narrator represents the liberal American as "the blandly benevolent rationalist" (448). Such a man cannot deal with cosmic irrationality and recoils from "more ominous and nihilistic truths about the universe" (453). Widmer dismisses the narrator's final exclamation as "a last sentimental gesture of the representative American confronted with the violation of his faith" (457).

Widmer presents his existential perspective as an opposition to the Marxist or more generally anti-capitalist view of the story. He dismisses such perspectives as inadequate in dealing with the story's complexity. According to Widmer, Melville's Wall Street works well as a "metaphysical metaphor of confinement and of barriers to understanding" but does not work as a propagandistic expression of abusive financial "power and manipulation" (447). Since Bartleby is indifferent to wealth, Widmer concludes that the story fails to target American capitalism and commercialism (446–7). Widmer's dismissal of a socioeconomic interpretation of "Bartleby" is only a more extreme expression of Leo Marx's argument that although "Bartleby's state of mind may be understood as a response to the hostile world of Wall Street" (Marx 619), "Melville does not exonerate the writer by placing all the onus upon society" (620). Both in Leo Marx's 1953 context and Widmer's 1969 context the underlying implication of an anti-socioeconomic interpretation expresses opposition to Marxist critics, first the popular Marxist criticism of the 1930s opposed by the original New Critics and later the resurgence of Marxist criticism during the cultural revolutions of the 1960s. Of course, an existential interpretation need not dismiss a socioeconomic interpretation (no surprise to Jean-Paul Sartre), but one can easily understand the either/or logic that would see within Bartleby's dead-wall revery *either* a recognition of the cosmic void (death, isolation, epistemological limitations, or the limits of love) *or* a confrontation with Wall Street as the ascending power of modern capitalism. Leo Marx's argument is that Bartleby *errs* in extending his interpretation of the wall *from* the socioeconomic to the existential: "What ultimately killed this writer was not the walls themselves, but the fact that he confused the walls built by men with the wall of human mortality" (622). However, few critics thereafter have been willing to argue that the story's meaning derives from Bartleby's misinterpretation of the walls. Since 1970, most criticism argues that whatever Bartleby sees in the walls is real and extends beyond the vision of the narrator.

Although both Leo Marx and Widmer respond to or anticipate a Marxist interpretation of "Bartleby," the first developed Marxist view does not appear until Louise K. Barnett's article in 1974. However, since Bartleby lacks proletarian consciousness, Barnett sees him as the "alienated worker who, realizing that his work is meaningless and without a future, can only protest his humanity by a negative assertion" (Barnett 379). According to Barnett, Bartleby sees the natural world as "equally constrained in the Tombs and on Wall Street" as the "man-made wall is omnipresent" (384). This may seem similar to Leo Marx until we see how Barnett reverses Marx's interpretation of the redemptive blades of grass by arguing that when Bartleby is imprisoned and still in his dead-wall revery, "the narrator can patronize him once more and encourage him to make the best of it" (384).

James C. Wilson extends the Marxist argument in 1981 and, in so doing, clarifies the way in which the Marxist argument is likely to oppose the existential interpretations. According to Wilson, the narrator "exposes Wall Street and its new religion of materialism, of which he and John Jacob Astor are members of a kind of priestly caste" (Wilson 338). Within the story, "this new religion posits money as its only value" (338). Thus, Bartleby's alienation and dehumanization result from the "prison of his socioeconomic system" (340). From an opposing perspective, Wilson, like Leo Marx, emphasizes the limitations of Bartleby's vision as he argues that Bartleby fails to make a connection "between his own individual alienation and the class alienation of the propertyless worker" (340). One might initially look at this statement and assume that Wilson has reached the same point as Leo Marx. However, the important distinction is that Leo Marx's Bartleby goes too far in giving meaning to the wall whereas Wilson's Bartleby does not go far enough. Whereas Marx's Bartleby makes the artist's mistake of extending his personal situation into "metaphysical problems which seem to be timeless concomitants of the condition of man" (Marx 619), Wilson's Bartleby lacks the capacity to connect his personal state and class struggle (Wilson 340). In both cases, Bartleby ends in despair, but the first is the isolated, egocentric artist while the second is the isolated, uninformed worker.

Naomi C. Reed summarizes a primary direction of "Bartleby" criticism in the past twenty years as she notes the movement of Marxist criticism from a "more thematic approach, which presents the story as illustrative of Marxist concepts, to rigorously historicist readings" (Reed 248). Since there is "no real evidence that Melville was familiar with Marx's writings at the time he composed 'Bartleby'," the emphasis of Marxist criticism has shifted to labor disputes in New York at the time of the story's publication (248). Reed's article (2004) extends the excellent scholarship of writers like David Kuebrich (1996), Richard R. John (1997), and Barbara Foley (2000) in providing a historical context for "Bartleby" that reveals Melville's awareness "that Wall Street was a hotbed of labor activism" and that he "knew of political debates about the rights of workers" (Reed 248). It is within this context that the story has been reevaluated. Kuebrich's article is particularly insightful in its application of Antonio Gramsci's concept of hegemony to the perspective of the narrator. According to Kuebrich, the lawyer is "self-deceived by the moral categories developed by nineteenth-century U.S. Christian culture as it accommodated itself to capitalism" (Kuebrich 396). Kuebrich believes that Melville uses the narrator to investigate the cultural denial of contradictions between exploitative self-interest and Christian values (396). Hegemony is thus at the core of the lawyer's narrative, and the narrator expects his readers to accept that capitalism and "its ideological underpinnings are not subject to question because they are commensurate with the rational or natural ordering of society" (404). I have elsewhere analyzed these "underpinnings" as derivations of the central principles proposed by Cicero in *The Offices*, thus explaining Bartleby's troubled gazing upon the bust of Cicero over the narrator's head.

Whether from the existential or Marxist direction, the past forty years have placed a great deal of emphasis upon the original subtitle, "A Story of Wall-Street." As an image of philosophical "blankness" or a study of socioeconomic systemic abuse, the world of walls has come to be seen as central to Melville's communication. Critics gaze upon the wall with Bartleby and typically question the narrator's inability or unwillingness to do so.

Communication

The one story element that receives as much attention as walls in the study of "Bartleby" is communication. We are introduced into the world of those who copy legal documents. In the epilogue, the narrator offers the rumor that Bartleby previously worked in the Dead-Letter Office. In the Tombs, the grub-man mistakes Bartleby for a "gentleman forger" ("They are always pale and genteel-like, them forgers" ["Bartleby" 670]). Once we consider these references to written documentation, we next consider the lawyer's narrative as another form of documentation. The final consideration becomes Bartleby's *refusal* to copy and his reticence versus the narrator's verbosity. We may then ask ourselves: who communicates more effectively, the narrator or Bartleby? How may more language say less and less language say more? How may silence become expression and expression become silence?

Early criticism was quick to equate Melville's biography with Bartleby's fate. Particularly stressed was his reaction to the public reception of *Pierre* since Melville was accused of insanity. Details such as the narrator's suspicion that Bartleby's diligence has caused damage to his eyes tempt the reader to consider the parallel to Melville's comparable diligence and similar family fears. Biographical encoding to Bartleby as resistant copyist may occur as an equivalent to Melville's resistance to commercial writing. Susan Weiner in her 1992 essay takes this parallel to a deeper level that asks us to consider Melville's reaction to language itself: "By the time Melville completed *Pierre*, he had become profoundly skeptical about the ability of language to penetrate beneath the surface of appearance and reveal something about the mystery underlying reality" (Weiner 91). Weiner builds upon the post-structural perspective of John Carlos Rowe (1982) and others when she focuses on semiotics and sees "Bartleby" as a story about language and its limitations: "The act of writing, which is an assertion of originality in *Pierre*, has been reduced to copying in 'Bartleby.' Similarly, the language of law has also become so rigid as to inhibit its flexibility in dealing with the most pressing conflicts of the period, particularly slavery" (92). Weiner is appropriately fascinated by the whole concept of "copy" from the epistemological doubt that may question the existence of creativity to the legal underpinnings of culture.

This range is reminiscent of the previously discussed opposition of existential and Marxist perspectives as it asks us to consider whether the focus is more on the human condition or the culture. In regard to culture, Weiner examines the law office and the specific work of the narrator as it reflects upon the larger culture: "By repetitiously writing the documents that encoded the laws of ownership or origin, the lawyer becomes a key element in maintaining the structure of the entire legal framework" (104). The problem at this level is the way in which law and language provide the framework for culture: "the written legal document is the surface expression of a reality that is decontextualized and refuses to consider any adaptation to special circumstances of an individual case" (105). Weiner presents cultural law as a language-based process through which reality is squeezed into ill-fitting boxes: "Exactitude substantiates truth and the copy comes to stand for the original" (105). This is a useful way of approaching the narrator's hegemony as well as officially documented law. Thus the "copyist" becomes all who repetitively document or "force" a reality and in so doing create a substitute for "what landscape painters call 'life'" ("Bartleby" 636).

However, a movement from the more sociological to the epistemological occurs when Weiner questions the human's, including the writer's, dependence upon language: "Melville undermines the whole notion of an abstract truth that can be contained in the finite material of language" (Weiner 105). Therefore, language itself becomes the ultimate source of deception: "Language is put to the task of creating surface illusion to stand for meaning" (111). One may thus argue that beneath the actual source of meaning (language) lies meaninglessness or the void. At this point, the implications of Weiner's argument carry the reader from protest of cultural rigidity to the void that lies beneath – in other words, again from the popular Marxist argument that Melville exposes the dangerous artifices of capitalistic class structure and ownership (the narrator's office and its production) to the existential realization that the word (or the wall) is also indicative of the blank/nothingness that underlies all meaning. Here again the suggestion is *not* that Bartleby's reticence is a reflection of his opposition to oppression and to his *inability* to see the true meaning that may lie beneath oppression (Leo Marx's compassion, Wilson's Marxist utopia, Weinstock's love letter), but rather the possibility that the final silence of the dead-wall revery is the final truth – death, meaninglessness. In this case, Bartleby's "language" of truth must move toward silence, just as we may assume that the more the narrator speaks/writes, the less he says. This possibility places Melville closer to Samuel Beckett than to any writer of his own generation.

Bartleby

A casual reading of "Bartleby" (or what one usually deals with in the college classroom) suggests that the first topic to consider in a discussion of the story is Bartleby himself – who is he and what is wrong with him? If the history of "Bartleby" criticism teaches us anything, it is the realization that consideration of the character of Bartleby is better left to a much later phase of analysis. The story's narrator misleads us into thinking that this is "A Study of Temperament" to quote a Kate Chopin subtitle and that the subject is Bartleby. Ironically, to the extent to which it is a study of temperament, the subject is the narrator. One can say very little with assurance about Bartleby's temperament. We know that the narrator knows little about Bartleby and understands him even less. Bartleby is the cipher that haunts the narrator and the void within which we all place our separate meanings.

"Haunting" is a concept that comes up often in "Bartleby" criticism. I once suggested that the story disguises a Gothic structure and that, within that structure, the narrator is haunted by a ghost – the perfect ghost intended to haunt this particular man (thus Bartleby's initial diligence and gentlemanly demeanor). The comparison I used was Poe's "The Fall of the House of Usher," and I still think this is useful if one is thinking in terms of a fictive construct and how characters play roles within such a construct. For example, if a student should ask why Bartleby will not leave the narrator's office, I would ask in turn why does not Roderick leave the House of Usher, and why does not Hester Prynne leave her New England village. Part of the explanation lies within the understanding of a Gothic construct – the haunted house or its equivalent – which envisions the human edifice as inescapable. Bartleby does not leave for the same reason the narrator shows up at the office on Sunday morning. The Gothic world is claustrophobic; to be haunted is to find no exit. To the extent to which all roads are closed, the human is held within a human edifice that associates with human dreams: the House of Usher is patriarchal lineage, her New England village is the City of God, and the narrator's office is the brave new world of American business. Nightmare derives from dream; without the dream, there is no true nightmare. Melville's mastery in "Bartleby" can be seen in watching the narrator's world, his "snug retreat," disintegrate, and Bartleby is the catalyst for this disintegration. The narrator's world, more a construct of mind than a specific place, does not literally crumble into a tarn, but as long as the narrator cannot stop telling his story, his office must remain what it is and not what he would like it to be. Like the House of Usher and Hester's village, it is a place that sucks away life rather than rejuvenating life (to be healed from the imagined effects of the Dead-Letter Office).

We will never be fully satisfied to see Bartleby as mere catalyst, nor should we be. We follow the clues of the dead-wall revery, the repetitive "prefer not to," or the gazing upon the bust of Cicero to glean what we can of a human character. We know that what we are given is suggestive and fragmentary, and from this, we either try to make a whole picture, or we conclude that the suggestive and fragmentary always is the whole picture (a very postmodern picture that questions the concept of identity).

For the sake of argument, I would like to consider the moment in which the narrator returns to his "old haunt," finds Bartleby sitting upon the banister, and directs Bartleby back into the office they have previously shared. The conversation that follows deserves more attention than it normally receives given that the "unwonted wordiness" of Bartleby "inspirited" the narrator (667). Essentially, the narrator introduces five possibilities of employment, followed by his invitation into his home. Bartleby rebuffs each idea and the final invitation with slight variations in his rejections. Of course, the narrator's expression of "unwonted wordiness" is comical given that Bartleby's six statements total one hundred words, but, relatively speaking, this is a verbal explosion from Bartleby. It does seem clear that we are to believe that Bartleby is actually thinking about each option, as though the narrator may hit upon the final solution that could bring Bartleby out of his stupor. The five options are:

(1) "re-engage in copying," (2) "a clerkship in a dry-goods store," (3) "a bar-tender's business," (4) "travel through the country collecting bills for the merchants," and (5) "going as a companion to Europe, to entertain some young gentleman with your conversation" (667). Wilson's Marxist perspective is one of the few analyses of this list. Wilson sees all but the last as "Wall Street approved forms of slavery" while "the last is simply ludicrous" (Wilson 344). The key to Wilson's response is expressed in the statement that these proposals reveal "the narrow limits of the lawyer's imagination" (343). This is logical and suits the Marxist perspective. The restrictions and even the absurdity of the narrator's list then mirror the narrowness of his own world. *He* can envision nothing beyond menial, dull jobs that match those of his own employees or positions that are absurd mismatches for Bartleby's character.

However, we might switch our focus and examine instead Bartleby's responses. He would "prefer not to make any change," sees "too much confinement" in a clerkship, would not like "at all" bartending despite not being "particular," would prefer to do "something else" rather than collect bills, finds being a companion on a Grand Tour lacking in something "definite" and would like to be "stationary," and to the final offer of the narrator's home, would "prefer not to make any change at all" (667). Despite what the narrator sees as maddening contradictions (How can one *choose* such stasis, yet dislike confinement?), Bartleby's responses do suggest that he is trying to discover something that will satisfy him, something that he may find rewarding. He has become resistant to change and movement, yet does not see himself as "particular." The narrator is not necessarily justified in equating "confinement" with desire to remain "stationary" or avoid change. This may suggest that Bartleby truly sees an unpleasant change in his confinement in the Tombs. One may argue that Bartleby vaguely envisions possibilities for an alternative life, but such possibilities do not surface within the lawyer's list.

We must then ask ourselves: is this because of "the narrow limits of the lawyer's imagination," or is this because such vague possibilities are not of this world? To say that Bartleby is not at home in the world can express Bartleby's individual frailty (suggesting a variety of psychological readings) or that the frailty of the narrator's world is defined by the narrator's limits or that the frailty of physical existence is expressed by the list. Any one of these possibilities can suggest a way of approaching the character of Bartleby: victim of himself, victim of capitalism, victim of life. I do see importance in this list mainly because within the fictive construct of the story, it is Melville's opportunity to extend to a world outside the narrator's office and the Tombs. In doing so, does he at least hint at an exit, an alternative to the stultifying environment of the narrator? I believe the answer is "no" – nothing within the framework of the story suggests such an exit to the Gothic edifice. The most revealing option is bill collecting in the country, which the narrator sees as a great opportunity for improving Bartleby's health (667). The "thud" to any romantic suggestion of nature's healing power is bill collecting – yet one more image of culture's dead documentation. "Stationary" and "definite" both suggest that Bartleby longs for permanence, for an absolute or ideal state, for the refreshing fixed point. The lawyer would seem to share this distant dream, given his frustration over losing a "life-lease of the profits" as Master of Chancery and having to settle for "a few short years" (636). This may suggest that Bartleby's dream is not of this world and that his state is similar to Hamlet's. However, the other options in interpreting Bartleby remain viable. For example, when the narrator finally offers his home as a refuge, some critics see this as the narrator's grand gesture – a moment in which he breaks through his own limitations – but to view it in this way, one must ignore what the narrator's home would be. He is the nameless bachelor whose home can offer nothing but momentary respite from his *real* life which is in his office. Despite the obvious generosity of the narrator, can this possibly be seen as an alternative for Bartleby? I can see no difference between bill collecting in the country and living in the narrator's home: both introduce particular dream images that are based upon the redemptive force of nature and the hearth, but both are negated by the qualifiers. Yet, here again, no argument can be settled between Marxist/existentialist readings. The story apparently offers no exit from the confines of a quiet, entropic nightmare, possibly because Melville has constructed the story to express what he sees as the inevitable limitations of human existence, or it may be because Melville has successfully limited the story to the restrictive vision of the narrator. So in the end we have returned to the wall and our shared gaze along with Bartleby.

Conclusion: On Teaching "Bartleby"

One of the finest critical essays ever written on American literature was Randall Jarrell's study of Robert Frost's "Home Burial." In a careful textual reading, Jarrell explains how the text contrasts the positions of the husband and wife as they react to the death of their child. Although both positions are given their due, Jarrell clarifies how Frost has constructed his poem so as to demonstrate a very real, harsh worldliness within the husband and, in so doing, justify the wife's recoil from him and his world. When I teach "Home Burial," a class will often divide down the middle in its support of either the husband or the wife. When students defend the husband, they usually emphasize that he tries to communicate and to achieve intimacy whereas she doesn't. My experience in teaching "Bartleby" is very similar. Classes will often divide evenly in their support of either the narrator or Bartleby and will argue their cases vehemently. Again, the lawyer scores points for trying. To be honest, I no longer encourage my students to take a position quickly in this regard. Although it can lead to lively discussion, once students take a position, they tend to dig in their heels. Instead, I prefer to read the lawyer's opening description of himself and his office – including that wonderful dash. I believe students need to think about how the author undermines the narrator's authority from the beginning of the story. (In my upper-division classes, I compare this to Melville's treatment of Captain Delano in "Benito Cereno," a man whose surprising survival reminds me of Mr. McGoo.) Once the reader has begun to grasp the complexity of the narrator's character, then consideration of such key matters as the symbolism of walls, the thematic treatment of communication, and the identity of Bartleby can better be considered. Of the wife's position in "Home Burial," Jarrell argues that Frost gives great weight to it, for there is something she has discovered that the reader is expected to contemplate. In other words, she goes where her husband cannot or will not go, and the reader is expected to share this deeper perception of the woman whose mourning has led her into a profound level of disillusionment. Yet, in the end, Jarrell notes that we can only follow her so far, for to follow her any further is to follow her into the grave. Thus, we are finally left holding back, ironically sharing something with the less perceptive husband. I would argue that in "Bartleby" our position is likely to be very similar. We can follow Bartleby by recognizing the limitations of the narrator. But at some point, we too must hold back and share our world with the narrator.

References and Further Reading

Barnett, Louise K. "Bartleby as Alienated Worker." *Studies in Short Fiction* 11 (1974): 379–85.

Bickley, R. Bruce, Jr. *The Method of Melville's Short Fiction.* Durham, NC: Duke University Press, 1975.

Foley, Barbara. "From Wall Street to Astor Place: Historicizing Melville's 'Bartleby.'" *American Literature* 72 (2000): 87–116.

Jarrell, Randall. "Robert Frost's 'Home Burial.'" *The Third Book of Criticism.* New York: Farrar, Straus & Giroux, 1962. 191–231.

John, Richard R. "The Lost World of Bartleby, The Ex-Officeholder: Variations on a Venerable Literary Form." *New England Quarterly* 70 (1997): 631–41.

Kuebrich, David. "Melville's Doctrine of Assumption: The Hidden Ideology of Capitalist Production in 'Bartleby.'" *New England Quarterly* 69 (1996): 381–405.

McCall, Dan. *The Silence of Bartleby.* Ithaca, NY: Cornell University Press, 1989.

Marx, Leo. "Melville's Parable of the Walls." *Sewanee Review* 61 (1953): 602–27.

Melville, Herman. "Bartleby the Scrivener: A Story of Wall-Street." *Pierre, Israel Potter, The Piazza Tales, The Confidence-Man, Uncollected Prose, Billy Budd, Sailor.* New York: Library of America, 1984. 635–72.

Reed, Naomi C. "The Specter of Wall Street: 'Bartleby, the Scrivener' and the Language of Commodities." *American Literature* 76 (2004): 247–73.

Rowe, John Carlos. *Through the Custom-House: Nineteenth-Century American Fiction and Modern Theory.* Baltimore: Johns Hopkins University Press, 1982.

Ryan, Steven T. "Cicero's Head in Melville's 'Bartleby the Scrivener.'" *English Language Notes* 43 (2005): 116–33.

———. The Gothic Formula of 'Bartleby.'" *Arizona Quarterly* 34 (1978): 311–16.

Springer, Norman. "Bartleby and the Terror of Limitation." *Publications of the Modern Language Association* 80 (1965): 410–18.

Weiner, Susan. *Law in Art: Melville's Major Fiction and Nineteenth-Century American Law.* New York: Peter Lang, 1992.

Weinstock, Jeffrey Andrew. "Doing Justice to Bartleby." *American Transcendental Quarterly* 17 (2003): 23–42.

Widmer, Kingsley. "Melville's Radical Resistance: The Method and Meaning of *Bartleby.*" *Studies in the Novel* 1 (1969): 444–58.

Wilson, James C. "'Bartleby': The Walls of Wall Street." *Arizona Quarterly* 37 (1981): 335–46.

4

Towards History and Beyond: Hawthorne and the American Short Story

Alfred Bendixen

No one in the first half of the nineteenth century did more to advance the American short story than Nathaniel Hawthorne. He transformed the historical tale into a significant literary form by skillfully incorporating Gothic elements in ways that led to penetrating psychological insights. He also wrestled with a culture that rarely supported the development of art and artists, producing significant fiction on this subject as well as engaging with the literary marketplace in ways that were both innovative and creative. If his original visions for his early works could have been realized, we would probably be praising him for inventing the modern short story cycle, which is certainly one of the most important forms of short fiction in the United States. Although he rarely receives credit for this achievement, he is also one of the chief inventors of the literary genre we now call science fiction. A full appreciation of his contributions to the American short story requires an understanding of his lifelong attempt to develop this form, his mastery of the historical tales, and his experiments with a wide range of other forms. This chapter provides a starting point for such an appreciation by offering three sections, one on each of these aspects of one of the most versatile and productive careers in American letters.

Hawthorne: A Portrait of an Artist

It is not surprising that an author whose most famous works deal with secret sins, strange obsessions, and various forms of repression and masochism should attract psychological speculation from biographers as well as psychoanalytical criticism.[1] The details of Nathaniel Hawthorne's life seem to invite a wide range of conjecture. It is difficult to ignore the fact that the first author to make the American past into the subject of complex art was born on the fourth of July, 1804, into a Salem family whose ancestors included both one of the judges in the witchcraft trials (John Hathorne) and a revolutionary war hero (Daniel Hathorne). Scholars have tended to emphasize the cruel judge and ignore the war hero. The author added a "w" to the spelling of the family name, a sign that some commentators interpret as an attempt to distance himself from his personal past, but may simply reflect a desire to make the spelling of the name conform to its pronunciation. Hawthorne never really knew his father, a ship's captain who spent much of the young boy's childhood away on voyages and perished abroad before his son reached his fourth birthday. Raised by his mother and sisters, who apparently doted on him, the young Hawthorne also received a great deal of support and attention from his mother's extended family, particularly an uncle, Robert Manning, a successful businessman. Thus, there may be biographical sources for his fiction's frequent concern with absent or oppressive father figures, with nurturing or destructive women, and with healthy or dysfunctional families. Although he had some formal schooling as well as work with tutors, the most important part of Hawthorne's pre-college education almost certainly came from his extensive reading during private moments. Indeed, his best fiction reveals a clear debt to the great allegorical tradition that stretches from Spenser's *Faerie Queene* to Bunyan's *Pilgrim's Progress* and two immensely popular forms of the British novel: the Gothic romances and Sir Walter Scott's historical novels.

By the time he graduated from Bowdoin College in 1825, Hawthorne had committed himself to a career as a writer. It would take him twelve years to have a book published under his own name, but scholars have demolished the old portrait of a shy, reclusive artist who withdrew from the world to produce brilliant masterpieces during solitary moments in a Salem study. During the years 1825–37, Hawthorne was actively struggling to make a place for his work in a literary marketplace that provided frequent calls for the creation of a genuinely American literature but little financial support. Publishers found it relatively easy to pirate British masterpieces and best-sellers without paying any royalties, and they generally expected American writers to provide subsidies or guarantees. Hawthorne had the resources to arrange for the anonymous publication of his first novel, *Fanshawe* (1828), but he soon regretted this decision, calling on his family and friends to burn their copies and never publicly acknowledging his authorship. He also attempted to market a collection of stories, *Seven Tales of My Native Land*, which may have been completed as early as 1825. His experiences with one printer proved so frustrating that Hawthorne recalled and may even have destroyed the manuscript. Nevertheless, he focused his literary energies on the creation of unified books of short stories, volumes that may have looked very much like the contemporary form we now call the short story cycle. The chief influence here is clearly Washington Irving, who had both invented the short story as an artistically developed work ideally suited to capturing the special qualities of American life and had demonstrated that these works could be marketed within the framework of carefully organized collections. In *The Sketch Book* (1819–20), Irving's American tales serve as a kind of comic counterpoint to the more sentimental meditations of a genial traveler in Great Britain. In his *Tales of a Traveller* (1824), the stories were grouped into thematic sections, including one which focused on literary life in England.

Many of Hawthorne's finest stories were originally intended to appear within the contexts of carefully organized books. One of these projected volumes, *Provincial Tales*, would have contained most of the great historical tales of New England that have established his current reputation as a master of the American short story. Although these pieces have almost always been read and valued as individual works, it is possible that they might have achieved an even greater impact when organized into a larger coherent pattern. Unfortunately, it is not possible to completely reconstruct *Provincial Tales* or even to determine with certainty which of the early tales would have been included. The situation is even more complicated with *The Story Teller*, a projected collection of descriptive sketches and tales inspired by a journey through the states of New Hampshire, Vermont, and New York that Hawthorne took in 1832. His plan involved an itinerant storyteller who would describe his travels, the stories he told on route to various audiences, and the reactions he elicited. Thus, the completed volume might have built up to an intriguing narrative that not only fused the distinctive qualities of the American landscape with the works of fiction they inspired, but also provided a larger inquiry into the role of storytelling in the United States. Hawthorne entrusted the manuscripts of *Provincial Tales* and *The Story Teller* to Samuel Goodrich and Park Benjamin, both of whom ignored whatever pattern of unity these volumes contained and printed individual tales and sketches anonymously in *The Token*, the *Salem Gazette*, *New England Magazine*, or *American Magazine*. Anonymous publication was the custom for most annuals like *The Token* and for many magazines of the time, a practice that benefited publishers like Goodrich, who was quite happy to be able to use multiple works by Hawthorne in a single issue without paying him very much. Park Benjamin's dismantling of *The Story Teller* reflects an almost complete disdain for whatever plan of organization the author had as well as a willingness to cut and add material to serve the purpose of magazine publication. Hawthorne ultimately had to accept literary hack work as a way to earn a living, agreeing in 1836 to edit *The American Magazine of Useful and Entertaining Knowledge*, a position that mostly entailed compiling extracts or preparing paraphrases from various publications for a promised salary of $500 a year. The bankruptcy of the publisher meant that he received only $20 after six months of work. He earned another hundred dollars by joining his sister, Elizabeth, in preparing *Peter Parley's Universal History, on the Basis of Geography* (1837) for the popular series of children's books that ultimately made Goodrich wealthy.

Hawthorne's first public success as an author came in 1837 with the publication of *Twice-Told Tales*, a collection of eighteen previously published stories and sketches, which appeared because a close friend secretly guaranteed the publisher against financial loss. Surprisingly, many of the stories that we now regard as his most important were not included. Hawthorne passed over such powerful works as "Roger Malvin's Burial" (1832), "My Kinsman, Major Molineaux" (1832), and "Young Goodman Brown" (1835) in order to make room for such genial sketches as "Sights from a Steeple" (1831), "A Rill from the Town Pump" (1835), and "Little Annie's Rambles" (1835). In compiling this volume, he clearly rejected his earlier plan of a carefully unified volume and decided to introduce himself to the literary world as a writer with a wide range of interests and moods, one who could entertain his audience with cheerful sketches as well as offer more disturbing, more challenging visions of reality with tales like "The Gentle Boy" (1832) and "The Minister's Black Veil" (1836). The strategy seems to have worked. Contemporary reviews often singled out the lighter sketches for praise, and the book sold well enough that Hawthorne was able to bring out an enlarged edition in 1842, which added seventeen more works but again emphasized a wide variety of moods and tones. The first two editions of *Twice-Told Tales* present the author as a genial moralist who occasionally immerses the reader into a surprisingly grim view of the world, but is just as likely to offer a conventional moral and a cheerful conclusion. Throughout the rest of his career, Hawthorne continually emphasized the importance of diversity in the production of books, often working hard to ensure that dark, tragic moments would be counterbalanced by lighter, comic elements.

Hawthorne's long apprenticeship in the unstable world of American literary publishing may have taught him the importance of winning over the broadest possible audience, but it also showed him how difficult it would be to make a living as an author. He became a regular contributor to the *United States Magazine and Democratic Review*, but he also sought political appointments and even hoped to be named the official historiographer for the South Seas expedition of 1838. He finally secured a post as a measurer of salt and coal in the Boston Custom House in 1839, a lucrative position that he held until 1841, when he resigned to join the utopian community of Brook Farm. During this period, much of his literary energy went into the production of books for children, a form that he had learned from Goodrich could be quite profitable if the author found the right balance between entertainment and education. Hawthorne employed his extensive knowledge of the past to produce a series of three books in 1840–1 that traced the history of New England from the first Puritan settlers to the time of the American Revolution: *Grandfather's Chair, Famous Old People*, and *Liberty Tree*. They were collectively entitled *The Whole History of Grandfather's Chair* when they were reprinted along with the inferior *Biographical Stories for Children* (1842) in the 1851 collection, *True Stories from History and Biography*. Hawthorne also fell in love with Sophia Peabody, whom he eventually married in 1842. His decision to join Brook Farm was based on the hope that a few hours of daily labor would provide him with a cottage and the financial security he needed both to maintain his identity as a writer and to start married life. The experience proved very disappointing. Although most biographers emphasize his basic lack of sympathy with the Transcendentalist idealists, Hawthorne is the only major American writer who devoted his entire life savings and eight months of his life to a utopian experiment.

When the Brook Farm episode ended in failure and a lawsuit, Hawthorne and his new wife moved into the Old Manse, the house in Concord, Massachusetts, where Emerson had written *Nature*. Life in the center of American Transcendentalism proved delightful to Hawthorne, who enjoyed being a part of a community of thinkers and writers and responded by enlarging the scope of his literary range. If the major short fiction of the 1830s tends to be a complex exploration of human psychology within the framework provided by the historical past, the stories of the 1840s show a new engagement with speculative visions of the future and with allegorical musings on the social and human condition. The writer who demonstrated that the American past could be a rich subject for short fiction now produced brilliant stories focusing on mad scientists ("The Birth-mark" [1843] and "Rappaccini's Daughter" [1844]) and apocalyptic visions of the end of the world ("The New Adam and Eve" [1843] and "Earth's Holocaust" [1844]). In short, in the 1840s, Hawthorne helped invent the genre we now call science fiction. He also developed a new interest in the possibilities of allegory and even contemplated a series to be called "Allegories of the Heart." It is in this period that he also writes some of his most interesting stories about the nature of art and artists, including "The Artist of the Beautiful" (1844).

By 1846, American publishing conditions had begun to improve and Hawthorne had established enough of a literary reputation that the firm of Wiley and Putnam brought out a new collection of his short fiction, *Mosses from an Old Manse*, in 1846. Although the volume was a commercial success and attracted thoughtful criticism, financial security still seemed out of reach. The birth of a daughter, Una, in 1844 and a son, Julian, in 1846 added to his financial responsibilities. When they lost the lease on the Old Manse in 1845, the Hawthornes moved back to Salem, where he gained a political appointment in 1846 as the surveyor of the Custom House, a post that enabled him to provide for his family but not to produce much writing. When the change in administrations led to his dismissal in 1849, Hawthorne faced the greatest financial crisis of his life and responded by re-energizing his literary career. The appearance of *The Scarlet Letter* in 1850 clearly established him as a significant American author and also marked his shift from short fiction to the novel, a form that he recognized would be more lucrative. Originally, he planned to include other tales in the volume, partly because he thought that *The Scarlet Letter* was not long enough for book publication and partly because he wanted to balance its tragic mood with lighter pieces, but his publisher persuaded him to provide only the novel and a long introductory sketch, "The Custom House." Hawthorne moved his family to Lenox, Massachusetts, from 1850 to 1852 and then back to Concord, where they purchased Bronson Alcott's former house, The Wayside. Hawthorne went on to produce two other novels, *The House of the Seven Gables* (1851), which he regarded as his best work, and *The Blithedale Romance* (1852), which was based on his experiences at Brook Farm. His literary success also led to the publication of *The Snow-Image, and Other Twice-told Tales* (1852), which collected tales from the previous twenty years, and expanded editions of both *Twice-Told Tales* (1852) and *Mosses from an Old Manse* (1854). He also continued to produce books for children; both *A Wonder-Book for Girls and Boys* (1851) and *Tanglewood Tales* (1853) retell the classic Greek myths within a frame narrative.

Nevertheless, Hawthorne had clearly decided to focus his literary energies on the novel and to abandon the short story, even explicitly telling one editor that a long story cost him much less "thought and trouble" than a collection of short tales

(Wright 440). He bid farewell to the form with a final satiric tale, "Feathertop" (1852), in which a witch attempts to transform a scarecrow into a gentleman, but discovers that he cannot survive after seeing himself in a mirror. In some sense, Hawthorne's most profitable book was the *Life of Franklin Pierce* (1852), the biography he wrote for the successful presidential campaign of his old college friend, because it resulted in his appointment as Consul to Liverpool. Although he produced relatively little writing during his years in the foreign service (1853–7), he was able to step down from this position with savings of over $30,000, a huge sum at that time and much more than he ever made from his literary earnings. He also collected material for a proposed English romance, but was never able to finish it to his satisfaction. Later travel in Italy, however, provided the background material for his final novel, *The Marble Faun* (1860), the best-selling of his books during his lifetime. His final years were marked by grief at the ravages wrought by the Civil War and by frustration at his inability to transform his English notes into a novel. He ended up using his English notes to produce a series of graceful essays that were eventually collected into a travel book, *Our Old Home* (1863). He died in 1863 while on a vacation tour with his old friend, Franklin Pierce.

Hawthorne and the Historical Tale

Hawthorne's current reputation as a writer of the short story rests largely on the historical tales he wrote in the 1830s, many of which were probably intended to appear within the framework of *Provincial Tales* or *The Story Teller*. Unfortunately, we can rarely be certain which tales would have appeared in which volumes and which might have been intended to stand alone. It seems likely that "Roger Malvin's Burial" (1832), "The Gentle Boy" (1832), and "My Kinsman, Major Molineaux" (1832) were designed for *Provincial Tales*, but scholars differ about which collection might have included two of his most famous and most anthologized tales, "Young Goodman Brown" (1835) and "The Minister's Black Veil" (1836).[2] Although we cannot fully reconstruct these projected works, we know how Hawthorne dealt with a broad expanse of American history in *The Whole History of Grandfather's Chair*, the three-volume history of New England he produced for children in 1840–1. Although largely ignored by most scholars, *Grandfather's Chair* provides a remarkably clear and detailed guide to Hawthorne's view of the basic facts of New England and to his larger conception of the meaning of American history. The individual chapters are carefully set within a frame narrative in which an elderly man recounts the history of New England from the first English settlers until the American Revolution by telling his grandchildren about the famous men and women who have occupied a family chair. The presentation of the grandfather as narrator and the children as a responsive audience who both react and ask questions reflects Hawthorne's ongoing concern with exploring the narrative relationship between storyteller and audience and with the role of storytelling in a democratic society.

In a larger sense, *Grandfather's Chair* is about the way in which a new nation fashions the facts of its history into a coherent shape, a mythology that creates a sense of national identity and affirms a specific set of defining values. It is not surprising that Hawthorne discovers sources for the American revolutionary spirit in the Puritans with stories that emphasize courage and perseverance and a desire for freedom. It is, however, surprising to discover a history for children that is filled with so many accounts of cruelty and needless human suffering. Some of the most vivid episodes in this history are stories of persecution: Grandfather speaks honestly and sometimes passionately about the banishments of Roger Williams and Anne Hutchinson, the tormenting of Quakers, the extermination of American Indians, and the accusation and execution of witches, as events for Americans to acknowledge with humility and shame while also remembering the nobler aspects of their past. Hawthorne's engagement with American history in *Grandfather's Chair* reveals a brave willingness to face the contradictions embedded in the national experience: the ways in which the New England pioneers seek freedom and justice for themselves but deny it to others form the narrative expression of a larger conflict between democratic ideals and historical reality.[3]

During his youth, Hawthorne undoubtedly heard the numerous calls for the development of a national literature, one that would exploit the dramatic potential of native materials and create brilliant comedies and moving tragedies out of specifically American experience. Of course, this literary nationalism was fundamentally patriotic, with an underlying assumption that the resulting literature would affirm the superiority of democratic values. But there were unpleasant facts in the way, including a history that encompassed slavery and persecution as well as real moments of courage and achievement. Some of Hawthorne's historical tales, perhaps most notably "Roger Malvin's Burial" (1832) and "The Gentle Boy" (1832), seem to provide very grim views of a psychologically repressive or even sadomasochistic culture. Others, mostly those that are less likely to be anthologized today, such as "The Gray Champion" (1835) and "Endicott and the Red Cross" (1838), appear remarkably patriotic in their affirmation of an heroic principle that is central to the Puritan spirit and ultimately culminates in the American Revolution. Hawthorne's grappling with the past involved a deep awareness of historical wrongs tempered by faith in the possibilities of the great democratic experiment. The vision of history expressed in *Grandfather's Chair* and some of Hawthorne's other works seems quite compatible with Hegel's view of the human past as a series of dialectical forces moving humanity ever forward. This sense of dialectic is probably clearest in "The May-Pole of Merry Mount," in which "Jollity and gloom were contending for an empire" (*Tales and Sketches* 360). Even though gloom wins, the story ends with both a marriage ceremony and the suggestion that a new synthesis has emerged which will temper the harshness of the Puritans. Of course, other tales seem to reject the notion of progress almost entirely. It is impossible to detect Hawthorne's view of American history from any single story, but it is important to remember that he conceived of most of his best historical tales as part of a larger whole, as elements of a larger vision that not only acknowledges past injustice but also insists on exploring its psychological dimensions while simultaneously expressing an underlying faith in the possibilities inherent in democratic life.

Any attempt to reconstruct *Provincial Tales* must rely on a good bit of speculation, but it is likely that the underlying view of American history that would emerge entails the same mixture of critique and affirmation that marks much of Hawthorne's works, and that each piece might assume greater resonance from its placement into a larger pattern. For instance, both "Young Goodman Brown" (1835) and "My Kinsman, Major Molineaux" (1832) are initiation stories in which a young male protagonist enters a symbolic realm and finds himself forced to confront the meaning of his own identity through a series of encounters with various authority figures. Of course, there are crucial differences between the two works. Brown enters a wilderness apparently prepared to sell his soul to the devil and leaves believing that the world that he has cherished for its superior virtues is hopelessly corrupt. Robin goes into a town with the belief that his life will be easy because of his social status as the nephew of an important man, but learns that he cannot define his identity this way in a revolutionary world. If Brown's experience encompasses the gloomy sensibility that Hawthorne and others of his generation ascribed to the Puritans, then the lesson Robin learns seems to be one fully appropriate to a new democratic order in which family connections and social positions must be less important than a shrewd youth's willingness to work hard. Yet, there are striking similarities embedded in the basic structure of the two tales. Both move from an opening that emphasizes historical reality, a setting in a specific time and place, into an increasingly surreal world in which the elements of setting seem to be projections of a terrifying landscape that is fundamentally psychological. Moreover, the male character's loss of innocence in both tales is tied to speculations about the moral purity or corruption of a female figure. Both characters fall asleep and awake to find their perceptions of the world radically transformed. In both cases, the climax of the initiation story is denoted by a shocking moment of recognition that leads to a kind of demonic laughter. The endings of both stories explicitly raise the question of whether the chief character has been dreaming. If we presume that these similarities are not coincidental but evidence of a carefully devised framework in which a recurrent pattern of images, motifs, and themes places the stories into conversation with each other, then we must conclude that *Provincial Tales* was intended to offer a complex dialogue about the meaning of the American experience as embedded in specific historical moments. If so, then we should attempt to place the stories back into conversation with each other as well as reading each tale as an individual literary artifact with its own internal integrity.

The resulting conversation is partly about the nature of American history as Hawthorne envisioned it, which seems to be a complex dialectic between aspirations for freedom and moments of repression, between the ideals of a democratic society and the realities of persecution, injustice, and psychic turmoil. Yet, an appreciation of the resulting discourse ultimately depends upon a fuller recognition of the ways in which Hawthorne's narrative artistry penetrates beneath the surface of the human psyche and resists simple conclusions. Along with Poe, Hawthorne deserves credit for transforming the American short story into a form capable of psychological investigation. While he is generally credited with inventing the short story, Washington Irving had a limited sense of the value of form and structure, viewing plot largely as a framework on which to display his materials and demonstrate his stylistic mastery. Hawthorne and Poe brought a greater commitment to plot structure, to form and shape, to the dramatic expression of climactic scenes, to a process in which the development of both character and setting became increasingly and perhaps inevitably psychological. There is a sense of dramatic shape to both "Young Goodman Brown" and "My Kinsman, Major Molineaux" that makes the movement from history to psychology possible: both stories are built around grand, almost operatic scenes of nightmare and revelation that compel the protagonists to abandon their own easy preconceptions about the world and their places in it. The difference, of course, is that Brown goes on a journey and then returns as a bitter and angry man while Robin enters a new world, discovers he is not welcomed on the terms he assumes, but is ultimately invited to stay. Although he presumably will stay in the town he has entered, psychologically speaking, Robin is still moving forward into the complex world of adult responsibility. On the other hand, Brown's movement home ends with psychological stagnation and an arrested development that is manifested in the depiction of the return to the town as a perverted replay of the journey into the wilderness and his peculiarly juvenile insistence on oversimplifying all questions of good and evil. In short, Goodman Brown and Robin Molineaux ultimately represent two different outcomes, two different possibilities for the human psyche in specifically American landscapes.

Hawthorne developed an aesthetic form that enabled the short story to explore moral dilemmas and psychological traumas as well as historical facts. When Irving's Rip Van Winkle retreats into the forest and ends up sleeping through the American Revolution, his motivation is largely limited to escaping the demands of a nagging wife. The journey away from the wife assumes many more dimensions in "Young Goodman Brown." In the opening paragraph, Brown steps into the street, but puts his head back to exchange a kiss with his wife, who is "aptly named" Faith (*Tales and Sketches* 276). Thus, the story opens on a threshold, informing the thoughtful reader that the story will be about a "threshold" in the life of the protagonist, a symbolic boundary that may or may not be finally crossed. It is only his head that Brown puts back, suggesting the unhealthy division between mind and body – or head and heart, as Hawthorne usually expresses it – that often marks the Gothic mode in nineteenth-century literature. For many readers, Faith is the thinnest of characters, defined simply by her allegorical name and pink ribbons, but that is because readers often make the same mistake that Brown does, the mistake of failing to listen to her. She has only a few lines but they are quite revealing:

> "Dearest heart," whispered she, softly and rather sadly, when her lips were close to his ear, "pr'y thee, put off your journey until sunrise, and sleep in your own bed to-night.

A lone woman is troubled with such dreams and such thoughts, that she's afeard of herself, sometimes. Pray, tarry with me this night, dear husband, of all nights in the year!" (276)

The lines reveal a richly complex woman, one with dreams and thoughts and fears, who speaks "softly and rather sadly" as she asks her husband to stay with her that night. Brown's failure to hear what she is trying to tell him becomes clear when we learn that just before turning the corner "by the meeting-house, he looked back, and saw the head of Faith still peeping after him, with a melancholy air, in spite of her pink ribbons" (276). Significantly, he sees only the head, not the body and not the complete woman, indicating both the limits of his perception and his inability to unite head and heart, mind and body. His words reinforce his failure to understand her, to accept her as a complex human being with fears and needs: "Well, she's a blessed angel on earth; and after this one night, I'll cling to her skirts and follow her to Heaven." This is bad theology in almost any religious scheme, including that of the Puritans, but it is also evidence that he has failed to acknowledge his wife as a real woman with a body, mind, and soul who wants her husband to listen to and care about her dreams, thoughts, and fears. In short, the story is ultimately about Brown's failure to understand Faith, his wife, as well as the religious concept of faith.

The opening prepares the reader to appreciate the carefully structured journey into and out of the forest, which for Hawthorne usually represents a moral wilderness free of human law and normal boundaries. As he moves into the woods, Brown gradually discovers the depravity, hypocrisy, and corruption of every representative of moral authority that he has ever admired. His guide may be the Devil assuming the shape of his grandfather or just a fabrication of his own twisted imagination. Certainly, the landscape becomes increasingly symbolic and psychological as the story builds to the witch's Sabbath at which Brown collapses after imploring his wife not to pledge her soul to the devil. After awakening from this trauma, Brown exits the forest and on the way home confronts and condemns each of the figures of moral authority that he met on the previous night. The man who entered the wilderness believing in a world filled with virtue leaves believing only in the corruption and depravity of everyone around him. Ultimately, he settles into a life of grief and sorrow with his wife and their posterity that will end only with death. The story that opens on the threshold of a Salem street at a certain moment of Puritan history moves from the world of historical fact into a symbolic realm filled with surrealistic imagery, psychological confrontation, and moral confusion, a symbolic realm that resists easy interpretation. Hawthorne's much-praised insistence on ambiguity even explicitly raises the issue of whether Brown has fallen asleep "and only dreamed a wild dream" (288). It is much too easy to say that it does not matter whether he was dreaming or not because the end result is a life of endless gloom. The author wants us to ponder the questions he raises and not dismiss them. He wants us to engage the multiple dimensions – both ontological and epistemological – of his fictional realms in all of their implications, which may be historical, theological, psychological, and oneiric.

As I suggested earlier, it is tempting to place "Young Goodman Brown" into conversation with "My Kinsman, Major Molineaux" and see young Robin's response to disillusionment as ultimately a healthy counterpart to Brown's regression into misery. Throughout the story, Robin repeatedly asks others for directions to his kinsman, a sign that he is asking the wrong question about the direction of his own future. By the end of the story, Robin has a mentor, a guide who will help him accept the adult world of work and personal responsibility and escape the juvenile world of easy judgment. While we are told about the gloom that follows Brown to his dying day, we leave Robin as a young man about to face the future without any presumptions of his right to a certain place in an endlessly fluid world. The ending is not about the closure of a life, but about a new beginning and new possibilities to create a meaningful identity in a complex and changing world. In some respect, Hawthorne's historical tales are about the ways in which individuals and nations grow to achieve complex, fluid, and life-affirming identities or regress into tyranny and grief.

The fascination with the formation or destruction of meaningful identity certainly shapes "Roger Malvin's Burial" (1832) and "The Gentle Boy" (1832), both of which focus on a special capacity for self-destruction within the American psyche. When he leaves his dying friend, Roger Malvin, to end his life alone in the wilderness and then misleads Roger's daughter, his future wife, into believing that he had provided a proper burial, Reuben Bourne finds himself almost accidentally falling into a life of secret shame and personal dishonor. The psychic burden of concealed guilt, a theme that occurs in many of Hawthorne's strongest works, leads the protagonist to undermine almost all opportunities for happiness and success and finally forces him to seek a new life for himself and his family in the frontier. In some sense, the psychic drama here points to a national myth, the idea of an America that continually provides the opportunity for new beginnings and fresh starts. Nevertheless, Reuben Bourne cannot find happiness in a simple change of place. He cannot remake himself and cannot even move forward into a new and healthier direction. Ironically, he finds himself compelled to return to the very place where he left his old friend and where he now accidentally shoots his own son in a perverted ritual of sacrifice and expiation. The return of the repressed[4] comes with a terrible price as the sins of the father are visited upon the son. The frontier becomes the site where past actions come back to haunt the present, not the place of new beginnings.

"The Gentle Boy," which provides a chilling portrayal of persecution and masochism, appears to have been among the most highly regarded of his early historical tales. It not only found a place in the first edition of *Twice-Told Tales* (1837), but also was published separately in a special edition, *The Gentle Boy; a Thrice-Told Tale* (1839), with illustrations by Hawthorne's future wife, Sophia Peabody. This exploration of the cruel mistreatment of Quakers focuses much of its attention on the victims of persecution, but that attention is not fully sympathetic. The title character, Ilbrahim, exemplifies the appealing innocence of childhood, but he is caught between Puritans and Quakers in a process that increasingly equates religious zealotry with sadomasochism. There are a number of crucial contradictions at the heart of the great democratic experiment that emerged from the American Revolution. The most obvious is the fundamental contradiction of a land of liberty occupied by slaveholders and slaves, but Hawthorne rarely deals explicitly with slavery in his fiction. "The Gentle Boy," however, clearly punctures New England's claim to be a refuge for those seeking freedom of religion by depicting the inhumanity of both persecutors and persecuted. The story exemplifies Hawthorne's fierce distrust of all extreme positions, but if there is a dialectic here, it certainly does not move to any meaningful synthesis. Ilbrahim's death redeems neither his fanatical mother nor persecuting Puritans. Although the passing of time brings a "spirit of forbearance," it is not marked by Christian mercy and genuine compassion, but by a variety of "superfluous sympathies" that enable the community to find a remarkably unimportant place for the woman they once tormented: "every one spoke of her with that degree of pity which it is pleasant to experience; every one was ready to do her the little kindnesses, which are not costly, yet manifest good will; and when at last she died, a long train of her once bitter persecutors followed her, with decent sadness and tears that were not painful, to her place by Ilbrahim's green and sunken grave" (*Tales and Sketches* 138). Both "Roger Malvin's Burial" and "The Gentle Boy" would have been part of the conversation about the meaning and future of American society that I believe is the foundation of the historical tales making up *Provincial Tales*, and they would have been among the most disturbing and pessimistic parts.

Hawthorne returned to the source material of American history in the unjustly neglected "Legends of the Province-House" (1838–9), a frame narrative featuring four tales told in a tavern which served as the mansion of the royal governors in colonial times. The first two accounts depict men whose arrogant opposition to New England freedom meets with apparently supernatural disapproval, while the final two focus on haughty women who become ghostly victims of a changing world. The first three are told by Bela Tiffany, a narrator who clearly supports the heroes of the revolution, but the final one is narrated by an old loyalist whose words, we are assured, have been filtered through the perspective of the more democratic frame narrator. The series begins with the promise of supernatural justice for the opponents of liberty and ends with profound sympathy for the loyalists who have lost everything except perhaps their illusions. One of the most remarkable facts about Hawthorne's treatment of the American Revolution is that he always insists on evoking empathy for the loyalists who opposed it and in the process lost almost everything. The final legend ends with John Hancock expressing a moment of compassion for the last loyalist and then proclaiming "We are no longer children of the Past!" (*Tales and Sketches* 677). The frame narrator has come to the Province-House seeking to be charmed and entertained by the truth of history, but finds himself forced to confront a past that entails much more than the "tinge of romance and historic grandeur" (639) he seeks to throw over the present, a past that includes pain and suffering as well as heroism and triumph. In the final sentence, he retreats from both the tavern and history, "being resolved not to show my face in the Province-House for a good while hence – if ever" (677). "Legends of the Province-House" preceded the writing and publication of *The Whole History of Grandfather's Chair*, but it would be the last historical tale for adults that Hawthorne would write for a decade. Although he returned to historical materials with his masterpiece, *The Scarlet Letter* (1850), he was moving into other terrains and other times.

Hawthorne Beyond History

A full appreciation of Hawthorne's contribution to the short story requires a larger recognition of his willingness to experiment with a wide range of subjects and forms and of his conscious attempts to expand the possibilities of short fiction.[5] Although now known mostly as the author of powerfully tragic tales set mostly in New England's past, Hawthorne was admired in his own time as a writer of many moods and diverse interests. Melville seized on only a small portion of them in his famous 1850 review of *Mosses from an Old Manse* when he proclaimed that Hawthorne said "No, in Thunder!" but other reviewers valued other aspects of his art. Although Poe linked Hawthorne to the German romantic, Ludwig Tieck, reviewers were much more likely to evoke comparison to Charles Lamb, the British writer of genial essays. In his review of the 1837 *Twice-Told Tales*, Longfellow largely ignored the powerful tales we admire today and singled out three sketches for special praise: "Sunday at Home," "Sights from a Steeple," and "A Rill from the Town Pump."[6] The sketch as a literary form currently receives almost no scholarly attention, but it was a well-established and immensely popular genre that had not only launched Washington Irving's career as an author but also went on to dominate American magazine publication for much of the nineteenth century. As a literary genre, it was, in fact, more established and more respected than the short story, a relative new-comer to literature. The requirements of the literary sketch also seem especially congenial to Hawthorne's talents and inclinations. While his tales rely on a strong sense of plot and structure, his sketches tend either to offer a pleasant ramble through a specific location or to assume a single vantage point from which the author provides a blend of precise visual description, moral reflection, and ironic commentary. The sketch allows a creative writer to assume an imaginative stance that relies more on a point of view than the telling of a story, more on the demonstration of a fine sensibility actively engaged in reading the world than on the development of narrative. Hawthorne produced sketches throughout his career, included significant numbers of them in his collections of stories, employed them to introduce both his collections and his novels, and ultimately found that this literary form enabled him to use the English material that he had been unable to shape into a romance to construct his final book, *Our Old Home*. His most important comments on his literary values and his own position as an American writer appear in the literary sketches that he used as introductions to his book. The inclusion of sketches also allowed him to ensure that his books had the wide variety of moods that he believed to be essential to maintaining the reader's interest in collections of short works.

His most ambitious attempt to shape a coherent book out of sketches and tales would have been *The Story Teller*, which we can only partly reconstruct through the fragments that were published out of context. It seems likely that the completed volume would have detailed the travels of an itinerant storyteller through a specifically American landscape (including the White Mountains of New Hampshire, and Niagara Falls, the Erie Canal, and old Ticonderoga in upstate New York), providing stories inspired by various scenes and events, and probably offering some account of the various audiences and their responses to his tales. According to his sister-in-law, Elizabeth Peabody, after the book was dismantled, Hawthorne lost interest in the individual stories "which had in their original place in the 'Storyteller' a greater degree of significance" (Wineapple 81). Given the care Hawthorne took with frame narratives throughout his career, this "greater degree of significance" might have come from the relationship of a specific narrative to the site that inspired it or the development of thematic patterns in which individual pieces form a kind of debate or conversation on various topics. For instance, some of the stories that were probably intended for the projected volume focus on a basic conflict between an unsettled life of roving ambition and the stable values of home and family. Both "The Ambitious Guest" (1835) and "The Great Carbuncle" (1837) are clearly connected to the White Mountains, and both emphasize the dangers posed by various abstract desires that remove individuals from the human connections offered by home, marriage, and family. If these works are placed in the context of other stories with similar themes, such as "The Wedding Knell" (1836) and "The Threefold Destiny" (1838), and perhaps even with the perverse violation of the marriage bond in "Wakefield" (1835), then it seems likely that Hawthorne was building towards a larger exploration of the value of home and the danger of any ambition or abstraction that cuts human beings off from what he later called "the magnetic chain of humanity" ("Ethan Brand," *Tales and Sketches* 1064). This strong affirmation of home is actually central to American travel writing in the early and mid-nineteenth century, much of which explicitly declares the chief purpose of travel to be the acquisition of a greater appreciation of one's own home and native land. This discovery of the importance of home and human connection might even have been the primary lesson that the narrator of *The Story Teller* finally learns as well as the one that is incorporated in many of its narratives.

It seems likely that one of Hawthorne's most impressive tales, "The Minister's Black Veil," might have been part of *The Story Teller*, because it clearly alludes to another story, "The Wedding Knell," suggesting that they were meant to be part of the same volume. If so, then the way the minister's act of putting on a veil separates him from his community and his fiancée would have been a crucial part of the book's larger study of the dangers of human isolation. Parson Hooper cuts himself off from his congregation by two acts, the wearing of the black veil and the refusal to explain his reasons for this strange act. The veil generates an amazing number of possibilities. A reader familiar with the conventions of the Gothic romance is likely to conclude that any tale about a minister with secret guilt must involve some kind of sexual transgression, probably with a parishioner, a plot element that eventually formed the basis of *The Scarlet Letter*. In his discussion of the tale, Edgar Allan Poe even identifies the parishioner as the woman in the coffin. Those wishing to emphasize the sexual implications of secret guilt also note that the donning of the veil enables the minister to escape the marriage bond as his fiancée refuses to marry a man who hides his face. Of course, the veil immediately raises the issue of perception because it obscures and darkens the vision of the minister as well as preventing others from perceiving whatever emotions or revelations might be expressed in his face. Nevertheless, in a very different way, the veil connects Parson Hooper to his parishioners, whose reactions often suggest that the veil actually reflects their secret guilt and hidden anxieties. The power of the veil lies in its ability both to provoke questions and to deny answers, to elicit interest in the minister while creating a barrier that isolates him. Ultimately, it is the veil's almost endless capacity to create a multiplicity of meanings that endows "The Minister's Black Veil" with extraordinary power. It is possible that it might generate even more meanings if we could restore it to its place within *The Story Teller*.

The framework Hawthorne devised for *The Story Teller* certainly would have been an important part of his lifelong fascination with the place of the literary artist in a democratic society. No American writer of fiction, except possibly Henry James, has devoted more attention to the artist, to the capacity of art to redeem or alienate, and to the inherent conflicts between meaningful aesthetic values and a materialistic culture. The projected volume would have integrated fiction and descriptive sketches within a framework that explored the relationship between author and audience, thus foregrounding the social role of narration. The book also would almost certainly have emphasized the special difficulties American writers faced in realizing an artistic vision. The traveling storyteller who appears in "The Seven Vagabonds" (1833) and "Passages from a Relinquished Work" (1834), the fragments that clearly would be among the earliest parts of the book, is remarkably cheerful and carefree as he embarks on his great adventure. The pieces, however, that probably were designed to appear towards the end of the volume, "Fragments from the Journal of a Solitary Man" and "The Devil in Manuscript," portray an author at the point of despair, one who burns his manuscripts and ends up setting the town on fire. The fragmentary nature of these pieces and the degree to which Hawthorne's framework has been destroyed make it impossible for us to make any final judgments, but it is difficult to see how the final fragments could lead to anything but the most pessimistic conclusions about the possibilities for the literary artist in America.

Hawthorne continued to devote much of his literary energy to exploring the nature of art and the artist, producing a number of intriguing stories about the power and limits of art. "The Prophetic Pictures" (1837) emphasizes the ability of a great artist to capture the true qualities of his subjects, including a capacity for murder. "Drowne's Wooden Image" (1844) explores the way in which a carver of ship figureheads creates an artistic masterpiece. A couple of stories offer insights into Hawthorne's view of his British and American contemporaries. "P's Correspondence" (1845) provides the comic ramblings of a deranged mind who fantasizes that several dead writers are still alive and bemoans the untimely death of literary figures who were really still alive and working. The allegorical visit recounted in the "The Hall of Fantasy" (1843) included some intriguing comments on other American writers in its magazine version, which were unfortunately deleted in book publication. Hawthorne's most fully developed and most impressive story about the role of art in materialistic America is "The Artist of the Beautiful" (1844), which uses the mode of science fiction to explore the power and limitations of art and the artist. In the act of creating a machine endowed with spiritual qualities, a mechanical butterfly, Owen Warland commits himself to the ideal of the Beautiful and separates himself from the earthly worlds of commerce and love. Annie, the woman he loves, marries Robert Danforth, a blacksmith who clearly embodies the brute force of a materialistic reality, and their child ultimately crushes the beautiful, but fragile butterfly that Warland has created. The story ends with a surprisingly transcendentalist affirmation of the ability of the true artist to rise above the crude reality of a money-loving world and take delight in the process of creation as intrinsically rewarding.

Hawthorne rarely gets the credit he deserves for helping to invent science fiction, but no other author of his time produced as many powerful works in this new genre. When he moved to Concord, Massachusetts, in 1842, he turned away from historical fiction almost entirely and focused his energy on new forms, including stories about scientists and the end of the world. This is partly because he was a serious writer actively seeking ways to expand the range of his talents as well as searching for forms that might be commercially viable. His turning towards the material of science fiction probably also reflects the intellectual atmosphere of Concord, which exposed him to a world of bold thinkers engaged in a variety of philosophical and cultural experiments, but also enhanced both his own natural distrust of disembodied thought and his basic skepticism about the idea of unlimited human progress. Another source of inspiration was clearly the Millerites, whose predictions about the Day of Judgment coming in 1843 or 1844 resulted in two impressive stories about the end of the world. In "The New Adam and Eve" (1843), the extinction of the human race is followed by the immediate creation of a new Adam and Eve, two innocents who wander the remains of a now deserted Boston, attempting to make sense of what they find and giving the author the opportunity for a wide range of moral reflections. "Earth's Holocaust" (1844) is much more pessimistic: the bonfire created to burn away all the "worn-out trumpery" of human folly also devours works of literature, philosophy, and scripture, and Hawthorne concludes that all efforts at human perfectibility are doomed to failure unless we figure out a way to purify the human heart. Hawthorne's fiction had always called for a holistic recognition of the importance of both head and heart, and much of the science fiction he produced explicitly calls for a greater recognition of the importance of the heart, of the emotional life, and of the need for all human beings to recognize and accept their limitations.

Hawthorne's scientists are usually victims of their own egoism who fail to under-stand the world they attempt to control and change. Their arrogance leads them into a cold-blooded violation of the human heart, which is usually represented by an experiment on a woman who personifies both the emotional component of human experience and the fragility of human life. "Dr. Heidegger's Experiment" (1837), the earliest of Hawthorne's experiments with the form we now call science fiction, focuses on an elixir that temporarily restores youth to a group of elderly friends. In "The Birth-mark" (1843), Aylmer's foolish and arrogant attempt to remove his wife's single physical blemish emphasizes our need to accept the limitations inherent in our mortality. These themes are developed most fully in the longest and most complex of Hawthorne's tales, "Rappaccini's Daughter" (1844), in which Giovanni falls in love with the mysterious Beatrice only to discover that she has been transformed into a poisonous creature by her father's scientific experiments. Another scientist offers an antidote, but it proves fatal to her. In this brilliant and intricately crafted work, Hawthorne is enlarging the boundaries of his fictional territory to permit a fuller, more complex engagement with multiple characters and the moral positions that they embody. The story ends by appearing to ask us to judge who is responsible for the death of Beatrice, but the final answer is really everyone. In "Rappaccini's Daughter," mistrust destroys love, the pretense to knowledge masks destructive pride, and the only shared value is the failure to accept moral responsibility.

Hawthorne's search for new literary forms in the 1840s also led him to experiment with the possibilities inherent in allegory, and he even toyed with the idea of a series of linked works that he planned to call "Allegories of the Heart." Although he later disparaged most of these works and his own tendency to indulge in allegory, he successfully transformed the allegorical world of Bunyan's *Pilgrim's Progress* into the brilliant satire of nineteenth-century life, "The Celestial Rail-road" (1843). These experiments in allegory should be seen as part of Hawthorne's continued attempt to explore and expand the possibilities of fictional form. This process of experimentation also led him to the retelling of classical myths for children in *A Wonder-Book for Girls and Boys* (1851) and *Tanglewood Tales* (1853). Hawthorne, the first major author to provide English versions of the Greek myths for children, introduced some important innovations. For instance, in the original versions of the Midas story, the king repents of his golden touch when he discovers that he can no longer eat, because the food he needs turns to gold. In Hawthorne's version, his renunciation comes because he accidentally turns his daughter into gold. We value Hawthorne today mostly for a relatively small part of his literary work, the romances and tales that enlarge our understanding of human psychology and history, but a full appreciation of his career and achievements requires greater recognition of the diversity of his literary interests and of his mastery of a wide range of literary modes.

NOTES

1   There are numerous biographical studies of Hawthorne, which take a variety of psychological viewpoints, but the books by Mellow and Wineapple listed in the References section provide the clearest guide to the available facts. The fullest Freudian study of his fiction remains Frederick Crews's brilliant book, but readers should know that Crews himself has repudiated both much of that book and Freudian approaches in general.

2   Alfred Weber, who has made the fullest attempt to reconstruct Hawthorne's *Story Teller*, believes that it would have contained "Young Goodman Brown" and that there is not enough evidence to place "The Minister's Black Veil" in it. These conclusions differ substantially from those developed later in this chapter, which share many of the views presented by Richard P. Adams in his article.

3　The ideas expressed here and throughout the section on history owe a great deal to Michael Bell's brilliant study of the historical tales. The fullest exploration of Hawthorne's extensive knowledge of the Puritan past may be found in Michael J. Colacurcio's impressive book. Roy Harvey Pearce's comments on Hawthorne's historical imagination remain invaluable.

4　For the fullest consideration of the idea of the return of the repressed and other Freudian concepts, please see the book by Frederick Crews cited in the References.

5　Nina Baym's *The Shape of Hawthorne's Career* provides the fullest overview of the many aspects of this literary career.

6　These reviews and more may be found in *Nathaniel Hawthorne: The Contemporary Reviews*, edited by John Idol, Jr., and Buford Jones.

REFERENCES AND FURTHER READING

Adams, Richard P. "Hawthorne's *Provincial Tales.*" *New England Quarterly* 30 (1957): 39–57.

Baym, Nina. *The Shape of Hawthorne's Career.* Ithaca: Cornell University Press, 1976.

Bell, Michael. *Hawthorne and the Historical Romance of New England.* Princeton: Princeton University Press, 1971.

Bell, Millicent. *Hawthorne's View of the Artist.* New York: New York State University Press, 1962.

Bell, Millicent, ed. *New Essays on Hawthorne's Major Tales.* New York: Cambridge University Press, 1993.

Colacurcio, Michael J. *The Province of Piety: Moral History in Hawthorne's Early Tales.* Cambridge, MA: Harvard University Press, 1984.

Crews, Frederick. *The Sins of the Fathers: Hawthorne's Psychological Themes.* New York: Oxford University Press, 1966.

Doubleday, Neil Frank. *Hawthorne's Early Tales: A Critical Study.* Durham, NC: Duke University Press, 1977.

Erlich, Gloria C. *Family Themes and Hawthorne's Fiction: The Tenacious Web.* New Brunswick, NJ: Rutgers University Press, 1984.

Feidelson, Charles, Jr. *Symbolism and American Literature.* Chicago: University of Chicago Press, 1953.

Fetterley, Judith. "Women Beware Science: 'The Birthmark.'" *The Resisting Reader: A Feminist Approach to American Fiction.* Bloomington: Indiana University Press, 1978. 22–33.

Fogle, Richard H. *Hawthorne's Fiction: The Light and the Dark.* Norman: Oklahoma University Press, 1964.

Gollin, Rita K. *Nathaniel Hawthorne and the Truth of Dreams.* Baton Rouge: Louisiana State University Press, 1979.

Hawthorne, Nathaniel. *Tales and Sketches.* New York: Library of America, 1982.

Idol, John, Jr., and Buford Jones, eds. *Nathaniel Hawthorne: The Contemporary Reviews.* New York: Cambridge University Press, 1994.

Male, Roy R. *Hawthorne's Tragic Vision.* Austin: University of Texas Press, 1957.

Martin, Terence. *Nathaniel Hawthorne.* Rev. edn. Boston: Twayne, 1983.

Matheisen, F. O. *The American Renaissance.* New York: Oxford University Press, 1941.

Mellow, James R. *Nathaniel Hawthorne in His Times.* Boston: Houghton Mifflin, 1980.

Miller, J. Hillis. *Hawthorne and History: Defacing It.* Cambridge, MA: Blackwell, 1991.

Pearce, Roy Harvey. *Historicism Once More.* Princeton: Princeton University Press, 1969.

Reynolds, Larry, ed. *A Historical Guide to Nathaniel Hawthorne.* New York: Oxford University Press, 2001.

Turner, Arlin. *Nathaniel Hawthorne: A Biography.* New York: Oxford University Press, 1980.

Von Frank, Albert J., ed. *Critical Essays on Hawthorne's Short Stories.* Boston: G. K. Hall, 1991.

Waggoner, Hyatt H. *Hawthorne: A Critical Study.* Rev. edn. Cambridge, MA: Harvard University Press, 1963.

Wineapple, Brenda. *Hawthorne: A Life.* New York: Knopf, 2003.

Wright, John W. "A Feathertop Kit." *Norton Critical Edition of Nathaniel Hawthorne's Tales.* Ed. James McIntosh. New York: W. W. Norton, 1987. 439–54.

5

Charles W. Chesnutt and the Fictions of a "New" America

Charles Duncan

By the end of the nineteenth century, the American short story had, of course, been firmly established. Washington Irving, Nathaniel Hawthorne, Edgar Allan Poe, and Herman Melville each "Americanized" to some extent the European models from which they had found source material or narrative pattern, or tone and diction. Later, figures such as W. D. Howells, Mary E. Wilkins Freeman, Sarah Orne Jewett, and Mark Twain offered fictions that particularized American characters and settings, often delivered in more distinctly "American" voices. But when Charles W. Chesnutt appeared on the American literary scene in the late nineteenth century, readers began to hear more extensively from previously muted American voices. While other writers had included African American and mixed-race characters, no other American writer had so assiduously (and so interestingly) probed the profound and growing diversity of the US and, indeed, the central role race has played (and continues to play) in the formation and evolution of the country. As the United States struggled to remake itself following the Civil War, Chesnutt – the first African American fiction writer to earn a national reputation – explored the complexities, origins, and consequences of that national remaking through his writings, particularly in his short stories. And while Chesnutt had new American stories to tell and new voices to deliver, his best work generally refits, and sometimes appropriates, traditional American narrative patterns and plots – the "plantation" story, the slave narrative, the sentimental love story, the local-color story, among others – in ways that both expand our national narrative and, at times, challenge and even subvert it. In doing so, Chesnutt contributed to the delineation of a new national narrative, one that still had at its core the Founding Fathers' democratic ideals but that was far more inclusive and complicated.

No figure could have been better prepared to articulate this "new," more diverse post–Civil War America, one in which African Americans (men at least) could, for the first time, vote and run for political office. Charles W. Chesnutt's life and works bridged many, if not all, of the seeming oppositions that defined, and in many ways continue to define, America. As a man of mixed race – he identified himself as African

American – who vowed in his journals to educate white readers about African Americans and who served as teacher and principal of a Normal school, Chesnutt offered readers nuanced accounts of both African Americans and white Americans of virtually every economic, social, and educational type. Similarly, he lived significant portions of his life in both the South (he resided in North Carolina for nearly twenty years) and the North, having moved to Ohio, where he spent the rest of his life, at age 26. Similarly, his fictions contain narrative and thematic oppositions as well – he explored the past and the present, often within the same text, the white and the black, the North and the South, and he generally did so in multiple voices, including various dialects.

In fact, Chesnutt's handling of voices defines, in many ways, his short fiction. In his efforts to re-narrate this new America, Chesnutt often uses embedded narratives – long, highly personal stories told in the individual voices of an array of characters with a range of education, background, and experience – as a primary storytelling method. Sometimes, these embedded narratives reflect the characters' attempts to re-form their families, as happens in a story such as "Her Virginia Mammy," in which the two women protagonists, according to Susan Fraiman, tell long personal narratives as a way to "piece together their common past" (446). At other times, the quoted narratives express resistance to the new America, as happens in "The Doll," in which a Southern politician tells a long, violent tale to illustrate his racial theories, especially in regard to the rights of African Americans. There's something undeniably compelling about Chesnutt's willingness to let so broad an assortment of characters – men and women, blacks and whites, Northerners and Southerners – speak for themselves, and in their own voices. And Chesnutt's skill at rendering the dialects and voices of so many disparate Americans likewise makes these stories resonate.

Generally speaking, Chesnutt's short stories can also be divided by setting. He sets roughly half of his short works, as well as most of his novels, in the South, most usually in North Carolina, the state in which he grew up after the Civil War. In "The Goophered Grapevine," the first of the conjure tales to be published (in the *Atlantic Monthly*, in 1887), the narrator, a transplanted Ohioan (like Chesnutt) who has moved to the South for health and business, describes his new milieu as "a quaint old town, which I shall call Patesville, because, for one reason, that is not its name" (*Conjure Woman* 3). Thus, the fictional Patesville (based explicitly on Fayetteville, North Carolina) becomes the setting for most of Chesnutt's "Southern" stories; having lived in and around Fayetteville for nearly twenty years, the author knew it well. He chose to locate most of the rest of his short fiction in a place familiar to him as well. Virtually all of his "Northern" fictions are set in "Groveland," Ohio, a fictionalized twin for Cleveland, the city in which he lived from 1884 until his death in 1932.

At first glance, many of Chesnutt's short stories, especially those about the ante- and postbellum South, probably seemed recognizable, even conventional, to many readers. Indeed, the dialect stories which earned Chesnutt his initial fame – published in the *Atlantic Monthly* beginning in 1887 and later collected into his first book, *The Conjure Woman*, in 1899 – came familiarly clothed. After all, readers had grown largely familiar with the so-called "plantation tradition" works of such writers as John

Pendleton Kennedy, Thomas Nelson Page, Joel Chandler Harris, and Thomas Dixon. Typically, such stories focused on idealized versions of the antebellum South, a place (and time) depicted nostalgically as simpler, and more honorable and orderly than modern life. Thus, plantation life is recalled, often by an ex-slave narrator who regales listeners – generally white characters and, broadly speaking, white readers – with tales of plantation life, including generally favorable descriptions of the relationships between slaves and masters created by the "peculiar institution." Interesting, too, is the fact that the stories told by the ex-slave characters, who speak in sometimes exaggerated dialect, often derive from African American folktales; both Page's *In Ole Virginia, Or Marse Chan and Other Stories* (1887) and Harris's *Uncle Remus: His Songs and Sayings* (1881), for example, drew on African American folktales for their "inside" narratives.

Several nineteenth-century African American writers, however, professed to having found plantation literature distasteful; there are many examples of attempts to respond to, parody, and rebuke such writings. Frederick Douglass's *The Heroic Slave* (1853), William Wells Brown's *Clotel; or The President's Daughter: A Narrative of Slave Life in the United States* (1853), Frances Watkins's *The Slave Mother: A Tale of the Ohio* (1856), and Paul Laurence Dunbar's *The Sport of the Gods* (1902) all, to greater or some extent, repudiate the racial and social claims implicit in plantation tradition literature.

Many scholars today similarly detect racially charged, even sinister messages underlying the plantation tradition. Figures such as Houston Baker, Amy Kaplan, and Kenneth Warren posit that authors in the tradition overtly attempt to reinforce racial (and often racist) stereotypes; Kaplan, for example, calls Page's *In Ole Virginia* "a collection of dialect stories narrated by a faithful ex-slave who reminisces nostalgically about 'dem good ole times.'" And Eric J. Sundquist suggests that the function of plantation tradition fiction goes far beyond idle nostalgia:

> The recreated plantation was a perfect topos for lamenting the loss of legitimate white mastery but also for demonstrating that, though legal slavery was gone, the forms and hierarchies of a clearly defined racial order, with its consequent economic privileges, could still be maintained. Plantation literature and culture did not simply demand a febrile return to the past; it was the deceptive screen for keeping contemporary African Americans in bondage to the whole white race, as Albion Tourgee had said in his brief for Homer Plessy. (Sundquist 287)

Thus, both nineteenth-century African American authors and modern scholars argue that the tradition perpetuated unflattering stereotypes of the past at best and attempted to maintain a racist social order at worst.

Why, then, would a reform-minded writer who identified himself as African American choose to work in what might have been for him an offensive literary form? Surprising though it may seem, the plantation tradition – and especially the frame story as popularized by Harris and Page – provided an ideal platform from which to try to advance Chesnutt's two primary goals as a writer: to earn money and to educate white readers about African Americans. In using such a well-established literary genre, one his late nineteenth-century readers found familiar and comfortable, Chesnutt would be able to accomplish both goals, despite their seeming inherent contradictions. The stories, that is, would allow him to attain popular success (*The Conjure Woman* did indeed become his best-selling book) by appealing to the expectations of readers captivated by nostalgic and quaintly exotic descriptions of the Old South; and the stories would simultaneously amend the attitudes of his white readers about slaves and the free African Americans who, by the end of the nineteenth century, had come to form a significant portion of the citizenry. The format thus allows Chesnutt to demythologize the patrician ideals that seem to inform the plantation tradition, and it likewise permits the sort of subtle and complex humanizing of African Americans that became a feature of virtually all of his writings. In addition, the stories, as Joseph McElrath, Jr., points out, are "dominantly comical in tone; [their] serious reflections ... are designed to elicit sympathy in a gentle manner" (*Critical Essays* 4). Such an approach no doubt reflects Chesnutt's own nature as well as his savvy.

Chesnutt obviously believed he could make productive use of the genre – he uses it to structure fourteen "conjure" stories (a significant share of his entire short story output), the seven collected in *The Conjure Woman* and seven others published between 1887 and 1925. Like some of his predecessors in the genre, Chesnutt bases many of these so-called "conjure" stories on African American folktales, and, as the title of his collection suggests, he imbues the tales with magic (or, as Julius calls it, "goopher"). The stories typically rest upon the interaction of three central characters: John, a white Ohio businessman who has moved to North Carolina after the Civil War to purchase and operate a vineyard; Julius, an ex-slave raconteur and now coachman who had lived and worked on the property when it had been a plantation; and Annie, John's wife, who seems to serve in many ways as the proxy for the kind of open-minded white reader Chesnutt hoped to cultivate. Each story typically opens with John as narrator of the "outside" story, but it is Julius's "inside" narrative – told in dialect – that forms the crux of the story. Each of Julius's tales recounts events on the plantation before the war, while John and Annie listen; after Julius concludes his tale, both figures typically comment on, interpret, question, and debate the merits – both literary and historical – of the tale (and Julius's telling of it). Perhaps the best description of the tales comes from John, who summarizes them this way:

> Some of these stories are quaintly humorous; others wildly extravagant, revealing the Oriental cast of the negro's imagination; while others, poured freely into the sympathetic ear of a Northern-bred woman, disclose many a tragic incident of the darker side of slavery. (*Conjure Woman* 40–1)

In "The Goophered Grapevine," the first story in *The Conjure Woman* collection, Chesnutt introduces the three central characters and, indeed, the governing paradigm of all fourteen of his conjure stories, and it certainly discloses a darker side of slavery than one might find in a traditional plantation tale. Having recently relocated from the North and in search of some land in North Carolina to cultivate, John and Annie decide to buy a plantation that has suffered from neglect since the Civil War, which had ended a considerable, if never specified, number of years earlier. There they meet Julius McAdoo, an ex-slave who has apparently been living on the plantation and subsisting in part by tending what's left of the vineyards on the property. As in all of the conjure stories, the frame story is narrated by John, a white Ohio businessman, while Julius narrates the "inside," or embedded, story. In short, Chesnutt developed a narrative paradigm which allows him both to counter romantic depictions of slavery but also – more interestingly – to explore his own fictionalized version of "Reconstruction"; here, as in the other conjure stories, blacks and whites, Northerners and Southerners come together and share stories of the past as they attempt to remake the country following the Civil War.

Thus, when Julius learns of John's plans to purchase the estate, he tells the couple, in dialect and without interruption, a long story about the plantation's pre–Civil War days. The tale recounts the grim consequences that accrue when the plantation owner, Mars Dugal' McAdoo, hires Aunt Peggy (the conjure woman of the title of the collection) to bewitch the vineyard as a means of preventing local slaves from stealing his grapes. The spell, which putatively causes anyone who eats the grapes to die within a year, works wonderfully well as a deterrent until Henry, a recently acquired slave unaware of the vineyard's "goophered" condition, eats some of the grapes. Moved to spare Henry, Aunt Peggy puts a protective spell on him, but one that conflates his physical well-being with that of the plants; in the summer, therefore, Henry and the vineyard thrive, while both are sapped of their energy in the winter. Recognizing Henry's magic-induced organic cycles, the plantation owner seeks to maximize profit by selling Henry every summer during his peak condition, and then buying him back in every winter, at a greatly reduced price, when Henry, like the plants, is frail and unproductive. This profitable enterprise eventually comes to an end when Mars McAdoo falls victim to a Yankee confidence man and his own greed; when he takes the Yankee's advice on how to exploit his land and slaves even more, the crops and Henry both die.

Julius's tale about Henry thereby literalizes the conflation of African American slaves and property, in this situation transforming a black man into the very land he works. Henry, that is, literally becomes just another crop that McAdoo cultivates, harvests, and profits from every season. With Henry functioning as little more than a disposable commodity – after Henry's death, McAdoo curses the Yankee only for costing him money – in the business of plantation ownership, Julius thus introduces John and Annie to an incisive lesson on the treatment of African Americans and the very economics of slavery in the Old South. It's no surprise, then, that "The Goophered Grapevine" and, indeed, virtually all of the conjure stories, focuses on the grim consequences of an economic system predicated on the buying and selling of humans. Julius stresses not only the tangible effects on the slaves, but he also emphasizes – as Annie repeatedly recognizes – how the system dehumanizes the white characters as well. After Henry's death, for example, Julius describes the slaveowner's responses: "'Mars Dugal' tuk on might'ly 'bout losin' his vimes en his nigger in de same year.

... He say he wuz mighty glad dat de wah come, en he des want ter kill a Yankee fer eve'y dollar he los' 'long er dat grape-raisin' Yankee'" (*Conjure Woman* 32).

Taken together, the plots of the conjure stories offer a range of tone and interpretive possibility. In stories such as "Po' Sandy" and "Dave's Neckliss," Chesnutt describes brutalities inherent in the slavery system that lead to psychological devastation, murder, and suicide. In the latter, for example, the title character takes a degrading punishment so much to heart that he ultimately kills himself. Clearly, Chesnutt intends for readers to find such events shocking. But other stories emphasize instead the more positive implications of blacks and whites – in the forms of Julius, John, and Annie – learning to live and work together in a new America. Although John often questions or even dismisses Julius's motives for telling his tales, Annie's interpretations of the tales often demonstrate not only her sympathy for those who had been enslaved but also a perceptive comprehension of the human motivations that pervade each tale. In many ways, the conjure tales look back critically on the antebellum South, but the stories also evoke more encouraging implications – the main characters may well represent the beginning of a new understanding of, and appreciation for, the "other."

Several of Chesnutt's other stories also borrow from familiar literary genres, only to be manipulated into a new form by the author. In "The Passing of Grandison," for example, Chesnutt once more appropriates, but modifies, another literary form, this one distinctly African American: the slave narrative. Charles T. Davis and Henry Louis Gates, Jr., define the slave narrative as "[t]he written and dictated testimonies of the enslavement of black human beings" (Davis and Gates xii), and the genre constituted a significant portion of the African American literary tradition well into the nineteenth century. As James Olney and others have pointed out, traditional slave narratives, which are generally autobiographical in form, have a number of shared characteristics: an account of the slave's life in bondage, a "description of successful attempt(s) to escape, ... guided by the North Star" (Olney 153), and a brief commentary on the ex-slave's life in the North. As with plantation tradition literature, nineteenth-century readers would have been familiar with slave narratives; thousands reached print in the United States before the Civil War. Black authors such as Frederick Douglass (about whom Chesnutt published a biography), Henry Bibb, William Wells Brown, Solomon Northrup, and Harriet Jacobs, among many others, published autobiographical accounts of their slave years. Traditional slave narratives have at their core a shared rhetorical goal – to convince white readers that slavery should be abolished.

By the time "The Passing of Grandison" reached print in 1899, of course, slavery had long since been abolished. Thus, Chesnutt clearly has another purpose in mind for the work. Although broadly comic in tone and far different in narrative strategies, the plot of "The Passing of Grandison" may nevertheless initially seem familiar to readers of slave narratives; it focuses, after all, on a particular slave, Grandison, who lives on a Kentucky plantation and who eventually escapes to the North; he even makes use of the North Star in one of his treks. That's where the similarity ends, though, as the rest of the story adds a farcical element to a genre not known for its use of comedy.

The action of the story derives from the attempts of the son of the plantation owner to "free" one of his father's slaves as a means of impressing his fiancée. But despite the young man's elaborate efforts – including secretly plotting with abolitionists and leaving Grandison alone (with a drawer full of "escape" money) for days at a time in a Boston hotel – Grandison proves unfailingly loyal to his masters, so much so that the son ultimately hires thugs to kidnap the slave and take him to "freedom" in Canada. Even that desperate measure works only temporarily as Grandison escapes *from* Canada, and in a startlingly ironic plot contrivance, uses the North Star to navigate (South!) back to captivity in Kentucky. Ultimately, however, Grandison proves not quite the model slave after all; having gathered his family, he re-escapes with them to the North, leaving his "master" deeply disappointed in the fidelity of his slaves. Easily one of Chesnutt's best stories, "Grandison" is both surprising and very funny, two traits not normally associated with slave narratives.

In refitting, more than thirty years after the abolition of slavery, the slave narrative form for a comic – though important – story, Chesnutt stays true, I think, to the rhetorical intentions of traditional slave narratives. While Douglass, Bibb, Jacobs, and other authors of "literal" slave narratives tried through their writings to convince presumably reasonable white readers to reconsider their views of slavery (and blacks in general), "The Passing of Grandison" asks later generations of white readers to do much the same, especially in terms of their regard for African Americans. For here's a story in which a stereotypically acquiescent and dim-witted slave – Chesnutt's depiction of Grandison for much of the story might make modern readers distinctly uncomfortable – ultimately outwits his "superiors" by engineering his escape and that of his family. Thus, while "The Passing of Grandison" certainly amuses, it also suggests that readers might have to reevaluate their views of African Americans. In the story, both the plantation owner and his son, relying on racial stereotypes, misread Grandison – Chesnutt seems to offer this story in the hope that it might convince his readers not to fall into the same trap.

In addition to stories about the South or escaping from the South, roughly half of Chesnutt's stories focus on the lives of Northerners, primarily, but not exclusively, African Americans and those of mixed blood. Indeed, two of his best works, "Her Virginia Mammy" and "The Wife of His Youth," focus on characters living and working in "Groveland," Chesnutt's fictionalized twin of Cleveland.

Typical of Chesnutt's "Northern" stories is "Her Virginia Mammy," a tale that, while in many ways an apparently conventional sentimental love story, is infused with such controversial topics as miscegenation, passing, and the consequences of slavery. First published in *The Wife of His Youth and Other Stories of the Color Line* in 1899, the story recounts a period in the life of Clara Hohlfelder, the adopted daughter of German immigrants who refuses to marry her fiancé, John, until she can verify the worthiness of her "blood" family. Clara's postponement of the marriage to a man of "pure" heritage – his genealogical roots include "the governor and the judge and the Harvard professor and the *Mayflower* pilgrim" (*Wife* 82) – derives from her fear that her origins won't favorably compare with his. During the course of the story, though, readers learn that the light-skinned Clara doesn't come from a poor white family, as she fears; rather, we and two of the three main characters discover (although Clara never does) that her "blood" mother is an ex-slave. When the two women meet and Clara's mother, Mrs Harper, learns of her daughter's predicament, she and Clara's fiancé choose to withhold the genealogical truth from her, thus insuring a "happy" ending – a marriage, but one between a white man and a black woman. The story thus seems to endorse miscegenation, a precarious position for a turn-of-the-century black writer to take.

Although not at all provocative in tone or mood, "Her Virginia Mammy" offers some of Chesnutt's most daring messages – that "blood" (and race) don't matter much and also that, perhaps, one's racial identity is not quite as secure as he or she may think. For Clara's happiness at the end of the story – now that she "knows" her ancestry – comes at high cost: her continued ignorance about the one issue she considers most important. Chesnutt thus seems to minimize the importance of "blood" and "heritage" and even the past, at one point having Clara's fiancé dismissing her concerns by saying, "For the past, we can claim no credit, for those who made it died with it. Our destiny lies in the future" (*Collected Stories* 118). Even more provocatively, though, Chesnutt seems to mock the very idea of a secure racial identity, as the story implicitly calls into question the unexamined assumptions about race and the past that his readers may have had.

Also set in "Groveland," "The Wife of His Youth" offers a similarly complicated view of the remaking of America at the micro, or family, level. In that story, Mr. Ryder – the "dean" of a society of socially and financially successful "individuals who were … more white than black" (Duncan, *Northern Stories* 65) and who look down on those of darker complexion – has decided to marry a young, very light-skinned woman. But he must reconsider those plans when his slave wife, who has been search-ing for him for twenty-five years, unexpectedly arrives on the day he intends to propose. Thus, Ryder must choose between reconnecting with his (slave) past and beginning a new life in the North with a new (younger, paler, and prettier) wife. Like so many of Chesnutt's works, "The Wife of His Youth" has at its core the very notion of storytelling, as Ryder's long-lost wife, 'Liza Jane, tells of her search for him in a long, uninterrupted narrative. Here, then, an ex-slave has the chance to articulate her life story as an embedded narrative in the midst of a story about the "New" North. Chesnutt thus uses this narrative arrangement to explore issues one finds throughout his short fictions: the ongoing consequences of slavery, the formation and re-formation of the American family, and the implications of race – which, in this case, have to do with intra-racial prejudice. In this and so many others of his Northern fictions – "A Matter of Principle," "Mr. Taylor's Funeral," and "White Weeds," to name only a few – Chesnutt examines race not as an abstraction but as it pervades the lives of Americans living in a nation struggling to redefine itself in the midst of a profound and ongoing "reconstruction."

Given the central, even defining role the issue of race plays in the author's short fictions, it's almost startling to find that perhaps Chesnutt's best short story, "Baxter's

Procrustes," makes no explicit mention of race whatsoever (although it's certainly possible to interpret the story as a racial allegory). "Baxter's Procrustes" traces the arc of a finely wrought practical joke perpetrated on snobbish book collectors who value the accoutrements of book publishing – wide margins, fine lettering, and exquisitely embroidered covers – far more than the textual contents. When Baxter, a poet whose biography very much resembles that of Chesnutt, decides to turn the pretensions of the Bodleian Club – a fictitious twin of the Rowfant Club, a society of book collectors in Cleveland to which Chesnutt belonged – against it, the resulting story offers a wide-ranging satire of book collectors, literary critics, and the reading public. Given absolute control over the publishing of his epic poem, *The Procrustes*, a publication the members of the Bodleian hope to profit from, Baxter instead publishes a volume of blank pages. The resulting ecstatic reviews – by club members who refuse to "cut" (or actually read) their copies of the book and thus reduce the profit they might realize – offer a hilarious send-up of a culture all too eager to value the trappings of a book (including the race of its author) over its content. While the story seems initially to mock a pompous subset of late nineteenth-century culture without having anything to do with race, one can nevertheless appreciate Chesnutt's satire on other levels as well; for Baxter is an author who, like Chesnutt, refuses to submit willingly to the Procrustean bed that his readers seem to insist upon. Like Chesnutt, Baxter can only try to redirect (and occasionally subvert) the expectations of readers far too comfortable with their preconceived notions of "America" and its stories.

It's tempting, finally, to assume that Charles W. Chesnutt's importance as an American short story writer derives primarily from the seeming oppositions he both embodied and addressed in his short fiction. A self-identified African American author (but of "mixed" heritage) who was born in the North but grew up in the Reconstruction South, Chesnutt did use his short fiction to explore, in intricate and complex ways, our national obsession with race. Most of his best short stories tended to focus on race both in broad, sociological terms – the outcomes, intended and unintended, of Reconstruction, the ongoing consequences of racialized thought, etc. – and its effects on individuals and, especially, families in an America trying to put itself back together following the Civil War. Ultimately, though, Chesnutt's depiction of our national reconciliation, while delivered through the prism of race, had more to do with his unique vision of an America – a country well schooled in invention – re-inventing itself all over again.

<h2 style="text-align:center">REFERENCES AND FURTHER READING</h2>

Andrews, William L. *The Literary Career of Charles W. Chesnutt.* Baton Rouge: Louisiana State University Press, 1980.

———. *To Tell a Free Story: The First Century of Afro-American Autobiography, 1769–1865.* Urbana: University of Illinois Press, 1986.

Brasch, Walter M. *Brer Rabbit, Uncle Remus, and the "Cornfield Journalist": The Tale of Joel Chandler Harris.* Macon, GA: Mercer University Press, 2000.

Chesnutt, Charles W. "Baxter's Procrustes." *Atlantic Monthly* 93 (June 1904): 823–30.

———. *Collected Stories of Charles W. Chesnutt*. Ed. and Intro. William L. Andrews. New York: Mentor, 1992.

———. *The Conjure Woman*. Boston: Houghton Mifflin, 1899.

———. *The Conjure Woman and Other Conjure Tales*. Ed. and Intro. Richard Brodhead. Durham, NC: Duke University Press, 1993.

———. "The Goophered Grapevine." *Atlantic Monthly* 60 (August 1887): 254–60. Rpt. in *Conjure Woman*. 1–31.

———. "Her Virginia Mammy." *Collected Stories*. 114–31.

———. "The Wife of His Youth." *The Wife of His Youth and Other Stories of the Color Line*. Boston: Houghton Mifflin, 1899. Ann Arbor: University of Michigan Press, 1968.

Chesnutt, Helen. *Charles Waddell Chesnutt: Pioneer of the Color Line*. Chapel Hill: University of North Carolina Press, 1952.

Davis, Charles T., and Henry Louis Gates, Jr., eds. *The Slave's Narrative*. Oxford: Oxford University Press, 1989.

Duncan, Charles. *The Absent Man: The Narrative Craft of Charles W. Chesnutt*. Athens: University of Ohio Press, 1998.

———. *The Northern Stories of Charles W. Chesnutt*. Athens: University of Ohio Press, 2004.

Fraiman, Susan. "Mother-Daughter Romance in Charles W. Chesnutt's 'Her Virginia Mammy.'" *Studies in Short Fiction* 22.4 (Fall 1985): 443–8.

Howells, W. D. "Mr. Charles W. Chesnutt's Stories." *Atlantic Monthly* 85 (May 1900): 699–701.

———. "A Psychological Counter-Current in Short Fiction." *North American Review* 173 (December 1901): 872–88.

Kaplan, Amy. "Nation, Region, and Empire." *Columbia History of the American Novel*. New York: Columbia University Press, 1991. 240–66.

Keller, Frances Richardson. *An American Crusade*. Provo: Brigham Young University Press, 1978.

McElrath, Joseph R., Jr., ed. *Critical Essays on Charles W. Chesnutt*. New York: G. K. Hall, 1999.

McElrath, Joseph R., Jr., and Robert C. Leitz III, eds. *"To Be an Author": Letters of Charles W. Chesnutt, 1889–1905*. Princeton, NJ: Princeton University Press, 1997.

McElrath, Joseph R., Jr., Jesse Crisler, and Robert C. Leitz III, eds. *Charles W. Chesnutt: Essays and Speeches*. Stanford, CA: Stanford University Press, 1999.

———. *An Exemplary Citizen: Letters of Charles W. Chesnutt, 1906–1932*. Stanford, CA: Stanford University Press, 2002.

McWilliams, Dean. *Charles W. Chesnutt and the Fictions of Race*. Athens: University of Georgia Press, 2002.

Olney, James. "'I Was Born': Slave Narratives, Their Status as Autobiography and as Literature." In Davis and Gates, eds., *The Slave's Narrative*, 148–75.

Sundquist, Eric J. *To Wake the Nations: Race in the Making of American Literature*. Cambridge, MA: Belknap Press, 1993.

Warren, Kenneth. *Black and White Strangers: Race and American Literary Realism*. Chicago: University of Chicago Press, 1993.

6

Mark Twain and the American Comic Short Story

David E. E. Sloane

As America's premier humorist and literary comedian, Mark Twain ranks among the great short story writers in the world. He is not the first great writer of comic short fiction in America; even Washington Irving, despite his importance, could not make that claim. Nor is he the last, if we recognize William Faulkner's use of the tradition or Woody Allen, more generally, but he is the focal point. Almost every critic sees Twain as a unique culmination of nineteenth-century American traditions of humor, as he will be treated here. In his writing, he gathers together comic modes from before his time, and his influence radiates down to current humor writers. To understand the tradition of the comic short story in America, then, we need to look back in American literary history and even to Europe. Mark Twain, however, is a central reference point for a historical view of the medium and the American context. Twain and the tradition represent national characteristics embodied in a broad generic form which was recognized as unique as early as the 1830s, if not before. Often, his expanded burlesques of townsfolk and roughhouse antics are accounted for by the Southwestern tradition, but his intellectual exaggeration and more sophisticated ethical ideas owe a great deal to the tradition of Northeastern humor, and the result is truly national.

British and European models for the comic short story or humorous episodic adventure abound. *The Travels and Surprising Adventures of Baron Munchausen* bulks large in references to Twain, to offer a single reference to a larger field of study. First among equals for British influences on American comic writers would be the episodic classic, Laurence Sterne's *Life and Adventures of Tristram Shandy, Esq.*, and from that we move easily to Rabelais, Cervantes, Montaigne, and Swift, among others. Dickens and Thackeray follow. *The Spectator* and *Vanity Fair* each had a role in developing the American satiric tradition, beginning with the sarcasm in Colonial and early Federal sources. On our own side of the Atlantic, Benjamin Franklin has to be recognized as one of our earliest comic storytellers. Whether in the neoclassic mode of "The Ephemerae" written for Madame Helvetius, or in the newspaper style of "The Witch Trial at Mount Holly" in 1730, his attitude and materials are distinctly American.

The first major recognition of the comic American short story by a British source was in 1830. Mary Russell Mitford, indefatigable English sketch writer and anthologist, collected "shorter American stories," many comic, in *Stories of American Life; by American Writers*, in three volumes, published in London by Henry Colburn and Richard Bently in that year. Washington Irving was omitted, "in spite of [a] few inimitable sketches ... his writings are essentially European" (iv). James Kirke Paulding, however, was well represented, along with Julian Verplank, James Hall, John Neal, N. P. Willis, and others; subjects ranged "from Otter-bag and Pete Fetherton, down to the fine lady in the Country Cousin, and Monsieur de Viellecour, most courtly of refugees" (v). Miss Mitford sought the "national and characteristic" by grasping "at the broadest caricature, so that it contained indications of local manners; and clutched the wildest sketch, so that it gave the bold outline of local scenery" (vi). The opportunistic Yankee traveler made his appearance in Verplank's "The Peregrinations of Petrus Mudd," along with reformed idlers, would-be profiteers who get their comeuppance, and oddly matched lovers and marital couples in J. K. Paulding's "The Little Dutch Sentinel." The literary pretender, in this case named Huggins, dies of mortification that his great work goes unappreciated (III. 225–30) in "Reminiscences of New York," a rambling review of the go-getter characters of the city, representative of its democracy. She also included the new American scene: Indians from the frontier wars were obvious, but so was the Washington profiteer-parvenu, in "Scenes in Washington," where characters criticize themselves as rough speakers of the "vernacular" and predatory representatives of the "gyneocracy," (II. 294) in recognition of the changing status of women. One comic sketch mentioned above displayed the American international traveler as a "go-getter," a theme that remained popular among humorists for the next century, and after. Mitford, however, missed one of the greatest works in this tradition, J. K. Paulding's "Jonathan Visits the Celestial Empire," in which a Yankee traveler traverses the world and Chinese society with a Newfoundland dog as first mate, and exposes the life of the city in terms that look forward to Twain's travels (rpt. in Sloane, *LHUNE* 50–62). Northeastern and Western stories are more literary in style than the rambunctious frontier tales to come out of the Southwest, but they are clearly American, nonetheless, and Twain owed his debt to the whole tradition, not just a part of it.

The frontier was a major presence, but so was the urban frontier of new social types. Miss Mitford's dismissal of Washington Irving slighted the school of Northeastern and Knickerbocker humor, some of it Boston-based or Down-East, which displayed not only unique history but, also, the new American urban scene in the Northeast, accompanied by greenhorns, naïve farmers ready for plucking, and Yankee democratic character-types and entrepreneurs seeking to perform not only locally but on a national and international scale. The widely recognized "Old Southwest" was the other crucial part of the range of new American experiences in literary comedy. Later scholars have corrected Mitford's dismissal of Irving. In their landmark collection, *The Humor of the*

Old Southwest, Cohen and Dillingham noted especially Irving's "The Legend of Sleepy Hollow" as an influence in the Southwest, where a bold roughhouse tradition subsumed it readily.

Thomas Chandler Haliburton, Canadian father of "Sam Slick," who himself figures in the history of the "North American" comic story, anthologized his counterparts from the States about twenty years after Miss Mitford. *Traits of American Humour by Native Authors* was published in London by Hurst and Blackett in 1852. Haliburton threw his net wider than had Mitford. He included many of the truly great and representative pieces of American Southwestern humor, which by that time had flowered. "The Shooting Match" and "The Horse Swap" by Augustus Baldwin Longstreet appeared, along with "Georgia Theatrics." Mike Fink and Davy Crockett were represented; William T. Thompson's "The Coon Hunt; or, a Fency Country," forerunner of the blizzard episode in *Roughing It*, appeared along with Thomas Bangs Thorpe's "The Big Bear of Arkansas," the signature story for the genre of Southwestern humor. Haliburton noted that their characteristics were distinctive. They were often presented as narratives by a somewhat vulgar or vernacular speaker. They usually featured local scenery and characteristics integrated into the action and helping to identify the experience. Almost always, they showed traits of regional dialect and local speech. American words and democratic phrases jostled more pretentious language and provided a formidable tool in depicting the horse swap, the fight, the swindler, and the urban bully. Last, but by no means least, they often registered vulgarity, greed, or entrepreneurialism. Haliburton recognized these stories as representative of the broader Yankee spirit of all Americans. "The Fastest Funeral on Record," by Francis A. Durivage, "The Big Bear of Arkansas," by Thomas Bangs Thorpe, "Peter Brush, the Great Used-up," by Joseph C. Neal, and an array of the best regional stories make this an impressive compilation across regional boundaries, and Haliburton's "Preface" is remarkable in laying out the dimensions of the American comic short story.

Haliburton found the stories not merely characterized as "regional," but more accurately described as local, rather than general in theme and topic. He found each region representing its own characteristics, as different as British, Irish, and Scottish, for which he substituted Yankee Northeastern, Southern, and Western. Appropriately, the first piece in his anthology is "My First and Last Speech in the General Court," which shows a blowhard Down-East farmer suffering comic retribution for his stuffy, bombastic oration to the Massachusetts legislature. It is followed by "Hoss Allen, of Missouri," "The Widow Rugby's Husband" by Johnson Jones Hooper, and Thorpe's "The Big Bear of Arkansas." Haliburton is at pains to show that every region took a hand, and the colorful characters of the frontier ventured both north and south of the Mason-Dixon Line, and off the far western end, as well.

Politics, courtship, and local swaps and commercial ventures make up much of the content of the genre Haliburton displays, the primary interests of nineteenth-century Americans and still largely dominant today. His major distinction emphasized the development of a new American language. The popular and vulgar voice was a primary characteristic, showing neologisms, Indian derivations, and sheer dialect inventions. He concluded his preface with a discussion of regional intonations and a lengthy table of peculiarly enunciated American words (Haliburton v–ix). He noted a large number of phrases from American politics ("to cave in," "a flash in the pan," to fizzle out"), Indian words ("hominy," "tapioca," "barbecue," "pow-wow"), Spanish ("canyon," "cavortin"), French ("calaboose," "bayou"), and the broader vowels of American English itself ("bar" for "bear," "thar" for "their," and a hundred others, which he lists).

Haliburton credits William T. Porter's racing paper, *The Spirit of the Times* (1831–61) as the primary source of American comic stories from their beginning, which he ascribes to the 1820s, although he also cites the earlier New York *Constellation*, as a comic paper of significance. "The Comic Paper Question," itself, is complicated because many comic periodicals appeared and disappeared rapidly. Periodicals fueled the growth of the American humorous story. Oral tales and reminiscences could be captured, written down, manipulated intellectually, and then be seen into print easily. Many of the Southwestern comic writers consciously intended to capture their era as a passing phenomenon. In the Northeast, the spirit was somewhat contained, particularly in focusing on social and economic issues while mostly omitting the more grossly physical that the Southwest embraced. Many of the major periodicals of the 1830–60 period were Northeastern, with the exception of the New Orleans *Picayune* and the St. Louis *Reveille*. Porter's *Spirit of the Times* was a New York racing paper aimed at the railroad car rather than the domestic parlor; horse swaps, sweaty, earthy women, vulgar speech, and even more vulgar action were accepted. Before Porter there were others. Most immediately coming to mind is George Helmbold's *Philadelphia Tickler*, from 1809 through 1813, and then again briefly after the close of the War of 1812, in 1816–17. Helmbold was happy to publish satiric sketches of Irish low-lifes and local politicos gone corrupt. When Joseph C. Neal began publishing his sketches of "City Worthies" in the *Pennsylvania Gazette* in the mid-1830s, he might well be considered to be taking up the earlier urban tradition. The New York *Knickerbocker* edited by Lewis Gaylord Clark was also a lively outlet for comic writers, but with a more literary turn than Porter's racing sheet, reflecting its antecedents in Washington Irving's and James Kirke Paulding's *Salmagundi* of the same period as Helmbold's venture.

The most eclectic of the early nineteenth-century anthologizers of American humor was the Philadelpia actor and comic writer W. E. Burton. As described by Edgar Allan Poe in "A Chapter on Autography," "Mr. BURTON is better known as a comedian than as a literary man; but he has written many short prose articles of merit, and his quondam editorship of the 'Gentleman's Magazine' would, at all events, entitle him to a place in this collection. He has, moreover, published one or two books." His most notable book came later: Burton's *Cyclopedia of Wit and Humor*, published in New York in 1858, is a major contribution. Burton offered four sections, "American" first, followed by Scottish, English, and Irish. The American section filled 480 pages in double-column small type, beginning with "The Maypole of Merrymount" in 1625. Washington Irving has two pieces. William Cox's wonderfully

modern "Steam," with its parody steam men living on the high pressure principle, is
included (rpt. in Sloane, *LHUNE* 63–9), along with Asa Greene's "Peter Funk,"
showing up a crooked auction. George P. Morris's "The Stage Competitors; or, a Tale
of the Road" (*LHUNE* 92–101) made the contest for passengers between "The
Monopoly" and "The People's Line" into raucous slapstick. The list is far more extensive than these brief mentions suggest.

Some of Burton's discoveries look forward to others later on. George P.
Burnham's "He Wanted to See the Animal" (272–3) is a sort of Yankee version of
Twain's "The Dandy Frightening the Squatter." Replace the steamboat with the
Boston printing office of *Littell's Living Age* on Tremont Street, replace the steamboat
admirers with an urban crowd including a rowdy wag or two, and set the country
greenhorn against an urban clerk. In this case, the fight is between the Greenhorn,
who thinks the "Age" is an animal and he needs to pay 25 cents to see it, like the
elephant he had seen yesterday, and common sense, as no one can figure out what the
rube wants. Finally, the wags tie firecrackers to his shirt-tails which start exploding
as another wag inside the building screams, "Look out! *The crittur's loose!*" The up-
country greenhorn is last seen streaking across Boston Common and into his seat on
a train, whistling out the window for the engine to "hurry it on." Action, dialect,
attitude, and setting are all American and all-American. The theme levels society, the
dialect localizes and regionalizes, the action is exaggerated slapstick, and the characters are pure American wise-guys, city folks, and rubes all mixed together.

Joseph C. Neal of Philadelphia, short-lived, but a clever and observant student of
Philadelphia urban low-lifes, figures prominently in many of the earlier anthologies.
His stories seem to invent the urban vulgar character. Peter Brush is typical of the
series of "City Worthies" Neal created. Before being hauled off by the night watch,
he soliloquizes:

> A long time ago, my ma used to put on her specs and say, "Peter, my son, put not your
> trust in princes;" and from that day to this I haven't done anything of the kind, because
> none on 'em ever wanted to borry nothing of me. ... [but], I can't get no office. Republics
> is ongrateful! ... I only wanted to be took care of, and have nothing to do but to take
> care of the public, and I've only got half-nothing to do! Being took care of was the main
> thing. ... This is the way old sojers is served. (rpt. in *LHUNE* 72–3)

"Orson Dabbs, the Hittite" is a tough who brags, "Now, look here – look at me
well, ... I'm a real nine foot breast of a fellow – stub twisted and made of horse-shoe
nails – the rest of me is cast iron with steel springs" (Neal 37). Neal's authorial voice
contrasted with his characters' reported speech, although he didn't employ the "frame"
of other authors. "Fydget Fyxington," his most widely reprinted story, is a classic
demonstration of the down-and-outer facing winter in the city. His dialect is raw and
vulgar, his needs are so basic as to be brutish, and he gladly disrupts the upper classes,
as in the concluding Ball, which he boisterously invades (Neal 207–22). Conflicting
cultures create "action" and interest using American materials.

The American Renaissance featured its own more formal literary humor, rather divorced from the descendental vulgarians by language and style, but demonstrating that allegorical and symbolic language and more transcendental intellectual concerns could also form the humorous story and infuse it with major themes. Hawthorne's "The Celestial Railroad," and "Feathertop" demonstrate these capacities. Poe's "The Man Who Was Used Up" went directly after military leaders running for office on the strength of their wounds. Melville's "Me and My Chimney" is now recognized as a clever metaphor for sexuality. Burton reprinted Hawthorne's "Mr. Higgenbotham's Catastrophe," Poe's "A Tale of Jerusalem," and Melville's "The Lightning-Rod Man."

The humor of the Old Southwest has been the most researched, most analyzed, and most reprinted of American comic short story genres. Haliburton, as noted above, presented several of the best. Burton added more; most notable were William Tappan Thompson, Madison Tensas, and John S. Robb, among a host of others. The signature story of the group, as noted earlier, is Thomas Bangs Thorpe's "The Big Bear of Arkansas," and the most notable venue was William Trotter Porter's racing newspaper, *The Spirit of the Times*, where the rougher, more vernacular stories were welcomed. "The Big Bear of Arkansas" is a frame story in which the narrator describes the unusual speech and story of a country hunter, admittedly green among sophisticated steamboat travelers on the Mississippi, but not so green at home in the forest and on the farm, he tells us. He then presents his story in his own dialect. Dialect, naïveté, grotesque, and somewhat bathroomy humor (he sights the bear at the last chase while his "inexpressibles" are down around his ankles) merge amid frontier scenes of lively hunting action. The Bear is elevated to the level of natural symbol, made a mystery by his continuous escapes from the hunters, and well he should be, according to the talker, considering that the events happened "in Arkansaw: where else could it have happened but in the creation State, the finishing-up country – a State where the *sile* runs down to the center of the 'arth, and government gives you a title to every inch of it? Then its airs – just breathe them, and they will make you snort like a horse. It's a State without a fault, it is" (Cohen and Dillingham 338). The statement by itself is a declaration of independence from the conventions of literary formulas and cultural restraint. Its emphatic power comes from the elements Mitford, Haliburton, Burton, and others, saw quite clearly: local language, energy and vitality, newness to the literary scene, abandonment of convention, natural and earthy experience expressing the new world frontier culture, a character acting and expressing all those tendencies in unexpected settings and in unexpected ways. All of these characteristics would be brought to their climax in Mark Twain.

Southwestern humor, as a genre, has been fortunate in the scholarly research it has attracted, chiefly Hennig Cohen and William Dillingham's *The Humor of the Old Southwest*. Walter Blair's *Native American Humor* also contains an excellent array of short stories and authors representing the Old Southwest, as in his selections and lengthy discussions of "The Beginnings," "Down East Humor," and "The Literary Comedians." Blair identifies George Washington Harris's Sut Lovingood as the highest achievement of antebellum humor in the South. Sut is coarse and earthy well beyond anything seen in the other regions. His low opinion of "human natur'" and "nat'ral born durn'd fools," of which he knows he is the chief, is justified by the vulgar stories he tells in low dialect. "Sut Lovingood's Daddy, Acting Horse," in the Cohen and Dillingham anthology, shows Sut's Dad stripping buff naked to plow his fields like the family horse but overdoing the thing by pretending to run away over a bluff into a creek:

> Thars nara hoss ever foaldid durn fool enuf to lope over eny sich place; a cussed muel mout a done hit, but dad warn't actin muel, tho' he orter tuck the karacter; hit adzactly sooted tu his dispersition, all but not breedin. I crept up tu the aidge, an' peep'd over. Thar wer dad's bald hed fur all the yeath like a peeled inyin, a bobbin up an' down an' aroun', an' the ho'nets sailing roun tuckey buzzard fashun, an' every onst in a while one, an' sum times ten, wud take a dip at dad's bald head. He kep' up a rite peart dodgin onder, sumtimes afore they hit im, an' sumtimes arterard, an' the warter wer kivered wif drownded ball ho'nets. Tu look at hit from the top ove the bluff, hit wer pow'ful inturestin, an' sorter funny; I wer on the bluff myse'f, mine yu. (Cohen and Dillingham 205)

Sut himself has a characteristic view of the action, and the action is low enough to justify him. In "Blown up with Soda," Sut is cured of his puppy-love for Sicily Burns when she slips him a powerful emetic and falls down laughing as his stomach acts like a "thrashin-meersheen with fightin bull-dorgs." He gets his revenge in "Sicily Burns's Wedding," which Twain borrowed later for a scene in *Personal Recollections of Joan of Arc*. He destroys the wedding with wild bulls and stinging bees. She says to him flatly, "Yu go tu hell!" (224–5) – strong language. The way is open for the wildest variety of effects, languages, and emotions. "Rare Ripe Garden-Seed" is a folksy story of the Appalachians where a man is bamboozled to think his bride's new baby comes four-and-a-half months after the wedding because of the effects of highly fertilized agricultural seed. The story is still alive in Vance Randolph's collection of Appalachian risqué stories, *Pissin' in the Snow*.

Augustus Baldwin Longstreet provided many of the best early Southwestern stories: "Georgia Theatrics," "The Drill," "The Fight," and "The Shooting Match" offer a panorama of backwoods behavior of the ring-tailed roarer, half-horse, half-alligator frontier types throughout the region. Oliver Hillhouse Prince's "The Militia Drill" was an inclusion in his *Georgia Scenes*, which was republished in American comic papers and later was taken into a European book on the Napoleonic wars, where Thomas Hardy found it, liked it, and plagiarized it in *The Trumpet Major*, creating a literary puzzle that took years to solve. This humor could travel if the dialect was altered and the scene masked.

Other Southwestern authors contribute their own characteristic stories to the genre. Johnson Jones Hooper's Simon Suggs, whose motto is "It's good to be shifty in a new country," fleeces a camp meeting in a sequence linked to the camp meeting scene in *Adventures of Huckleberry Finn*. Joseph G. Baldwin, John S. Robb, William Tappan

Thompson – particularly in his character Major Jones – and Henry Clay Lewis, the Louisiana swamp doctor, all expanded dimensions of the genre.

Twain built his technique out of a vast array of such cultural materials available as reprints in newspapers, as books reprinted by firms like T. B. Peterson in Philadelphia, and as word-of-mouth stories. He honed his style for fifteen years before his notorious frog jumped to national prominence as a throw-away newspaper piece, where it was published after failing to arrive East in time to go into Artemus Ward's *Travels Among the Mormons*, a fortunate accident which made the story and Twain's authorship stand alone. Ward had burst on the national scene as a burlesque old showman modeled on P. T. Barnum, as colored by the fictional hick town, Baldinsville, Indiana. Ward traveled, interviewed celebrities, including the Prince of Wales and Abe Lincoln, upbraided political and social radicals, and spoke in the curdled voice of ignorant democracy, the worst fear of old Whigs burst into fantastic flower, as unabashedly entrepreneurial, idealistic, and go-getter money-grubbing as Barnum himself. Ward created the naïve, deadpan sarcastic voice that Twain made into the world's conscience at the turn of the century with such short pieces as "To the Person Sitting in Darkness" and "King Leopold's Soliloquy." Twain's management of irony and sarcasm owes Ward more than just a passing debt.

In "How to Tell a Story," Twain laid out four parameters of the short story for vocal telling, attributing three of them to Ward. Elizabeth Oakes Smith (Mrs. Seba Smith) had covered the same territory in an earlier "How to Tell a Story" in *Graham's Magazine* (22, 33–5) in January 1843 (rpt. in Sloane, *LHUNE* 132–7). Stories must be offered in the right setting, she suggested, unhurried, and aimed at psychological involvement. She then offered a hunting story with a long lead into a quickly delivered line that was somewhat parallel to Twain's technique of pause and surprise. Understanding how storytelling was practiced in America was an ongoing interest. The brilliant but naïve digressive progress of the action became one of its outstanding features. Varied social and human ironies were drawn into events and descriptions, seemingly unintended, but central to the humor of the piece. Twain's later brief essay needs to be taken cautiously, tempting though the title may be to explain Twain's craft. It is actually a vehicle to carry his beloved "The Golden Arm." Twain embarrassed his daughter by telling it to her friends, but he needed more scaffolding to present it to a general public. His four rules of storytelling provide that. Also, of course, they are oriented toward vocal telling. Nevertheless, three out of the four criteria derived from Artemus Ward were the naïf as narrator, the deadpan, and the pause. The story lulls the reader until the sudden surprise ending.

These Yankee traits do much to explain how the shock ending and change of mood works, but they do little to explain the social ideals lying at the base of the action and the surprises explaining the achievement of Charles Farrar Browne, and, even more important, how Twain rose above him. Crucial to Ward's writing, as in his brief letters in *Artemus Ward in London* (1867), was the addition of a sense of history, as in the case of Prince Albert or Prince Napoleon. In London, at the Tower of London, he observes that traitors are an unfortunate class of people because they failed to bust a country, and so are not heroes. The irony depends on the "snapper," which is, for the literary comedians, the equivalent of the pause in importance. For a brief second the reader's intellectual wheels churn while the conflicting ideas are untangled, and then the laugh comes. Twain was a master at developing snapper lines and then topping snapper lines with even more snapper lines, developing more power than Ward. He took over the "Is he dead?" joke in *The Innocents Abroad* from a brief Ward story and makes not only a rebuttal of Columbus, Michelangelo, and European guides at the hands of American vandals, but also transmutes it into a sarcastic theme of practical incredulity that runs all the way to the Capuchin Convent mortuary in Rome. He builds out by extending the snapper into a motif. In doing this, he creates a persona that can tell stories as both experience and imagination at the same time. This quality rises above Maine or Arkansas. He is free to bring a moral dimension within his persona and make it believable as an intellectual fact. Some of those traits are Yankee greenhorn traits, some are Southwestern frontier behavior, but the leap is to the level of intellectual puzzle that each story represents – the realism that makes us accept the premises of the most unlikely stories almost from the first word. Vulgar voice and regional–local tendency, even in his broader pieces, are mixed on an intellectual palette which can roam across varied themes, national boundaries, ethical issues, egregious entrepreneurialism, national pride, democratic politics, and, ultimately, the standing in the world of the two key issues in all his work: humanity and moral responsibility.

The English noted the "lawlessness" of Twain's humor, and Twain perfected this quality in the American humorous short story. The quality we have just identified is what makes the English respond as they do. Everything mixes together like Huck Finn's chowder pot, elements from vulgar to universal, from physical to conceptual, from beast to man and back again. The Bible and other literary works, euphemism, swear-words and camp language resonate against each other in the voices in which the stories are told and in the mouths of their characters. Jokes and one-liners, slapstick, and moral fable rub together in story after story. *Blackwood's Magazine* flatly labeled Twain for this quality: "Mark Twain is a bull in the china-shop of ideas" (Sloane, *MTH* 183). *Blackwood's* sneered that the hilarity of Twain's humor and its incongruities would quickly fade away. They were wrong. His fusion had jumped the divide between popular writing and great writing.

"The Notorious Jumping Frog of Calaveras County" (1865) is a local California gold nugget that formed the base of Mark Twain's literary fortune. By the standards set forth by Miss Mitford and Judge Haliburton, it offers all the characteristics of the true American comic story. The dialect and character are preeminently "local." Jim Smiley takes over the storytelling after a very brief framing comment by the author tying the story to Artemus Ward in the East. We are quickly prepared for a long digressive amble through local history as it buzzes through the brain of a garrulous drunkard in a country store. Bows are made to the national political scene in the naming of the fighting bulldog Andrew Jackson and the Frog, Dan'l Webster. Edgar Branch has documented an immense number of references to local figures around San

Francisco, and to some readers the story was even more local than it appears now. All America greeted the story, William Dean Howells reported, with "universal joy." Americans loved it because it is them: eager as puppydogs, egregiously enthusiastic, naïve, and democratic. If any piece must be chosen as representative, therefore, of the American comic short story, "Jumping Frog" should be the first nominee. Indeed, Twain played with the motif many times throughout the rest of his career, and it served him well in identifying him with the West, as a new "voice," willing and able to perform in local voice and setting and with characteristic American events, in this case a classic American swindle, worthy of both Yankee sharpers and the Southern horse-swap, a truly representative piece.

The tag-line is the refrain, "I don't see no p'ints about that frog, that's any better'n any other frog." The sentence is the ultimate democratic statement in vernacular language. In a democracy, virtue is elected from the ranks, as we already knew from the fate of the "20 Minute Nag" and the bull-pup Andrew Jackson. Smiley's jumping frog is not able to produce results that win. He retains his status as a great comic figure because he loses it at the polls of performance. Henry Nash Smith characterizes the language and values as vernacular, and we might narrow this to vulgar, regionally dialectal, and local. This piece is typical of Twain's brilliant mastery of words and phrases with unique sounds advancing a statement of foolish entrepreneurialism gone awry. Angel's Camp becomes immortal, and the piece takes on that air of classic literature which is both rooted in the immediate fact but also reflective of universal lines, dare I say, of beauty, and Smiley becomes, as Keats describes in "Ode on a Grecian Urn," that still-unravished bride of garrulousness, forever chasing and being chased by the skeptical stranger and his lost bet. The story is full of echoes of earlier stories in the tradition, from the race, to the tricky stranger, to the long-winded vulgar story in local language. Even the frog-catching theme as a scam had been recounted in Henry Finn's "The Frog Catcher" (Burton 80). But Twain's piece is unique. Setting and language correspond in a local American setting. Damage from a bar-room bet is minor, 40 dollars; in a low-class vulgar setting, a naïf gets his comeuppance, but no more than that. Pain is minimized, not exaggerated. The story is the thing. Smiley merges the mysteriousness of the big bear and the entrepreneurialism of the universal Yankee and makes both into an illusion.

"Cannibalism in the Cars" is a second, seemingly very different, Twain piece that adds an important dimension to understanding the American comic story. The British recognized it at once; its original publication was in London's *Broadway Journal*, but Twain had published three or four newspaper pieces in St. Louis with the same style in 1867. The satire on democratic institutions is woven into nature seemingly flawlessly, as "Nature must yield" the floor of the snow-bound railroad car to the parliamentary determinations of starving passengers deciding who will be eaten first to serve the greater good. Discussing human body and character traits as culinary edibles is a brilliant comic exercise manipulated to exaggerate parliamentary quirks and euphemisms. It is a slapstick story of literary comedy in which the jokes are intellectual and verbal rather than realistic. The fun of the reading is to see how Twain continues to expand what is, after all, a metaphor for egocentrism to bring it to a climax which reflects American political experience. Although some unsophisticated readers take the story seriously, the fanciful railroad story packs a sarcastic political message that is pure intellectual fantasy.

"Scotty Biggs and the Parson" demonstrates a third mode of blending comic story traditions that occurs in Twain's work. It could be considered somewhat like the ancient "flyting," that escalating verbal conflict between two heroes (backwoods or otherwise) that often leads to a frontier fight, complete with half-horse, half-alligator eye-gouging and other elements of Southwestern fun. In classic Twain fashion the rhetoric keeps escalating on each side. The form is in place. Important differences also appear, however, and the "action" of the story takes the comedy in another direction. Instead of challenging each other, both parties are seeking to cooperate and resolve the differences that disrupt communication. It might be that Scotty is a disrupter and vulgarian, but he is not attacking authority, and the parson, laboring under his own language burden, does not take it so. No one has to back down or fight. The language is interpretative, not boastful, and, if anything, is deferential. Finally, the colorful backwoods figure successfully breaks through the barriers and is welcomed into the formal religious authority *with his frontier characteristics intact and welcome*. Twain has created an elastic world that is neither static nor hostile and has populated it with men of good will who are still uniquely regional or representative of differing social castes. The comedy is intellectual rather than physical, although the status of the corpse is a physical complexity. Twain is writing more in a Northeastern mode, but with Southwestern materials, describing a Western experience in language that is vulgar and dialectal, representing both region and class differences.

Twain has rounded up the strengths of all the conventions and brought them to a higher form. These stories have permanence; they deal in universals; their metaphors for democracy and greed are elaborated through local characters and language, yet they represent the broadest lines of human experience ... and they are funny. It is hard to imagine a higher fusion of elements than Twain has accomplished in these stories and in a handful of others, but Twain may achieve it in the character of "Aunt Rachel," the fictional persona playing against "Misto' C" in "A True Story," one of a handful of outstanding American short stories encompassing Hawthorne's "Young Goodman Brown," Poe's "The Fall of the House of Usher," Melville's "Billy Budd," Irving's "The Legend of Sleepy Hollow," and Thorpe's "The Big Bear of Arkansas," and "The Notorious Jumping Frog of Calaveras County."

"A True Story, Repeated Word for Word as I Heard It" belongs in the top rank of stories written in a uniquely American voice – or any voice, for that matter. The narrator of the frame story appears only in a couple of lines, but they are crucial in making an American social statement. "Misto' C" says he thought the storyteller of the inside story had never experienced grief. "Aunt Rachel," the colored servant, based on the real servant of the Cranes at Quarry Farm in Elmira, New York, Mary Ann Cord, reveals that she was "bawn down 'mongst de slaves" and responds to the supposedly off-hand remark with her story, enriched by her dialect and her personal identifying phrase, "I wa'n't bawn in de mash to be fool' by trash! I's one o' de ole Blue Hen's Chickens, I is." Twain worked hard on the dialect, and the important phrase triggers the climax of the interior story, so its employment is powerful. Aunt Rachel unwinds her tale of slave abuse and Civil War loss: her husband and seven children are sold away from her. She will only see *one* of her children, Henry, again. The "Blue Hen's Chickens" phrase is comic linguistic differentiation of style and local personality, which also represents a majestic philosophical position in the story's climax, for her son Henry, a grown man, recognizes her, bringing her the most supreme moment of joy in her life. She concludes, "Oh, no, Misto C—, I hain't had no trouble. An no joy!" The revelation of character fulfills every definition of greatness at all levels, from Miss Mitford's regard for incident and unique language and setting to our own recognition of heroic character displayed in the American historical context. Twain revealed to his friend William Dean Howells, who published the story in the prestigious *Atlantic Monthly* magazine, that he had reordered the story and altered many dialectal variants. Twain told Howells that the story was a little out of his line, but Howells responded that he would gladly publish many more like it. The American comic story had reached its finest and most characteristic expression.

Although Twain represents the high-water mark of the comic short story tradition, other writers made major contributions in their own styles, and the writing goes on. William Faulkner proved adept at modernizing the Southwestern tradition. The wits at the Algonquin "Round Table" formed a coterie producing humor in a unique *New Yorker* style that bears its own special cachet. Woody Allen and Kurt Vonnegut immediately come to mind as contemporary practitioners. The local color movement of the 1870–90 period is largely composed of stories conforming to this tradition. The opinion of many analysts seems to be that the present time is one where mechanical media create homogeneity. For a tradition with such clear roots in unique local traits, so clearly identified by both foreign and native critics in language, setting, and action, the American comic short story might seem to have come to its highest point with Mark Twain's "A True Story." The stories of Garrison Keillor, however, suggest that reports of the death of the tradition may be greatly exaggerated.

REFERENCES AND FURTHER READING

Blair, Walter. *Native American Humor*. New York: Chandler/Harper & Row, 1960.

Branch, Edgar M. "'My Voice is Still for Setchell': A Background Study of 'Jim Smiley and His Jumping Frog.'" Rpt. from *PMLA* in Sloane, ed. *Mark Twain's Humor*, 3–29.

Burton, William E. *The Cyclopedia of Wit and Humor*. 1858. New York: D. Appleton, 1875.

Clemens, Samuel L. [Mark Twain]. *Mark Twain/ Collected Tales, Sketches, Speeches, & Essays/1852–*

1890, 1891–1910. 2 vols. Ed. Louis J. Budd. New York: Library of America, 1992.

Cohen, Hennig, and William Dillingham, eds. *The Humor of the Old Southwest, Third Edition*. Athens: University of Georgia Press, 1994.

Haliburton, Thomas Chandler, ed. *Traits of American Humour/ by Native Authors*. London: Hurst & Blackett, 1852.

Howells, William Dean. *My Mark Twain*. New York: Harper, 1910.

Mitford, Mary Russell, ed. *Stories of American Life; by American Writers*. 3 vols. London: Henry Colburn & Richard Bently, 1830.

Neal, Joseph C. *Charcoal Sketches; or, Scenes in the Metropolus*. Philadelphia: E. L. Carey & A. Hart, 1838.

Sloane, David E. E. *American Humor Magazines and Comic Periodicals*. Westport, CT: Greenwood Press, 1987.

———. *The Literary Humor of the Urban Northeast, 1830–1890*. Baton Rouge: Louisiana State University Press, 1982. (Cited in the text as *LHUNE*.)

———. *Mark Twain's Humor: Critical Essays*. New York: Garland, 1993. (Cited in the text as *MTH*.)

Smith, Henry Nash. *Mark Twain: The Development of a Writer*. Cambridge, MA: Harvard University Press, 1962.

7
New England Local-Color Literature: A Colonial Formation

Josephine Donovan

On April 3, 1834, Harriet Beecher Stowe (1811–96) published "A New England Sketch" in *Western Monthly*, thus inaugurating the New England – indeed, the American – local-color tradition. The story was later retitled "Uncle Tim" in Stowe's pioneering local-color collection, *The Mayflower; Or, Sketches of Scenes and Characters among the Descendants of the Pilgrims* (1834). The story, conveniently, presents a paradigm of the classic local-color work, which, by definition, is characterized by its realistic focus upon a particular geographical locale, its native customs, its physical and cultural environment, and its regional dialect. As in much local-color fiction, Stowe's story portrays the local region positively, set in counterposition against threatening influences of modernity. The clash between the older vernacular culture and the modern is represented in this story by a conflict between Uncle Lot Griswold, who speaks in dialect and exhibits extensive knowledge of local customs and ways – *mētis* – and, on the other hand, a young educated "modern" figure James Benton, who speaks in standard English and is headed for college, a formative institution of modernity. As James is courting Uncle Lot's daughter, he has to overcome the older man's skepticism about his cocky confidence and claims to authority. In the process, however, it is James who comes to appreciate the wisdom of the native, "who had the strong-grained practical sense, the calculating worldly wisdom of his class of people in New England" (Stowe 36).

In addition to *The Mayflower*, Stowe, who is best known for *Uncle Tom's Cabin* (1852), published several local-color novels, most notably *The Minister's Wooing* (1859), *The Pearl of Orr's Island* (1862), and *Oldtown Folks* (1869). Her successors in the New England local-color school included Rose Terry Cooke (1827–92), whose stories, like Stowe's, are set principally in Connecticut; Sarah Orne Jewett (1849–1909), a Maine writer considered the greatest of the local colorists; and Mary E. Wilkins Freeman (1852–1930), whose works are set in Vermont and Massachusetts. Also important were Annie Trumbull Slosson (1838–1926), Elizabeth Stuart Phelps Ward (1844–1911), Rowland Robinson (1833–1900), Alice Brown (1857–1948), and Celia Thaxter (1835–94), though the last was primarily a poet and essay writer.

Probably the best of the local-color stories are to be found in Cooke's *Somebody's Neighbors* (1881) and *Huckleberries Gathered from New England Hills* (1891); Freeman's *A Humble Romance and Other Stories* (1887), and *A New England Nun and Other Stories* (1891); and Sarah Orne Jewett's *Deephaven* (1877), *The Country of the Pointed Firs* (1896), and several of her story collections, including *Old Friends and New* (1879), *Country By-Ways* (1881), and *A White Heron and Other Stories* (1886).

The New England local-color school produced several stories that may indeed be considered masterpieces of the genre, such as Cooke's "Alcedama Sparks; Or, Old and New" (1859), "Miss Lucinda" (1861), "Freedom Wheeler's Controversy with Providence" (1877), "Mrs. Flint's Married Experience" (1880), "Clary's Trial" (1880), "Some Account of Thomas Tucker" (1882), and "How Celia Changed Her Mind" (1891); Freeman's "A Wayfaring Couple" (1885), "A New England Nun" (1887), "Sister Liddy" (1891), "Christmas Jenny" (1891), "A Poetess" (1891), and "Old Woman Magoun" (1905). In addition to *The Country of the Pointed Firs*, which Willa Cather designated one of three American works destined for immortality (the others being *A Scarlet Letter* and *Huckleberry Finn*), Jewett's master stories include "A White Heron" (1886) – probably the most famous of the American local-color stories – "The Courting of Sister Wisby" (1887), "Miss Tempy's Watchers" (1888), "The Flight of Betsey Lane" (1893), "The Only Rose" (1894), "Martha's Lady" (1897), and "The Foreigner" (1900).

The heyday of the local-color movement was the latter half of the nineteenth century, a period during which Jackson Lears notes the United States underwent a "second industrial revolution" (in *No Place of Grace: Antimodernism and the Transformation of American Culture, 1880–1920* [1981]), entailing the rise of "organized corporate capitalism" and a concomitant "rationalization of economic life," and the imposition of Enlightenment modes of "technical 'rationality'" on much that had been unregulated theretofore. "The process of rationalization" ushered in by modernity "did more than transform the structure of economic life," Lears asserts, "it also affected the structure of thought and feeling" (Lears 9–10). It was this ideological colonization that the local colorists wrote against and/or in negotiation with, often affirming instead the value of non-standardized, idiosyncratic, *local* tradition.

Sarah Orne Jewett's story "The Flight of Betsey Lane" (1893), an acknowledged *locus classicus* of her work, encapsulates the conflict between the modern and the premodern in nearly allegorical form. It is set at the time of the 1876 Centennial (of the Declaration of Independence) Exposition in Philadelphia, which showcased the latest technological innovations, signifying the ascendancy of capitalist modernity and the ideological colonizations it imposed upon premodern rural life-worlds. The eponymous protagonist is an elderly woman who lives in a "poor-house" in rural New England. She conceives a desire to visit the Centennial and, thanks to a financial windfall, is able to make what is in effect a pilgrimage to the exposition. Betsey is enlightened and excited by the new inventions she sees there, but the author also points up the urban anomie that has accompanied modernity by remarking how an animated Betsey stood out against the "indifferent, stupid crowd that drifted along

... seeing ... nothing" (Jewett, *Pointed Firs* 188). In the end, Betsey returns to her rural community – where "people knew each other well" (183) – to live out her life with her friends. The story affirms, therefore, the virtues of rural *Gemeinschaft* even while acknowledging the positive aspects of modernity, in particular, the liberties it affords women, for, in making the trip by herself Betsey is, in effect, rehearsing her own "declaration of independence."

Local-color literature emerged in Ireland – then a British colony – in the early 1800s as a colonial literature, Maria Edgeworth's *Castle Rackrent* being acknowledged as the founding work in the genre. Like other colonial literatures, local-color literature "emerged ... out of the experience of colonization and asserted [itself] by foregrounding the tension with the colonial power, and emphasizing ... differences from the assumptions of the imperial center" (Ashcroft et al. 2). More often than not, colonization of non-Western countries by Western powers entailed – indeed was ideologically justified by – the imposition of modernity upon colonized natives (the "white man's burden"). Most of the native cultures in Africa and Asia seized and colonized by the imperial Western powers in the nineteenth century were premodern, oral cultures deemed by the colonizers to be inferior to Western modes of modernity. Similarly, in the construction of modern nation-states, regions within states were culturally colonized, that is, held up as inferior to externally imposed cultural standards of modernity, to which regional natives were urged instead to conform.

With the imperial power representing and enforcing modernity, the indigenous author, writing from the standpoint of the colonized, Edward Said notes, often expressed a "negative apprehension ... of 'civilized' modernity," celebrating instead premodern traditions (Said 81). Such was the case with regionalist writers within states, the local colorists; schooled in the perspectives of modernity by virtue of education or class background, they were also knowledgeable about native local culture, which as a rule they affirmed in opposition to modernity. In their case the opposition was more cultural than overtly political in nature, as the bearers of modernity to US regions, for example, were not (except in the case of the South) conquering armies but rather the ideological instruments of the modern nation-state in alliance with capitalist industrialism. Local-color writers thus evince the "double vision" that Bill Ashcroft et al. note as characteristic of the postcolonial author (26): keeping one eye on the hegemonic authority and the other on the native subject, translating, in effect, from the latter to the former.

Modernity, therefore, refers to the way of life and thinking that accompanied the emergence of capitalist industrialism as the dominant economic system in seventeenth-century Western Europe and modern science as the dominant epistemology. Articulated in the philosophical systems of the Enlightenment, modernity found political expression in the formation of the modern nation-states during the seventeenth to nineteenth centuries. These states were organized around major metropolitan centers (London, Paris, Boston/New York/Washington) where the bureaucratic apparatuses were located that enforced the governing standards, rules, tastes, and norms of modernity upon regional locales, which often had variant norms that were rooted in local tradition and lore. Metropolitan control was facilitated by the imposition of a standard national language, thus reducing provincial dialects to the status of deviant and inferior.

The process of standardization and normalization imposed by the advocates of modernity was rooted in the philosophical premises of Cartesian rationalism, themselves reflective of the adoption of the Newtonian scientific paradigm in the seventeenth century, which effected what Edmund Husserl labeled the "mathematization of the world" (Horkheimer and Adorno 25). The reduction of reality – including biotic life-forms and the social life-world – to its quantitative properties rendered it machine-like; elided in the process were qualitative, subjective properties, such as color, taste, and emotion. Transforming nature "into mere objectivity," Newtonian-Cartesian epistemology occasioned "the disenchantment of the world" (Max Weber's term) and the "extirpation of animism," according to Frankfurt School critics Max Horkheimer and Theodor Adorno (5), who viewed the Enlightenment paradigm as a dominative model imposed upon the manifold forms of social and biotic life, requiring the "subdual of difference, particularities" (22). Necessarily, all that did not fit into the quantitative normalizing grid of the scientific model was marginalized, that is, rendered anomalous or invisible, which meant, in the case of deviant humans, voiceless. In the impartiality of scientific knowledge "that which is powerless has wholly lost any means of expression" (23). Thus were certain standards of human behavior established as norms and others characterized as deviant by emerging social sciences, such as sexology.

In its negotiation with the ideological colonizations of modernity, local-color literature nearly always mediates the colonizer–colonized dialectic through class positions: the colonized equates to the peasant, folk, native society whereas the colonizer is upper-class, urban, and located outside the region. Often the writer enjoys an intermediate location between the colonizing metropole and the native region; by virtue of class, education, or travel, having some familiarity and often acceptance of modern norms and ideas but also having intimate knowledge and often emotional roots and attachments to premodern ways of being.

An example of a story where the author approaches the rural premodern world satirically, from a metropolitan perspective, is Rose Terry Cooke's "Miss Lucinda" (1861). In so doing, however, she provides enough sympathetic information about her protagonist that the contemporary reader may disengage from the story the ethos of Lucinda, seeing it in counterposition to the metropolitan disciplinary knowledge endorsed by the author that would colonize Lucinda and her world in a process of normalization.

Like many of the protagonists in nineteenth-century women's local-color literature, Lucinda is an eccentric middle-aged spinster who lives happily in a separate, marginal rural world. Her main companions are her animals, and her main occupation is tending them, her house, and her garden. The story is set during the Civil War, in what the narrator calls the "Disuniting States," evincing the federal versus regional dialectic central to American local-color literature.

In "Miss Lucinda" the disciplinary process is effected by a French dancing master, Monsieur Jean Leclerc, whose name, "the clerk," suggests the bureaucratic functionary whose chief historical mission has been to impose rationalizing disciplines upon the populace. His French origin unintentionally highlights that the normalizing disciplines that were encroaching upon rural eccentricity by mid-century were rooted, as noted, in Cartesian Enlightenment rationalism.

Leclerc enters Lucinda's world when he helps her recapture a pig who had gotten loose. Lucinda's relationship with her animals, he feels, is too undisciplined, a view the author shares. Indeed, the animals lived in Lucinda's house on equal terms with their owner: "her cat had its own chair ... her dog, a rug and basket" and her blind crow, a "special nest of flannel and cotton." (Cooke 156).[1] Lucinda does not believe in imposing a hierarchical disciplinary grid upon her creatures. She felt "that animals have feelings ... and are of 'like passions'" with people and that they have souls (162–3). The author feels that Lucinda's undisciplinary practice is out of line (162–4).

Once Leclerc is installed in Lucinda's house (he had injured himself during the pig chase and was being nursed back to health by her), he begins disciplining her animals. He commences by "subduing" her German spaniel, Fun; the narrator cites (apparently non-ironically) a legitimizing proverb: "'Women and spaniels,'" the world knows, 'like kicking'" (168). Leclerc then takes on Lucinda's other dog, Toby. "[A] few well-timed slaps, administered with vigor, cured Toby of his worst tricks: though every blow made Miss Lucinda wince, and almost shook her good opinion of Monsieur Leclerc" (169). Leclerc also has her pet pig slaughtered when he becomes too unmanageable.

The taming process is not only applied to the animals but also to Lucinda herself. A crucial episode in the story concerns Lucinda's dancing lessons. Dancing here represents metonymically an alien discipline to which the rural woman tries awkwardly to conform. The other students laugh at the odd outfits she wears to the lessons, signifying her non-conformity; her "peculiar" practice of the steps is a further sign of her deviance (176). During this period her animals are neglected, suggesting a betrayal of her native life-world as she attempts to assimilate to new life patterns. The denouement of the story is that she and Leclerc marry, and the final authorial note is one of ridicule against Lucinda for her "sentimental" views of animals. Lucinda's subdual may thus be interpreted as reflecting the process by which homogenizing, normalizing institutions were gaining hegemony over rural deviancy in the nineteenth-century Western world.

In the first of his lectures in *Power/Knowledge*, Foucault advocates searching for "subjugated knowledges." "[I]t is through the re-appearance of ... these local popular knowledges, these disqualified knowledges, that criticism performs its work" (Foucault 82). The knowledge Foucault has in mind is "a particular, local, regional knowledge, a differential knowledge incapable of unanimity" (82); it is a "minor" knowledge (85). The critic's job, he suggests, is to "emancipate historical knowledges from [their] subjection" within "the hierarchical order of power associated with science" and to render these silenced knowledges "capable of opposition and of struggle against the coercion of a theoretical, unitary, formal and scientific discourse" (85). The "local knowledge" evinced in "Miss Lucinda" is a nonhierarchical, "undisciplined," "disordered," premodern perspective governed by animism (animals are of "like passions" with people).

In their discussion of the ideological ascendancy of the Cartesian/Newtonian paradigm – the "mathematization of the world" – Horkheimer and Adorno point to the confrontation between the witch Circe and Odysseus in Homer's epic allegorically as a representation of this process. Circe turns Odysseus's men into pigs; the pig was a sacred animal to Demeter, which connects Circe to this ancient cult (Horkheimer and Adorno 71). "Miss Lucinda" may be seen as a reversal of this ancient story; it is not the Greek goddess who is triumphant in this story with her "insurrectionary" holistic knowledges but rather the representative of modern mathematizing, unitary discourse, the French dancing master.

The literature of the nineteenth-century New England local-color school, which was dominated by women, records in one of its principal subtexts the clash between dominant, colonizing, mathematizing disciplines and the rural, eccentric culture Foucault saw as having counterhegemonic potential. Scores of stories concern marginal communities peopled by deviant, often witch-like women who live in predisciplinary peace with their animals in a green-world environment. At times the authors were sympathetic to the characters whose lives were being erased by the encroaching disciplines. At other times the authors seem to ally with the forces of "progress," as Cooke does in "Miss Lucinda," joining in the colonization of their characters.

In *Discipline and Punish* Foucault identifies the prison as the model disciplinary grid to which other modern institutions such as hospitals, asylums, etc. conform. In the first volume of his *History of Sexuality*, Foucault focuses upon the emergence of pseudo-scientific disciplines such as sexology, which "entomologized" sexual lifestyles into species and subspecies of deviance, thus ideologically colonizing people's life-world.

Many of the works of Sarah Orne Jewett concern a resistance to this colonization. By the mid-1880s the views of sexologists, such as Richard von Krafft-Ebing in the *Psychopathia Sexualis*, were well known. The latter work is a series of "case studies" of people who were "tainted with antipathic sexual instinct" (Krafft-Ebing 205). Oliver Wendell Holmes's parody of the term *antipathy* in his 1885 novel *A Mortal Antipathy* suggests the extent to which Krafft-Ebing's theories had been popularized.

Jewett's novel *A Country Doctor* (1884), a local-color work, is one example of a repudiation of the Krafft-Ebing notion of deviance, sexology being a signal instance of the Foucauldian normalizing discipline.[2] The main character, Nan Prince, has the earmarks of what Krafft-Ebing called a "viragint," a species of woman who adopted a "mannish" style and was attracted to other women. While Nan does have a crush on a female class-mate (which Jewett sees as normal), she was not "the sort of girl who tried to be mannish" (Jewett, *Country Doctor* 160). Nevertheless, like Krafft-Ebing's "female urning" (another species of female deviant), Nan is a tomboy: she "may chiefly be found in the haunt of boys. She is their rival in play... . Love for art finds a substitute in the pursuits of the sciences" (Krafft-Ebing 399). Similarly, Nan (who becomes a physician) displays a "lack of skill and liking for female occupations" (419) and has a "bold and tomboyish style" (420). In one of the central episodes of the novel Nan quickly responds in a crisis and sets a man's dislocated shoulder while her suitor stands helplessly by, feeling "weak and womanish, and somehow [wishing] it had been he who could play the doctor" (*Country Doctor* 266). In this novel Jewett was resisting the normalizing discipline of sexology, affirming instead the right of women to follow their own "deviant" bent.

An even more powerful rejection of normalization occurs in Jewett's "An Autumn Holiday" (1881). This story concerns Daniel Gunn, a retired militia captain, who "got sun-struck" and comes to believe he is his dead sister Patience (Jewett, "Autumn Holiday" 153). He begins wearing her clothes, adopting her feminine manners, and participating in traditionally female activities, such as the sewing bees of the Female Missionary Society. In short, he is a transvestite (though Jewett does not use this or any other label to classify him). Rather than ship their old neighbor off to an asylum, however, the villagers decide to accommodate him. One woman even decides to make him a dress in his size because his sister's clothes are a tight fit. Rather than force him, therefore, into a prefabricated form, the form is adjusted to him – unlike the situation in "Miss Lucinda," where she is forced to conform. The story was originally entitled "Miss Daniel Gunn" but somewhere in the federalizing, normalizing editorial process it got changed to the more respectable "Autumn Holiday." Yet Jewett's central point in this story is to endorse acceptance of deviance. Despite their bemusement, the townspeople are compassionate toward Daniel and do not stigmatize him as "other." This story represents a signal example of local resistance to normalizing disciplines of the type identified by Foucault.

Much of Jewett's work is indeed devoted to a defense of eccentricity and deviancy. In *The Country of the Pointed Firs*, Mrs. Todd, the protagonist, repeatedly sticks up for the community's "strayaways": "I never want to hear Joanna laughed about" (*Pointed Firs* 103), she warns when the eccentric hermit Joanna's story is broached. Significantly, her comments follow upon a discussion lamenting the increasing conformity, standardization, and homogenization in American life. Her interlocutor Mrs. Fosdick observes: "What a lot o' queer folks there used to be about here, anyway, when we was young, Almiry. Everybody's just like everybody else now" (101). Mrs. Todd agrees:

Yes ... there was certain a good many curiosities of human natur' in this neighborhood years ago. There was more energy then, and in some the energy took a singular turn. In these days the young folks is all copy-cats, 'fraid to death they won't be all just alike; as for the old folks, they pray for the advantage o' bein' a little different. (102)

In "The Courting of Sister Wisby" (1887) a local herbalist, Mrs. Goodsoe, also blames mass transportation and communication systems: "'t was never my idee that we was meant to know what's goin' on all over the world to once. … [I]n old times … they stood in their lot an' place, and were n't all just alike, either, same as pine-spills" ("Sister Wisby" 59).

Jewett also has various characters who repudiate the claims of modern medicine, affirming instead the virtues of the ancient feminine practice of herbology. Mrs. Todd, the herbalist in *Pointed Firs*, is one example; although she has an amicable relationship with the local doctor, it is likely that he is an "irregular" physician of the order of Jewett's own father, who respects herbal lore and is himself skeptical of the scientific bent in modern medicine. Even more explicit in her rejection of modern disciplines – especially modern medicine – is the herbalist noted above, Mrs. Goodsoe, who claims that modern doctors may be "bilin' over with book-larnin' [but they're] … truly ignorant of what to do for the sick. … Book-fools I call 'em" (57). Mrs. Goodsoe espouses in effect a theory of bio-regionalism: illness should be treated with regionally grown remedies: "[F]olks was meant to be doctored with the stuff that grew right about 'em; 't was sufficient and so ordered" (59). As in *Pointed Firs*, Mrs. Goodsoe's position is mediated through a more modern narrator who challenges and occasionally demurs from her views. But, as in *Pointed Firs*, the narrative frame by no means dominates the rural perspective. Indeed, one senses, as in *Pointed Firs*, a kind of self-irony occurring: the limitations of the narrator's "modern" view is also being ironized as circumscribed and limited; she concludes by lamenting the modern "world [which is] foolish enough to sometimes undervalue medicinal herbs" (68).

Many Jewett stories may thus be read as affirming an alternative to the colonizing disciplinary grids of modern industrial culture, conceived dialectically as a negative criticism of the homogenizing, federalizing tendencies of the modern world. Local-color literature in general may thus be seen as a "minor literature" – as defined by French critics Gilles Deleuze and Felix Guattari (in *Kafka: Pour une littérature mineure* [1975]) and applied to Jewett by Louis Renza in *"A White Heron" and the Question of Minor Literature* (1984) According to Deleuze and Guattari, a hallmark of minor literature is that it is written in a "deterritorialized language." To write from such a position means "to find one's own point of underdevelopment, one's own patois, one's own third world." (*Kafka* 33; author's own translation). Renza claims Jewett's works can be seen as representing "'points of nonculture and underdevelopment, the zones of a linguistic third world' intent on sabotaging the major language of American patriarchal culture" (Renza 35).

Jewett's and the other local colorists' use of "patois" or dialect throughout their work defiantly affirms the solidity and reality of this colonized linguistic realm – notwithstanding the fact that Jewett's frame narratives are in standard English (while she herself probably spoke in a Maine dialect). One might argue that such a use of a "normalizing" frame might serve to set off the dialect as deviant, if not inferior, but the frames in Jewett's work do not dominate or erase the embedded dialects; they rather serve to accentuate them, even to elevate them much as a picture frame highlights the picture it encases or a setting enhances a gem. Such a frame says: "different but valuable." It affirms – indeed, emphasizes – the ontological presence of the items scored. The embedded dialect also often serves to ironize the frame language, rendering it less authoritative, less "normal," much as the narrator's "modern" viewpoint in *Pointed Firs* and other works is undercut as authoritatively dominant by indigenous premodern views.

Other practices, customs, and characters of premodern rural culture are similarly rendered ontologically present in Jewett's treatment. A work like *Pointed Firs* is a veritable catalogue, for example, of use-value production practices from Mrs. Todd's herbal preparations to the fisherman Elijah Tilley's knitting. Dunnet Landing is not a world of capitalist entrepreneurs engaged in economic imperialism. Mrs. Todd does charge for her herbs and presumably also charges rent of her tenant, but the relationship between the two quickly eclipses economic roles, operating finally in terms of kinship relation. Dunnet Landing is in fact largely a subsistence economy, close to being an exemplar of the premodern gift economy, governed as it is by kinship ties and codes of hospitality. Most of the economic exchange in the work is through gifts, and most of the products exchanged are handcrafted. The increasing dominance of factory-made goods is lamented by another Jewett character, a tailoress, the title character in "Miss Debby's Neighbors" (1883), who complains of how people are now buying "cheap, ready-made clothes," which has the effect of making everyone look alike. "She always insisted ... that the railroads were making everybody look and act of a piece, and that young folks were more alike than people of her own day" ("Miss Debby" 191).

In the same story the urban narrator, expressing the viewpoint of modernity with its emphasis on unifying hypotaxis, offers a complaint that the indigenous speaker's method "of going around Robin Hood's barn between the beginning of her story and its end can hardly be followed at all" (191). The indigenous narrator is uneducated and her narrative style reflects the oral mentality that A. R. Luria famously identified in illiterate peasants, who resisted organizing material into deductive or hypotactic patterns. In his study of oral culture, *Orality and Literacy* (1982), Walter J. Ong lays out several features that characterize oral thought and expression, among them that it is "additive rather than subordinative," "aggregative rather than analytic," "redundant or 'copious,'" "empathetic and participatory rather than objectively distanced," and "situational rather than abstract" (Ong 36–49). All of these features readily describe the narrative technique not just of Miss Debby but of the numerous indigenous Jewett characters who narrate tales within her stories. In this way aspects of oral culture are embedded or transcribed in print in Jewett's and other local colorists' work – another instance of the author serving as mediator between two cultures – oral and print, premodern and modern.

Many, if not all, of Jewett's and other local colorists' embedded narrators similarly speak in the fashion Ong describes, using primarily parataxis, and at the extreme (as in "Miss Debby's Neighbors") losing the unifying hypotactic thread of the narration. Significantly, in this story it is the modern author – urban, literate, and educated – who criticizes this round-about narrative tendency, looking vainly for some sort of deductive climax.

Many of Jewett's stories, for example, are constructed in layers of narration where an outsider narrator from the metropole comes to a rural region, and encounters an insider who tells her tale paratactically in vernacular idiom. This technique is used most famously perhaps in *Pointed Firs* but may also be seen in such masterful stories as "The Courting of Sister Wisby" (1887) and "An Autumn Holiday" (1881).

In "Sister Wisby," for example, an urban I-narrator, wandering in the country (the first few pages read indeed like a nature essay), encounters the herbalist Mrs. Goodsoe, who is in the process of gathering "mulleins," an herb. The two engage in a meandering, gossipy conversation in which the herbalist reveals herself to harbor the typically antimodern attitudes noted above. Her grasp of local knowledge or *mētis* is immediately apparent: when the urban narrator (who speaks in standard English, as opposed to Mrs. Goodsoe's dialect) asks whether the herbalist plans to gather the herb pennyroyal, she is immediately put down: "'Pennyr'yal!' repeated the dear little old woman, with an air of compassion for inferior knowledge; ''tain't the right time, darlin'. Pennyr'yal's too rank now. But for mulleins this day is prime'" ("Sister Wisby" 57). When the narrator offers to help her cut the mullein, Mrs. Goodsoe tells her how: "'Now be keerful, dear heart … choose 'em well. There's odds in mulleins same's ther is in angels'" (57). The narrator "listened respectfully" (57), while Mrs. Goodsoe rambles on anecdotally, finally (two-thirds of the way through the story) reaching the main story about "Sister Wisby," which is sparked by a discussion of another herb, "Goldthread."

"An Autumn Holiday" similarly starts out as a nature essay, an I-narrator wandering the countryside with her dog. Eventually (four pages into the story) she comes upon a house where she finds two women spinning wool. They stop and chat with the visitor and after several shorter anecdotes the main tale emerges (more than halfway through the story), which concerns the transvestite "Miss Daniel Gunn."

Mrs. Goodsoe's insistence that the herbs be locally grown points to a central tenet of the community ethos celebrated in *Pointed Firs* and other local-color works. In this preindustrial, predisciplinary environment, time is not measured by the clock, goods are not appreciated for their abstract exchange value, and people are not uprooted and homogenized through mass media stereotypes. Rather, they remain rooted in their own eccentric (de)territory; their produce comes from their own familiar environment – Mrs. Todd grows her own herbs and/or gathers them from well-known local habitats. She ministers to people as individuals with histories and not in accordance with abstract symptoms and diagnoses.

In her work Mary E. Wilkins Freeman focuses less on the alternative community seen in Jewett's work and more on the resisting practices of women whose life-worlds are being threatened by the intrusion and imposition of alien disciplinary forces. Several concern critiques of asylums. "Sister Liddy" (1891) is set in an "almshouse" where the poor – young and old – and the insane are kept. One of the inmates, Polly Moss, a sadly deformed woman, tells stories about her fictitious well-to-do sister. Her fantasies constitute a kind of "anticipatory illumination," an imagined alternative to her own benighted, confined existence. "A Mistaken Charity" (1891) concerns the escape of two sisters, one deaf and the other blind, from an asylum, back to their own home, the details of which are lovingly beheld. In the asylum they had been forced to wear uniforms, which include caps that the sisters despise. "[N]othing could transform these two unpolished old women into two nice old ladies. They did not take kindly to white lace caps and delicate neckerchiefs" (Wilkins [Freeman], *Humble Romance* 244). When they leave, they place the caps defiantly on bedposts, thus repudiating the imposition of sameness. Two other Freeman stories – "Bouncing Bet" (1900) and "The Elm Tree" (1903) – concern rejections of asylum life.

In several Freeman stories the lives of women who are living peacefully with their animals or children are violated by the intrusion of an alien authority who destroys their world. Often the authority figure resembles the modern social worker– bureaucrat who has the power to intervene in people's private life-worlds. In "Brakes and White Vi'lets" (1887) a girl's father claims custody from her grandmother, using a medical theory that the grandmother's home is too damp and will bring about consumption. He thus removes the child; the grandmother has the choice of moving to an alien environment with the girl or remaining in her beloved home. She finally decides to move, requesting wistfully that "a root of white vi'lets an' some brakes" be dug up, "so I kin take 'em with me" (*Humble Romance* 117) – a pathetic attempt to keep one's local roots with one even while conceding their destruction.

"A Gatherer of Simples" (1884) similarly concerns a rural "yarb woman," an herbal- ist, who informally adopts a child only to have her urban grandmother claim custody of her so she can be raised properly. The child runs back to her adoptive mother, however, and the grandmother dies, so the story ends happily. "Old Woman Magoun" (1905) is a tragic version of a similar plot. Here again it is a grandmother who is raising a granddaughter; in this case, it is the father who claims custody when the child is entering puberty. He thinks the grandmother is raising her too narrowly; she thinks he intends to sell the child into prostitution. To save her, the grandmother allows her to eat the poisonous berries of the deadly nightshade, which kill her. Thus, the old woman is willing to use her local knowledge of herbs perversely, to save the child from being inscribed in the circulatory system of patriarchal power/knowledge, which entails the exchange of women.

In "A Poetess" (1891), another poignant Freeman story, the alien discipline that destroys the title character's life-world is that of aesthetic criteria. Betsey Dole, another impoverished spinster, lives happily in her green-world bower, which is "all a gay spangle with sweet-peas and red-flowering beans, and flanked with feathery asparagus" (Wilkins [Freeman], *New England Nun* 140). Betsey's calling is writing poetry, particularly verse for local consumption, occasional mourning poetry, which she writes to console neighbors who are grieving. Her reward comes not from having her work praised by distinguished critics or published in famous journals – and thus being stamped in the currency of academic literary discourse – but rather in the emotional comfort it brings her friends. Unfortunately, however, she learns that a local clerical authority, a minister, has branded her work as sentimentalist trash.

Accepting his verdict, she burns all her work and soon dies. The silence and erasure imposed upon this woman by a translocal discipline could not be more graphic. A final aspect of the local colorists' resistance to the colonizations of modernity may be found in their ecologically sensitive treatment of nature and animals. (For a fuller discussion of this issue see Mayer, *Naturethik und Neuengland-Regionalliteratur: Harriet Beecher Stowe, Rose Terry Cooke, Sarah Orne Jewett, Mary E. Wilkins Freeman* [2004].) Jewett's resistance to capitalist and industrial development of the natural world is clearly stated in a number of letters. Perhaps her most poignant and moving state- ment of this position comes in an 1892 letter: "The other day quite out of the clear sky a man came to Mary with a plan for a syndicate to cut up and sell the river bank all in lots... . Sometimes I get such a hunted feeling like the last wild thing that is left in the fields" (Fields 90). In a much earlier letter (1877) Jewett similarly remarks, "Berwick ... is growing and flourishing in a way that breaks my heart" (Cary 36).

In several stories Jewett expressed intense empathy with the natural world, even to the point of explicitly endorsing an animistic theory of nature; see especially "An October Ride," "A Winter Drive," and "River Driftwood," which were collected in *Country By-Ways* (1881). But Jewett's most powerful story of "cultural resistance" to colonization is her justly famous "A White Heron."

The story concerns a confrontation between the rural premodern world of Sylvia, a young girl who lives with her grandmother in an isolated woodland, and the world of modernity represented by an urban scientist, an ornithologist, who invades her peaceful green sanctuary looking for a rare white heron he hopes to kill and stuff for his collection. That the ornithologist has a scientific, classificatory, "entomologizing" purpose (to reprise Foucault's term) highlights his status within the text as an avatar of modernity. His perspective is that of the quantifying, objectifying gaze of modern science. He sees the bird as an object to be scrutinized and colonized within the scientific paradigm of species and subspecies of *Avis*.

The girl, on the other hand, is preliterate and uneducated in the perspectives of modernity; she has an animist view of nature. Its creatures are alive to her as pres- ences, as "persons." "There ain't a foot o' ground she don't know her way over," her grandmother explains, "and the wild creatur's counts her one o' themselves. ... Last winter she got the jay-birds to bangeing here" (Jewett, *Pointed Firs* 165). That Jewett grants equal ontological status to the creatures of the natural world may be seen in several other works in which she evinces a desire to give voice, to articulate the "language" of the non-human. In "River Driftwood," for example, the narrator meditates:

> Who is going to be the linguist who learns the first word of an old crow's warning to his mate ... ? [H]ow long we shall have to go to school when people are expected to talk to the trees, and birds, and beasts in their own language! ... Is it science that will give us back the gift, or shall we owe it to the successors of those friendly old saints who talked with the birds and fishes? (Jewett, *Country By-Ways* 4–5)

Jewett's anti-modern answer is clear: it is not science. Her resistance to its dominative colonizing claims is manifest as she continues,

> It is not necessary to tame [creatures] before they can be familiar and responsive; *we can meet them on their own ground*. ... Taming is only forcing them to learn some of our customs; we should be wise if we let them tame us to make use of some of theirs. (5; emphasis added)

Jewett proceeds to envisage a day of "universal suffrage ... when the meaning of every living thing is understood, and is given its rights and accorded its true value" (6).

In "A White Heron" Sylvia, though inarticulate, has a similar viewpoint; and although she is attracted initially to the ornithologist and interested in his knowledges, and he stimulates her to expand her horizons (literally: she climbs a tree looking for the bird and sees the ocean in the distance, something she had never done before); she nevertheless is distressed by his willingness to destroy the natural world in order to learn more about it. She "would have liked him vastly better without his gun; she could not understand why he killed the very birds he seemed to like so much" (166). Also disturbing is the way in which the ornithologist is willing to exploit the girl's knowledge of the birds for his own purposes. The corruptness of his instrumental treatment of Sylvia is further emphasized when he offers her money, in a sense bribing her, to reveal the location of the white heron. The unholy alliance between modern science and capitalism is tacitly acknowledged in this moment.

In the end Sylvia takes a stand and refuses to reveal the bird's location to the ornithologist, thus saving the bird's life and upholding the claims of the premodern, animist, *local* world of rural Maine as against the modernist imperative.

> No, she must keep silence. What is it that suddenly forbids her and makes her dumb? ... The murmur of the pine's green branches is in her ears, she remembers how the white heron came flying through the golden air and how they watched the sea and the morning together, and Sylvia cannot speak; she cannot tell the heron's secret and give its life away. (171)

Sylvia cannot speak but her author does, giving voice to the inarticulate people – human and non-human – of rural Maine, telling their story, that it not be erased, that its claim to ontological status be upheld against the colonizing, extirpating forces of modernity.

NOTES

1 Cooke also wrote several stories that depicted rural people positively, especially her "Polly Mariner" stories. An earlier version of this discussion of Cooke's story appeared in Donovan, "Breaking the Sentence."

2 Earlier versions of this discussion of Jewett and modernity appeared in Donovan, "Nan Prince" and Donovan, "Local-Color Literature and Modernity."

REFERENCES AND FURTHER READING

Ashcroft, Bill, Gareth Griffiths, and Helen Tiffin. *The Empire Writes Back: Theory and Practice in Post-Colonial Literatures*. London and New York: Routledge, 1989.

Cary, Richard, ed. *Sarah Orne Jewett Letters*. Waterville, ME: Colby College Press, 1967.

Cooke, Rose Terry. *"How Celia Changed Her Mind" and Selected Stories*. Ed. Elizabeth Ammons. New Brunswick, NJ: Rutgers University Press, 1986. 151–81.

Deleuze, Gilles, and Felix Guattari. *Kafka: Pour une littérature mineure*. Paris: Editions de Minuit, 1975.

Donovan, Josephine. "Breaking the Sentence: Local-Color Literature and Subjugated Knowledges." *The (Other) American Traditions*. Ed. Joyce Warren. New Brunswick, NJ: Rutgers University Press, 1993. 226–43.

———. "Local-Color Literature and Modernity: The Example of Jewett." *Tamking Review* 38.1 (December 2007): 7–25.

———. "Nan Prince and the Golden Apples." *Colby Library Quarterly* 22.1 (March 1986): 17–27.

———. *New England Local Color Literature: A Women's Tradition*. New York: Ungar, 1983.

Fields, Annie, ed. *Letters of Sarah Orne Jewett*. Boston: Houghton Mifflin, 1911.

Foucault, Michel. *Power/Knowledge: Selected Interviews and Other Writings, 1972–1977*. Ed. Colin Gordon. New York: Pantheon, 1980.

Freeman, Mary E. Wilkins. *Selected Stories of Mary E. Wilkins Freeman*. Ed. Marjorie Pryse. New York: W. W. Norton, 1983.

Horkheimer, Max, and Theodor W. Adorno. *Dialectic of Enlightenment*. Trans. John Cumming. 1944. Rpt. edn. New York: Continuum, 1988.

Jewett, Sarah Orne. "An Autumn Holiday." *Country By-Ways*. Boston: Houghton Mifflin, 1881. 139–62.

———. *The Country of the Pointed Firs and Other Stories*. Ed Willa Cather. Garden City, NY: Doubleday, 1956. (In this edition, however, three stories written later were interpolated into the original text of *The Country of the Pointed Firs*.)

———. *A Country Doctor*. Boston: Houghton Mifflin, 1884.

———. "The Courting of Sister Wisby." *The King of Folly Island and Other People*. Boston: Houghton Mifflin, 1888. 50–80.

———. "Miss Debby's Neighbors." *The Mate of the Daylight and Friends Ashore*. Boston: Houghton Mifflin, 1884. 190–209.

———. "River Driftwood". Boston: Houghton Mifflin, 1881. 1–33.

Krafft-Ebing, Richard von. *Psychopathia Sexualis, with Especial Reference to the Antipathic Sexual Instinct*. Trans. F. J. Rebman. New York: Medical Art Agency, 1906.

Lears, Jackson. *No Place of Grace: Antimodernism and the Transformation of American Culture, 1880–1920*. New York: Pantheon, 1981.

Mayer, Sylvia. *Naturethik und Neuengland-Regionalliteratur: Harriet Beecher Stowe, Rose Terry Cooke, Sarah Orne Jewett, Mary E. Wilkins Freeman*. Heidelberg, Germany: Winter, 2004.

Ong, Walter J. *Orality and Literature*. London: Routledge, 1988.

Renza, Louis A. *"A White Heron" and the Question of Minor Literature*. Madison: University of Wisconsin Press, 1984.

Said, Edward W. "Yeats and Decolonization." *Nationalism, Colonialism and Literature*. Eds. Terry Eagleton et al. Minneapolis: University of Minnesota Press, 1990. 67–95.

Stowe, Harriet Beecher. "A New England Sketch." In (under the title "Uncle Lot") *Regional Sketches: New England and Florida*. Ed. John R. Adams. New Haven, CT: College and University Press, 1972. 31–55.

Westbrook, Perry D. *Acres of Flint: Sarah Orne Jewett and Her Contemporaries*. Rev. edn. Metuchen, NJ: Scarecrow Press, 1981.

Wilkins [Freeman], Mary E. *A Humble Romance and Other Stories*. 1887. Rpt. New York: Garrett Press, 1969.

———. *A New England Nun and Other Stories*. New York: Harper, 1891.

8

Charlotte Perkins Gilman and the Feminist Tradition of the American Short Story

Martha J. Cutter

When Charlotte Perkins Gilman (1860–1935) initially attempted to place her short story "The Yellow Wallpaper" (1892) in the prestigious magazine *Atlantic Monthly*, then editor Horace Scudder rejected it with a terse note: "I could not forgive myself if I made others as miserable as I have made myself!" (Golden 3). Eventually the story was published in *New England Magazine* but then virtually ignored for over seventy-five years, until it was republished by Elaine Hedges in a Feminist Press edition in 1973. Yet today Gilman's story has garnered more critical attention for its feminist themes than perhaps any other short story by an American writer; it is taught frequently in American literature courses, has received an abundant amount of scrutiny by literary scholars, doctors, and historians, and has been adapted for radio, the stage, television, and film. To grasp the continuing prominence of this work in the feminist tradition of the American short story, we must place it in the context of Gilman's other short fictions and within the larger history of American women's feminist short story writing. Gilman's story, while certainly unique, carried forward a number of themes that other writers have dealt with concerning women and language, women and masculine authority, women and the natural environment, and the material and historical basis of women's oppression. The continuing popularity of "The Yellow Wallpaper," then, can be linked to the way it articulates archetypal and enduring themes about the causes and resolutions of women's social, economic, and linguistic oppression – issues which continue to be ambiguous and unresolved, even in our own era.

American Women's Feminist Short Story Writing at the Turn of the Century

With its frank confrontation of male authority and its graphic depiction of the pernicious effects of medical treatments that infantilize and sicken women, "The Yellow Wallpaper" seems to be a unique text. Yet numerous women short story writers at the turn of the century confronted, with less graphic detail, similar questions, embedding historical controversies within their texts and sometimes refashioning limiting stereotypes of feminine identity and voice. During this era, two images of women's identity competed with each other: the "True Woman" (or "domestic saint"), who was supposed to be pure, pious, domestic, subservient, and silent, and the "New Woman," who was financially independent of men, more outspoken, less domestic, and less subservient to male authority. According to Sarah Grand, who is thought to have coined the "New Woman" term in an essay in *North American Review* in 1894, man has "set himself up as a sort of god and required us to worship him, and, to our eternal shame be it said, we did so" (Grand 272). However, Grand believes that women are now rebelling – they are beginning to think for themselves, to look at the world with their own eyes, and they are becoming more articulate (274–6). It would be simplistic to suggest that women writers from this time period always depict the triumph of the New Woman over the True Woman; however, many of their texts do investigate the potential freedom that the new image might offer.

In "The Revolt of 'Mother'" (1890), for example, Mary Wilkins Freeman (1852–1930) portrays a "good" domestic saint in her main character Sarah Penn, a woman who spends virtually every minute of the story caring for her family and their home – cleaning, cooking, sewing, dusting, and helping her husband. But when Sarah learns that her husband is building a new barn instead of the house he has been promising her for more than forty years, she revolts. While he is away on a business trip, she moves all of the family's possessions into the newly finished barn and makes it their home, stabling the horses and cows in the old house. She also asserts her right to think and speak for herself, telling the town minister: "I'm goin' to think my own thoughts an' go my own ways, an' nobody but the Lord is goin' to dictate to me unless I've a mind to have him" (Freeman 310). In confronting both her husband and her minister's authority, Sarah enacts a double challenge to the ideal of true womanhood, which required piety (towards God and religious figures) and submissiveness (towards male authority in general). And her revolt is successful. Throughout the story, when Sarah tries to plead for the new home, her husband Adoniram ignores her, but at the end he finally hears what she has been saying all along: "'Why, mother,' he said, hoarsely, 'I hadn't no idee you was so set on't as all this comes to'" (313). Through creative rearrangement of the space of the home into the barn, Sarah merges her world with her husband's, and finally finds a voice that can be heard by, and even counter, male authority.

Stories published after "The Revolt of 'Mother'" continue to show the subtle challenges turn-of-the-century women writers presented to male authority and its silencing of women. "A Jury of Her Peers" (1917), by Susan Glaspell (1876–1948), details the investigation by an all-male sheriff's posse of the murder of a husband. The men suspect the wife might have committed this crime, but can find no motive. In the meantime, the women who accompany the men to the scene of the crime – the house where the couple lived – find one damning piece of evidence: the woman's pet canary, mournfully buried in a box, after its neck has been broken. Based on this and other signs, the women conclude that Minnie Foster has been abused by her husband, that he killed her pet, and that she eventually killed him. Yet they cover up the evidence carefully, resisting the male authority of the sheriff and acquitting the woman of her crime. The female "jury" of the town challenges patriarchal authority. The women also bring Minnie's silent suffering into language, making it articulate through the narrative they weave around her.

Like Freeman, Alice Dunbar-Nelson (1875–1935), an African American writer, also illustrates the necessity for women to speak out; in so doing, they sometimes change not only their own self-definition but enhance men's growth and development. In "Ellen Fenton" (c. 1900–10) for example, a good housewife embarks on a journey of self-discovery after twenty-two years of married life because she finds herself discontented (Dunbar-Nelson 35). In a direct homage to Gilman's "The Yellow Wallpaper," Ellen sits "a long while as if reading the wallpaper" and discovers that "she had not become acquainted with herself" (35). As Ellen changes, so does her husband, who also goes through a "metamorphosis" and learns to be a "real companion and comrade" (50) to his wife. Stories such as this one indicate that the New Woman and her new voice may be met, at times, by a New Man who hears her story.

Women from other ethnic groups also consider how race impacts the struggle for self-definition and voice. In many of Sui Sin Far's (Edith Eaton's, 1865–1914) short stories collected in *Mrs. Spring Fragrance* (1912), for example, women must come to terms with how society grants them a secondary place due to both race and gender. In "Its Wavering Image," a young mixed-race woman named Pan is tricked by her white boyfriend Mark Carson into revealing rituals of the Chinese community; Carson then publishes these secrets in a newspaper for which he writes. After usurping the voice of the Chinese community, Mark Carson then also attempts to speak *for* Pan, telling her, "You are not [Chinese]. You are a white woman – white" (66). But Pan finally finds her voice and recovers the cultural heritage Carson has attempted to take from her: "I would not be a white woman for all the world. You are a white man. And *what* is a promise to a white man!" Interracial unions frequently end disastrously in Sui Sin Far's fiction, perhaps suggesting that within the dominant (white) male culture, ethnic women are doubly disempowered by race and gender, and they will not find voice or self-definition. Yet stories such as "Mrs. Spring Fragrance" suggest that Chinese American women can find voice and self-definition within their own communities. The title character in "Mrs. Spring Fragrance" writes about Americans: "As she walked along she meditated upon a book which she had some notion of writing. Many American women wrote books. Why should not a Chinese? ... The American people were so interesting and mysterious" (28). Sui Sin Far slyly implies here that ethnic women will not be exotic objects of the white and/or male gaze, but will instead turn their own gaze on to the white community, revealing *its* mysteries and secrets. In so doing, these women will find mediums of expression that are specific to Chinese American subjectivity.

The stories discussed above foreground concerns about women's voice and self-definition in a patriarchal (and racist) world that devalues their needs, refuses to allow them to speak, and turns them into objects of language who are spoken about, rather than speakers or subjects in their own right. Is language itself, as Gilman and other feminist linguists have contended, patriarchal, male-centered, or "androcentric"? One of the reasons "The Yellow Wallpaper" has been such a popular feminist text is because of its careful and full investigation of such questions – even if, as we shall see, it does not necessarily provide an easy resolution to them.

The Problem of Feminine Voice: Gilman's "The Yellow Wallpaper"

Turn-of-the-century women writers often imply that in the world they inhabit, language is gendered as masculine, and as "belonging" to speakers who are male and white. Language, as Gilman says, is "androcentric," relegating women to the place of prepositions: "[Woman] has held always the place of a preposition in relation to man. She has been considered above him or below him, before him, behind him, beside him, a wholly relative existence – 'Sydney's sister,' 'Pembroke's mother' – but never by any chance Sydney or Pembroke herself" (*The Man-Made World* 20). Linguistically, women are defined through their relationship to the male subject, but do not possess an identity and voice of their own: "Even in the naming of other animals we have taken the male as the race type, and put on a special termination to indicate 'his female,' as in lion, lioness; leopard, leopardess; while all our human scheme of things rests on the same tacit assumption; man being held the human type; woman a sort of accompaniment and subordinate assistant, merely essential to the making of people" (20). Language may initiate a process whereby some individuals are granted voice and identity (or, to use a more modern term, subjectivity), while others are defined as silent and subordinate objects; therefore, the speaking or writing subject is defined as inherently masculine, while the silent object or blank page is inherently feminine.

"The Yellow Wallpaper" forcefully confronts the issue of women's confinement within patriarchal language and male-authored medical discourse. The female narrator, suffering from a "temporary nervous depression – a slight hysterical tendency" (4), is forbidden by her physician husband to engage in any intellectual activity, including her own writing. She is also subjected to an actual medical treatment – S. Weir Mitchell's (1829–1914) infamous "rest cure," in which intellectual women were forbidden to read and write, and forced to rest, eat, and spend time with their babies – which only makes her mental condition deteriorate. Shut up in a large attic room that used to be a nursery, she resorts to first "reading" the yellow wallpaper and later writing her own secretive narrative about the hulking, cowering woman she believes she sees behind the bars of the paper. Ultimately, the narrator determines to free this woman, and in a burst of energy, strips the wallpaper off the walls. In so doing, she becomes the other woman; by the end of the story she claims, "I've got out at last ... you can't put me back" (19). Paradoxically, the narrator also has a rope to tie the woman, should she try to escape. Finally, the narrator uses this rope to tie herself securely (presumably to the bed, the only object of furniture left in the room). She creeps around the perimeter of the room, fitting her shoulder into a narrow groove that has been worn in the wall by a previous occupant. When her husband sees her he faints, so that she has to "creep over him every time" (19) she completes a rotation of the room. On the one hand, the narrator appears to achieve some sort of triumph, causing the icon of male authority (her husband/doctor) to faint dead away. But what sort of "triumph" is this? The narrator seems completely insane; moreover, she is now physically constrained by a rope and her confinement within patriarchal authority seems all the more assured.

The narrator's descent into insanity is caused, to some extent, by the "cure" to which she is subjected, which infantilizes her and robs her of the tasks she most enjoys – reading and writing. The story may also be interpreted as being about the way masculine language (symbolized by the doctor/husband) attempts to confine women within its patriarchal sentence (symbolized by the husband's verdict that his wife may not leave the room and resume her normal activity of writing). Set against this masculine, authoritative discourse (which is portrayed as rational, ordered, and logical) is women's language, embodied by the yellow wallpaper with its disordered and illogical, yet ultimately more creative, patterns. Paula Treichler reads the story as a clash between masculine and feminine discourse in which the wallpaper represents women's writing or women's discourse and the woman in the wallpaper represents a vision "of women that becomes possible only after women obtain the right to speak." As a symbol, the yellow wallpaper therefore "stands for a new vision of women – one which is constructed differently from the representation of women in patriarchal language" (Treichler 64). In part, then, the story concerns a clash between opposing modes of discourse: one mode is authoritative, ancestral, and dominant, and the other is new, impudent, and prophetic (64). Yet the narrator's escape from "the sentence" does not lead to a permanent liberation, as Treichler further explains; although the narrator has made manifest the nature of women's condition, she is still locked in a room and bound by a rope (74). The social and material conditions the narrator has diagnosed must change before she can be free.

Further, the narrator only escapes from patriarchal discourse through a radical deconstruction of her own self. Caught between modes of discourse which are figured as opposite – the rational and the imaginative, the logical and the illogical, the sane and the insane, the masculine and the feminine – the narrator's personality splits; she forms two warring psyches that mirror the discursive modes that surround her. Through identification with the wallpaper and the woman in it, she creates a subversive personality that tries to help the woman escape, one that so identifies with the woman in the wallpaper that she *becomes* this unruly presence. This subversive feminine self strips off the wallpaper and ultimately claims: "I've got out at last ... you can't put me back" ("Yellow Wallpaper" 19). This self works with the woman in the wallpaper to free all women: "I pulled and she shook. I shook and she pulled, and before morning we had peeled off yards of that paper" (17). This self opposes patriarchal authority and her rebellion seems to succeed, at least momentarily; the husband faints when he sees this new, subversive self.

Yet in the final scene, there is also a self that attempts to escape from subjugation by incorporating the oppressor's views. Prisoners placed in positions of authority will sometimes tyrannize other inmates more than the jailers; identification with the oppressor becomes a psychological strategy of self-preservation. So while the narrator forms a feminine personality matching that of the woman in the yellow wallpaper, she also forms a masculine one inculcating patriarchal values. This personality constantly wars with the wallpaper, attempting – and failing – to "master" it, to impose sequence on it. Finally, it is this oppressor self that agrees to the incarceration of the prisoner in the wallpaper, and to its own incarceration:

> If that woman does get out, and tries to get away, I can tie her! ... I am securely fastened now by my well-hidden rope – you don't get *me* out in the road there! ... Here I can creep smoothly on the floor, and my shoulder just fits in that long smooch around the wall, so I cannot lose my way. (18)

As Linda Wagner-Martin comments, although the latter half of the story seems to move toward the protagonist's liberation, this freedom is ultimately false: "The woman does not dance or skip or fly, common images for the state of freedom. She only *creeps*, a derogation of the more positive word *crawls*, which is not itself a very positive movement" (61). The oppressor self accepts her confinement within the house of patriarchy, and her creeping, imprisoned, alienated status within patriarchal language.

Trapped between the subversive patterns of the yellow wallpaper and her husband's rational discourse, between the masculine and feminine sides of her personality, the narrator forms two incompatible identities that mirror two oppositional discursive modes. Finally, in the warring between these two opposed linguistic modes, her personality and voice are erased by madness. Gilman's text articulates what were for her – at this time – irresolvable oppositions between the feminine and the masculine, between a language that is freeing and one that constrains.

Some critics have conflated Gilman with her semi-autobiographical character, and indeed there are many parallels: Gilman did suffer from post-partum psychosis after the birth of her daughter, she was subjected to S. Weir Mitchell's rest cure, she did spiral down towards insanity, and she did (like the narrator) write about these experiences. Yet Gilman eventually recovered from her mental illness. What saved her, specifically, was writing. Gilman abandoned S. Weir Mitchell's rest cure, went back to her work, and wrote frequently about mental and physical illness. She also authored feminist fictions that depict a more successful resolution of the conflict between masculine language and feminine voice. Short stories such as "An Honest Woman" (1911), "Mrs. Beazley's Deeds" (1911), and "Dr. Clair's Place" (1915) insert an unruly feminine subject into masculine language. This angry subject breaks apart patriarchal discourse by traversing boundaries, by refusing to silence herself, and by telling stories that critique and rewrite the gaps of patriarchal history.

Writing a Cure for Women's Silencing: Gilman's Later Short Fictions

Written almost twenty years after "The Yellow Wallpaper," Gilman's short story "An Honest Woman" illustrates that women can learn to use language effectively, but also that they can come to understand and manipulate the underlying processes whereby meaning is created and linguistic authority is granted. The story begins with a conversation that seems to reveal women's secondary status in language and culture. Two men discuss Mary Main, the owner of a successful boarding hotel. While one man – Abramson – talks and talks about Mary, saying, "There's an honest woman if ever there was one!" (75), the other man – Burdock – only feeds him an occasional question:

> "I've got a high opinion of good women," [Abramson] announced with finality. "As to bad ones, the less said the better!" and he puffed his strong cigar, looking darkly experienced.
> "They're doin' a good deal towards reformin' 'em, nowadays, ain't they?" ventured Burdock.
> The young man laughed disagreeably. "You can't reform spilled milk," said he. "But I do like to see an honest, hard-working woman succeed."
> "So do I, boy," said his companion, "so do I," and they smoked in silence. (76)

For Abramson, women are words in men's mouths, and men have the ability to stereotype and define them as angels or whores, "good women" or "ruined" ones. Notably, however, Burdock is rather silent; he is aware that some women escape men's categorizations.

As Burdock knows, Mary Cameron Main is not, in actuality, a "good" woman. A flashback reveals that Mary had an adulterous affair and bore a child out of wedlock. After Mary's lover abandons her, she realizes she is "ruined": "'I suppose I am a ruined woman,' she said. She went to the glass and lit the gas on either side, facing herself with fixed gaze and adding calmly, 'I don't look it!' ... The woman she saw in the glass seemed as one at the beginning of a splendid life, not at the end of a bad one" (82). This moment of mirroring reflects a radical swerve from the patriarchal plot, a moment in which women are encouraged to comprehend the artificiality of the linguistic categories used to define them, and to break from these categories.

In this scene, Mary also comprehends the rules of her culture's "language game": men control and manipulate language, authoring women's destiny through their words; women are silent, passive agents within language – created by language, rather than creators of it. But at this crucial juncture, Mary rejects the rules of this language game as it has been played. She moves to another town, dresses in black, and when asked about her husband presses her handkerchief to her eyes and says only, "He has left me. I cannot bear to speak of him" (83). Literally, she classifies her husband as unspeakable, but on a more metaphoric level, this statement demonstrates that Mary has discerned that she need not be passively constructed by patriarchal words, but rather can actively and consciously engage in the linguistic processes that shape how she is received. In short, Mary has become a person who not only uses language, but who also understands and intervenes in its functioning.

Mary demonstrates her linguistic ability most clearly when her former lover returns and threatens to blackmail her by revealing her "fallen" status to her boarders, saying he could "shatter [her life] with a word" (85). Mary merely smiles patiently at Main and states: "You can't shatter facts, Mr. Main. People here know that you left me years ago. They know how I have lived since. If you try to blacken my reputation here, I think you will find the climate of Mexico more congenial" (86). Mary takes a calculated risk, asserting that her actions have constructed a world that transcends the linguistic categories that normally would be applied to her. The battle is played out over and within language. Mr. Main tries to force Mary to abide by the rules of the old language game, while Mary asserts a new reality in which she is judged by her actions, rather than by outdated and sexist linguistic categories. Mary's confidence in her own abilities finally convinces Mr. Main that her reality is more credible, and he gives up his plan. Furthermore, Mary's new reality is affirmed by the external frame of the story, in which a silent observer – the male character Burdock – overhears the entire story yet does not reveal Mary's secret (86). The story finally illustrates that while masculine language may claim to construct women, an understanding of language's functioning gives women the ability to reconstruct themselves and create a supportive community in which they are judged by their actions, rather than by patriarchal stereotypes.

"Mrs. Beazley's Deeds" (1911) also critiques systems of language that disempower women, but in this text Gilman indicates even more explicitly how women's voices can transform discursive structures (such as the system of law). The story concerns a woman completely cut off from discourse, so much so that she is reduced to getting information through holes in the floor, as the story's opening vividly depicts: "Mrs. William Beazley was crouching on the floor of her living-room over the store in a most peculiar attitude. It was what a doctor would call the 'knee-chest' position; and the woman's pale, dragged out appearance quite justified this idea. She was as one scrubbing a floor and then laying her cheek to it, a rather undignified little pile of bones, albeit discreetly covered with stringy calico" (207). Mrs. Beazley is reduced to a pale "little pile of bones" crouching without dignity before the superior linguistic power of her husband. But Maria Beazley is also disempowered in her personal situation, for she is married to a lazy, tyrannical man who overworks her and beats their children. Mr. Beazley forces his family to live over the store he runs, rather than in the more spacious house his wife owns. Mr.

Beazley is now on the verge of selling this home, Maria's last piece of property, and Maria is listening at the hole in the floor in a desperate attempt to get information about this transaction.

With the help of a clever female attorney, Maria is eventually able to subvert this transaction, retake her maternal property, and divorce her husband. Language is central to her struggle for control, for Maria must overturn both a patriarchal discourse that has been used to silence her, and a patriarchal story that has erased her agency. Mr. Beazley is a discursive tyrant who exercises complete control over his wife's access to information and knowledge. When she asks questions about the legal documents (deeds) he continually forces her to sign or when she tries to protest his actions, he simply ignores her: "Mr. Beazley minded her outcry no more than he minded the squawking of a to-be beheaded hen" (208). Mrs. Beazley's speech is not even considered to be human "language," but rather the "squawking" of an animal. Marie Beazley believes herself to be completely disempowered by her husband's physical, legal, and discursive power. At this juncture, she appears to have no voice that can be heard by anyone.

Yet Mrs. Beazley does find her voice and she does find a listener to hear her tale in Miss Lawrence, the lawyer who comes to board with the family. When she finally does tell her story to her friend, Mrs. Beazley states she is telling "no great story" (213). It is simply the sad tale of her life, a tale full of sound and fury, but ultimately signifying little because, as Mrs. Beazley declares, "girls don't know nothin'!" (214). It is not even a unique story for, as she states, most of the women she knows are "near dead" (212) from overwork. Yet in telling this story, Maria begins to swerve from the patriarchal plot, the language game that insists women remain silent and disempowered. The act of telling her story to a friend (which is, after all, an act of authoring her story) and the act of asking for advice (which is, after all, a way of asking how the story can be changed) destabilize the text's prior construction of Maria Beazley. When Miss Lawrence learns that Mr. Beazley has been putting his property in his wife's name to shield it from creditors, she helps Maria take legal action to gain control of it. So one day Mr. Beazley returns from a business trip to find that his store and house have been sold, his wife and children have left him, and his money has been withdrawn from the bank. Most importantly, Mr. Beazley no longer wields linguistic power over his wife, as Miss Lawrence informs him: "Any communication you may wish to make to her you can make through me" (219). Clearly, this is a legal change, but also a linguistic one. And language is the key to Maria's empowerment – authoring her story is the first step toward freedom, a step that enables all the others.

Gilman also depicts women taking command over their stories in "Dr. Clair's Place" (1915). Medical discourse is reconfigured in this piece, and so Gilman comes full circle, revising the patriarchal story that initially caused her breakdown into a narrative of women learning to read and write their way to mental health. S. Weir Mitchell's "rest cure," of course, prescribed that women do nothing but eat, rest, and raise their children; women were also confined to their homes and allowed little exercise. In "The Yellow Wallpaper" the narrator initially longs to be out walking in the garden – in "those mysterious deep-shaded arbors, the riotous old-fashioned flowers and the bushes and gnarly trees" ("Yellow Wallpaper" 7) – but she is seldom allowed to do so. So it seems important that in Dr. Clair's treatment, women are not kept confined in any way but are instead rejuvenated through intellectual activity and through physical regimens that include hiking, climbing, swimming, and sleeping outdoors under the stars ("Dr. Clair's Place" 287).

The husband/doctor in "The Yellow Wallpaper" authoritatively diagnosed his wife's disease and dictated its course of treatment; moreover, when she tried to protest, he only ridiculed her concerns. Conversely, in "Dr. Clair's Place" the patient (Octavia Welch) plays a participatory role in diagnosis and treatment: "Dr. Clair came in twice a day, with a notebook and pencil, asking me many careful questions; not as a physician to a patient, but as an inquiring scientific searcher for valuable truths. She consulted me in a way, as to this or that bit of analysis she had made; and again and again as to certain points in my own case" (286). This active, collaborative, language-based therapy helps the patient understand her disease and participate in its cure. The story concludes with Octavia's statement that she is now an employee of Dr. Clair and "a well woman" (288). Quite literally, then, the patient grows from someone who has a diagnosis inflicted upon her, to someone who can diagnose herself.

As we have seen, "The Yellow Wallpaper" depicts a frightening antagonism between a feminine subject and the masculine world of authoritative patriarchal and medical discourse she inhabits. Gilman resided for part of her life in this frightening world, but unlike her protagonist she did not go insane. Instead, she wrote short stories such as "An Honest Woman," "Mrs. Beazley's Deeds," and "Dr. Clair's Place" that renovate language. Like Gilman herself, Gilman's unruly women insist on controlling and at times even creating the language that describes them, rather than being created by it. As the next section illustrates, women writers from our time period continue to examine how women can amend patriarchal (and racist) languages and find unique modes of identity.

Carrying Forward the Tradition of Protest: Contemporary Feminist American Short Story Writers

As Gilman's later fictions suggest, women may find voice by understanding exactly how and why they have been silenced, and/or by becoming part of a feminist community that allows them to tell and retell, fashion and refashion, their stories until they become authorized. They may also find voice, Gilman suggests in "Dr. Clair's Place," by inhabiting the natural world, or by creating a balance and harmony between nature and culture. Stories by contemporary writers show women achieving freedom through a feminine community that can only exist when women find equilibrium between the natural and "man-made" worlds. Some of these stories depict a coexistence between women and nature that rewrites not only the mechanical quality of patriarchal society but also its erasure of women's voices.

In an homage to, but also revision of, "The Yellow Wallpaper," Pat Murphy's "Women in the Trees" (1990) tells of a battered wife who sees imaginary women in the trees around her house, women who invite her to "stay with us" (Murphy 263). For the abused young wife of the story, the trees offer safety and community, absent from her real life. They also offer a way to reclaim her mode of expression. To her husband, she has lied in order not to be beaten, or been silent: "So you stopped stating your opinion, and he called you stupid because you had nothing to say" (258). The young woman cannot find expression in traditional (male-centered) language, even though, like the narrator of "The Yellow Wallpaper" she tries to write: "You have a red notebook. ... Sometimes you write in your notebook, trying to tell the truth. ... The truth is a slippery thing, as elusive as the women in the trees" (263). One night, to escape a beating, the woman runs and hides in her favorite tree. There, after a long night of fear, she either dies or finds an ambiguous freedom and voice: "Your body is stiff and you are starting to wonder what to do. 'Leave it' the oak women say. 'Come with us.' ... You stand up and look back at the small body, curled in the fork of the tree. ... You feel the wind in your hair" (267). The protagonist joins the community of women in the trees, leaving behind her body. In so doing, she appears to find a truth-telling voice: "But you will not be sorry, not sorry ever again. Eventually, you will forget how to lie. And then you can come back down" (267). Overtly paralleling, but also rewriting, the ending of "The Yellow Wallpaper" in which the narrator appears to go insane yet triumphs over her doctor/husband, in Murphy's short story the narrator finds community through other women and nature. Unfortunately, as in Gilman's story, it is unclear whether the woman actually *survives* to speak aloud her new vision of selfhood, to articulate the new mode of language she appears to have found.

Two other contemporary short stories typify how women can invest in natural, ecological, and feministic communities that move beyond patriarchy; these stories parallel, yet also rewrite, the linguistic struggle encoded in "The Yellow Wallpaper." In Estela Portillo Trambley's "If It Weren't for the Honeysuckle ..." (1975) three women – Beatriz, Sofía, and Lucretia – are abused by their mutual lover/husband, a man named Robles. But they form a community together, building a house and caring for the plants and vegetables that grow around them, living in harmony with nature. One night when Robles returns drunk and ready to beat and rape the youngest woman, the other two poison him with a naturally growing plant they have discovered, thereby insuring their own liberation and the preservation of the natural community they have created. Like the woman in Murphy's story, they also find a voice in/through nature: "I believe in the greenness of the earth. Listen! The river's singing again. Can't you hear it?" (Trambley 69). While in "The Yellow Wallpaper," the narrator finally does not want to be in the natural world ("you don't get *me* out in the road there! ... I don't want to go outside" [18]), in Trambley's story the women discover community, power, and voice by growing plants, caring for the land, and creating a home together. Gilman's concerns about women and language are, in a sense, transplanted to the natural world, where they can grow, flourish, and have a more positive outcome.

Similarly, in Sandra Cisneros's "Woman Hollering Creek" (1991) the legend of La Llorona – or the weeping woman – is rewritten so that women find voice within it and within the natural world. In most versions of the original Mexican legend of La Llorona, a woman is abandoned by her husband, and in revenge she drowns her children; she then spends eternity wailing for them alongside the river in which they died. In the original myth, then, women are defined through men and children, and they have no voice outside of lamentation for the "crimes" they commit. Cisneros's short story, however, revises this myth when a female character named Felice helps an abused pregnant woman named Cleófilas escape from her husband:

> But when they drove across the *arroyo* [river bed], the driver opened her mouth and let out a yell as loud as any mariachi. ... Every time I cross that bridge I do that. Because of the name, you know. Woman Hollering. *Pues* [then], I holler. ... That's why I like the name of that *arroyo*. Makes you want to holler like Tarzan, right? ... Who would've? Pain or rage, perhaps, but not a hoot like that one Felice had just let go. (Cisneros 55–6)

Felice refuses the pejorative association of the creek – its story of an evil woman who destroys herself and her children. Instead, she transforms the creek into a symbol of her (and women's) independence from patriarchal dictates; yelling loudly like a "mariachi" or "Tarzan," she converts "rage or pain" into joy. Finally, her joy is transferred linguistically to Cleófilas, who also appears to find a way out of the patriarchal plot that has silenced her: "Then Felice began laughing again, but it wasn't Felice laughing. It was gurgling out of [Cleófilas's] throat, a long ribbon of laughter, like water" (56). Silenced throughout the story by her abusive husband, Cleófilas achieves articulation and a transmuting of pain with the help of the natural world – the beautiful river bed – and another woman (Felice).

"The Yellow Wallpaper" articulates a conflict between masculine and feminine modes of discourse, and between a male authority which defines women in limiting ways and a feminine need for more commodious modes of self-definition. It sets out these conflicts in graphic detail, but it does not resolve them. However, as seen in these contemporary short stories, the questions raised by "The Yellow Wallpaper" are vivid in our own era, when women still must struggle against pejorative patriarchal myths and a language that seems to be androcentric, or man-made. On many levels, "The Yellow Wallpaper" is an archetypal text for women short story writers, but they constantly transform and transfigure it. Rather than being confined in the room of Gilman's infamous nursery, with its seething yellow wallpaper, they move out into the external world of feminine and natural community – the world of riotous flowers, gurgling natural creeks, and startling oak trees filled with female forms that welcome them into a renovated linguistic community and innovative modes of self-definition.

References and Further Reading

Bauer, Dale. "Cultural and Historical Background." *The Yellow Wallpaper by Charlotte Perkins Gilman*. Ed. Dale Bauer. Bedford Cultural Edition. New York: St. Martin's Press, 1998. 3–27.

Christensen, Carolyn, ed. *A New Woman Reader: Fiction, Articles, and Drama of the 1890s*. Peterborough, ON: Broadview, 2001.

Cisneros, Sandra. *Woman Hollering Creek and Other Stories*. New York: Vintage, 1991.

Cott, Nancy. *The Bonds of Womanhood: "Woman's Sphere" in New England 1780–1835*. New Haven: Yale University Press, 1977.

Cutter, Martha J. "Frontiers of Language: Engendering Discourse in 'The Revolt of Mother.'" *American Literature* 63.2 (1991): 279–91.

———. "Smuggling Across the Borders of Race, Gender and Sexuality: Sui Sin Far's *Mrs. Spring Fragrance*." *Mixed Race Literature*. Ed. Jonathan Brennan. Stanford: Stanford University Press, 2002. 137–64.

———. *Unruly Tongue: Identity and Voice in American Women's Writing, 1850–1930*. Jackson: University Press of Mississippi, 1999.

———. "The Writer as Doctor: New Models of Medical Discourse in Charlotte Perkins Gilman's Later Fiction." *Literature and Medicine* 20.2 (2001): 151–82.

Dunbar-Nelson, Alice. "Ellen Fenton." Ca. 1900–1910. *The Works of Alice Dunbar-Nelson*. Vol. 3. Ed. Gloria Hull. New York: Oxford University Press, 1988. 33–50.

Freeman, Mary Wilkins. "The Revolt of 'Mother.'" 1890. *Selected Stories of Mary E. Wilkins Freeman*. Ed. Marjorie Pryse. New York: W. W. Norton, 1983. 293–313.

Gilman, Charlotte Perkins. "Dr. Clair's Place." 1915. *Herland, The Yellow Wall-Paper, and Selected Writings*. Ed. Denise Knight. New York: Penguin, 1999. 280–8.

———. "An Honest Woman." 1911. *The Charlotte Perkins Gilman Reader*. Ed. Ann J. Lane. New York: Pantheon, 1980. 75–86.

———. *The Man-Made World, or Our Androcentric Culture*. New York: Charlton, 1911.

———. "Mrs. Beazley's Deeds." 1911. *Herland, The Yellow Wall-Paper, and Selected Writings*. Ed. Denise Knight. New York: Penguin, 1999. 207–20.

———. "The Yellow Wallpaper." 1892. *The Charlotte Perkins Gilman Reader*. Ed. Ann J. Lane. New York: Pantheon, 1980. 3–20.

Glaspell, Susan, "A Jury of her Peers." *Women in the Trees: US Women's Short Stories about Battering and Resistance*. Ed. Susan Koppelman. Boston, Beacon Press, 1917. 76–93.

Golden, Catherine. "One Hundred Years of Reading 'The Yellow Wallpaper.'" *The Captive Imagination: A Casebook on "The Yellow Wallpaper."* Ed. Catherine Golden. New York: Feminist Press, 1992. 1–23.

Grand, Sarah. "The New Aspect of the Woman Question." *North American Review* 158.448 (March 1894): 270–6.

Hill, Mary A. *Charlotte Perkins Gilman: The Making of a Radical Feminist 1860–1896*. Philadelphia: Temple University Press, 1980.

Murphy, Pat. "Women in the Trees." *Women in the Trees: U.S. Women's Short Stories About Battering and Resistance*. Ed. Susan Koppelman. Boston: Beacon Press, 1996. 256–67.

Poirier, Suzanne. "The Weir Mitchell Rest Cure: Doctor and Patients." *Women's Studies* 10 (1983): 15–40.

Shumaker, Conrad. "Realism, Reform, and the Audience: Charlotte Perkins Gilman's Unreadable Wallpaper." *Arizona Quarterly* 47 (1991): 81–93.

Sui Sin Far [Edith Eaton]. *Mrs. Spring Fragrance and Other Writings*. Ed. Amy Ling and Annette White-Parks. Urbana: University of Illinois Press, 1995.

Trambley, Estela Portillo. "If It Weren't For the Honeysuckle ..." 1975. *Rain of Scorpions and Other Stories* 1975. Tempe: Bilingual Press, 1993, 47–70.

Treichler, Paula A. "Escaping the Sentence: Diagnosis and Discourse in 'The Yellow Wallpaper.'" *Tulsa Studies in Women's Literature* 3.1–2 (1984): 61–77.

Wagner-Martin, Linda. "Gilman's 'The Yellow Wallpaper': A Centenary." *Charlotte Perkins Gilman: The Woman and Her Work*. Ed. Sheryl Meyering. Ann Arbor: UMI Research Press, 1989. 51–64.

Welter, Barbara. "The Cult of True Womanhood, 1820–1860." *American Quarterly* 18.2 (1966): 151–74.

9

The Short Stories of Edith Wharton

Donna Campbell

In 1925, reflecting on the work that had won her critical and popular acclaim during her long career, Edith Wharton compared fiction writing to another subject about which she already knew a great deal: money. "There is a sense in which the writing of fiction may be compared to the administering of a fortune," she wrote. "True economy consists in the drawing out of one's subject of every drop of significance it can give" (*The Writing* 43). Born in 1862 to a socially prominent New York family, Wharton had known the advantages of wealth all her life, and the values of economy and thrift that she proposes here seem at first those of the "Old New York" of her fiction, a world in which careful expenditure and a lack of ostentation distinguish the true aristocrats from the newly rich who try to crash their way into Old New York society. But Wharton's comment was born of hard-won experience, not inherited prejudices; as she writes in her memoir *A Backward Glance* (1934), she had taught herself to become a professional writer, when, in completing *The House of Mirth* on a demanding schedule, she learned the "discipline of the daily task, that inscrutable 'inspiration of the writing table'" (*A Backward* 941). Although Wharton's reputation as an author rests largely on classic novels such as *The House of Mirth* (1905), *Ethan Frome* (1911), *The Custom of the Country* (1913), and *The Age of Innocence* (1920), the eighty-six short stories she published during her career not only echo the themes of her longer works but demonstrate her mastery of short fiction.[1] As Gary Totten has shown in a recent analysis, several factors have delayed equal recognition for the short fiction. Among these are twentieth-century critical prejudices about women as inferior authors (for example, Wharton was often cast as a minor Henry James), the preference for Wharton's novels over her short stories, and critical preferences for experimental modernist techniques in fiction rather than the realist style that Wharton employed. Of criticism on Wharton's short fiction, a handful of stories, including "The Other Two," "Roman Fever," and the ghost stories, have received the bulk of the attention.

But if critics were slow to recognize their worth, Wharton knew that her stories were good, as she intimated to Elisina Tyler shortly before her death (Totten 118).

In addition to her sixteen novels and her books of travel writing and poetry, Wharton published ten collections of short stories during her lifetime and had written a preface and a new story for the eleventh, *Ghosts*, before her death in 1937. Her stories range from classic comedies of manners such as "The Other Two" through marriage and divorce tales, artist stories, historical romances, social satires, and, not least, a handful of Gothic-inflected ghost stories now considered among her best. Because Wharton employed all of these forms throughout her long career, Barbara White asserts that "[t]he stories of any particular time period resemble each other more than the art or marriage or ghost stories of another era" (White xiii) and should be considered together. White defines these eras as the "early stories," twenty-four of which were published between 1891 and 1902; the "middle period" of thirty-five stories published between 1902 and 1914; and the "later period" composed of the twenty-six stories published from 1915 to 1937 (xiii). A brief discussion of Wharton's theories of short fiction, followed by an analysis of representative stories, shows the artistry – and economy – with which Wharton used the forms of short fiction.

Although Wharton's critical essays, notably *The Writing of Fiction*, have been treated respectfully by critics, most agree that her essays on fiction reveal less than they might about the true foundations of her art. For example, *The Writing of Fiction* has been characterized by Penelope Vita-Finzi as "confused and repetitious" (Vita-Finzi 46), and the bulk of her critical prose has been seen, somewhat more charitably, as "limited in its reach and not intellectually as adventurous as that of some of her contemporaries" by Frederick Wegener (*Edith Wharton* 30). Both critics acknowledge, however, that Wharton took the obligations of writing about her craft seriously and that she had considered at length the problem of writing short fiction.[2] In chapter 2 of *The Writing of Fiction*, "Telling a Short Story," Wharton credits French and Russian writers such as Flaubert, Maupassant, and Turgenev with perfecting the modern short story, but she also praises the English and American writers Hawthorne, Poe, "Stevenson, James, and Conrad" (*The Writing* 27). The difference between the novel and the short story, Wharton explains, is not merely one of length; rather, "the situation is the main concern of the short story" as "character [is] of the novel" (37), a difference that emphasizes the necessity for observing "two 'unities'" (34) of time and point of view. For Wharton, the control of point of view is essential, and she frequently uses nested frame stories (the narrator hears a story from another person, who in turn heard it from a third, and so forth) to achieve the right balance of intimacy and distance. Wharton also varies the gender of her point of view characters. As Elsa Nettels has observed, "Of the twenty-two first-person narratives in the two-volume *Collected Stories*, nineteen have male narrators" (Nettels 245), but stories such as "Souls Belated" and "Roman Fever" use limited omniscience rather than the first person to render the intense emotions of their female characters.

Wharton believed that structure and technique were as important as point of view. The first page of a short story must not only contain the kernel of the whole but must also arrest the reader's attention. Wharton illustrates this principle, which she calls the story's "attack," with an anecdote from Benvenuto Cellini's *Autobiography*, in which Cellini and his father, sitting by the hearth, saw a salamander in the fire, after which the father boxed the boy's ears so that he would always remember the sight. But a sensational opening does not in itself make a good story, for, Wharton continues, "it is useless to box your reader's ear unless you have a salamander to show him," the salamander being the "living, moving *something*" that animates the tale (*The Writing* 40). Even with a "salamander" to show the reader, technique and above all time are necessary for a story's development. Like Henry James, who thought that novelists like H. G. Wells and Arnold Bennett squeezed out "to the utmost the plump and more or less juicy orange of a particular acquainted state" (James 132) yet substituted the "squeezing" of excessive detail for the shaping of material that constitutes "true technique", Wharton contends that the best stories are those that have been "worked over" like the best chocolate or "completely blent" like a rich sauce until perfection is achieved (*The Writing* 41). That Wharton couched the intangible process of creating art in such tangible and mundane terms – spending one's money, seeing a salamander, or blending a rich sauce – suggests the evident concern she had for demystifying the process for her readers.

Less vivid than her analogies but equally significant are the connections between Wharton's ideas and those of other writers. For example, Wharton's insistence on the importance of achieving a striking effect and the conscious application of techniques to enhance this effect owes much to Edgar Allan Poe, who discusses these elements in his review of Hawthorne's *Twice-Told Tales* and in "The Philosophy of Composition." To these two requirements, Wharton adds a third, that of "economy of material" (42), in a manner that recalls Ernest Hemingway's "iceberg theory." In *Death in the Afternoon*, Hemingway writes, "If a writer of prose knows enough about what he is writing about he may omit things that he knows and the reader, if the writer is writing truly enough, will have a feeling of those things as strongly as though the writer had stated them" (Hemingway 192). Wharton's insistence on an opening that "shall be a clue to all the detail eliminated" and on a story "stripped of detail and 'cleared for action'" (41) suggests a similar economy of approach.

Wharton also pays an unusual amount of attention to the genre of the supernatural tale, devoting a full section of the chapter to ghost stories. She implies that the limits of the short story are most strongly tested in this form, with its Poe-like emphasis on producing an effect and evoking fear in one's readers. Instead of artist stories like "The Figure in the Carpet" or "The Real Thing," she singles out Henry James's "The Turn of the Screw" for praise, noting its ability to evoke "simple shivering animal fear" (32). Wharton's theory of the short story may seem in retrospect less than revolutionary, but her willingness to admit the ghost story as a legitimate form and to see it as embodying some of the best characteristics of a good short story is unconventional. For Wharton, supernatural fiction not only provides a different set of challenges – in satisfying the reader's desire for verisimilitude and probability – but also permits the expression of violence, cruelty, and extreme emotions in a manner at odds with the more constrained surfaces of her artist and marriage tales.

The stories of the early period, from 1891 when Wharton published her first story, "Mrs. Manstey's View," through 1902 when she published her first novel, *The Valley of Decision*, are more varied in subject matter and point of view than those written later. For example, although Wharton is usually associated with stories set in New York or Europe, several tales written before 1900, including "A Coward," "April Showers," and "Friends," take place in small towns of the sort that Wharton would later satirize as Undine Spragg's home town of Apex in *The Custom of the Country*. "Friends," with its plot of a jilted young woman who behaves generously to her rival, even suggests the local color stories of Mary E. Wilkins Freeman and Sarah Orne Jewett, as Barbara White, Janet Beer, and others have pointed out. Although Wharton was later to regard her early stories as "the excesses of youth" and to resist her editor Edward Burlingame's effort to include them in her first volume of stories, *The Greater Inclination* (1899) (*Letters* 36), these stories represent Wharton's experimentation in currently fashionable modes of expression that she would adopt temporarily and later abandon, such as the story structured as a dialogue or playlet ("Copy: A Dialogue") and the ironic fable.

Stories such as "The Valley of Childish Things" and "The Fullness of Life" are part of the 1890s vogue for ironic fables, a form that Ambrose Bierce adopted for his *Devil's Dictionary* and Stephen Crane employed in the poems in *The Black Riders* and *War is Kind*. "The Fullness of Life," which Wharton later described as "one long shriek" (*Letters* 36), is also a reaction to a nineteenth-century theme; as Alfred Bendixen notes, it is "Wharton's response to those nineteenth-century fictions, most notably Elizabeth Stuart Phelps's *The Gates Ajar*, which imagined a heavenly refuge from earthly griefs" (Bendixen 7). "The Fullness of Life" depicts an unnamed woman being welcomed into the afterlife by the Spirit of Life. The woman explains her marriage by saying that "a woman's nature is like a great house full of rooms" but that in her "innermost room ... the soul sits alone and waits for a footstep that never comes."[3] Given a choice, however, between a new partner who is a "kindred soul" (*Collected Short Stories* I. 20) and waiting for her husband, who annoys her because he does not understand her and because his boots creak, she chooses the latter because "it would break his heart not to find me here when he comes" (20). The theme of being "tied to an inferior partner"[4] that informs later novels such as *Ethan Frome* and *The Age of Innocence* is prefigured in this fable, but in this early work, the character does not share the reader's awareness of the situation's tragedy. By contrast, in Wharton's later fiction, character and reader alike understand the tragic consequences of the character's choice, as when Newland Archer contemplates what his life will be without Ellen Olenska but stays with his wife, May Welland.

The two volumes of stories that Wharton published before 1902, *The Greater Inclination* (1899) and *Crucial Instances* (1901), also include a variety of short story forms and subjects, including several "artist stories," among them "The Rembrandt," "The Moving Finger," "The Portrait," and "The Recovery." Like those of Henry James, which they frequently resemble, the "artist stories" often feature a painter, writer, or critic caught in a dilemma between preserving his integrity by being true to his art and selling out either for the sake of a higher good, such as compassion, or as a means to greater material comforts. A subset of these stories, such as "Copy" and "Expiation," satirize the process of selling out and the literary marketplace's hunger for sensationalism. The artist stories suggest that art is able to represent the truth faithfully but that artists who conceal the truth or betray their artistic vision, however good their initial motives may be, are generally harmed by doing so. For example, in "The Portrait," Lillo, a painter, is commissioned to paint a portrait of Alonzo Vard, a corrupt political boss whose only good qualities are brought out by the faith that his daughter has in him. When Lillo brilliantly renders the terrible truth of the man that he sees into the portrait and tries, too late, to conceal the truth by painting over the portrait, the daughter recognizes her father for what he really is. "The Rembrandt" poses the theme of truth in art versus human compassion in a different manner. Asked by his young cousin Eleanor Copt to assess the Rembrandt owned by the elderly and impoverished Mrs. Fontage, the narrator takes pity on the old woman and lies about its value, telling her that it is a treasure. After various complications, he purchases it for the museum of which he is a board member, only to have his taste called into question by the director. Upon being reassured that the narrator knows that the Rembrandt is worthless and that this was a case of philanthropy, not bad judgment, the director informs the narrator that they have purchased the Rembrandt and are giving it to him in recognition for his services. The sentence for betraying artistic ideals is in this case humorous and ironically appropriate, since the narrator and his highly trained aesthetic sense will have to endure the sight of the bad Rembrandt every day, but even such a worthy cause as the rescue of an elderly widow merits some form of punishment when artistic integrity is compromised. In "The Moving Finger," the artist Claydon is responsible for another sort of philanthropy: he continues to repaint the portrait of Mrs. Grancy, who died young, so that her grief-stricken widower can see her grow old with him. Here, too, art reveals a truth almost despite the artist's intentions: at one point, Mr. Grancy learns that he is dying because he sees the truth about his health in his wife's portrait, for "it was the face of a woman *who knows that her husband is dying*" (*Collected Short Stories* I. 310). In these stories, art speaks truth despite the best efforts of human beings to bend the truth to their own ends, an idea that also resonates in later stories such as "The Verdict" and, most memorably, "The Eyes."

Three other significant stories of Wharton's early period also anticipate themes and subjects in her later work: "Souls Belated," "The Duchess at Prayer," and "The Angel at the Grave." "Souls Belated" nominally takes place in Italy, but its actual locale is the country that Newland Archer imagines in *The Age of Innocence* when he tells Ellen Olenska that he wants to be with her in a place where "nothing else on earth will matter" (*Age of Innocence* 174). "Oh, my dear – where is that country? Have you ever been there?" Ellen responds, adding that those who have tried to find it found themselves in a place like the "old world they'd left, but only rather smaller and dingier and more promiscuous" (174–5). In "Souls Belated," Lydia Tillotson also tries to find that country by eloping with her lover, Ralph Gannett, only to find that the conventions of marriage from which she had fled constitute the only protection from the more sordid world that Ellen Olenska describes. The two live as a married couple and fear being unmasked as unmarried lovers, yet Lydia, clinging to the idealistic vision of lovers who remain together only out of love and not out of duty, refuses to marry

Gannett even when her divorce is made final. When the flashy, vulgar Mrs. Cope, who has eloped with her aristocratic lover, tries to blackmail Lydia by insinuating that they are both in "the same box" (*Collected Short Stories* I. 119) of illicit romance and pretense, Lydia realizes to her horror that instead of scorning respectability, as she had prided herself on doing, she has embraced it, thus betraying her ideals by clinging to the same "keep-off-the-grass morality" (122) that she had fled when she left her husband. Trapped by her own hypocrisy, she wants to flee again and to leave Gannett behind, since to marry Gannett and become respectable would imply that she had never been his mistress in the first place, a pretense abhorrent to her. But convention is once again too strong for Lydia: as Gannett watches from the window, Lydia, trying to escape, hesitates and then turns back before boarding the boat that would take her away from Gannett.

Wharton uses the railroad, which unlike the boat follows a fixed and immovable course, to signify the inescapable nature of the lovers' fate: the story begins in a railway car as the lovers try to avoid "the thing" (105) – Lydia's divorce decree and the question of their marriage – and it ends with the promise of another railway journey as Gannett looks up the train times for Paris, where, as the lovers have discussed earlier, they can be married. Despite Lydia's assertions of freedom and unconventionality, the course of illicit love that they have chosen carries them along as inexorably as the railway cars in which they travel together to the country that, as Ellen Olenska sees, does not exist. With these enclosed spaces, they are trapped not only by love but by a painfully acute awareness of silences and, on Lydia's part, of the "famine-stricken period when there would be nothing left to talk about" (105). The supposed happy ending of Paris and marriage, which would be the stuff of dreams for an adventuress like Mrs. Cope, is thus a confession of defeat for Lydia and her idealism. Yet marriage does serve a purpose: it displaces the inevitable boredom of two people living together from each other onto the institution of marriage itself, as Lydia implies when she tells Gannett that "the nakedness of each other's souls" is too much to bear without the buffer of marriage's dreary round of "children, duties, visits, bores" (125). Gannett's fitful attempts at writing make it clear that the marriage, however imperfect or tedious, also provides a haven for lovers tired of endless journeys and endless subterfuge and a space within which to work and live.

"The Duchess at Prayer" likewise features unhappy lovers and also introduces another important theme in Wharton's work, that of the young woman who is dominated by an older man. Often taking the form of a father–daughter story in which the daughter is unable to escape the father's powerful will, as in "The House of the Dead Hand," the motif also appears in the form of a powerful elderly husband dominating his young wife, as in "Confession" and "Kerfol." In Wharton's contemporary stories, the abuse is primarily emotional, but in stories of the past narrated in the present, like "The Duchess at Prayer," the violence is physical and horrific. In a plot that echoes Robert Browning's "My Last Duchess," in which a visitor is shown the portrait of the Duke's first wife by the husband who has murdered her, Wharton's narrator is shown the sixteenth-century Bernini statue of the Duchess Violante, whose name fittingly evokes both "violence" and the "violation" visited upon her by her sadistic husband. Like the courier in Browning's poem, the narrator is told the story of a young duchess, neglected by an elderly husband, who falls in love with a young man, the Cavaliere Ascanio. For their trysts, the lovers choose a crypt that holds the remains of St. Blandina, the patron saint of young girls, who was tortured to death, a fitting symbolic commentary on the Duchess's plight. Suspecting their affair, the Duke presents his wife with a statue of herself and orders that it be placed over the crypt, thus walling Ascanio up alive. Unable to rescue Ascanio without confessing their affair, the Duchess falls ill and dies, after which the statue reveals the truth of her feelings through its horrified expression, a supernatural transformation effected as the statue blocks the door and presumably hears the moans of the dying Ascanio. "The Duchess at Prayer" shares with the artist stories the idea that art reveals truth, but the grisly, Poe-like motif of live burial also provides a symbolic equivalent of the death-in-life marriages that occur in other Wharton stories.

A variation of this theme of the older man repressing a young woman occurs in "The Angel at the Grave," in which Paulina Anson's devotion to the reputation of her grandfather, the minor Transcendentalist Orestes Anson, keeps her entombed in his house. A votary to his memory, Paulina experiences psychological rather than physical live burial, yet she accepts her imprisonment willingly. After she rejects marriage to a young man, Hewlett Winsloe, who refuses to live in Anson's house after their marriage, Paulina eventually finds consolation in preparing a massive biography of her grandfather. But rejecting the living in favor of the dead has its drawbacks, among them a shift in literary fashions that has rendered Anson's writings irrelevant. Like many of Wharton's later characters, Paulina recognizes the uselessness of her sacrifice and the psychic vampirism that claims her youth and vitality: "I gave up everything ... to keep *him* alive" (*Collected Short Stories* I. 257). Ironically, one of Anson's minor writings is rediscovered as a key piece of evolutionary theory, and Corby, the young researcher who discovers it, praises her for saving Anson and work that would otherwise be "irretrievably lost" (257). Such affirmation convinces Paulina that her devotion has not been in vain, and, as she turns "back into the empty room she looked as though youth had touched her on the lips" (258). As the use of the simile "as though" suggests, however, youth has not, indeed cannot, touch Paulina on the lips again, and the room to which she returns is "empty," as her life has been. Janet Beer has argued that the story's account of replacing vaporous religious and philosophical rhetoric with "the empiricism of evolutionary processes" (Beer 128) reveals that "Paulina's act of memorialisation" has been "validated" (129) by Corby's arrival and that she escapes "specimen status" through her acts of preservation. In an evolutionary scheme of things, Paulina now fits a useful niche through the ideas that she has preserved and can transmit, and she can thus be beneficial to the evolution of human knowledge. But when her fate is viewed on the individual, personal level – the fate of the individual being of no interest to the forces of evolution – the ambiguous last sentence suggests that living for someone else's ideas is a muted pleasure at best and a useless sacrifice at worst.

The story collections of Wharton's middle period, which include *The Descent of Man, and Other Stories* (1904), *The Hermit and the Wild Woman, and Other Stories* (1908), and *Tales of Men and Ghosts* (1910), contain some of her best work. In addition to artist tales ("The Verdict," "The Potboiler," "The Daunt Diana"), historical romances ("The Letter," "A Venetian Night's Entertainment") and relationship stories ("The Dilettante," "The Letters," "The Reckoning"), these collections include some stories with more humor, such as the social satires "The Mission of Jane" and "The Other Two." Although it has received less modern critical attention than "The Other Two," "The Mission of Jane" was a favorite of William Dean Howells, who shortly before his death in 1920 asked Wharton if he could reprint it in *The Great Modern American Short Stories: An Anthology*. In "The Mission of Jane," the Lethburys, a couple gradually growing apart, adopt a baby, Jane, a "preternaturally good child" (*Collected Short Stories* I. 371) who grows into a self-righteous young woman. Through the adoption theme, the story comes down heavily on the "nature" rather than "nurture" side of the nature–nurture debate, since nothing in the easygoing Lethburys' existence prepares them for the kind of overbearing conscientiousness that Jane employs with them. In a humorous reversal of the usual oppressive father-dominated daughter scenario of other stories, the burden of Jane falls especially heavily on Mr. Lethbury, who instead of dominating Jane is dominated by her. Under Jane's regime of perfect housekeeping the Lethburys can never relax, and they hold their breath as a suitor appears, hoping that Jane will marry and leave them. She does, and the two Lethburys happily go out to dinner together, for Jane "had fulfilled her mission after all: she had drawn them together at last" (379). "The Mission of Jane" provides an ironic twist on several conventional pieties of American life, among them its obsession with health and cleanliness, its confidence that parents naturally love their children, and its belief that the molding of children's characters is solely in the parents' control. Wharton satirizes the scientific housekeeping movement of the era by showing how Jane reorganizes the household along scientific and hygienic principles, and she represents ironically the conventional belief that children bring a couple together.

"The Mission of Jane" also satirizes the advice-ridden popular magazines that promoted rules of cleanliness, structured time, household economy, and moral righteousness as absolute values; what would happen, it asks, if all of those virtues were not only achievable but packaged in one person who governed everyone else according to her ideas? Jane is a poster child for the kind of modern childrearing practices promoted by reformers such as Charlotte Perkins Gilman, as Frederick Wegener notes ("Charlotte Perkins Gilman, Edith Wharton" 144), but her lack of a "fusing grace" (*Collected Short Stories* I. 373) of human feeling makes her perfection intolerable to her parents and most others.

"The Other Two" presents an equally satiric look at a social phenomenon: serial divorce. Newly returned from his honeymoon, Waythorn glows with the pride of possession as he gazes on his bride, Alice, who is twice divorced and has "married up" with each succeeding husband. Throughout the story, minor incidents link Waythorn to his predecessors and make interaction with them unavoidable: the illness of Lily, Alice's daughter by her first husband, Mr. Haskett, means that Haskett must make regular visits to Waythorn's house, while the illness of a partner in Waythorn's firm, Sellers, leaves Waythorn as the logical choice to negotiate a deal for Gus Varick, Alice's second husband. In a pattern repeated in each section of the story, Waythorn's sense of exclusive ownership is immediately undercut by a reference to one of her earlier two marriages. Wharton's use of language in the story resonates with the sexual overtones of his bride's previous intimacy with others, relationships that Waythorn cannot quite bring himself to admit. The "softly-lighted room … full of bridal intimacy" that he notices with pride loses that quality as Alice tells him that Haskett must visit Lily at their home, saying "I'm afraid he has the right" – of access to Lily's presence now, and, in years past, of access to Alice's body (*Collected Short Stories* I. 382). Waythorn once again begins to yield "to the joy of possessorship" as Alice serves him coffee, and once again his sense of possessorship suffers a blow when he sees that Alice pours cognac in his coffee without asking him, for this is the way that Varick, not Waythorn, takes his coffee. As Alice's actions continue to remind him of her former husbands, Waythorn begins to put more effort into constructing the history of her past relationships than into building his current relationship with her. He envisions Haskett and Alice living in cheap small-town splendor, with a pianola and a copy of *Ben-Hur* in the parlor, and marvels, not altogether admiringly, at her adaptation to New York society and her "studied negation" of her past. Although Varick's infidelities had given Alice cause for a "New York divorce," a sign of virtue, a chance allusion by Varick makes Waythorn realize that "a lack of funds had been one of the determining causes" (387) of his and Alice's divorce. Alice inadvertently confirms this impression when she reveals a vulgar interest in wealth and social advancement by disparaging Haskett: "It's not as if he could ever be a help to Lily" (391). Waythorn realizes that despite the comic vulgarity of Haskett's "made-up tie attached with an elastic" (389), the man himself is genuine precisely because of this vulgarity, a badge of his small-town roots. Alice's ability to adapt to various environments, usually an admirable evolutionary advantage, is by contrast a kind of deception that masks her ambitious social climbing. With flawless tact, she speaks to Haskett but lies to Waythorn about it, remembers Varick's preferences in coffee-drinking, sits next to Varick unbidden without betraying any nervousness, and glides through each situation with a "pliancy" that begins to "sicken" Waythorn (393). As is revealed through her mercenary comment, her manners derive from a conscious adaptation to her surroundings rather than from the spontaneous responses of the finer nature that Waythorn at first attributes to her.

Throughout the story Wharton juxtaposes three rhetorical registers: Waythorn's private flights of fancy over his ownership of Alice, which he couches in the language of the stock market ("discounts" and "shares"); the scrupulously polite yet loaded language ("he has the right") that he, Alice, and her former husbands use to converse with one another; and the unspoken language of gesture and the body. The language of the body undercuts the abstract language of the other registers with constant material reminders of Alice's former intimacy with her husbands. She is, Waythorn decides, "as easy as an old shoe – a shoe that too many feet had worn" (393), a simile with loaded overtones of sexual promiscuity. Despite his dismay at Alice's elasticity, Waythorn begins to adjust both his thinking and his rhetoric: in place of his primitive pride of ownership, he is now a modern "member of a syndicate," a stockholder who "held so many shares in his wife's personality" along with "his predecessors" (393). His complete acceptance occurs when, after returning home one day, he finds both Varick and Haskett in the library. Waythorn offers them cigars and even offers Varick a light from his own cigar, a gesture of intimacy, as Alice enters the room. Never losing her perfect composure, she offers them all a cup of tea, and as "the two visitors ... advanced to receive the cups she held out," Waythorn "took the third cup with a laugh" (396). Like Lizzie West of "The Letters," who decides to accept her marriage as it is after learning that her husband has read none of the letters she sent him and has married her for her money, or Mr. Mindon, who accepts his wife's infidelity in "The Line of Least Resistance," Waythorn decides to settle for the marriage he has instead of pining for the marriage that he thought he had. Confronted with a situation of multiple marriages that modern civilization has rendered acceptable, Waythorn chooses the civilized solution. He completes the repression of his primitive instincts of ownership and accepts that he can never have more than a one-third share of Alice, sexually, emotionally, or even socially, and he uses the modern tool of a sense of irony, which occasions his laugh, to seal the process.

The stories of Wharton's later career, from 1915 until her death in 1937, appeared in six collections: *Xingu and Other Stories* (1916), *Here and Beyond* (1926), *Certain People* (1930), *Human Nature* (1933), *The World Over* (1936), and *Ghosts* (1937). Among these are stories lampooning consumer culture ("Charm Incorporated" and "Permanent Wave"), social satires ("Xingu" and "After Holbein"), stories of empire ("A Bottle of Perrier," "The Seed of the Faith"), and ghost stories ("Mr. Jones," "All Souls"). One of the most frequently anthologized stories of this period, "Roman Fever," may be Wharton's definitive statement of women's rivalry for the affection of another person, a theme most notable in *The Age of Innocence, The Reef,* and *The Old Maid,* although it occurs in other works as well. Like "The Other Two," the story is structured in a series of progressive revelations by two New York society matrons, the imperious Mrs. Alida Slade and her quieter friend Mrs. Grace Ansley. The pair sit and talk on the terrace of a restaurant overlooking the Roman forum while waiting for their daughters, Mrs. Slade's demure Jenny and Mrs. Ansley's brilliant Barbara, who are rivals for the same eligible man, a piece of exposition that sets in motion the revelation of other rivalries between women in the past. The more dominant of the two, with "high color and energetic brows" (*Collected Short Stories* II. 834), Mrs. Slade reflects that the two have "lived opposite each other – actually as well as figuratively – for years" (835). As the sun sets and the two gaze out on the ruins of the Roman past, Mrs. Slade begins to probe the less visible ruins of the past that she has shared with Mrs. Ansley when the two were rivals for the affections of Delphin Slade. Recalling that a jealous great-aunt of Mrs. Ansley's had sent her younger sister to the Colosseum at night and that the girl had died of "Roman fever," Mrs. Slade reveals that she had played a similar trick on Mrs. Ansley in their youth. Wanting to be sure of Delphin Slade before their marriage, Alida Slade had sent a note ostensibly from him to Grace Ansley asking that Grace meet him at the Colosseum.

Thus far, the conversation has been Mrs. Slade's one-sided attack on Mrs. Ansley, who metaphorically fends off the attack by keeping a set of knitting needles between herself and Mrs. Slade, as Alice Hall Petry has suggested; she keeps her emotions in check by knitting, and thus controlling, a skein of "red silk" that suggests the passionate intensity of her feelings. When Mrs. Slade recites the letter that Delphin had supposedly sent and reveals that she had been its sender, Mrs. Ansley drops her knitting, and also her defenses, to engage in the fencing match of words that Mrs. Slade has provoked. The balance of power shifts as Mrs. Ansley reveals that she had answered the letter and had met Delphin at the Colosseum. Unable to bear Mrs. Ansley's comment "I'm sorry for you," Mrs. Slade tries once again to gain the upper hand, stating that she had had Delphin Slade for twenty-five years and that Mrs. Ansley "had nothing but that one letter that he didn't write." "I had Barbara," Mrs. Ansley replies, and "move[s] ahead of Mrs. Slade toward the stairway" (843) symbolically moving ahead in their ancient rivalry as well. Rachel Bowlby contends that the revelation in "Roman Fever" may actually be merely a statement of fact that Mrs. Ansley had the brilliant Barbara to sustain her while Mrs. Slade has had to make do with the angelic Jenny, but the clues that Wharton has scattered throughout the story point to a concealed pregnancy, including Mrs. Ansley's illness and her sudden marriage to Horace Ansley two months after her visit to the Colosseum by moonlight. "Girls are ferocious sometimes ... [g]irls in love especially," Mrs. Slade admits, trying repeatedly to explain how she could expose Grace Ansley to possible death, and her incessant goading of Mrs. Ansley suggests that that ferocity is present even in "ripe but well-cared-for middle age" (833). Beneath the veneer of civilization and lack of passion implied by the women's wealth, social status, manners, and age lurk the primitive emotions and drives that Mrs. Slade and Mrs. Ansley display as they run the gamut of jealousy, competition for status, a drive toward dominance, and the impulse to protect their offspring and to see their genes survive. The story's evocation of modernity – the Count whose attentions both daughters desire is an aviator – is merely a cover for the sexual rivalry that spans three generations.

Wharton's ghost stories also address the ferocity and primitive emotions inherent in human beings. Wharton had begun publishing ghost stories as early as "The Lady's Maid's Bell" (1902), and one of her finest stories, "The Eyes" (1910), is the product of her middle period, but the late period ghost stories are among the best examples of her theory of deriving significance from an economical handling of material. According to Margaret McDowell, Wharton's later ghost stories are more ambiguous and less intent on linking the appearance of a ghost to "some recognizable breach of morality" (McDowell 312) than her earlier ones. Another difference, however, is that the events in these late stories gain in force and terror as the supernatural element causes physical as well as psychological harm – the terrorizing of an elderly woman and the breaking of her ankle in "All Souls," a husband's disappearance in "Pomegranate Seed," and the murder of a housekeeper in "Mr. Jones." Moreover, several ghost stories revisit situations from Wharton's earlier career. The early New England stories lend their settings to some altogether darker stories, "Bewitched" and "The Young Gentlemen," which question "the nature of Americanness" (Beer 132) and the nation's unsavory history of ties to European imperialism, according to Janet Beer. Similarly, "The Eyes" recasts the artistic integrity theme of the earlier artist stories into a dark parable of predation. Culwin, a Jamesian figure with impeccable literary taste who likes young and "juicy" men (*Collected Short Stories* II. 116), tells his attractive friend Phil Frenham about the vision of "a man's eyes" with "thick and red-lined lids" (120); they are, he concludes, eyes that "belong to a man who had done a lot of harm in his life, but had always kept just inside the danger lines" (120). The visions occur on two occasions when Culwin is dishonest: the first when he promises to marry his cousin Alice Nowell, primarily to inherit her fine house; and the second when he lies about the literary merit of the work of Gilbert Noyes, a young man with whom he is infatuated. The visions of the eyes cease when he behaves ethically by breaking off his engagement to Alice and telling Noyes the truth about his lack of talent. But Culwin's vampiric attraction to handsome young men has not changed, and the eyes have not vanished for good. When Culwin lays his "gouty hands" (130) on Frenham's shoulders, clutching the younger man with a gesture of grotesque eroticism, Frenham and the narrator see the eyes in the mirror and realize that they are, and were, Culwin's. Culwin, however, "scarcely" recognizes his reflection, gazing at the eyes not with remorse for the harm he has done but with "a glare of slowly gathering hate" (130). Far from accepting responsibility for the harm he has done, Culwin rejects the vision of himself in the mirror. A narcissist, he has for years sought his own reflection in the eyes of the beautiful young men he cultivated and discarded, but a true reflection of his character is abhorrent to him. Like the statue in "The Duchess at Prayer" or the portrait in "The Portrait," the reflection gives Culwin a picture of the truth: that he has been the artist of his own corrupt character and that his greatest work of art has been his own deceptive and destructive self-portrait.

"All Souls" likewise revisits a theme from earlier stories. In its depiction of an elderly woman living alone who is beset by changes to her surroundings, it loosely resembles "Mrs. Manstey's View," yet the strong and vigorous Sara Clayburn seems at first only a distant echo of the helpless Mrs. Manstey. As Sara goes for a walk on All Souls' Eve, she meets a mysterious woman who claims that she is going to visit a servant at Whitegates, Sara's home; shortly thereafter, Sara falls, breaks her ankle, and is ordered to bed by the doctor. When she awakens, she is terrified to find that the house is deserted and the electricity is off. The next day, her loyal maidservant Agnes disclaims any knowledge of the deserted house, saying that Sara must have been feverish. On the next All Souls' Eve, Sara appears on the narrator's doorstep, claiming that she does not want to repeat the experience and will never live in the house again. The narrator hypothesizes that the woman whom Sara saw was a "fetch" who had come to summon the servants to a witches' coven. Critics have seen biographical echoes in this story; as Annette Zilversmit notes, Wharton's house The Mount, unlike most Berkshires estates, had white gates (Zilversmit 317), and Jenni

Dyman and Karen J. Jacobsen see in the desertion of the servants Wharton's own fears about such an event, with Jacobsen tying the issue to anxieties about class resentment. Reading the stories through the theory that Wharton was an incest victim, Barbara White considers the story as yet another example of the incest theme, with the disembodied and insinuating male voice coming from the crystal radio set evoking repressed memories of a sexual abuser. The story's Gothic elements are also controversial, with Kathy Fedorko finding it a "dark Gothic abyss" of "sexuality, death, [and] loss of control" (Fedorko 160) and Janet Beer and Avril Horner judging the Gothic elements so excessive as to constitute a parody of the Gothic, using "comedy and the supernatural to unsettle conventional values and beliefs" (Beer and Horner 285).

As Gianfranca Balestra points out, however, the story did not always end with the narrator's explanation of witchcraft and the "fetch," which some critics have thought a weakness in it. According to Balestra, the manuscript shows that Wharton had originally ended the story with Sara's flight from the house and had added the witchcraft explanation later "for the use of the magazine morons" who presumably would not be satisfied with the indeterminate nature of the story's events (Balestra 21). In fact, virtually all the events of the story can be explained by resorting to Agnes's commonsense explanation that Sara had suffered a fever and become delirious; for example, the male voice coming from the crystal set would not have been loud enough to hear without electrical amplification. But despite the narrator's insistence on Sara's reliability and his or her own (the narrator's gender is never specifically stated), the witchcraft explanation is ultimately as unsatisfying as the original indeterminate ending that refuses to explain the events, which is perhaps Wharton's point. "All Souls" illustrates the factors that Wharton considered the necessary conditions for the ghost story: an absence of "the wireless and the cinema" that might cause the "ghost instinct" (*Ghost Stories* 8) to atrophy; a presumably English-descended pair of characters, for ghosts appear to those who hear the "hoarse music of the northern Urwald" (8) and not the "Latin" peoples who see ghosts; and "two conditions abhorrent to the modern mind: silence and continuity" (9), in which the sparse and ambiguous supernatural events can multiply and do their work of "send[ing] a cold shiver down one's spine" (11). For Wharton, as for the modernists, less is more, ambiguity is more potent than an accumulation of details, and an "economy of material" produces the greatest effect, principles nowhere more evident than in her ghost stories.

Considered as a whole, Edith Wharton's short stories constitute a body of work as varied and complex as that of her novels. Although a few of the stories, such as "Permanent Wave" or "The Introducers," seem more like pat "magazine stories" than thorough explorations of character or theme, most have a subtlety of approach and a quality of insight that place them among her best work. In addition, some stories are sketches for or companion pieces to the novels, as "Autre Temps ..." anticipates the situation in *The Mother's Recompense*, "The Lamp of Psyche" provides an early version of characters in *The Old Maid*, and "Souls Belated" elaborates on a concept later alluded to in *The Age of Innocence*. Although she did not write linked stories in the manner of Sarah Orne Jewett's Dunnet Landing stories or Margaret Deland's tales of Old Chester,

Wharton returned several times to the same themes and situations, among them fathers and daughters, mothers and sons ("The Pelican," "Her Son"), artistic and intellectual integrity, the inescapability of the past, which appears in ghost stories like "Pomegranate Seed" as well as in "Confession," and the struggle of primitive emotions with the civilized veneer necessary to modern life. If the stories meet Wharton's criterion of having a subject that "contain[s] in itself something that sheds a light on our moral experience" (*The Writing* 24), through her treatment of the material, they also capture something of the tempo of modern life, with its uncanny, disorienting, and sometimes violent dislocations of human beings from their surroundings, from their comforting conceptions of themselves, and from each other.

NOTES

1   Apparently omitting "Les Metteurs en Scène," the "slightly improved French version" of "The Introducers" (White 77), Barbara White puts Wharton's total number of short stories at eighty-five: twenty-four in the early period, thirty-five in the middle period, and twenty-six in the late period (xv–xvi). In his *Collected Short Stories of Edith Wharton*, R. W. B. Lewis apparently includes "Les Metteurs en Scène" in giving the total number as eighty-six (vii). Neither counts "Bunner Sisters," a long short story or novella written in the 1890s but first published in *Xingu* (1916).

2   For Wharton's correspondence with her publishers about *The Writing of Fiction*, see Frederick Wegener, "Edith Wharton and the Difficult Writing of *The Writing of Fiction*" (*Modern Language Studies* 25.2 [1995]: 60–79).

3   "The Fullness of Life" in *The Collected Short Stories of Edith Wharton* I. 12–20, at p. 14. Subsequent references are to this two-volume edition and will be cited in the text.

4   Blake Nevius uses this term in describing *Ethan Frome* in *Edith Wharton, a Study of Her Fiction* (Berkeley: University of California Press, 1953), 126.

REFERENCES AND FURTHER READING

Balestra, Gianfranca. "'For the Use of the Magazine Morons': Edith Wharton Rewrites the Tale of the Fantastic." *Studies in Short Fiction* 33.1 (1996): 13–24.

Beer, Janet. *Kate Chopin, Edith Wharton, and Charlotte Perkins Gilman: Studies in Short Fiction.* New York: St. Martin's Press, 1997.

Beer, Janet, and Avril Horner. "'This Isn't Exactly a Ghost Story': Edith Wharton and Parodic Gothic." *Journal of American Studies* 37 (2003): 269–85.

Bendixen, Alfred. *Haunted Women: The Best Supernatural Tales by American Women Writers.* New York: Ungar, 1985.

Bowlby, Rachel. "'I Had Barbara': Women's Ties and Wharton's "Roman Fever.'" *differences* 17.3 (2006): 37–51.

Dyman, Jenni. *Lurking Feminism: The Ghost Stories of Edith Wharton.* New York: Peter Lang, 1996.

Fedorko, Kathy A. *Gender and the Gothic in the Fiction of Edith Wharton.* Tuscaloosa: University of Alabama Press, 1995.

Hemingway, Ernest. *Death in the Afternoon.* New York: Scribner, 1960.

Jacobsen, Karen J. "Economic Hauntings: Wealth and Class in Edith Wharton's Ghost Stories." *College Literature* 35.1 (2008): 100–27.

James, Henry. "The New Novel." *Henry James: Literary Criticism. 1914.* Ed. Leon Edel. New York: Literary Classics of the United States, 1984. 124–59.

McDowell, Margaret B. *Edith Wharton.* Boston: Twayne, 1990.

Nettels, Elsa. "Gender and First-Person Narration in Edith Wharton's Short Fiction." *Edith Wharton: New Critical Essays*. Eds. Alfred Bendixen and Annette Zilversmit. Garland Reference Library of the Humanities, 914. New York: Garland, 1992. 245–60.

Petry, Alice Hall. "A Twist of Crimson Silk: Edith Wharton's 'Roman Fever.'" *Studies in Short Fiction* 24.2 (1987): 163–6.

Totten, Gary. "Critical Reception and Cultural Capital: Edith Wharton as a Short Story Writer." *Pedagogy* 8.1 (2008): 115–33.

Vita-Finzi, Penelope. *Edith Wharton and the Art of Fiction*. New York: St. Martin's Press, 1990.

Wegener, Frederick. "Charlotte Perkins Gilman, Edith Wharton, and the Divided Heritage of American Literary Feminism." *The Mixed Legacy of Charlotte Perkins Gilman*. Eds. Catherine J. Golden and Joanna Schneider Zangrando. Newark: University of Delaware Press–Associated University Press, 2000. 135–59.

———. *Edith Wharton: The Uncollected Critical Writings*. Princeton: Princeton University Press, 1996.

Wharton, Edith. *A Backward Glance: Novellas and Other Writings*. Ed. Cynthia Griffin Wolff. New York: Literary Classics of the United States, 1990. 767–1068.

———. *The Age of Innocence: Authoritative Text, Background and Contexts, Sources, Criticism*. Ed. Candace Waid. New York: W. W. Norton, 2003.

———. *The Collected Short Stories of Edith Wharton*. Ed. R. W. B. Lewis. 2 vols. New York: Scribner, 1968.

———. *The Ghost Stories of Edith Wharton*. New York: Simon & Schuster, 1997.

———. *The Letters of Edith Wharton*. Eds. R. W. B. Lewis and Nancy Lewis. New York: Collier Books, 1989.

———. *The Writing of Fiction*. 1st Touchstone edn. New York: Simon & Schuster, 1997.

White, Barbara A. *Edith Wharton: A Study of the Short Fiction*. Twayne's Studies in Short Fiction, 30. New York: Twayne, 1991.

Zilversmit, Annette. "'All Souls': Wharton's Last Haunted House and Future Directions for Criticism." *Edith Wharton: New Critical Essays*. Eds. Alfred Bendixen and Annette Zilversmit. New York: Garland, 1992. 315–29.

Part II
The Transition into the New Century

10

The Short Stories of Stephen Crane

Paul Sorrentino

Though Stephen Crane is best known as the author of *The Red Badge of Courage* (1895), he was a prolific writer who wrote three novels, half of another, three novellas, two collections of poetry, and more than 100 short stories and sketches within about ten years. Arguably the most important American writer during the 1890s, he experimented with various narrative techniques and created a truly distinctive style marked by irony, impressionistic responses to reality, and characters with limited perspectives, their "own little cylinder of vision" (*Tales, Sketches, and Reports* 683),[1] through which to interpret reality. Whether he was writing about the impact of immigration and urbanization on New York City, the disappearance of the frontier in the West, conflict during recent or imaginary wars, or the absurdity of life – whether in a city, on the battlefield, or in the wilderness on land or at sea – Crane's short stories reflect major forces that transformed American culture in the last part of the nineteenth century.

Part of his attraction to writing short stories was financial. Constantly in debt, he received payment for a story much more quickly than he did for a novel, and the increasing number of magazines in the 1890s created a steady market for stories. He had a good sense of what was marketable. For example, he wanted to publish "An Ominous Baby" during the economic depression of 1893 because "the present time – during these labor troubles – is the best possible time to dispose of it" (Wertheim and Sorrentino, *Correspondence* I. 56; subsequent references to this edition are cited as *Correspondence*), and he wrote "A Grey Sleeve" to capitalize on the popularity of sentimental war stories. As Willa Cather recalled after meeting Crane in 1895, "[h]e gave me to understand that he led a double literary life; writing in the first place the matter that pleased himself, and doing it very slowly; in the second place, any sort of stuff that would sell" (Cather 15).[2]

Deciding what to include in a discussion of his stories is difficult, however, because he used the terms *tale*, *sketch*, and *short story* interchangeably. A "sketch" is typically a brief composition focusing on a single scene or incident with little, if any, development of character or plot; like an artist's sketch, it can be a rough draft for a more finished product. A "tale" is a short narrative with simple development, but both terms have been used loosely, as in the titles of Dickens's elaborate novel, *A Tale of Two Cities*, or Washington Irving's collection of essays and tales, *The Sketch Book*. Similarly, when writing about New York City in 1894, Crane mentioned to Hamlin Garland that he had "fifteen short stories in my head and out of it" that could "make a book" (*Correspondence* I. 65); but two years later in a letter to his brother William, he announced the proposed title of the book as " 'Midnight Sketches' " and described its contents as "stories," "short things," and "some fifteen or twenty short sketches of New York street life and so on" (I. 265, 266).[3] Crane's looseness in terminology was not simply carelessness, for he blurred the traditional distinction between the factual reporting of journalism and the imaginative recreation of reality in fiction. Though he worked as a journalist, he was, as Amy Lowell observed, "the last man in this world who should have attempted newspaper writing" (Lowell xx), for he questioned a writer's ability simply to report objectively. Assigned to cover a newsworthy incident, he had little interest in reporting facts and preferred to record impressionistically his response to them. Although Crane professed "that the most artistic and the most enduring literature was that which reflected life accurately" (*Correspondence* I. 230), his reliance on disjointed plots, shifting perspectives, and limited points of view implies epistemological uncertainty and the existence of multiple realities.[4] The typical length of a tale, sketch, or short story made these literary forms attractive to a writer for whom brief glimpses of life reflected a philosophical perception of reality as fragmented, disconnected, and ephemeral. Even in his longer work – e.g., *The Red Badge of Courage*, *Maggie: A Girl of the Streets*, or "The Monster" (1898) – short chapters function as flashing glimpses of an ever-changing reality.[5]

His earliest known short story, written when he was 13 or 14, is "Uncle Jake and the Bell-Handle," a slight piece about naïve country folk who come to the city to sell turnips and buy farm supplies. Its focus on irony, self-deception, and appearance vs. reality foreshadows distinctive traits in Crane's major work. Crane's first important venture into prose fiction grew out of camping trips near Port Jervis in Sullivan County, New York, that he and friends took in summer 1891. With titles such as "A Ghoul's Accountant" and "An Explosion of Seven Babies," the Sullivan County stories (1892) are at times surrealistic and often rely on slapstick, tall tales, or the macabre for effect. The stories focus primarily on the "little man," who travels around the countryside vainly making pompous proclamations and assaulting normal occurrences of nature that he misreads as being variously animistic, hostile, or tranquil. In "Four Men in a Cave" he explores a cave "because its black mouth gaped at him," when in reality the threatening "mouth" is merely "a little tilted hole" (*Prose and Poetry* 489); in "The Mesmeric Mountain," he thinks he must conquer a mountain with glaring eyes and "red wrath" (515) that is supposedly chasing him, but in reality it is merely a mountain; and in "The Black Dog: A Night of Spectral Terror," he confronts the "sperrit" (502) that howls when someone is near death, though the spirit is only a hungry, mangy dog that smells food cooking. Throughout, the little man is a blustering, egotistical character whose self-righteous poses belie his vanity and whose puffed-up ego repeatedly gets deflated.

Crane characterized the Sullivan County pieces as "little grotesque tales of the woods which I wrote when I was clever" (*Correspondence* I. 111), but he soon "renounced the clever school in literature" in order to develop a more truthful "little creed of art" that "was identical with the one of Howells and Garland" (I. 63). Though minor, these fictional pieces typify Crane's later treatment of irony, nature, and humanity. One need merely think of Henry Fleming's arrogance in *The Red Badge of Courage*, the harrowing experience of four men struggling to survive in a hostile universe in "The Open Boat," or the irony that exists in practically all of his fiction, to realize that Crane was developing his major themes in these stories.[6] Of particular note, however, is Crane's concern with what will become a hallmark of his writing: a blurring of lines between fact and fiction as he incorporated fact, folklore, and legend into his narrative. In "Not Much of a Hero," for example, he juxtaposes three contradictory interpretations of a famous Indian fighter's life in order to raise questions about the nature of biographical evidence; and in "Sullivan County Bears," he concludes that "it is difficult to reconcile the bear of fiction with the bear of reality" (*Tales, Sketches, and Reports* 219).. In "The Way in Sullivan County: A Study in the Evolution of the Hunting Yarn," Crane consciously draws attention to himself as an artist and as an interpreter of tall tales recounted to him by local residents: He is "the unoffending city man" who "seizes his pen and with flashing eye and trembling, eager fingers, writes those brief but lurid sketches which fascinate and charm the reading public while the virtuous bushwhacker, whittling a stick near by, smiles in his own calm and sweet fashion" (220–1). Despite being aware of the hyperbole in the tales recited to him as fact, he accepts that "[i]n a shooting country, no man should tell just exactly what he did. He should tell what he would have liked to do or what he expected to do, just as if he accomplished it" (221). Viewed differently, the statement is a commentary on the creative process in fiction. A simple reporting of facts does not create meaning or have significance. Only through the recollection of facts that have been shaped imaginatively does one get to some sort of truth. Given these observations, it is not surprising that labels such as "story," "sketch," and "tale" are inadequate for categorizing the Sullivan County pieces. This instability of labels is similar to larger attempts to categorize Crane's literary technique, for he was, as Daniel G. Hoffman recognized, "a literary chameleon, writing in almost every fashion then prevailing: naturalism, impressionism, psychological realism, local color, native humor" (Hoffman 273).

Like the Sullivan County pieces, Crane's New York City sketches and stories, written while he was living there from 1892 to 1894, also blur fact and fiction. Rather than merely reporting factually his first-hand exploration of slum life, he conveyed his experience impressionistically. In "An Experiment in Misery" a saloon is a monster with "ravenous lips," and a flophouse has human stench "like malignant diseases with wings" and a locker with "the ominous air of a tombstone" (*Prose and Poetry* 539, 541, 542). In "The Men in the Storm," a wealthy shop owner, smug and complacent in

his cozy store during a blizzard, "stood in an attitude of magnificent reflection …
slowly stroked his moustache with a certain grandeur of manner, and looked down at
the snow-encrusted mob" of homeless people outside his window (581). Similarly, the
newspaper article "When Every One is Panic Stricken" with a sub-headline reading
"A Realistic Portrait of a Fire" would seem to be an eyewitness account of an actual
fire in a tenement house at midnight, but it is actually an impressionistic reconstruction of what it would be like to experience one. More clearly fictional are three stories
about Tommie, Maggie's baby brother who dies, in *Maggie: A Girl of the Streets*. Two
of the stories deal with economic disparity. In "A Great Mistake" Tommie is caught
attempting to steal a lemon from a fruit stand, and in "An Ominous Baby" he fights
with a wealthy child who refuses to share his toy with him. In "A Dark-Brown Dog"
Tommie's drunken father throws the family dog out the window. Although Crane
empathized with social outcasts because he understood their condition firsthand, he
never moralized about them. Unlike his literary mentors, Hamlin Garland and
William Dean Howells, he never formulated convictions about the causes of social
injustice. His aesthetic aim was to set forth reality as truthfully as possible, and he
considered preaching "fatal to art in literature" (*Correspondence* I. 230).

The theme of conflict in Crane's urban fiction gets treated comically and tragically
in his Western stories. After the abridged version of *The Red Badge of Courage* appeared
in December 1894, Irving Bacheller hired Crane as a special correspondent to travel
to the West and Mexico and to report on his experiences. Bacheller had been impressed
with Crane's powers of observation in the novel and the positive response of readers
to it. Crane left for four months starting in late January 1895. His literary output
consisted of a number of stories and journalistic sketches that undercut the romanticized view of the West as depicted in dime novels popular at the time. In "The Bride
Comes to Yellow Sky" (1898), Jack Potter, rather than being an adventurous hero, is
an awkward, middle-aged marshal who suddenly decides to get married. As the train
brings the newlyweds home, so too does it bring what marriage represents – family,
domesticity, refinement – everything that the once rugged West lacked. As a symbol
of technological and cultural progress, "[t]he great Pullman was whirling onward
with such dignity of motion that a glance from the window seemed simply to prove
that the plains of Texas were pouring eastward. Vast flats of green grass, dull-hued
spaces of mesquite and cactus, little groups of frame houses, woods of light and tender
trees, all were sweeping into the east, sweeping over the horizon, a precipice" (*Prose
and Poetry* 787). With a primitive frontier being swept away, the environment was
geographically and culturally at a turning point and the beginning of something new.
Given the end of one era in American history and the dawn of another, it is appropriate that the name of the town be associated with renewal, for "the hour of Yellow
Sky, the hour of daylight, was approaching" (789).

Despite the rapid advancement of civilization across the continent, Scratchy Wilson
still believes that a gun is man's best friend and disputes are settled not in court but
on the street. In the past, Marshal Potter protected the town from Wilson's games of
comic violence, but now that Potter is married, he no longer wants to play. The

potential for a shootout at the end of the story is immediately defused when Scratchy discovers that Potter lacks a gun. Attempting to goad him into a fight, Scratchy sneers, " 'If you ain't got a gun, why ain't you got a gun?' ... 'Been to Sunday-school?' " (797). But when Scratchy learns that his relationship with Potter has been forever changed because of the marriage, this "simple child of the earlier plains" (798) struggles to accept that their ritualized game is "all off now" (798). Scratchy drags his feet, creating funnel-shaped tracks in the sand that visually depict an hour glass recording the inevitable passing of time and an era.

Whereas "The Bride Comes to Yellow Sky" treats the end of the West comically, "The Blue Hotel" (1898) dramatizes the tragic consequences of holding on to it in a naturalistic universe. During a raging snowstorm that symbolizes the violent nature of humanity, three travelers are forced to spend a night in a desolate prairie town. Because the Swede has come West with distorted expectations, the Easterner observes that "this man has been reading dime-novels, and he thinks he's right out in the middle of it – the shootin' and stabbin' and all" (*Prose and Poetry* 809). During a card game at the hotel, the Swede unexpectedly announces that someone is going to kill him. When he becomes drunk, he brutally beats up Johnnie after accusing him of cheating; and when he gets into another fight, a gambler stabs him. Given the Swede's boisterous behavior, it seems appropriate that his corpse, "alone in the saloon, had its eyes fixed upon a dreadful legend that dwelt a-top of the cash-machine. 'This registers the amount of your purchase' " (826). Though the legend implies that the Swede got what he paid for, in the concluding section of the story the Easterner announces that the Swede was indeed correct in accusing Johnnie of cheating and not totally to blame for his own death.

Although the universe is bleak in "The Blue Hotel," Crane does not simply conclude that humans are amoral creatures controlled by deterministic forces over which they have no control; instead, he is interested in what happens when people misread each other, when communication breaks down, and when individuals ignore the natural and ethical consequences of their actions. Though the Swede misreads the West because of his fondness for dime novels, he recognizes Johnnie's deception in the card game, and his attempt to leave the Palace Hotel soon after arriving reveals that he correctly senses the potential for violence there. Other characters are no better at reading reality than he is. When they have trouble understanding the Swede, Johnnie dismisses him flippantly – "I don't know nothin' about you ... and I don't give a damn where you've been" (803) – and the cowboy reduces him to a racist stereotype: " 'It's my opinion ... he's some kind of a Dutchman.' It was a venerable custom of the country to entitle as Swedes all light-haired men who spoke with a heavy tongue" (809).

Although the Swede believes that he is fated to die in the Palace Hotel, it oversimplifies the matter, as the Easterner asserts, to conclude that only the gambler is responsible for his death. Legally, he is because he killed the Swede; but morally (as depicted in grammatical terms), the gambler is not "a noun" but "an adverb": He is not the sole doer of the action but rather someone who modified an action already

begun by others – the "five of us" – all of whom have contributed to the tragic
outcome of the story (827). Though Scully appears to be a congenial host taking care
of his customers' needs, his motives are purely financial. To entice customers to his
hotel, he is "a master of strategy" who "work[s] his seduction" (799) on prospective
customers, "practically [makes] them prisoners" (800), and paints his hotel a garish
blue so that it is the first building seen after leaving the train station. Like his father,
Johnnie also cares only about his own interests. His immediate reaction to charges of
irresponsibility is denial. When his father accuses him of troubling the Swede, Johnnie
decries defensively, " 'Well, what have I done?' " (806), a question that foreshadows
the last line of the story. Before the travelers arrive at the Palace Hotel, the mood is
already tense because of a card game between Johnnie and a farmer. Though the narrator does not mention the cause of their disagreement, the farmer's "air of great
impatience and irritation" (800) implies that the farmer also suspects Johnnie of
cheating, lending credence in hindsight to the Swede's charge. Similarly, though the
cowboy denies any responsibility for his actions, he goads Johnnie a half dozen times
during the fight to "Kill him" (817). Although the Easterner feebly tries to stop the
fight, he too joins the cowboy and Scully in "a cheer that was like a chorus of triumphant soldiery" (818) when Johnnie hits the Swede. Who, then, is responsible for the
Swede's death? Whereas the law says that the gambler must serve three years in prison
for his crime, "We, five of us, have collaborated in the murder of this Swede" (827).

The Easterner's sudden revelation about Johnnie's cheating raises the question of
how to interpret the ending: Should it be read as an affirmation of the need to assume
responsibility for one's actions, is it an ironic statement about the ultimate meaninglessness of any human action in an amoral universe, or is it simply a tacked-on ending
that unnecessarily complicates what seems obvious: the Swede is responsible for his
own death? The multitude of critical responses is a tribute to a rich, complex story
that defies easy categorization and that captures the modern existentialist dilemma:
Do questions of moral responsibility have any significance in an absurd, disjointed
universe? Crane's treatment of the question may at least partly explain Ernest Hemingway's famous quotation about major influences on modern American literature: "The
good writers are Henry James, Stephen Crane, and Mark Twain. That's not the order
they're good in. There is no order for good writers. ... Crane wrote two fine stories.
'The Open Boat' and 'The Blue Hotel.' The last one is the best" (*Green Hills* 22).

Besides "The Bride Comes to Yellow Sky" and "The Blue Hotel," other fine
Western stories explore themes of chance, primitivism vs. civilization, and misap-
prehension of reality. In "The Five White Mice" (1898) – a story about a dice game,
a circus, and a near shootout in which "[n]othing ... happened" (*Prose and Poetry* 771)
– the New York Kid learns that chance is the controlling factor in human events. In
"Moonlight on the Snow" (1900), a sequel to "The Bride," Tom Larpent, a highly
literate protagonist, exposes the greed of fellow townspeople who fear that the image
of a Wild West town will hurt the commercial growth of their town. And in "One
Dash – Horses" (1896), a blanket separating Richardson from outlaws symbolizes
humanity's limited understanding of veiled reality. Like a number of Crane's other

characters, including the seasoned veterans in his war stories and the men in "The Open Boat" (1897), characters in the Western stories – e.g., Larpent, the New York Kid, and Richardson – act with what Hemingway would later characterize as "grace under pressure," the ability to act stoically and resolutely during times of stress. Though this behavior does not guarantee survival, as shown by the death of Bill in "A Man and Some Others" (1897), it is the proper conduct in a world in which individuals have little, if any, control.

Crane's desire to transform his own experience into fiction, as he does in his urban and Western stories, is nowhere more evident than in the *Commodore* episode in early January 1897. Crane dramatized his near-death experience on the filibustering boat into a feature newspaper article and two short stories, "The Open Boat" and "Flanagan and His Short Filibustering Adventure" (1897). The article, "Stephen Crane's Own Story" (1897), recounts the fateful voyage and in the last two paragraphs condenses a number of details pertaining to the bravery of the captain and the oiler, the capsizing of the dinghy in the breakers, and the oiler's death; however, Crane says nothing in his "own story" about the ordeal on the dinghy after the *Commodore* sinks: "The history of life in an open boat for thirty hours would no doubt be very instructive for the young, but none is to be told here now" (*Prose and Poetry* 883). Following the newspaper account, Crane wanted to celebrate the heroism of his fellow seamen, but he first needed to make sense of the whole experience before he transformed it into fiction, for as the subtitle of "The Open Boat" states, it was "[a] Tale Intended to be after the Fact, Being the Experience of Four Men from the Sunk Steamer 'Commodore.'" To insure he had captured the experience completely, he showed his manuscript to Edward Murphy, captain of the *Commodore*, because, as he told him, "I want to have this *right*, from your point of view" (Paine 168, 170).

Rather than simply report factual details surrounding the experience, Crane explored its social and metaphysical implications. The first sentence – "None of them knew the color of the sky" (*Prose and Poetry* 885) – makes clear that perspective is central to the story. More specifically, the story fluctuates between the point of view of four men in the boat, whose focus is strictly on the "walls of water" and "barbarously abrupt and tall" waves that threaten their survival, and an omniscient author, whose view "from a balcony, [would make] the whole thing … weirdly picturesque" (885, 886). Out of necessity the men divide up their duties: the oiler and correspondent row, the cook bails out water from the boat, and the captain, whose arm is broken, controls the tiller. Their situation is made worse by an argument between the cook and correspondent about the likelihood of rescue, by the vulnerability of a boat that seems no bigger than "a bath-tub," and by the "loud swishing" of a shark moving like "a monstrous knife" near them (885, 900, 901).

When the men believe they will soon be rescued, they smoke cigars, drink from their supply of water, and relax "with an assurance … shining in their eyes" (892). This hope, however, is quickly undercut, for they soon realize that rather than living in an orderly world that can assure salvation, they are isolated victims floating in an irrational cosmos. Angry at his fate, the correspondent complains that "[t]he whole affair is absurd" (894). In an indifferent universe symbolized by a "high cold star" and a tower looking like "a giant, standing with its back to the plight of the ants," there is no spiritual court of appeals to lodge a complaint about unfair treatment, about "the struggles of the individual," about life itself (902, 905).

Despite their bleak existence, the men develop a "subtle brotherhood" (890) of trust and concern. The correspondent recalls a poem about a dying soldier that he was forced to memorize in school. At the time it meant nothing to him; but now, possibly facing his own death, he realizes that literature, here in the form of a poem about comradeship, can help him find meaning in an indifferent universe. As the dinghy finally gets close to shore, this comradeship is augmented by a bystander who, "like a saint" with "a halo about his head," pulls the exhausted men from the breakers and by a community of people with blankets, clothing, coffee, "and all the remedies sacred to their minds" (909). Ironically, the oiler, the best swimmer, dies before getting to shore. The story ends with peaceful imagery of the night and ocean and a realization that now the four men "felt that they could then be interpreters" (909). Despite their own insignificance in an indifferent universe, they have learned the value of solidarity and compassion.

Like "The Open Boat," in "Flanagan and His Short Filibustering Adventure" a fili- bustering boat develops engine trouble before sinking, insurgents get seasick, and a crewman drowns in the breakers. Flanagan's assignment as captain is an initiation into filibustering. He is successful in getting the insurgents and munitions to Cuba and in avoiding getting captured by the Spanish; but when his crew is forced to abandon ship, people on shore view the sudden appearance of lifeboats on the horizon as an entertaining spectacle rather than an occasion for rescue and comfort. Like other Crane stories – e.g., "The Five White Mice," "An Episode of War," and "War Memories" – an ironic ending deflates a character's attempt to understand his experi- ence. When Flanagan's corpse washes ashore, indifferent spectators avoid it for fear of getting their shoes and clothing wet in the surf. As the narrator laments in the last line of the story, Flanagan's heroic effort will remain forgotten in the annals of history: "[t]he expedition of the *Foundling* will never be historic" (*Prose and Poetry* 925). Despite Crane's effort to make sense of the *Commodore* incident in three ways – as his "Own Story," as the "Experience of Four Men," and as an "Adventure" – the harrow- ing nightmare remained with him for the rest of his life. On his deathbed, as Cora Crane recalled, "My husbands [*sic*] brain is never at rest. He lives over everything in dreams & talks aloud constantly. It is too awful to hear him try to change places in the 'open boat'!" (*Correspondence* II. 655–6).

Crane explored the "rage of conflict" (*Correspondence* I. 228) not only in the city, out West, and on the sea but also on the battlefield. His war fiction falls into three chronological periods: stories written loosely about the Civil War before he had wit- nessed combat, those written after having experienced it in Greece and Cuba, and those written about an imaginary war between two countries.[7]

To capitalize on the success of *The Red Badge of Courage*, S. S. McClure sent Crane to Virginia in late January 1896 to tour Civil War battlefields for a series of sketches about major battles for McClure's literary syndicate, but nothing came of the project. Instead, Crane wrote short stories about the war but soon realized that he could not sustain the narrative intensity of the novel. Fearing he had "used [himself] up in the accursed 'Red Badge,'" he wrote, "[p]eople may just as well discover now that the high dramatic key of *The Red Badge* cannot be sustained (*Correspondence* I. 161, 191). Most of the stories, which comprise Crane's first period of war fiction and appear in *The Little Regiment and Other Episodes of the American Civil War* (1896), lack the imaginative quality often found in his great fiction. In "The Veteran," a sequel to *The Red Badge of Courage*, Henry Fleming dies trying to rescue animals in a burning barn. "An Indiana Campaign," a humorous account of mistaken identity concerning the theft of chickens, was rejected by the *Atlantic Monthly* because "in substance it is somewhat too slight for our more or less serious pages" (*Correspondence* I. 226). In "A Grey Sleeve," which capitalized on the popularity of sentimental wartime love stories, a nascent romance develops between a dashing Union officer and a Southern belle. Although Crane once characterized their behavior "charming in their childish faith in each other," they were "a pair of idiots," and "A Grey Sleeve" was "not in any sense a good story" (I. 180, 171). In "Three Miraculous Soldiers" another Southern heroine helps three Confederate soldiers escape from the enemy. Despite its sentimentality, its treatment of the theme of limited perception – at one point the heroine's vision is literally restricted to what she can see through a knothole – is what James Nagel has called "one of the most remarkably limited narrative perspectives in American literature" (Nagel 48). The title story, "The Little Regiment," lacks plot and character development, but its use of color, contrasts between art and nature, and blurring of fact and fiction are reminiscent of Crane's best literary impressionism.

Two stories during Crane's first period of war fiction, "A Mystery of Heroism: A Detail of an American Battle" (1895) and "An Episode of War" (1899), deserve special attention. In "A Mystery of Heroism," the sixth story in *The Little Regiment*, Fred Collins risks his life during an artillery battle to try to bring back a bucket of water for his comrades; but when one lieutenant tries to take a drink, another playfully jostles his elbow and knocks the bucket to the ground, spilling the water. Given the ending of the story, is Collins a hero for risking his life to get water for his comrades, or is he a fool carelessly motivated by pride? One might argue that his decision to comfort a dying officer suggests his empathy for fellow humans, but his action, what-ever motivates it, is for naught. Perhaps the emptiness of the bucket symbolizes the emptiness of his action – and by extension, if actions have no meaning, abstractions such as courage and bravery seem ultimately meaningless as well. Hemingway would later echo the same sentiment when Frederic Henry, wearied from the ultimate use-lessness of war in *A Farewell to Arms*, says, "I was always embarrassed by the words sacred, glorious, and sacrifice and the expression in vain. ... Abstract words such as glory, honor, courage, or hallow were obscene" (*A Farewell to Arms* 184, 185). For many of Crane's and Hemingway's characters, the final question is: what is the proper mode of conduct in a chaotic universe?

Like "A Mystery of Heroism," "An Episode of War" is one of Crane's finest war stories. A lieutenant is shot in the arm while apportioning coffee beans for his troops. As he heads for the field hospital, an increasingly widened perspective of "many things which as a participant in the fight were unknown to him" (*Prose and Poetry* 672) represents metaphorically the shift in his attitude towards battle and life in general. When he reaches the hospital – appropriately located in a schoolhouse, a place where one goes to learn – he sees a wounded man, resigned to his condition, calmly smoking a pipe. After the lieutenant's arm is amputated, he returns home to his family grieving "at the sight of the flat sleeve" (675); however, like the pipe smoker, he recognizes a wound as a badge of mortality and stoically accepts his own insignificance in the universe.

Whereas Crane's war fiction before 1897 consists mostly of impressionistic studies of fear and isolation or sentimental treatments of war, during his second period, which is marked by his first experience of combat, he soon learned that "the 'Red Badge' [was] all right" (Conrad 11).[8] Out of the Greco-Turkish War came *Active Service* (1899), a novel that uses war primarily as the setting for a domestic comedy of manners, and "Death and the Child" (1898), a superb short story that explores the nature of conflict and heroism.

Peza, a young Italian correspondent of Greek descent, has been assigned to report the war. Like Henry Fleming in *The Red Badge of Courage*, Peza's view of war is based on his naïve imagination and an inflated sense of self-importance. The immediacy of war and the sight of dead and wounded, however, force him to confront his illusions about combat. Even though Peza tries to defend his actions or ignore the consequences of his behavior, the narrator constantly undercuts him. When Peza deserts the spectral soldier, the narrator quickly chastises him for being "surely craven in the movement of refusal" (*Prose and Poetry* 957); and when he attempts to get a better viewpoint of the battle by standing on "a pillar" "surveying mankind, the world" (958) – an image in which he ironically resembles a statue commemorating some military hero – dust gets into Peza's eyes, literally and figuratively suggesting his own limited point of view. In contrast are the perspectives of experienced soldiers, who accept the drudgery of war as essential to its outcome, and a deserted child, whose confused parents, in the terrifying rush of innocent peasants to flee the battle, have forgotten their son and left him in a hut on a hill. Like Peza, the boy misreads the reality of war and interprets it only from the limited perspective of a child familiar with games and the actions of shepherds tending to a flock of animals. In the final section of the story, which juxtaposes the perspectives of Peza and the child, Peza finally acknowledges the illusion of an inflated ego and accepts his own insignificance in the grand scheme of the universe.

Sick and tired for much of the time, Crane produced little fiction based on the Greco-Turkish War. His experience in Cuba, however, was different. Of the more than 200 reporters, photographers, and artists who covered the Cuban phase of the Spanish-American War, Crane was among the two or three most famous – and arguably the best. His experience led to a collection of eleven war stories, *Wounds in the*

Rain (1900), in which he continued to develop innovative narrative techniques and to explore the complex nature of courage and sacrifice; but unlike his earlier war fiction, these stories are more firmly grounded in current social and political issues and reveal Crane's admiration for seasoned, professional veterans who did their task in combat dutifully and stoically.

In "The Price of the Harness," Crane criticizes the constant attention paid in the American press to colorful volunteer regiments such as Theodore Roosevelt's Rough Riders at the expense of the common regular soldiers, who, in "Marines Signaling under Fire at Guantánamo," calmly stand up in the line of fire to call in artillery shells from nearby ships. Similarly, "The Second Generation" criticizes nepotism and class privilege as the basis for a military commission. War also produces absurdist humor when a drunken soldier suddenly begins singing a medley of songs during combat in "The Sergeant's Private Madhouse"; and in "God Rest Ye, Merry Gentlemen," "This Majestic Lie," and "The Lone Charge of William B. Perkins," Crane satirizes incompetent correspondents and debunks yellow journalism.

Besides treating the war realistically and satirically, Crane experiments with innovative narrative techniques in *Wounds in the Rain*. Certainly one of his most stylistically and thematically complex stories is "The Clan of No-Name," which he called "a peach. I love it devotedly" (*Correspondence* II. 379). Its complex plot, frame structure, shifting time schemes and points of view, and indeterminacy of meaning foreshadow postmodernism. Equally as original is the little-known masterpiece "War Memories," which seamlessly blends journalistic dispatches with impressionistic glimpses of combat. Unlike other autobiographical accounts of the Spanish-American War that focus on factual summaries of military details and major events, Crane adopts the persona of a correspondent named Vernall, who struggles with ontological and linguistic questions about the nature of reality.

Throughout, Vernall acknowledges the inability to capture objective truth, "the real thing," because " 'war is neither magnificent nor squalid; it is simply life, and an expression of life can always evade us. We can never tell life, one to another, although sometimes we think we can' " (*Tales of War* 222). Vernall struggles to control his own story. Occasionally, he realizes that "[he has] forgotten to tell you" (247) an important detail; at other times, in trying to recall simple details about his experience in Cuba, he has only a "vague sense" or "vague impression" (248, 259) of his war memories – certainly a contrast to Theodore Roosevelt's autobiographical *The Rough Riders*, in which the author appears to have total recall of even the smallest detail. As a result, the chronology in "War Memories" is complex. Vernall's inability to control his narrative is further complicated by his implied conversation with an unnamed voiceless interlocutor who wants the narrator to tell heroic stories about Rough Riders and the military details about the famous battles at Las Guásimas and the San Juan hills – the kind of narrative that Roosevelt and others wrote. This narrative battle between an uncertain narrator and an audience demanding romantic accounts of glorious deeds highlights the ontological and linguistic difficulties in trying to capture "the real thing" in the act of storytelling itself.

Vernall learns that language cannot ultimately articulate what is real about war – or anything. By the end of the story, all he can say with certainty is that "[t]he episode was closed. And you can depend upon it that I have told you nothing at all, nothing at all, nothing at all" – and yet paradoxically he gives us a disturbing glimpse at an "overwhelming, crushing, monstrous" reality so different from that in other accounts of the Spanish-American War (263, 254). One of America's greatest accounts of war, "War Memories" foreshadows Hemingway's artistic dictum in *Death in the Afternoon* to get "the real thing" (2) in writing as well as postmodern narratives of the Viet Nam War, most notably Michael Herr's *Dispatches* (Robertson 174).

Crane's final set of war stories," The Spitzbergen Tales" (1899), was written during the last year of his life. The four stories depict an imaginary war between two fictious countries, Spitzbergen and Rostina, and focus on an infantry regiment called the "Kicking Twelfth." Read together, the stories have a narrative progression, and in three of them the main character is Lieutenant Timothy Lean. In "The Kicking Twelfth" Lieutenant Lean defeats the enemy from Rostina despite suffering heavy losses. In "The Shrapnel of Their Friends," the regiment accidentally comes under artillery fire from one of its own batteries during a second engagement with the enemy. In "And If He Wills, We Must Die," the mood is more bleak, with a graphically described slaughter of a squad of Spitzbergen soldiers defending a house at the front of the enemy lines. With Crane's typical irony, the battle was unnecessary, for a courier had been sent with orders for the squad to retreat, but he had been killed before he could reach the house.

The best of the Spitzbergen tales, "The Upturned Face," recounts the burial of a soldier during combat. In terms of technique, "The Upturned Face" is practically unlike any of his other war stories. A number of the basic elements of fiction – in particular plot, setting, visual imagery, and point of view – have been kept to a minimum. The narrator is detached, and there is almost no action, no description of where the characters are, or no clear sense of what time of day it is. Typically, Crane's stories rely on visual images to help convey mood, theme, and character; however, here there are few: the dead man's face, his clothing, and his few possessions. Instead Crane focuses on aural and tactile imagery: the attempt to avoid touching the corpse and the sound of dirt dropping on to it. The story is the best example of Crane's late prose style – characterized as "lean, open, and sardonically understated" by James B. Colvert – which allows him to refine "his essentially mythic sense of war so severely that it seems all but absent except in the broad context of his characteristic feeling for the ambiguous crossing of horror and humor in a dreamlike suspension of the movement of time" (Colvert "Stephen Crane: Style as Invention" 131).

"The Upturned Face" epitomizes Crane's final statement about the horror of war. Lieutenant Lean and the adjutant struggle to maintain dignity and propriety during a ceremonial burial of a comrade. They discover, however, that any attempt to assign significance to a ceremony – indeed, any ceremony – is meaningless in a chaotic universe. Nevertheless, humans need to adhere to a code of conduct, what George W. Johnson calls Crane's "metaphor of decorum" (Johnson 250). Though humans are trapped between "an unknowable world and incongruous ceremonies," says Johnson, they still believe in these ceremonies because this allows them to "accept incongruities which would otherwise overwhelm [their] imagination" (251, 253). A code of conduct maintains at least a semblance of order and civility. In his war fiction, Crane has moved from Henry Fleming's self-absorbed, romanticized view of combat in *The Red Badge of Courage*, through the larger social and historical concerns of war in *Wounds in the Rain*, to the final suspension of humanity between an unknowable universe and incongruous rituals. In this sense, Crane is a precursor of what will become a dominant theme in twentieth-century fiction: the sense of isolation and alienation in an inhospitable world.

Starting in summer 1897, Crane began writing stories about an imaginary town named Whilomville. Crane used the archaic word *whilom*, meaning "formerly," to suggest stories about the past or "once upon a time." Thirteen of the fifteen stories focus primarily on children and are based partly on Crane's childhood in Port Jervis, New York, where he lived from ages 6 to 11. With the exception of the novella "The Monster," the tone is often ironic, humorous, and idyllic, with occasional hints of more serious issues dealing with race, religion, and social identity.

The children in Whilomville go to school, wander the countryside, pretend to be cowboys or pirates, develop crushes, and get in trouble. They have a secure home life, especially Jimmie Trescott, who appears in all but one of the stories and whose parents can afford a cook and a servant. Despite a gently comic tone, the children's world has its own fears, conflicts, and meanness. As a group they are often uncivilized. When Homer Phelps does not use the proper password during a game of war in "The Trial, Execution, and Burial of Homer Phelps," he is condemned to a mock trial and execution, the price he must pay to be part of Willie Dalzel's gang. Because he chooses at first not to "play it the right way" (*Prose and Poetry* 1230), he is ostracized from the group and is accepted back only after Jimmie Trescott shows him how to play the game properly. Like Homer, Johnnie Hedge in "The Fight" is another outsider who, after moving to Whilomville, establishes his position in the gang by fighting with, and defeating, Jimmie and Willie Dalzel. The sequel to this story, "The City Urchin and the Chaste Villagers," also deals with power and social rank. In beating the gang leaders, Johnnie has upset the established order of the children's society so that "the world was extremely anxious to know where to place the newcomer" (1249). Willie, however, fights with Johnnie in order to reassert his authority within the gang. The fighting ends only when Johnnie's mother, the "supreme power" (1255), breaks it up.

Though adults function as figures of ultimate authority, they occasionally find the children's behavior amusing. In "Lynx-Hunting" – which reintroduces Crane's most famous character, Henry Fleming from *The Red Badge* and "The Veteran" – Jimmie Trescott and his friends hunt a lynx, even though they do not know what it looks like, because it is "their romance of the moment – whether it was of Indians, miners, smugglers, soldiers, or outlaws" (*Prose and Poetry* 1169). When Jimmie accidentally shoots a cow that he mistakes for a lynx, Henry and his farmhand "laughed themselves helpless" (1173). Likewise, in "The Carriage-Lamps" Jimmie gets in trouble when he secretly obtains a pistol and accidentally breaks lamps in the carriage house. Though he is confined to his room as punishment, his friends concoct a highly imaginative, romantic scheme to rescue him in which they portray such characters as "the Red Captain," "Hold-up Harry, the Terror of the Sierras," and "a prisoner in yon – in yond – in that there fortress" (1214, 1213, 1212). Like the adults in "Lynx-Hunting," Jimmie's father finds the children's behavior so amusing he forgets about any further punishment.

The stories also capture the excitement and sometimes painful embarrassment of puppy love. In "The Lover and the Tell-Tale," Rose Goldege, the tell-tale, catches Jimmie writing a love letter to Cora, who also appears in "The Angel-Child" and "The Stove," and promptly announces her discovery to the rest of the children. When the "yelping demoniac mob" baits Jimmie "like little blood-fanged wolves" (*Prose and Poetry* 1186), a fight breaks out, and he is punished by having to stay after school. As he returns to his seat, he sees "gloating upon him the satanic black eyes of the little Goldege girl" (1188). In "Showin' Off" Jimmie becomes infatuated with another girl, but his attempt to impress her runs into a problem when Horace Glenn, the protagonist of "His New Mittens," comes by riding an early version of a bicycle called the velocipede. When the two boys argue about who can ride faster, Horace challenges Jimmie to ride into a ravine but then remembers that he never lets anyone else ride his velocipede. When Horace gets taunted into accepting his own challenge, he accidentally falls into the ravine, getting hurt and wrecking his bike. Neither boy ends up showing off to anyone.

Other stories in the collection illustrate additional childhood anxieties. In "Making an Orator" Jimmie Trescott dreads having to speak in front of his class and for two weeks manages to pretend he is sick on each Friday, the day that students must recite a memorized passage. By the third Friday, however, he is forced to attend school. When it is his turn to declaim, he can deliver only a mangled version of Tennyson's "The Charge of the Light Brigade." He is temporarily relieved when the teacher tells him to sit down, with the expectation that he will be better prepared next Friday, but the story ends with the likelihood that Jimmie's anxiety about public speaking will be longlasting. In "Shame" Jimmie is treated like a "social leper" by his peers when he shows up at a picnic with sandwiches in a lunch pail: The boys "were not competent to care if he had brought his luncheon in a coal bin; but such is the instinct of childish society that they all immediately moved away from him" (*Prose and Poetry* 1200). And in "A Little Pilgrim" (also published as "A Little Pilgrimage"), Jimmie learns about the hypocrisy of substituting the external trappings of religion for its spiritual core. When the Presbyterian Sunday school he attends suddenly decides to use its money to help victims of a recent earthquake instead of spending it on a Christmas tree, Jimmie is worried he may miss out on Christmas festivities and switches to the Sunday school of the Big Progressive Church, only to discover that this church, not to be outdone by the former, decides also to do without a Christmas tree.

Though Crane's *Whilomville Stories* is not widely known, it captures realistically the joys and traumas of growing up in rural America. Crane had no desire to write in a popular earlier tradition of stories that romanticized children as angelic heroes and heroines and moralized upon their behavior. Indeed, whether he was writing about hometown children, the urban poor, Western cowboys, or individuals facing traumatic experiences at sea or on the battlefield, Crane was a groundbreaking writer of short stories who strove "to observe closely, … to set down what I have seen in the simplest and most concise way[,] … . [and to be] very careful not to let any theories or pet ideas of my own be seen in my writing. Preaching is fatal to art in literature. I try to give to readers a slice out of life; and if there is any moral or lesson in it I do not point it out. I let the reader find it for himself" (*Correspondence* I. 230). This desire to show "readers a slice out of life" exemplifies the fragmented vision of reality that J. Hillis Miller has identified as a key characteristic of modern literature (Miller 3ff.).[9]

It is easy to forget how much Crane accomplished so quickly. From the minor fictional episodes about Sullivan County in 1892, to the masterful "The Open Boat" in 1897, and finally to the immensely innovative "The Clan of No-Name" and "War Memories" in 1899 – a passage of only seven years – Crane developed his craft more quickly than any other American writer. Indeed, if one compares his work in general to that of other nineteenth-century writers, the contrast is remarkable. Whereas Crane had completed two pioneering novels, *Maggie* and *The Red Badge*, before he was 23, Melville did not publish *Moby-Dick* until he was 32, Hawthorne was 46 when *The Scarlet Letter* appeared, and Twain was 49 at the time that the *Adventures of Huckleberry Finn* came out. Though it is mere speculation to guess what direction Crane's work might have taken had he not died at the age of 28, one could reasonably argue that of all the American writers who died young, no one had more potential to become one of the country's great writers than Stephen Crane.

NOTES

1 For a comprehensive treatment of the "cylinder of vision" in Crane's work, see Holton, *Cylinder of Vision*. For additional commentary on Crane's short stories, see Wolford, *Stephen Crane*, and Schaefer, *A Reader's Guide*.

2 The conflict resulting from Crane's "double literary life" is a major theme of *The Third Violet*. See Sorrentino, "Stephen Crane's Struggle."

3 The book publication of these pieces further complicated the issue. In the British edition of *The Open Boat and Other Stories* (London: Heinemann, 1898), nine of the New York City pieces were grouped under the title "Midnight Sketches." They were excluded in the

American edition, *The Open Boat and Other Tales of Adventure* (New York: Doubleday & McClure, 1898), in which the word *Tales* in the title has replaced *Stories*.

4 For a discussion of the literary implications of Crane's epistemology, see Dooley, *The Pluralistic Philosophy*, and Robertson, *Stephen Crane*.

5 This preference for brevity may also explain the shortness of Crane's poems. The average length is about ten lines.

6 As James B. Colvert notes about "The Mesmeric Mountain" in "Stephen Crane's Magic Mountain," "The relation of the fable to *The Red Badge* is obvious. It is at once a summary of the plot of the novel and an expansion of the

metaphor by which Henry interprets his victory. There are the familiar elements – the terror and rage of the hero, the hallucinatory imagery, the antagonism of Nature, the delusive victory, the heroics, the narrator's ironic commentary. ... The meaning of the fable is amplified elsewhere in Crane's fiction. The Swede in 'The Blue Hotel,' his mind swarming with terror at the threat of an unknown menace is, we discover, really at war with himself and an angry Nature. ... And again we find the symbols of the fable in 'The Open Boat,' the story of the correspondent's anguished speculation about the meaning of an ambivalent Nature" (Colvert "Stephen Crane's Magic Mountain," 100–1, 104).

7 Crane also wrote a number of war sketches and dispatches, and *Great Battles of the World*

(1901) contains eight articles on major battles; however, Kate Lyon, Harold Frederic's mistress and a friend of the Cranes, did the research and wrote most of the eight articles.

8 Conrad, Crane's closest literary friend in England, wrote a sentimental reminiscence of their relationship as the introduction to Beer's biography. Though the introduction is an important reminiscence, Beer fabricated letters and incidents for what is now recognized as an unreliable biography. For the impact of Beer's book on Crane scholarship in the twentieth century, see Wertheim and Sorrentino, "Thomas Beer"; Clendenning, "Thomas Beer's *Stephen Crane*"; and Sorrentino, "The Legacy of Thomas Beer."

9 I am indebted to Wolford (*Stephen Crane: A Study of the Short Fiction* xii) for making this connection.

References and Further Reading

Cather, Willa. "When I Knew Stephen Crane." *Stephen Crane: A Collection of Critical Essays*, ed. Maurice Bassan. Englewood Cliffs, NJ: Prentice-Hall, 1967. 12–17.

Clendenning, John. "Thomas Beer's *Stephen Crane*: The Eye of His Imagination." *Prose Studies* 14 (1991): 61–80.

Colvert, James B. "Stephen Crane's Magic Mountain." *Stephen Crane: A Collection of Critical Essays*. Ed. Maurice Bassan. Englewood Cliffs, NJ: Prentice-Hall, 1967. 95–105.

———. "Stephen Crane: Style as Invention." *Stephen Crane in Transition: Centenary Essays*. Ed. Joseph Katz. Dekalb: Northern Illinois University Press, 1972. 127–52.

Conrad, Joseph. Introduction to Thomas Beer, *Stephen Crane: A Study in American Letters*. New York: Knopf, 1923. 1–35.

Crane, Stephen. *Stephen Crane: Prose and Poetry*. New York: Library of America, 1984.

———. *Tales of War*. Vol. 6 of *The Works of Stephen Crane*. Ed. Fredson Bowers. Charlottesville: University Press of Virginia, 1970.

———. *Tales, Sketches, and Reports*. Vol. 8 of *The Works of Stephen Crane*. Ed. Fredson Bowers. Charlottesville: University Press of Virginia, 1973.

Dooley, Patrick K. *The Pluralistic Philosophy of Stephen Crane*. Urbana: University of Illinois Press, 1993.

Hemingway, Ernest. *Death in the Afternoon*. New York: Scribner, 1932.

———. *A Farewell to Arms*. New York: Scribner, 1929.

———. *Green Hills of Africa*. New York: Scribner, 1935.

Hoffman, Daniel G. "Stephen Crane's First Story." *Bulletin of the New York Public Library* 64 (1960): 273–8.

Holton, Milne. *Cylinder of Vision: The Fiction and Journalistic Writings of Stephen Crane*. Baton Rouge: Louisiana State University Press, 1972.

Johnson, George. "Stephen Crane's Metaphor of Decorum." *Publications of the Modern Language Association* 78 (1963): 250–6.

Lowell, Amy. Introduction to *The Black Riders and Other Lines*. Vol. 6 of *The Works of Stephen Crane*. Ed. Wilson Follett. New York: Knopf, 1926. ix–xxix.

Miller, J. Hillis. *Poets of Reality*. Cambridge, MA: Harvard University Press, 1965.

Nagel, James. *Stephen Crane and Literary Impressionism*. University Park: Pennsylvania State University Press, 1980.

Paine, Ralph D. *Roads of Adventure*. Boston: Houghton Mifflin, 1922.

Robertson, Michael. *Stephen Crane, Journalism, and the Making of Modern American Literature*. New York: Columbia University Press, 1997.

Schaefer, Michael. *A Reader's Guide to the Short Fiction of Stephen Crane*. New York: G. K. Hall, 1996.

Sorrentino, Paul. "The Legacy of Thomas Beer in the Study of Stephen Crane and American Literary History." *American Literary Realism* 35 (2003): 187–211.

———. "Stephen Crane's Struggle with Romance in *The Third Violet*." *American Literature* 70 (June 1998): 265–91.

Wertheim, Stanley, and Paul Sorrentino, eds. *The Correspondence of Stephen Crane*. 2 vols. New York: Columbia University Press, 1988.

———. "Thomas Beer: The Clay Feet of Stephen Crane Biography." *American Literary Realism 1870–1910* 22.3 (1990): 2–16.

Wolford, Chester L. *Stephen Crane: A Study of the Short Fiction*. Boston: Twayne, 1989.

11
Kate Chopin

Charlotte Rich

After attending a convention of the Western Association of Writers in Indiana in 1894, Kate Chopin wrote an essay in which she described the works of Midwestern authors such as James Whitcomb Riley as limited by their provincialism, their earnestness, and "a clinging to past and conventional standards.".[1] Fiction, Chopin wrote, should instead represent "human existence in its subtle, complex, true meaning, stripped of the veil with which ethical and conventional standards have draped it." This reflection provides a key to much of Chopin's short fiction, published in several periodicals and newspapers of her day as well as in two collections, *Bayou Folk* (1894) and *A Night in Acadie* (1897), particularly her recurrent depictions of women who deviate, in varying ways, from dominant ideologies of gender in their era. Chopin's short stories, often set in the rich, multicultural contexts of the Creole and Acadian communities in Louisiana, invite analysis on many levels, including their location within the regionalist tradition and their engagement with racial and class issues. However, her canon is particularly notable for its exploration of how women who transgress conventions of female behavior, or at least recognize their restrictions, contend with the society that prescribes such mores. In so doing, Chopin's fiction engages repeatedly with the concept of the New Woman – a newly emancipated, progressive female ideal arising in the 1890s that challenged Victorian notions of the domestic, submissive True Woman.[2] What makes her short fiction distinctive in its treatment of this figure is how her female characters' conflicts with society often arise from acknowledgment of their emotional and erotic needs, which Chopin portrayed in a light that was too candid for many readers. However, in keeping with her own dislike of didacticism, Chopin's fiction does not provide a prescriptive answer to the Woman Question. Instead, reserving judgment of her characters, Chopin depicts various modes of fulfillment for women, both conventional and unconventional, throughout her stories.

Such themes permeate Chopin's entire body of short fiction, from her earliest writings to her final stories.[3] In fact, her earliest creative piece, a fable from her commonplace book written sometime between 1867 and 1870, addresses the issue of self-definition, a theme which reverberated through her career to the infamous novel she published thirty years later, *The Awakening.* "Emancipation. A Life Fable" tells of a beautiful beast born in a cage; though he enjoys a placid life under the "care of an invisible protecting hand" (*Complete Works* 37), one day he sees that the door of his cage stands open. After going repeatedly to the door, he leaps out: "On he rushes, in his mad flight, heedless that he is wounding and tearing his sleek sides – seeing, smelling, touching of all things; even stopping to put his lips to the noxious pool. ... So does he live, seeking, finding, joying, and suffering" (37–8). While the creature in this fable is male, his experiences presage those of many of Chopin's female protagonists in later works; the "awakening" to wider opportunities, the departure from the metaphoric cage, and the willingness to suffer in pursuit of knowledge are important thematic elements in several of her stories. Moreover, Chopin's use of cage symbolism in this tale anticipates a pervasive metaphor in late nineteenth-century literature of the New Woman: the bird that is either caged or allowed to soar free.[4]

Chopin's two earliest published stories, "Wiser Than a God" (1889) and "A Point at Issue!" (1889), explore a recurrent topic of her short fiction, marriage, in contrasting ways that underscore her varying treatments of that institution, especially its impact upon women. The first story deals with the conflict between marriage and a career for a New Woman, while the second explores the possibility of a marital model which provides a new "space" for its partners. In "Wiser Than a God," Paula Von Stolz is a would-be virtuoso pianist who subsists by performing for society parties. She falls in love with George Brainard, a wealthy young man, but when he proposes to her, she explains that she is not interested a society marriage, asking him, " 'Is music anything more to you than the pleasing distraction of an idle moment? Can't you feel that with me, it courses with the blood through my veins?' " (46). In rejecting the role of leisure-class wife in favor of a musical career, Paula anticipates another New Woman artist, opera singer Thea Kronborg in Willa Cather's novel *The Song of the Lark* (1915). George convinces Paula to see him again, but he arrives at her home to learn that she has left for Germany to pursue her studies. Years later, newspapers report that the "renowned pianist, Fräulein Paula Von Stolz, is resting in Leipsic, after an extended and remunerative concert tour" (47). With her is her former music professor, Max Kuntzler, who, also in love with Paula, followed her "with the ever persistent will ... that so often wins in the end" (47). Indicating the constraints of leisure-class marriage for some women, Chopin's story asserts that the only possible partner for her heroine is a man who respects her need to pursue an artistic career.

In "A Point at Issue!" the kind of progressive union that Paula Von Stolz favors is portrayed through the marriage of Charles and Eleanor Faraday, but with consequences that instead suggest its limitations, at least for some. Eleanor has diverged from the typical lives of young women in Plymdale through her intellectual pursuits, and Charles, a professor of math at the local university, finds in her "his ideal woman." Chopin's narrator notes his pleased surprise that she is "possessed of a clear intellect. ... She was that *rara avis*, a logical woman – something which Faraday had not encountered in his life before" (49), invoking popular beliefs about the female mind that underlay criticism of the intellectual activities of the New Woman.[5] Indeed, many arguments against higher education for women arose in the late nineteenth century from assumptions of female intellectual inferiority and the fear that rigorous study would damage women's reproductive capabilities.[6] Despite such cultural deterrents, Charles and Eleanor vow to marry and to live according to a new "companionate" ideal, and they scandalize the community of Plymdale in agreeing that Eleanor should study French in Paris, where her husband will join her each summer.

Meanwhile, Charles befriends two very different women who illustrate Chopin's pattern of juxtaposing progressive and traditional female characters, as Per Seyersted has noted.[7] Margaret Beaton resembles the stereotypical New Woman of popular satire; she is "slightly erratic, owing to a timid leaning in the direction of Woman's Suffrage" (52), and she wears garments that, "while stamping their wearer with the distinction of a quasi-emancipation, defeated the ultimate purpose of their construction by inflicting a personal discomfort that extended beyond the powers of long endurance" (52–3).[8] Likening Margaret to bloomer-wearing feminists of the nineteenth century, the narrator mocks her earnestness in contrast to her prettier sister Kitty, who "[clamored] for no privileges doubtful of attainment and of remote and questionable benefit" (53) and who captures Charles's attention.

Eleanor unhappily suspects her husband of romantic distraction, and after Charles arrives in Paris, she suggests that they return to America, admitting to her jealousy: "'I have found that there are certain things which a woman can't philosophize about, any more than she can about death when it touches that which is near to her'"(58). Charles, pleased, kisses his wife as he thinks, "'I love her none the less for it, but my Nellie is only a woman, after all'" (58). In contrast to the conclusion of "Wiser Than a God," this text thus dismisses the possibility of a "new" kind of marriage emphasizing individuality, and conventional assumptions about gender prevail, at least in the mind of Eleanor's husband, for failing to articulate one's feelings in a logical manner means being "only a woman." However, Chopin does not satirize Eleanor's inability to live in a companionate marriage; rather, this story depicts her as someone for whom that ideal does not lead to contentment. Indeed, "A Point at Issue!" expresses a theme throughout much of Chopin's fiction: that a woman's own sense of what makes her happy is most important, whether it be as an independent artist or intellectual or as a housewife and mother.

Another early story by Chopin contains the more radical implication that marriage is not for all women, an idea taken up in several New Woman novels. Her sole attempt at historical fiction, "The Maid of Saint Phillippe" (1891), has received scant critical attention, perhaps because Chopin thought it an unsuccessful venture.[9] Set in the Missouri territory during the 1760s, the story tells of Marianne Laronce, a buckskin-clad, rifle-toting young woman who is more content hunting in forests than at home caring for her aged father, and who in the course of the story responds to two marriage proposals. She first refuses an offer to move to the new settlement of Saint Louis with fellow colonist Jacques Labrie, saying that she cannot force her father to leave the land where his wife lies buried. Soon after, a French soldier, Captain Vaudry, offers the young woman a luxurious life back in France " '[w]here you shall wear jewels and silks and walk upon soft and velvet carpets' " (122). Marianne refuses, and when Vaudry presses his case, she responds:

> "I will not look into your eyes … with your talk and your looks of love – of love! You have looked it before, and you have spoken it before till the strength would go from my limbs and leave me feeble as a little child. … Go away to your France and to your treacherous kings; they are not for me." (122)

Though the story is set in the eighteenth century, Marianne's response is significant in its critical perspective on ideals of love and marriage in Chopin's own era. In refusing to allow love to weaken her into a "feeble" infant or invalid, Marianne rejects a feminine response to love often portrayed in nineteenth-century sentimental fiction. Instead, Chopin appropriates an archetype for male protagonists in American literature through the conclusion of the story; Marianne resolves to live among the Cherokees, declaring, " 'Hardships may await me, but let it be death rather than bondage' " (122). The bondage that she rejects is not only the incipient political oppression of the English in her region but also the constraints of marriage, and she literally turns away from potential husbands and patriarchal protectors:

> While Vaudry sat dumb with pain and motionless with astonishment; while Jacques was hoping for a message; while the good curé was looking eagerly from his door-step for signs of the girl's approach, Marianne had turned her back upon all of them. With gun across her shoulder she walked up the gentle slope; her brave, strong face turned to the rising sun. (122–3)

In portraying the response of the local priest as well as those of Marianne's suitors in this scene, Chopin suggests how he is not only a surrogate father figure but also an emblem of Catholicism, a religion that Chopin often presented as constricting to women.[10]

Marianne thus turns from the constraints of her culture to the wilderness, though it contains the civilization of Native Americans whom both French and English settlers often saw as "Other." She does so in the manner of Cooper's Natty Bumppo and his literary descendants, such as Melville's Ishmael and Twain's Huck Finn, and Barbara Ewell calls this conclusion a "narrative cliché" (Ewell 81). However, Chopin's conclusion hardly conforms to the pattern that Leslie Fiedler noted throughout American literature in depicting a *woman* leaving society to enter the wilderness. Moreover, Marianne's rejection of Vaudry and of her culture reflects gender ideology in Chopin's own era. In declining to let him adorn her with jewels and live under a "treacherous" patriarchy, she metaphorically eschews another institution: the economic dependence of women in middle-class marriage which Charlotte Perkins Gilman criticized in *Women and Economics* (1898) and which Chopin later explored in *The Awakening*. Even Chopin's Marianne, in a narrative set in the eighteenth century, recognizes the problematic basis of the union that Vaudry describes, and as a questioning of nine-teenth-century notions of marriage, "The Maid of Saint Phillippe" is an early example of the theme to which Chopin would return more explicitly in her most famous text.

Complementing these treatments of the institution of marriage, other stories from the earlier years of Chopin's career explore the subject of divorce. Her interest in this topic extends from her first novel, *At Fault* (1890), through two stories written in 1893 to her English translation in 1894 of Guy de Maupassant's story "A Divorce Case." In that text, a lawyer defends his client's desire to divorce her husband because of the latter's perverted behavior, and a theme emerges that also appears in Chopin's work: the sense that an individual is entitled to divorce if he or she is unhappy in marriage, regardless of religious and social prejudice.[11] Like many works treating the ideals of the New Woman, Chopin's fiction reflects a growing sense at the close of the nineteenth century that the Victorian temple of matrimony was not as ideal and eternal an institution as once thought.

"Madame Célestin's Divorce" (1893) and "In Sabine" (1893) both question the idea of the marriage bond as indissoluble, echoing the New Woman's challenge of that institution in its patriarchal form, but they also exemplify the varied ways in which Chopin treated such controversial issues. In "Madame Célestin's Divorce," a lawyer tactfully urges his charming neighbor to divorce her husband. Célestin goes off for months at a time, forcing her to support the family; worse still, he may abuse her. At first she considers Lawyer Paxton's advice, though she is warned against it by her family, her priest, and even the bishop, as she tells Paxton: "'It would move even you, Judge, to hear how he talk' about that step I want to take. ... How it is the duty of a Catholic to stan' everything till the las' extreme'" (278). The infatuated lawyer daydreams about someday marrying Madame himself, but he soon learns that Célestin has returned and promised to "turn over a new leaf." Madame's "unusually rosy" face that morning (279) may suggest that a satisfying sexual relationship with her husband makes her willing to continue the marriage. Nonetheless, at the small influence of a promise of improvement from her husband, this female character capitulates to the admonitions against divorce from her family, her church, and her society.

Chopin's story "In Sabine" makes a clearer case for the necessity of the right to divorce through the abusive behavior of an alcoholic, Bud Aiken, toward his wife, 'Tite Reine. Grégoire Santien, on a visit to Bud's Sabine parish homestead, senses the husband's cruelty when he notes the once-vivacious girl's frightened air.[12] 'Tite Reine awakens Santien that night with a frantic appeal for help, confessing that Bud abuses her both physically and psychologically. Santien is appalled at her situation, and while Bud is in a drunken stupor, he facilitates the young woman's escape back to Natchitoches. Though 'Tite Reine does not possess stereotypical characteristics of the New Woman, her tale treats an issue that some women of that era brought into public discussion: an individual's expectation of love and respect in marriage and, conversely, the need for a way out of a union that lacks these qualities.

Chopin also introduced in her early stories a common trope of narratives of the New Woman: women with longings for a world beyond their narrow environments.

For example, "The Going Away of Liza" (1891) tells of a young wife who left her husband and rural community after reading novels depicting scenes of urban leisure that made her yearn for a "'higher life'" (112). Like the heroines of novels such as Dreiser's *Sister Carrie*, Chopin's idealistic protagonist is drawn to the opportunities of the American city. However, Liza-Jane's venture apparently took her in the opposite direction of a higher life, for her husband lashes out angrily when an acquaintance implies that his wife has succumbed to sinful ways, and her appearance upon her meek return is telling: "Liza-Jane stood a hunted and hungry thing in the great glow of the firelight. ... Her cheeks were not round or red as they had been. Whatever sin or suffering had swept over her had left its impress upon her plastic being" (114). After momentary hesitation, he accepts his wife again, and the story's conclusion responds conservatively to the New Woman's emancipationist ideals: a woman's desire to expand her boundaries has been destructive, but redemption is possible through a return to married domesticity. This text demonstrates the varied ways in which Chopin's fiction treats such ideals; while some of her stories daringly assert the protagonists' wayward desires and unconventional values, others focus instead on the price that such transgressions may incur.

For example, "Dr. Chevalier's Lie" (1891) offers no redeeming alternative for another young woman whose attempt at independence fails, and the story suggests that the end to which she comes is all too common. A doctor, after hearing a gunshot in the "unsavory quarter" where he keeps his office, goes to the scene of the crime, noting the usual appearance of "groups of tawdry, frightened women bending over the banisters ... not a few shedding womanly tears; with a dead girl stretched somewhere, as this one was" (147). This time, he recognizes the corpse; he remembers receiving hospitality in a cabin during a hunting trip from parents "proud as archangels of their handsome girl, who was too clever to stay in an Arkansas cabin, and who was going away to seek her fortune in the big city" (147). Though the young woman, like Carrie Meeber, had idealistic views of the city, she was likely a victim of the business of seducing female newcomers to secure them for houses of prostitution.[13] The doctor fabricates a story for her parents that she died of a fatal disease. Among his associates, it is whispered that Dr. Chevalier made burial arrangements for a "woman of ill repute," and though society considers cutting him, it does not.

The conclusion's reference to the prurient interest and moralizing of Dr. Chevalier's peers reflects Chopin's own dislike of individuals who would impose moral standards on all. However, the neutral tone of the conclusion characterizes much of her fiction; the narrator does not editorialize upon society's thought of cutting Chevalier, nor whether it was ethical for him to lie to the girl's parents about her death. Such objectivity, especially in treating such controversial material as prostitution, adultery, and venereal disease, made it difficult for Chopin to publish stories like "Dr. Chevalier's Lie," "The Going Away of Liza," and "Mrs. Mobry's Reason," and is likely why she never attempted to place "The Storm," a story of adultery with a similarly objective conclusion.[14] Finally, though "Dr. Chevalier's Lie" does not contain moral comment on prostitution, it offers a realistic picture of what might happen in the nineteenth century to a naïve girl who went to the city in search of greater opportunities. In this sense, the story illuminates the gap, for many nineteenth-century women, between the optimistic ideals of the New Woman and the actual limitations of their circumstances.

Another early story, "Caline" (1892), which later appeared in the collection *A Night in Acadie*, presents a variation on the theme of a young woman longing for greater experiences. One day a rural Acadian girl is fascinated to watch elegant passengers dismounting a nearby train at the news of engine trouble, and one of the men draws Caline's likeness in a sketchbook. She thereafter becomes preoccupied with the grand "city in the south" to which these passengers are traveling, and she finds employment in New Orleans as a maid-of-all-work. She is excited by the colorful city, but after a few weeks, Caline weeps at the realization that "it was not the great city and its crowds of people she had so eagerly sought; but the pleasant-faced boy, who had made her picture that day under the mulberry tree" (248). Here, Caline has not left home in search of the opportunities that Liza-Jane and the girl in "Dr. Chevalier's Lie" sought; rather, she realizes that what she has awakened to is the desire for love.

For a related group of characters from other early stories by Chopin, realization of unfulfilled needs is tied to a newly awakened sexuality, a theme to which she would return repeatedly, most notably with *The Awakening*. One example is "A Shameful Affair" (1891), which tells of a young woman, Mildred Orme, who spends her time "loung[ing] with her Browning and Ibsen" (131) while on vacation at the farm of the Kraummer family. She is physically attracted to a young farmhand who passes by the porch: "His fair hair was disheveled. His shoulders were broad and square and his limbs strong and clean" (131). One day, when she finds him fishing at the river, he kisses her passionately on the mouth and departs, leaving Mildred shocked but wondering, "why was that kiss the most delicious thing she had known in her twenty years of life?" (134–5). She receives a friend's letter telling her that an eccentric acquaintance, Fred Evelyn, is working the soil that summer on the Kraummer farm. When Mildred encounters the "Offender" himself, he apologizes for his behavior, asking forgiveness, and her answer hints at Mildred's own realization: "'Some day – perhaps; when I shall have forgiven myself'" (136). The story exhibits a candor in describing Mildred's sexual awakening – and her acknowledgment of it – that presages Chopin's treatments of female sexuality in such later stories as "The Storm." Moreover, "A Shameless Affair" portrays a character who upholds two qualities associated with the New Woman: intellectual interests and acknowledgment of sexuality.

Another young woman's initiation into sexuality is portrayed in Chopin's story "A Harbinger" (1891), which interrogates Victorian gender standards for sexual love and marriage. An artist falls in love with a model whom he paints one summer, and he fondly recalls Diantha's erotic awakening: "Her violet eyes were baby-eyes – when he first came. When he went away he kissed her, and she turned red and white and trembled. As quick as thought the baby look went out of her eyes and another flashed into them" (145). When the artist returns the next summer, he wonders if she "would quiver red and white again when he called her his sweet own Diantha," but finding her coming out of the church at her wedding, he regretfully realizes that he was only "the harbinger of love" (146). This story, in contrast to the more conservative ideas represented in "The Going Away of Liza," contradicts the Victorian notion that a "proper" young woman experienced the sexual dimension of love only in marriage. Here, Diantha has an affair, or at least a flirtation that awakens her capacity for physical desire, but goes on to marry another man. This story thus presents a more realistic picture of female sensuality than was typical of the literature of Chopin's day.

Other stories from Chopin's earlier career also treat the theme of a woman's acknowledgment of her sexuality. In "A Respectable Woman" (1894), Mrs. Baroda is bewildered by her erotic response to her husband's friend, Gouvernail. She is intrigued by their houseguest's courteous, slightly aloof air, and one night, as Gouvernail joins her and talks of his life, she is clearly distracted:

> She was not thinking of his words, only drinking in the tones of his voice. She wanted to ... touch him with the sensitive tips of her fingers upon the face or lips. She wanted to draw close to him and whisper against his cheek – she did not care what – as she might have done if she had not been a respectable woman. (335)

She is tempted to tell her husband about this interlude, but decides that "there are some battles in life which a human being must fight alone" (336). Mrs. Baroda leaves the house and returns after Gouvernail has left, but several months later she proposes that he visit again. When her husband congratulates her on overcoming her dislike, she responds "laughingly, after pressing a long, tender kiss upon his lips, 'I have overcome everything! you will see'" (336). With Chopin's characteristic ambiguity, whether what Mrs. Baroda has "overcome" is merely her previous dislike of Gouvernail or an ethical inhibition about adultery is unclear. Even if the former interpretation is correct, the fact that she internally acknowledged her attraction to a man other than her husband reflects the theme of sexual assertion in many of Chopin's works that challenge conventional ideals of nineteenth-century womanhood.

The importance of erotic satisfaction for a woman is also central to one of Chopin's stories treating the color line, "La Belle Zoraïde" (1893). In the story, a black servant, Manna-Loulou, tells Madame Delisle the tale of Zoraïde, a light-skinned lady's maid who refused to marry the mulatto manservant whom her mistress, Madame Delarivière, had selected for her. Zoraïde was in love with Mezor, a dark-skinned field laborer, and when Madame refused to allow her to marry him, Zoraïde pointed out her hypocrisy: "'Doctor Langlé gives me his slave to marry, but he would not give me his son. Then, since I am not white, let me have from out of my own race the one whom my heart has chosen'" (305). Though the couple were forbidden to meet, Zoraïde became pregnant, and Madame had Mezor sold into another state and took away the infant after the delivery, telling her that the child had perished. When Zoraïde's grief turned into insanity, Madame brought Zoraïde's little "griffe" girl back from her plantation, but the slave mother rejected her child. Though Manna-Loulou's nightmarish story inspires some pity in her young mistress, Madame Delisle's sympathy is limited to the child and is backhanded at that: "'Ah, the poor little one, Man Loulou, the poor little one! better she had died!'" (307).

While this story is not about the New Woman of the 1890s, the experience of Zoraïde has metaphoric significance for other women of her century. Women's rights activists in the nineteenth century often invoked analogies between women and African Americans as oppressed groups. Manna-Loulou, a slave herself, tells a subversively cautionary tale against a particular evil of slavery, lack of choice in marriage, which brings to mind a more sinister counterpart: lack of any choice, for many female slaves, over how their bodies were used sexually. This story emphasizes the importance of such romantic and sexual agency and, although the circumstances of female slaves were certainly the most unjust for women in the nineteenth century, this issue extends to the lot of all women whose desires were thwarted by social deterrents. While the story also explores the importance of the maternal bond, "La Belle Zoraïde" is perhaps Chopin's grimmest treatment of the consequences of a woman's being denied choice in romantic fulfillment.

Though Chopin's fiction reveals a preoccupation with themes of female agency and independence that were the touchstones of the New Woman, her work does not present progressive or activist women solely as positive emblems of social change, as shown in her satirical description of Margaret Beaton in "A Point at Issue!" In two other early stories, Chopin also presents a critical view of women of her day who organized not only for their own rights but to improve the world. Georgie McEnders, the protagonist of "Miss McEnders" (1892), is a wealthy young woman devoted to social improvement; her schedule is typical of the reform-minded New Woman: "Three-thirty – read paper before Woman's Ref. Club. Four-thirty … Join committee of ladies to investigate moral condition of St. Louis factory girls" (204). She visits the home of Mademoiselle Salambre, the seamstress for her bridal trousseau, because she has heard whispers concerning the woman's character. Her suspicions are confirmed when she sees that the woman has a child with her whom she protests, unconvincingly, belongs to a neighbor. When Georgie self-righteously asks "Mademoiselle" why she calls herself so, the latter's reply suggests the realities of being a "fallen woman": "'For the reason that it is more easy to obtain employment. For reasons that you would not understand. … Life is not all *couleur de rose*, Mees McEndairs'" (206). Georgie takes her business away, but Mlle. Salambre the next day confronts her, suggesting that she go out and ask passersby how her father made his money, and adding that her fiancé "'is not fit to be the husband of a self-respecting bar-maid'" (209). Georgie investigates and learns of her father's unethical business dealings, while she realizes that her husband-to-be is equally capable of indiscretions of a sexual nature.

Miss McEnders has had an awakening very different from those of Mildred Orme and Mrs. Baroda, but an awakening nonetheless – in this case, to the presence of sin where she least expected to find it and the consequent impossibility of making moral judgments about others' lives. This story illustrates a common characteristic of Chopin's short fiction: objective narrative depiction of individual moral choices, with critical treatment reserved only for those who would judge others. As far as the New

Woman is concerned, Chopin's story portrays one version of this figure – those who wished to achieve public influence through social reform work – but only to show how this reform-minded New Woman must "clean up" at home first to avoid hypocrisy. Moreover, "Miss McEnders" dramatizes the gap between middle-class women who worked to improve society and other women who worked to support themselves, facing circumstances that the former group might not appreciate.

Chopin's story "Loka" (1892) contains a more light-hearted but equally pointed satire on lady philanthropists. Loka, a half-breed Choctaw girl from an abusive home, has been fired from her job at a local saloon, and the Band of United Endeavor meets to decide her fate. The girl is taken to the meeting and inspected by the Band's condescending members: "The minister's wife reckoned she might be sixteen. The judge's wife thought that it made no difference. The doctor's wife suggested that the girl have a bath and change before she be handled, even in discussion" (212). The ladies find Loka a post as help in a respectable household where they hope she will learn responsibility and have "good moral training beside" (213). However, rather than the Band's endeavors, it is the influence of the Padues' affectionate baby that causes the Indian girl at the conclusion to withstand the urge to run away to her old ways.

While these two stories suggest the susceptibility of social reform–minded New Women to hypocrisy or prejudice, much of the fiction Chopin published throughout the mid-1890s tends toward her characteristic objectivity in portraying varieties of female experience. Several stories continue Chopin's pattern of depicting varied means of fulfillment for women without asserting the superiority of any one choice, with such contrasting possibilities presented by two characters within one story or even within one character. One example is "Lilacs" (1894), which concerns Adrienne Farival, an opera singer and career-oriented New Woman who returns from Paris each spring to visit the convent school she attended as a girl. The nuns look forward to her visit, especially one named Sister Agathe. However, this year the Mother Superior refuses to allow Adrienne to visit, and Sister Agathe weeps as she watches the stunned woman walk away from the convent. The story implies that Adrienne, a successful artist, has a licentious lifestyle that perhaps prompts her need to return periodically to her religious roots; a glimpse of her life in Europe reveals Adrienne discussing a male admirer with her maid while wearing negligée and "reclining indolently in the depths of a luxurious armchair" (361) and calling for liquor and cigarettes when she invites in her suitor. In this context, she might be seen as one of the bohemian New Women of the decadent 1890s.

It is this lifestyle that prompts the Mother Superior to bar Adrienne from the convent, but Chopin's narrator judges neither the life of Adrienne nor that of Sister Agathe in presenting their incompatibility. Though the routines of convent life did not interest Chopin,[15] her close childhood friend Kitty Garesché chose this vocation, and it has an appeal that speaks to Adrienne, despite her worldly sophistication.[16] Moreover, though Sister Agathe is unhappy at the loss of Adrienne's visits, it is not necessarily because they have awakened her to pleasures of the secular world; indeed, what most pleases her during Adrienne's visits is the latter's resumption of convent-school ways. However, Chopin treats critically Sister Agathe's repression of her feelings at the conclusion of the work, implying that ultimately, both women's lives lack balance.

This contrast between the spiritual and the sensual in the life choices that women make is also the focus of a tale from 1895, "Two Portraits," or "The Nun and the Wanton," which Chopin intended to include in a final story collection, *A Vocation and a Voice*, that was accepted but never published by Herbert S. Stone and Company.[17] In this work, Chopin describes two different destinies for a young woman, Alberta, one worldly and the other religious. Alberta the wanton has a body "too beautiful to be beaten – it was made for love"; she "gives her love only when and where she chooses" and "does not know shame or reserve" (463). On the other hand, Alberta the nun dedicated her life to religion at "the age when with other women the languor of love creeps into the veins and dreams begin" (464). Though she is the most saintly woman in the convent, her experiences are described in sensual terms; during meditation she feels an "oblivious ecstasy" from which she must be roused. In contrast to "Lilacs," this story implies that the nun has a happier life than the wanton; while the sensual Alberta contemplates suicide and carries a knife as "she is apt to be vixenish" (363), the spiritual Alberta is awash in celestial love, filled with rapture at visions of her Savior. However, like "Lilacs," this story suggests that the extremes of the two women's lives might be mediated to attain happiness.

In a variation on this theme, Chopin's widely anthologized story "Athénaïse" (1895) presents alternative possibilities for satisfaction in a woman's life through the growth of one character. As the story opens, Athénaïse has left her husband and returned to her family, declaring that "'I can't stan' to live with a man ... his coats an' pantaloons hanging in my room; his ugly bare feet – washing them in my tub, befo' my very eyes, ugh!'" (431).[18] Cazeau retrieves her, but Athénaïse escapes again, this time to New Orleans. Settling in a boarding house, she seeks employment and befriends fellow boarder Gouvernail, the journalist who also appears in "A Respectable Woman" and *The Awakening*. She becomes dependent on the courteous man for company, and one evening, when he finds her distraught and homesick, he comforts her in a brotherly manner.

A few days later, Athénaïse learns that she is pregnant with Cazeau's child, and this discovery stimulates a radical change in her, described in sensual terms: "Her whole being was steeped in a wave of ecstasy. When she ... looked at herself in the mirror, a face met hers which she seemed to see for the first time, so transfigured was it with wonder and rapture" (451). Moreover, Athénaïse's view of Cazeau has dramatically changed: "She half whispered his name, and the sound of it brought red blotches into her cheeks. ... Her whole passionate nature was aroused as if by a miracle" (451). Upon her return home to Cazeau, "As he clasped her in his arms, he felt the yielding of her whole body against him. He felt her lips for the first time respond to the passion of his own" (454). Despite this surprisingly erotic description of the couple's reunion, the essentially orthodox message of the story – that Athénaïse, after a brief attempt at "freedom," finds profound satisfaction in motherhood, a conventional nineteenth-century ideal of female fulfillment – is likely what enabled Chopin to publish this story in the *Atlantic Monthly* in 1896 and as part of her collection *A Night in Acadie*.

As Per Seyersted has suggested, Chopin presents ambiguously this seemingly traditional means of Athénaïse's finding happiness. Asserting that her initial "'sense of hopelessness, of the futility of rebellion against a social and sacred institution' is supported by the story's symbolism," he cites Cazeau's remembrance of capturing an escaped slave as metaphoric of her fate (*Kate Chopin* 113–14). However, the story is also ambiguous in light of the ideals of New Womanhood; the conclusion indicates that marital happiness is possible, but Athénaïse's discovery of it is presented both conventionally *and* unconventionally for Chopin's time. Athénaïse may indeed anticipate satisfaction in the selfless role of a mother, but the conclusion suggests that she will also find happiness through her newly acknowledged sexuality, a part of human nature that Chopin's work often presents as an essential influence on the actions of individuals.

In contrast, other stories from the middle phase of Chopin's career present a more pessimistic view of the possibility of marital happiness, particularly when sexual needs remain unfulfilled. Again, the narratorial tone varies throughout Chopin's treatments of this theme; for example, "The Kiss" (1894) describes with cynical humor a woman's desire to wed for money while having a lover for sexual fulfillment. Nathalie, after her marriage to a wealthy but unattractive man, expects another suitor to treat her as seductively as before, but he refuses, pointing out that she cannot have it both ways. The narrator sardonically comments, "Well, she had Brantain and his million left. A person can't have everything in this world, and it was a little unreasonable of her to expect it" (381). The ending of the story, however, is sobering; Nathalie will have luxury, but not marital happiness.

The darker story "Her Letters" (1894) describes the consequences when another woman carries out her adulterous intentions, with the implication that such defiance of the marriage bond causes tragedy. In this story, a wife has kept her lover's letters hidden in her writing-desk. Knowing she is fatally ill, she cannot bring herself to burn them; instead, she leaves a note stipulating that, if the letters are found, they be destroyed unread. After her death, her husband finds the letters, and though tempted to read them, he throws them in the river. However, he becomes preoccupied with their import, and he gradually drives himself insane searching for evidence of her infidelity. Finally, the man's misery leads him to drown himself in the same river, his mind filled with impressions that anticipate the final scene of *The Awakening*: "Only the river knew. … it told him nothing, but it promised all. He could hear it promising him with caressing voice, peace and sweet repose. He could hear the sweep, the song of the water inviting him" (405). As in Chopin's novel, the water is anthropomorphized into a seductive lover which may provide a sensuous escape from the husband's unhappy reality.

Such later works by Chopin as "The Storm" and *The Awakening* treat the fact of adultery more objectively, but what William Dean Howells referred to only as "guilty love" is shown in "Her Letters" to hurt those that it betrays, as well as those that commit it. However, Emily Toth notes that Chopin "pondered moral questions in her fiction," and that "what was considered 'moral' for a woman was often reduced simply to physical 'chastity' – a problem in the story 'Her Letters' " (*Kate Chopin* 252). This story may treat adultery in a more critical light than does "The Storm," but it also raises another issue: the cultural deterrents to divorce or separation, particularly for women, that could lead to adultery. Indeed, Chopin's works often raise questions of morality, but they do not provide definitive answers to them.

Two widely anthologized stories from the middle phase of Chopin's career, "The Story of an Hour" (1894) and "A Pair of Silk Stockings" (1897), also portray women who acknowledge needs of the self, though these are not erotic needs. However, in doing so, these women defy the cultural expectation of selflessness for Victorian womanhood, and both of their stories end pessimistically. "The Story of an Hour" depicts Louise Mallard's recognition of her desire for freedom after learning that her husband has died in a train wreck. She is so delighted at the prospect of "spring days, summer days, and all sorts of days that would be her own" (354) that when Mr. Mallard arrives home alive, she dies of shock. That shock is more likely at the sudden loss of this opportunity for freedom than at the sudden appearance of her husband. Chopin's narrative stance illuminates the theme of this story, with a famously ambiguous final comment: "When the doctors came they said she had died of heart disease – of joy that kills" (354). While the narrator may echo in earnest the doctors' words to suggest that a woman would be so happy at her husband's return that she would die of shock, thus complying with Victorian views of women as defined by their relation to husband or family, the narrator more likely ironically implies that the woman's joy sprang from her newfound freedom, and that what killed her was the destruction of that joy through her husband's reappearance.

On the other hand, in "A Pair of Silk Stockings," a young widow, Mrs. Sommers, impulsively spends on herself the fifteen dollars she had allotted for her children's needs, purchasing silk stockings, new shoes, gloves, magazines, a restaurant lunch, and theatre tickets. As she rides home after her one day of indulgence, the woman's pale face reveals the futile longing "that the cable car would never stop anywhere, but go on and on with her forever" (504). Neither Mrs. Sommers nor Mrs. Mallard possesses stereotypical characteristics of the New Woman; they do not smoke cigarettes, ride bicycles, or have "advanced ideas." However, their inner conflicts resemble those that many real and fictional New Women encountered; they must mediate the gap between cultural expectations of selfless absorption in husband and children and the fulfillment of their own desires.

Continuing to reflect this theme, Chopin's stories from the late 1890s introduce a triad of women who defy social rules of varying gravity. The consequences of these transgressions also vary, underscoring the lack of moral agenda in Chopin's treatment of controversial topics. In "An Egyptian Cigarette" (1897), the narrator's rebellion is merely her smoking, an "unladylike" habit Chopin herself enjoyed and refused to give up in response to censorious readers.[19] The protagonist, while attending a meeting of a women's club, receives some cigarettes from a male friend who has visited Cairo. The box is covered with "glazed, yellow paper" (570), associating the cigarettes with the decadence of yellow-backed novels and the fin-de-siècle publication *The Yellow Book*, to which Chopin subscribed. She goes into her friend's smoking-room to sample a cigarette, glad to escape the "incessant chatter" of her female peers (571). The woman's preference for smoking in a masculine space over the club meeting suggests her unconventionality, and her attitude corresponds to Chopin's experience as a brief member of Charlotte Eliot's prestigious Wednesday Club in St. Louis.[20]

Inhaling the smoke, the speaker begins to hallucinate that she is in a desert, having collapsed with exhaustion and despair after following a neglectful lover. She drags herself to a river, and as she sinks beneath the water her senses are filled with rich impressions: "Oh! The sweet rapture of rest! There is music in the Temple. And here is fruit to taste. ... The moon shines and the breeze is soft" (572). She awakens from her trance feeling that she has "tasted the depths of human despair" (572), and though she briefly wonders whether the other cigarettes might hold pleasant visions, she destroys the remainder, telling her friend that she is "'a little the worse for a dream'" (573). For all her wish to escape the mundanity of the club meeting, the protagonist's desire to experience a different world has not brought pleasure. Indeed, the story conservatively treats her "unwomanly" experimentation, implying that the cigarettes contain more than just tobacco.[21] Her decadent adventure with the cigarette has allowed the woman to glimpse only misery, not euphoria.

In contrast, in "The Storm" (1898), the consequences of another woman's defiance of societal convention are paradoxically less serious. This story follows such works as "A Shameless Affair," "A Harbinger," and "A Respectable Woman" in its treatment of erotic initiation and the controversial ideal of sexual freedom often associated with New Women. However, "The Storm" is bolder in its depiction of such matters than the earlier tales. Chopin also treated the topic of sexual awakening in a story written between those works and "The Storm," "A Vocation and a Voice" (1896), although that narrative describes a young man who is initiated by a gypsy girl, Suzima, and who, after becoming a priest, flees the monastery to rejoin her. A sensual young woman who neither feels shame over nor suffers for her sexual acts, Suzima is an antecedent for Calixta in "The Storm."

Calixta, in contrast to her incarnation as a young coquette in the story's prequel, "At the 'Cadian Ball" (1892), is now a wife and mother, but her seductive ways have not disappeared, as her former suitor Alcée Laballière finds when he takes refuge in her home during a storm while her family is away. She staggers into his arms during the thunder, and "as she glanced up at him the fear in her liquid blue eyes had given place to a drowsy gleam that unconsciously betrayed a sensuous desire" (594). After the explicitly described scene of their adultery, the two part, Calixta laughing as she watches him ride away. When her husband and son return, she is pleased to see them. Alcée writes to his wife encouraging her to remain on vacation, and she is also pleased, for "devoted as she was to her husband, their intimate conjugal life was something which she was more than willing to forego for a while" (596). Thus, everyone is happy at the end of the story, unlike the tragedies wrought by fictional adulteresses such as Anna Karenina and Emma Bovary, and, as with several stories by Chopin, the tale unapologetically acknowledges female sexuality, in contrast to dominant gender ideologies of her day. Moreover, this tale excludes narratorial comment on Calixta's act, again demonstrating Chopin's tendency toward objectivity about moral issues in her fiction.

Chopin's late story "Charlie" (1900) contains one of the most independent of Chopin's protagonists, a young woman who violates several conventions of nineteenth-century Southern womanhood. Charlotte Laborde, or Charlie, first appears in the story after having been out riding her horse, sporting cropped hair and "a costume of her own devising ... which she called her 'trouserlets'" (639). Like the female protagonist in an earlier story entitled "The Unexpected" (1895), Charlie also rides a bicycle, an emblem of the New Woman's liberation. Furthermore, she enjoys the unladylike hobby of shooting at targets, but after accidentally grazing the arm of a visitor to the Laborde plantation, she agrees to enter a convent school and learn more feminine ways. Working to "transform herself from a hoyden to a fascinating young lady" (658), she is near her goal when she receives news that her father has been injured. She rushes home and, finding that his arm must be amputated, stays on to manage the plantation admirably. When a young friend, Gus Bradley, declares his love for her, she confesses her mutual feelings, but also asserts her desire to keep working. As with Paula Von Stolz in "Wiser Than a God," it appears that Charlie will only enter into a "new" or companionate marriage that allows her to have non-domestic pursuits.

Despite her many fictional portraits of women like Charlie Laborde who defy convention, Chopin's stories also contain characters who adhere to nineteenth-century codes of feminine behavior, as well as to Creole and Catholic mores, suggesting that the New Woman's progressive or radical ideas do not suit all women. For example, in "A Lady of Bayou St. John" (1893), the protagonist considers entering into an adulterous relationship while her husband is away in the Civil War. However, she receives news of her husband's death, and when her suitor comes after an appropriate interval to ask for her hand, she refuses him. Madame Delisle has dedicated her life to her dead husband, explaining that he "'has never been so living to me as he is now'" (301), and she spends the rest of her life worshiping his memory as a proper Catholic widow. The conclusion of Chopin's story "Regret" (1894) also adheres to dominant Victorian notions of female identity in valorizing the maternal impulse. Aurélie is a middle-aged woman who once refused marriage and "had not yet lived to regret it" (375). However, when she cares for a neighbor's children for two weeks, her maternal instinct blossoms as she grows to love them. The conclusion contains perhaps the most poignant scene in Chopin's stories: when Aurélie is alone after the children leave, she weeps at the opportunity for motherhood she once declined.

Similarly, two of Chopin's tales focus on women as objects of the male gaze and, while their treatment of this conception is ironic, they suggest the women's complicity with this dominant ideal in one degree or another. In "A Mental Suggestion" (1896), the intellectual Pauline Edmonds, who wears eyeglasses and is "possessed of an investigating turn of mind," appears to a male character, Faverham, as "the type of woman that [he] detested. Her mental poise was a rebuke to him; there was constant rebuff in her lack of the coquettish, the captivating, the feminine" (548). However, during an experiment with hypnosis, he becomes attracted to Pauline, and she becomes a pretty woman, from another male character's perspective, after she falls in love with and marries Faverham: "There was color in her face whose contour was softened and embellished by a particularly happy arrangement of her brown hair. The pince-nez which she had substituted for the rather formidable spectacles ... lent it a piquancy that was very attractive" (554). Pauline is thus "feminized" when she replaces her intellectual enthusiasm with a more conventional object of affection, though Chopin qualifies this view by filtering it through a male perspective. The resulting dramatic irony calls attention to such assumptions and, as with stories such as "The Story of an Hour," Chopin utilizes point of view to illuminate the themes of the story. The protagonist of Chopin's story "Suzette" (1897) also reifies the cultural idealization of women in the nineteenth century as passive objects to be admired for their beauty, perceiving herself merely as an object of the male gaze. Hearing that a suitor has drowned, Suzette is barely disturbed by this news as she anticipates being seen by a handsome cattle-driver who often passes her window. Unfortunately, he does not notice her, and the narrator dryly notes Suzette's distress: "He had not looked at her! He had not thought of her! He would be gone three weeks – three eternities! and every hour freighted with the one bitter remembrance of his indifference!" (559). The tone of this story is clearly critical of Suzette, but perhaps also of the culture that influences her attitude.

Moreover, besides these examples of more conventional female characters in Chopin's fiction, and aside from her sympathetic portrayal of Charlie Laborde, Chopin depicts few examples of women working outside the home, and these women often do so out of financial need or to provide for others rather than for their own satisfaction. For example, in Chopin's final story, "The Impossible Miss Meadows" (1903), a poor young woman is invited to visit a wealthy family, the Hyleighs. Miss Meadows's confession to Evadne Hyleigh that " 'a nursery governess is about all I'm equal to, ma'm. ... Indeed me pride's all gone' " (688) reveals her unhappiness and shame at being alone in the world, forced to make her own way. Similarly, the protagonist of Chopin's late story "Polly" (1902) works as a bookkeeper but willingly resigns her position after her marriage. When she receives a bequest from a relative with the injunction to use the money rather than save it, Polly buys household items for her parents, adhering to the feminine code of selfless dedication to family. Likewise, Elizabeth Stock is the town postmistress in "Elizabeth Stock's One Story" (1898), but she uses her earnings to provide schooling for her sister's children. In fact, as she reveals in the course of the "one story" she ever wrote, Elizabeth would have liked to pursue a more personally satisfying career as a writer. These examples of characters who adhere to Victorian ideas of femininity rather than to the progressive ideals of the New Woman, particularly in their selflessness, illustrate the tendency of Chopin's fiction not to suggest a single model of fulfillment for women.

As the wide variety of stories discussed above indicates, Chopin's short fiction that treats the theme of female defiance of social codes ranges broadly in tone. But as the long-debated, ambiguous conclusion of *The Awakening* also demonstrates, she did not provide a clear solution to the widely debated Woman Question of her day. In fact, Chopin did not see lasting value in "social problem" literature concerning specific contemporary issues; in an 1894 review of Hamlin Garland's literary manifesto *Crumbling Idols*, which praised authors such as Henrik Ibsen, she wrote:

> Human impulses do not change and can not so long as men and women continue to stand in the relation to one another which they have occupied since our knowledge of their existence began. It is why Aeschylus is true, and Shakespeare is true to-day, and why Ibsen will not be true in some remote to-morrow, however forcible and representative he may be for the hour, because he takes for his themes social problems which by their very nature are mutable. (693)

Chopin's short fiction does reflect her cultural moment of the 1890s in that it frequently embodies the historical and literary phenomenon of the New Woman, and, indeed, her work is distinctive within that genre for its candid acknowledgment of female sexuality. However, Chopin resists turning her tales of women in conflict with their society's gender expectations into "social problem" literature with a specific agenda. Treating her female characters with restrained objectivity, and avoiding judgment of their choices in keeping with her dislike of didacticism or polemic, she insists above all else upon the importance of seeking an authentic self, be that through conventional or controversial means.

NOTES

1 "The Western Association of Writers," originally published in *Critic* (July 7, 1894); *The Complete Works of Kate Chopin*, ed. Per Seyersted (Baton Rouge: Louisiana State University Press, 1969, rpt. 1993), 691. Page references to Chopin's works hereafter cite this edition and appear in the text.

2 Defined by her commitment to various types of independence, the stereotypical New Woman was college educated and believed in a woman's right to work in traditionally masculine professions; in the United States, in particular, she often sought a public role in occupations that would help to "improve society." The New Woman championed women's right to the vote, to economic autonomy, and to the right to prioritize intellectual or artistic aspirations over marriage and domestic concerns. She was often an advocate of "rational dress" and fond of exercise. If the New Woman chose to marry, she was associated with the concept of companionate marriage, in which husband and wife regarded each other with equal respect and shared responsibilities, while after the turn of the century she was associated with greater sexual freedom. For further discussion of the New Woman phenomenon in literature, see Ardis, *New Women, New Novels*; Fernando, *"New Women" in the Late Victorian Novel*; Cunningham, *The New Woman and the Victorian Novel*; Ledger, *The New Woman*; Smith-Rosenberg, *Disorderly Conduct*; and Tichi, "Women Writers and the New Woman."

3 Contrary to popular myth, Chopin continued writing after the censure of *The Awakening*;

see Thomas, "'What Are the Prospects for the Book?'" 36–57, on how Chopin's final years were mythologized by the literary marketplace of her day and how such misrepresentations were perpetuated in twentieth-century scholarship.

4 Besides *The Awakening*, other American novels that employ imagery of the New Woman as a bird include Elizabeth Stuart Phelps's *The Story of Avis* (1878), Ellen Glasgow's *The Wheel of Life* (1906), and Willa Cather's *The Song of the Lark* (1915).

5 See "Women's Education: 'Maddest Folly Going,'" in Marks, *Bicycles, Bangs and Bloomers*, 90–116, on satirical arguments against higher education for women, some of which proceeded from assertions of female intellectual inferiority (102–3).

6 See Woloch, *Women and the American Experience*, on the influence of Edward Clarke's book *Sex in Education* (1873), which asserted that "mental activity drew blood from the nervous system and reproductive organs. Higher education, therefore, could cause mental collapse, physical incapacity, infertility, and early death" (278).

7 Seyersted, in *Kate Chopin*, states that the theory that Chopin loved her husband yet also felt "emancipationist urges" would explain why her fiction "frequently opposes a woman who stays home and one who strikes out, and why she advocates no 'best way' to live for a female" (173).

8 See Marks, *Bicycles, Bangs, and Bloomers*, for satirical depictions of the New Woman in American and British cartoons, poetry, and editorials of the 1890s.

9 Several earlier critics dismiss the story; Seyersted concurs with Daniel Rankin's assessment of the story in 1932: "Only in 'The Maid of Saint Phillippe' … did she turn to an historic event, and the result was disastrous" (*Kate Chopin* 82). In book-length studies of Chopin, both Peggy Skaggs (57) and Barbara Ewell (80) find the story a weak anomaly among her work. However, Emily Toth has recently asserted its significance as Chopin's reflection on the life of her great-great-grandmother in "Kate Chopin Thinks Back Through Her Mothers."

10 Chopin deals with the effects of Catholicism on women not only in *The Awakening* and her first novel, *At Fault*, but also in stories including "Madame Célestin's Divorce" (1893), "A Lady of Bayou St. John" (1893), "A Sentimental Soul" (1894), and "Two Portraits" (1895).

11 Chopin herself was known to oppose religious and social prejudice against divorce; see Toth, *Kate Chopin* 266.

12 Chopin's naming the parish "Sabine" has historical resonance for the brutality that 'Tite Reine suffers. The Sabines inhabited a region of Italy subjugated by the Romans around 290 BCE; an event often depicted in classical art is the rape of the Sabine women, when Romulus, who needed wives for his soldiers, lured the men away and allowed the soldiers to have their way with the women.

13 See Schneider and Schneider, *American Women in the Progressive Era*, 137–8, for discussion of this phenomenon.

14 Chopin's story "Mrs. Mobry's Reason" (1891) describes how young love is destroyed by hereditary insanity apparently caused by inherited syphilis, as Emily Toth notes in *Kate Chopin* (198–9). Toth also observes that "The Going Away of Liza" was rejected twelve times before it was accepted for publication (200).

15 Chopin comments in an entry from May 22, 1894, of a diary, reprinted in *A Kate Chopin Miscellany*, ed. Seyersted and Toth, that when asked by a friend, "'Would you not give anything to have [a nun's] vocation and happy life,'" she responded, "'I would rather be that dog,'" pointing to one nearby (92).

16 In "The Search for Self in Kate Chopin's Fiction" Patricia Hopkins Lattin similarly notes that Adrienne has two identities, "the sophisticated, jaded woman of the world and the ascetic identity she assumes two weeks of the year when she goes to the convent" (228), contending that she is seeking a "rebirth" in each visit.

17 See Toth, *Kate Chopin* 373.

18 In "Kate Chopin Thinks Back Through Her Mothers" Toth theorizes that this story is Chopin's meditation on the life of her maternal grandmother, Mary Athenaïse Charleville Faris, who likewise "had gone into marriage naively and been wounded by it" (18).

19	See Chopin's comments in a late essay, "On Certain Brisk, Bright Days" (1899): "'Do you smoke cigarettes?' is a question which I consider impertinent, and I think most women will agree with me. Suppose I do smoke cigarettes? Am I going to tell it out in meeting? Suppose I don't smoke cigarettes. Am I going to admit such a reflection upon my artistic integrity, and thereby bring upon myself the contempt of the guild?" (723).

20	Toth notes that Chopin joined the Wednesday Club as a charter member in December 1890, but the club became increasingly regimented, and by the end of 1892, Chopin "had decided to be a loner, not a clubwoman"

(*Kate Chopin* 207). Toth cites possible reasons for Chopin's departure: preference not to join a specific section; dislike of the emphasis on structure, organization, and committees; or dislike of the emphasis on social uplift (209).

21	The use of opium was associated with the 1890s Decadent movement in the arts, as were such New Woman authors as Anglo-Irish author George Egerton, as Elaine Showalter notes in her introduction to *Daughters of Decadence* (x). Showalter asserts that Chopin's story, which she includes in this anthology, "describes an erotic hallucination brought on by smoking a yellow opium cigarette" (xi).

References and Further Reading

Ardis, Ann. *New Women, New Novels: Feminism and Early Modernism*. New Brunswick, NJ: Rutgers University Press, 1990.

Chopin, Kate. *The Complete Works of Kate Chopin*. Ed. Per Seyersted. Baton Rouge: Louisiana State University Press, 1969, rpt. 1993.

Cunningham, Gail. *The New Woman and the Victorian Novel*. New York: Harper & Row, 1978.

Ewell, Barbara. *Kate Chopin*. New York: Ungar, 1986.

Fernando, Lloyd. *"New Women" in the Late Victorian Novel*. University Park: Pennsylvania State University Press, 1977.

Lattin, Patricia Hopkins. "The Search for Self in Kate Chopin's Fiction: Simple Versus Complex Fiction." *Southern Studies* 21 (Summer 1982): 222–35.

Ledger, Sally. *The New Woman: Fiction and Feminism at the Fin de Siècle*. Manchester: Manchester University Press, 1997.

Marks, Patricia. *Bicycles, Bangs and Bloomers: The New Woman in the Popular Press*. Lexington: University Press of Kentucky, 1990.

Schneider, Dorothy, and Carl J. Schneider. *American Women in the Progressive Era, 1900–1920*. New York: Facts on File, 1993.

Seyersted, Per. *Kate Chopin: A Critical Biography*. Baton Rouge: Louisiana State University Press, 1969.

Seyersted, Per, and Emily Toth, eds. *A Kate Chopin Miscellany*. Natchitoches, LA: Northwestern State University Press, 1979.

Showalter, Elaine. "Introduction." *Daughters of Decadence: Women Writers of the Fin-de-Siècle*. New Brunswick, NJ: Rutgers University Press, 1993.

Skaggs, Peggy. *Kate Chopin*. New York: Twayne, 1985.

Smith-Rosenberg, Carroll. *Disorderly Conduct: Visions of Gender in Victorian America*. New York: Knopf, 1985.

Thomas, Heather Kirk. "'What are the Prospects for the Book?' Rewriting a Woman's Life." *Kate Chopin Reconsidered: Beyond the Bayou*. Eds. Lynda S. Boren and Sara deSaussure Davis. Baton Rouge: Louisiana State University Press, 1992. 36–57.

Tichi, Cecelia. "Women Writers and the New Woman." *Columbia Literary History of the United States*. Gen. Ed. Emory Elliott. New York: Columbia University Press, 1987. 589–606.

Toth, Emily. *Kate Chopin: A Life of the Author of The Awakening*. New York: William Morrow, 1990.

———. "Kate Chopin Thinks Back Through Her Mothers: Three Stories by Chopin." *Kate Chopin Reconsidered: Beyond the Bayou*. Eds. Lynda S. Boren and Sara deSaussure Davis. Baton Rouge: Louisiana State University Press, 1992. 15–25.

Woloch, Nancy. *Women and the American Experience*. New York: Knopf, 1984.

12

Frank Norris and Jack London

Jeanne Campbell Reesman

Frank Norris (1870–1902) and Jack London (1876–1916) were leading proponents of "naturalism," a French-influenced new school of American fiction at the beginning of the twentieth century, along with their contemporaries Stephen Crane and Theodore Dreiser. American literary naturalism flourished between the 1890s and the 1920s. As a term in philosophy, art criticism, and literary criticism, "naturalism" has a long history, but its meaning is still in debate. Is naturalism, as Norris believed, a form of romanticism? (Norris, "A Plea" 75). Or is naturalism merely a branch of realism – a "heightened" realism "infused with pessimistic determinism," as Donald Pizer describes it? (*Realism and Naturalism* 11). In which competing and conflicting ways does naturalism refer to nature? In its emphasis upon power, survival, and biology, does it constitute materialistic determinism, as London thought? How does its use of sensationalism reflect its documentary function? As in their novels, the short fiction of Norris and London furnishes dramatic examples of engagement with these questions.

Both Émile Zola and Hippolyte Taine, French originators of naturalism in mid-nineteenth-century France, used the terms *realism* and *naturalism* as if they were identical, as did Gustave Flaubert. Realism expanded in the nineteenth-century novels of France, Russia, Britain, and the United States, attempting to offer an objective view of everyday life that would constitute a new mimesis to replace the imaginative subjectivity of the Romantics. The novel genre itself had developed in the preceding two centuries out of the rising middle class, and the realistic novel became the standard of the genre. A detached point of view and everyday subjects seemed appropriate to cultures increasingly inhabited by the bourgeois class, which venerated scientific and social innovation and expected a literature to reflect their more enlightened age.

Naturalism was no less a development of the middle class, but a different (and poorer) middle class that included the voices of outspoken social critics such as Zola, whose naturalism depicted the lives of the poor at the mercy of pitiless and illimitable forces in biology and society, with themes of power and survival. In the preface to

Thérèse Raquin (1868), Zola compares the naturalist writer's portrayal of his characters to a surgeon dissecting a corpse, and elsewhere he classifies literature as a social science. Though far from an idealist, he did believe that the novelistic exposure of the real conditions of survival in the world could help right political and economic wrongs. With this aim his authorial descendants, Norris the "muck-raker" and London the socialist, would heartily agree.

Naturalists employed a documentary, photographic use of detail in a way quite different from the leisurely details of the realist novel, befitting its different use of data and its affinities to journalism, sociology, and the new intellectual and social challenges of Karl Marx, Sigmund Freud, and, most of all, Charles Darwin and his theories of natural selection and evolution. It is important to note the relationship of naturalism to the new art of photography. But naturalism had its influences from the arts, as well: one of Zola's school-friends was Paul Cézanne, and through him, remarks Lilian Furst, Zola was introduced to Impressionist painters who chose subjects from contemporary reality set in the natural changing play of color and light (Furst and Skrine, *Naturalism* 5). The new world was able to see more than before, but the powerful capitalist classes of the dawning century were not interested in seeing everything. Naturalist writers arose to bring attention to those excluded realities.

Realistic plots work toward the restoration of order, often with a character's proper location in a class hierarchy; if minor crises lead to a major confrontation, it is followed by resolution. In naturalistic novels the plot line may lead us fervently to desire order or at least stasis, but instead of a climb upwards, naturalistic characters confront crises and are destroyed. A realistic theme might suggest that good will ultimately prevail, but in naturalistic novels, often in contradistinction to an author's own political ideals, humans are doomed by biological, social, and economic forces beyond their control. Whereas the realist novels of the nineteenth century may attack social mores and manners, they are rarely as critical of society as naturalist novels, which are interested in exposing the seamier sides of society's underpinnings. At the turn of the century, this included one's genetic ancestry and one's race or gender, thought to predetermine a given individual's traits, whether physical or mental health, sexuality, criminality, or other tendencies, so that characters were seen as doomed from within and without. With its clearer set of social doctrines, a more clearly restricted period in literature (approximately 1890–1920), and location largely in just two countries, France and the United States, naturalism sharply focused its critiques of the industrial wealth of the bourgeoisie and articulated a sense of lower-class despair in the face of economic and biological forces seen as too powerful to be reformed, as was the hope of the liberal-minded in the nineteenth century and the dream of the New World. Yet American "naturalism" was never really a school; that is, aside from reading each other's books, naturalists in the United States held forth no mutual doctrine, as did naturalists in Europe.

One must remember that as tempting as it is to assign romanticism, realism, and naturalism to different domains, one must be cautious. British Romantic poets expressed belief in naturalness and spontaneity so as to give "a powerful new impetus to the study of nature" by scientists, Furst notes (*Naturalism* 3–4). Just as American transcendentalists popularized the romantic conception of reality as organic, scientists were led to observe and record related physical phenomena more carefully. And realism, perhaps unwittingly, tended to open the doors to new realms of knowledge difficult to assess by traditional Victorian standards.

Few naturalist heroes are heroic by traditional definition. In naturalist fiction there is usually a great distance between a protagonist and his creator, and in recognizing that distance, readers are called upon both to experience alienation and to share the larger view of the author, which may be merely to mourn or to observe the effects upon the hapless protagonist, or even, as in Norris's work, to see the entire situation as tragicomedy. Pizer has insisted upon idealism as an ingredient of naturalist writing to be located in the author's, if not character's, point of view: "Whether in a Huck Finn beleaguered by a socially corrupted conscience yet possessed of a good heart, or a Carrie grasping for the material plenty of life yet reaching beyond as well, in these and other works the late nineteenth-century American realists and naturalists continued to maintain the tension between actuality and hope which in its various forms has characterized most Western literature since the Renaissance" (Pizer, *Realism and Naturalism* xiii). Naturalism has been criticized as inconsistent because it degrades humans as merely victims of internal and external forces beyond their control, while at the same time identifying qualities that could elevate or lower individuals. For Pizer the problem is solved by recognizing *tragic* themes in naturalist novels (Pizer, *Twentieth-Century* x). He identifies "a compensating humanistic value ... which affirms the significance of the individual." Although the individual may be a cipher in an amoral world, "the imagination refuses to accept this formula as the total meaning of life." Indeed, in his memorable definition: "Naturalism reflects an affirmative ethical conception of life, for it asserts the value of all human life by endowing the lowest character with emotion and defeat and with moral ambiguity, no matter how poor or ignoble he may seem." The "vast skepticism" of the naturalist hero, as Pizer calls it, affirms the "worth of the skeptical or seeing temperament, of the character who continues to look for meaning in experience even though there probably is no meaning" (Pizer, *Realism and Naturalism* 11–12, 37). One can see this happening in Stephen Crane's "The Open Boat," wherein the only saving value of the men's struggle with the sea is their realization of their dependence upon each other, their community.

The trick for the naturalist author, then, is to distance the naturalist protagonist from the reader, like Zola's "corpse," but also to offer some sort of possible response to his plight. This blend of skepticism with humanism is sometimes carried out successfully by naturalists, and sometimes not. In many well-known cases, such as Zola's *Thérèse Raquin,* Norris's *McTeague,* Dreiser's *Sister Carrie* (1900), or London's *Adventure* (1911), human life is unremittingly bleak, and anything resembling an "ideal" is hard to spot.

The naturalistic hero's tragic condition differs from that of Aristotle's classic tragic hero, who has already reached his full stature and is brought low through a fall, for the naturalistic hero's potential for growth is never allowed to develop – he does not understand himself before or after the forces that caused his fall. As Pizer puts it: "wrenched by their desires or by other uncontrollable circumstances from their grooved but satisfying paths," these protagonists "fall from midway" (*Realism and Naturalism* 37). Such a definition of tragedy is perhaps America's true epic literature, with heroes such as Miller's Willy Loman or Dreiser's Hurstwood – or even Crane's Henry Fleming. Furst praises the naturalist narrator's attempts at finding meaning in the "fortunate fallacy" of naturalism (Furst and Skrine, *Naturalism* 52–3). Thus there is no purely "naturalist" text, and there is no agreement on what that might look like. And the pursuit of meaning may be only a fallacy. Naturalism, as a rule, tends to ask questions and cast doubts rather than arrive at resolution. If one were purely a naturalist, one would have no reason to create a work of literature or art, which, after all, represents an attempt at dialogue with an audience, an affirmative humanistic value.

Naturalist subject matter ranges from the cosmic questioning of Crane's awed and terrified young Union soldier Fleming in *The Red Badge of Courage* (1895) to Norris's and Upton Sinclair's exposés of the enormous power of capitalism in California's agricultural valleys and Chicago's slaughterhouses in *The Octopus* (1901) and *The Jungle* (1906). Though human nature seems inevitably to go wrong, it can sometimes also be saved in rugged environments where "civilized" notions such as self-gain are no longer useful, as in Crane's "The Open Boat." Paradoxically, where only "primitive" ideas of community prevail, group survival takes precedence over individual wants, and the civilized vices of pride and self-aggrandizement find no place. As the unnamed protagonist of "To Build a Fire" learns, too late, the motto of the Northland is "Never Travel Alone."

The most important force behind naturalism was Darwinian thought. Life as a series of events governed by natural selection, proposed in Darwin's *Origin of Species* (1859) and *The Descent of Man* (1871), suggested that the strong survive and the weak are destroyed: this notion ran counter to received religion and genteel morality, including social reformism. The middle classes and the Church were incensed at Darwin. Was nature only a set of deterministic forces working upon humans, invisible in contemporary time and discerned only by science? Were human beings only animals determined by heredity, environment, and the pressures of the moment? This was to deny free will and responsibility for human actions. Any action would merely be the inescapable result of physical forces and conditions totally beyond one's control and hence seemingly without meaning (see Furst and Skrine, *Naturalism* 18).

Herbert Spencer influenced naturalist writers with his applications of Darwin's ideas to society. "Social Darwinism" identified hereditary reasons why some would succeed in the new global society of the twentieth century, and some not. Norris and London, in particular, wrote stories that dwelt upon hereditary influences, but their real interest was the Darwinian concept of adaptability. Though they sometimes impose racial or biologically "degenerate" stereotypes, especially Norris, naturalist writers are rarely outright so much *racists* (especially as compared to non-naturalist authors of their day, such as Kipling), who have always existed, but more accurately *racialists*. That is, they, and London in particular, did not so much attack other races as subscribe to what was called "race science" in the late nineteenth and early twentieth centuries, the accepted "scientific" ideas on race of their day, particularly when it came to such ideas as eugenics and nativism. These ideas were taught at the best universities of the day, including the University of California at Berkeley, and Stanford. The patrician Norris could be quite dismissive of ethnic "others" and was not above the crudest stereotypes. He often seeks romantic, philosophic, and biological explanations for situations that later writers would view as social in nature. In *McTeague: A Story of San Francisco* (1899), Norris's characterizations of Mac as the son of an Irish drunkard and of Trina as the product of Swiss-German "peasant" stock, not to mention Maria Macapa's Mexicanness and Zerkow's stereotypical Jewishness, are supposed to speak for themselves.

London presents a thornier problem with race. As a socialist and member of the working class, he embraced the equality of humankind and attacked capitalists worldwide, but he also entertained a strong attraction to powerful individualist figures. In his short stories London nearly always attacks racism, often making the hero the non-white character, but in some of his novels and public essays he is as viciously racist as the worst social Darwinist, particularly about Asians. Short stories with memorable non-white heroes include "The House of Pride," "Mauki," and "The Mexican." Novels of particularly leaden racism include *A Daughter of the Snows* (1901), *Adventure* (1912), and *The Mutiny of the Elsinore* (1914). London's handling of race is an easy predictor of a work's quality: he is a much better writer in the short fiction; in the novels the more racism, the weaker the book. Norris's and even more so London's contradictions point to the ferment of complex ideas that characterized the turn of the century and helped create the naturalists and sustain their questioning of social realities.

The works of Zola were a heavier influence on Norris, who had studied in Paris and who wrote essays about him, than on London, but both display Zolaesque features. Zola's twenty-volume *Rougon-Macquart* series (1871–93) presented the life of one extended family during the Second Empire. Zola had a great interest in heredity as the dominating force in human destiny, corroborated by his friend Hippolyte Taine's assertion that humans are a product of race, place, and time; yet despite his belief in heredity, the humane is never missing in his work. He agreed with Edmond Goncourt: *"seuls, disons-le bien haut, les documents humains font les bons livres"* ("only human documents make good books, let's say it loud and clear") (preface to *Les Frères Zemgano*, quoted in Furst and Skrine, *Naturalism* 13–14). The phrase "human document" was picked up and used by other realists and naturalists, from Sarah Orne Jewett to Jack London. Zola wrote about all classes, choosing the conditions of heredity and environment as the organizing principles of characters, in the end, demonstrating that all people are fundamentally similar, for better or worse. Zola's naturalism thus rejects the notion of heroism and the (romantic) extraordinary individual.

The work of nineteenth-century British novelist Thomas Hardy and the German naturalist playwrights notwithstanding, the story of naturalism was really a French and American one. That naturalism never caught on in Victorian and Edwardian England was a result of a more conservative national entitlement system and its imperialistic supports. Zola's agonized depiction of the lower classes seemed overly *French* and overly *revolutionary* to English readers. The British disliked naturalism's reluctance to make moral judgments. Darwinian doctrines further alienated them. The French may have envisioned themselves as a second generation of realists, but the British had their *own* realism without what they regarded as Zola's "depressing view of man and his 'filthy' method" (Furst and Skrine, *Naturalism* 30–3).

Howells, James, and Twain, all born in the 1840s, appear to have been among the last believers in the very possibility of objective realism in the American novel. The next generation of naturalists were more open to Zola's ideas because they sprang from what Pizer calls a "struggle to survive materially rather than to prevail morally," with fiction as the means of exploring economic, social, and sexual worlds in terms of survival (Pizer, *Twentieth-Century* 3–5). Between the Great Panic of the 1890s, which left unheard-of masses of people out of work, and the terrors of World War I, there developed literature of fragmentation, as naturalism and early modernism mingled loss of meaning with the horrors of war. But unlike modernism in its early forms, naturalism recognized and embraced popular culture. Unlike what became "high" modernism, naturalism was a literature for the masses to accompany the broadening of other forms of popular art, such as photography and film. The popularity of some of the naturalist writers certainly hurt them with critics – including London, Dreiser, and Steinbeck, most notably.

Many of the naturalists, including Crane, Norris and London, began in journalism. Led by the Hearst Syndicate, newspapers depicted the shocking lives of the poor in the manner of Jacob Riis in *How the Other Half Lives*, first published in *Atlantic Monthly* in 1899–1900. In the same issue appears Norris's "Comida: An Experience in Famine," about civilian war victims in Cuba, and London's short story "An Odyssey of the North," the tale of the deadly impact of white miners upon the Indians of the Yukon. Riis and the "muckraker" journalists, including Crane in his novel *Maggie: A Girl of the Streets, A Story of New York* (1893), documented the slums. Norris's *McTeague* related the inevitable social decline of its characters due to their greed and fear of poverty. London's *The People of the Abyss* (1903), a study of the poor of London's East End, is a forerunner to later sociological works such as Herbert Asbury's *The Gangs of New York* (1928). Naturalists offered a full range of racial and class complexities in the post–Civil-War landscape.

London wrote essays on Poe and other writers from a naturalist point of view, but Norris was the earliest and most organized critical thinker on naturalism; his premature death in 1902 robbed his readers of further development in his theories. In "Zola as a Romantic Writer" (1896), Norris discounts William Dean Howells's realism as that of people "who live across the street from us," people of "small passions, restricted emotions, dramas of the reception-room, tragedies of an afternoon call, crises involving cups of tea" (Norris, "Zola as Romantic Writer" 85). For Norris, Howells is uninteresting insofar is he is not passionate or romantic. Crane satirizes Howellsian "teacup tragedies" in the sardonic closing scene of "The Monster," his disturbing story of middle-class gentility confronted with its own racism, when the doctor's wife stares at the empty teacups from her failed party as her husband relates the fate of their black servant, Henry, horribly disfigured while rescuing their son from their burning house.

Naturalism is "not an inner circle of realism," says Norris. Quite the contrary:

> To be noted of M. Zola we must leave the rank and file, either to the forefront of the marching world, or fall by the roadway; we must separate ourselves; we must become individual, unique. The naturalist takes no note of common people, common as far as their interests, their lives, and the things that occur in them are common, are ordinary. Terrible things must happen to the characters of the naturalistic tale. They must be twisted from the ordinary, wrenched out from the quiet, uneventful round of every-day life, and flung into the throes of a vast and terrible drama that works itself out in unleashed passions, in blood, and in sudden death.

Characters may be "common," but what happens to them cannot be: "These great, terrible dramas no longer happen among the personnel of a feudal and Renaissance nobility, those who are in the fore-front of the marching world, but among the lower – almost the lowest – classes; those who have been thrust or wrenched from the ranks who are falling by the roadway" (Norris, "Zola as Romantic Writer" 86–7).

Norris could have formed an "intellectual" school of thought, but didn't, and because of the brevity of his career it is hard to guess what he may have done had he lived longer. Norris's most significant contribution in his non-fiction essays is to outline how he hopes to meld the realism of Balzac and Flaubert with the demands of a new American and an even newer West Coast, Pacific Rim world. Rather than try to promote Zola's uncompromising exactitude or fit Zola's naturalism with the New England realism of Howells, Norris was drawn to Zola's mixed naturalist ethics of identity, befitting the young Western writer's possibilities. This quality Joseph M. McElrath, Jr., describes as Norris's "celebrative description" of naturalism as a "pluralistic and tolerant orientation" (McElrath, *Dictionary* 172–3, 177–8; see also Norris, "Frank Norris's Weekly Letter").

Norris's *The Octopus* makes an interesting comparison with London's *The Call of the Wild*. Both take place in the wide open spaces of the West rather than in the tenements of San Francisco; they are both "epics" in the sense that they are mythic tales with mythic structures; they both address the failures in the American Dream and in modern American society even as they celebrate the regenerative quality of the land. Like Norris, London reflects in his "naturalistic romances," as Jacqueline Tavernier-Courbin calls them, the romantic and the mythic dimensions of survival, though London's symbolic landscapes and archetypes are a far different thing from Norris's half-hearted nod to the romantic in the conclusion of *The Octopus*; the paean to "the Wheat" strikes many readers as an embarrassing evasion of the massacre that has gone before. The longer and more complex *Octopus* – with its social criticisms of capitalism and human greed diffused by romanticism, especially in the conclusion, and by the dreamy sub-plots of the poet/protagonist Presley and the reveries of the wanderer Vanamee – lacks the sheer force of the argument and the personal story of *The Call of the Wild*. In contrast, Norris's *McTeague* might suggest the parallel of London's psychopathological intensity in *The Sea-Wolf* (1904).

Both *McTeague* and *The Call of the Wild* offer intense emotional focus playing out in life-or-death situations, portraying in graphic terms the effects of greed – their characters must live or die by the rule of gold. In a strange way, as both protagonists, Mac and Buck, become unproductive members of society, they become their "true" selves (as is also the case with Vanamee, though probably not of Presley). Mac loses his dental practice and, as Michael Bryson notes, he also "loses the ability to produce, and thus own, his self" and reverts to an atavism (Bryson 5). Within that field, many of Norris's themes and symbols in *McTeague* would find parallels and mirrorings in the patterning of *The Call of the Wild*. Critical elements in each book involve such key naturalistic concerns as the nature of the self; heredity and environment in shaping lives versus free will; Darwinistic ideas concerning an individual's ability to adapt to environment; awareness of the human capacity for animalistic and brutal behavior; patterns of dominance and submission; survival of the individual versus survival of the community or species; a sense of the land as exploited, whether mined in California or in the Klondike. They share a certain skepticism as to the place of humankind as superior to all other creatures, man as Zola's "human beast" instead of what McElrath describes as "a noble creature superior to others in the instinct-governed animal kingdom" (*Frank Norris Revisited* 36). Yet whereas Mac's story is a story of degeneration, Buck's becomes, through his own "authorship" of his destiny, one of regeneration and freedom, though this cannot take place within the realm of the civilized, modern world.

In contrast to *McTeague* and *The Octopus,* or London's *Martin Eden* (1909), for that matter, in *The Call of the Wild* the presence of romance and tragedy do not interfere with the indictment of modern capitalistic society nor distill the concentrated naturalistic bleakness, the "white silence" of Nature that is, in the end, the only arbiter of survival – impartial, uncaring, ever-evolving Nature. In *McTeague* this silence surrounds the dumbfounded and doomed dentist, having murdered his wife and his friend for the gold he lusts after, now finding himself handcuffed to a corpse in the middle of the white-hot Death Valley. But Mac has no understanding of how he got there, and he hears no call to a new self. His final confrontation with Nature is his end, symbolized by the dead canary. Buck in *The Call of the Wild* escapes the machinery of men that is fueled by the desire for gold, the machinery that kidnapped and sold him into slavery, and in the end he embraces the stern facts of the frozen North instead. His is a joyous leap into the future, an embrace of his destiny, and not a handcuff.

These novelistic echoes and counter-movements between naturalists Norris and London are sharply crystallized in a pair of short stories that are among their author's best: Norris's "*Fantaisie Printanière*" (1897) and London's "The Apostate" (1906). Like Crane, Norris and London also died young, but despite their short careers they each produced scores of short stories in the popular magazines of the day, in addition to their novels. These are two gems.

Norris, though better known for his novels, *McTeague, The Octopus, The Pit* (1903), and *Vandover and the Brute* (1914), was a talented and prolific writer of short stories, though they are mostly unknown today. These early works feature Norris's sharp observations of life on the streets and in the parlors of San Francisco and other new urban settings. Norris published sixty short stories in the San Francisco literary magazine *The Wave* from 1891 to 1898. This magazine appealed to readers who were educated, upper middle-class, and inclined to enjoy iconoclastic and satiric pieces, especially when they violated social taboos left over from the past (and from the East Coast). His use of strong detail in *The Wave* stories demonstrates his growing knowledge of the city and its ways, as well as his experimenting with subject, point of view, dialogue and dialect, tone, and theme in fiction, much derived from his journalistic perspective.

Norris's stories run the gamut of genres and parodies of genres. "The Jongleur of Taillebois" (1891), one of his earliest written works, is an epic set in medieval France, wherein his characters confront murderous and vengeful ghosts. Many of his tales are humorous sketches filled with dialect humor, but many are brutally naturalistic and somber in tone, offering scathing critiques of economic and political power structures in the modern city and countryside. Like *The Octopus*, "A Deal in Wheat" looks closely at the effects of rampant capitalism from various political and class viewpoints. Realizing he is only a cog in a game played by the power brokers, a Kansas wheat farmer is ruined by market traders in Chicago. "A Deal in Wheat" suggests what Norris might have done had he completed his proposed trilogy with a third novel after *The Octopus* and *The Pit*. Because of his political exposés of capitalists, Norris, like Upton Sinclair, was called a "muck-raker" for his sensationalistic attacks. But his writings were a factor in attempts to make the Congress act to curb the grotesque excesses he portrays. "A Deal in Wheat" is highly typical of Norris's insistence upon repeating themes of injustice and class consciousness. One can appreciate his influence upon contemporary and later writers such as London, Dreiser, Fitzgerald, and Steinbeck.

Other stories display strong evidence both of Norris's naturalism and also of his romantic sense of the primal, the healthy, the rural, as opposed to the corrupt, the urban, the effete. However, like London, Norris also sees "Nature" not only as that which inhabits the forest or the countryside, but also nature as *human* nature, a much more frightening apparition, with all of its seemingly senseless, unnatural cruelties. Like "A Deal in Wheat," several of his stories contain in embryonic form ideas that would later be treated maturely in his novels. For example, the gold in "Judy's Service of Gold Plate" foreshadows the use of that element as a symbol for greed in *McTeague*. But most closely related to McTeague and to his overall naturalistic vision is "*Fantaisie Printanière*," which seems like a partial draft for *McTeague* that was never used in the novel, but that in itself offers a sardonically bleak portrait of the lower class as well as some unsettling questions about authorial intention and reader response.

Like Crane and Dreiser, Norris often seeks to disorient the reader and help him or her into a new sensibility. Though many of his stories are quite genteel, others continue to shock. "*Fantaisie Printanière*" is one of these. As McElrath has noted, on the one hand, it appeals to a reader's *petit bourgeois* sympathy with "the unfortunate" as well as a voyeuristic, superior sense of spectatorship at their melodramas, similar to the dual sense we get at Crane's portrait of slum life in *Maggie: A Girl of the Streets* (1893) coupled with his tongue-in-cheek portrait of Maggie's mother (see: www.georgetown.edu/faculty/bassr/heath/syllabuild/iguide/norris.html). Despite the desperate situation of the two abused women in "*Fantaisie Printanière*," the fact that they quarrel over their husbands' wife-beating skills invites us to examine Norris's own shockingly humorous point of view on their struggles; that is, is Norris's lack of disapproval evidence of decadence on his part, or is he trying to poke fun at the typical Victorian moral smugness when it came to helping the poor? Does he wish to show how the sins of the men (who are at first the feuding pair) are visited upon those under their power (their wives, who take up their own feud, thereby settling the men's)? Or is his use of the absurd point of view aiming at something else, a sense of the meaninglessness of life, an idea that evolved out of the failures of Victorianism and Western values and the advent of modernism and naturalism? We should feel outraged at the characters' sadomasochism, and we might, but we also cannot escape the sardonic humor of the narrator. Norris could write tragedy, and he did, in *The Octopus*, but, as in *McTeague*, in this story he offers an alternate response to horror. Yet what kind of reader would find the situation actually comic?

The words Norris uses to describe the neighbors, the McTeagues and the Ryers, evoke a dismal atmosphere: their "squalid" block lies at "the disreputable end" of Polk Street. A huge red gas drum at the gas works nearby leaks a "nasty brassy foulness" into the air, compounded with "the odors of cooking from the ill-kept kitchens, and the reek of garbage in the vacant lots" ("*Fantaisie*" 175). And the stench is still there in the end, after the story's shocking events have unfolded in the Ryers' tiny, filthy kitchen, as dirty a space as the motivations of the characters.

In *McTeague* we witness the decline and fall of Mac the dentist due to the greed and violence that destroy his marriage, friendships, career – and ultimately three lives including his own. If we follow *McTeague*'s chronology, this story seems to occur at some point after his loss of his dental parlors and during his alcoholic attempts at escaping the downhill slide his life has taken. In this story the men and women are beaten down by a variety of factors we infer are primarily social, but also others that are also all-too-recognizably human: like Zola, Norris gives us human beings struggling fundamentally to survive, and this struggle give rise to the human failings of fear, false pride, and venality, as well as to alcoholism and wife-beating. This is the human drama at its basest, its stupidest. McTeague's neighbor, Ryer, has also been banished from a career by sheer greediness and a sociopathic lack of regard for society: he was censured by the Board of Health for feeding his hogs on "poultices obtained from the City and County Hospital" (*McTeague* 175). The adulteration of food by unscrupulous capitalists was one of the era's great scandals, as witnessed by Upton Sinclair in *The Jungle* (1906).

Like warring primitive tribesmen, McTeague and Ryer carry on a feud, which Norris satirizes by a comparison to the Capulets and the Montagues, a feud which arose from a bar-room brawl over how the lines of latitude and longitude converge at the poles, a fitting argument for people to have who are trapped in their own spaces without any understanding of themselves, let alone the larger world around them. Ryer beats his wife when sober; McTeague when drunk. Norris's description of these beatings leaves nothing to the imagination: McTeague uses fists, feet, and a club, while Ryer employs rawhide and a rubber hose filled with gravel – "his nature demanded a variety of sensation" (176). Unlike the "colossal, clumsy" blows of the dentist, Ryer fancies himself more a gentleman, and as a result "Ryer was cruel, McTeague only brutal" (177), this an invitation to gentlemen readers to consider the difference.

The only sign of spring *"Fantaisie Printanière"* offers is the appearance of three dandelions that sprout "in the vacant lot behind the gas works," drawn upwards by spring warmth which also makes the garbage stink even more and the men stay out to drink. Trina and Mrs. Ryer usually come out on such a day to share the "hated ritual" (177) of washing, not a rite of spring. Instead of singing nymphs or warbling birds, we heard these two "calling shrilly to one another as their backs bent and straightened over the scrubbing-boards" (177). When Mrs. Ryer does not show up, Trina goes through a hole in their fence and into the Ryers' kitchen to investigate.

Ryer has beaten Mrs. Ryer the night before with a trunk strap, as has McTeague, who came after his wife with fists and hurled boots. Trina finds Mrs. Ryer black and blue and miserable; for the first time they talk about their beatings. But their empathy soon transforms into envy and pride, and they argue over which husband is the most effective batterer! They taunt each other over "'little scars, little flesh wounds like that!'" as Trina "loftily" observes of Mrs. Ryer (179), until "suddenly they tore at each other like infuriated cats" (181), the comic and racist allusion to the (Irish) Kilkenney cats not lost on Norris's readers. They are broken up by the amused husbands, who are able to amend their own feud in raucous laughter at their wives: "'Fightin' over our fightin' them' bellowed McTeague." "'Mac, this does beat the carpet, sure,'" observes Ryer. The source of the women's outrage was Mrs. Ryer's calling Trina "a drab," and Trina's retort that "'my kitchen wasn't a place for pigs to live in,'" as Mrs. Ryer puts it (181). Despite the relocation of the feud to the wives, "both men continue to thrash their wives in the old ratio – McTeague on the days when he is drunk (which are many), Ryer on the days he is sober (which are few)" (183).

The story is clearly influenced by a Darwinian view of human survival in which atavism – or animalistic characteristics – are revealed. As McElrath observes, the influence of Freud may also be detected, inasmuch as Freudian psychology identified the dark, unconscious motivations for seemingly unexplainable behaviors (see www.georgetown.edu/faculty/bassr/heath/syllabuild/iguide/norris.html). Perhaps, as Zola and London also supposed, there was an "abysmal brute" within all of us. The McTeagues and the Ryers certainly appear to be driven by uncontrollable violence on the part of the men and equally perverse submission to violence by the women. They are primitives in the sense that they behave like brutes; it is as though, in Freudian terms, they are all id but fool themselves into believing they are all super-ego. Like

London, Norris described the lowest classes as animal-like, and like London he recognized the terrible destruction in their lives wrought by alcohol. In the poisonous
and hopeless atmosphere of fear in their households and, one infers, in the entire
lower-class world they inhabit, things will only end in death, with no possibility for
positive change. Norris predicts the despairing absurdism and nihilism of the modernists in the next generation. His mocking, grotesquely light-hearted tone suggests
the Sweeney poems of Eliot and parts of *The Waste-Land* (1925), as it also points
toward the dark humor and amoral existentialism of *Waiting for Godot* (1953).

One also notes the ethnic and racial stereotypes at play: McTeague is Irish and
Ryer is German. These groups were not considered quite white or fit for democratic
self-government on the American model at the turn of the century; their troubles and
peccadilloes were the subject of cartoons and dialect jokes in all the newspapers. These
and other immigrant groups were thought of as lazy, dirty, and drunk. These stereotypes are repellent today, but in Norris's day they were approved by readers such as
those of *The Wave* who actually had little knowledge of the lower classes. He certainly
departs from the earnest social reform writings of the previous generation, such
as those of Rebecca Harding Davis, and resembles in his pessimism and distance
his contemporary Ambrose Bierce (see www.georgetown.edu/faculty/bassr/heath/
syllabuild/iguide/norris.html).

The most important influence upon Norris's amoral naturalism is, of course, Émile
Zola, whom he deeply admired and imitated. All human life, he would have agreed
with Zola, is open to the writer; nothing need be hid. In tracing the story of his
doomed lovers in *Thérèse Raquin*, Zola says, "I simply applied to two living bodies the
analytical method that surgeons apply to corpses" ("Preface" 23).

Unlike Norris's, London's short fiction is still widely read and taught. Stanford
University Press issued *The Complete Short Stories of Jack London* in 1993, offering for
the first time a complete scholarly collection. New editions and critical studies of his
short fiction continue to be published in ever-increasing numbers, so that although
his stories have remained popular around the world, they are occasioning a renewal
of interest from American critics and professors. Like *"Fantaisie Printanière,"* "The
Apostate" offers a portrait of slum life as a place of brutality, poverty, meaningless
labor, domestic violence, and family breakdown. London's portrait of factory and
working-class life is as depressing as Norris's, but in contrast to Norris's story,
London's allows the naturalistic hero – shown in his full misery and fully at the mercy
of economic forces he cannot control – an escape into nature in a Transcendental
moment of self-determination.

Ironically, as in *Adventures of Huckleberry Finn*, in London's tale apostasy to society
means a renewal of a spirit of freedom and new possibilities for living. As with
Norris's story, the title is ironic. London lived an early life remarkably similar to his
child-laborer hero, while Norris was a spectator of poverty in San Francisco, having
been raised in an upper-middle-class home and well educated at home and abroad.
Paradoxically, London offers a sense of hope, an idealistic and romantic sense of hope,
whereas Norris's narrator seems a hardened cynic, laughing at his debased characters.

Also, while Norris uses small spaces and presents a generally claustrophobic sense of space into which progress will not enter, London uses time, as represented in the light and dark imagery, to delineate the days and nights of the life of his hero. The darkness into which Johnny escapes in the end is a reversal: this darkness he has chosen and it is the way toward his eventual freedom in the daylight to come.

One of London's most provocative portraits of social injustice, "The Apostate" presents a semi-autobiographical hero, a half-starved boy named Johnny, a child laborer who seemingly exists only to work in a garment factory and bring his meager earnings home to his mother and brother. After becoming ill and spending an uncharacteristic number of days at home – in fact, actually seeing the daylight after having risen before dawn and returned home after dark for so many years – Johnny experiences two revelations in feverish clarity. First, he calculates the number of movements his body has made in his years of toil (a reference perhaps to the "time and motion" studies of Frederick Taylor in *The Principles of Scientific Management* [1911]). Second, he experiences an epiphany of nature as he observes day after day recovering on his porch a small spindly tree growing through the sidewalk. In the end, despite his mother's protestations that he get back to work so that his younger brother will be spared child labor, with his vision of the tree he bolts, jumping into an empty box-car on a freight train headed into the countryside. He lies back in the empty box-car: "The engine whistled. Johnny was lying down, and in the darkness he smiled" (London, *Complete* 1129). There is perhaps no clear resolution, in the sense that we know what happens to Johnny, but this is more resolution than "*Fantaisie Printanière*," to say the least, and it is a positive ending for Johnny, one is sure. Like Eliot's Fisher King at the end of *The Waste Land*, Johnny at least hears the thunder and smells the rain approaching, as it were.

London praised the value of hard work, but detested what he saw as "wage slavery," the kind of back-breaking, endless, low-paid physical labor he experienced working in a cannery, a rope factory, a boiler room, a laundry, and elsewhere as a boy. Johnny is no more than a machine, literally a cog in the system:

> He worked mechanically. When a small bobbin ran out, he used his left hand for a brake, stopping the large bobbin and at the same time, with thumb and forefinger, catching the flying end of twine. Also, at the same time, with his right hand, he caught up the loose twine-end of a small bobbin. These various acts with both hands were performed simultaneously and swiftly. Then there would come a flash of his hands as he looped the weaver's knot and released the bobbin. There was nothing difficult about weaver's knots. He once boasted he could tie them in his sleep. And for that matter, he sometimes did, toiling centuries long in a single night at tying an endless succession of weaver's knots. (1115)

Johnny is praised by the overseer for his accuracy and speed:

> Some of the boys shirked, wasting time and machinery by not replacing the small bobbins when they ran out. And there was an overseer to prevent this. He caught Johnny's neighbor at the trick, and boxed his ears.

"Look at Johnny there – why ain't you like him?" the overseer wrathfully demanded.

Johnny's bobbins were running full blast, but he did not thrill at the indirect praise. There had been a time … but that was long ago, very long ago. His apathetic face was expressionless as he listened to himself being held up as a shining example. He was the perfect worker. He knew that. He had been told so, often. It was a commonplace, and besides it didn't seem to mean anything to him any more. From the perfect worker he had evolved into the perfect machine. (1116)

"And small wonder," the narrator observes. There has never been a time when Johnny was not "in intimate relationship with machines." He was born on the factory floor:

Twelve years before, there had been a small flutter of excitement in the loom room of this very mill. Johnny's mother had fainted. They stretched her out on the floor in the midst of the shrieking machines. A couple of elderly women were called from their looms. The foreman assisted. And in a few minutes there was one more soul in the loom room than had entered by the doors. It was Johnny, born with the pounding, crashing roar of the looms in his ears, drawing with his first breath the warm, moist air that was thick with flying lint. He had coughed that first day in order to rid his lungs of the lint; and for the same reason he had coughed ever since. (1116)

The birth scene reinforces London's portrait of Johnny's family life as similarly mechanical and unfeeling. His mother is willing to sacrifice him to spare his brother and treats him like a machine she must keep sending to work. As Norris distinguishes between "house" and "home" in *Fantaisie Printanière* ("The Ryers' home [or let us say, the house in which the Ryers ate and slept], adjoined the house in which the McTeagues ate and slept" [175–6]), Johnny's house is no home. For example, his only memory of his father is as follows:

This particular memory never came to Johnny in broad daylight when he was wide awake. It came at night, in bed, at the moment that his consciousness was sinking down and losing itself in sleep. It always aroused him to frightened wakefulness, and for the moment, in the first sickening start, it seemed to him that he lay crosswise on the foot of the bed. In the bed were the vague forms of his father and mother. He never saw what his father looked like. He had but one impression of his father, and that was that he had savage and pitiless feet. (*Stories* 1123)

As in *"Fantaisie Printanière,"* home life and social life (like work life) is lived under cruelly restrictive paradigms of manhood and womanhood as well as class, taken to a ridiculous extreme of what passes for pride among the lowly. Johnny, for example, should be proud of his efficiency according to the factory foreman, and proud to be the breadwinner for his family according to his mother.

Yet Johnny finds neither pride nor joy in life, only miserable toil. Like the two couples in Norris's story, he is locked into a seemingly inescapable prison of behaviors he seems powerless to resist, both family and social pressures:

[H]is consciousness was machine consciousness. Outside this his mind was a blank. He had no ideals. ... He was a work-beast. He had no mental life whatever; yet deep down in the crypts of his mind, unknown to him, were being weighed and sifted every hour of his toil, every movement of his hands, every twitch of his muscles, and preparations were making for a future course of action that would amaze him and all his little world. (1124)

When Johnny finally bolts, we sense that whatever he finds on the open road, it will be better than what he has left. Yet the dilemma remains: was this "fair" to his mother and brother? Such a lingering question parallels Norris's conundrum about how to "take" the McTeague/Ryer situation, whether comic or something else. Like Norris, London believed in the regenerative powers of the countryside and the deleterious effects of urban squalor. Both authors choose titles for their stories that are ironically at odds with their content. Norris's title, which translates to "Spring Fantasy," evokes the genres of the pastoral, the lyric, the lovers' reverie, hardly the tone set by the story. London's title describes someone who loses his faith, but the ending is a life-saving affirmation. Both titles point to what is not: for faith in either the family system modeled by the McTeagues, Ryers, and Johnny's family, or in the industrial system that destroys them all, would be faith in false and dangerous ideals.

REFERENCES AND FURTHER READING

Berkove, Lawrence. "The Romantic Realism of Bierce and Norris." *Frank Norris Studies* 15 (1993): 13–17.

Bryson, Michael. "Glands, Perverts, and Misers: Economics of Dominance and Submission in Relation to Productive and Unproductive Labor in Frank Norris' *McTeague*." <www.brysons.net/academic/mcteague.html>.

Campbell, Donna. "'One Note of Color': The Apprenticeship Writings of Frank Norris." *Frank Norris Studies* 25 (1998): 3–5.

Davison, Richard Allan. "Zelda Fitzgerald, Vladimir Nabokov and James A. Michener: Three Opinions on Frank Norris's *McTeague*." *Frank Norris Studies* 9 (1989): 11–12.

Dickey, James. *Introduction to "The Call of the Wild," "White Fang," and Other Stories, by Jack London*. Ed. Andrew Sinclair. New York: Penguin, 1981. 7–16.

Duncan, Charles. "Where Piggishness Flourishes: Contextualizing Strategies in Norris and London." *Frank Norris Studies* 14 (1992): 1–6.

Eby, Clare. "Of Gold Molars and Golden Girls: Fitzgerald's Reading of Norris." *American Literary Realism* 35 (2003): 130–58.

Foner, Philip S. *Jack London: American Rebel*. New York: Citadel Press, 1947.

Furer, Andrew. "'Zone-Conquerors' and 'White Devils': The Contradictions of Race in the Works of Jack London." *Rereading Jack London*. Eds. Leonard Cassuto and Jeanne Campbell Reesman. Stanford: Stanford University Press, 1996. 158–71.

Furst, Lilian R., and Peter N. Skrine. *Naturalism*. London: Methuen, 1971.

Furst, Lilian R., and Peter N. Skrine, eds. *Realism*. London: Longman, 1992.

Howard, June. *Form and History in American Literary Naturalism*. Chapel Hill: University of North Carolina Press, 1985.

Howells, William Dean. "The Prudishness of the Anglo-Saxon Novel." *Criticism and Fiction*. New York: Harper & Brothers, 1891.

Labor, Earle, and Jeanne Campbell Reesman. *Jack London*. Rev. edn. Twayne US Authors Series. New York: Macmillan, 1994.

Lawlor, Mary. "Naturalism in the Cinema: Erich Von Stroheim's Reading of *McTeague*." *Frank Norris Studies* 8 (1989): 6–8.

London, Charmian Kittredge. *The Book of Jack London*. 2 vols. New York: Century, 1921.

London, Jack. "The Apostate." *When God Laughs.* New York: Macmillan, 1906. Rpt. in *The Complete Short Stories of Jack London.* Eds. Earle Labor, Robert C. Leitz, III, and I. Milo Shepard. Stanford: Stanford University Press. 1112–29. All quotations used in text are taken from this edition.

———. *The Call of the Wild.* New York: Macmillan, 1903.

———. "The White Silence." *The Son of the Wolf.* Boston: Houghton Mifflin, 1900.

London, Joan. *Jack London and His Times.* Seattle: University of Washington Press, 1968.

McElrath, Joseph R., Jr. "Frank Norris." *Dictionary of Literary Biography.* Vol. 71, *American Literary Critics and Scholars, 1880–1900.* Eds. John W. Rathbun and Monica M. Green. Detroit: Gale Research, 1988. 168–79.

———. *Frank Norris Revisited.* New York: Twayne, 1992.

———. "Frank Norris and *The Wave*: 1894." *Frank Norris Studies* 1 (1986): 4.

———. "Frank Norris and *The Wave*: 1895." *Frank Norris Studies* 3 (1987): 4.

McElrath, Joseph R., Jr., ed. "Special Issue: Perverted Tales." *Frank Norris Studies* 15 (Spring 1993).

Norris, Frank. *Complete Edition of Frank Norris.* 10 vols. Garden City, NJ: Doubleday, Doran, 1928.

———. "*Fantasie Printanière*." *The Wave* 16 (November 6, 1897): 7. Rpt. in *The Apprenticeship Writings of Frank Norris 1896–1898.* Vol. 2: *1897–1898.* Eds. Joseph R. McElrath, Jr., and Douglass K. Burgess. Philadelphia: American Philosophical Society, 1996. 175–83.

———. "Frank Norris's Weekly Letter." *Chicago American* (August 3, 1901). Rpt. in *Frank Norris's McTeague.* Ed. Donald Pizer. New York: W. W. Norton, 1977. 275–7.

———. *McTeague: A Story of San Francisco.* New York: Doubleday and McClure, 1899.

———. "A Plea for Romantic Fiction." *Boston Evening Transcript* (December 18, 1901). Rpt. in

The Literary Criticism of Frank Norris. Ed. Donald Pizer. Austin: University of Texas Press, 1964. 75–8.

———. "Zola as a Romantic Writer." *The Wave* (June 27, 1896): 3. Rpt. in *The Apprenticeship Writings of Frank Norris, 1896–1897.* Eds. Joseph R. McElrath, Jr., and Douglas K. Burgess. Philadelphia: American Philosophical Society, 1996. 85–7.

Pizer, Donald. "The Biological Determinism of *McTeague* in Our Time." *American Literary Realism* 29.2 (Winter 1997): 27–33.

———. "Frank Norris's *McTeague*: Naturalism as Popular Myth." *ANQ* 13.4 (2000): 21–6.

———. *Realism and Naturalism in Nineteenth-Century American Literature.* Rev. edn. Carbondale: Southern Illinois University Press, 1984.

———. *Twentieth-Century American Literary Naturalism: An Interpretation.* Carbondale: Southern Illinois University Press, 1982.

Reesman, Jeanne Campbell. *Jack London: A Study of the Short Fiction.* New York: Twayne, 1999.

———. "'Never Travel Alone': Naturalism, Jack London, and the White Silence," *American Literary Realism, 1870–1910* 29.2 (1997): 33–49.

Starr, Kevin. "Introduction." *McTeague: A Story of San Francisco by Frank Norris.* New York: Penguin, 1994.

Tavernier-Courbin, Jacqueline. *The Call of the Wild: A Naturalistic Romance.* New York: Twayne, 1994.

Walcutt, Charles C. *American Literary Naturalism: A Divided Stream.* Minneapolis: University of Minnesota Press, 1956.

Werner, Mary Beth. "'A Vast and Terrible Drama': Frank Norris's Domestic Violence Fantasy in *McTeague*." *Frank Norris Studies* 19 (1994): 1–4.

Zola, Émile. "Preface" to the 2nd edition of *Thérèse Raquin*. 1868. Rpt. in *Thérèse Raquin* by Émile Zola. Trans. Leonard Tancock. London: Penguin, 1962. 21–8.

13

From "Water Drops" to General Strikes: Nineteenth- and Early Twentieth-Century Short Fiction and Social Change

Andrew J. Furer

I perceived that the whole energetic, busy spirit of the age tended wholly to the Magazine literature – to the curt, the terse, the well-timed, and the readily diffused, in preference to the old forms of the verbose, the ponderous and the inaccessible.

– Edgar Allan Poe (1844?)

I became a socialist, first, because I was born a proletarian and early discovered that for the proletariat socialism was the only way out; second ... I discovered that socialism was the only way out for art and the artist.

– Jack London (1911)

Not surprisingly, given the United States' radical birth, American literary figures have long exploited fiction's power to convey messages of social change, deploying both novels and short stories, the latter peculiarly suited to the task as they are, in Poe's phrase, "terse ... well-timed, and ... readily diffused" (qtd. in Levy 17). The two major eras of the short story parallel the two great upsurges of American reform impulses: the mid-nineteenth century, which saw the rapid growth of the temperance, abolitionist, and women's rights movements, as well as the multiplication of utopian communities such as Brook Farm, Oneida, and Amana, and the late nineteenth and early twentieth centuries, during which Progressivism, Populism, and many other reform movements, large and small, appeared, including socialism, suffragism, modern hygiene reform, labor reform, anti-imperialism, and trade unionism, among others. Not coincidentally, these eras are also the major periods of the American magazine's development, in which reformist non-fiction and fiction frequently appear side by side in such publications as *Harper's*, *Century Magazine*, the *Atlantic Monthly*, and *Everybody's Magazine*. Between 1820 and 1860, the number of magazines grew from under 100 to nearly 600.[1] Subsequently, from 1885 to 1905, the number grew from 3,300 to over 6,000.[2]

In the following pages, we will see the ways in which American short fiction between 1830 and 1920 engages with issues central to nineteenth- and early twentieth-century reform movements, and the manner in which tropes of domestic influence that dominate earlier reform fiction begin, in the Progressive Era, to be supplemented – or in some cases, supplanted – by masculinist ones such as those of battle and direct resistance, on the one hand, and feminist anti-domestic tropes, on the other.[3]

Temperance was one of the largest mid-nineteenth-century reform movements; in 1835, the American Temperance Society had a membership of 1.5 million, 10 percent of the free population (Young 4). The results of this crusade were also impressive: between 1830 and 1850 per capita consumption of alcohol declined by a factor of four. This movement was one of the first in which men and women appear to have participated in equal numbers – in the 1820s and 1830s, women, active in both mixed and all-female societies, constituted approximately 50 percent of all those engaged in the crusade against alcohol (Mattingly 4).[4] Indeed, this movement can be seen as one of the first through which women took a public, social role, albeit behind a mask of domestic concerns.

Writers such as Lucius Marcellus Sargent (whose "My Mother's Gold Ring" [1833] was among the most popular temperance stories), Lydia Howard Huntley Sigourney, Caroline Hyde Butler (Laing), Harriet Beecher Stowe, Elizabeth Cady Stanton, Louisa May Alcott, and many others published powerful temperance stories in both general interest and temperance magazines, as well as in the popular temperance gift books.[5]

Women writers, such as Sigourney, often described their stories against drink as "water drops" (Mattingly xi), of which her "The Intemperate" (1833) – first published in pamphlet form, and then in 1834 in a gift book – provides a paradigmatic early example. The protagonist, Jane Harwood, enters her marriage with high hopes, but soon finds herself in a horrific, precarious situation in which her husband may become violent at any time, putting the family at risk, a situation that eventually leads to her son's death: "Harshness, and the agitation of fear, deepened the disease which might else have yielded. The timid boy, in fear of his natural protector, withered away like a blighted flower" (Sigourney 40). Such sentimental, overwrought language is typical of temperance fiction, and more generally, of course, of that produced by Hawthorne's "hordes of scribbling women," who wrote most of the era's bestsellers. "The Intemperate" aptly illustrates the adage that absolute power corrupts absolutely, as well as the increased danger to dipsomaniacal husbands' wives who move away from friends and extended family, a not uncommon event in the age of Manifest Destiny. Jane emerges as both victim and heroine, nobly bearing up under the despotism of her husband, a frequent theme in women's temperance fiction, one much appreciated by its predominantly female readership. Ultimately, however, she is left with a life-long "sacred and deep-rooted sorrow – the memory of her erring husband and the miseries of unreclaimed intemperance," a sorrow the author hopes will be burned into her reader's memories (Sigourney 45), provoking them to fight this social evil themselves.

Butler's "Emma Alton" (1850), first published in a gift book, tells an even more tragic story, that of a young bride and newborn babe destroyed by an intemperate husband, who is subsequently jailed for murdering another man (though not for abusing his family). Along the way, while a few pity Emma, many "[point] the finger at the *drunkard's wife*," even though she is, as Butler declares, "the innocent sufferer of her husband's vices!" (Butler 25). The narrator closes the story by attempting to lead the reader to join her in her sorrow, declaring, after witnessing Emma's funeral, "as the hot tears gathered, [that] 'thou art yet another victim at the shrine of intemperance!'" (30). It is worth noting that although most victims of intemperance were working-class, most characters in temperance fiction are middle- or lower middle-class, a clear attempt by these writers to engage their predominantly bourgeois audience through the hoary rhetorical strategy of appealing to their self-interest and instinct of self-preservation – the implied motif of "this could happen to you!" runs through many such stories.

Whereas Sigourney's and Butler's stories show the destruction of the husband as well as the suffering of the wife and children, Sargent's "My Mother's Gold Ring" illustrates the salvation of both husband and wife, the former being inspired by others who have "taken the pledge," though initially, in place of the pledge, the husband uses a ring. In this story husband and wife share equally in the triumph over intemperance, perhaps a reflection of the author's gender. That is to say, both male and female agency prevail here, not merely the latter. Speaking to an abstemious neighbor, the husband declares:

> "For five months, instead of the pledge, I have in every trial and temptation – and a drinking man knows well the force and meaning of those words – I have relied upon this gold ring, to renew my strength, and remind me of my duty to God, to my wife, to my children, and to society. ... [The ring] ... has proved, thus far, the life-boat of a drowning man." (Sargent 23)

Here a symbol of domestic attachments, its rhetorical force doubled by referencing both wife and mother, rescues the intemperate, another recurring temperance theme. Sargent attempts to extend the reach of his domestic theme by urging his readers to convey the story beyond the realm of the family, not merely within it. He prefaces his story by urging the reader, "When you have read it, if, among all your connexions [*sic*] and friends, you can think of no one, whom its perusal may possibly benefit – and it will be strange if you cannot – do me the favor to present it to the first little boy that you meet. He will, no doubt, take it home to his father and mother. If you will not do this, throw it in the street, as near to some dram-seller's door, as you ever venture to go" (Sargent iii–iv). His intent is clear: speed the message of temperance by any means necessary.

One of the best-known mid-nineteenth-century fiction writers was, of course, Harriet Beecher Stowe. Most readers, however, are probably unaware that she first used domestic tropes in temperance fiction before famously applying them nearly a decade later in the cause of abolition in *Uncle Tom's Cabin* (1852). For example, in "The Coral Ring" (1843) – first published in a gift book, and later reprinted in *Godey's*

Lady Book – she demonstrates the power of women to achieve social change through domestic influence, though in this case, between cousins:

> It was not more than a week before the news was circulated that even George Elliot had signed the pledge of temperance. There was much wondering at this sudden turn among those who had known his utter repugnance to any measure of the kind, and the extent to which he had yielded to temptation; but few knew how fine and delicate had been the touch to which his pride had yielded. (Stowe 217)

This is the same "fine and delicate" touch wielded by the Senator's wife in *Uncle Tom's Cabin,* and the wife-narrator in Sargent's "My Mother's Gold Ring," though extended slightly beyond immediate family. The implication in such stories is clear: if every female relative, close or distant, were to wield this delicate weapon of hearth and home, intemperance would be rapidly wiped out.

Temperance fiction, while highly popular in antebellum America, did not lose its appeal after the war, as evidenced by Louisa May Alcott's "Silver Pitchers" (1876), published shortly after the establishment of the Woman's Christian Temperance Union, an organization for which Alcott later served as her local chapter's corresponding secretary (Mattingly 218–19).[6] Here, Alcott echoes Stowe's emphasis on the efficacy of women's domestic power to achieve social change through the tale of a close-knit group of girls (friends rather than sisters, as in *Little Women* [1868]), who come to the conclusion that young women should "use our youth, our beauty, our influence for something nobler than merely pleasing men's eyes, or playing with their hearts" (Alcott 241). As Priscilla, one of the girls, notes, speaking directly to this theme: "We [girls] can't preach and pray in streets and bar-rooms, but we may at home, and in our own little world show that we want to use our influence for good" (Alcott 222), a power that saves several men and, by implication, their families.[7] By showing the influence of a group of women – the "Silver Pitchers" society, meant to symbolize a pitcher of water – on their families and friends, rather than focusing on a single family, Alcott not only brings her readers inside homes similar to their own, like Sigourney and Butler, but also presents a compelling case for the efficacy of temperance societies. Alcott and Stowe, like other temperance writers, relying heavily on the trope of female domestic influence, provide a variation on the theme of "the hand that rocks the cradle rules the world."

The effects of reform texts are, of course, manifestations of what Jane Tompkins in *Sensational Designs* calls their cultural work. Often, as just illustrated, a gentle female hand achieves such work. While the ameliorating effect of domestic influence is one of the most widely used strategies of mid-nineteenth-century reform fiction, it is less frequently and less sentimentally used in later reform stories of social change, as we shall see below in Jack London's socialist fiction and Jacob Riis's tenement stories, among other examples.

One notable feature of the major mid-nineteenth-century reform movements is the degree to which they overlap, particularly in the case of women, who were not only a major part of the temperance crusade, but were also significant participants in abolitionism. Although much major abolitionist writing was non-fiction, such as the works of Frederick Douglass, Harriet Jacobs, William Lloyd Garrison, Theodore Weld, and Wendell Phillips, there was also a steady stream of abolitionist novels and stories, of which *Uncle Tom's Cabin* is merely the best known. While male abolitionist leaders such as Garrison or Weld founded or edited many of the major abolitionist periodicals, in 1841 one of the most prolific reform writers of the era, Lydia Maria Child, became editor of the *Antislavery Standard*.[8] Child wrote both fiction and non-fiction addressing issues relating to all three major reform movements (though her main interests were in women's rights and abolitionism), as well as less popular ones, such as Native American rights.[9] As Carolyn L. Karcher notes, Child was a household name in her time, as well known to Americans as her Thanksgiving song, "Over the river, and through the wood, / To grandfather's house we go" (*A Lydia* 1).

"Slavery's Pleasant Homes" (1843) is one of Child's most powerful anti-slavery stories. Drenched in irony, a common technique in reform fiction, this text, among other horrors, features a scene in which a fragile, beautiful pregnant woman is flogged to death. Having disobeyed her jealous master, and continued to see her slave lover, Rosa

> exasperated their master beyond endurance. He swore he would overcome her obstinacy, or kill her; and one severe flogging succeeded another, till the tenderly-nurtured slave fainted under the cruel infliction, which was rendered doubly dangerous by the delicate state of her health. Maternal pains came on prematurely, and she died a few hours after. ("SPH" 241)

Child, like Stowe, Alcott, and others discussed above, uses the domestic and maternal to tug at readers' heartstrings, in this case compelling them to identify with the racial Other.

This story further rouses our outrage by dramatizing the sexual exploitation of slave women by their masters, and slavery's destruction of all human ties. George, her slave lover, asks her: "'Rosa, where were you last night?'... 'Oh ...' said she with bitter anguish, 'what *can* I do? I am his *slave*'" (240). She subsequently attempts to avoid her master, but the result is that her lover is sent away and they are forbidden to see each other, "under penalty of severe punishment" (240). Child closes her narrative with heavy irony. After George confesses to killing his master, the newspapers announce a "*'Fiend-like murder.* Frederic Dalcho, one of our most wealthy and respected citizens, was robbed and murdered last week, by one of his slaves'" (242). Of course, the real *"Fiend-like murder"* is Dalcho's heartless destruction of Rosa and her unborn child, an act sure to raise abolitionist sympathies in her readers.[10]

Deploying a somewhat more elegant form of irony, Stowe, in "The Two Altars; or, Two Pictures in One" (1851), published a year before *Uncle Tom's Cabin*, and, like the longer work, a response to the Fugitive Slave Law, juxtaposes two vignettes. The first shows a white family's sacrifices in 1776 in support of soldiers fighting the British, while the second portrays a black family destroyed by enforcement of the new law. The story concludes: "the man is bid off, and the hammer falls with a last crash on his heart, his hopes, his manhood, and he lies a bleeding wreck on the altar of Liberty! Such was the altar in 1776; such is the altar in 1850!" (Stowe, "Two Altars" 182). Stowe shows us a retrograde movement in politics and morality, a decline from Revolutionary ideals, implicitly urging us to recapture them.

Clearly, women were deeply invested in anti-slavery and abolitionism, partly, it seems, because many, such as Child and the Grimké sisters, saw that black slaves and women had much in common, since women's rights were nearly as limited in this period as those of slaves.[11] Until they were married, nineteenth-century women were under the "protection" of their fathers and/or brothers. In nearly every state, women, after marriage, were subject to coverture laws, derived from English Common Law. As stated in Blackstone's *Commentaries on the Laws of England* (1765): "By marriage, the husband and wife are one person in the law; that is, the very being and legal existence of the woman is suspended during the marriage."[12] Not only did a woman's premarital property become her husband's, but also any property accumulated subsequently, including wages and inheritances. Furthermore, until 1850, wife beating with a "reasonable instrument" was legal in nearly all states – the parallels to slavery are quite clear.

Similarly, as suggested by our earlier discussion of temperance fiction, women's experience in the temperance movement led them to feel that the safety of women and children necessitated the former's independence.[13] Such conclusions, derived from experience with both abolitionism and temperance, contributed significantly to the development of the Women's Rights movement, whose first major achievement was the Seneca Falls Convention. Organized by Elizabeth Cady Stanton and Lucretia Mott, this gathering culminated in a "Declaration of Sentiments," signed by 300 women and men, which was essentially a plea – modeled on the Declaration of Independence – for an end to discrimination against women in all spheres of society.[14] (Subsequently, after 1850, annual national conventions were held.) While such activists as Margaret Fuller turned out powerful non-fiction tracts such as *Woman in the Nineteenth Century* (1845), others, such as Betsey Chamberlain and Jane Sophia Appleton, used fiction to urge a reform of gender roles.

In Chamberlain's "A New Society" (1840) the narrator falls into a daydream, and then is handed a paper titled "Annual Meeting of the Society for the Promotion of Industry, Virtue, and Knowledge" (91). Among the resolutions of this society are: "1. *Resolved.* That every father of a family who neglects to give his daughters the same advantages for an education which he gives his sons, shall be expelled from this society, and be considered a heathen" (91), and "4. … That the wages of females shall be equal to that of males, that they may be enabled to maintain proper independence of character" (91). Chamberlain thus advocates an economic gender equality that still has not been achieved a century and a half later, while urging a gender-blind attitude toward education, whose full success was not achieved until the passing of Title IX in 1972.[15] The narrator subsequently reads in the document that, as of 1860 (two decades in the future, of course), two-thirds of America's population belongs to this Society, projecting Chamberlain's hopes for the rapid attainment of a just relation between the genders.

In Appleton's "Sequel to the 'Vision of Bangor in the Twentieth Century'" (1848), published the same year as the Seneca Falls Conference, the narrator, as in "A New Society," begins to dream, and finds herself in a utopia among whose qualities is a markedly more egalitarian attitude toward women than that evidenced during the Victorian era, as her "guide" states:

> "Woman is no longer considered as a mere object for caresses and pretty words. … *Your* age *fondled* woman. *Ours* honors her: You gave her *compliments.* We have given her *rights.* Your contemporaries … looked upon woman as a mere *adjunct* to man. As merely the … 'angel to soothe *his* sorrows, the wife to adorn *his* fireside'. … We regard her as *complete in herself.*" (Appleton 251–2)

Again, we see a radical emphasis on female autonomy and independence at the height of the era of the Cult of True Womanhood. Anticipating Charlotte Perkins Gilman's ideas in such works as *Women and Economics* (1898), *The Home: Its Work and Influence* (1903), and *The Man Made World or Our Androcentric Culture* (1911), Appleton, through her utopia's "eating houses," among other innovations, suggests that shared domestic duties and collective kitchens and laundries would allow women to improve their intellectual powers and help them achieve economic independence. Her narrator observes that in this twentieth-century utopia, "no fear of the world's smile cramped … [women's] vigorous intellect, and no visions of 'blue stockings' repressed the soul that *would* be free" (263). Such freedom, however, in reality would not be achieved for some time, as the fate of Kate Chopin's Progressive Era heroine in "Story of an Hour" (1894) reveals, as we shall see below.

As these two examples suggest, mid-nineteenth-century literary agitation for women's rights found utopian fiction a congenial genre, a tradition continued much later in Gilman's *Herland* (1915). Here is thus another moment of overlapping agendas, as such antebellum visionary texts also engage with broader reform issues encapsulated in the utopian experiments of the era. Appleton's story, for example, exemplifies such Fourieristic ideas as communal living, which was among those that motivated the Brook Farm founders (ideas later satirized in Hawthorne's *A Blithedale Romance* [1852]).

Women's Rights, temperance and utopian fiction continue in the postwar period, often persisting in the use of domestic tropes of social change, as we have already seen in Alcott's "Silver Pitchers," for example. Nonetheless, after 1880, new sub-genres of social change stories began to become popular, such as pro-labor fiction. Interestingly, however, even this industrial genre has its roots in the earlier period. A few years before the Civil War, Herman Melville struck two blows for workers' rights, though characteristically complex and ambiguous: the highly canonical

"Bartleby the Scrivener" (1853), and the lesser known "The Paradise of Bachelors and the Tartarus of Maids" (1855).

Scholars have provided many readings of Bartleby, from the economic and epistemological to the ethical (nihilism) and even the biological (Bartleby as anorexic).[16] It seems clear that even though Bartleby's occupation is technically white-collar, scrivening is a repetitive, tedious endeavor, differing little from industrial factory work in its soul-destroying effects. Thus, Bartleby's refrain of "I would prefer not to" (112) suggests, among other things, a critique of and resistance to the relentless, mindless work imposed on the masses by industrial capitalism, and the difficulty of effective resistance. Bartleby ultimately withers away in jail – his only route of opposition leads to isolation and self-destruction.

Two years later, Melville continued his critique in "The Paradise of Bachelors and the Tartarus of Maids," inspired by a visit to a paper mill near Pittsfield in January of 1851. Though characteristically Melvillean in its symbolic complexity, the story's sympathy for the worker is evident: the first factory denizen the narrator meets has a face "pale with work," and an eye "supernatural with unrelated misery" (219). Anticipating both Rebecca Harding Davis's and Jack London's portrayals of the dehumanizing effects of industrial labor, Melville, through the dull rhythm of repetitious diction, shows us workers who have become their product, as London's Johnny becomes the machine he works on in "The Apostate" (1906/1911) (see p. xxx, below): the narrator soon encounters rows of "blank-looking girls, with blank, white folders in their blank hands, all blankly folding paper" (220). Echoing Emerson – "Things are in the saddle, / And ride mankind" ("Ode, Inscribed to William Ellery Channing" {1846, ll. 50–1}) – and anticipating Thoreau – "But men labor under a mistake" (*Walden* 261) – Melville tells us that, "Machinery – that vaunted slave of humanity – here stood menially served by human beings. ... The girls ... [were] ... mere cogs to the wheels" of this mechanized edifice that turns rags into paper (221). Fear of what machines will to do humanity in an industrial age permeate the text. "The Tartarus of Maids" continually associates the factory with the devil and death – it is located in "Devil's Dungeon," and is described as a "whited sepulcher" (216). The narrator is quite direct about what the factory girls' work is doing to them, telling us with Melvillean dark irony and punning that, "through consumptive pallors of this blank, raggy life, go these white girls to death" (223).

A few years later, Rebecca Harding Davis, in *Life in the Iron Mills; or, The Korl Woman* (1861), took up the cause of workers' rights.[17] According to Jane Atteridge Rose, Davis's story, initially published anonymously in the *Atlantic Monthly*, "confronted readers with their own ignorance and challenged their complacency" (35). Unlike the often genteel, or at least genteelly represented, subjects of much temperance fiction, Davis's subjects are likely to repel her middle-class readers. However, she boldly attacks her topic head-on, inviting the reader into the steelworkers' horrific lives, challenging them not to flinch at the spectacle of their twisted bodies and disfigured souls: "This is what I want you to do. I want you to hide your disgust, take no heed to your clean clothes, and come right down with me, – here, into the thickest of the fog ... and foul effluvia" (13). The narrator describes the lives of the workers as "incessant labor, sleeping in kennel-like rooms, eating rank pork and molasses, drinking – God and the distillers only know what; with an occasional night in jail, to atone for some drunken excess" (15). Depicting the main female character, Deborah, the narrator states that she looks like a "limp, dirty rag, – yet not an unfitting figure to crown the scene of hopeless discomfort and veiled crime: more fitting, if one looked deeper into the heart of things, at her thwarted woman's form, her colorless life, her waking stupor" (21). Using rhetorical questions (as revealed by the plot), Davis asks the reader, "was there nothing worth reading in this wet, faded, thing ... ? no [*sic*] story of a soul filled with groping passionate love, heroic unselfishness, fierce jealousy?" (21). Combining the techniques of realism, sentimentalism, and the classic strategy in slave narratives of using personal, emotional, and familial identification to engage her readers' sympathies, thus refamiliarizing the apparent "Other," Davis equates Deborah's expression of unrequited love to that on the "rarest, finest of women's faces" (22). She then asks the reader, "Are pain and jealousy less savage realities down here in this place I am taking you to than in your own house or your own heart ... ? *The note is the same, I fancy, be the octave high or low*" (22, 23; emphasis added). Similarly, Davis presents us with a working-class figure, Wolfe, whose korl sculptures reveal that exceptional, artistic natures can be hidden amidst the grim and "hard, grinding labor" (25) of the workers' quotidian existence.[18] She thereby bridges the gap between middle-class reader and working-class subject, yet never lets the former forget the malformed body and spirit inflicted on the latter:

> Think that God put into this man's soul a fierce thirst for beauty, – to know it, to create it; to *be* [original emphasis] – something, he knows not what, – other than he is. There are moments when a passing cloud ... a kindly smile, a child's face, will rouse him to a passion of pain, – when his nature starts up with a mad cry of rage against God, man, whoever it is that forced this vile, slimy life upon him. With all this groping, this mad desire, a great blind intellect stumbling through wrong, a loving poet's heart, the man was by habit only a coarse, vulgar laborer. ... Be just: when I tell you about this night, see him as he is. (25)

Nonetheless, through the mouth of one of her upper-class characters, Davis warns that if conditions do not change, the working classes, out of need, "will [throw] up their own light-bringer ... their Cromwell, their Messiah" (39). A man like Wolfe, she implies, could lead a revolution, or found a new faith.

Twenty years later, with millions more workers like Wolfe and Deborah having entered the labor force, perhaps the most significant period of reform in the United States began.[19] During the Progressive Era, a multiplicity of reform movements flourished, as society underwent rapid urbanization and industrialization. The population doubled to 100 million, of whom close to 20 million were immigrants (mostly from Southern and Eastern Europe), the largest influx in American history. In 1907 alone 1.25 million immigrants arrived; by 1910, nearly 15 percent of all Americans were foreign-born, and in some Eastern cities, more than half the population consisted of immigrants and their children. In 1900, one-third of all Americans lived in cities of 8,000 or more; by 1910, nearly half the population lived in urban areas. The number of urban areas of 100,000 or more increased from twenty-five during the final decades of the nineteenth century to nearly three times as many by 1916.

Such expansion, however, was accompanied by significant growing pains. In 1890, 11 million of the nation's 12 million families earned less than $1,200 per year; of this group, the average annual income was $380, well below the poverty line. Over the next decade, the economy was shaken by two major panics, in 1893 and 1897, even as "trustification" proceeded; by 1900 there were seventy-five trusts worth 10 million dollars or more, with as many as a thousand mergers a year at the turn of the century. This period was also the era of American Imperialism, during which conti-nental Manifest Destiny was extended overseas, leading to the Spanish-American War (including the takeover of Cuba and the Philippines) and the annexation of Hawaii.[20] Such changes led to both reform and violent resistance, including the rise of unionism, exemplified by the founding of the American Federation of Labor (1881), the United Mine Workers (1899), and the International Workers of the World (1905), as well as by the Haymarket riot (1886), the Pullman railroad (1894), and Lawrence textile workers' (1912) strikes, and the Ludlow massacre (1914), during which the National Guard fired machine guns at a workers' encampment in Colorado. Between 1881 and 1905, over 37,000 strikes occurred throughout the country; by 1911, union member-ship was five times what it had been in 1897. This period also saw the founding of significant anti-racist organizations such as the NAACP (1909), which accompanied the beginning of the Great Migration (mass movement of blacks from rural South to urban North), the Society of the American Indian (1911) and the Japanese Association of America (1908).

The era's reform movements, in addition to trade unionism and the pursuit of minorities' rights, included the Anti-Saloon League (a continuation of the mid-nineteenth-century temperance movement);[21] the Settlement House Movement (Hull House opened in 1889); Regulationism (dedicated to controlling prostitution; over 200 of the largest cities closed their red-light districts between 1912 and 1920); hygiene reform, including the pure food and birth control movements; socialism (Eugene V. Debs's tally in presidential elections went from 402,283 in 1904 to 900,672 in 1912, reaching the largest total ever for a socialist candidate in American history, at a time when the population was only 90 million); Women's Suffrage/women's rights; anti-trust agitation; anti-imperialism; anti-lynching; slum reform; the conservation movement (e.g. the establishment of the National Park system under Teddy Roosevelt); and the City Beautiful Movement.

Among the many successes of Progressive Age reform were the 190 million acres of land added to national forests and protected from development between 1900 and 1908; the opening of higher education to women (47 percent of college students were women by 1920); near universal school attendance (enrollments reached 86 percent by 1920); the passing between 1900 and 1916 by most states of minimum working age laws (and limitation of hours of work to less than ten); the Pendleton Civil Service

Act (1883), which rooted out corruption in the Civil Service; the Interstate Commerce Act (1887), which created the first true federal regulatory agency; the New York State Tenement House Act (1901); the Pure Food and Drug Act (1906); the Meat Inspection Act (1906); the Antiquities Act (protection of Native American "antiquities") (1906); the Mann Act (1910; formally known as the "White-Slave Traffic Act"), which criminalized transportation of women across state lines "for the purpose of prostitution or debauchery, or for any other immoral purpose"; the 16th Amendment (income tax) (1913); the 17th Amendment (popular election of Senators) (1913); the Federal Reserve Act (1913); the Federal Trade Commission Act (1914); the Clayton Antitrust Act (1914); the Child Labor Act (1916, though overturned in 1918 by the Supreme Court), which prohibited products of child labor to be sold across state lines; the Adamson Act (1916), which instituted an eight-hour work day for railroad workers; the 18th Amendment (Prohibition) (1919); and the 19th Amendment (Women's Suffrage) (1920).

One of the most powerful genres of social change fiction in this period was anti-capitalist fiction, which focuses on such topics as industrial working conditions, the exploitation of farmers, the corrupt practices of industrialists, and life in the tenements. Stylistically, such stories appear in dystopian, utopian, and realist form. Perhaps the era's most successful writer of such radical short fiction was Jack London, whose stories often parallel the arguments of his many lectures on socialism – lectures that inspired such headlines as, "One of the World's Great Authorities on Socialism Analyses Campaign Made in Behalf of Eugene V. Debs" (*San Francisco Examiner* November 10, 1904: 3) – and whose fiction was highly praised by Lenin, Trotsky, Debs, Big Bill Haywood, and Bukharin. Such stories fit several genres, ranging from science fiction and horror to realism.[22] Among the most well-known of these is "The Apostate" (1906), partly based on London's experience working in a jute mill at age 16. The protagonist, Johnny, is turned into both machine and beast by industrial work; he is an exploited child forced into the world too soon, prematurely old, yet never having been allowed to grow up. Although only a few years older than his siblings, having gone to work in a factory aged 7, at 16, he was "very old, while they were distressingly young" ("Apostate" 124). Johnny, in fact, was born among machines, on the factory floor, foreshadowing his destiny, "drawing with his first breath the warm moist air that was thick with flying lint. He had coughed that first day in order to rid his lungs of the lint; and for the same reason he had coughed ever since" (122); here London echoes Melville, in "Tartarus of Maids," when the latter describes how in the paper factory "the air swam with the fine poisonous particles [of lint], which from all sides darted, subtilely [*sic*] ... into the lungs" (Melville, "Tartarus" 222). From "the perfect worker [Johnny] had evolved into the perfect machine. ... There had never been a time when he had not been in intimate relationship with machines" ("Apostate" 121–2). Johnny, naturalistically shaped by his environment, embodies the dehumanizing, yet highly efficient mode of work that Frederick Winslow Taylor called for five years later in *The Principles of Scientific Management*: "All waste movements were eliminated. Every motion of his thin arms, every movement of a muscle in the thin fingers, was swift and accurate … his mind had gone to sleep … He was a work-beast" (127, 128, 129).

Throughout the story, London describes him as either brute or machine, the two poles of the inhuman.[23] Johnny is stunted both physically and mentally; when he finally rebels, and leaves the factory to become a hobo, as London himself did in 1894, all of his humanity has been drained out of him by industrial work. The eloquence of London's call for child labor reform is perhaps most evident in his final description of Johnny, a description that also could easily be applied to Davis's steelworkers: "He did not walk like a man. He did not look like a man. He was a travesty of the human. It was a twisted and stunted and nameless piece of life that shambled like a sickly ape, arms loose-hanging, stoop-shouldered, narrow-chested, grotesque and terrible" (134). Our sympathy is roused for Johnny's plight here not primarily through sentimental or domestic techniques, but rather by London's directly confronting us with the dehumanizing effects of industrial labor. Although Johnny, unlike such later London anti-capitalist protagonists as Ernest Everhard or Freddie Drummond, does not violently resist the forces of capital, his heretical abandonment of it is as much of a direct confrontation (hence his mother's horror and shock) as throwing a bomb or beating a scab would be.

Other notable anti-capitalist stories of London's include "The Dream of Debs" (1909/1914), "South of the Slot" (1909/1914), and "The Strength of the Strong" (1911/1914). The first describes through the eyes of a wealthy man a successful general strike that paralyzes the country; at the end he states, "I never want to see another one. It was worse than a war … the brain of man should be capable of running industry in a more rational way" ("Debs" 1277–8). The second shows the conversion of a repressed, upper middle-class sociology professor, Freddie Drummond, into his fiery working-class alter ego, Bill Totts. Drummond at first adopts this persona as a disguise to further his research into labor–capital disputes; eventually, however, he leaves his former self behind, disappearing "into the labor ghetto" ("Slot" 1594), symbolizing the superior vigor and eventual triumph of the working classes over their oppressors. In later years, "no more lectures were given in the University of California by one Drummond and no more books on economics and the labor question appeared over the name of Frederick A. Drummond. On the other hand, there arose a new labor leader, William Totts" (1594). London implies that forever after, Drummond/Totts will violently resist the oppression of capitalism, beating up scabs and capital's enforcers, the police, at every turn: "A rush of three [policemen] … locked with Bill Totts in a gigantic clinch, during which his scalp was opened up by a club, and coat, vest and half his starched shirt were torn from him. But the three policemen were flung far and wide … and … Totts held the fort" (1593). The third story is a socialist parable that answers Rudyard Kipling's anti-socialist story "Melissa" (1908) by showing that the "strength of the strong" is not that of the "superman," but rather that of cooperation: when such cooperation is achieved, says a member of the tribe, " 'nothing will withstand us, for the strength of each man will be the strength of all men in the world' " ("Strong" 1578). All of these stories exploit the masculinist tropes of battle and conflict – rather than those of domesticity – to show their readers the most effective path to social change, namely to fight for one's beliefs.

Other writers of Progressive Era anti-capitalist fiction include Hamlin Garland, whose *Main-Traveled Roads* (1891) contains a number of anti-capitalist stories, such as "Under the Lion's Paw," which illustrates the greed endemic to capitalist specula-tion. Haskins, a farmer, having been rescued by a fellow farmer, Council, works hard to improve a farm leased to him by Butler, a local speculator: "no slave in the Roman galleys could have toiled so frightfully and lived … There is no despair so deep as the despair of a homeless man or woman … It was the memory of this homelessness, and the fear of it coming again, that spurred … Haskins and Nettie … to such fero-cious labor during that first year" (234–5). After their work has substantially improved the farm, Butler nearly doubles the purchase price and gives Haskins no credit for his improvements, baldly declaring, "'the land has doubled in value, it don't matter how. … Never trust anybody, friend. … Don't take me for a thief. It's the law. The reg'lar thing. Everybody does it'" (239). Under capitalism, the "lion," Garland is saying, such exploitation of the downtrodden is routine.

As suggested above, one of the major issues addressed in workers' rights stories was the living conditions of the poor, some of which, like the London texts previously discussed, or those in James Oppenheim's *Pay Envelopes* (1911), indict the capitalist system, and others of which, like those in Jacob Riis's *Neighbors: Stories of the Other Half* (1914), and *Children of the Tenements* (1903), suggest the need for change, but within the system. Riis deliberately blurs the line between fact and fiction, a powerful rhetorical strategy for convincing the reader of the urgency of social change. Both of his fiction collections include prefaces that stress that – for the most part – he has merely changed individual and place names in his texts. He expects that his readers will be more likely to be influenced by "true stories" (a common stratagem in reform fiction), than they were by his wildly successful journalistic exposé, *How the Other Half Lives* (1890).[24]

In "The Problem of the Widow Salvini," from *Neighbors*, Riis emphasizes the intractability of tenement life and its dominant form of work, sweated labor, which he calls "industrial slavery" ("Salvini" 57), describing three "curses of the tenement" (59): home sweat work, lodgers crammed into tiny apartments, and child labor. In "What the Christmas Sun Saw in the Tenements" from his 1903 collection, he pounds home the grimness and tragedies of life among the tenements through several vignettes, including that of a little girl, "barefooted and in rags" (Riis, "Sun" 134) sent to procure a pint of beer for her mother, clearly a corruption of domestic purity. Later, she returns to a tenement apartment, "windowless, airless, and sunless, but rented at a price that a millionaire would denounce as robbery" (136). As the narrator notes, "There are no homes in New York's poor tenements" (139). Continuing with a miniature fictional-ized version of his tenement travelogue in *How the Other Half Lives,* he then vividly depicts young white girls enslaved to the opium pipe in Chinatown (142), concluding his story with a view of Potter's Field, implying the premature, nameless end to tene-ment lives, through "the shadows of countless headstones that bear no names, only numbers" (148). He thus both draws in his readers through reference to a common and usually joyous, experience, Christmas, and then savagely undermines their expectations, hoping to propel them to clamor for reform. These are conventional sentimental representations of the powerless poor, quite different from London's Johnny. Working-class life is grim in both texts, but Johnny is not helpless; he acts. London – unlike Riis – wants to rely not merely on the goodwill of the middle class, but also on workers' own actions.

Oppenheim's *Pay Envelopes* collection is often equally melodramatic. Its preface, "Troubles of the Workshop," baldly states the critique dramatized by its stories: "the murder of men through twelve-hour days, child labor, and unprotected machinery; the struggle between labor and capital; the fights for sanitation" ("Troubles" 11), and proclaims the necessity for fiction dedicated to social change, a need convincingly illustrated by many of the writers we have been discussing: "In America, we must interpret one race to another; one class to another; one type to another, before we will ever feel that all have the same essential humanness" (14). In Oppenheim's view – supported by many writers' use of the tropes previously discussed (domesticity, for example) – stories aimed at social change engage in acts of class translation to bring middle-class readers into the working-class's world.

For Oppenheim, such interpretation can involve the provoking of both sympathy and fear in the reader. In "The Great Fear," Oppenheim elicits readers' sympathies by telling the tale of a young couple with a new baby (an effective subject for reform fiction, as we saw in Butler's "Emma Alton") devastated by unemployment, leading them to the verge of what Jack London calls the "social pit" in works such as *The People of the Abyss* (1902). The author continues to use well-worn tropes of the domestic to engage his readers, yet he also begins to add masculine tropes of at least the threat of violence. The couple's "great fear" is the fear of unemployment and starvation, yet the story also conveys the idea that, according to the husband, workers are " 'slaves – *slaves*' "; and that, if changes aren't made, " 'this country better look out' " (26). This statement reveals a double meaning in the title: the workers fear unemployment, but so should middle- and upper-class readers, lest they be confronted by Riis's "Man with a Knife" (*Other Half* 207).

Many writers of the period produced short stories meant to address problems of race and ethnicity in a society that was becoming ever more rapidly multicultural. Interestingly, in addition to many non-Protestant or non-white writers invested in interpreting their own cultures for a predominantly Protestant Euro-American audience, one of the most eloquent voices of anti-racism – despite his reputation otherwise – is Jack London. Indeed, he seems to have written nearly as many anti-racist stories as anti-capitalist ones; London's protest fiction, like his work as a whole, covers multiple topics, on multiple levels.[25]

As I have discussed at length in " 'Zone-Conquerors' and 'White Devils': The Contradictions of Race in the Works of Jack London," London's attitudes towards race are complex and conflicted. London was, as it were, constituted by a series of contradictions: superman socialist, racist/anti-racist, etc. In many of his stories (and it is more often in his stories than his novels that this is the case), he displays profound sympathy, and even outrage, at the ways in which Euro-Americans have exploited, and often destroyed, non-whites. Among his nine or so anti-racist stories, several of the most notable are "Chun Ah Chun" (1912/1914), "Koolau, the Leper" (1909/1912) and "The Mexican" (1911/1913).[26]

The first of these explodes the kind of anti-Chinese attitudes manifested by the Chinese Exclusion Acts, by illustrating the brilliance and power of its title character: "He was essentially a philosopher, and whether as coolie, or multi-millionaire and master of many men, his poise of soul was the same" ("Chun Ah Chun" 1455). A man of great vision, Chun imagines Honolulu as a modern city with electricity while it is still a primitive sandblasted settlement set on a coral reef. London also shows that, contrary to popular belief, the Chinese can become part of the American melting pot; while Chun Ah Chun himself retires to China, his children, among whom "the blend of races was excellent" (1458), go to Harvard, Oxford, Yale, Mills College, Vassar, Wellesley, and Bryn Mawr, living the American dream.

In "Koolau, the Leper," another Hawaiian tale, London illustrates the devastating effects on native peoples of Western colonialism and imperialism, producing a text that is both anti-racist and anti-imperialist. Koolau states: "Because we are sick they take away our liberty. We have obeyed the law. We have done no wrong. And yet they would put us in prison. Molokai is a prison. ... They came like lambs, speaking softly. ... To-day all the islands are theirs" (164). Amplifying these views, a former judge, Kapalei, proclaims:

> "The sickness is not ours. We have not sinned. The [white] men who preached the word of God and the word of Rum brought the sickness with the coolie slaves who work the stolen land. I have been a judge. I know the law and the justice, and I say to you it is unjust to steal a man's land, to make that man sick with the Chinese sickness, and then to put that man in prison for life." (167)

The title character refuses to be sent to Molokai, and shows his superiority to the Euro-American soldiers sent to capture him by killing dozens of them and evading capture, keeping his freedom, and his rifle, until he dies of leprosy, surrounded by the natural beauty of his native island, in an area not yet despoiled by whites.

In "The Mexican," a story that is both anti-capitalist and anti-racist, the eponymous character shares not only an indomitability of spirit with London's Anglo-Saxon heroes like Martin Eden, Ernest Everhard, and Wolf Larsen, but also their physiological power (if not their size; the protagonist here is wiry, rather than bulky). Felipe Rivera has a "deep chest," tough-fibred flesh, an "instantaneousness of the cell explosions of the muscles, [and] ... fineness of the nerves that wired every part of him into a splendid fighting mechanism" (306). Furthermore, London is careful to note that "Indian blood, as well as Spanish, was in his veins" (300). Rivera, like Koolau, is a tragic figure – a sympathetic fellow revolutionist says, " 'he hates all people. ... He is alone. ... lonely' " (295).

Nonetheless, he is admirable both in his strength and in his ideals: he is a boxer who fights for money to help fund a socialist revolution in Mexico. Although his fellows in his revolutionary cell, the Junta, are unaware of how Rivera gets money to bring them, they are well aware of his force and dedication: " 'To me he is power – he is the wild wolf, – the striking rattlesnake,' " says one. To another, " 'He is the Revolution incarnate'. ... 'He is the flame and spirit of it, the insatiable cry for vengeance ...' " (295). In Rivera's ultimate fight – upon which $5,000 and the guns necessary to start the revolution depend – he finds that "[a]ll Gringos were against him, even the referee" (308), who counts long seconds when his opponent is down, and short seconds when Rivera himself is down. Through his strength and quick intelligence, and his keen senses, however, he triumphs over the whites' conspiracy of unfairness. (London refers to Rivera's handlers, who are all white and strangers, as "scrubs," a phrase he uses elsewhere as a derogatory term for mixed breeds.) Although his opponent is one of the top fighters in the game, "the coming champion," and helped by "the many ways of cheating in this game of the Gringos" (303), Rivera is something much more, an "Übermensch": although only a boy of eighteen, "he had gone through such vastly greater heats that this collective passion of ten thousand throats, rising surge on surge, was to his brain no more than the velvet cool of a summer twilight" (312). Furthermore, like Ernest Everhard in *The Iron Heel* (1908), Rivera is a superman devoted to the cause of the masses. He does not fight for himself; rather, "resplendent and glorious, he saw the great, red Revolution sweeping across his land. ... He was the guns. He was the Revolution. He fought for all Mexico" (309). After Rivera wins the bout, the narrator declares, "The Revolution could go on" (313). London thus uses a highly unusual genre, boxing fiction (which he invented), through which to convey his message of socialist, anti-racist social change. Here, the heroism of individual combat is supposed to engage readers in the cause of social justice.

As previously indicated, London was unusual in being a white, Protestant promoter of racial justice in this period. There were, however, many non-Anglo Saxon fiction writers – more than in any earlier period – active in the Progressive Era, who came not only from European ethnic groups such as the Jews, Irish, German, Scandinavians, and so on, but also from non-white groups such as African Americans, Chinese Americans, Native Americans, and Chicanos. Such writers as Charles Chesnutt, Abraham Cahan, Sui Sin Far, Zitkala-Ša, and Maria Cristina Mena tried to teach the Euro-American audience for such magazines as *Harper's,* the *Atlantic Monthly,* and *Everybody's Magazine* about the significance of their cultures and the injustices perpetrated against them, hoping to influence readers to change their views and become active combatants in "the good fight."

Chesnutt, interestingly, often simultaneously addresses both a black and white audience in his social change fiction. In "The Wife of His Youth" (1898), first published in the *Atlantic Monthly,* for example, he simultaneously shows his white readers the levels of sophistication and success many blacks have already achieved, hoping to undermine their racist, primitivist preconceptions, while reminding his black audience that in striving to better themselves in a white society, they should never forget their "blackness," symbolized by the main character's slave wife, whom he has conveniently forgotten amidst his postwar success.

Abraham Cahan, a Russian Jewish socialist and labor advocate and longtime editor of the *Jewish Daily Forward*, in stories such as "A Sweatshop Romance" (1898), demonstrates to his Gentile readers that the apparently alien Russian Jewish hordes "invading" America by the millions are nonetheless composed of individuals that resemble themselves in their quotidian concerns. In this story, he uses a love triangle plot in an industrial workplace to draw in his readers – a return to sentimental, if not domestic, rhetorical stratagems in the fiction of social change. Here, such tropes are placed in a solidly working-class milieu, as opposed to the middle-class context of most antebellum authors of social change fiction, such as the temperance writers.

Sui Sin Far (Edith Maude Eaton), the first Asian American writer to publish fiction in the US ("The Chinese Ishmael" [1899]), also returns to sentimental and domestic themes in "Mrs. Spring Fragrance" (1910/1912), not only to emphasize the similarities of the Asian Other to whites, but also to attack the paranoid, xenophobic Chinese Exclusion Acts.[27] Interestingly, even this political premise, not just the text's love theme, is conveyed through a vehicle of the domestic, a letter from wife to husband, which while sometimes heavily ironic – "And murmur no more because your ... brother ... is detained under the roof-tree of this great Government. ... Console him with the reflection that he is protected under the wing of the Eagle, the Emblem of Liberty" (21) – is nonetheless intimate and affectionate ("Your ever loving and obedient woman ..." [22]), not unlike those that her white readers undoubtedly wrote to their spouses. However, although her plot deals with matchmaking and the definition of love, as her Chinese American characters negotiate the line between their American and Chinese identities, Far also deploys masculinist images, including among her characters Kai Tzu, as "stalwart as any young Westerner," noted "amongst baseball players as one of the finest pitchers" in California (17).

Another writer from a marginalized group, Maria Cristina Mena, one of the earliest published writers of Latino fiction, after Maria Amparo Ruiz de Barton, also uses romance to critique race relations. In "The Education of Popo," published in the *Century Magazine* in March 1914, a teenage Mexican boy falls in love with a visiting young American woman in her twenties, Alicia, recently estranged from her fiancé. Popo's family goes to great lengths to please the American family, importing "American canned soups" and breakfast cereal (47) and much more, a blatant reference to American arrogance, and a veiled one to imperialism; rather than accepting Mexican culture, they impose their own on their hosts, who feel it important to indulge them. The American family, the Cherrys, treat their hosts condescendingly, and Alicia, blond and draped with a "generous measure of diamonds" (57), encourages Popo, exploits his affections, and then returns to her American fiancé, Edward Winterbottom, after he shows up in Mexico unexpectedly. At the story's conclusion Edward self-importantly assumes he is paying Popo the highest compliment by declaring that the Mexican youth is "worthy of being an American" (62). Alicia, meanwhile, describes Popo's behavior as "his Indian revenge" (62), while also stereotyping him as an emotional Latin (61). The allusions to American racist, imperialist arrogance, though hidden beneath a sentimental plot and language, are unmistakable. Alicia takes what she wants from the Mexican boy, and leaves; meanwhile, Popo denounces her "treacherous falseness" (61). While demonstrating the sophistication of Popo's upper middle-class family to her white American readers, depicting an elegant ball given by Governor Arriola (58), Popo's father, Mena also rebukes them for their racism and arrogance, albeit in the sugar-coated form of a travel romance. She wants her Anglo readers to acknowledge the significance of Mexican culture, and to cease interfering.

It seems clear that certain Progressive Era female writers, like Far and Mena (and some male, such as Cahan), continue to pursue social change via the sentimental and the domestic. Others, however, such as Zitkala-Ša (Gertrude Simmons Bonnin), a mixed race Lakota Sioux author, use stories of conflict and violence to achieve their aims. In "The Soft-Hearted Sioux" (1901), published in *Harper's*, the author shows the destructiveness of Euro-Americans' attempts to Christianize Indians, and to use starvation to force them on to reservations. The narrator, a Sioux who left his people as a teenager to attend a mission school, is eventually sent back to try to convert them, an endeavor at which he has little success. The fact that he is never named is significant, since it allows him to stand in for the thousands of Native Americans assimilated by the mission schools. When he returns home to his people, he immediately feels estranged from them, even from his own parents. Sitting with them, he thinks, "I did not feel at home ... far apart in spirit our ideas and faiths separated us" (120–1).[28] While preaching, he is attacked by the medicine man – whose views seem clearly endorsed by the author – who reminds him of the injustices of the whites, declaring that his dress is that of the "foreigner" who "'bound a native of our land, and ... kindled a fire at his feet'" (122). He continues, turning to his people, "'Why do you sit here giving ear to a foolish man who could not defend his people because he fears to kill, who could not bring venison to renew the life of his sick father? With his prayers, let him drive away the enemy! With his soft heart, let him keep off starvation'" (122), accusations echoed by the narrator's family (123), since his assimilation has rendered him unfit to hunt for meat for his starving, ill father. Finally, he is driven to steal a cow, but chased by the farmer, he commits murder to escape, only to find that his father has perished while he was away. He is then arrested, and, as the story concludes, awaits execution at the hands of white law. The story is a plea to white readers to understand the plight of Native Americans, and to get the Euro-American government and society to cease attempting to impose their values on them.

The following year, Zitkala-Ša published a story that addresses themes of both racial pride and women's rights, "A Warrior's Daughter" (1902). On the one hand, as she strove to do in much of her fiction and non-fiction, the author tries to convey to her white audience the dignity and significance of her tribal culture, as well as the intimate particulars of daily life among the Sioux, details designed, as with Sui Sin Far, to lead her readers to see the racial Other's humanity.[29] At the beginning of the story, Tusee is very young, with a "childish faith in her elders" and a "child's buoyant spirit" (134), much loved by her parents and uncles; this is one of the few moments in the story where the author relies on domestic tropes. At the same time, however, she shows her readers the fierce pride of her people and their traditions – Tusee's father has won by ferocious "heroic deeds" many privileges, showing that the Sioux's cultural conventions are equivalent to the heroic traditions valorized by Western culture – and uniquely preaches a feminist message via violent conflict and the application of female physical strength and bravery.

As I argue in "'A Mighty Power Thrills Her Body': Zitkala-Ša's 'A Warrior's Daughter' and Natural Feminism," Tusee speaks to the aspirations of many other American women of the time, regardless of ethnic or racial background, who fought to escape from the constraints of the Cult of True Womanhood. On the one hand, Tusee exemplifies the superiority of Native American women to overcivilized, hyper-feminized Euro-American women, especially in their alternative sex role as warrior women; on the other, Tusee is a model for what all American women can achieve if they break free of Victorian notions of femininity (Furer, "Natural Feminism"). After the brief vignette set during Tusee's childhood, the narrative focuses on her transformation into a warrior woman as an adult. When her lover is captured in battle, and no men volunteer to go after him, Tusee single-handedly rescues him. First, she uses her feminine attractiveness as a young woman to lure away her lover's captor. Appearing to flee seductively, she then lets him catch her, at which point she whirls, announces herself as his enemy, and kills him with a single knife thrust, having previously prayed for her warrior-father's heart to be planted within her "strong to slay a foe, and mighty to save a friend" (Zitkala-Ša, "Daughter" 137). Next, Tusee disguises herself as an old woman to pass unnoticed to where her lover is being kept, and then reveals herself to him, frees him, and takes him back to safety. Particularly notable in the text are the brilliance of Tusee's disguises, and the fact that she uses both traditional feminine and masculine modes of behavior to achieve her goal, culminating in a significant feat of strength. The story culminates with a moment of significant role-reversal, at least as her contemporaries would have perceived it: "'Come!' she whispers, and turns to go; but the young man, numb and helpless, staggers nigh to falling. The sight of his weakness makes her strong. A mighty power thrills her body. Stooping beneath his outstretched arms grasping at the air for support, Tusee lifts him upon her broad shoulders. With half-running, triumphant steps she carries him away into the open night" (140). This ending, while highly unusual in its redefinition of the feminine, is not surprising in the context of the author's life. In 1901, writing to her fiancé, Native American activist Carlos Montezuma, she asks combatively, "Am I not an Indian woman as capable in serious matters and as thoroughly interested in the race – as any one or two of you men put together? Why do you dare leave me out?"[30]

"A Warrior's Daughter," of course, was part of a flood of feminist fiction that appeared during the Progressive Era, far outstripping its antebellum counterpart in volume. Writers such as Kate Chopin, Charlotte Perkins Gilman, and Jack London, among others, attempted to redefine gender roles in an age during which women were going to college and entering the workforce in far greater numbers than ever before (see p. 196, above).[31] Between them, Gilman and Chopin published dozens of feminist stories, questioning the traditional gender roles of wife and mother, of which the former's "The Yellow Wallpaper" (1892) and the latter's "The Story of an Hour" (1894) are highly representative.[32]

Over the past several decades, Gilman's text has become one of the most well-known, widely taught short stories of the period. This much interpreted semi-autobiographical story about a woman suffering through S. Weir Mitchell's "rest cure" under the doubly patriarchal supervision of her physician-husband John (and with the agreement of her brother, also a doctor), was intended to save women from being driven crazy, which it apparently did, according to Gilman's "Why I Wrote 'The Yellow Wallpaper'" (1913). The narrator indicts her husband and Mitchell, by writing "John is a physician, and *perhaps* – … *perhaps* that is one reason I do not get well faster" ("Wallpaper" 31). The story condemns not merely Mitchell's misogynist cure, which prohibited women from writing and from thinking deeply, but also a society whose broader concept of women's role quashes what Gilman, in the story, as well as in her highly influential *Women and Economics* (1898) suggests is a fundamental human need, "the creative impulse, the desire to make, to express the inner thought in outer form … 'I want to mark!' cries the child" (*W&E* 116–17). The narrator is infantilized and dehumanized by the strictures put on her mental and physical activity. Locked in a nursery with barred windows and a bed bolted to the floor much of the time, with a "schedule prescription for each hour in the day" ("Wallpaper" 33), she eventually crawls around the room (like a baby), obsessed with the room's wallpaper, which she sees imprisoning and even strangling women. Her captivity, and the repression of her humanity and creativity, eventually drive her mad. Gilman shows us that her only path to freedom from patriarchal oppression, other than suicide, which she also contemplates – "to jump out the window would be admirable exercise" (46) – is to go mad, a Pyrrhic victory highlighted by John's fainting spell upon seeing her crawling around the room: "Now why should that man have fainted? But he did, and right across my path … so that I had to creep over him every time!" (47). In addition to rejecting second-class status for women, Gilman also uses the story, along with several of her non-fiction works (see p. 193, above) to suggest the radical idea that not all women are suited to be mothers: "It is fortunate Mary is so good with the baby. Such a dear baby! And yet I *cannot* be with him, it makes me so nervous" (34). Gilman wants women to be free to create intellectually, not just biologically. More than just a text of mental hygiene reform, "The Yellow Wallpaper" represents an effort to show Gilman's audience the extremely urgent need for radical reform of traditional gender roles.

Chopin, like Gilman, sees significant problems with society's traditional constructions of woman as wife and mother. While she is best known for *The Awakening* (1899), in the years prior to its publication she focused primarily on short fiction. In "The Story of an Hour," first published in *Vogue* as "The Dream of an Hour" (1894), Mrs. Mallard, the protagonist, at first reacts to the news of her husband's sudden death with terrible grief, followed by exhaustion. Soon, however, she feels something coming into her consciousness, and begins to whisper " 'free, free, free!' " after which, in place of her former "repression" (138), she begins to feel gloriously alive: "Her pulses beat fast, and the coursing blood warmed and relaxed every inch of her body" (138). What follows is a manifesto of female independence: "she saw ... a long procession of years to come that would belong to her absolutely ... she would live for herself. There would be no powerful will bending hers" (138). Although there is no question that she loves her husband – what could love, "the unsolved mystery, count for in face of this possession of self-assertion which she suddenly recognized as the strongest impulse of her being! ... 'Free! Body and soul free!' She kept whispering" (138–9) – it is plain that married life has stifled her, transforming her into a slave. Subsequently, she murmurs "a quick prayer that life might be long. It was only yesterday she had thought with a shudder that life might be long" (139) (clearly the concerns of Seneca Falls have not yet been addressed, despite the passing of half a century). Chopin implies that death might be better than marriage, at least from a wife's perspective.

Tragically, however, Mrs. Mallard's freedom is short-lived; she goes downstairs, only to encounter her husband, who had been far from the accident, as it turns out. Seeing him, she lets out a "piercing cry" and falls dead. Chopin, having told her story in mostly unironic manner up to this point, concludes it with a savage inversion: "When the doctors came they said she had died of heart disease – of joy that kills" (139). Of course, the truth is, she has died of a broken heart, having lost the intoxicating freedom she had so briefly enjoyed. Chopin and Gilman reject the domestic, both as trope and social structure, using anti-domestic themes to drive home to their readers the injustice and inhumanity of *fin-de-siècle* women's roles.

Although not all writers discussed here would agree with Jack London's claim that "socialism was the only way out for art and the artist" (Charmian London 528), they would agree that the short story can be an effective weapon with which to impel the nation in the direction of social justice. From temperance and workers' rights fiction to stories of Native American resistance and Euro-American exploitation, American writers in the nineteenth and early twentieth centuries, utilizing tropes of both domesticity and violent conflict, found short fiction a highly congenial genre for expressing their desire for change.

NOTES

1 See Frank Luther Mott, *A History of American Magazines: 1741–1850*, 341–2, and Mott, *A History of American Magazines: 1850–1865*, 4–5. According to Mott, as many as 5,000 magazines were active in this period. He quotes the *Illinois Monthly Magazine* 1.302 (April 1831), as proclaiming that "this is the golden age of periodicals" (qtd. in Mott, *A History: 1741–1850*, 341).

2 See Mott, *A History of American Magazines: 1885–1905*, 11–12. According to Mott, including failed publications, mergers, etc., nearly 11,000 magazines were published during this period.

3 This chapter is designed to present a broad overview of the short fiction of social change between 1820 and 1918. For extended deep analysis of the stories noted here, the reader

will need to look elsewhere. (See "References and Further Reading" below, for some useful critical works and collections.)

4 In fiction, however, women appear to predominate, as a casual survey of temperance magazines and gift books reveals. Interestingly, among the men who did produce such work was Walt Whitman, albeit in long form, not surprisingly – a novel, rather than short stories. In 1842, he published *Franklin Evans, or The Inebriate: A Tale of the Times*, which seems to have sold as many as 20,000 copies (Whitman, *Franklin Evans*, ed. Castiglia and Hendler xiii). According to Mark Walhout, later in life, Whitman liked to joke about his novel. He told Horace Traubel that he had written the novel for money "'with the help of a bottle of port or what not.' Another version had Whitman penning the novel in Tammany Hall with the help of gin cocktails from the nearby Pewter Mug" (Walhout 39). Such tales, however, according to Walhout, are not credible. Apparently, Whitman both preached and practiced temperance throughout his life. As a journalist, for example, he reported positively on Temperance events in New York. He also composed an unfinished sequel to *Franklin Evans* called *The Madman* (Walhout 39).

5 Because temperance fiction is not widely known today, we will examine multiple texts here. Concerning Sargent, see Mattingly, ed., *Water Drops from Women Writers: A Temperance Reader* (17 n.6). According to Mattingly, women temperance writers were able to be more open about their dissatisfaction with "woman's place" than many other writers of the time. They addressed topics which other fiction writers, and even male temperance writers, dared not, "not only general equality between the sexes and violence against women but also prejudicial societal attitudes towards victims of male assault and abuse, a woman's right to her own body, marital infidelity, and the imperative for women to focus on their own needs" (5).

6 Later temperance fiction, published by writers including Elizabeth Stuart Phelps, Frances Ellen Watkins Harper, and Marietta Holley, well into the late nineteenth and early twentieth centuries, increasingly took the form of novels, rather than short stories, as the post-1880 works excerpted in Mattingly's anthology indicate. One possible reason for this was the decreasing number of temperance gift books and temperance magazines being published. According to Frank Luther Mott, most of the latter survived only a few years, and only two major ones survived more than a decade past the Civil War (Mott, *A History of American Magazines: 1850–1865*, 210); meanwhile, relatively few new ones were started in the later era.

7 As Mattingly notes, older women led the temperance crusade in public, as well as at home; here, Alcott suggests a way in which young women and girls could add their voices to the crusade, albeit in a more domestically restricted manner. The "Silver Pitchers" society is a local, informal one; Alcott thus implies that the proliferation of independent, small-scale informal groups of younger women would be a useful supplement to large-scale organizations such as the WCTU, run by adult women.

8 Garrison refers to her as early as 1829 as "the first woman of the republic" (qtd. in Karcher, ed., *A Lydia Maria Child Reader* 1).

9 See, for example, her story "Willie Wharton" (*Atlantic Monthly* 11 [March 1863]: 324–45), reprinted in Karcher, ed., *A Lydia Maria Child Reader*.

10 "Charity Bowery" (1839), while supposedly an interview, according to the author, shows parallel themes. It relates the life story of a slave woman, a narrative that effectively demonstrates that even the kindest of slaveowners cannot ultimately diminish the horrors of slavery. Charity has such a master, but after his death, she is inherited by her mistress, "a divil!" This woman proceeds to sell away Charity's children, one by one, something her master had promised never to do. These sales occur even though Mrs. McKinley, the mistress, knows that Charity is doing outside work to save up to buy her children back. Indeed, her mistress repeatedly turns down Charity's offers, even when the latter is able to pay "market value."

11 See, for example, Angelina Grimké, *An Appeal to the Christian Women of the South* (1836).

12 The passage continues, "or at least is incorporated and consolidated into that of her husband under whose wing, protection, and *cover* she performs everything; and is therefore called ... a *feme-covert*." One partial exception was Mississippi after 1839, when the state granted women the right to hold property in their own name, although only with their husbands' permission. As time passed, other states slowly began to modernize these laws; in 1848, New York passed a Married Woman's Property Act that gave wives some control of their property – by the 1860s, nearly a dozen additional states had passed similar legislation.

13 An interesting minor reform convergence connects temperance activism and women's rights in the person of Amelia Bloomer, who was both the editor of the temperance magazine *The Lily* and one of the major American proponents of "rational dress" for women.

14 "The Declaration of Sentiments" (1848) is quite a radical document, even by twenty-first-century standards: "When, in the course of human events, it becomes necessary for one portion of the family of man to assume among the people of the earth a position different from that which they have hitherto occupied, but one to which the laws of nature and of nature's God entitle them, a decent respect to the opinions of mankind requires that they should declare the causes that impel them to such a course. We hold these truths to be self-evident: that all men and women are created equal; that they are endowed by their Creator with certain inalienable rights; that among these are life, liberty, and the pursuit of happiness; that to secure these rights governments are instituted, deriving their just powers from the consent of the governed. Whenever any form of government becomes destructive of these ends, it is the right of those who suffer from it to refuse allegiance to it, and to insist upon the institution of a new government, laying its foundation on such principles, and organizing its powers in such form, as to them shall seem most likely to effect their safety and happiness. Prudence, indeed, will dictate that governments long established should not be changed for light and transient causes;

and accordingly all experience hath shown that mankind are more disposed to suffer while evils are sufferable, than to right themselves by abolishing the forms to which they are accustomed. But when a long train of abuses and usurpations, pursuing invariably the same object, evinces a design to reduce them under absolute despotism, it is their duty to throw off such government, and to provide new guards for their future security. Such has been the patient sufferance of the women under this government, and such is now the necessity which constrains them to demand the equal station to which they are entitled. The history of mankind is a history of repeated injuries and usurpations on the part of man toward woman, having in direct object the establishment of an absolute tyranny over her. To prove this, let facts be submitted to a candid world. He has never permitted her to exercise her inalienable right to the elective franchise. He has compelled her to submit to laws, in the formation of which she had no voice. He has withheld from her rights which are given to the most ignorant and degraded men – both natives and foreigners. Having deprived her of this first right of a citizen, the elective franchise, thereby leaving her without representation in the halls of legislation, he has oppressed her on all sides. He has made her, if married, in the eye of the law, civilly dead. He has taken from her all right in property, even to the wages she earns. He has made her, morally, an irresponsible being, as she can commit many crimes with impunity, provided they be done in the presence of her husband. In the covenant of marriage, she is compelled to promise obedience to her husband, he becoming, to all intents and purposes, her master – the law giving him power to deprive her of her liberty, and to administer chastisement. He has so framed the laws of divorce, as to what shall be the proper causes, and in case of separation, to whom the guardianship of the children shall be given, as to be wholly regardless of the happiness of women – the law, in all cases, going upon a false supposition of the supremacy of man, and giving all power into his hands. After depriving her of all rights as a married woman, if single, and the owner of property, he has taxed her to support a government which recognizes her only when her property can be made profitable to it. He has monopolized nearly all the profitable employments, and from those she is permitted to follow, she receives but a scanty remuneration. He closes against her all the avenues to wealth and distinction which he considers most honorable to himself. As a teacher of theology, medicine, or law, she is not known. He has denied her the facilities for obtaining a thorough education, all colleges being closed against her. He allows her in church, as well as state, but in a subordinate position, claiming apostolic authority for her exclusion from the ministry, and, with some exceptions, from any public participation in the affairs of the church. He has created a false public sentiment by giving to the world a different code of morals for men and women, by which moral delinquencies which exclude women from society, are not only tolerated, but deemed of little account in man. He has usurped the prerogative of Jehovah himself, claiming it as his right to assign for her a sphere of action, when that belongs to her conscience and to her God. He has endeavored, in every way that he could, to destroy her confidence in her own powers, to lessen her self-respect, and to make her willing to lead a dependent and abject life. Now, in view of this entire disfranchisement of one-half the people of this country, their social and religious degradation – in view of the unjust laws above mentioned, and because women do feel themselves aggrieved, oppressed, and fraudulently deprived of their most sacred rights, we insist that they have immediate admission to all the rights and privileges which belong to them as citizens of the United States" (Elizabeth Cady Stanton, *A History of Woman Suffrage* 70–1).

15   Subsequently, a man enters the room and reads the same document that the narrator has been perusing, and states " 'O happy America! Thrice happy land of Freedom! Thy example shall yet free all nations from the galling chains of mental bondage; and teach to the earth's remotest ends, in what true happiness consists!' " (Chamberlain 91).

16   Since this story, unlike those discussed above, is very widely known, I will not summarize it here.

17   At twenty magazine pages in its original form, *Life in the Iron Mills* certainly qualifies as short fiction, though it is sometimes referred to as a novel.

18   Korl is the waste product of steel refining processes.

19   Some historians use 1890 as the start of this era. However, since a number of significant reforms such as the Pendleton Civil Service Act (1883) and the Interstate Commerce Act (1887) were passed prior to this date, and since events such as the founding of the American Federation of Labor (1886), the introduction of the secret ballot system (1888), and the start of the Settlement House movement (Hull House, 1889), occur during the 1880s, I have chosen 1880 as the period's start date. For similar reasons, a number of major monographs on the period, such as Robert Wiebe's *The Search for Order: 1877– 1920,* and Nell Irvin Painter's *Standing at Armageddon: The United States, 1877–1919,* start their coverage before 1890, as do certain institutions, such as the National Women's History Museum (www.nwhm.org/exhibits/womenindustry_intro.html).

20   Additional changes include the invention of the automobile, airplane, radio, and phonograph, as well as motion pictures and air conditioning. By 1915, 2.5 million cars were in use, while the number of telephones increased twenty-five times. Moreover, there were significant upheavals in gender roles in the Progressive Era: in the 1880s and 1890s women flocked to colleges in ever-increasing numbers, and when they graduated, tended to choose careers over marriage: from 1889 to 1908, for example, 55 percent of Bryn Mawr women did not marry, while 62 percent undertook graduate training (Smith-Rosenberg 281). Women also entered the professional workforce in increasingly large numbers; during this period, women made up as much as 25 percent of the national labor force, with women between the ages of 15 and 24 forming the largest proportion of this group (Evans 130).

21   Temperance reform thus continued, as previously noted, though it did not produce as

much significant literary work as it did earlier in the nineteenth century.

22 A partial listing of London's anti-capitalist short fiction would include, in addition to those discussed here, "The Minions of Midas" (1901/1906), "A Curious Fragment" (1907), and "Goliah" (1910).

23 For more on the tropes of the brute and machine in American naturalism, see June Howard, *Form and History in American Literary Naturalism*, and Mark Seltzer, *Bodies and Machines*.

24 It would not seem coincidental that this is also the period at the end of which Bernarr Macfadden, physical culture advocate, and self-made publishing tycoon, invented the "true crime" and "true romance" type of magazine, with which he had enormous success.

25 Topics of his works include: adventure, agriculture, alcoholism, androgyny, animal training (and rights), architecture, assassination, astral projection, big business, boxing (he invented boxing fiction), bullfighting, crime, dreams, ecology, economics, ethics (esp. situational), evolution, fantasy, feminism, folklore, gambling, gold-hunting, hoboing, imperialism, labor, leprosy, mental retardation, mythology, penal reform, political corruption, poverty, prize fighting, psychology, the publishing industry, racism, revolution, seafaring, science, science fiction, socialism, spiritualism, stockbreeding, surfing (which he introduced to the American public), travel, war, wildlife, and writing itself.

26 For additional examples of London's anti-racist and/or anti-imperialist stories, see, for example, "The Seed of McCoy" (1909/1911), "Aloha Oe" (1908/1912), "The Inevitable White Man" (1910/1911), and "The Chinago" (1909/1911).

27 Sui Sin Far was born in England, but moved with her family to the US at the age of 7. The Chinese Exclusion Acts were a series of three

acts passed from 1882 to 1902 that limited and ultimately prohibited Chinese immigration, and put ever tighter restrictions on those already residing in the US, including prohibiting them from becoming citizens.

28 Zitkala-Ša directly expresses her views on the importance of holding fast to native religion in a non-fiction piece drenched in the racial politics of resistance, "Why I Am a Pagan" (1902).

29 It is important to remember, however, that like Far, and many other writers from marginalized groups, Zitkala-Ša in both her life and her fiction is also interested in trying to figure out how to be simultaneously a part of both her racial subculture and the dominant Euro-American culture, how to negotiate the fluctuating boundaries of "double-consciousness," to borrow Du Bois's term for African Americans' dilemma.

30 From John William Larner, Jr., ed. *The Papers of Carlos Montezuma, M.D.* [Microfilm edn.]. Wilmington, DE: Scholarly Resources, 1983. Reel 1 of 9 reels.

31 Unlike Chopin and Gilman, who devoted not only novels, but also numerous short stories to feminist themes, London focused on the former genre for his New Woman works (e.g., his first novel *A Daughter of the Snows* [1902], as well as *Burning Daylight* [1910], and his last novel published during his lifetime, *Little Lady of the Big House* [1916]), devoting relatively few short stories to what he called, in *Daughter of the Snows*, "the new womanhood." For more on London's typically conflicted attitudes toward women and changing gender roles, see my "Jack London's New Woman: A Little Lady with a Big Stick" (1994).

32 This idea was paralleled by Thorstein Veblen in *The Theory of the Leisure Class* (1899) and *The Instinct of Workmanship and the State of the Industrial Arts* (1914).

REFERENCES AND FURTHER READING

Alcott, Louisa May. "Silver Pitchers." 1876. In Mattingly, ed., *Water Drops from Women Writers: A Temperance Reader*, 219–49.

Appleton, Mrs. M. L. [Jane Sophia]. "Sequel to the 'Vision of Bangor in the Twentieth Century.'" 1848. *Voices from the Kenduskeag*. Eds. Cornelia

Crosby Barrett and. Mrs. M. L. (Jane Sophia) Appleton. Bangor: David Bugbee, 1848. 243–65.

Barnett, Louise K. "Bartleby as Alienated Worker." *Studies in Short Fiction* 11 (Fall 1974): 379–95.

Butler, Carolyn Hyde. "Emma Alton." 1850. In Mattingly, ed., *Water Drops from Women Writers: A Temperance Reader*, 22–30.

Cahan, Abraham. "A Sweatshop Romance." 1898. *Yekl and the Imported Bridegroom and Other Stories of Yiddish New York*. New York: Dover, 1970. 188–202.

Cane, Aleta Feinsod, and Susan Alves, eds. *American Women Writers and the Periodical, 1837–1916: "The Only Efficient Instrument."* Iowa City: University of Iowa Press, 2001.

Chamberlain, Betsey. "A New Society." 1840. *Nineteenth-Century American Women Writers: An Anthology*. Ed. Karen L. Kilcup. Oxford: Blackwell, 1997. 90–1.

Chesnutt, Charles W. "The Wife of His Youth." 1898. *Collected Stories of Charles W. Chesnutt*. Ed. and Intro. William L. Andrews. New York: Penguin, 1992. 102–13.

Child, Lydia Maria. "Charity Bowery." *The Liberty Bell*. Boston: Massachusetts Anti-Slavery Fair, 1839. 26–43.

———. "Slavery's Pleasant Homes." 1843. *A Lydia Maria Child Reader*. Ed. Carolyn Karcher. Durham, NC: Duke University Press, 1997. 238–42.

———. "Willie Wharton." *Atlantic Monthly* 11 (March 1863). 324–45.

Chopin, Kate. "The Story of an Hour." 1894. *Women Who Did: Stories by Men and Women, 1890–1914*. Ed. Angelique Richardson. New York: Penguin, 2002. 137–9.

Davis, David Brion, ed. *Antebellum Reform*. New York: HarperCollins, 1967.

Davis, Rebecca Harding. *Life in the Iron Mills and Other Stories*. Ed. and Intro. Tillie Olsen. New York: Feminist Press, 1985.

Evans, Sara. *Born for Liberty: A History of Women in the United States*. New York: Free Press, 1997.

Far, Sui Sin (Edith Maude Eaton). "The Chinese Ishmael." *Overland Monthly* (July 1899): 43–9.

———. "Mrs. Spring Fragrance." 1910/1912. *Mrs. Spring Fragrance and Other Writings*. Eds. Amy Ling and Annette White-Parks. Urbana: University of Illinois Press, 1995. 17–41.

Furer, Andrew J. "'A Mighty Power Thrills Her Body': Zitkala-Ša's 'A Warrior's Daughter' and Natural Feminism." *The Genders of Naturalism*. Ed. Andrew J. Furer. Durham, NC: Duke University Press, in press.

———. "Jack London's New Woman: A Little Lady with a Big Stick." *Studies in American Fiction* 22.2 (1994): 185–214.

———. "'Zone-Conquerors' and 'White Devils': The Contradictions of Race in the Works of Jack London." *Rereading Jack London*. Eds. Leonard Cassuto and Jeanne C. Reesman. Stanford: Stanford University Press, 1996. 158–71.

Garland, Hamlin. "Under the Lion's Paw." *Main-Travelled Roads*. Boston: Arena, 1891. 217–240.

Gilman, Charlotte Perkins. "The Yellow Wallpaper." 1892. *Women Who Did: Stories by Men and Women, 1890–1914*. Ed. Angelique Richardson. New York: Penguin, 2002. 31–47.

———. "Why I Wrote 'The Yellow Wallpaper.'" *The Forerunner* (October 1913): 19–20.

———. *Women and Economics: A Study of the Relation between Women and Men*. 1898. Ed. Carl N. Degler. New York: Harper Torchbooks, 1966. (Cited in the text as *W&E*.)

Ginzburg, Lori D. *Women in Antebellum Reform*. New York: Harlan Davidson, 2000.

Grimké, Angelina. *An Appeal to the Christian Women of the South*. 1836. New York: Ayer, 1969.

Hapke, Laura. *Labor's Text: The Worker in American Fiction*. New Brunswick, NJ: Rutgers University Press, 2001.

Howard, June. *Form and History in American Literary Naturalism*. Chapel Hill: University of North Carolina Press, 1985.

Howe, Daniel Walker. *What Hath God Wrought: The Transformation of America, 1815–1848*. New York: Oxford University Press, 2007.

Karcher, Carolyn, ed. *A Lydia Maria Child Reader*. Durham, NC: Duke University Press, 1997.

———. *The First Woman in the Republic: A Cultural Biography of Lydia Maria Child*. Durham, NC: Duke University Press, 1998.

Kilcup, Karen L., ed. *Nineteenth-Century American Women Writers: An Anthology*. Oxford: Blackwell, 1997.

Levy, Andrew. *The Culture and Commerce of the American Short Story*. Cambridge: Cambridge University Press, 1993.

London, Charmian Kittredge. *The Book of Jack London*. 2 vols. New York: Century, 1921.

London, Jack. "The Apostate." 1906/1911. *The Portable Jack London*. Ed. Earle Labor. New York: Viking Penguin, 1994. 118–35.

———. "Chun Ah Chun." 1912/1914. *The House of Pride. The Complete Short Stories of Jack London*. Vol. 2. Eds. Earle Labor, Robert C. Leitz, III, and I. Milo Shepard. Palo Alto, CA: Stanford University Press, 1993. 1455–66.

———. "The Dream of Debs." 1909/1914. *The Complete Short Stories of Jack London*. Vol. 2. Eds. Earle Labor, Robert C. Leitz, III, and I. Milo Shepard. Palo Alto, CA: Stanford University Press, 1993. 1261–78.

———. "Koolau, the Leper." 1909/1912. *The Portable Jack London*. Ed. Earle Labor. New York: Viking Penguin, 1994. 164–77.

———. "The Mexican." 1911/1913. *The Portable Jack London*. Ed. Earle Labor. New York: Viking Penguin, 1994. 291–313.

———. "South of the Slot." 1909/1914. *The Complete Short Stories of Jack London*. Vol. 2. Eds. Earle Labor, Robert C. Leitz, III, and I. Milo Shepard. Palo Alto, CA: Stanford University Press, 1993. 1580–94.

———. "The Strength of the Strong." 1911/1914. *Complete Short Stories of Jack London*. Vol. 2. Eds. Earle Labor, Robert C. Leitz, III, and I. Milo Shepard. Palo Alto, CA: Stanford University Press, 1993. 1566–79.

———. "What Life Means to Me." 1906. *The Portable Jack London*. Ed. Earle Labor. New York: Viking Penguin, 1994. 475–82.

McCall, Dan. *The Silence of Bartleby*. Ithaca: Cornell University Press, 1989.

Mattingly, Carol, ed. *Water Drops from Women Writers: A Temperance Reader*. Carbondale: Southern Illinois University Press, 2001.

Melville, Herman. "Bartleby, the Scrivener." 1853. *Herman Melville: Selected Tales and Poems*. Ed. Richard Chase. New York: Holt, Rinehart & Winston, 1950. 92–131.

———. "The Paradise of Bachelors and the Tartarus of Maids." 1855. *Herman Melville: Selected Tales and Poems*. Ed. Richard Chase. New York: Holt, Rinehart & Winston, 1950. 206–29.

Mena, Maria Christina. "The Education of Popo." 1914. *The Collected Stories of Maria Christina Mena*. Ed. and Intro. Amy Doherty. Houston: Arte Público Press, University of Houston, 1997. 47–62.

Mott, Frank Luther. *A History of American Magazines: 1741–1850*. Cambridge, MA: Harvard University Press, 1957.

———. *A History of American Magazines: 1850–1865*. Cambridge, MA: Harvard University Press, 1957.

———. *A History of American Magazines, 1885–1905*. Cambridge, MA: Harvard University Press, 1957.

Nagel, James, ed. *Anthology of the American Short Story*. Boston: Houghton Mifflin, 2008.

Oppenheim, James. "The Great Fear." *Pay Envelopes*. New York: B. W. Huebsch, 1911. 21–46.

———. "Troubles of the Workshop: A Skippable Preface." *Pay Envelopes*. New York: B. W. Huebsch, 1911. 9–15.

Painter, Nell Irvin. *Standing at Armageddon: The United States, 1877–1919*. New York: W. W. Norton, 1987.

Reesman, Jeanne C. *Jack London: A Study of the Short Fiction*. New York: Twayne, 1999.

Richardson, Angelique, ed. *Women Who Did: Stories by Men and Women, 1890–1914*. New York: Penguin, 2002.

Riis, Jacob. *How the Other Half Lives*. 1890. New York: Dover, 1971.

———. "The Problem of the Widow Salvini." *Neighbors: Stories of the Other Half*. New York: Macmillan, 1914. 48–62.

———. "What the Christmas Sun Saw in the Tenements." *Children of the Tenements*. New York: Macmillan, 1903. 133–49.

Rose, Jane Atteridge. *Rebecca Harding Davis*. New York: Twayne, 1993.

[Sargent, Lucius Manlius]. *My Mother's Gold Ring* [pamphlet]. 8th edn. Boston: Ford & Damrell, 1833.

Seltzer, Mark. *Bodies and Machines*. New York: Routledge, 1992.

Sigourney, Lydia Howard Huntley. "The Intemperate." 1833. In Mattingly, ed., *Water Drops from Women Writers*, 31–45.

Simal, Begona. "'A Wall of Barbed Lies': Absent Borders in Maria Cristina Mena's Short Fiction." *Border Transits: Literature and Culture across the Line*. Ed. Ana M. Manzanas. Amsterdam: Rodopi, 2007. 147–80.

Smith-Rosenberg, Carroll. *Disorderly Conduct: Visions of Gender in Victorian America*. New York: Oxford University Press, 1986.

Stanton, Elizabeth Cady. *A History of Woman Suffrage*. Vol. 1. Rochester, NY: Fowler & Wells, 1889.

Stowe, Harriet Beecher. "The Coral Ring." 1843. In Mattingly, ed., *Water Drops from Women Writers*, 209–17.

———. "The Two Altars; or, Two Pictures in One." 1851. *Anthology of the American Short Story*. Ed. James Nagel. Boston: Houghton Mifflin, 2008. 173–82.

Thoreau, Henry David. *Walden, or, Life in the Woods*. 1854. *The Portable Thoreau*. Ed. Carl Bode. Rev. edn. New York: Penguin, 1964.

Tompkins, Jane. *Sensational Designs: The Cultural Work of American Fiction, 1790–1860*. New York: Oxford University Press, 1985.

Walhout, Mark. "Whitman the Temperance Novelist." *Books and Culture* 13.5 (2007): 38–9.

Whitman, Walt. *Franklin Evans, or The Inebriate: A Tale of the Times*. Eds. Christopher Castiglia and Glenn Hendler. Charleston, NC: Duke University Press, 2007.

Wiebe, Robert. *The Search for Order: 1877–1920*. New York: Hill & Wang, 1967.

Young, Michael P. *Bearing Witness against Sin: The Evangelical Birth of the American Social Movement*. Chicago: University of Chicago Press, 2007.

Zitkala-Ša (Gertrude Simmons Bonnin). "The Soft-Hearted Sioux." 1901. *Zitkala-Ša: American Indian Stories, Legends, and Other Writings*. Eds. and Intro. Cathy N. Davidson and Ada Norris. New York: Penguin, 2003. 118–26.

———. "A Warrior's Daughter." 1902. *Zitkala-Ša: American Indian Stories, Legends, and Other Writings*. Eds. and Intro. Cathy N. Davidson and Ada Norris. New York: Penguin, 2003. 130–42.

———. "Why I Am a Pagan." *Atlantic Monthly* 90 (1902): 801–3.

Part III
The Twentieth Century

14

The Twentieth Century: A Period of Innovation and Continuity

James Nagel

The history of the short story in the twentieth century takes place against a backdrop of enormous social change and international conflict. It begins in a horse-drawn era before the first flight of the airplane, prior to popular radio broadcasts, previous to women having the right to vote. It ends in a computer age of astonishing technological advancements, of people walking on the moon, of prosperity and longevity undreamed of only a century ago. There were more dramatic alterations to the nature of human existence in this period than the world had ever experienced before, and it had enormous impact on the psychic quality of American life, a transformation recorded in short fiction.

In literary terms, the period begins in aesthetic continuity and ends in transformation of subject and theme, albeit not dramatically in methodology. Throughout the decades there were numerous attempts at experimentation, at polyphonic prose, at Dadaistic incomprehension, at fragmentary notations, at genre bending, but the dominant form of short fiction remained essentially Realistic, driven by character, plot, theme, and narrative method. Indeed, the fiction of 2000 in most important ways greatly resembled that of 1900.

In the early years of the century, the prevailing modes of the 1890s continued to dominate. O. Henry's formulaic tales were enormously popular, despite the scandal of his personal life, and "The Gift of the Magi" and "The Ransom of Red Chief" were anthologized for decades. But entertaining stories of that mode were quickly supplanted by darker fare. Naturalistic impulses predominated, driven by a spirit of social reform and characterized by omniscient narration, lower-class or even grotesque characters, plots that moved unrelentingly toward the expression of Deterministic forces, and dehumanizing imagery derivative of an animalistic or mechanized conception of the universe. Characters in such stories do not so much act as are acted upon, making them the impotent victims of forces beyond their control. Jack London's nineteen volumes of stories emphasize these ideas. His most famous story, "To Build a Fire," stresses the inferiority of human reason to a dog's instinct when facing survival in the frozen north, and other stories, such as "The White Silence," involve the acceptance of inevitable death, an idea that drives "The Law of Life" and "Love of Life" as well. London's stories are powerfully negative and pessimistic, but they had an impact on literature that lasted throughout the century.

Frank Norris is perhaps better known for his novels than for his short fiction, but "A Deal in Wheat," concerning the socioeconomic effects of commodities speculation on the lives of poor people, has become a classic and is widely regarded as the quintessential example of economic Determinism. His other stories, including "His Sister" and "The Guest of Honor," have not been so widely regarded but still exemplify his approach to fiction. Theodore Dreiser wrote a good number of memorable stories in this tradition: "The Lost Phoebe," "Curious Shifts of the Poor," and "The Second Choice," for example, are built on the theme of the diminished lives of the poor. Paul Lawrence Dunbar's "The Lynching of Jube Benson" portrayed the injustice of racial discrimination in depicting an innocent African American hanged by a lynch mob. Anzia Yezierska captured the lives of urban Jewish immigrants in the tenements of New York in "The Fat of the Land" and "My Own People." Sherwood Anderson wrote some of the best Naturalistic fiction of the era not only in his landmark *Winesburg, Ohio* stories but in companion works such as "Death in the Woods" and "The Door of the Trap." James T. Farrell's "Helen, I Love You" follows the adolescent theme of Anderson's story, but Farrell was capable of writing much richer fiction in the Naturalistic mode, as in the treatment of racism in "For White Men Only" and "The Fastest Runner on Sixty-First Street." He eventually published fifteen volumes of short stories. Erskine Caldwell's work is related to Farrell's in its exploration of racism and poverty. "Candy-Man Beechum" is remarkable for its representation of the African American vernacular, and "Kneel to the Rising Sun," which depicts a Southern lynching, explores race relations from a white perspective.

Perhaps the culmination of the Naturalistic tradition in fiction comes with John Steinbeck and Richard Wright, not simply for their great novels *The Grapes of Wrath* and *Native Son* but for their stunning stories as well. Steinbeck was a master of the form, as exhibited in "The Chrysanthemums," a wrenching revelation of longing, of the submerged life of a farm woman. "The Harness" depicts domination by a wife, and the stories in *Pastures of Heaven* show the harsh realities of agrarian life in the Salinas valley. The four related stories that comprise "The Red Pony" are some of Steinbeck's best writing. Poignant, tough, and undeniably "real," they show, in gripping drama, the severe existence of rural folk in the 1930s. Wright's Naturalistic stories present Deterministic forces, including a racist social environment and a vague "Fate," as overpowering influences that compel the tragedies of his African American characters. These themes are played out most dramatically in the stories included in *Uncle Tom's Children*, especially "Big Boy Leaves Home," "Down by the Riverside," and "Long Black Song." His later stories contain some of the existential themes that emerged in the conclusion of his sensational novel *Native Son*, and these controversial ideas lead to Wright's break with the Communist Party. Perhaps the finest of these late works is "The Man Who Lived Underground," based in part on Dostoevsky's *Notes from Underground*.

If Naturalism largely collapsed by 1940 under the weight of its own unsustainable assumptions, Realism flourished throughout the century. A movement that not only portrayed life in the light of common day, with believable characters and situations, Realism also placed moral culpability on individual characters making the decisions that directed their lives, whereas Naturalism diverted responsibility to Deterministic forces. The inception of Existentialism in the 1920s, especially John Paul Sartre's argument that people create themselves every day and are thus accountable not only for what they do but for what they are, did not allow for the diffusion of guilt in tragic events. But Realism also emphasized less dramatic situations in American life, ordinary conflicts, family interactions, the appreciation of the beauty in Nature.

Early in the century, Willa Cather quickly established herself as an outstanding writer of Realistic short fiction. Each of her three volumes of stories contains memorable work, beginning with "Paul's Case," "A Wagner Matinee," and "The Sculptor's Funeral" from *The Troll Garden* (1905). These depictions of the importance of Art in a mercantile American society established her literary reputation. "Coming, Aphrodite," from *Youth and the Bright Medusa*, and "Neighbor Rosicky," from *Obscure Destinies*, demonstrated her continued mastery of the form. One of her early works, "The Bohemian Girl," anticipates much of *My Antonia!*, Cather's novelistic masterpiece.

Many of Cather's themes are carried forward in Edith Wharton's stories, beginning with "Mrs. Manstey's View" in 1891, which deals with a frustrated artist. Wharton's best work is also decidedly Realistic in method and theme, although many of her tales deal with marriage and domestic issues, the best of which are "The Other Two," about divorce and remarriage, and "Roman Fever," about a illicit affair and the child born from it. "Xingu" is a satiric piece aimed at high culture, and Wharton's ghost stories, including "The Lady's Maid's Bell" and "Afterward," give yet another dimension to her work. Ring Lardner's short fiction was immensely popular in the early twentieth century. Featuring the vernacular, and dealing with such commonplace situations as a barber shop or minor-league baseball, his work captured the attention of the American public. "Haircut" endured in anthologies throughout the century, but some of even the best of his stories have been largely forgotten, including "The Golden Honeymoon," "A Busher's Letters Home," an epistolary tale, and "Some Like Them Cold."

Post–World War I Modernism changed American fiction in fundamental ways. The experimentation in prose that accompanied the Imagist movement brought a tendency for sparse prose, direct language, and frank depictions of the sensations of life. As the practitioners of the tradition moved from London to Paris, the American expatriates became exposed to a new style of writing. No one was more influenced by the trend than Ernest Hemingway, whose aesthetic evolved in the early 1920s under the influence of Ford Madox Ford, Ezra Pound, and others who had been Imagists the decade before. To this new method of rendering fiction Hemingway added the social and intellectual concerns of the decade: the devastation of the war, the loss of confidence in the institutions that had directed social values in earlier times, and the collapse of religion and customs that formed the core principles for earlier generations. Most of his protagonists have been wounded in some important way, and many of them, having lost faith in traditional values, strive to establish new codes to guide their behavior.

Hemingway expressed these new ideas from the beginning of his mature fiction, depicting a frank but cruel sexuality in "Up in Michigan," suicide in "Indian Camp," unhappy marriage in "The Doctor and the Doctor's Wife," adolescent sexuality in "Ten Indians," and abortion in "Hills Like White Elephants." To these harsh domestic issues he added the psychological consequences of violence in "A Way You'll Never Be," the aftermath of wounding in "In Another Country," the lingering impact of war even when the fighting ended in "Soldier's Home." Death was a theme in Hemingway's African stories, as in "The Snows of Kilimanjaro" and "The Short, Happy Life of Francis Macomber," and the emptiness of life forms the thematic center of "A Clean, Well-Lighted Place," one of the great stories in English.

F. Scott Fitzgerald's work focused primarily on the domestic issues of the Jazz Age, but his finest story, "Babylon Revisited," deals with life in Paris after the war. Other stories, "Winter Dreams," "Absolution," and "The Rich Boy," for example, stress the psychological struggles of adolescence and the desire of the central characters to be accepted into the country-club set. The varied and complex fiction of William Faulkner transcends simple description, but his best work takes place in Yoknapatawpha, a fictional county in Mississippi containing characters who reappear in multiple works. Among his finest stories are those that capture the value struggles of poor whites, as in "Barn Burning"; African Americans attempting to survive in Southern society, an issue in "That Evening Sun" and "The Fire and the Hearth"; and the multi-layered collapse of "aristocratic" whites in such works as "A Rose for Emily." Many stories develop other themes, such as the vanishing wilderness and the loss of its moral instruction, as does "The Old People," "Delta Autumn," and Faulkner's finest effort in short fiction, "The Bear," a complex story that combines many of his central themes: the mythological ritual of hunting for a young white boy guided by an elderly man of color, the disappearing delta forest, the haunting moral legacy of slavery, the interactions of people across the social strata. No other writer captured such depth in his portrayal of a region as did Faulkner, and no one employed more complex strategies of narrative method, structure, and thematic development than he did in his remarkable stories and novels.

Anzia Yezierska followed the work of Abraham Cahan in portraying the travails of Jewish immigrants to the New World, although with a special emphasis on the plight of urban women. In "The Fat of the Land," for example, a mother battles poverty and despair only to find in her old age that the economic advances her family has made have left her empty, longing for the close-knit society of her younger years. "Children of Loneliness" deals with the loss of family, "Wild Winter Love" with suicide. One of her last stories, "A Chair in Heaven," returns to the idea that financial enrichment does not bring contentment and inner peace. In the later years of the century, Jewish writers were a dominant force in American letters for several decades. The period featured the fine stories of Philip Roth, especially those in *Goodbye, Columbus*, such as "Defender of the Faith"; Saul Bellow, who won a Nobel Prize for Literature; Cynthia Ozick; Bernard Malamud; and Isaac Bashevis Singer. Their collective impact was immense, and it expanded and deepened American fiction.

The African American stories of Charles Chesnutt, Jessie Faucet, Paul Lawrence Dunbar, Alice Dunbar-Nelson, and Frances Ellen Watkins Harper in the nineteenth century were followed in the twentieth by the fiction of Jean Toomer, Langston Hughes, and Zora Neale Hurston. Toomer's *Cane* from 1923 was hailed as a masterpiece, and "Blood Burning Moon" has been widely anthologized throughout the many decades since. Langston Hughes, known primarily as a poet, was also a prolific writer of short fiction, publishing ten volumes in the form. "Slave on the Block" shows white people fascinated with African American culture, a common theme during the Harlem Renaissance. His "Simple" stories, about Jessie B. Semple, capture the vernacular, folkways, and tone of black life, as does "Possum, Race, and Face." Zora Neale Hurston, trained in anthropology, concentrated on portraying the folklore, language, and local traditions of the deep South in such stories as "The Conscience of the Court," "Sweat," and "Under the Bridge."

Other African American writers contributed to the genre in the years that followed, most notable among them were James Baldwin (whose "Sonny's Blues" and "This Morning, This Evening, So Soon" are among his best-known works) and Ernest Gaines (whose "The Sky is Gray" opens his collection *Bloodline*). Amiri Baraka's *Tales* (1967) is composed of both stories and poems in an experimental configuration similar to that of Toomer's *Cane* in 1923. Ralph Ellison contributed numerous stories in addition to *Invisible Man,* for which he is best known, and some of them, "Flying Home," for instance, have been widely anthologized. Gloria Naylor's story cycle *The Women of Brewster Place* established her credentials in the genre, as did Jamaica Kincaid's short fiction in the *New Yorker,* later brought together in *Annie John*. Toni Morrison's stories are immensely popular, and frequently anthologized, if often overshadowed by her award winning novels. Similarly, Alice Walker is famous for *The Color Purple*, but her story "Everyday Use" is read by millions of college students. James Alan McPherson's "Of Cabbages and Kings" is also widely known along with Toni Cade Babara's "The Lesson." At the end of the twentieth century, the African American story remained a vibrant and vital force in literature.

Many other ethnic groups have emerged to forge important contributions to the form as well. In Native American fiction, for example, Sherman Alexie instilled new energy into the form with such stories as "The Lone Ranger and Tonto Fistfight in Heaven" and "Because My Father Always Said He Was the Only Indian Who Saw Jimi Hendrix Play 'The Star-Spangled Banner' at Woodstock." Louise Erdrich, whose natural genre is the collection of inter-related stories, has become famous for *The Beat Queen* and *Love Medicine*, a volume often misinterpreted as a novel. "The Red Convertible" is one of her most often anthologized tales. Leslie Marmon Silko's "Yellow Woman" and "Storyteller" are complex narratives with a thematic edge often missing in Erdrich's work. Susan Power, educated in the Ivy League, and holding a law degree, brought an intellectual rigor to the story in such works as "Morse Code."

Asian American writers have also enriched American literature with their stories, perhaps the most famous of which are those in Maxine Hong Kingston's *Woman Warrior* and the sixteen stories that make up Amy Tan's *The Joy Luck Club*, of which "Four Directions" and "Rules of the Game" are among the most widely read. Hisaye Yamamoto's *Seventeen Syllables* consists of short fiction about the Japanese internment experience during World War II, the best of which is perhaps "The Legend of Miss Sasagawara," a stunningly insightful psychological portrait. Frank Chin's work introduced a new defiant tone to Asian American writing. In such stories as "The Only Real Day" and "Railroad Standard Time," his fiction establishes an angry protagonist who insists on abolishing stereotypes and expressing an assertive personality who dominates, rather than simply persists, in society. Gish Jen has developed a broad following for her portrayal of Chinese American families in "Who's Irish," for example, and the emergence of Yiyun Li in 2005 with "The Princess of Nebraska" revealed an immigrant writer who can, with sensitivity and grace, depict issues of ethnicity and sexual preference with great artistic skill.

Latino writers also contributed to the richness of American literature. Sandra Cisneros burst on the scene with a dramatically poetic volume of fictional vignettes, *The House on Mango Street*, which won the Before Columbus American Book Award. More mythological in scope are the stories in *Woman Hollering Creek*. Judith Ortiz Cofer draws on her Puerto Rican background to enrich her short fiction, as she did in the award winning "Nada," which shows the anguish of death in war. Much of her work bends genres into semi-autobiographical, creative non-fiction, but, throughout, she mixes humor with tragedy, bitter resentment of racism with the satisfaction of functioning in American society. Helena María Viramontes uses her fiction to express social protest against the social and sexual forces that oppress Chicana women in California, as she does in "The Cariboo Cafe" from *The Moths and Other Stories*. Her second volume of stories was entitled *Paris Rats in E. L. A.* Julia Alvarez used her background in the Dominican Republic to introduce new characters experiencing an old theme, immigrants going through the process of assimilation. The four sisters in the fifteen stories that comprise *How the Garcia Girls Lost Their Accents*, for example, deal with language acquisition, cultural loss, familial strife, and romance in a new society.

Throughout the century important writers emerged who addressed other kinds of concerns. Flannery O'Connor, for example, wrote about her native South in such masterpieces as "A Good Man is Hard to Find," and Eudora Welty addressed the same region in such landmark stories as "Petrified Man." John Updike placed his stories in New England and the mid-Atlantic states, as did Andre Dubus, both writers capturing domestic dramas in their compelling stories. Dubus's "Killings" received a great deal of attention after it was made into a Hollywood motion picture entitled *In the Bedroom*. Garrison Keillor addressed his short fiction to his native Minnesota and the mythical town of Lake Wobegone. In a vast number of brief vignettes, all closely related to the oral tradition, he dealt humorously yet poignantly with the ordinary situations of small-town life. Tim O'Brien sprang from the same area, but his work is focused on the moral confusion and conflict surrounding the war in Viet Nam, and his stories in *The Things They Carried* are brilliant evocations of the ethical compromises in combat, all contained in such works as "The Sweetheart of the Song Tra Bong." Robert Olen Butler's short fiction mirrors that of O'Brien. Rather than tracing Americans in action in Southeast Asia, Butler deals with Vietnamese who have immigrated to Louisiana in the aftermath of the war. His characters still carry the war with them, in their memories, dreams, and family tragedies.

In essence, the late twentieth century enjoyed the fruition of the American story, a richness beyond measure. From the controlled minimalism of Raymond Carver's "Cathedral" and the finely crafted components of Susan Minot's *Monkeys* to the experimentation in such Donald Barthelme stories as "Views of My Father Weeping" or John Barth's "Night-Sea Journey," the potential of the genre seems limitless. Bobbie Ann Mason is perhaps less innovative in form but richer in her explorations of human emotion in everyday situations, as in "Shiloh" and "A New-Wave Format." The stories of Bharati Mukherjee, such as "The Tenant" or "A Four-Hundred-Year-Old Woman," are a reminder that immigration to the New World is an ongoing process, and new citizens continue to enrich the culture of the United States now as they did in the late nineteenth century. To be sure, short fiction in twentieth-century America has left a rich and complex legacy, one filled with impressive artistry, social conflict, and enormous potential for sustained innovation, and it is one that is only beginning to be explored and understood.

15
The Hemingway Story

George Monteiro

In a 1950 front-page review of Ernest Hemingway's *Across the River and Into the Trees* in the *New York Times Book Review* the writer John O'Hara proclaimed that the book's author was the most important writer in the English language since the death of Shakespeare in 1616. The reaction to O'Hara's statement was immediate and loud. In fact, O'Hara's opinion achieved such notoriety, and was so long-lasting, that a full ten years later O'Hara was still trying to explain what he had meant in insisting on Hemingway's great historical importance.

> The various circumstances that have made him the most important are not all of a purely literary nature. Some are anything but. We start with a first-rate, original, conscientious artist, who caught on because of his excellence. The literary and then the general public very quickly realized that a great artist was functioning in our midst. Publicity grew and grew, and Hemingway helped it to grow, not always deliberately but sometimes deliberately. He had an unusual, almost comical name; he was a big, strong, highly personable man. He associated himself, through his work, with big things: Africa, Italy, Spain, war, hunting, fishing, bullfighting, The Novel, Style, death, violence, castration, and a teasing remoteness from his homeland and from the lit'ry life. All these things make you think of Hemingway, and each and all of them add to his importance, that carries over from one writing job to another. I have a theory that there has not been a single issue of the Sunday Times book section in the past twenty years that has failed to mention Hemingway; his name is a synonym for writer with millions of people who have never read any work of fiction.[1]

Born in 1899, in Oak Park, Illinois, Ernest Hemingway was the son of Clarence and Grace Hall Hemingway. He was educated in the public schools of Oak Park, where, in addition to his studies, he played football and wrote for school publications. Upon graduation he was hired as a cub reporter for the *Kansas City Star*. In May 1918 he joined the Red Cross ambulance corps, arriving in Italy a few weeks later. Wounded at the front in early July, he returned to Oak Park a war hero. After the war he worked for a time in and around Chicago and later for a Toronto newspaper. On September 3, 1921, he married Hadley Richardson. His commitment to a literary career can be considered to have begun at that time, starting out, mainly, with short stories.

That he would commit himself fully to the task of becoming a professional writer was the single great choice behind Hemingway's decision in 1921 to leave for Europe. He was 22 years old, and he was eager to try Paris, the home then of such famed exiled writers as Gertrude Stein, James Joyce, and Ezra Pound. In December 1921, Ernest and Hadley sailed from New York on the *Leopoldina*. He was to spend most of the decade in Europe; by the time he returned to the United States he had become famous, mainly as the author of the novels *The Sun Also Rises* and *A Farewell to Arms*. By 1927 he had divorced Hadley and married Pauline Pfeiffer. He had also published *In Our Time* (1925) and *Men Without Women* (1927). Five years after publishing *Winner Take Nothing* (1933), he collected the three separate volumes of stories and added to them a handful of other pieces – four stories written after 1933: "The Snows of Kilimanjaro" (1936), "The Short Happy Life of Francis Macomber" (1936), "The Capital of the World" (1936), and "Old Man at the Bridge" (1937); one early story previously bypassed for commercial publication, "Up in Michigan" (1923, *Three Stories and Ten Poems*); and *The Fifth Column*, a play set in Civil-War Spain – to make up *The Fifth Column and The First Forty-Nine Stories* (1938), the only collective gathering of his stories to appear during his lifetime. After Hemingway's death, on July 2, 1961, in Ketchum, Idaho, there appeared two other collections of his short fiction, *The Fifth Column and Four Stories of the Spanish Civil War* (1969), containing previously published but uncollected stories, and *The Nick Adams Stories* (1972), containing stories previously published in *In Our Time*, *Men Without Women* and *Winner Take Nothing*, along with unpublished stories and fragments. Still subject to debate is whether or not *A Moveable Feast* (1964), the first of Hemingway's works to appear after his death, is more profitably read as a memoir of Hemingway's Paris years or as a collection of stories and sketches in which the names of characters and places are real – a story cycle that melds fact and fiction.

Hemingway's apprenticeship as a serious writer of short stories cannot be fully traced, let alone documented. It is known that upon arriving in Europe late in 1921, he began to write fiction that he tried assiduously to publish, with little success. Then nearly all of his early short stories were lost in December 1922. A valise containing nearly all the stories he had written to that date was stolen from his wife while she was carrying them to Hemingway, who was in Lausanne. Just how many stories were lost has never been determined. Three stories from that period that did survive – "Up in Michigan," "Out of Season," and "My Old Man" – achieved print in Hemingway's first book, *Three Stories and Ten Poems*, issued in 1923 in Paris by Contact Publishing Company in a first printing run of only 300 copies.

As Hemingway's earliest known work in the genre, these three stories deserve more than passing attention. "My Old Man," among the most derivative of Hemingway's stories, parodies, in an honorific way, the style and subject matter of characteristic stories by Sherwood Anderson and Ring Lardner. It is written from the point of view of a boy who never fully understands the nature or the import of his "autobiographical" tale about his life with his father, a jockey, at the European racetracks. The father's true character reveals itself in the story the callow youth tells in the familiar puzzled style defined and nurtured by Anderson in his racetrack stories and elsewhere. Like Anderson, Hemingway follows a pattern of initiation that leaves the boy more experienced in the raw ways of the world but barely more perceptive. Like Lardner, Hemingway chooses to center on an adolescent "tough," one living in a know-it-all world, and speaking that world's language, but knowing very little, and, at the end, having what he started out knowing brought into doubt. "Up in Michigan," a story that Hemingway's first trade publisher would not permit him to include in _In Our Time_, tells the story of a young woman's first sexual experience. The story again deals with an initiation that leaves the central character seemingly more experienced but actually less knowledgeable and in greater confusion. She never realizes the extent to which she has romanticized the young blacksmith, or that the rough sex on the hemlock planks of the dock is tantamount to the rape others would see in it. The word "it" – in definite and indefinite senses – appears throughout the story, often standing for "sex." This substitution/omission works aesthetically, however, because sex is precisely what the young woman, given her background, would repress. The way she displaces her own sexual attraction in favor of other details is rendered in the following passage, foreshadowing as it does the much later statement, "She was frightened but she wanted it. She had to have it but it frightened her": "Liz liked Jim very much. She liked it the way he walked over from the shop and often went to the kitchen door to watch for him to start down the road. She liked it about his mustache ... She liked it very much that he didn't look like a blacksmith. ... One day she found that she liked it the way the hair was black on his arms and how white they were above the tanned line when he washed up in the washbasin outside the house. Liking that made her feel funny" (62, 59).[2] Horace Liveright, Hemingway's first trade publisher, was not the only one to find "Up in Michigan" too "outspoken" for publication. Gertrude Stein thought so too, telling its author that the story was "_inaccrochable_," meaning that it was the equivalent of a painting that could not be "hung" for public display. That it was Stein who admonished Hemingway is somewhat surprising, for in its stylistic rhythm and repetition of words in only slightly varied sentences, "Up in Michigan" epitomizes the early influence of Stein's writing, notably in _The Making of Americans_ and _Three Lives_, on Hemingway's short fiction.

"Out of Season," set in Italy, is a story of a small world in which everyone is out of sorts and everything is out of sync. The old guide drinks so much that he cannot fulfill what is required to ensure the success of the fishing venture on which the young couple embarks. To start with, the fishing, out of season, is illegal. But because they have forgotten the lead sinkers the fishing itself goes awry. Yet this, superficially the guide's mishap and misfortune, merely reflects the true burden of the story, which is to show just what the couple's spiritual weather is like. The woman is out of sorts, as is the man, and their relationship is out of sync. The story ends with the drunken guide's promise that things will go better the next day. It's a fond hope, though, for the young man has the last word: "I may not be going, said the young gentleman, very probably not. I will leave word with the padrone at the hotel office" (139).

Hemingway's second book, with a printing of 170 copies, appeared in 1924. Brought out by the Three Mountains Press in Paris, *in our time* (the contents of which, a year later, would be incorporated into *In Our Time*) consists of eighteen prose chapters. The book was one volume of "The Inquest" (1923–4), a series of avant-garde titles edited by Ezra Pound, which included work by Pound, Ford Madox Ford, and William Carlos Williams, among others. Manuscript material now in the Hemingway Collection at the John F. Kennedy Library shows that Hemingway was trying to name the sub-genre to which these pieces belonged. Before he settled on the rubric "chapter" for the pieces published in *in our time*, he tried out "episodes" and "unwritten stories." Later readers, responding more directly to their inclusion in *In Our Time*, have chosen to call them by different names, for example, "inter-chapters," "vignettes," and "miniatures." Probably begun as exercises in condensing the raw materials of narrative, most of them attempt to convey the emotional and spiritual ambience of a single incident. For its value as an example of Hemingway's early realistic prose, it is instructive to look at one of them. Here is the whole of chapter 1:

> Everybody was drunk. The whole battery was drunk going along the road in the dark. We were going to the Champagne. The lieutenant kept riding his horse out into the fields and saying to him, "I'm drunk, I tell you, *mon vieux*. Oh, I am so soused." We went along the road all night in the dark and the adjutant kept riding up alongside my kitchen and saying, "You must put it out. It is dangerous. It will be observed." We were fifty kilometers from the front but the adjutant worried about the fire in my kitchen. It was funny going along that road. That was when I was a kitchen corporal. (*Complete Short Stories* 65)

It is a piece of naturalistic prose, told in the first person, in which nothing seems to happen. Years later, in 1935, Hemingway would publish *Green Hills of Africa*, a book of travels in which he "attempted to write an absolutely true book to see whether the shape of a country and the pattern of a month's action can, if truly presented, compete with a work of the imagination" (v). In both instances, in the chapters of *in our time* and the experimental narrative of *Green Hills of Africa*, Hemingway was working toward stretching fiction in the direction of actuality. In chapter 1, as elsewhere – first in *in our time* and then at intervals throughout his career (see, for example, the motives and incidents that run through the hero's mind in "The Snows of Kilimanjaro") – he tests the dramatic possibilities of what might be termed a *memorate*: an image or sensation or a small complex of the two that seemingly persists in the author's or his narrator's memory. Here, in chapter 1, we find many of the familiar characteristics of Hemingway's early prose: short sentences; simple, ordinary language; repetition and redundancy; the occasional use of a foreign phrase, the general meaning of which is clear from the context. And, of course, there is war as subject. Other chapters focus on bullfighting and crime as well as war. The tenth chapter treats, in a radically foreshortened way, materials that Hemingway later developed into his war novel of depression and spiritual numbness, *A Farewell to Arms*. When he included it in *In Our Time*, presenting it no longer as a chapter but as a story, he titled it "A Very Short Story." He also turned chapter 11 into a story, entitling it "The Revolutionist." Such conversions may have resulted from Hemingway's recognition that they were different from the other sixteen untitled chapters in *in our time* or, more likely, from his need to expand his first full collection of short stories. In any case, to put together *In Our Time*, Hemingway was compelled to gather all of his available fiction from his two previous books, along with the stories he had written since the loss of that notorious suitcase. For "Up in Michigan" he was able to substitute "The Battler," written for the volume and not previously published.

Besides the fifteen chapters referred to above, *In Our Time* includes thirteen stories, one of which is presented in two parts. Beginning with the 1930, second edition of the book, all subsequent editions begin with an introductory piece, at first labeled "Introduction by the Author" but subsequently given the permanent title "On the Quai at Smyrna." But in the1925 edition the book had begun with "Indian Camp." Few writers have opened a first collection of stories with a more powerful or characteristic piece. "Indian Camp" can be looked at, from one point of view, as an overture of themes that both permeate the rest of volume and announce the concerns of much of Hemingway's subsequent work. It presents as a child the Nick Adams who had already appeared briefly in Hemingway's work as a soldier wounded on the Italian front (chapter 7 of *in our time*). The narrative, although in the third person, reveals the central consciousness of the child, the reader usually seeing only what the child sees. The boy's rite of passage takes place when his father, a physician, takes the boy along to attend an Indian woman in labor and has the boy "assist" him (he jokes that the boy is his "interne"). Under primitive conditions and using rudimentary implements, the father delivers the baby, a boy. Exhilarated, he boasts that this one is "for the medical journal," only to discover that the baby's father, lying quietly in the upper bunk, has cut his throat from ear to ear. O. Henry, still very much in vogue at the time, might well have ended the story here at the moment of the shocking discovery that the "proud" father has committed suicide. Hemingway does not. He follows the doctor and his son out into the dawn as they row across the water away from the camp and back home. Nick continues to ask questions – about women, suicide, and death – and his father continues to answer those questions as best he can. And what does Nick, who has witnessed such pain and suffering, finally conclude? "In the early morning on the lake sitting in the stern of the boat with his father rowing, he felt quite sure that he would never die" (70). Nick will live on to learn to accept the fact that he, too, will suffer the common doom; but at this moment it is his child's belief of personal immortality that quiets him before the act of violence to which he has just been exposed.

Nick as child, adolescent, and adult appears in six other stories in *In Our Time*: "The Doctor and the Doctor's Wife" (*Transatlantic Review*, 1924), which focuses on the character of Dr. Adams as revealed in unpleasant encounters with a workman and with his own wife and a concluding meeting with his son; "The End of Something," which dramatizes the end of a young love relationship over which hovers the competing claim of adolescent male companionship; "The Three Day Blow" ("the greatest drunk story in the language," John Berryman once said in conversation), which shows two boys taking themselves seriously and self-importantly at a time when Nick is depressed at having broken up with his girl friend; "The Battler," a brief tale in which Nick, while riding the rails, runs into a punch-drunk ex-prizefighter traveling with a black man who acts as his keeper; "Cross Country Snow" (1925), which presents Nick, recently married, on a skiing vacation in Europe with a friend, lamenting that the responsibilities attending marriage and imminent parenthood will bring to an end the pleasures of "bumming" around at will; and "Big Two-Hearted River" (1925), a story of the adult Nick fishing alone in Michigan's Upper Peninsula.

"A Very Short Story" and "The Revolutionist" were first published as chapters in *in our time*; "My Old Man" and "Out of Season" had appeared in *Three Stories and Ten Poems*; "Mr. and Mrs. Elliot" (1924–5), which also caused Hemingway problems with his publisher, satirizes the domestic life and sleeping arrangements of a desiccated poetaster given to drinking white wine in the evening and writing reams of poetry during the night. The satirical mode of this story is uncharacteristic of Hemingway's early fiction. "Soldier's Home" treats with simple power the theme of the returning war veteran's disgust and despair. Returning too late to receive even the hero's fleeting welcome, he drops, depressingly, into a world in which nothing works for him. Everything causes him more trouble than it is worth. Back from the war, the soldier discovers, home is no longer home as he had known it.

More subtly than does "Up in Michigan," "Cat in the Rain" presents a crisis in the emotional needs of a young woman. The story is set in Europe. On vacation, presumably, a young American man reads in bed, while his wife (presumably) looks out at a cat caught in the rain. She leaves the room intending to get the cat, but by the time she gets outside, the cat is gone. Later the hotelkeeper, having witnessed her unsuccessful search, sends her another cat, "a big tortoise-shell" one. The woman's need for a cat, while her husband lies in bed, suggests what is missing in their relationship; so too does her attraction to the hotelkeeper, expressed in the author's characteristic style of repetition and syntactical variation in short sentences: "He stood behind his desk in the far end of the dim room. The wife liked him. She liked the deadly serious way he received any complaints. She liked his dignity. She liked the way he wanted to serve her. She liked the way he felt about being a hotel-keeper. She liked his old, heavy face and big hands" (130).

An early reader of "Big Two-Hearted River" called it a purely naturalistic story in which nothing happens; there is no action. No one did more than Hemingway to teach readers to see the drama inherent in the telling of such stories in which "nothing happens." On the surface, the narrative tells of one man's journey over familiar terrain to a place where he will pitch his tent for a few days of fishing for trout in a stream he has fished in the past. In focused detail Hemingway unfolds his story of a man returning to a place and an activity that is deeply meaningful to him. Everything Nick Adams does he does carefully, exactly as it should be done, from pitching his tent and cooking his food to threading a grasshopper to bait his hook. Nick places great value on technique and expertise, but things do not go as smoothly as he would like. Just as he finds the land around him burnt and the grasshoppers scorched black from the fire, he too finds himself spoiling his immediate pleasures by thinking thoughts he had tried hard to repress. Indeed, there is tension running through the narrative which is intended to orchestrate the theme of tension threatening the psychological balance of the young man returning to old haunts and finding that they seem to harbor new and unnamed ghosts he has brought with him. Not for nothing, apparently, does he put off going into the swamp, rejecting the place where fishing would be "a tragic adventure." Nick's world is a world of pressure. Even from the bridge over the river Nick sees tension and quiet force in each trout's holding itself fast in the stream:

> Nick looked down into the clear, brown water, colored from the pebbly bottom, and watched the trout keeping themselves steady in the current with wavering fins. As he watched them they changed their positions by quick angles, only to hold steady in the fast water again. Nick watched them a long time.
>
> He watched them holding themselves with their noses into the current, many trout in deep, fast moving water, slightly distorted as he watched far down through the glassy convex surface of the pool, its surface pushing and swelling smooth against the resistance of the log-driven piles of the bridge. (163)

D. H. Lawrence was the first critic to suggest that *In Our Time* was unified in a unique way. He called it "a fragmentary novel" – "a series of successive sketches from one man's life." If the book does "not pretend to be about one man," it is nevertheless exactly that, he insists; for "these few sketches are enough to create the man and all his history: we need know no more."[3] A related critical idea that has affected the ongoing publication of Hemingway's stories involves the life of Nick Adams, boy and man. Eleven years after Hemingway's death, *The Nick Adams Stories* appeared. This volume reprints all previously published Nick Adams stories (including chapter 7 of *in our time*), several unfinished and/or rejected fragments from manuscript, and two previously unpublished stories, "Summer People" and "The Last Good Country," that were determined to be in more-or-less finished form. The sequence of the stories follows, insofar as his age can be determined, Nick's life from childhood to his mid-to-late thirties. The book adds little to Hemingway's reputation as a short-story writer, a fact indirectly acknowledged by the publisher's blurb, which says only that the collection includes "Eight New *Additions* Hitherto Unpublished" (emphasis added).[4]

After the favorable critical reception of *In Our Time*, Hemingway chose to follow up his triumph with *Torrents of Spring*, a work that not only parodies the novel form but satirizes contemporary fiction, particularly Sherwood Anderson's. It was published in 1926 by Scribner's, which became Hemingway's regular publisher. *The Sun Also Rises*, a second novel, was published later in the same year. By 1927 Hemingway had in hand enough new short stories to warrant a second collection. Echoing the titles of Robert Browning's *Men and Women* and Ford Madox Ford's *Women and Men* (Ford's book appeared in Pound's "Inquest" series, as did the 1924 *in our time*), Hemingway called his book *Men Without Women*, explaining wryly to his editor, after he had listed the stories he proposed to include in the volume, that the title was meant to indicate that "in all of these" stories, "almost, the softening feminine influence through training, discipline, death or other causes [is] absent" (*Letters* 245).

The first story in the volume is "The Undefeated," a more complex treatment of the material on bullfighting appearing in the chapters of *In Our Time* and a complementary back-story for the Pedro Romero episodes of *The Sun Also Rises*. It is the first of his stories to probe deeply into the limits of professionalism, a theme that interested Hemingway all his life. The aging professional, still recovering from a goring, is given the chance to perform in a nocturnal, a nighttime bullfight. He requests the services of an experienced picador, a friend who will help him. The performance goes well enough at first (though the fighter's efforts are not appreciated by the third-string newspaper critic). But the bullfighter runs into difficulties, not of his own making, and he is severely gored. And in the final scene, as he lies in the infirmary waiting for surgery, he implores his friend, the picador, not to cut off his pigtail. It is the symbol of his profession.

"The Undefeated" dramatizes the tragic situation in which the bullfighter, weakened through wounding and aging, is not able to overcome his bad luck in drawing bulls he can no longer master. Hemingway finds pathos and poetry in the bullfighter's desperate attempts to meet his standards as a torero and preserve his personal integrity. At the end the bullfighter breathes deeply into the anaesthesia, ready for surgery. He is the first of those heroes who are destroyed but not defeated – a theme that Hemingway returns to often, most famously in *The Old Man and the Sea* (1952).

The human value of performing professionally – being "pretty good in there" (272) – is the major theme of "Today is Friday," which is included in this collection as a story in the form of a one-act play. Hemingway sets his piece historically in Jerusalem on the first Good Friday. The characters, besides a tavern keeper, are the Roman soldiers who have carried out the execution of Jesus and now, at the end of their working day, stand around talking over the day's events. Not yet suffused with historical Christianity, mythology or legendry, Jesus emerges in the eyes of some of the Romans, not as an outlaw or a man obsessed by a vision but as a courageous performer under extreme duress. In "Fifty Grand" (1927) Jack Brennan breaks with the code of fairness in prizefighting in asserting his own personal, largely implicit, sense of morality. Knowing he cannot win an honest fight, he bets heavily against himself only to have his opponent deliberately foul him in an attempt to throw the fight. The old fighter, double-crossed, fouls his opponent and is disqualified, thereby losing both the fight and his championship. But through crossing and double-crossing, the outcome of the fight is the same as it would have been had it been fought squarely; besides, the old fighter has won his bet. The complex issue of "outlaw" morality reappears in *To Have and Have Not* (1937), a novel developed out of two narratives, "One Trip Across" (*Cosmopolitan*, 1934) and "The Tradesman's Return" (*Esquire*, 1936), both published originally as short stories.

Hemingway's working title for "The Killers" (*Scribner's*, 1927) was "The Matadores," linking the story to bullfighting. Set in a town outside of Chicago, it tells the story of two hit men waiting in a lunchroom for their victim, and can be seen as a particularly sardonic parody of the professional's performance of an ugly, ritualized killing that misfires – if only for the time being. Nick Adams is the link between the two parts of the story: he witnesses the visit and the departure of the hit men, after which he hurries off to warn the intended victim of his danger. Because of his presence at these events, the point of the story is often seen to be that he has been affected by what he has experienced. As such, the story becomes, like the earlier "Indian Camp" and "The Battler," the rendering of still another milestone episode in Nick Adams's worldly education. Still other milestones in that journey, both earlier and later ones, appear in *Men Without Women*, including: "Ten Indians," which focuses on the boy's discovery of adolescent sexual infidelity; "Now I Lay Me," the concluding story in the volume, which takes up a neurotic, war-wounded Nick terrified that if he goes to sleep at night his soul will disappear from his body never to return; and "In Another Country" (1927), a first-person narrative in which the narrator goes unnamed. This last story presents us with another of Hemingway's professionals – this time an Italian army officer, formerly a fencer, who now comes for machine-rehabilitation of his wounded hand. He does not believe that the machine will have any efficacy. Yet, despite his belief that the only thing a man can do for himself is to keep from putting himself in a position to lose what he values, and despite the bitter, unexpected death of his young wife, he continues to come for the treatments that he knows cannot help him.

In what has proven to be, especially in recent years, the most topically interesting story in the collection, however, Nick Adams is absent. "Hills Like White Elephants" (1927), in some ways, takes up the theme of heterosexual conflict and complexity of earlier stories, such as "Up in Michigan," "Out of Season," and "Cat in the Rain." In a tightly controlled story in which setting and image brim with potentially symbolic meaning, especially for the woman, whose frustration and anger motivates the dramatic focus, two persons sit at a table in a railroad station bar. The story is told mainly through conversation between two troubled and discomfited people. There is talk but no agreement. The young man, identified as an American, is agitated; the woman is nervous, out of sorts. They argue at some length, as they await their train, but avoid naming the thing that plagues them. The reader begins to sense what the unnamable thing is when the conversation suddenly turns away from open bickering and bitchy talk:

"Should we have another drink?"
   "All right."
   The warm wind blew the bead curtain against the table.
   "The beer's nice and cool," the man said.
   "It's lovely," the girl said.
   "It's really an awfully simple operation, Jig," the man said. "It's not really an operation at all."

The girl looked at the ground the table legs rested on.

"I know you wouldn't mind it, Jig. It's really not anything. It's just to let the air in."

The girl did not say anything.

"I'll go with you and I'll stay with you all the time. They just let the air in and then it's all perfectly natural." (212)

The man is right; it's not really an operation. The current synonym – procedure – is meant to allay fears, reduce trepidation. But the increasingly disturbing note in the scene lies not only in what the man proposes for the woman, but in the irony emanating from his presentation of the procedure as "perfectly natural." There's a subtle transvaluation going on here that goes beyond the ethics or morality of what the girl has agreed to undergo. It is the human potential for so considering, for whatever human reason, valid or not, what is, neutrally speaking, an unnatural act and so domesticating it that it can appear to be entirely natural. It may well be, as has been argued, that the girl fears her own death. But the story seems to resonate beyond that possibility to the recognition of a greater death, that of personal sympathy and the humanistic spirit. The horror lies almost as much in how they talk about what is to be done as in any contemplation of the consequences of the proposed operation itself.

In the fall of 1929 Hemingway published his second major novel, *A Farewell to Arms*, followed three years later by *Death in the Afternoon*, a hefty volume telling the historical and contemporary story of the Spanish bullfight, along with what amounted to his *ars poetica*. In 1933 appeared *Winner Take Nothing*, a third collection of short fiction, which would prove to be the last such volume of uncollected and new stories to appear during Hemingway's lifetime. Hemingway's title (playing on the phrase "winner take all") echoes the epigraph for the book, lines that he wrote himself in pseudo-Elizabethan speech: "Unlike all other forms of lutte or combat the conditions are that the winner shall take nothing; neither his ease, nor his pleasure, nor any notions of glory; nor, if he win far enough, shall there be any reward within himself."[5] He had never been interested in pyrrhic victories, and too often, he felt, unalloyed victories were impossible (the young Pedro Romero's heroics in and out of the arena in *The Sun Also Rises* constituting an exception), but personal achievement in the face of defeat was a matter he had already treated and would do so again. But in *Winner Take Nothing* Hemingway's overarching theme seems to be that there really are no winners for there is nothing to win. The book opens with "After the Storm" (1932), a story that deals with a sunken ship and its salvageable contents. It is told from the first-person point of view of a Key West tough whose language and outlook make him a forerunner of Harry Morgan, the outlaw hero of "One Trip Across," "The Tradesman's Return," and *To Have and Have Not*. Although the narrator's failure to profit from his discovery of the submerged ship at least superficially embodies Hemingway's overall theme for the volume, it was not the story he wanted to place as his lead. His choice for that spot was "The Light of the World," a story he later insisted was "a very fine story about whores – as good or better a story about whores than Maison Tellier" by Maupassant (*Letters* 393), but his editor, arguing that placing it first "would play into the hands of his critics, who would again accuse him of using a 'small-boy wickedness of vocabulary' simply for its shock effect," talked him into leading with "After the Storm."[6] What Hemingway did not argue is that "The Light of the World" was a Nick Adams story, and that taken with "Fathers and Sons," another Nick Adams story, which he insisted from the start must close the volume, they would have given the collection a frame similar to the one employed in *In Our Time*. The third Nick Adams story in *Winner Take Nothing*, "A Way You'll Never Be," again deals with a soldier, still psychologically jittery and jumpy, though he has largely recovered from his physical wounds.

The collection is filled out with a mixture of stories on familiar Hemingway themes and stories that constitute new departures, "The Mother of a Queen" (bullfighting), for example, but "Homage to Switzerland" (1933) (Americans in Europe as targets for satire, recalling, in its ambience, the earlier story, "A Canary for One" [1927]), "One Reader Writes" (a lonely-hearts letter), and "Wine of Wyoming" (1930) (reminiscent of Turgenev's *A Sportsman's Sketches*, a Hemingway favorite). "A Natural History of the Dead" was an anecdote he culled from *Death in the Afternoon*. This story is in two parts: an essay on dying, the combat dead, and the absurdities of the self-proclaimed humanists of the day, followed by a dramatized incident exemplifying the moral complexities of triage at a battlefield dressing station. This interest in the professionalism of physicians (and its limitation and breakdown under duress), seen as early as "Indian Camp" and *A Farewell to Arms*, resurfaces in "God Rest You Merry, Gentlemen" (1933). Set in Kansas City, this story centers on the reactions of two ambulance surgeons to the situation of a boy who, out of a deep Pauline sense of sinning against purity, mutilates himself. The story draws complexly on Christian materials, as does "The Light of the World," in which Hemingway tests the Christian notion of charity, as expressed in Jesus's imprecation to those who would honor him that they do so by extending charity "unto the least" of humankind. Do the obligations of charity extend to the whore, large as "a hay mow"? Does it apply to the "sisters," exemplified in men who put lemon juice on their hands to keep them white and soft?

Filial and parental relationships, a staple in Hemingway's work from "Indian Camp" to the posthumously published novel *Islands in the Stream* (1970), inform two stories in *Winner Take Nothing*: "A Day's Wait" and "Fathers and Sons." "A Day's Wait," which Hemingway insisted was transcribed directly from experience, is structured around a surprising revelation. A sick child has confused a Fahrenheit temperature reading for centigrade and consequently thinks he is at death's door. This tightly controlled story presents an indelible image of the child as "a little man" whose tight-lipped bravery as he faces death gives way, after the mistake over temperatures is discovered and cleared away, to crying "very easily at little things that were of no importance." In "Fathers and Sons" Nick Adams, now aged 38, has a son of his own. The roles of son to father in "Indian Camp" and "The Doctor and the Doctor's Wife" are repeated, but now it is Nick who would coach and teach the child who wants to know about his grandfather. If we go by age, this is the oldest Nick we meet in Hemingway's fiction.

The theme of heterosexual conflict and complexity is again taken up in "The Sea Change" (1931), but with a twist that is particularly interesting for Hemingway. As in "Hills Like White Elephants," the story takes place in a bar. The woman is about to leave the man for someone else. They argue until the man says angrily, "'I'll kill her'" (302). After more arguing, the woman walks away. The man's reaction to what is happening is the focal point of the story. It ends with a note on his behavior after the woman has left. He talks to the barman and then, insisting that he is "a different man," stares at himself in the mirror. Even the potential for irony in the barman's closing observation, "You must have had a very good summer," does not detract from the story's shift away from the woman's sexual choice to the man's narcissism (304).

Published in *Scribner's Magazine* as "Give Us a Prescription, Doctor" (1933), "The Gambler, the Nun, and the Radio" is a Depression story about the illusions and delusions that are humankind's opiates. The neurotic, jumpy hospital patient whose central consciousness structures the narrative lists them: religion, music, economics, patriotism, sexual intercourse, drink ("an excellent opium"), the radio ("a cheap one"), gambling, ambition, new forms of government, and bread ("the real, the actual, opium of the people") (367). The opiate he, a writer, does not mention, is writing. There is much in this significant story that recalls the Hemingway most familiar to readers – the hospital setting; the frazzled, neurotic center of consciousness; the expressions of anxiety and despair. Never a favorite with critics, it continues to suffer from critical and interpretive neglect.

Hemingway's most memorable story of despair, however, is the widely anthologized "A Clean, Well-Lighted Place" (1933). Told in the third person, the story is set in Spain, first in a cafe and then, briefly, in a bar. Its principal is a so-called "old waiter" who first converses with a younger colleague and then has a brief exchange with a barman. What is revealed is that the two cafe waiters see life differently. The younger one has what he calls "confidence"; the older one does not (290). They talk about an old man who drinks at the cafe, revealing that he has tried to commit suicide but was saved by a niece who feared for his soul. The reader gradually discovers that it is the "older waiter" the author would have us attend to. He questions himself: "What did he fear? It was not fear or dread. It was a nothing that he knew too well. It was all a nothing and a man was nothing too. It was only that and light was all it needed and a certain cleanness and order. Some lived in it and never felt it but he knew it all was *nada y pues nada y nada y pues nada*" (291). Then, in one of the most famous passages in all of Hemingway's writings, he breaks into a nihilistic parody of the Christian prayer: "Our *nada* who art in *nada*, *nada* be thy name thy Kingdom *nada* thy will be *nada* in *nada* as it is in *nada*. Give us this *nada* our daily *nada* and *nada* us our *nada* as we *nada* our *nadas* and *nada* us not into *nada* but deliver us from *nada*; *pues nada*" (291). The waiter has replaced with "nada" nouns and verbs that suggest things and attributes – father, heaven, hallowed, come, done, earth, heaven, day, bread, forgive, trespasses, forgive, enemies, lead, temptation, evil, and amen (so be it). From the waiter's point of view, alone or collectively they add up to nothing. Belief in the existence of such entities, like belief in the efficacy of prayers to the Lord or the Virgin, are – to borrow terms from "The Gambler, the Nun, and the Radio" – opiates of the people. The story ends with a characteristic irony as the waiter wryly dismisses his despairing thoughts: "After all, he said to himself, it is probably only insomnia. Many must have it" (291).

In 1935 Hemingway published *Green Hills of Africa*, an account of his experiences on a big-game hunting trip he had taken with his second wife, Pauline. He explained that the book was an experiment in writing intended to bridge the worlds of factual experience and fictional creation; that is, he had invented neither characters nor incidents, but had selected his material and so shaped it to see if a work of fact could compete with a work of fiction on the latter's own grounds. Out of that African safari also came the germ for two stories that would become virtually synonymous with the name of Hemingway: "The Short Happy Life of Francis Macomber" (*Cosmopolitan*, 1934) and "The Snows of Kilimanjaro" (*Esquire*, 1936). No other work of fiction by Hemingway has been more critically controversial as "The Short Happy Life of Francis Macomber." That it is a tightly controlled narrative of the title character's coming of age – a psychological baptism in which he behaves courageously in the face of potential violent death – has seldom been questioned (although one critic was disturbed that Hemingway had chosen, at certain moments, to write from the point of view of the lion). Rather, the controversy has waxed, at times hotly, over the precise nature of Mrs. Macomber's character and whether or not, when she kills her husband, she has committed murder. The narrative overall seems to indicate that Margot Macomber, who uses infidelity and a sharp tongue to humiliate her diffident and at times cowardly husband into subservience in what has obviously been a disastrous marriage, might very well murder a husband whose conquest of his fear of the animals he hunts is emblematic of his acquisition of control over the way he will live his life. But in one sentence describing what Wilson, the white hunter, calls, sardonically, "the manner of the accident" (28), Hemingway set interpretive hares that are still running. "Macomber had stood solid and shot for the nose, shooting a touch high each time and hitting the heavy horns, splintering and chipping them like hitting a slate roof, and Mrs. Macomber, in the car, had shot at the buffalo with the 6.5 Mannlicher as it seemed about to gore Macomber and hit her husband about two inches up and a little to one side of the base of his skull" (28). The immediate aftermath of this "accident" is that the guide bullies and taunts the woman who is "crying hysterically." In an exchange replete with irony, he tells her, "Of course it's an accident," but then asks her accusingly, "Why didn't you poison him?" (28). When the author was asked about the matter, he said that he simply did not know, that he could have found out but did not want to probe deeper into the case. As the guide says, there will be an inquest (and indeed in *The Macomber Affair*, a 1947 film based on the story, the entire narrative is presented within the framing situation of an inquest) that will, through legal procedure, decide whether Macomber's death was accidental or homicidal. But Hemingway chose to stop short of such an inquest, because the legal determination, whatever the verdict, would be beside the point. Hemingway ends his story with mystery, not the detective's, but the psychological moralist's. When this hard woman unexpectedly collapses into hysteria and falls into subservience before the white hunter, the reader witnesses the uncovering of a depth in Mrs. Macomber's character that even she had not expected or feared. Can she, let alone the reader (or the author), ever know whether in her heart of hearts she had not only been capable of murdering her husband but, in the only way that morally and personally counts, had actually done so?

"The Snows of Kilimanjaro," Hemingway's most complexly arranged narrative and his most consciously symbolic story up to that time, dramatizes the final hours in the life of a failed writer who finds himself dying from infection as he futilely awaits the plane that would fly him out of this hunting encampment to the medical treatment that could save his gangrenous leg and his life. Except for the exchanges between the writer and his attending wife, the narrative consists of a long self-examination on the part of the writer in which he mixes memories of incidents and personages with judgments of his past. Printed in italics, these memories, the reader soon discovers, are biographical, constituting materials that the backslider writer, having betrayed his talent, has hitherto failed to turn into art. Recognizing and facing up to his self-deluding rationalization for marrying into the tribe of "the rich" and living among them, namely that he would study them so that he could write about them, the writer *in extremis* confesses to himself.

To get at the matter, Hemingway employs a double-ending, first, an apocalypse in which the writer experiences the arrival of the salvific airplane and which ends with his perception that he is going directly to the square top of Kilimanjaro, and secondly, closing out the narrative, a bit of symbolic naturalism, in which his wife could see the writer's "bulk under the mosquito bar but somehow he had gotten his leg out and it hung down alongside the cot. The dressings had all come down and she could not look at it" (56). At the last, the act of writing gets the moral right. Notation no longer even matters. At his death the author is once again a writer – a minimalist "telescoping" his "stories" into a paragraph or two.[7] The mystery of the leopard whose carcass, dried and frozen, was found close to the western summit of Kilimanjaro (as indicated in the epigraph) lends itself to unresolved interpretations, both naturalistic and apocalyptic. About the nature of the writer's final, if implicit, judgment of himself, however, there is no doubt; he has become the writer he should have been all along, once again composing his stories.

Hemingway's African stories were not collected in book form until 1938, when Scribner's published *The Fifth Column and the First Forty-Nine Stories* (1938). The "first forty-nine stories" included, besides "Macomber" and "Snows," and the stories from the three collections, *In Our Time, Men Without Women,* and *Winner Take Nothing,* as well as "Up in Michigan" (1923) and two stories set in Spain: "Old Man at the Bridge" and "The Capital of the World," the latter telling the story of a mock bullfight, held in a restaurant, in which a young boy, "full of illusions," is accidentally killed. Nearly all the short stories Hemingway had published to date were included in this volume.

In hand, however, he had another four stories of the Spanish Civil War – "The Denunciation" (1938), "The Butterfly and Tank" (1938), "Night Before Battle" (1939), and
"Under the Ridge" (1939) – which were collected only after Hemingway's death. In
1969 Scribner's issued them, along with Hemingway's play, as *The Fifth Column and
Four Unpublished Stories of the Spanish Civil War*, a title that contradicts the fact that
these stories had all appeared in journals in the 1930s.

The 1938 preface that Hemingway wrote for *The First Forty-Nine Stories* concludes
with the statement that the author "would like to live long enough to write three
more novels and twenty-five more stories. I know some pretty good ones" (4). He did
produce and publish the three novels – if included among them is *The Old Man and
the Sea*, the novella for which he received the Pulitzer Prize, along with *For Whom the
Bell Tolls* (1940) and *Across the River and Into the Trees* (1950), the story of a US Army
colonel's last days in Venice. The posthumous publication of his works includes the
novels *Islands in the Stream* (1970), the account of a painter's domestic relationships
and wartime exploits, and *The Garden of Eden* (1986), a story of psychological disintegration culled from manuscripts relating to Americans living in France in the 1920s,
as well *True at First Light* (1999), African materials put together by his son, Patrick
Hemingway. But "twenty- five" was a number he did not begin to approach. Towards
that number he left two fables, "The Good Lion" (1951, *Hemingway Reader*), in which
a lion drinks martinis at Harry's Bar in Venice, and "The Faithful Bull" (*Fortune*,
1951), several uncollected stories, such as "Nobody Ever Dies!" (*Cosmopolitan*, 1939),
and two stories that appeared in the November 1957 *Atlantic Monthly* (under the
heading "Two Titles of Darkness,") "A Man of the World" and "Get a Seeing-Eyed
Dog," and a few other unpublished stories. Although there were indications, especially
after Hemingway was awarded the Nobel Prize for Literature in 1954, that there
would be a new edition of his collected stories (Hemingway even went so far as to
write an introductory piece, "The Art of the Short Story," which remained unpublished until it appeared in the *Paris Review* in 1981), no such collection materialized
in Hemingway's lifetime.

Only in 1987, in fact, did Scribner's issue an enlarged edition of Hemingway's
short fiction. As the publisher's preface acknowledges, there had "long been a need
for a complete and up-to-date edition of the short stories of Ernest Hemingway."
Unfortunately, this publication was not that long-needed edition. *The Complete Short
Stories of Ernest Hemingway* was misnamed, for not all of Hemingway's stories were
included, while excerpts from unpublished manuscripts of unfinished novels were.
The stories from *The Fifth Column and the First Forty-Nine Stories* volume were included,
along with "The Denunciation," "The Butterfly and the Tank," "Night Before Battle,"
"Under the Ridge," "Nobody Ever Dies!," "Get a Seeing-Eyed Dog" (a sequel to "The
Sea Change"), "A Man of the World," "The Summer People," and "The Last Good
Country," the final two first published in *The Nick Adams Stories*. From the novel *The
Garden of Eden*, itself an editorial arrangement of extracts from an unpublished manu-
script, the editors culled "An African Story." The two fables "The Good Lion" and
"The Faithful Bull" were included, as well as "One Trip Across" and "The Tradesman's

Return," both published in magazines as short stories but later incorporated into the novel *To Have and Have Not*. To these were added new stories edited from manuscript. Some, "Landscape with Figures," "I Guess Everything Reminds You of Something" (about a father and son), "Great News from the Mainland" (another father and son story), and "Black Ass at the Cross Roads," were identified as short stories. Others, such as "A Train Trip," "The Porter," and "The Strange Country" were identified as excerpts (of several chapters, in some instances) from unfinished novels. But some published work is excluded – "The Mercenaries," "Crossroads," and "The Ash Heel's Tendon" (early stories included in Peter Griffin's 1990 biography, *Along with Youth*), two anecdotes told to the "Old Lady" in *Death in the Afternoon*, and high-school juvenilia.[8]

In his last years Hemingway prepared a book-length manuscript of reminiscences of his Parisian years in the 1920s. Published posthumously, *A Moveable Feast* was edited, in part, by his widow, Mary Welsh Hemingway, whom he had married in 1946, shortly after divorcing his third wife, Martha Gellhorn. Included is a preface by Hemingway, dated "San Francisco de Paula, Cuba 1960," in which he writes: "For reasons sufficient to the writer, many places, people, observations and impressions have been left out of this book. Some were secrets and some were known by everyone and everyone has written about them and will doubtless write more" (in mode the work is memorial). But that it is entirely a record of what actually happened, however selective, is called into question by the sentences which conclude this short preface. "If the reader prefers, this book may be regarded as fiction," offers the author, who continues, slyly cautioning, "but there is always the chance that such a book of fiction may throw some light on what has been written as fact" (*Moveable* v). Only the names of persons and places are real, he might have said, the incidents making up the narrative are imaginary – perhaps. If one chooses not to disregard the implications of Hemingway's prefatory statements, one is then confronted with the interesting possibilities in how to regard, describe, and assess the work. It can, of course, be regarded as a book of sketches and portraits deriving from remembered facts, described as a memoir, and evaluated for its fidelity to observation and its reliability as record. It is replete with acidic and not so acidic pictures of by-now historical personages such as Gertrude Stein, Ford Madox Ford, Zelda and Scott Fitzgerald, Ezra Pound, and Hadley Richardson Hemingway. But consider for a moment this possibility: suppose Hemingway had substituted fictitious names for the real ones, as he had in the final version of *The Sun Also Rises*, that earlier account of Paris (and Spain) in the 1920s, would there be any point in denying that in *A Moveable Feast* he had written his final collection of short stories? Once again (as always, but particularly in *In Our Time*) he has combined fully developed stories ("A Matter of Measurements"), paired stories ("Miss Stein Instructs" and " '*Une Génération Perdue*' ") and sketches ("Shakespeare and Company") within a structure that successfully conveys an archetypal story of the loss of a golden age, of a young artist's fall from a second innocence. It is less an account of a young man's adventures than a portrait of the man as young artist. Much of what Hemingway is up to in *A Moveable Feast* he reveals in the opening story, "A Good

Café on the Place St.-Michel." This simple, direct narrative moves from an account of "bad weather," "a sad, evilly run café" (3), and the dirty and sour smells of certain parts of Paris to a dramatized episode in "a pleasant café, warm and clean and friendly" (5), where the author takes a notebook out of his pocket and a pencil and writes a story. It turns out that the story he writes is one his readers will recognize as "The Three Day Blow." He tells us that since, on the day he writes, "it was a wild, cold, blowing day it was that sort of day in the story" (5). Moreover, the boys in the story were drinking and this made the author so thirsty he ordered "a rum St. James." "This tasted wonderful on the cold day," he writes, "and I kept on writing, feeling very well and feeling the good Martinique rum warm me all through my body and my spirit" (5). When he looks up from his notebook, he watches a very pretty girl with hair as "black as a crow's wing and cut sharply and diagonally across her cheek" (5). He wishes that he could put her into the story he is writing, but he cannot. She must wait her turn until, thirty-five years later, she surfaces in the story we are now reading.

If "A Good Cafe on the Place St.-Michel" does not reveal the mysteries of good writing, Hemingway does tell the reader that the facts of memory are only one ingredient, sensitivity to immediate experience and present ambience being equally important. This story, leading off the collection, serves to caution the reader of *A Moveable Feast* not to take incidents, events, and characters therein displayed as strictly adhering to what actually happened at the time, but as instances, it may be, of a higher, fictional truth. It is an artist's tenet, one that Hemingway would have his readers apply to all the writing he cared about. He was always pleased, as he said elsewhere, that critics, when trying to distinguish those stories he invented from those he had transcribed from actuality and memory, seldom did so accurately. His stories were of both kinds. He wrote some stories "absolutely as they happen," he claimed – "Wine of Wyoming," "One Reader Writes," "A Day's Wait," "The Mother of a Queen," "The Gambler, the Nun, and the Radio," and "After the Storm" – while others he invented – "The Killers," "Hills Like White Elephants," "The Undefeated," "Fifty Grand," "The Sea Change," and "A Simple Enquiry." "*Nobody* can tell," he boasted, "which ones I make up completely" (*Letters* 400).

The author's purpose, in any and every instance, was to create his narrative such that the places and personages he rendered would be truer to his readers than their own actuality. The problem, though, as the author saw it, was that critics were invariably too ready to read the author's biography directly out of his fiction. In *A Moveable Feast* he turns their question around: he challenges them not to look for the actuality behind the stories but, if they will look for such things, the invention that went into them. If Hemingway wanted all the stories in *In Our Time*, for instance, "to sound as though they really happened" (400), can it not be said of the stories of actuality in *A Moveable Feast* that he wanted them all to sound as though they were really invented? This melding of fact and fiction in Hemingway's best writing has always interested his readers. In the end it did not much matter to him or, for the most part, to his readers. After all, dissolving the boundaries between imagined reality and recorded imagination enabled him to write *A Moveable Feast*.

Hemingway's work remains vital. He was the innovator of an unmatched style, a shrewd chronicler of his times, a close observer of child and adolescent life, an anatomist of pain, courage, and cowardice, and a poet of aging and death. He liberated the American short story from the constrictions imposed by the plot-driven formula culminating in a final wry twist that marked so many American stories in the early decades of the twentieth century. Rather than playing up to the smaller ironies in single incidents (the so-called O. Henry ending), Hemingway's stories delineate a world in which the fact of human existence is itself discovered to be inherently ironic.

Of the short stories Hemingway most cared about, which included both the recalled and invented sort, we have his own list. In his preface to the *First Forty-Nine Stories*, excluding those stories he considered even then to have been overly anthologized ("The Undefeated," "Fifty Grand," "The Killers" among them, one surmises), he names seven: "The Short Happy Life of Francis Macomber," "In Another Country," "Hills Like White Elephants," "A Way You'll Never Be," "The Snows of Kilimanjaro," "A Clean Well-Lighted Place," and "The Light of the World." His readers would undoubtedly add other titles to this list ("Indian Camp" and "Soldier's Home," for example), but none, one surmises, would omit any of those named by Hemingway, a clutch of stories that rank undeniably among the finest and most influential in the English language. Writers such as J. D. Salinger, Norman Mailer, John Updike, Oscar Hijuelos, Raymond Carver, Antonio Lobo Antunes, and Joyce Carol Oates, to name only a few that come readily to mind, have acknowledged their indebtedness to Hemingway. But let the last word go to a contemporary writer in Brazil. In an interview published in 2002, over forty years after Hemingway's death, Ana Maria Machado was asked to name those writers "from other countries" who had influenced her. "At age nineteen, I discovered John Dos Passos, Steinbeck, Fitzgerald, Faulkner, and Hemingway," she answered. "From these last two I've read all they have written many times over. It was pure passion, especially Hemingway, whom I consider one of that very select group of writers who have thoroughly mastered their craft. He is a writer I would like to emulate someday; his ability to give voice to the land, whether in Pamplona, the Gulf of Mexico or Africa, is truly astonishing. He is so humble amid nature, and his quietness allows nature to speak for itself in his works."[9]

NOTES

1 *Selected Letters of John O'Hara*, ed. Matthew J. Bruccoli (New York: Random House, 1978), 348. In 1950 O'Hara had evoked a flurry of protest when he wrote: "The most important author living today, the outstanding author since the death of Shakespeare, has brought out a new novel. The title of the novel is *Across the River and Into the Trees*. The author, of course, is Ernest Hemingway, the most important, the outstanding author out of the millions of writers who have lived since 1616" (*New York Times Book Review*, September 10, 1950: 1).

2 Quotations from Hemingway's stories come from *The Complete Short Stories of Ernest Hemingway*, The Finca Vigía Edition (New York: Scribner's, 1987).

3 D. H. Lawrence, Review of *In Our Time*, *Calendar of Modern Letters* 4 (April 1927): 72–3.

4   Scribner's followed Philip Young's plan for the book, but decided not to use his critical introduction, preferring a much shorter preface; see Philip Young, "Big World Out There: The Nick Adams Stories," *Novel: A Forum on Fiction*, 6 (Fall 1972): 5–19, and "Posthumous Hemingway, and Nicholas Adams," in *Hemingway In Our Time*, eds. Richard Astro and Jackson J. Benson (Corvallis: Oregon State University Press, 1974), 13–23. As early as 1930 Granville Hicks asserted that any study of Hemingway's portrayal of the "spiritual history" of the hero must start with Nick Adams ("The World of Hemingway," *New Freeman* 1, March 1930: 40–2).

5   This epigraph appears on the title-page of all editions of *Winner Take Nothing* but is absent from the collective editions of Hemingway's stories.

6   It is Maxwell Perkins's warning that Carlos Baker quotes in *Ernest Hemingway, A Life Story* (New York: Scribner's, 1969), 241.

7   Typical of Harry's final "stories," echoing the content and style of the sketches Hemingway first published in *in our time* and incorporated into *In Our Time*, is the following:

> He remembered long ago when Williamson, the bombing officer, had been hit by a stick bomb some one in a German patrol had thrown as he was coming in through the wire that night and, screaming, had begged every one to kill him. He was a fat man, very brave, and a good officer, although addicted to fantastic shows. But that night he was caught in the wire, with a flare lighting him up and his bowels spilled out into the wire, so when they brought him in, alive, they had to cut him loose. Shoot me, Harry. For Christ sake shoot me. They had had an argument one time about our Lord never sending you anything you could not bear and some one's theory had been that meant that a certain time the pain passed you out automatically. But he had always remembered Williamson, that night. Nothing passed out Williamson until he gave him all his morphine tablets that he had always saved to use himself and then they did not work right away. (53)

8   Two additional stories, "Philip Haines Was a Writer" and "Lack of Passion," edited from manuscript, appeared in the Spring 1990 issue of *The Hemingway Review* (9: 1–93).

9   Glauco Ortolano, "An Interview with Ana Maria Machado," *WLT: World Literature Today*, 76 (Spring 2002): 112. Best known for her children's books, Ana Maria Machado has done distinguished work in several literary genres. The range of writers influenced by Hemingway is further suggested by the admiration of the novelist James Lee Burke, who lists Hemingway's collected stories among his top five books from which "to learn style and the creation of character" and that of the mystery novelist Robert B. Parker, the creator of the private eye Spencer, who lists Hemingway among his major influences, "particularly the short stories" – *The Reader's Companion*, compiled by Fred Bratman and Scott Lewis (New York: Hyperion, 1994), 36, 48.

References and Further Reading

Beegel, Susan F., ed. *Hemingway's Neglected Short Fiction: New Perspectives*. Tuscaloosa: University of Alabama Press, 1992.

Benson, Jackson J., ed. *New Critical Approaches to the Short Stories of Ernest Hemingway*. Durham, NC: Duke University Press, 1990.

DeFalco, Joseph. *The Hero in Hemingway's Short Stories*. Pittsburgh: University of Pittsburgh Press, 1963.

Flora, Joseph M. *Ernest Hemingway: A Study of the Short Fiction*. Boston: Twayne, 1989.

———. *Hemingway's Nick Adams*. Baton Rouge: Louisiana State University Press, 1982.

———. *Reading Hemingway's Men Without Women: Glossary and Commentary*. Kent, OH: Kent State University Press, 2008.

Hemingway, Ernest. *Three Stories and Ten Poems*. Paris: Contact, 1923.

———. *in our time*. Paris: Three Mountains Press, 1924.

———. *In Our Time*. New York: Boni & Liveright, 1925.

————. *Men Without Women*. New York: Scribner, 1927.

————. *Winner Take Nothing*. New York: Scribner, 1933.

————. *The Fifth Column and the First Forty-nine Stories*. New York: Scribner, 1938.

————. *The Hemingway Reader*. Ed. Charles P. Moore. New York: Scribner, 1953.

————. *A Moveable Feast*. New York: Scribner, 1964.

————. *The Fifth Column and Four Stories of the Spanish Civil War*. New York: Scribner, 1969.

————. *The Nick Adams Stories*. New York: Scribner, 1972.

————. *Selected Letters 1917–1961*. Ed. Carlos Baker. New York: Scribner, 1981.

————. *The Complete Short Stories of Ernest Hemingway* (The Finca Vigía Edition). New York: Scribner, 1987.

Johnston, Kenneth G. *The Tip of the Iceberg: Hemingway and the Short Story*. Greenville, FL: Penkevill, 1987.

Montgomery, Constance Cappel. *Hemingway in Michigan*. New York: Fleet, 1966.

Reynolds, Michael S., ed. *Critical Essays on Ernest Hemingway's* In Our Time. Boston: G. K. Hall, 1983.

Smith, Paul. *A Reader's Guide to the Short Stories of Ernest Hemingway*. Boston: G. K. Hall, 1989.

Smith, Paul, ed. *New Essays on Hemingway's Short Fiction*. Cambridge: Cambridge University Press, 1998.

16
William Faulkner's Short Stories

Hugh Ruppersburg

"I'm a failed poet," Mississippi novelist William Faulkner told an interviewer in 1955. "Maybe every novelist wants to write poetry first, finds he can't and then tries the short story which is the most demanding form after poetry. And failing at that, only then does he take up novel writing."[1] Despite his claim that he valued poetry over fiction, and short stories over novels, Faulkner spent most of his time and energy writing novels, and novels are the foundation of his reputation. Still, Faulkner wrote a number of remarkable stories during his career, some among the finest English language stories in the twentieth century. They include such often-anthologized stories as "A Rose for Emily" (1930), "Barn Burning" (1939), and "That Evening Sun" (1931). A number of lesser known but equally fine stories may also be named, "Mountain Victory" (1932), "Red Leaves" (1930), and "Pantaloon in Black" (1940) among them. These reflect Faulkner's literary art at its best. Even though he once said that "I never wrote a short story I liked," Faulkner was an accomplished writer of short fiction.[2]

Faulkner's stories can be considered in three different ways. First, they are works to be read and studied on their own merits. Second, they are a crucial element of Faulkner's work as a novelist. Faulkner tended to write his novels in discrete chunks of narrative. Rather than developing monovalent, linear plot lines, he used shifts in narrative voice and chronology to build his stories. In "A Rose for Emily," his best-known story, an unnamed member of the community relates the life of Emily Grierson. We know he is a community member because he refers to himself and the community viewpoint with the collective "we," and he often comments on what community members thought or believed. He begins the story with Emily's funeral and then moves back in time to describe the events of her life, especially those that account for her curious standing in the town: her father's death, her relationship with Homer Barron, the reaction to the smell that briefly envelops her house, her china-painting lessons, and her resistance to property taxes. The important events of her life are told in brief episodes. The story concludes by coming again to Emily's death and then moves forward to a macabre discovery made shortly after her funeral. The novel *Light in August* (1932) is built in a similar but more complex fashion. Sometimes the narrator appears to be a member of the community; sometimes a character; sometimes a more objective authorial narrator. Each narrator's story composes a different chunk of narrative. The novel also develops at least three major plot strands involving three major characters. Each character's story is narrated in episodic fashion, interwoven with, contrasted against, the stories of the other characters. The point is that although Faulkner thought of himself as a novelist, he built many of his novels out of episodes that bear a significant resemblance to short stories.

It is not surprising that many of Faulkner's novels began as stories. Faulkner said that *The Sound and the Fury* began with a story he called "Twilight."[3] Elements of *Light in August* and *Sanctuary* both had their inception in a story called "The Big Shot," which featured an early version of the character Gale Hightower. "Barn Burning," with its primal image of the innocent boy turned away from the front entrance to a grand Southern mansion, was initially intended as the opening chapter of *The Hamlet*. All three of the novels in Faulkner's Snopes trilogy are episodic, incorporating a number of previously published stories, such as "The Hound" (1931) and "Spotted Horses" (1931), which became part of *The Hamlet* (1940), and "Centaur in Brass" (1932) and "A Mule in the Yard" (1934), which were incorporated in *The Town* (1957).

Third, and finally, following the examples of James Joyce's *Dubliners*, Sherwood Anderson's *Winesburg, Ohio*, and Ernest Hemingway's *In Our Time*, Faulkner organized several of his collections of short fiction so as to create thematically coherent units. This is especially true in his first story collection *These 13* (1931), and to a lesser extent in *Doctor Martino and Other Stories* (1934). In *Go Down, Moses* he built an intricately structured novel out of a series of chapters originally written as stories. When the publisher added the words "and other stories" to the novel's title in its first printing, Faulkner expressed irritation, insisting that what he had written was a novel, not a collection of stories.[4] *The Unvanquished* (1938) is also built from a sequence of stories originally published in the *Saturday Evening Post*.

Faulkner published four volumes of short fiction during his lifetime: *These 13*, *Doctor Martino and Other Stories*, *Knight's Gambit* (1949), and *Collected Stories of William Faulkner* (1950). This list does not include *The Big Woods* (1955), which collected previously published hunting stories, some of which Faulkner revised for the volume. After his death, several volumes of early newspaper sketches appeared, but the most significant publication was *Uncollected Stories of William Faulkner* (1979), which included a number of previously unpublished stories as well as others that had been published but never collected.

Faulkner's short fiction is an important aspect of his art, and an important avenue toward a wider understanding of his work as a whole. In this discussion, I want to examine several examples of Faulkner's best short fiction. These stories were written during the years 1931 to 1935, when Faulkner wrote most of best stories. (In fact, Faulkner's "great" period in short fiction can be narrowed to the years 1930 to 1932.)

The stories I will discuss appeared in the 1950 volume *Collected Stories of William Faulkner*, where Faulkner collected most of his short fiction published up to that year, including all the stories that appeared in *These 13* and *Doctor Martino and Other Stories*. A few truly great Faulkner stories are missing from *Collected Stories* because they were published as parts of novels, primarily "The Old People," "The Bear," "Pantaloon in Black," and "Delta Autumn," which were part of *Go Down, Moses*. I would argue that "The Bear" is really a short novel, or novella, rather than a short story,[5] and that the other stories in *Go Down, Moses* (with the exception of "Pantaloon in Black," one of Faulkner's greatest stories) benefit from the larger context the novel provides – they work better as stories or chapters within the novel than as stories that stand alone. The stories in *Knight's Gambit* are also missing, but they are not among his best works of short fiction. With those exceptions, *Collected Stories* contains all his important short fiction and provides excellent testimony to the scope of his achievement in the genre.

The individual works in *Collected Stories* address the same social and natural world that Faulkner portrayed in his novels, explore the same themes, and employ the same literary strategies and devices. In general, they are more tightly and modestly focused than the novels, somewhat less ambitious in style and theme, and, with a few notable exceptions, less innovative. At the same time the stories offer a view of Faulkner's world that confirms, deepens, and broadens the portrait offered in the novels. In particular, the stories in the first two sections, "The Country" and "The Village," provide more information about and explorations into the location and time period of such novels as *The Sound and the Fury* (1929), *As I Lay Dying* (1930), *Sanctuary* (1931), and *Light in August* (1932). The stories of "The Wilderness" section narrate the early history of Yoknapatawpha County, focusing especially on the Indians who lived in the region and from whom Thomas Sutpen bought his hundred square miles of land ("Sutpen's Hundred") in *Absalom, Absalom!* (1936). Although Faulkner alludes in *Absalom* to some of the events in these stories, none of his longer works addresses the Native American history of Yoknapatawpha in as much detail as these stories. Likewise, stories in "The Wasteland" section reflect Faulkner's interest in pilots and aviation of the post–World-War I generation. That subject occupied an important place in the early novels *Soldiers' Pay* (1926) and *Sartoris* (1929),[6] but in the stories of "The Wasteland" as well as in such stories as "Honor" (included in "The Middle Ground" section that follows "The Wasteland") Faulkner offers a glimpse into the importance that aviators of the World War I generation had for him and his view of the modern world. They provide context as well for the novel *Pylon* (1935), whose air show aviators are presented as lost citizens of a contemporary Southern wasteland world. In general, Faulkner's short fiction fills in missing spaces in his imagined narrative of Yoknapatawpha County.

The opening section of stories, entitled "The Country," addresses those characters and situations in backwoods rural life that many people associate most closely with Faulkner, especially in such novels as *Light in August*, *As I Lay Dying*, and *The Hamlet*. Among these stories, "Barn Burning," which opens the section, rises above the others and stands as one of Faulkner's best. Its image of an embittered older man and his innocent son who are confronted by a black servant at the front door of a Southern mansion is central to Faulkner's work in the 1930s, and to his sense of social conflict in the South. The boy is overwhelmed by the image of the house: "he saw the house for the first time and at that instant he forgot his father and the terror and despair both ... *Hit's big as a courthouse* he thought quietly, with a surge of peace and joy whose reason he could not have thought into words" (*Collected Stories* 10). The events of "Barn Burning" are recast and retold in the opening pages of *The Hamlet*, for which Faulkner initially intended the story as the first chapter. In *Absalom, Absalom!* the turning point in the main character Thomas Sutpen's life comes when as a young boy he sees a large, white-columned Southern mansion for the first time and is turned away from its front entrance by a black servant. A number of generally similar episodes occur elsewhere in Faulkner's work, but it is significant that this image has its most powerful representation in short story form.

The mansion in "Barn Burning" is not only a focus of social conflict, but also of social change. The boy's father Abner has been accustomed to an individualistic, frontier existence in a world where the frontier has all but vanished. He moves from one sharecropping arrangement to another, leaving as soon as he becomes bored or the landowner he works for makes some demand that he regards as unreasonable. Abner insists on remaining unrepentant and unreconstructed. He resists all efforts to make him conform, to civilize him. He is also fundamentally hostile to the upper-class white Southerners who inhabit the grand houses that symbolize the material wealth and success he will never have. The mansion confronts him with his own lack of success, his poverty, his powerlessness. It also confronts him with an emblem of the civilized and civilizing world – an agent of encroaching social gentility. Abner automatically lashes out against agents of change and order. The efforts of the black servant to keep him from entering Major De Spain's house only ensure that he will seize the first opportunity to rebel. In fact, the black servant, who clearly looks down on the lower-class white man, is the element in the story that conveys to Ab Snopes and his son most clearly that they occupy the lowest rungs on the ladder of social class, privilege, and power.

"Barn Burning" is written in the intense rhetorical style that characterized much of Faulkner's work during the major period of his career. Its narrator essentially inhabits the consciousness of the main character, the boy named Colonel Sartoris Snopes ("Sarty), describing what he sees, feels, and thinks. Although some of Faulkner's child narrators are characterized entirely by their innocence, Sarty has reached a transition point in his life. He is old enough to recognize his father for what he is, and sufficiently moved by the image of the grand white house to understand the values and progress it signifies. Two courtroom scenes in the story stand in contrast to Abner's brutal encounters with the man who owns the white house, and with Abner's decision to burn down the barn, a symbol of order and of the agricultural economy that has come to dominate the North Mississippi area where the story is set. Sarty is torn between blood loyalty to his father and recognition that his father is a relic of a distant past, a dead end. Ultimately, Sarty warns the owner of the white-columned house, Major De Spain, that his father plans to burn down his barn. The story ends ambiguously: Abner has either been captured or shot to death by Major De Spain, while Sarty has run away, bearing the guilt of his decision to betray his father and ally himself, however obliquely, with what the grand white house represents. At the same time he willingly confronts the future that lies before him (both the "dark woods" and the "liquid silver voices of the birds"): "He went on down the hill, toward the dark woods within which the liquid silver voices of the birds called unceasing – the rapid and urgent beating of the urgent and quiring heart of the late spring night. He did not look back" (25).

Michael Millgate in *The Achievement of William Faulkner* suggests that the place-ment of "Barn Burning" as the first story in *Collected Stories* established "patterns of conflict which echo throughout the volume – white vs. Negro, poor vs. rich, family vs. outsiders – and ... themes which also recur: the opposition between the emotional ties of home and family and the urgent need for escape and self-determination, the complexities of the father–son relationship, the tension between social values and those which are primarily moral or aesthetic" (*Achievement* 270–1). Many of the basic themes of Faulkner's fiction – class struggle, change, coming of age, order versus disorder – are encapsulated in "Barn Burning" and appear in different and varied forms throughout *Collected Stories*. Many of Faulkner's stories center in some way on the changes taking place in the American South during the late nineteenth and early twentieth centuries. In "Barn Burning" the last vestiges of frontier are disappearing, replaced by an agricultural economy and a political structure governed by courts and laws. The desires of men such as Abner Snopes to live free and unmolested by codes of social, economic, and political order are fast being thwarted. Sarty's gradual dis-covery of his father's true nature in "Barn Burning," along with the choices it forces on him, gives the story much of its force and poignancy.

Faulkner uses child narrators on several other occasions to describe and comment on older adult characters who struggle against the forces of order and conformity, or who at least stand in contrast to these forces. In "Uncle Willy," for example, a child narrator admires an adult character, a pharmacist, who resists the town's efforts to cure his drug addiction. "That Evening Sun" is narrated by Quentin Compson, remembering as an adult events that took place when he was about 10 years old. His sister Caddy, little brother Jason, and his parents, all from *The Sound and the Fury*, appear as minor characters in the story, which is focused primarily on the fear of a black woman named Nancy. Nancy is married to a man named Jesus who she fears plans to murder her out of anger and jealousy that she has become pregnant with another man's child (possibly a white Baptist deacon's child). The story portrays her fears and her efforts to find help from the Compson family. It is apparently set around 1890, a year corresponding with early events in *The Sound and the Fury*. That the story is told from a future vantage point is made clear by Quentin's two-paragraph intro-duction, which remarks on the change that has come to the town, the paved sidewalks, the telephone poles that have replaced trees, the city laundry that has replaced the Negro women of some fifteen years before: "balanced on their steady turbaned heads, bundles of clothes tied up in sheets, almost as large as cotton bales, carried so without touch of hand between the kitchen door of the white house and the blackened washpot beside a cabin door in Negro Hollow" (289). The implication is not only that the narrator himself has grown older in years and understanding but that the town has progressed, and that the story being told is of an older time.

Nancy is portrayed as illiterate, hysterical with fear, an occasional prostitute, and probably a cocaine addict. Her lifestyle and her murderous husband isolate her from other members of the black community, who are nearly as afraid of her husband as she is. Moreover, her status as prostitute and drug addict make her a moral pariah. Her race, social class, and lack of education further separate her from the white members of the community, specifically the Compson children and their parents. Mr. Compson, in particular, seems totally at a loss to help Nancy. He does not know what to do and at the height of her terror essentially abandons her, advising her to go to sleep. Mrs. Compson sees Nancy's problem as an inconvenience. And the children simply do not understand. What most fundamentally isolates Nancy, above and beyond questions of race or class or literacy, is her conviction that she faces death and therefore divine judgment. The Jesus whom she fears is not merely the husband Jesus who may enter her house and cut her throat, but the Divine Jesus, who will judge her sinful behavior and cast her down to hell. Her position as a helpless and irrational person places her in a category similar to that of the children, who sense but do not understand her fear and who also have no comprehension of her problems with her husband or of her fear of death and damnation. Their innocent ignorance creates an additional layer of isolation in the story.

"That Evening Sun" is a literal horror story. Nancy believes that her murderer lurks in the ditch outside her shabby house. The children can tell only that she is afraid, and they are young enough not to be bothered by her fear. Moreover, as Jason repeatedly points out, Nancy is "only a nigger" and therefore someone who doesn't matter.

It is difficult to think of any character in Faulkner's fiction as profoundly isolated as Nancy. Her fear is existential, a profound apprehension of the nothingness of her life, and the core of the horror that penetrates the story is that there is no way to assuage her fear, no way, as the helplessness of the Compson parents and the indifferent ignorance of their children illustrate, even to understand it. Even though this story begins as a framed narrative – told in retrospect by an adult narrator about a childhood memory, it is significant that the frame does not close when the story ends. Instead the story concludes by focusing on Nancy's fear and the children's gradual loss of interest in her fear as their indifferent father leads them away from her house back towards the light and safety of their white-columned house, where fear and death and a vengeful Jesus do not intrude, at least as far as the children are aware.

Immediately preceding "That Evening Sun" in *Collected Stories* is one of Faulkner's most effective comic stories, "That Will Be Fine" (1935). It uses a narrator similar to Quentin in the previous story, although this time the narrator is even younger, around seven years old, and there is no clear evidence of a frame or that the story is told from a future vantage point. The narrator is so young, in fact, that on occasion the story verges on caricature. In "That Evening Sun" part of the terror stems from the fact that the narrator is recalling a time when he was just old enough to sense Nancy's terror. In "That Will Be Fine" comedy stems from the fact that the young narrator understands virtually nothing that goes on around him. When Uncle Rodney hires the boy to watch out for the husband of a woman with whom he is having an affair, the boy thinks his uncle is "in business" with the woman. When his mother and aunt weep after discovering their brother has absconded with a large portion of the family fortune, the boy merely describes the fact, taking no special note of what appears to be a common event. He even fails to recognize at the end of the story that the object being carried by the men back to his grandparents' house is his dead uncle. The boy does not know that his uncle is a philandering adulterer and probably an alcoholic who has by fraud, forgery, and outright theft lost much of the family fortune.

The boy's innocent point of view also cloaks darker elements of the story, which ends with the uncle's death. All the boy can think about are the quarters his uncle has offered him for helping out, and the boy mistakes the gunfire that kills his uncle for Christmas fireworks going off in a nearby town. In fact, the boy's moral ignorance, not to mention his greed, suggests that he shares some traits in common with his uncle. Told through the boy's viewpoint, "That Will Be Fine" is a hilarious story of a wild and carefree uncle whom the boy admires and loves. Told from the point of view of the boy's older relatives, who must deal with the consequences of Rodney's behavior (a perspective that is at least implied), the story of adultery, theft, fraud, and murder is tragic. Its success depends on the adult reader's corrective reactions to the child narrator's descriptions. The adult reader recognizes and understands what the boy cannot see. Faulkner often depends on his adult readers to provide the correcting perspective to his narratives. This is especially true in the early pages of *The Sound and the Fury*, when Caddy Compson climbs the pear tree to look through the window at the funeral of her grandmother. (Although the family in "That Will Be Fine" is not the Compson family, Uncle Rodney resembles the alcoholic, philandering Uncle Maury of *The Sound and the Fury*.)

Faulkner uses the child's point of view in a number of his stories and novels, from *As I Lay Dying* and *The Unvanquished* to much of *Go Down, Moses* and *The Reivers* (1962). In "A Justice" (1931), which appears in "The Wilderness" section of *Collected Stories*, Faulkner employs Quentin's juvenile viewpoint once again, though in this story the viewpoint serves only to emphasize the ancient nature of the tale of Ikkemotubbe and Sam Fathers that is being told and has no particular organic relation to the main narrative. A similar narrative viewpoint is at work in "Uncle Willy" (1935), where a young narrator and his friends admire a middle-aged pharmacist's resistance to the efforts of the townspeople to civilize him and cure him of his drug addiction. The boys see their own rebelliousness as analogous to the older man's and fail to understand that his problems are of an entirely different order than their own. "That Evening Sun" and "That Will Be Fine" depend on the essential function of point of view, without which the stories would be fundamentally different. Their primary effects – whether tragic or comic – stem from the limited perspective from which the main character views the events of the story.

A number of Faulkner's stories focus on the isolation of characters. Certainly, this is a central theme of "That Evening Sun" and even of "Barn Burning," where Abner Snopes is isolated by class, poverty, and his self-conditioned resistance to any form of control or order. Faulkner often used the plight of African American characters to represent the theme of isolation that he saw as a basic condition of modern existence. We have already seen that theme in "That Evening Sun," and it occurs again in "Pantaloon in Black" in *Go Down, Moses*. Isolation is important as well for the slave at the center of the story "Red Leaves," published in 1930 in the *Saturday Evening Post* and collected in *These 13*. "Red Leaves" is a companion story to "A Justice," which also appeared in *These 13*. Both stories chronicle the Indian history of Yoknapatawpha County that lies in the background of *Absalom, Absalom!* While "A Justice" is a framed narrative, told to Quentin Compson by Sam Fathers as he talks about his parentage and how the Indians came to acquire slaves, "Red Leaves" is narrated externally and is focused on the efforts of two Indians to capture an escaped slave. The chief of the tribe has died, and the slave who belonged to him is to be killed and buried along with the chief's horse and hound. From the viewpoint of the two Indians, the slave (and slavery in general) is an inconvenience. Although they respect the slave's determination to escape, they also view him as nothing more than chattel. Although the story does not present the slave's point of view, it makes clear, through his desperate attempts to escape, and through his fear at the story's end, that he is another of Faulkner's hapless, isolated characters, trapped by circumstance and history. The comic aspects of the story – focused on the Indians – are counterbalanced by the slave's fear. Faulkner has genuine sympathy for the slave and shows his plight clearly, along with the indifference of the Indians to his status as a human being desperate to escape death. However, contemporary readers may have difficulty recognizing Faulkner's sympathy for what it is, nor may they see the humor in the difficulties Indians experienced in owning slaves. In both "Red Leaves" and "A Justice" Faulkner shows through his satiric portrayal how the Indians were corrupted by the materialism of white settlers and the ownership of slaves.

One cause of the slave's isolation in "Red Leaves" is his powerlessness. Mr. Compson in "That Evening Sun" is powerless to assuage Nancy's terror because he lacks empathy, does not understand her, and therefore cannot communicate with her. The opening section of "Dry September" (first published in *Scribner's* in 1931 and collected in *These 13*) is narrated from the perspective of another character isolated by powerlessness, a barber named Hawkshaw (also the main character in "Hair"), but in this case powerlessness results from moral cowardice as well as social circumstances that the barber cannot alter. In the story a black man named Will Mayes is rumored to have attacked a white woman named Minnie Cooper. The woman is known as an eccentric spinster, and rumors about her might not normally be trusted, except that in this case the rumor that she has been attacked by a black man seizes precedence over rationality. As soon as the story is told, everyone automatically believes it – because the culprit is a black man.[7] When Hawkshaw expressed doubt that Will

Mayes could have committed such a crime ("He's a good nigger" [169]), a "hulking youth in a sweat-stained silk shirt" answers, "Won't you take a white woman's word before a nigger's?" It is not a woman's hysteria that dominates the story but instead the racist hysteria of the white men who band together to lynch Will Mayes. Few stories by Faulkner or any other writer so painfully describe the racism of a small provincial town. The story is composed of five sections, each a contrast to the section that follows or precedes it: Hawkshaw's impotent claims that Will Mayes is innocent contrast with the vicious certainty of other townsmen that he is guilty; Minnie Cooper's social ostracism in the town as an old maid contrasts with the terror of Will Mayes; the brutality of the character McLendon, who participates in the lynching, clashes with the fear of his own wife. The story does not describe the lynching, just as it does not describe the supposed crime against Minnie Cooper. By allusion, contrast, and indirection, Faulkner implies a set of circumstances that led to the murder and that stand in a more general way for the condition of the town as a whole. Sexual repression and abuse, racism, despair, frustration, and moral weakness are interwoven in the story, perhaps Faulkner's most scathing indictment of racism and its consequences.

Many of the stories in "The Middle Ground" section of *Collected Stories* do not represent Faulkner's best work. Still, they illustrate the diversity of his range. Two stories – "Wash" and "Mountain Victory" – do stand out as major works. Both, in different ways, are by-products of Faulkner's work on *Absalom, Absalom!*[8] "Wash," published in 1932, recounts events leading to the death of Thomas Sutpen, the novel's main character. Beginning *in medias res* like "A Rose for Emily," it describes Wash Jones's relationship with and murder of Sutpen, the same events told in chapter 7 of the novel. The story explores from Wash's point of view events that are described more objectively in the novel, where Wash Jones is a minor character, an accessory to the narrative. Wash serves in the novel as a reminder of Sutpen's origins in the mountains of West Virginia and shows by his role in the story how, following the end of the Civil War and the decline of his fortunes, Sutpen's life has come, in effect, full circle. In the story Wash is the main focus, and the events of Sutpen's final day recede into the background of the more central concern with Wash, his romantic illusions about Sutpen, and the betrayal he feels when he hears the man compare his granddaughter Milly to a horse. Events that occupy only a few paragraphs in the novel are fully developed in the story. While Wash takes pride in his friendship with Sutpen, whom he idealizes as a paragon of courage and chivalry, he realizes after the man fathers a child on his granddaughter and then shows indifference to the child's birth that the friendship has meant nothing to Sutpen, and that all the pride and self-importance Wash has taken from it are meaningless.

"Wash" explores the same themes of class conflict and identity as "Barn Burning," but from the viewpoint of a man at the end of his life rather than a boy on the verge of adulthood.[9] While Sarty's experience frees him from the self-destructive, hopeless existence of his father to face an uncertain future, Wash's illumination about the true nature of his relationship with Sutpen leaves him nothing but a rusting scythe and the "wild glaring eyes of the horses and the swinging glints of gun barrels, without any cry, any sound" (550). The story's ending, where Wash runs towards the waiting guns and horses and his own obliteration, is his ironic reenactment of the glorious wartime valor that he imagined for Sutpen. Like Nancy at the end of "That Evening Sun," and even Abner at the end of "Barn Burning," Wash is an extreme example of isolation imposed by social and class-based circumstances.

Isolation is also a theme in the Civil War story "Mountain Victory." Written in 1931, published in the *Saturday Evening Post* in 1932 and later collected in *Doctor Martino and Other Stories*, "Mountain Victory" seems a product of Faulkner's early work on the material that would become *Absalom, Absalom!* Set in the mountains of Tennessee shortly after the end of the Civil War, the story focuses on Major Saucier Weddell, who is traveling towards his home in Mississippi in the company of his servant and former slave Jubal. Weddell seeks shelter for the night in the cabin of Unionists. They are immediately suspicious of him, and one of them, a former Union soldier, threatens to kill the visitor. The story emphasizes the regional, ethnic, social, and cultural barriers that divide its characters. At first the family takes Weddell for a white Confederate officer. Then the brother Vatch thinks Weddell is black because of his dark complexion, but Weddell explains that he is Choctaw, the son of an Indian chief and a European mother. The lower-class poverty of the mountain family contrasts with the wealth and social pretensions of Weddell as well as his servant, who mimics his master. The family resents Weddell, because he was a Confederate officer, because of his wealth, because of doubts about his race, because of his servant. Moreover, Weddell comes from the Mississippi planter class, while the mountain family scrabbles for a living as best they can. Two members of the family, a young boy named Hule and his sister, unnamed and about 20, are attracted to Saucier. To the girl he strikes a dashing figure to which she is sexually drawn and in whom she sees a possible escape from her mountain family. The boy sees in Weddell what Sarty Snopes saw in the white-columned house of Major De Spain in "Barn Burning." He both respects and resents Weddell, and in the end he warns the man of his brother's murderous intentions and even mounts Weddell's horse to confuse his brother. As a result, his brother mistakes the boy for Weddell and shoots him. James Ferguson, in his book *Faulkner's Short Fiction*, sees the issue of moral choice as a central theme in the story, which he compares in this regard to "Barn Burning."[10] Weddell has had ample warning to leave the mountain before dawn, but he stays to care for Jubal, who has passed out from drinking moonshine. Weddell knows what is about to happen to him, but he avoids taking steps to save himself, as if he wants to be killed. The same can be said for the boy Hule, who knows that his brother will shoot at whatever rider sits astride Weddell's horse.

As in "Dry September," "Mountain Victory" employs shifting narrative viewpoints to convey the different attitudes of characters in the story, moving from Jubal to Weddell to the girl to an uninvolved narrator. Weddell's social pretensions, and his fatigue, prevent him from taking action to save himself. The fear and terror in the story stem from the foreknowledge of the characters of what is to happen to them, and from their inability or unwillingness to try to escape that fate. In a sense the story presents a parabolic portrait of the class, regional, and racial prejudices that led to the Civil War and that will lead to further troubles after its end. But its main emphasis falls on Weddell, the certain extinction he knows he faces, and his unwillingness to avoid that fate.

Although Faulkner is best known as a writer of stories like "Mountain Victory," "Barn Burning," "A Rose for Emily," and "That Evening Sun" – which address the same subjects and materials as his best-known novels – he wrote other stories that explore concerns decidedly less regional and more contemporary. Two closely related stories, "Honor" (1930) and "Artist at Home" (1933), are about adultery. "Golden Land" (1935) satirizes Hollywood, in the same general vein as Nathanael West in *Day of the Locust*, likely reflecting opinions Faulkner developed during his screenwriting stints in California. The stories in the final section of *Collected Stories*, "Beyond," also do not represent Faulkner's best work, with the exception of "Carcassonne" (1931), but they reach beyond Yoknapatawpha to encompass concerns with war and life in Europe following the war. They are decidedly pessimistic, and despite the fact that Faulkner's Nobel Prize Speech in 1950 expressed confidence that "man will not only endure, he will prevail," these stories express a more guarded attitude. That Faulkner collected them together in the final section of the volume perhaps expressed his Cold War concerns about the future of the human race.

Two Faulkner works that did not appear in *Collected Stories* or *Uncollected Stories* deserve consideration as short fiction. One is the Compson Appendix written for Malcolm Cowley's *The Portable Faulkner* in 1946. This retelling of the Compson story in *The Sound and the Fury* stands alone from the novel as an independent and separate work. It was not intended as an additional section of the novel (in paperback editions of which, for several years, it was included) and instead was written as a kind of genealogy of characters connected to the Compson family, The appendix extends the Compson story nearly fifteen years past the novel's conclusion and meditates on the nature of time and history. Its famous and somewhat ambiguous conclusion, "They endure," looks forward to the final statement of the Nobel Prize. One other work worth considering as a short story is "Mississippi," an autobiographical essay published in *Holiday* magazine in 1954 that bears a relation to the prose sections on Mississippi history in the 1951 novel *Requiem for a Nun*. As several critics have noted, there are clear fictional elements in this work, which blends memoir, fact, and fiction. Although Faulkner's fiction is often said to have become more traditional, less experimental, following 1940, both these works may be regarded as innovative, experimental examples of the short story form.

NOTES

1 Interview with Jean Stein vanden Heuval, 1955, in *Lion in the Garden: Interviews with William Faulkner 1926–1962*, eds. James B. Meriwether and Michael Millgate (New York: Random House, 1968), 238.

2 Interview with John K. Hutchens, 1948, in *Lion in the Garden* 59.

3 Joseph Blotner, *Faulkner: A Biography* 209–10; see also "An Introduction to *The Sound and the Fury*," *Mississippi Quarterly* 26 (Summer 1973): 413.

4 *Selected Letters of William Faulkner*, ed. Joseph Blotner (New York: Random House, 1977), 284.

5 In an interview with John K. Hutchens, Faulkner said that he did not consider "The Bear" a short story because "A short story is 3000 words or less. Anything more is, well, a piece of writing" (*Lion in the Garden* 59). In a class discussion at the University of Virginia, he elaborated on the same point: "the short story is conceived in the same terms that the book is. The first job the craftsman faces is to tell this as quickly and simply as I can, and if he's good, if he's of the first water, like Chekhov, he can do it every time in two or three thousand words, but if he's not that good, sometimes it takes him eighty thousand words" (March 11, 1957, class

discussion, in Gwynn and Blotner, eds., *Faulkner in the University* 48).

6 The full-length and preferred version of *Sartoris* was published in 1973 as *Flags in the Dust*, the original title (New York: Random House).

7 A similar phenomenon occurs in *Light in August* when the rumor begins to spread that Joe Christmas has killed Joanna Burden.

8 James B. Carothers, in "Short Story Background of *Absalom, Absalom!*" in Skei, ed., *William Faulkner's Short Fiction* 129–37, identifies a significant number of stories that contributed in some way to the novel. These include "The Big Shot," "Mistral," "Evangeline," "That Evening Sun," "A Justice," and the stories that became *The Unvanquished*.

9 For a discussion of the relationship between these stories, see Jacques Pothier, "Black Laughter: Poor White Short Stories Behind *Absalom, Absalom!* and *The Hamlet*," in Skei, ed., *William Faulkner's Short Fiction* 173–84.

10 James Ferguson, *Faulkner's Short Fiction* 78; see also 154, 174.

REFERENCES AND FURTHER READING

Blotner, Joseph. *Faulkner: A Biography.* 1 vol. edn. New York: Random House, 1984.

Cowley, Malcolm, ed. *The Portable Faulkner.* New York: Viking Press, 1946.

Faulkner, William. *Collected Stories of William Faulkner.* New York: Random House, 1950.

———. *Doctor Martino and Other Stories.* New York: Harrison Smith & Robert Haas, 1934.

———. *Knight's Gambit.* New York: Random House, 1949.

———. *These 13.* New York: Jonathan Cape & Harrison Smith, 1931.

———. *Uncollected Stories of William Faulkner.* Ed. Joseph Blotner. New York: Random House, 1979.

Gwynn, Frederick L., and Joseph L. Blotner, eds. *Faulkner in the University: Class Conferences at the University of Virginia, 1957–58.* Charlottesville: University of Virginia Press, 1959.

Ferguson, James. *Faulkner's Short Fiction.* Knoxville: University of Tennessee Press, 1991.

Grimwood, Michael. *Heart in Conflict: Faulkner's Struggles with Vocation.* Athens: University of Georgia Press, 1987.

Millgate, Michael. *The Achievement of William Faulkner.* New York: Random House, 1966. 259–75.

Skei, Hans. *William Faulkner: The Novelist as Short Story Writer.* Oslo, Norway: Universitetsforlaget As, 1985.

———. *William Faulkner: The Short Story Career. An Outline of Faulkner's Short Story Writing from 1919 to 1962.* Oslo, Norway: Universitetsforlaget As, 1981.

Skei, Hans, ed. *William Faulkner's Short Fiction: An International Symposium.* Oslo, Norway: Solum Forlag, 1997.

17
Katherine Anne Porter

Ruth M. Alvarez

The enduring literary reputation of Katherine Anne Porter (1890–1980) rests upon her brilliant short fiction, rather than her only full-length novel. As Porter lived through all but twenty years of the twentieth century, the record of her life and work documents some of the most important historical events of that century. Born and reared in rural Texas, she spent a large portion of the first three decades of her life in rapidly growing urban centers in the state – San Antonio, Houston, Corpus Christi, Dallas, and Fort Worth. She began to work as a writer during World War I; she and several of her women friends participated in the struggle for women's right to vote; she survived the influenza epidemic of 1918; she lived through Prohibition and its repeal; she stood witness to the execution of Sacco and Vanzetti; she was in Germany when Hitler was rising to power; and she agonized through World War II. She was in Hollywood as the red scare that later led to blacklisting began to emerge; she lived through the Korean War, the Army-McCarthy hearings, the Civil Rights Movement, the assassinations of John Kennedy, Martin Luther King, and Robert Kennedy, the rise of feminism, and the successful moon landings of American astronauts.

Porter's reputation as a literary artist was established in the decade of the 1920s, when her circle of friends and acquaintances in New York City was largely literary. Some members of her social circle in this period, Allen Tate, Robert Penn Warren, and Malcolm Cowley, are canonical figures in American literature. Porter's growing reputation and her distinguished friends enabled her to develop an ever-widening circle of important friends and acquaintances over the course of her life. She encouraged and befriended American writers, Eudora Welty, Flannery O'Connor, William Humphrey, William Goyen, and Peter Taylor, who produced significant works of literature.

Porter appeared on the American literary scene a few months after she came to New York City in late 1919. There she met individuals who held responsible positions in publishing and began writing for periodicals whose readers constituted a national as opposed to a local or regional audience. Armed with a contract to ghostwrite *My Chinese Marriage*, a book that was to appear serially in the national magazine *Asia*, Porter left her job as a movie publicist in November 1920 and traveled to Mexico in search of materials she could use to support herself as a writer of both fiction and non-fiction. In Mexico, she completed *My Chinese Marriage* as well as pieces that were published in newspapers and periodicals in Mexico and the United States (*El Heraldo de Mexico*, New York *Call*, *Magazine of Mexico*, *Christian Science Monitor*, *Freeman*).

Although she returned to the United States in late 1921 and eventually to New York City by early 1922, it wasn't until after her second trip to Mexico in Spring 1922 that Porter broke into the literary mainstream with "Where Presidents Have No Friends," published in *Century Magazine* (July 1922). Five months later her first piece of mature fiction, "María Concepción," was published in that same magazine. By November 1924, she was established enough as a writer to become a regular reviewer for the *New York Herald Tribune* (later reviewing for *New Republic*, *New Masses*, and *New York Evening Post*). Between July 1923 and Spring 1930, Porter published eight more short stories (two more in *Century*, two in *transition*, and others in *New Masses*, *Gyroscope*, *Second American Caravan*, and *Hound & Horn*). Six of these stories were published in her first book, *Flowering Judas* (1930). At the time of her death in 1980, Porter had published another four volumes of short fiction, *Flowering Judas and Other Stories* (1935), *Pale Horse, Pale Rider: Three Short Novels* (1939), *The Leaning Tower and Other Stories* (1944), and *The Collected Stories of Katherine Anne Porter* (1965), which won both the National Book Award and the Pulitzer Prize in 1965. Her full-length novel *Ship of Fools*, a best-seller and the basis for a popular movie, was published in 1962. The publication of two collections of essays and occasional writings, *The Days Before* and *The Collected Essays and Occasional Writings of Katherine Anne Porter*, came in 1952 and 1970. *The Never-Ending Wrong*, the account of her participation in the protests prior to the executions of Sacco and Vanzetti, appeared in 1977.

"Go Little Book," the brief introduction to *Collected Stories*, asks of "the reader one gentle favor": "Please call my works by their right names: we have four that cover every division: short stories, long stories, short novels, novels." This volume brought together twenty-six of the thirty-one works of fiction Porter had published by 1965. It did not include her only full-length novel, *Ship of Fools*, nor did it include four derivative stories she had published in 1920.[1] An additional story, "The Spivvelton Mystery," subsequently published in *Ladies' Home Journal* in August 1971, had been written in 1930. Using the "right names" Porter prefers for her work, *Collected Stories* includes short stories, long stories, and short novels, although she refers to these works collectively as "stories" throughout the introduction. Excluding her only mystery story, "The Spivvelton Mystery," the remaining thirty works of short fiction she published during her lifetime fall into four general categories: four early derivative stories, six stories set in Mexico, eleven stories and two short novels set in the South,[2] and five stories and two short novels of the twentieth-century wasteland.[3] This chapter will focus on the seventeen short and long stories Porter set in Mexico and the South. These two groups of stories are essential parts of her canon. With the Mexican stories, set in what she named her "familiar country" ("Why I Write About Mexico," *Collected Essays* 355), she made her debut as a literary artist on the New York scene. In Mexico, she found a subject for her fiction as well as "a feeling for art consanguine" with her own ("Why I Write About Mexico," *Collected Essays* 356). However, when she turned to the South, the "native land of [her] heart" (" 'Noon Wine': The Sources," *Collected Essays* 470), for the characters and settings of her fiction, she found her métier.

The publication of "María Concepción," the first of Porter's six short stories set in Mexico, marked the beginning of Porter's career as a literary artist. "María Concepción" has roughly the same plot as her early derivative story "The Adventures of Hadji", a wife's triumph over her unfaithful husband. In both stories, the husbands are awed by the seemingly supernatural powers of their wives. The earliest work Porter claimed as part of her canon, "María Concepción" was written as a direct result of her first two visits to Mexico (November 1920 to autumn 1921 and April to June 1922). Intrigued by descriptions of the country, its culture, and its history recounted by Mexican friends and acquaintances she encountered in New York City in 1919–20, Porter found in Mexico both aesthetic theories and subjects for her literary and journalistic work. The work that grew out of her Mexican visits brought Porter recognition and respect in New York literary circles. Published in *Century* in December 1922, the story is one of only seven of the twenty-six in *Collected Stories* that appeared in four of the collections of her work published during her lifetime.[4] Like all her other work written after her first visit to Mexico, it is markedly different from her previous work. What came before is either apprentice work or journalism, none of it rising much above competent professionalism.

"María Concepción," whose central character is an indigenous Mexican woman, was an outgrowth of Porter's 1920–2 experiences in Mexico and her reading on Mexican history and culture. Porter met William Niven, the model for Givens in the story, during her first week in Mexico in November 1920. A mineralogist who came to Mexico around 1891, Niven soon discovered the remains of a pre-Hispanic city in the state of Guerrero and turned to archaeology, excavating pre-Hispanic sites in Mexico for forty years. At one of these sites north of Mexico City, Azcapotzalco, Porter visited in 1920–1 and herself dug artifacts from the earth. Her acquaintance with Manuel Gamio also informs the story. His *Forjando Patria* (1916), credited with launching social anthropology in Mexico, was followed in 1922 by the monumental two-volume *La Poblacion del Valle de Teotihuacán*, a study of the ancient civilization and modern inhabitants of this region, like Azcapotzalco, north of Mexico City. Details of the setting of "María Concepción" are drawn from sites Porter had observed as well as from generalizations about Teotihuacán from Gamio. The story's setting is on the outskirts of Mexico City, perhaps Azcapotzalco. Porter depicts a valley and mountains not unlike that of Gamio's descriptions of the locations at Teotihuacán. In his outline of the contemporary architecture there, Gamio had described the organ cactus fences and jacales which are featured prominently in Porter's story. His characterization of the "pagan Catholicism" of Teotihuacán with its "extreme religiosity " and "fanaticism"[5] is skillfully portrayed in Porter's delineation of the practices of María

Concepción; the remnants of pagan beliefs are briefly sketched in the figure of Lupe, the old medicine woman. Although only alluded to in passing, the problems of high infant mortality and illiteracy delineated by Gamio are also represented by Porter. The primarily agricultural economy of Teotihuacán, into which bee-keeping was introduced by Gamio's program, as well as the town's production of pottery and other small arts and crafts for supplemental income are mirrored in Porter's story. These details help to structure Porter's sympathetic portrait of an indigenous woman's triumph over her philandering husband and her rival for his affection.

"The Martyr," the second of Porter's Mexican stories to appear, like "María Concepción," was published in *Century* (July 1923) during her third Mexican sojourn (June–September 1923). The central character Rubén is "the most illustrious painter in Mexico," who is creating a mural with twenty monumental figures of his sadistic model Isabel when she leaves him for her lover, a rival painter. In this light satire, Rubén, who eats himself to death, is "martyred" by his unrequited love for Isabel. The other major character in the story is a newspaper and magazine caricaturist friend of Rubén, who makes satiric drawings of Rubén and, after Rubén's death, gathers material for an intimate biography of him. Other than the studio of Rubén, the other important locale in the story is "The Little Monkeys" café where Rubén dies. These characters and locations are directly related to Porter's Mexican observations and experiences. Rubén, Isabel, and Ramón are modeled on Diego Rivera, his first wife Lupe Marin, and Miguel Covarrubias or another of the contemporary caricaturists whom Porter knew. Porter had visited Rivera's studio in 1922 as well as the famous café of artist Jose Clement Orozco's brother, Los Monotes, a favorite gathering place for Mexican artists. Rubén, a representative of the Mexican artists Porter knew, romanticizes Isabel and makes self-deluding assertions that he is dying for love, when, in fact, he is indulging the vice of gluttony. This work satirizes the self-serving, materialistic, opportunistic male artists of Mexico. However, it also parodies man the martyr in all his self-pitying, self-indulgent glory.

"Virgin Violeta" was the third and last of Porter's stories to be published in *Century* (December 1924). In it, the title character watches the formalized courtship of her older sister Blanca and their poet cousin Carlos under a framed depiction of the " 'Pious Interview between the Most Holy Virgin Queen of Heaven and Her Faithful Servant St. Ignatius Loyola,' "[6] while the mother of the girls dozes off and on. When Carlos follows Violeta into another room and attempts to kiss her, she becomes frightened and repels his advance despite her romantic fixation on him and his poetry. Confused by the exchange, Violeta subsequently becomes hysterical when he tries to give her a goodnight kiss in front of her mother and sister.

"Virgin Violeta" may be a disguised self-portrait. Porter conceived a child in the spring of 1924 and experienced a still birth in December 1924, when "Virgin Violeta" was published. As she wrote it, she must have confronted her deepest feelings about sexuality and its consequences, including the sexual urges and fears she had experienced when she herself was, like Violeta, "nearly fifteen." Her experiences during her marriage to the adulterer John Henry Koontz, consummated shortly after her sixteenth birthday, included physical and verbal abuse. Her pregnancy may also have triggered memories of another deeply disturbing incident of her sexual history. According to Porter's friend Mary Louis Doherty, Nicaraguan poet Salomón de la Selva and Porter "had an affair ending in an abortion in 1921 when he was living in a little house on Calle Guanajuato" in Mexico City.[7] The story is both a self-portrait of Violeta-Porter and also a caricature of a particular man, Carlos-Salomón de la Selva, who represents the rapacious sexuality of all men, especially the ones Porter had specific reason to despise (her first husband and lovers who had impregnated her). Porter's pregnancy and the death of her nearly full-term infant in the fall and winter of 1924 brought her face-to-face with the issues of womanhood explored in the story. The subject of sexuality was one Porter would continue to explore throughout her life.

"Flowering Judas" published in *Hound & Horn*, the little magazine founded by Lincoln Kirstein, in its April–June 1930 issue is one of Porter's most studied and anthologized short stories. Although Porter consistently claimed that this story was written in one night, it came out of the Mexican material she had begun gathering in 1920 and may have had its genesis in the "portrait of Yúdico," one of the "Four Portraits of Revolutionaries" outlined as a portion of a projected book.[8] By 1927, she was describing the book project as "a novel of Mexico" with the title "Thieves' Market." This particular story did not reach its final form until shortly before she sent it to Richard Blackmur of *Hound & Horn* on November 29, 1929.[9] The story's protagonist, Laura, a *gringa* in Mexico to support the revolution, attends union meetings, and visits prisoners of her "own political faith" and men hiding from firing squads. Laura's month-long ordeal, consisting of nightly serenades by the corrupt, corpulent revolutionist Braggioni, comes to an end when he callously dismisses the apparent suicide of Eugenio, one of his followers. Set in Laura's apartment in Mexico City where Braggioni attempts to seduce her with guitar playing and singing, the story ends when Braggioni returns to his forgiving wife and Laura retires and dreams of Eugenio. The figure of Laura, who is based on the physical appearance of Porter's friend Mary Doherty, is another of Porter's self-portraits. Other real-life models for characters in the story include Mexican politicians Samuel Yúdico and Luis Morones as well as foreign agitators Roberto Haberman and J. H. Retinger, one of Porter's former lovers. Braggioni's return to his wife and his granting her forgiveness for her faithfulness suggest that faithlessness is the norm in this perverted world, that faith is a sin for which one must atone. Braggioni's vision of the future, which he recites in the "hypnotic" voice" of his political oratory, predicts the reign of anarchy, the absence of government and order. Furthermore, Braggioni is the embodiment of sensual delight in "Flowering Judas," whom Laura fears both because of the sexual threat he poses as well as for the threat of death his cult of anarchy offers. The final visual image in the story, Eugenio as a skeleton serving Laura the Host in a parody of the sacrament of Communion of her Catholic faith, suggests the desiccation of Laura's beliefs. Her creeds – religious, political, and romantic – have lost their power to effect her salvation. Laura, like the title character of T. S. Eliot's "Gerontion" (three lines of which Porter had suggested as the epigraph for the story), is impotent and living in memories which in sum mean nothing, "a dry brain in a dry season."

"Hacienda" and "That Tree," the last two of Porter's Mexican stories, were written and published after her last period of semi-permanent residency in Mexico (April 1930 to August 1931). The month before her arrival there, she signed contracts with Harcourt, Brace for a collection of six of her short stories as well as a novel of Mexico entitled "Thieves' Market." The firm decided upon a limited edition of 600 copies of *Flowering Judas*, calculated to create a demand for her novel that it planned to publish in the fall of 1931, a year after the September 1930 publication of the collection. However, Porter never fulfilled the contract for the novel, and "Hacienda" and "That Tree" were completely new works of fiction unrelated to the never completed novel of Mexico.

Porter characterized the original, non-fiction version of "Hacienda" as "only an article"; it had been intended as an American outsider's observation of Mexican life, an attempt to assess the changes since 1920, when the revolution had triumphed. By November 1931, when Porter had sent the manuscript of this version of "Hacienda" to *Scribner's*, Porter had relocated to Europe, where she maintained her residence for five years. When the piece was rejected by *Scribner's*, Porter sent it to *Virginia Quarterly Review*, where it was published in October 1932. It is based on an actual trip Porter made to the pulque Hacienda Tetlapayac, northeast of Mexico City in the Mexican state of Hidalgo. The Russian film director Sergei Eisenstein had journeyed there with his crew and his Mexican government entourage in early May 1931 to film the second of four major stories of an ambitious work, tentatively entitled *Que Viva Mexico!*, which was being financed by Upton Sinclair and other wealthy investors.

Eisenstein had initially come to Mexico in early December 1930 and had aroused such curiosity and apprehension that he, his party (assistant director Grigori Alexandrov, cameraman Eduard Tissé, and business manager Hunter Kimbrough, who was Sinclair's brother-in-law), and several Mexican artists were arrested on December 21, 1930, although they were soon released. Adolfo Best-Maugard and Roberto Montenegro, Mexican friends of Porter, were among the Mexican government's advisors to Eisenstein during the period, from late December through late April 1931, when parts of *Que Viva Mexico!* were filmed in five separate Mexican locations. Eisenstein returned briefly to Mexico City between each of these location sessions, and, during a visit of Eisenstein's party to Mexico City, he met Porter, who was invited to visit the filming at Hacienda Tetlapayac in mid-July 1931. If Porter did, indeed, visit the hacienda on the day on which an Indian actor accidentally killed his sister, she must have spent July 15–17, 1931, at Tetlapayac. Based on the evidence of the non-fiction version, she must have traveled to the hacienda by train in the company of Alexandrov and Kimbrough, met the Indian male lead of the movie on the train, and encountered Eisenstein, Tissé, Best-Maugard, Don Julio Saldivar (the heir to the owner of the hacienda), Don Julio's "wife," and "some sort of assistant to the art adviser"[10] at the hacienda after her arrival.

The controversy over Eisenstein's loss of control of his Mexican film and the September 1933 release of *Thunder Over Mexico*, a film edited from some of Eisenstein's footage by Hollywood producer Sol Lesser, may have precipitated Porter's decision to revise "Hacienda" as fiction for publication in a fine press edition, by Harrison of Paris, a publishing venture of two of the friends she had made since relocating to Europe, Barbara Harrison and Monroe Wheeler. This version, completed in May 1934, appeared in December 1934; it shows evidence of exposure to *Thunder Over Mexico*, as scenes and characters drawn from the film are new introductions. Although the point of both versions is that the Mexican revolution has changed nothing, the revised version is both more despairing and more personal. It clearly articulates Porter's disillusionment and her fascination with death. The concluding dialogue of both versions of the story is spoken by the Indian who drives the narrator-Porter away from the pulque hacienda and urges her to return in ten days "when the green corn will be ready, and ... there will be enough to eat again!" Here Porter alludes to the Aztec festival of Xilonen, during which the eating of new corn was initiated after a maiden representing the Goddess of Young Corn was sacrificed.[11] Instead of the strictly controlled Aztec ritual in which all participated solemnly, the sacrifice has been transmuted into a domestic murder with implied incest and/or homosexuality. The executioner is not an official priest but rather a young Indian who is the victim's brother. The nobility do not share with the poor their feast, but rather remain aloof. The drinking of pulque is not regulated and restricted to the elders as a privilege of old age, but rather is encouraged in all in order to suppress the hunger of the underclass both for food and for freedom.

Completed in January 1934, "That Tree," Porter's last overtly Mexican story was published in July 1934 in *Virginia Quarterly Review*. She made significant revisions to it for the October 1935 publication of *Flowering Judas and Other Stories*, a revised edition of the first collection expanded from six to ten stories. Porter probably met novelist and journalist Carleton Beals, the model for the central figure of the story, in Mexico City in 1923. Beals had come to Mexico in the summer of 1918 and by 1923 had taught school, written and published poetry, spent two years in Europe, and written and gotten accepted for publication books on Fascism and Mexico. By 1935, he was well known for his articles and books on Latin America.

An "important journalist, an authority on Latin-American revolutions and a best seller" (*Collected Stories* 66) is the central figure. He repeats, as a dramatic monologue, the highlights of his life from about 1917 to 1930 to a shadowy listener who is his guest for at least four rounds of drinks over the course of an evening. Although the journalist may be intended as a caricature of Carleton Beals, it suggests a skillful self-portrait of Porter in 1935, an American artist who had come to realize that a regulated life and hard work were as essential to literary success as to ordinary middle-class comfort. In "That Tree," Porter implies that adherence to the cult of "Sacred Art" was no guarantee of success and often proved to offer fraudulent enticements. Where in "Hacienda," Porter satirized artists who strove for material success, in "That Tree", there is something as tawdry about failing to sell out as there is in selling out. The distaste for or disgust with Mexico that had touched "Hacienda" is pervasive here. Written and then revised after more than three years of residence in Europe, the story could be set in any country where expatriate Americans search for romantic adventure and art evolves into self-seeking careerism.

The heart of Porter's canon and arguably her best work are the eleven stories and two short novels set in the South, that she characterized in her essay "'Noon Wine': The Sources" as "stories of my own place, my South," "the native land of my heart" (*Collected Essays* 470). When she turned away from her "familiar country" and the Mexican subjects that she had claimed to be truly her own, Porter began to focus on her own personal and American experiences as a source of fiction. The results of her efforts constitute a statement about her country and her time. She first attempted to do this in "Holiday," a story created in late 1924 about the time of "Virgin Violeta" but not published until 1960 (*Atlantic Monthly*, December 1960). Porter's withdrawal from New York City to the Connecticut countryside in late 1924 in order to escape her personal problems apparently precipitated this meditation on the time when she, like the story's narrator, "was too young for some of the troubles [she] was having" (*Collected Stories* 407) – her Spring 1913 withdrawal to a farm outside Houston to recover from gynecological surgery and to contemplate her unhappy first marriage. When "Holiday" was drafted in 1924, Porter was pregnant and emotionally vulnerable as a result of a broken love affair. The "holiday" of the title refers not only to the narrator's holiday from her troubles but also the holiday from household drudgery the disabled Muller daughter Ottilie takes at the conclusion of the story. Although the narrator is the central figure in the story, Ottilie functions as her double or surrogate. "Holiday" shares with "Virgin Violeta" an exploration of the roles and experiences of women and a concern for an abused or threatened young woman. The story depicts the archetypal events in the life of a woman: birth, marriage, and death. The depiction of the Muller women creates a composite view of traditional women's roles in the early twentieth century, when such roles were being challenged and repudiated by Porter and her New York women friends. The most salient aspect of women's work depicted in "Holiday" is the sheer hard work and drudgery. However, more significant is the story's examination of women who, by choice or circumstance, are outside society's defined patterns: the narrator, by virtue of her self-awareness and intellect, and the maimed Ottilie. The narrator and Ottilie are "both equally the fools of life, equally fellow fugitives from death" (*Collected Stories* 435) who, because of their freakishness, cannot or will not fulfill the traditional roles of women.

The central concern of "Holiday" is death: its inevitability and the quite natural human fear of it. In the closing scene of the story, the narrator attempts to take Ottilie, who had been left behind, to the burial of her mother. Instead, she turns off the "main travelled" road (*Collected Stories* 435) and on a brief holiday, when Ottilie's despair turns to laughter on the bright, beautiful spring day. Ottilie's changed emotions evoke an epiphany in the narrator: she realizes she has escaped death "for one more day at least" (435). Although Ottilie represents the inescapable suffering and death in the garden of the world, the narrator realizes that death is as inevitable as the sun's westward course, but that one must savor the evanescent beauty of life. The narrator's withdrawal to the Muller farm has been motivated by her desire to escape her troubles, an escape from the reality and complexity of a more sophisticated and urban life. But despite her attempts to escape painful reality in the apparent paradise of the Muller farm, the narrator encounters it during her Arcadian retreat. The lesson to be drawn from the narrator's springtime holiday can be found in the example of Ottilie's short holiday from her daily drudgery. The narrator realizes that it takes courage to face the painful reality of life, that labor, suffering, and death are humankind's lot.

"He" was the first of Porter's stories set in the South to receive publication. For this work, Porter drew on her memories of the country poor she had observed in the South and elsewhere. The mere fact that it appeared in *New Masses*, "the principal organ of the American cultural left from 1926 onward,"[12] suggests that it can be read from a political perspective. Although the story drew on Porter's experiences and observations in rural Texas, it was written during the period when her radicalism was at its apogee. In August 1927, Porter had traveled to Boston and participated in the demonstrations to protest the executions of Sacco and Vanzetti. Published in October 1927, only two months after the executions, "He" is a miniature drama illustrating the exploitation of the worker. It depicts the decline and disintegration of a Southern family of poor whites, the Whipples, that is mirrored by the decline of their unnamed simple-minded second son. Although the boy and his mother are the central figures, Porter deliberately dehumanizes him; throughout, he is referred to only by the third person masculine pronoun. Themselves members of the underclass, the Whipples' exploitation of their son is cold and calculating, like that of the contemporary capitalists excoriated in *New Masses*. During the course of the story, the boy declines from robust physical health into permanent invalidism. Because he is not fully able to understand risks to his well-being, his parents take advantage of him, assigning to him dangerous tasks that they or his siblings cannot or will not perform. When his health is broken, the Whipples abandon him to the care of strangers at the County Home.

When "He" was revised for inclusion in *Flowering Judas* in 1930, the significant change Porter made was to capitalize all references to the Whipples' second son throughout the text as if he were the Deity, thus making the story of the boy's martyrdom more universal by implicit reference to the story of Christ. In addition, this revision makes use of a commonplace of proletarian fiction and journalism – proletarian writers made use of religious characters and stories to draw morals and parallels to the economic and political struggles of their own time. Porter amplifies the power of the concluding scene of the story, in which the sobbing boy is wrapped tightly in the arms of his weeping mother, by alluding to a common subject of religious art, the sorrowful Virgin holding the body of Christ after its removal from the cross. This portrait of the Southern proletariat, intended at least partly as a vehicle of protest, remains an enduring work of art.

The appearance of Porter's shortest story "Magic" in the summer 1928 issue of *transition* marked her debut in the highly regarded "little magazines" of the era.

"Magic" was in illustrious company in that issue. The cover illustration was by Pablo Picasso; the first piece of fiction in it was a "continuation" of James Joyce's work in progress, *Finnegans Wake*. Other contributors included some of Porter's New York friends: Malcolm Cowley, Slater Brown, Kenneth Burke, Robert Coates, Matthew Josephson, John Herrmann, and Genevieve Taggard. Written in early 1927, "Magic" was based on a story purportedly told to Porter in New Orleans by a mulatto maid who had worked in a Basin Street house. In a 1955 letter to her publisher Donald Brace, she called it "a little low-life gloss on the gay New Orleans" known by Amy, a character in her "Old Mortality."[13] Apparently witchcraft was very much on her mind in 1927. In a letter of September of that year, Porter associated snooping "around Voodoo doctors in Louisiana" with "Cotton Mather and the Witchcraft delusion," Mather being the subject of a never-published biography on which Porter began work at this time.[14]

The narrator of the story is the mulatto laundress and personal maid of Madame Blanchard, to whom the maid tells the story of a prostitute named Ninette, who is virtually imprisoned by the madam of a New Orleans "fancy house." The story, like "He," has political overtones. Ninette's relationship with the cheating madam is directly analogous to the plight of workers caught in involuntary economic servitude. The prostitutes receive only a "very small little" of their total earnings (*Collected Stories* 39), get into debt, and are brought back by the police or men hired by the madam if they try to escape without paying their debts. Eventually when Ninette tries to leave, she is brutally expelled but drawn back when the madam and her Creole cook work a New Orleans charm. Submerged undercurrents in the story reflect Porter's own experiences – brutal beatings suffered during her first marriage and the suggestion of abortion or miscarriage.

"The Jilting of Granny Weatherall," the second of her stories to be published in *transition* (February 1929), may have been written in February 1928 when Porter was in Salem, Massachusetts, researching her biography of Cotton Mather. It must have been seen before publication by Matthew Josephson, who was at that time both Porter's lover and a contributing editor to *transition*. It explores, like "Holiday," two of Porter's favorite subjects, women's roles and death, but with a narrower focus, the character of Ellen Weatherall, rather than the composite of the Muller women. However, in it, the depiction of these subjects is a more despairing and negative story. Mrs. Weatherall has lived into a time in which the old verities and constants on which she had grounded her life have been altered beyond recognition. Although modeled her on her paternal grandmother, the title character also drew on Porter's own experiences.

"The Jilting of Granny Weatherall" explores death and its meanings. In this story, however, there is no affirmation of life and its eternal continuity as had been implied in "Holiday." Here the traditional roles of women – wife, worker, mother, and daughter – seem devoid of meaning. As she had been jilted by her first bridegroom sixty years before, Mrs. Weatherall is jilted by the divine bridegroom on her deathbed. The story repudiates the traditional domestic role for women. Mrs. Weatherall had chosen such a role and had discovered on her deathbed that the promises held out to those making that choice are not fulfilled. This despairing view angrily rejects the consolations offered to women who choose the traditionally proscribed role – not only will faith in romance fail them, but religion will as well. Instead of a final reckoning with the Christian God and triumphant entry into paradise, Mrs. Weatherall's life ends with her own willful snuffing out of her life. Jilted by George, who, as St. George in religious art, would slay evil or paganism to win a maiden for the faith, Mrs. Weatherall never is secure in her faith and, despite her best efforts, succumbs to unbelief at the moment of death.

"The Fig Tree," not published until June 1960 in *Harper's* and included as one of the "Old Order" stories in *Collected Stories* in 1965, was written in Salem, Massachusetts, in 1928[15] and very likely revised during or after her March to August 1929 residence in Bermuda. Only "Holiday" and "The Jilting of Granny Weatherall" among Porter's previous stories had drawn from the intimate details of Porter's own life in Texas, the material she was to mine so successfully for her Old Order stories. The setting of the story draws from Porter's recollections of her grandmother's house in Kyle, Texas, as well as from the family farm between Austin and San Marcos where Porter summered with her family through 1902.

The earliest among Porter's stories to feature her fictional alter ego, Miranda, the story is narrated from the third person limited point of view of Miranda, the central intelligence. The youngest of three siblings, the character is very young; apparently, she does not yet attend school. The fig groves of her grandmother's town house and farm in the country and individual low branched fig trees are the vehicles through which Miranda gains knowledge of life and death that allows her to allay her fears of death. In the fig grove in town, she misinterprets the singing of the tree frogs as the cry of an animal buried alive; in the fig grove at Cedar Grove, the farm, she learns the true source of this sound. Unable to understand death, particularly that of her mother, Miranda performs ritual burial rites of her own devising for "any creature that didn't move or make a noise, or looked somehow different from the live ones" (*Collected Stories* 354). Because her family departs for Cedar Grove before Miranda has been able to complete her ritual burial of a dead chick, she imagines that she had buried the chick alive. Until her Great-Aunt Eliza explains the true origin of the sound "Weep, weep" (356), Miranda fears retribution, as she has learned to expect swift punishment for not conforming to her grandmother's strict code of conduct.

The contrast of the fig tree and the dead chick, of life and death, parallel the contrast of Miranda's grandmother and great-aunt in the story. The grandmother represents the traditional Southern woman confined by gender to a figurative straitjacket, a symbolic death in life or live burial, something which Miranda implicitly fears and rejects. The depiction of Great-Aunt Eliza is life affirming and expansive, a clear repudiation of the precepts of Southern womanhood into which Miranda's grandmother, father, and Aunt Nannie, the family's black retainer, have tried to circumscribe Miranda. This traditional model threatens to bury Miranda alive; her imagining that she has buried the chick alive projects her own fears of becoming a conventional woman as defined by her family. Great-Aunt Eliza is a significantly different kind of Southern woman, who has clearly rejected the traditional woman's role for one she has carved out for herself. Neither her appearance, nor her occupations, nor the objects identified with her suggest anything genteel or well-bred. She enacts the traditional masculine occupations of supervisor and scientist. Not beautiful and ladylike, Eliza is a guide and role model for Miranda, illuminating an alternate path for her, as she guides Miranda through the darkened fig grove holding her hand (*Collected Stories* 361). Miranda is in "a fog of bliss" at the conclusion of "The Fig Tree" not only because she comes to realize that she had not buried alive the baby chick at the town house. She also has learned that there is at least another model of womanhood, less suffocating, confining, and constrained than that posed by her grandmother. She has observed that a woman can both play her biological role determined by gender and have an active, meaningful self-fulfilling life.

Porter originally conceived of the other six stories published in *Collected Stories* under the heading "The Old Order" as a portion of a novel to be titled "Midway of This Mortal Life." She sent "60 odd pages" of the novel, titled "Legend and Memory," to her publisher Donald Brace in April 1934.[16] The surviving portions of this manuscript among Porter's papers consist of forty-two pages, forty of which comprise clean typescripts of three stories: "The Grandmother" (first published as "The Source" in *Accent*, Spring 1941), "The Circus" (first published in *Southern Review*, July 1935), and "The Old Order" (first published in *Southern Review*, Winter 1936, retitled "The Journey" in *Collected Stories*). In the manuscript, these stories are numbered I, III, and IV, respectively. From evidence in Porter's correspondence, it is also possible to determine the other stories missing from this manuscript ("The Witness," "The Grave," and "The Last Leaf") as well as the numbering on them (II, V, and VI, respectively). These last three stories were the first among them to be published, appearing in *Virginia Quarterly Review* in January and April 1935.

Porter planned for the entire novel to be set in the period between 1700 and 1918. An unnumbered page of the "Legend and Memory" manuscript indicates that the "scene is laid in the southern states of the United States of America, time, between 1827 and 1903" and further asserts, "these fragments have not been selected at random, but run consecutively, making a unified, if not complete, story in themselves."[17] Porter further explained her method and plan in a May 31, 1934, letter to Charles A. Pearce of Harcourt, Brace:

> In This Legend and Memory manuscript, I have begun to use Time, past present and future as a means of showing each character as the whole sum of himself at any given moment: this is to say, the grandmother is old, but the child she was is still present in her memory, herself as child is shown beside her grand-daughter as child, and the old people live over within themselves every stage of themselves from infancy to their present.
>
> ["The Grave"] really is the first step towards the future out of the past Miranda has lived in all her childhood.[18]

The six Old Order stories return to the characters and setting that Porter had created for "The Fig Tree" and later described as "my past and my own house and my own people – the native land of my heart" ("'Noon Wine': The Sources," *Collected Essays* 470). Four of these characters, Miranda, her grandmother Sophia Jane, and two black former slaves, Aunt Nannie and Uncle Jimbilly, each appear as the central figure in at least one of the individual stories of the sequence.

The grandmother is truly "The Source," the title of the first of the Old Order stories. Her memory is the source of the family legends that she recounts, passed on to Miranda, who, in turn, remembers and recounts them as well as her own memories of the grandmother and other family elders, who "all talked and behaved as if the final word had gone out long ago on manners, morality, religion, even politics" ("'Noon Wine': The Sources," *Collected Essays* 471). "The Source" depicts the yearly trip the grandmother makes to her farm in the country, where her three unnamed grandchildren are sent after school is closed. Although her son Harry, the father of the three children, is annoyed at the upsets and inconveniences of these annual visits, the grandmother's arrival has a salutary effect on the place and its inhabitants. Observing that "everything is out of order" (*Collected Stories* 322), she directs the cleaning and refurbishing of the Negro huts, the making of new clothes for the Negro men, women, and children, the cleaning and setting to order of the main house, and sees that that same "restoring touch" is applied to the barns, smokehouses, potato cellar, and "every tree or vine or bush" (324). In addition, she soothes dozens of small injuries and complaints arisen since her last visit. Her dominion extends to the three mother-less grandchildren who loved her as their "only reality" but felt that she was a "tyrant" from whom "they wished to be free" (324). The visit culminates with her ritual of riding her "weary, disheartened old" saddle horse Fiddler (324) and an "easy stroll in the orchards with nothing to do," as, with nothing more to restore to order, she can return to "the place in town," "which no doubt had gone somewhat astray in her absence" (325). Although the grandmother chooses to believe that "she herself walked lightly and breathed as easily as ever," the ironic third person narrator subtly suggests that the old order, which she represents, is declining, like Fiddler and herself, to its certain end (325).

Uncle Jimbilly, who appears briefly in "The Fig Tree," is the central character in "The Witness." His testimony is of slavery, and he recounts both legendary tales and his own memories of the hardships and horrors of slavery. Bent, stiff, and hobbled by many years of building, mending, replacing, and repairing things, Uncle Jimbilly, a former slave, tells the three children, identified by name as Miranda, Paul, and Maria, bloody tales of torture and death in slave times. Both his person and his stories make the children feel guilty, but they retain a measure of skepticism about his personal suffering and the accuracy of his slave narratives. They observe that he "had got over his slavery very well. Since they had known him, he had never done a single thing that anyone told him to do" (*Collected Stories* 341). In addition, the veracity of slave legends is called into question by his "exorbitant" threats of murder and mayhem, "that not even the most credulous child could be terrified by them" (342). But slavery and the plight of Southern Negroes is not the central concern of "The Witness." That concern is death, the profound and ubiquitous theme of many of Porter's short stories. Uncle Jimbilly carves miniature tombstones for the small beasts and birds the children bury with "proper ceremonies" and replies when prompted that "thousands and tens upon thousands" perished in slave times (341, 342). In his own person, he bears witness to the physical deterioration and certain death to which all of humanity is subject.

Miranda is the central intelligence in "The Circus." Like her grandmother, Miranda is attending her first circus in the company of a large party that includes her nuclear family and about a dozen members of her extended family – great aunts, first and second cousins, an uncle, and an aunt – on the occasion of a family reunion. Significantly, Miranda is "fearfully excited" before she notices "the bold grinning" stares of "roughly dressed little boys peeping up" the skirts of female members of her party (*Collected Stories* 344). This vaguely sexual threat colors Miranda's reaction to the high wire act of a man dressed in a Pierrot costume: when she realizes that he could be injured or killed, she covers her eyes, screams, and cries. Her father and grandmother order Miranda's Negro servant minder, Dicey, to take the hysterical girl away. As they depart, a dwarf "made a horrid grimace at her, imitating her own face" and, after Miranda struck at him, followed this with "a look of haughty, remote displeasure, a true grown-up look" (345). When the remainder of the family party returns from the circus, Miranda learns what she has missed and is maliciously taunted for "spoiling the day for Dicey" (346). Bursting into tears again, Miranda is taken away, falls asleep, and is awakened by a nightmare: "the bitter terrified face of the man in blowsy white falling to his death … and the terrible grimace of the unsmiling dwarf" (347). It is Dicey, not her father or grandmother, who responds to Miranda's screams, but Dicey can do little to address Miranda's inchoate fears of sexuality and death.

The single most important story in the Old Order sequence is "The Journey." Indeed, most of the sequence's "legend and memory" resides in this story set in the period between 1827 and 1901, the life span of Porter's paternal grandmother, which is assigned both specifically and by inference to the fictional Sophia Jane, Miranda's grandmother. Although the story opens when the grandmother and her former slave Nannie are in "their later years," it limns their parallel life journeys. While fitting together "scraps of the family finery" into more or less useful household furnishings, their conversation and recollections can be pieced together by the reader into a fairly complete family history (*Collected Stories* 326). Born to a genteel slaveowning family in Kentucky, Sophia Jane received Nannie as a gift as a child of five. Both marry at seventeen to men deemed suitable by Sophia Jane's elders. Sophia Jane marries her second cousin Stephen; and "Nannie was married off to a boy she had known ever since she came to the family, and they were given as a wedding present to Miss Sophia Jane." Their ensuing "grim and terrible race of procreation" results in eleven births for Sophia Jane and thirteen for Nannie (334). When Nannie nearly dies of puerperal fever after the births of each of their fourth children, Sophia Jane nurses both the children, experiences a "sensual warm pleasure" "missed in the marriage bed," and, henceforth, "resolved never again to be cheated" by "giving her children to another woman to feed" (334).

Wounded and ruined in the Civil War, Sophia Jane's "selfish, careless, unloving" husband dies, having used her dowry and property for "wild investments in strange territories: Louisiana, Texas" (335, 337). "Left so," Sophia Jane moves her nine children, Nannie and her three sons, Uncle Jimbilly, and two other Negroes, first to Louisiana where "she sold out at a loss," and finally to "a large tract of fertile black land in an almost unsettled part" of Texas (337, 338). By dint of her merciless driving of herself, her children, the Negroes, and the horses, the grandmother is able to build a "stronghold … for the future of her family" (337). Taking on "all the responsibilities of her tangled world, half white, half black, mingling steadily," Sophia Jane comes to despise men – the young male relatives whose "headstrong habits" resulted in the birth of mixed-blood children in the Negro quarters, her husband and her sons who "threw away" family assets and married women of whom she did not approve (337, 339). Revitalized by taking on her son Harry's three motherless children, she begins "life again, with almost the same zest, and with more indulgence," only to drop dead suddenly on a visit to the home of one of her sons in far western Texas (339–40). Through the story of Sophia Jane's journey through life, Porter explores the roles and experiences of women – Sophia Jane is a daughter, belle, wife, mother, and grandmother. The story also examines the culture of the American South, with its history of slavery, miscegenation, defeat in the Civil War, and postwar poverty. Finally the story explores the subjects of death and sexuality, the universal concerns to which Porter returned again and again.

Miranda is the central character in "The Grave," the fifth of the Old Order stories in the 1934 manuscript. In it, sexuality and death, the unstated "fathomless terrors" that "subjugated" Miranda in "The Circus," are overtly linked (*Collected Stories* 347). Although narrated in the third person, "The Grave" depicts a remembered incident from Miranda's life, specifically 1903, when she was nine years old. Walking in "a market street in a strange city of a strange country" "nearly twenty years later," the "episode of that far-off day leaped from its burial place before her mind's eye," evoked by the heat and smell of "mingled sweetness and corruption," like that on the day of the remembered episode (367). The main action of the story takes place on the day on which Miranda and her twelve-year-old brother Paul took a break from hunting rabbits and doves to explore the empty graves of their paternal grandfather and other "oddments" of Kentucky relatives in what was formerly the family cemetery on their grandmother's first farm (362). Miranda finds a silver-colored screw head for a coffin in her grandfather's grave, while Paul unearths a "thin wide gold ring carved with intricate flowers and leaves" (363). After the children trade their finds, Miranda loses interest in shooting after she places the gold ring on her thumb. Contemplating the glittering ring, Miranda becomes aware of the conflict between the mores of the "old order" and her father's "simple and natural" common sense (365). Corncob-pipe smoking old crones had chided her for breaking the "the back country" "law of female decorum" with her "summer roughing outfit" of overalls, shirt, straw hat, and sandals, attire that her father had defended as utilitarian and economical (364). Her feelings turning against the masculine clothing, Miranda wishes to return to the farmhouse to bathe and "put on the thinnest, most becoming dress she owned," experiencing "vague stirrings of desire for luxury … founded on family legend of past wealth and leisure" (365).

Her reverie is interpreted when Paul shoots a pregnant rabbit, and they examine it together. Seeing the rabbit fetuses, Miranda understands, "what she had to know," that she, like the rabbit, can bear young, and that knowledge makes her "quietly and terribly agitated" (367). Her brother's subsequent actions also worry her and make her unhappy – he hides the rabbit carcasses and swears Miranda to secrecy. The unstated lesson is that female sexual activity, which may result in pregnancy, is something she "ought not to do," "an important secret" to be kept between herself and Paul, her male guide (367). Miranda's epiphany brings understanding that pregnancy and childbirth can result in death, the unspoken cause of the death of her mother. If "The Grave" does depict "the first step towards the future out of the past Miranda has lived in all her childhood,"[19] is the reader to conclude that Miranda will reject the traditional roles of wife and mother? Her attitude toward her dolls provides a clue: "for though she never cared much for her dolls she liked seeing them in fur coats" (366); she would rather contemplate dolls as aesthetic objects than play mother to them.

The sixth and last of the Old Order stories in the "Legend and Memory" manuscript is "The Last Leaf." The "last leaf" of the title is Nannie, the grandmother's black contemporary, originally bought as a playmate and servant when Sophia Jane was five years old. Having spent "all their lives together," they were "unable to imagine getting on without each other" (*Collected Stories* 330). In "The Fig Tree," "The Source," and "The Journey," she is the stock figure of Southern fiction and legend, "the faithful old servant … , a freed slave" (*Collected Stories* 349). Many of the "facts" of her biography, including the birth date Sophia Jane assigned to her and recorded in the family Bible (June 11, 1827), are narrated in "The Journey." However, in "The Last Leaf," as the last remnant of the old order surviving into changing times, she escapes the restrictions imposed on her by virtue of her gender and her race.

Nannie asserts her independence after she is nearly physically worn out by more than seven decades of serving Sophia Jane and her family. Even for a period of time after Sophia Jane's death, she remained the maternal and domestic mainstay for Sophia Jane's son Harry and his three motherless children. Maria, "the elder girl," later observed that they "went on depending on her as they always had, letting her assume more burdens and more, allowing her to work harder than she should" (*Collected Stories* 348). When the opportunity arises, she asks for and receives "a house of her own," "a little cabin across the narrow creek" (348). Although the members of her "white family" had the place cleaned, repaired, and outfitted for her, they are "surprised, a little wounded," and "put upon" that she moved away from them (349). Her move transforms her; she forsakes the black and white dresses, aprons, and caps of a house servant for a blue bandanna and corncob pipe, the proper attire for what she becomes, "an aged Bantu woman of independent means" (349). Contentedly sitting "in the luxury of having at her disposal all of God's good time there was in this world," Nannie is a rebuke to her white family's "complacent" belief that she "was a real member of the family, perfectly happy with them" (351, 349).

Having rejected the role of a servant normally assigned to one of her race, she refuses to be confined by gender. The reader learns, in this last story in the 1934 Old Order sequence, "that Uncle Jimbilly and Aunt Nannie were husband and wife." Their "marriage of convenience" arranged by others "had dissolved itself between them when the reasons for it had likewise dissolved." In modern times, "blood and family stability" are no longer important reasons for marriage, nor are arranged marriages the norm (*Collected Stories* 350). Comfortably ensconced in her cabin, Aunt Nannie refuses to resume the traditional female role subservient to men, "pointedly" dismissing Uncle Jimbilly's attempt at insinuating himself into her private realm, "I don' aim to pass my las' days waitin on no man. ... I've served my time, I've done my do, and dat's all" (351).

The story also exposes how the antebellum South's unwritten codes defining race and gender roles brought unanticipated negative consequences in the early twentieth century. The exploitation and subjugation of women and African Americans are as deleterious to the oppressors as to those whom they oppressed. Accustomed to having servants, leisure, and luxury, members of the ruling class became lazy and self-indulgent, unable to properly care for their property and assets or to find profitable work. In "The Last Leaf," Harry and his children flounder without Nannie to sustain and support them.

> They were growing up, times were changing, the old world was sliding from under their feet, they had not yet laid hold of the new one. They missed Nannie every day. As their fortunes went down, and they had few servants, they needed her terribly. They realized how much the old woman had done for them, simply by seeing how, almost immediately after she went, everything slackened, lost tone, went off edge. Work did not accomplish itself as it once had. They had not learned how to work for themselves, they were all lazy and incapable of sustained effort or planning. They had not been taught and they had not yet educated themselves. (*Collected Stories* 349–50)

The story also hints at one of the root causes of the weakness of the Southern men so clearly delineated in "The Journey," "smothering matriarchal tyranny" (*Collected Stories* 351). Petted, spoiled, and indulged by women of both races from birth, the males of the Old Order are profligate, weak, and infantilized. Women restricted by virtue of their gender to a narrow realm of influence, exert their power indirectly. In "The Last Leaf," Nannie "gets the better of" Sophia Jane's proud and stiff-necked son Harry by reminding him of her service to the family as his wet nurse. Despite the knowledge that he knew that "this was not literally true," he submits to her, "being of that latest generation of sons who acknowledged, however reluctantly, however bitterly, their mystical never to be forgiven debt to the womb that bore them, and the breast that suckled them" 351). The reader may draw the conclusion that both women and men "can be oppressed by familial relationships."[20]

Porter's fiction set in the South and Mexico, as well as that depicting the sick, grotesquely dislocated culture of the twentieth century, is both particular and universal. It makes use of and examines the particular places and individuals that she knew and the historical events that she experienced and witnessed. Her work is set in Mexico City, Hacienda Tetlapayac, and a pre-Hispanic archaeological site in Mexico; in the agrarian South, rural New England, and cities (New York, New Orleans, and Denver) of her own country; in Berlin; and on board a ship sailing from Mexico to Berlin. Her characters draw on individuals she knew or observed in Mexico, members of the paternal side of her family, her spouses and lovers, and inhabitants of the rural Texas community where she grew up as well as those observed in the cities and other places where she resided during her adult life. Her work documents her experience of the changes wrought by historical events as well as the epochal events themselves; these include the Civil War, the Mexican Revolution, World War I, women's suffrage, and the rise of the Nazis in Germany. However, making use of the personal and particular, Porter explored universal subjects and themes: art and the artist, religion, race, gender, sexuality, death, and the inevitability of decay and change.

In a 1953 letter, Porter summarized her understanding of the artist's role: "The artist must work some order into … 'his little handful of chaos.' … Life is one bloody, horrible confusion, and the one business of the artist is to know it, admit it, and manifest his vision of order in the human imagination" ("Ole Woman River," *Collected Essays* 278). Porter strove to produce fiction that expressed issues and ideas that were central to the concerns of humankind. It was her view that art should observe and expose the impossible conditions of the world in which humans live, that it should provide a guide for poor, suffering humanity. She was interested in raising important questions for her readers to ponder, to arouse the intellect and the emotions, to confront apathy and indifference. She suggested no solutions but rather pointed to some of the problems of human existence. Enduring works of art, her stories are evidence of her success at what she once called her "vocation and fate" ("You Are What You Read" 248).

> In the face of such shape and weight of … misfortune, the voice of the individual artist may seem perhaps of no more consequence than the whirring of a cricket in the grass; but the arts do live continuously, and they live literally by faith; their names and their shapes and their uses and their basic meanings survive unchanged in all that matters through times of interruption, diminishment, neglect; they outlive governments and creeds and societies, even the very civilizations that produced them. They cannot be destroyed altogether because they represent the substance of faith and the only reality. They are what we find again when the ruins are cleared away. And even the smallest and most incomplete offering … can be a proud act in defense of that faith. ("Introduction to the 1940 edition of *Flowering Judas and Other Stories*," *Collected Essays* 457)

NOTES

1   The four derivative stories are "The Shattered Star" (*Everyland*, January 1920), "The Faithful Princess" (*Everyland*, February 1920), "The Magic Ear Ring" (*Everyland*, March 1920), and "The Adventures of Hadji: A Tale of a Turkish Coffee House" (*Asia*, August 1920).

2   The two short novels set in the South are "Noon Wine" (*Story*, June 1937) and "Old Mortality" (*Southern Review*, Spring 1937). Both were subsequently collected in *Pale Horse, Pale Rider* in 1939.

3   These works represent Porter's attempt "to achieve in the way of order and form and statement in a period of grotesque dislocations in a whole society when the world was heaving in the sickness of a millennial change" ("Introduction to the 1940 edition of *Flowering Judas and Other Stories*," *Collected Essays and Occasional Writings of Katherine Anne Porter* 457; hereinafter cited as *Collected Essays* in the text). The five stories include "Rope" (*Second American Caravan*, 1928), "Theft" (*Gyroscope*, November 1929), "The Cracked Looking Glass" (*Scribner's*, May 1932), "The Downward Path to Wisdom" (*Harper's Bazaar*, December 1939), and "A Day's Work" (*Nation*, February 10, 1940). The two short novels are "Pale Horse, Pale Rider" (*Southern Review*, Winter 1938) and "The Leaning Tower" (*Southern Review*, Autumn 1941).

4   The other six include "He," "Magic," "The Jilting of Granny Weatherall," "The Witness," "The Grave," and "The Journey."

5   Manuel Gamio, *Introduction, Synthesis and Conclusions of the Work* 40.

6   "Virgin Violeta," *The Collected Stories of Katherine Anne Porter* 22–3. Hereinafter quotations

from this collection of Porter's short stories will appear in the text cited as *Collected Stories*.

7   Thomas F. Walsh, *Katherine Anne Porter and Mexico* 64.

8   Katherine Anne Porter to Freda Kirchwey, September 8, 1921, Papers of Katherine Anne Porter, Special Collections, University of Maryland Libraries. Hereinafter cited as KAP Papers in the text.

9   KAP to Richard Blackmur, November 29, 1929, in *The Hound & Horn Letters*, ed. Mitzi Berger Hamovitch, 127.

10   "Hacienda," *Uncollected Early Prose of Katherine Anne Porter*, eds. Alvarez and Walsh, 270.

11   Hubert Howe Bancroft, *Native Races of the Pacific States of North America* III, 359.

12   Barbara Foley, *Radical Representations: Politics and Form in U. S. Proletarian Fiction, 1929-1941*, 65.

13   KAP to Donald Brace, January 30, 1955, KAP Papers.

14   KAP to Isidore Schneider, September 11, 1927, KAP Papers.

15   KAP to Gay Porter Holloway, March 5, 1928, KAP Papers; KAP to Josephine Herbst, undated but written in Salem, c. 1928, Papers of Josephine Herbst, Beinecke Library, Yale University.

16   KAP to Donald Brace, April 9, 1934, KAP Papers.

17   "Legend and Memory," KAP Papers.

18   KAP to Charles A. Pearce, May 31, 1934, KAP Papers.

19   "Legend and Memory," KAP Papers.

20   Jane Krause DeMouy, *Katherine Anne Porter's Women* 136.

REFERENCES AND FURTHER READING

Alvarez, Ruth M., and Thomas F. Walsh, eds. *Uncollected Early Prose of Katherine Anne Porter*. Austin: University of Texas Press, 1993.

Bancroft, Hubert Howe. *Native Races of the Pacific States of North America*. 5 vols. New York: Appleton, 1874–6.

DeMouy, Jane Krause. *Katherine Anne Porter's Women: The Eye of Her Fiction*. Austin: University of Texas Press, 1983.

Foley, Barbara. *Radical Representations: Politics and Form in U. S. Proletarian Fiction, 1929–1941*. Durham, NC: Duke University Press, 1993.

Gamio, Manuel. *Introduction, Synthesis and Conclusions of the Work: The Population of the Valley of Teotihucán*. Mexico City: Talleres Graficos de la Nación, 1922.

Givner, Joan, ed. *Katherine Anne Porter: Conversations*. Jackson: University Press of Mississippi, 1987.

———. *Katherine Anne Porter: A Life*. Athens: University of Georgia Press, 1991.

Hamovitch, Mitzi Berger, ed. *The Hound & Horn Letters*. Athens: University of Georgia Press, 1982.

Herbst, Josephine. Papers. Beinecke Library, Yale University, New Haven, CT.

Porter, Katherine Anne. "The Adventures of Hadji: A Tale of a Turkish Coffee House." *Asia* 20 (August 1920): 683–4.

———. "The Circus." *Southern Review* 1 (July 1935): 36–41.

———. *The Collected Essays and Occasional Writings of Katherine Anne Porter*. New York: Seymour Lawrence/Delacorte, 1970.

———. *The Collected Stories of Katherine Anne Porter*. New York: Harcourt, Brace, 1965.

———. "The Cracked Looking-Glass." *Scribner's* 91 (May 1932): 271–6, 313–20.

———. "A Day's Work." *Nation* 110 (February 10, 1940): 205–7.

———. "The Downward Path to Wisdom." *Harper's Bazaar* 2731 (December 1939): 72–3, 140, 142, 144–5, 147.

———. "The Faithful Princess." *Everyland* 2 (February 1920): 42–3.

———. "The Fig Tree." *Harper's* 220 (June 1960): 55–9.

———. "Flowering Judas." *Hound & Horn* 3 (April–June 1930): 316–31.

———. *Flowering Judas*. New York: Harcourt, Brace, 1930.

———. *Flowering Judas and Other Stories*. New York: Harcourt, Brace, 1935.

———. "The Grave." *Virginia Quarterly Review* (April 1935): 177–83.

———. "Hacienda." *Virginia Quarterly Review* 8 (October 1932): 556–69.

———. *Hacienda*. New York: Harrison of Paris, 1934.

———. "He." *New Masses* 3 (October 1927): 13–15.

———. "Holiday." *Atlantic Monthly* 206 (December 1960): 44–56.

———. "The Jilting of Granny Weatherall." *transition* 15 (February 1929): 139–45.

———. "The Leaning Tower." *Southern Review* 7 (Autumn 1941): 219–79.

———. *The Leaning Tower and Other Stories*. New York: Harcourt, Brace, 1944.

———. "Magic." *transition* 13 (Summer 1928): 229–31.

———. "The Magic Ear Ring." *Everyland* 2 (March 1920): 86–7.

———. "María Concepción." *Century* 105 (December 1922): 224–39.

———. "The Martyr." *Century* 106 (July 1923): 410–13.

———. "Noon Wine." *Story* 10 (June 1937): 71–103.

———. "The Old Order" (later published as "The Journey"). *Southern Review* 1 (Winter 1936): 495–509.

———. "Old Mortality." *Southern Review* 2 (Spring 1937): 686–735.

———. "Pale Horse, Pale Rider." *Southern Review* 3 (Winter 1938): 417–66.

———. *Pale Horse, Pale Rider: Three Short Novels*. New York: Harcourt, Brace, 1939.

———. Papers. Special Collections, University of Maryland Libraries, College Park, Md.

———. "Rope." *The Second American Caravan*. Eds. Alfred Kreymborg, Lewis Mumford, and Paul Rosenfeld. New York: Macaulay, 1928. 362–8.

———. "The Shattered Star." *Everyland* 2 (January 1920): 422–3.

———. "The Source." *Accent* (Spring 1941): 144–7.

———. "That Tree." *Virginia Quarterly Review* 10 (July 1934): 351–61.

———. "Theft." *Gyroscope* (November 1929): unpaged.

———. "Two Plantation Portraits: 'The Last Leaf.'" *Virginia Quarterly Review* 11 (January 1935): 88–92.

———. "Two Plantation Portraits: 'Uncle Jimbilly'" (later published as "The Witness"). *Virginia Quarterly Review* 11 (January 1935): 85–8.

———. "Virgin Violeta." *Century* 109 (December 1924): 261–8.

———. "You Are What You Read." *Vogue* 164 (October 1974): 248.

Stout, Janis. *Katherine Anne Porter: A Sense of the Times*. Charlottesville: University Press of Virginia, 1995.

Unrue, Darlene Harbour, ed. *Critical Essays on Katherine Anne Porter*. New York: G. K. Hall, 1997.

———. *Katherine Anne Porter: The Life of an Artist*. Jackson: University Press of Mississippi, 2005.

———. *Truth and Vision in Katherine Anne Porter's Fiction*. Athens: University of Georgia Press, 1985.

Walsh, Thomas F. *Katherine Anne Porter and Mexico: The Illusion of Eden*. Austin: University of Texas Press, 1992.

18

Eudora Welty and the Short Story: Theory and Practice

Ruth D. Weston

Eudora Welty (1909–2001) was awarded many prizes for her fiction, including her first Guggenheim in 1942 and the Pulitzer in 1973; and she received many other honors, including the *Légion d'Honneur Français* in 1996. Welty's work has attracted a perceptive and appreciative cadre of scholars, beginning with the editors of the *Southern Review*, who published some of her first stories. One of those editors was Robert Penn Warren, whose early essay "The Love and Separateness in Miss Welty" not only identified a major theme in her fiction but also began the close reading that is necessary for its full appreciation. He also, "at the risk of incompleteness, or even distortion," named an important theme in her fiction, that of "Innocence and Experience." In "A Still Moment," the naturalist Audubon loves the snowy heron he finds along Mississippi's Natchez Trace; but he must kill the beautiful bird to fully know it, to see and paint it accurately, and thus to share it. Warren sees in this situation "an irony of limit and contamination" (Warren 46; Welty, *Collected Stories* 189–99). For Audubon, it is also the artist's dilemma: "that the best he could make would be … a dead thing and not a live thing, never the essence." He realizes his essential isolation: he can never share his vision fully. Lorenzo, the evangelist who encounters Audubon along the Trace, has a similar experience; however, he sees the heron as God's love "come visible," but then taken away. He "could understand God's giving Separateness first and then giving Love to follow and heal in its wonder; but God had given Love first and then Separateness, as though it did not matter to Him which came first. Perhaps it was that God never counted the moments of Time. … Time did not occur to God." Other major modernist themes voiced here are alienation, ambiguity, and the preoccupation with time, especially differing perceptions of time. Welty most often develops the theme of Love and Separateness in terms of human relationships, especially the tensions between individuals and family or community, and of the risks inherent in the bonds of love and in breaking those bonds. "A Curtain of Green," the title story of her first collection, refers to the "curtain" of wild vegetal growth that Mrs. Larkin grows to shield her from further hurts of the world after her husband's death; but it also suggests Welty's stated objective in writing fiction: "to part a curtain ... that falls between people, the veil of indifference to each other's presence, each other's wonder, each other's human plight" (Welty, *Eye of the Story* 355).

In spite of the popularity of Welty's memoir-like autobiography, *One Writer's Beginnings*, and the prizes awarded her novels, she thought of herself as "more of a natural short story writer," as she told Alice Walker (Prenshaw, *Conversations* 132).[1] Indeed, *The Robber Bridegroom* and *The Ponder Heart* are more nearly novellas; and both *Delta Wedding* and *The Optimist's Daughter* began as short stories. Her short story cycle *The Golden Apples* has been called the very center of her canon (Pitavy-Souques, "Blazing Butterfly" 537), and it is in the tradition of the short story that Welty's literary legacy is greatest. She is, in fact, one of a select few short story writers whose essays are quoted by theorists of the genre. Susan Lohafer writes that, historically, "the ones who theorized about stories were the ones who wrote them: Poe, Chekhov, Henry James, H. E. Bates, Frank O'Connor, Eudora Welty".[2] Both Welty's short stories and her theoretical essays about fiction manifest aspects of the genre as it is described by some of its finest practitioners, including its mixture of realism and lyricism, its formal aesthetic patterning, and its focus on the nature of storytelling. These aspects, of course, overlap and complement each other in the fiction.

Charles E. May notes that "despite the 'new realism' introduced by Chekhov, Joyce, and Anderson early in the century, the short story still retained its links to its older mythic and romantic forms"; Eudora Welty is among the writers he lists who combine traits of this new realistic style of such writers as Hemingway and Babel with the more mythic style of Faulkner and Dinesen (May 19).

Welty often pointed to the lyric basis for the short story (*Eye of the Story* 108). The vocabulary that describes the lyric/realist nature of the modern short story comes from several sources, two of the most important of which are James Joyce and his American counterpart, Sherwood Anderson. Joyce's *Dubliners* illustrated his lyric concept of the "epiphany," a momentary manifestation of some truth revealed to a character; and Anderson's *Winesburg, Ohio*, like Joyce's "The Dead," revealed the short form as one that "focused more on lyric moments of realization than linear events" (May 59). Welty's theory and practice suggest that her understanding of the lyric/realist style derives not only from the tradition of Joyce and Anderson but in large part from Anton Chekhov, especially in terms of their mutual use of the technique that one of Chekhov's early critics called his "impressionistic" tendencies.[3] The aspects of literary impressionism that enhance Welty's stories include her pervasive use of vivid sensory "brush strokes" to suggest a character's fleeting impressions of reality from various perspectives and at significant moments. She also creates discontinuous narrative sequences in dreams, memory, or other altered states of consciousness; these passages depict psychological realism, to be sure, but they also suggest the fragmentary or ambiguous nature of modern life. Nor it is beside the point that a Welty story must be seen at the remove of thoughtful consideration of the whole before understanding can begin to coalesce, just as an Impressionist painting must be viewed from a certain distance, so that the viewer's eye may complete the artist's work.

The short story's focus on a single impression, also one of Edgar Allan Poe's famous dicta, is consistent with what Ernst Cassirer called "mythical thinking ... [in which] the entire self is given up to a single impression, is 'possessed' by it and, on the other hand, there is the utmost tension between the subject and its object, the outer world" (Cassirer 33). In her essay "Place in Fiction," Welty speaks to the lyric attributes of such mythopoeic thinking when she declares that the arts of writing and painting are very close, asserting that "impressionism brought not the likeness-to-life but the mystery of place onto canvas." She reinforces that concept in terms of a literary "canvas," as well as that of the lyric/realist nature of the modern short story, with her comment that her story "No Place For You, My Love," from *The Bride of the Innisfallen and Other Stories*, was "a realistic story in which the reality *was* mystery." And yet, always sensitive to the natural world, Welty's stories evince her photographer's eye for the realistic detail (*Eye of the Story* 118, 114).

Lyric Realism in "Flowers for Marjorie"

From early on, commentaries on Welty's fiction have remarked its mixture of lyricism and realism. In "Flowers for Marjorie" (*Collected Stories* 98–106), from her first collection, *A Curtain of Green*, lyric realism is manifest in the racing emotions and fragmented sense perceptions of the unemployed and desperate Howard, after he has murdered his pregnant wife and fled into New York's bleak streets where, ironically, he is awarded the key to the city. The story begins in mundane, real time, with the almost naturalistic description of the feet of men exhausted from seeking work during the Great Depression. Welty observed and photographed such despair, both as a junior publicity agent for the federal Works Progress Administration in Mississippi during the 1930s, and also in New York City.[4] The opening scene in "Flowers for Marjorie" is similar to that in Welty's photograph *Union Square, New York, 1930s*, in which people sit on a park bench between two "bracketing clocks [that] show the time to be 3:35 ... [suggesting that] they have no jobs to command their awareness of time" (Pollack and Marrs 248). Those clocks are like the many images in "Flowers for Marjorie" that contrast natural time with artificial time, as they clearly identify Welty with other great modernist writers for whom the theme of time is crucial, and who often use narrative distortion of time to reveal a character's perception of time as moving either faster or slower than "clock time." "The time as we know it subjectively," Welty explains, "is often the chronology that stories and novels follow: it is the continuous thread of revelation" (*One Writer's Beginnings* 69).

By the end of section one in "Flowers for Marjorie," the as yet unnamed protagonist has mostly kept his eyes shut against the world around him, as well as against the thought of his waiting wife. When Howard runs back to their apartment, having given up looking for a job, he must confront Marjorie, who is a comforting presence like their Mississippi home; but at the same time she is a mocking reproach to him in his unfruitful search. Unlike the pessimistic Howard, Marjorie is expectant in two ways: pregnant and hopeful for the future, in spite of their current plight. He finds her as composed as ever, looking perhaps as if the "excess of life in her rounding body" leads her to ignore him. After the story's opening in realistic prose, the reader enters lyric space and time, in which every gesture, every detail of vocabulary and pattern of language, is significant. At the level of language, historical, literary, and cultural meanings can well up in a single word or image, as Welty suggests by her remark, "We start from scratch, and words don't" (*Eye of the Story* 134). At the level of plot, the theory of narrative time includes Frank O'Connor's idea that in the short story, "since a whole lifetime must be crowded into a few minutes, those minutes must be carefully chosen indeed and lit by an unearthly glow, one that enables us to distinguish present, past, and future as though they were all contemporaneous" (O'Connor 22). In the first of three flower scenes in the story, Howard sees a pansy Marjorie has found on a morning's walk and placed in the buttonhole of her coat. The flower radiates with just such an "unearthly glow"; and in Howard's imagination its "dark red veins and edges ... [begin to] assume the ... curves of a mountain on the horizon of a desert, the veins becoming crevasses, the delicate edges the giant worn lips of a sleeping crater." Peter Schmidt reads the scene, especially the "giant worn lips" image, as evidence of Howard's fear of women and his sense of entrapment. Indeed, Howard is one of many Welty characters – male and female – who struggle against feelings of entrapment.[5]

When Marjorie asks if Howard has eaten, he is enraged that she, who seems so self-assured, has the temerity to ask about "his hunger and weakness!" His response is to stab her with a kitchen knife and to go again into the city, where he wanders in an almost Joycean phantasmagoria of artificial gratifications. But New York City's mocking façade of commercial plenty is ironically contradicted in Howard's imagination by the wastelandian images of a desert, a crater, and a burning flower. Howard himself is "ablaze with horror" from his day's experiences, one of which is noticing the subway sign that threatens: "God sees me," recalling the wastelandian scene from F. Scott Fitzgerald's *The Great Gatsby*, in which a huge eye on an optician's billboard ad looms over an ash pit. After the murder, Howard is so devoid of feeling that he does not even notice when he is hit by a bicycle. With ironic timing, it is now that he experiences two windfalls: first, a slot machine jackpot; then red roses and the key to the city. He runs back to Marjorie in a surreal state, thinking perhaps that he himself is the one dead.

Howard's confusion between reality and his imagination contributes to what Danièle Pitavy-Souques calls a Welty character's "doubling upon one's self ... [which is] true not only of 'moments,' but of the short stories themselves as structures." In one of the most insightful comments on Welty, Pitavy-Souques goes on to say that the stories in *The Golden Apples* "are built on this endless reflection, which doubles and doubles again. There are two parts or two movements in each story that are based on the ambiguity between a real experience and a dreamed one, between asserted reality and hypothetical reality" ("Technique as Myth" 265). Howard's ambiguous death-in-life state is also suggested by the fact that as he nears his apartment "his breath was gone." He "stop[s] still" on the sidewalk when he comes across the stopped clock he had thrown out the window because it had "ticked dreadfully" after he stabbed Marjorie in the heart. When he re-enters their room, only the dead roses seem to have life, as they exude their scent. In this second of three flower scenes, Howard strokes not Marjorie's body but the roses; and then he "knew ... that everything had stopped." Her lifelike form continues to lean against the window; but where she had earlier had "perfect balance," now her balance, like his breath, is gone; and the con-verse is also true: his balance and her breath are gone. An additional irony is the fact that, in one of Welty's most recognized symbols of openness to life, the open hand, Marjorie's hand lies open, even in death. The images of death – all of which describe Howard, not Marjorie – continue to accumulate, as he reports her death to a police-man on the street below and then "burie[s] his eyes, nose, and mouth in the roses."

What Joyce called "the curve of an emotion," which paints the "portrait of the artist" (258), defines the character of Howard as it arcs between the poles of life and death in his mind, dictating the aesthetic shape of the story. Welty employs the ancient Homeric narrative pattern of wandering and return; but she doubles the pattern, with a second action that is an ironic reversal of the first. Howard moves, mentally and physically, away from life in the apartment where his wife reminds him of home, out into an inhospitable world that has killed his spirit. On his first return, he who is "dead" kills one who is literally full of life. He then makes a second voyage out and a second return, to face the actual and spiritual death he has perpetrated.[6] In the third flower scene, when he starts to go back into the house with the policeman, the roses he has won at Radio City fall to the ground and children take them up and wear them. If this final action seems anticlimactic, it is the kind of purposeful anti-climax that O'Connor called, in Turgenev's "Byezhin Prairie," one of "supreme art-istry." It is not the expected ending – of justice done to a murderer, perhaps – but one like that which O'Connor says elicits a "shudder ... before the mystery of human life" (O'Connor 51–2). "Flowers for Marjorie" is one of Welty's stories in which, as Ruth M. Vande Kieft says, "the separateness triumphs over the love" (303).

Aesthetic Structure in "The Winds"

As Welty matured as an artist, she continued to experiment with the lyric technique, often to convey a character's sense of inner landscape, revising fiction's classic curve of plot action, which becomes, in the lyric story, more nearly an aesthetic structure that reveals a character's rising and falling emotions. In her second collection, *The Wide Net*, Warren noticed that "on the first page, with the first sentence, we enter a special world ... in which we are going to live until we reach the last sentence of the last story." Quoting the opening of "First Love" (*Collected Stories* 153–68), another story set on the Natchez Trace – "Whatever happened, it happened in extraordinary times, in a season of dreams" – Warren called the stories in *The Wide Net* "a tissue of symbols which emerge from, and disappear into, a world of scene and action which, once we discount the author's special perspective, is recognizable in realistic terms" (Warren 43, 50). This generalization is also exemplified in "The Winds" (*Collected Stories* 209–21), which depicts the realism of seasonal changes in terms of an equinoctial storm and, in terms of the author's perspective, the inner storm caused by a young girl's move from childhood to adolescence and sexual awareness. The story is composed of a series of lyric moments, experienced by both the protagonist and the reader, that shape its aesthetic structure.

Although not part of a short story cycle, like *The Golden Apples*, with its recurring characters and setting, *The Wide Net* includes several stories set on the Natchez Trace. Moreover, the volume coheres in subtle ways around a wide net of language and imagery that reveals Welty's sense of the essential mystery and allure of the world, including human life. In some ways, life in a Welty story is always set in "a season of dreams." "The Winds" opens with a passage that connects it with "First Love" in terms of their mysterious settings in extraordinary times, both of which involve weather. When Josie is awakened in the night by the wind, she mistakenly personifies it as the cheerful sounds of teenagers on a hayride on the old Natchez Trace, also known as Lover's Lane. Both stories depict inner and outer environments, and their language invites a closer comparison of the two. Whereas Josie is lifted from her bed in "The Winds," it is the Mississippi River that "shuddered and lifted from its bed" in "First Love"; and instead of a little brother who talks in his sleep in "The Winds," it is the river itself that is the "somnambulist" in "First Love." Josie and her town are undergoing a cyclic change in "The Winds," while in "First Love," the whole world seems to be "in a transfiguration." Even the historical Natchez Indians in "First Love" are represented in "The Winds" by Will, who screams in his dreams "like a wild Indian."

Welty's stories are often judged "difficult" and in need of an ideal reader who is willing to bring to the story an imaginative capacity equal to that of the writer: to brave the difficulties inherent in the short story form, to find its meaning and its beauty. She acknowledges such difficulties as she describes Katherine Mansfield's "Miss Brill," linking aspects of the lyric style (such as Chekhov's "impressionism" or O'Connor's "unearthly glow") with the story's aesthetic structure (shape). Welty says that Mansfield's story is imbued with a lyric style that often proves an obstruction to readers. Yet she explains that such obstructions may constitute the narrative reticence that is part of its artistic beauty (*Eye of the Story* 88, 105). Some narrative obstructions are what Austin M. Wright calls "inner recalcitrance" and "final recalcitrance" in the short story. The first kind is "a general recalcitrance common to all short works … [whereby] attention to the parts … implies … the arresting of notice at every significant point." Final recalcitrance, such as is found in the Joycean epiphany, "is an obstacle to artistic comprehension caused by the seemingly premature placing of the end, an effect of incompleteness, requiring the reader to look back, recalculate, and reconsider, so as to satisfy the expectation of wholeness that he has brought to the story" (Wright 120–1). One aspect of Welty's style is her use of such recalcitrance to alter a reader's expectations. Harriet Pollack argues that "Welty's strategy ... for shaping and educating the reader ... is to temporarily hinder his progress through the work. ... Her style demands that he gain perspective on his own first impressions, and coerces him to become more familiar with the limited range of possibility that is in the text" (Pollack 499). For example, in pointing out the long unnoticed or denied political content of Welty's fiction, Pollack and Suzanne Marrs assert, "Her play with and obstruction of all kinds of old stories and story expectations resisted and altered their meanings" (Pollack and Marrs 4).[7]

When "The Winds" was first presented to Welty's agent, he was "in a kind of bewilderment" about it; but editor Mary Lou Aswell of *Harper's Bazaar* proved to be an ideal reader (Kreyling, *Author and Agent* 68–9). The story is a poetic version of a psychological study of memory and memory's function in the longings for both the past and the future. Gail Mortimer argues that in "The Winds" Welty characterizes memory as "above all, preserving experience and something of its original wonder, ... [but that this idea] was gradually supplanted by Welty's emerging understanding that memory, like language itself, does not simply record but actually *structures* experience" (Mortimer 144). "The Winds" does, in fact, reveal the memory doing its structural work. The story illustrates Welty's concern with aesthetic structure in terms of a character's inner (psychological) and outer worlds, which Welty says she tries to connect as closely as possible (*Eye of the Story* 99, 94). "The Winds" follows the movement of the young protagonist's mind, as the fifteen unnumbered sections of the story alternate between the present reality (outside) and Josie's world of imagination (inside).

The first and longest passage of the story establishes the scene during a late summer storm, during which Josie's father has awakened the family to go downstairs and wait out the storm together. The description of the equinoctial storm is permeated by dream images that often seem surreal. Michael Kreyling asserts that Welty's "Dali-esque ... [image of] 'curtains ... like poured cream' ... direct[s] the story's shifting register from reality to dream ... [and that the surrealist imagery] signals that ... [Josie's] path into the life of the artist has already been taken" ("History and Imagination" 595). To Josie, "the stairway gave like a chain, the pendulum shivered in the clock." For her, it is a miniature descent into a dangerous underworld, when ordinary time is suspended, a world that excites her imagination. In the midst of the storm, Josie looks for an older girl who lives across the street. Josie's fast-beating heart is matched by the "pulse of the lightning," and her mental and physical awakening to the onset of adolescence is suggested by the throbbing light.

As the first section ends, the fitfully dozing girl dreams of the passing summer. She fantasizes about her slightly older neighbor, who has already reached the magic season of sexual maturity; yet she also holds on to the childhood represented by the dying summer. The language of this section is that of fairy tale and myth. Josie whispers, "I am thine eternally, my Queen," to the golden-haired Cornella, the enticing neighbor who has been "transformed by age" and who, to Josie, is as glamorous

as a fairy-tale princess. Section two opens with Josie's dual longing for the summer
gone by and for the future represented by Cornella. Her conflict is expressed in unsettling images of flying creatures that obscure her present vision, images that anticipate
those in the pivotal mirror scene of "The Burning," from Welty's *The Bride of
the Innisfallen and Other Stories*. Josie's bittersweet memory includes all the winged
creatures she has chased during the summer: "June-bugs, ... lightning-bugs, ...
butterflies, ... bees in a jar." But whatever Josie's sense of the present or coming
"tempest," of things "bitter" or "fierce," she welcomes the unknown future with open
hands. The similar, but more violent, images in "The Burning" symbolize the radical
change being wrought by the Civil War, for the South and for the slave Delilah. Thus,
a reader who knows the significance of such images in the later story will understand
their importance in "The Winds" for establishing the theme of violence that, in
Welty's fiction, usually threatens any life change, especially the move into sexual
maturity. Throughout her canon, Welty designs the outer structure of a narrative,
along with its supporting images, to reflect inner states of mind.

In section two, the rhythm of change increases, until Josie's mind moves several
times a page between past and present, dream and reality. Section three consists of
only three lines, illustrating the three separate worlds inhabited at the same moment
by Josie, her father, and her sleeping brother:

> "There! I thought you were asleep," said her father.
> She turned in her chair. The house had stirred.
> "Show me their tracks," muttered Will. "Just show me their tracks."

Josie remembers walking alone, one summer afternoon, through the park where
there was a Chinese dragon. She is brave enough to touch the stone dragon; but
then, against the dragon's curse, she calls on Cornella, who has become for her what
Ernst Cassirer calls a "momentary deity." "Every impression that man receives, every
wish that stirs in him, every hope that lures him can affect him thus religiously,"
Cassirer asserts. "Just let spontaneous feeling invest the object before him ... with an
air of holiness, and the momentary god has been experienced and created ... and for
only one subject whom it overwhelms and holds in thrall" (Cassirer 17–18). "Thou
art like the ripe corn, beautiful Cornella," Josie chants to her chosen deity. Later, as
she drags her shoe-box boat down the sidewalk, Josie invests Cornella with specific
mythic stature, imagining that Cornella might become a tree, as did the mythic
Daphne, to save herself from Apollo. The reader will better appreciate the significance
of this passage, in which stasis is chosen over the active pursuit of a possibly dangerous sexual adventure, in the light of the final vision of stasis versus action at the end
of the story.

Section eight, the structural center of the story, brings a complete stop to the
clamor of the storm and the images of the past. It is a still moment, as if her home
were in the eye of a hurricane. Will is still talking in his sleep; but their mother
shushes him and their father raises his hand and cautions the children to listen. Until

now, Josie's thoughts have alternated between present and past; but here the narrative dynamic changes, as she lies still and dreams of her future. It is not a new paragraph but only an ellipsis following the word "future" that signals the shift to section nine, when Josie imagines

> ... the sharp day when she would come running out of the field holding the ragged stems of the quick-picked goldenrod. ... When would the day come when the wind would fall and they would sit in silence on the fountain rim, their play done, and the boys would crack the nuts under their heels? If they would bring the time around once more, she would lose nothing that was given, she would hoard the nuts like a squirrel. (*Collected Stories* 219)

What one might notice first about this passage is its fast cadence, which then slows. From the previous still center of the story, the storyteller now moves to a new emotional dimension through what Northrop Frye calls "associative rhythms," such as "sound-links," "ambiguous sense-links," and "memory-links very like that of the dream." Characteristic of the lyric story, as in poetry, Frye asserts, such poetic rhythms are mostly "below the threshold of consciousness" (Frye 271–2). In the first few lines of the passage, the alliterative crackling of consonants and bits of rhyme in "sharp," "stems," "quick-picked," and "thrust" create sound-links that join with the present participles "running" and "bringing" to enhance the vision of enthusiastic movement. This positive sense, however, is soon undercut by the negative connotations, as well as the downbeat rhythms, of "fall," "silence," "done," "under," "lose," and "nothing." Modifying the whole are the rhythmic repetitions of soft and plaintive "w" and sibilant "s" sounds, especially in the clause "When would the day come when the wind would fall and they would sit in silence," in which the sonorous vowels of "would" and "come" enhance the vaguely ominous mood.

The goldenrod, which is the color of Cornella's hair but also a sense-link to the scepter, suggests that it is to this "momentary deity" that Josie would make an offering of flowers. In that future time, "when the wind would fall," the momentous change would be over; and Josie would be an adult who could "sit in silence" with her beloved. The last two sentences of the passage present adult options for her, through the ambiguous sense-links of nuts and squirrels. She could sit passively, in the face of male action of cracking nuts; or she could exert control by saving the nuts, thus preventing male violence against something she values. The passage is charged with sexual politics, and with tension between action and stasis.

At the end of section eleven, in which Josie asks to hold a fur muff (a sexual symbol also in "The Bride of the Innisfallen") that has been put away for the summer, her father gives her a kiss, which triggers a memory that suddenly seems crucial to her. It is an evening Chautauqua performance that Josie remembers, when Cornella is across the room, passionately listening to the music. Both girls are entranced by a young woman who plays a cornet. Josie's first reaction to the memory of that night is chagrin that she could have forgotten "what was closest of all." What follows is a delimiting narrative strategy that can educate the reader about possible meanings. It is neither Cornella nor the storm that is of greatest significance to Josie but, rather, her memory of an artist. Reflecting the story's theme of transition, the music of the trio of female Chautauqua musicians includes "a little transition to another key." When the cornetist plays a solo, Josie is as delighted as if "morning-glories had come out of the horn." The passage is charged not only with positive sexual images – of Josie's being "pierced with pleasure" by the phallic instrument of the cornetist and "the striving of the lips" – but also with negative cultural and narrative implications from the ideas of "stale ... expect[ations]" and "old shelter[s]." Heightening the association between the passionate artist (the cornetist) and Josie's current passion (Cornella) is the fact that Welty changed the trumpet in the earlier version of the story, entitled "Beautiful Ohio," to the cornet of "The Winds" (Mark, "Pierced with Pleasure" 109–10),[8] creating a sound-link between "Cornella" and "cornet" – perhaps a transition from one kind of passion to another. The cornetist herself is described in terms of a humming-bird, a term Welty often employs for her wanderer-artist characters, and which was the basis for the original title of "The Wanderers," the final story in *The Golden Apples*. Josie remembers that the cornetist and the traveling show of memory seemed to lead to "a destination [that was] being shown her." Thus, the memory helps Josie to re-invent the past in terms of what now seems most important and to put into perspective her changing life. On the dark sleeping-porch after the storm, it seems to Josie that "a proclamation had been made in the last high note of the lady trumpeteer." Now that she realizes "what was closest of all" about the summer, the "last high note" of a wandering artist may influence the way she responds to the second "sign" – in another kind of note – at the end of the story.

It is revealing to consider the final sections of the story in the light of Wright's idea of "final reticence," or what Lohafer calls "preclosure." Should Welty have ended "The Winds" after section thirteen, it would have been a far different story. In this brief section, two claps of thunder bracket the father's clapping of his hands. He then declares, "It's over," essentially performing a god-like calming of the storm: "From then on there was only the calm steady falling of rain." Accordingly, the repeated trochees in "only," "steady," and "falling" effect the rhythm of a downbeat. But although Josie's parents might think she is sleeping, in section fourteen she is actually thinking of Cornella, of the lady cornetist's lips, and of "all that was wild and beloved and estranged, and all that would beckon and leave her, and all that was beautiful." Josie is determined to follow wherever they lead. Had the story ended here, the curve of emotion would reflect female openness and anticipation. Poetic scansion of these sentences reveals a wild mixture of predominately upbeat iambs and dancing trisyllabic metric feet, for example, "outside/was all/that was wild/and beloved/and estranged." Yet both of these "false endings," which are feasible options, prepare the reader's expectations, only to have them altered by the actual closure. In fact, they do the reader a service. As Lohafer explains, "It's a common strategy. The false ending highlights the true ending, isolating what we mean by resolution, by fulfillment of design, by the achievement of a vantage point from which the whole story reveals its contour and point."[9]

In the final section it is morning, but the night has left a mysterious second sign for Josie to find: a fragmentary note with the name Cornella on it, including the message: "O my darling ... when are you coming for me?" This ending so mystified early readers that Welty, "astonished," explained it to her agent: "Maybe by its coming exactly at the end, it acquired a special obscurity. I wanted it to balance the whole story ... (which concerned the commonplace & specified longing & grief to come)" (Kreyling, *Author and Agent* 70). Thus, the actual closure brings neither the reassurance of a child's security in her family nor the unchecked, promiscuous joy of youthful anticipation. Instead, it offers a cautionary note. Both positive and negative images in the story's closure attest to the reality of an ordinary day, which is full of signs for one who can see: a sunny day but, after the storm, bedraggled leaves on the trees. Neither has human nature changed, for her brother is still "digging in his old hole to China." Josie's coming of age is affirmed, but in troubling images. Cornella's house now "looked as if its old age had come upon it at last." The most important sign, the note, suggests the possibility that Cornella's future life could read like what Nancy K. Miller calls, in the eighteenth-century novel, a "heroine's text";[10] thus, it offers Josie an altered – less enticing – view of Cornella, as a heroine who waits passively for a hero, who may not come, or if he comes may expect her to accept a prescribed role. The reader should heed two details that limit critical interpretation of the story: that Josie's memory of the cornetist supersedes, in her mind, that of Cornella; and that the memory includes Josie's sense that her coming of age means that waiting is over. The curve of Josie's emotion – rising and falling, racing and pausing, as she heeds and selects from her memory – has decreed the aesthetic structure of the story.

The Voice of the Storyteller in "Music from Spain"

The lyric voice of the storyteller often connects with the aesthetic structure of the short story through narrative frames, in which there are tellers and listeners, and sometimes stories within stories. The short story corresponds to the ancient lyric – the song of one singer (one lyre) – as the teller corresponds to that very subjective ancient singer. Crucial to the short story's form and content is its focus on the very nature of storytelling and, thus, on the voice of the one who tells: who stands apart, observes, and "sings." Frank O'Connor has famously described this teller as "the lonely voice" in his book of that title. Elizabeth Bowen imagines the storyteller on a "stage which, inwardly, every man is conscious of occupying alone." Wendell Harris notes that the short story's essence is "to portray the individual person, or moment, or scene in isolation ... [and is thus] the natural vehicle for the presentation of the outsider, but also for the moment whose intensity makes it seem outside the ordinary stream of time ... or outside our ordinary range of experience." Welty, who creates both outsider characters and extraordinary moments, explains the organic connection between the alienated speaker (content) and narrative obstruction (style), in her comments on

Hemingway's "Indian Camp": Hemingway's "obscuring and at the same time reveal-ing" use of dialogue in the story, she says, is the result of his wishing to show that "something is broken in two; language slips, meets a barrier, a shadow is inserted between the speakers."[11]

In spite of the ancient concepts of lyric (subjective) and dramatic (objective) modes as separate and distinct, and of Welty's belief that a short story usually is lyrical, she also sees story writing in terms of drama; and, indeed, her fiction is often adapted for stage or film.[12] She achieves a confluence of the lyric and the dramatic in many ways, in both short stories and novels, especially through the lonely voice of the outsider. Some of these lonely voices are the first-person narrators of "Why I Live at the P.O.," "Circe," and *The Ponder Heart*; others are the multiple voices in near-total dialogue narratives, such as "Lily Daw and the Three Ladies," "Petrified Man," "Powerhouse," and *Losing Battles*. In "Shower of Gold," Katie Rainey, although an emotional outsider in her community, supplies a communal point of view that has an effect similar to that of the first-person-plural narrator in Faulkner's "A Rose for Emily." Some narra-tive voices are presented more obliquely, as in "The Winds," through a character's thoughts, dreams, or memories. Characters isolated in unusual ways, such as deaf-mutes in "The Key" and "First Love," result in the creation of some of Welty's most "obstructionist" narratives. Noel Polk observes that the narrative voice in "Old Mr. Marblehall," who lives a double life as Mr. Bird, "moves freely and fluidly in to and out of Marblehall's mind in ways that make it difficult to determine the story's point of view" (Polk 557). As several scholars have shown, clearly one of Welty's major subjects, which in large part determines her style, is the nature of storytelling, and of communication – that is, of language and limits – between characters, as well as between artist and reader.[13]

"Music from Spain" (*Collected Stories* 393–426) is a major story in *The Golden Apples*, a volume united by, among other devices, the imagery of language and limits, of walls and other barriers.[14] In this story, Eugene MacLain spends a day wandering through San Francisco in the company of a Spanish guitarist with red fingernails. Neither speaks the other's language, whether it is the difference between English and Spanish or, as Rebecca Mark believes, "the difference between the language of the dominant conventional culture and the language of the artist – between the language of society and the language of love" (Mark, *Dragon's Blood* 222).[15] Yet the language barrier does not hinder a companionship that helps each man through a personal crisis during the day. The dual protagonists have in common the facts that neither is native to San Francisco, that each has slapped a woman that morning and then ventured alone into the city, and that each has a secret he cannot share. Ironically, Eugene, a native Mis-sissippian, who has lived in San Francisco for years, does not at first perceive a con-nection to the foreigner. The story of Eugene and the Spaniard is told by an ostensibly third-person narrator, who nonetheless most often sees through Eugene's eyes. That story is framed by the story of Eugene and Emma, told by a triple combination of third-person narrator, limited point-of-view narrator, and Eugene's unmediated thoughts and verbalizations. That, in turn, is framed by the story of Eugene in the context of family and community in Mississippi, told by a variety of tellers in the surrounding stories of *The Golden Apples*.

Of that larger story, which includes the exploits of Eugene's wandering Aengus-like, father, King MacLain, who is continually searching for Yeats's "golden apples of the sun," a few telling glimpses are seen here. And indeed, the evocations of Mississippi are not peripheral to the story. Eugene, in fact, is a pale version of his father; and he is emotionally scarred by the notoriety accorded the elder MacLain in the Mississippi town Morgana. The difference seems to be that King ran toward the world and life, while Eugene has been running away. He is in some ways like the protagonist in Welty's "Old Mr. Marblehall," whom Polk has compared with Poe's alienated "Man of the Crowd," and with Henry James's John Marcher, who is "waiting for experience, meaning, significance, to fall on him from somewhere else," and with T. S. Eliot's J. Alfred Prufrock, who is "afraid to assert himself against his own meaninglessness" (Polk 557, 564).

After a year's unexpressed, thus unshared, pain over their child's death, Eugene has unaccountably slapped his wife, Emma, at the breakfast table. The visibly structured story of seven sections follows Eugene from his front door "down ... the street like the sag of a rope that disappeared into fog; then through the city, up into the hills, and back home." As he walks, Eugene recognizes the artist he and Emma had seen in concert the previous night; and the mutual adventure of the two men begins when he pulls the Spaniard out of harm's way on a busy street. It may have been the only heroic thing he has ever done, as the man's imminent danger is a transforming moment, when "a gate opened to Eugene ... [and he] sprang forward as if to protect his own." Actually, the impetus for the adventure may have begun during the guitarist's performance the previous night, when the music had engendered in Eugene "a deep lull in his spirit. ... He felt a lapse ... in some visit to a vast present-time." The memory of this experience the next morning causes him to decide that he cannot go, as usual, to his job as a watch repairman.

Section IV, the center of the story, comes at noon, when the two men have an extravagant lunch and then resume their odyssey, climbing to up the cliffs at Land's End. They seem to be enjoying the day; yet negative images begin to accumulate, including the accidental death of a pedestrian. As they walk, Eugene reexamines his relationship with Emma, blaming her for the death of their little daughter, Fan. Welty's narrative never enters the mind of the Spaniard, and he speaks only one word to Eugene: "*Mariposa*," identifying a wild lily by the Spanish word, which means butterfly, but also is a common term for a gay man. Eugene's voice is heard through the feelings he expresses aloud and those expressed silently in his thoughts; in fact, the repetition of "Eugene felt" or "He felt" happens so often that a dramatization of the story was at first presented with the title "He felt."[16] Thus the story demonstrates Welty's idea that the writer "can never stop trying to make feeling felt" (*Eye of the Story* 105). Eugene's self-dialogue begins with the morning's slapping incident and slowly works back to the cause of his pain. He wonders why he has struck Emma. But then, in an italicized passage, he argues with himself: "*Why not strike her? And if she thought he would stay around only to hear her start tuning up, she had another think coming."* This more strident voice reveals not only a different scenario but a different, submerged, persona – one that aspires to a more forthright, if clichéd, mode of expression. The relationship between Eugene and Emma, who was previously his boarding-house landlady, is suggested when Eugene thinks, "If he had wanted to kill her, he would have had to eat everything on her table first, and praise it." For Eugene, the slap has seemed like "kissing the cheek of the dead," because their common mourning for their child had estranged them. It is not until section V that Eugene can articulate his specific grievance: "Your little girl ... said, 'Mama, my throat hurts me,' and she was dead in three days. You expected her mother would watch a fever, while you were at the office. ... But you never spoke of it, did you?"

Several voices across the city contribute to the story's theme of barriers or divisiveness, versus ways of escape or openness. Walking by a bar, Eugene hears, *"Open the door, Richard!"* The streetcar conductor shouts "Divisadero!" The ordinarily comforting sight of fire escapes – everywhere in San Francisco since the Great Fire – through associational logic morph into images of entrapment, which cause him to pause outside the bar, to hear again the song about openings. The song brings a memory of music from back home in Mississippi. This older memory and his next recollection of his present crisis in which he has struck his wife, together with his identification with "a sprawled old winehead sleeping up here far away from his kind," all combine to prompt an emotional crisis – a feeling of "secret tenderness toward his twin, Ran MacLain, whom he had not seen for half his life. ... Was all well with Ran? ... For ... he might have done some reprehensible thing." Eugene "half fainted upon the body of the city, the old veins, the mottled skin of pavement. Perhaps the soft grass in which little daisies opened would hold his temples and put its eyes to his." Here is another realistic image that transforms itself into a lyric one: a surrealistic image of city streets personified as an older (lover's? father's?) body that Eugene imagines holding him as he faints. But it is also a psychologically realistic mind-link with his twin, who, in "The Whole World Knows," actually does a reprehensible thing. Not to be ignored are the several references to "half" things ("half his life," "half fainted," "half-lifted across the street"), which suggest the loss incurred by separating twins, but also the possibility that he has lived a sort of half-life since his self-exile to San Francisco. That this is the low point in Eugene's day is confirmed by the death wish at the end of the passage, for the grass and daisies are imagined as covering and pressing down on him, as if he were in the grave. Carey Wall also sees him dealing with death in this story: "Eugene MacLain enters the season of dying," Wall says, "[He] assimilates his daughter Fan's death ... as a part of his own death ... [which, however, is also] to assimilate her love of life. ... When the Spaniard whirls him about at Land's End, he and Eugene retrieve the child in Eugene ... [and] life is validated within the inevitable movement toward death" (Wall 103).

The crisis will pass quickly for Eugene, much as it does for Mrs. Larkin in "A Curtain of Green," at the touch of rain. But Eugene has the additional touch of the Spaniard, who, acting the part of the parent/lover, "patted him and straightened him up. ... And rain fell on them." Then, as he and the Spaniard climb over rocks and look out over the sea in a beating wind, Eugene remembers a recurring dream, in which he is in bed with a sleeping Emma. In his dream he seems to be trying to swallow the huge stem of a cherry. This passage and the succeeding one, in which the Spaniard holds Eugene up in the air, combine to precipitate the moment outside of time that brings relief for both men. The dream's phallic image of the huge and growing stem in Eugene's mouth, together with the exhilaration of the men at the edge of the cliffs, has prompted several readings that demonstrate sensual/sexual content. "This is Eugene's real homecoming," Mark says, "his discovery of his own body, his own sexuality, and his release from social convention. ... Eugene thinks 'My dear love comes,' and the Spaniard makes a loud emotional cry." (*Dragon's Blood* 225–6). Mortimer, while acknowledging the sensual content, also sees Eugene's Perseus-like wrestling with the Minotaur-like Spaniard as occasion for Eugene's regeneration (*Daughter of the Swan* 102).[17]

However, another part of the sensual content of the dream is Eugene's feeling that he has "the world on his tongue." This image of a round object on the tongue recalls Welty's description of a very sensual connection she made as a child between herself, the natural world, and words to describe that world. It is the moon she remembers in *One Writer's Beginnings*: "The word 'moon' came into my mouth as though fed me out of a silver spoon. Held in my mouth the moon became a word. It had the round-ness of a Concord grape Grandpa took off his vine and gave me to suck out of its skin and swallow whole, in Ohio" (10). Until his hilltop exultation, it has been only in dreams that Eugene has experienced sensual passion; in this dream, Welty has given him the tactile vision of a budding artist.

For a moment, at least, Eugene finds relief in self-expression – to a stranger on the cliff; but the Spaniard himself remains a mystery. Eugene has realized that the guitar-ist's seeming detachment during last night's concert was only "the outer semblance of passion." Now, as he lights a cigarette on the cliff overlooking the Pacific Ocean, the Spaniard's face muscles "grouped themselves in hideous luxuriousness"; and in the midst of images like those describing the passionate jazz musician in Welty's "Powerhouse," the guitarist erupts in "a terrible recital": "a bullish roar opened out of him." Eugene, who has never spoken of his own sorrow, is astonished at "a man laying himself altogether bare like that." Yet the passage suggests a profound link between the two men: they share the very human traits not only of repressed passion, but also of doubleness, such that they seem almost alter egos, or mirror images, in terms of passion and control in their lives. The guitarist pours his passion into his music, but in a highly controlled fashion; whereas Eugene, who spends his days regu-lating clock time, manages his emotions in a way that David Kaplan has identified as "silent outbursts [which] occur in Eudora Welty's fiction when a character's impulse to strong expression is checked by circumstances that make such expression impossible."[18] In other words, they are safely voiced in the text as narrated thoughts, or either in words spoken to himself or to one who cannot possibly understand him. Eugene's astonishment comes from his own lifelong inability to "lay bare" the desires of his heart, much less pursue them passionately, as does the Spanish guitarist. At last, after the Spaniard is "flung out at [him], like the apples of Atalanta," he becomes both the storyteller and his own listener; and he achieves a purging oral outburst. The Spaniard has also shown him how to express joy, but he cannot sustain it. The story ends not in this moment of expansive openness, but back in Eugene and Emma's upstairs apartment, where nothing has changed. His extraordinary experience goes unnoticed, except for his missing hat. The final, overriding, image is not of a sensual experience for Eugene but, rather, of his sitting meekly at the kitchen table, listening to his wife and Mrs. Herring, and watching Emma "pop the grapes in." "Music from Spain" is a major reason Thomas J. McHaney calls *The Golden Apples* "Eudora Welty's chronicle of human longing" (113).

Welty employs the lyric/realistic technique in both short stories and novels, as I have argued elsewhere ("Lyric Novelist" 29–31). Especially in the works of her maturity, this technique contributes to the aesthetic structure of a story: delineating, through visible images that relate to inner states, the curve of emotion that is traversed by a character who is in some way an outsider, and who is often outside of ordinary time. The voice of the storyteller, as it rises and falls with that curve, and with the corresponding environment and terrain of outer reality, defines the shape of the story. In her essay "Words into Fiction," Welty says, rather mysteriously, about fiction in general, "The words follow the contours of some continuous relationship between what can be told and what cannot be told" (*Eye of the Story* 143–4). Understanding the techniques of lyrical realism, aesthetic structure, and the storyteller's many voices enables the reader to negotiate the barriers of Welty's narrative obstructions and sense the true aesthetic shape of the story. Neither is it beside the point to remember that, whether in fiction or non-fiction, Welty is always writing about the artistic process and the passionate artist as outside observer of the world.

NOTES

1   For accounts of Welty's publishing history, see Noel Polk, *Eudora Welty: A Bibliography of Her Work* (Jackson: University Press of Mississippi, 1994); Suzanne Marrs, *The Welty Collection: A Guide to the Eudora Welty Manuscripts and Documents at the Mississippi Department of Archives and History* (Jackson: University Press of Mississippi, 1988); and Michael Kreyling, *Author and Agent*.

2   Lohafer, "Introduction to Part I." In Lohafer and Clarey, eds., *Short Story Theory at a Crossroads*, 3.

3   Quoted in May (51). For an examination of the confluence between Welty and Chekhov, see Jan Nordby Gretlund, *Eudora Welty's Aes-*

thetics of Place (1994; rpt. Columbia: University of South Carolina Press, 1997).

4   See especially her *One Time, One Place* (New York: Random House, 1971) and *Photographs* (Jackson: University Press of Mississippi, 1989).

5   Schmidt (57–8) sees in this image "a profoundly threatening vision of the female body – especially its genitalia – as a devouring landscape." He also notes that Howard's sense of time is artificial, while Marjorie's is "associated with her biorhythms." See also Weston, *Gothic Traditions*, for a book-length study of Welty's images of entrapment and relevant narrative techniques.

6 Or is the murder imagined, as was the earlier violence? See Kreyling, "Modernism in Welty's *A Curtain of Green*," in Turner and Harding, eds., *Critical Essays*, 24.

7 For an extended analysis of Welty's narrative reticence and altered story expectations in her final collection, see Weston, "Reticent Beauty," 42–58.

8 Mark sees in "The Winds" "not a tale of choice but a story of female sexual fulfillment and power embodied in both of Josie's muses, the cornetist and Cornella."

9 Lohafer, "Preclosure and Story Processing," in Lohafer and Clarey, eds., *Critical Essays*, 249.

10 Miller, *The Heroine's Text: Readings in the French and English Novel, 1722–1782* (New York: Columbia University Press, 1980), x. Miller defines "the heroine's text ... [as] a locus of commonplaces about woman's identity and woman's place ... [and thus] the inscription of a female destiny."

11 Bowen, quoted in May (123) (ellipses May's); Harris, quoted in May (13–14); *Eye of the Story*, 90.

12 *Eye of the Story*, 108; Prenshaw, ed., *More Conversations*, 77. Dramatizations include the Broadway production of *The Ponder Heart* in 1956 and a recent PBS movie version of it, as well as stage and film versions of many other stories.

13 See, for example, Pollack, "Words Between Strangers"; and Merrill Maguire Skaggs, "Eudora Welty's 'I' of Memory," in Turner and Harding, eds., *Critical Essays*, 153–65.

14 See Kreyling, *Welty's Achievement of Order*, 77–105, for an analysis of the organic integrity of *The Golden Apples*.

15 Mark links this passage with one in Joyce's *Ulysses* on the topic of Spanish passion.

16 "He felt ..." was first staged as a work in progress for the Eudora Welty Society at the American Literature Association conference in San Francisco, in May 2004, starring Brenda Currin and Phil Fortenberry, directed by David Kaplan. A complete version of the show was performed at the 92nd Street Y in New York City, April 11, 2005, under the title of "A Fire Was In My Head."

17 Pitavy-Souques, in "Technique as Myth," 258–68, has brilliantly shown that *The Golden Apples* as a whole is framed, and given shape and perspective, by both Celtic and Greek myth, especially the Perseus story.

18 Kaplan, "Silent Outbursts and Silenced Outbursts in Eudora Welty's Fiction." Unpublished paper, n.d. (2004). Kaplan is an independent theatre director and writer (see *Eye of the Story* 105).

REFERENCES AND FURTHER READING

Cassirer, Ernst. *Language and Myth*. Trans. Susanne K. Langer. 1946. Rpt. New York: Dover, 1953.

Frye, Northrop. *Anatomy of Criticism: Four Essays*. 1957. Rpt. Princeton: Princeton University Press, 1990.

Joyce, James. *A Portrait of the Artist as a Young Man*. 1916. Rpt. in *"A Portrait of the Artist as a Young Man": Text, Criticism and Notes*. Ed. Chester G. Anderson. Viking Critical Library. New York: Viking Penguin, 1968.

Kreyling, Michael. *Eudora Welty's Achievement of Order*. Baton Rouge: Louisiana State University Press, 1980.

———. *Author and Agent: Eudora Welty and Diarmuid Russell*. New York: Farrar, Straus & Giroux, 1991.

———. "History and Imagination: Writing 'The Winds.'" *Mississippi Quarterly* 50 (1997): 585–99.

Lohafer, Susan, and Jo Ellyn Clarey, eds. *Short Story Theory at a Crossroads*. Baton Rouge: Louisiana State University Press, 1989.

McHaney, Thomas L. "Eudora Welty and the Multitudinous Golden Apples." 1973. Rpt. in Turner and Harding, eds., *Critical Essays*, 113–41.

Mark, Rebecca. *The Dragon's Blood: Feminist Intertextuality in Eudora Welty's "The Golden Apples."* Jackson: University Press of Mississippi, 1994.

———. "Pierced with Pleasure for the Girls: Eudora Welty's 'The Winds,'" *Journal of Contemporary Thought* 7 (1997): 107–22.

May, Charles E. *The Short Story: The Reality of Artifice*. Studies in Literary Themes and Genres, 4.
New York: Twayne, 1995.

Mortimer, Gail L. *Daughter of the Swan: Love and
Knowledge in Eudora Welty's Fiction*. Athens: University of Georgia Press, 1994.

O'Connor, Frank. *The Lonely Voice: A Study of the
Short Story*. 1963. Rpt. New York: Harper
Colophon, 1985.

Pitavy-Souques, Danièle. "A Blazing Butterfly:
The Modernity of Eudora Welty." *Mississippi
Quarterly* 39 (1986): 537–60.

———. "Technique as Myth: The Structure of *The
Golden Apples*." *Eudora Welty: Critical Essays*. Ed.
Peggy Whitman Prenshaw. Jackson: University
Press of Mississippi, 1979. 258–68.

Polk, Noel. "Welty, Hawthorne, and Poe: Men of
the Crowd and the Landscape of Alienation."
Mississippi Quarterly 50 (1997): 553–65.

Pollack, Harriet. "Words Between Strangers: On
Welty, Her Style, and Her Audience." *Mississippi Quarterly* 39 (1986): 481–505.

Pollack, Harriet, and Suzanne Marrs, eds. *Eudora
Welty and Politics: Did the Writer Crusade?* Baton
Rouge: Louisiana State University Press, 2001.

Prenshaw, Peggy Whitman, ed. *Conversations with
Eudora Welty*. 1984. Rpt. Jackson: University
Press of Mississippi, 1998.

———. *More Conversations with Eudora Welty*.
Jackson: University Press of Mississippi, 1996.

Schmidt, Peter. *The Heart of the Story: Eudora
Welty's Short Fiction*. Jackson: University of
Mississippi Press, 1991.

Turner, W. Craig, and Lee Emling Harding, eds.
Critical Essays on Eudora Welty. Boston: G. K.
Hall, 1989.

Vande Kieft, Ruth M. "Further Reflections on
Meaning in Eudora Welty's Fiction." 1982.
Rpt. in Turner and Harding, eds., *Critical
Essays*, 296–309.

Wall, Carey. "Collective Life, Liminality and
Sexuality in Welty's *The Golden Apples*; or
Out-of-Individuality Sexual Work." *Journal of
Contemporary Thought* 7 (1997): 91–106.

Warren, Robert Penn. "The Love and the Separateness in Miss Welty." 1944. Rpt. in Turner and
Harding, eds., *Critical Essays*, 42–51.

Welty, Eudora. *The Collected Stories of Eudora Welty*.
New York: Harcourt Brace Jovanovich, 1980.

———. *The Eye of the Story: Selected Essays and
Reviews*. New York: Random House, 1978.

———. *One Writer's Beginnings*. Cambridge, MA:
Harvard University Press, 1984.

Weston, Ruth D. "Eudora Welty as Lyric Novel-
ist: The Long and the Short of It." *The Late
Novels of Eudora Welty*. Eds. Jan Nordby
Gretlund and Karl-Heinz Westarp. Columbia:
University of South Carolina Press, 1998.
29–40.

———. *Gothic Traditions and Narrative Techniques
in the Fiction of Eudora Welty*. Baton Rouge:
Louisiana State University Press, 1994.

———. "Intimacy Between Strangers: The
Sensual Texts of Eudora Welty." *Journal of
Contemporary Thought* 7 (1997): 79–89.

———. "Reticent Beauty and Promiscuous Joy:
Textual Framing in Eudora Welty's *The Bride of
the Innisfallen and Other Stories*." *Southern Literary
Journal* 32 (2000): 42–58.

Wright, Austin M. "Recalcitrance in the Short
Story." In Lohafer and Clarey, eds. *Short Story
Theory*, 115–29.

19

The Short Stories of F. Scott Fitzgerald: Structure, Narrative Technique, Style

Kirk Curnutt

It has become something of an unfortunate obligation when writing about the 160-plus short stories that F. Scott Fitzgerald published during his lifetime to acknowledge his tenuous place in the canon of American short fiction. Although "Babylon Revisited" (1931) is a staple of high-school and undergraduate anthologies, and while the expired copyrights on his earliest and most popular tales have resulted in a slew of new editions of *Flappers and Philosophers* (1920) and *Tales of the Jazz Age* (1922), Fitzgerald remains at best a tangential presence in most histories of the form. From Henry Seidel Canby and Alfred Dashiell's *A History of the Short Story* (1935) through Austin Wright's *The American Short Story in the Twenties* (1961) to Arthur Voss's *The American Short Story: A Critical Survey* (1973) and, most recently, Charles E. May's *Short Story Writers* (2008), he either goes unmentioned entirely or is referenced as a counterpoint to Ernest Hemingway's more central contributions to the genre's development. This is not to deny, of course, that there have been excellent full-length examinations of Fitzgerald's stories. Alice Hall Petry's *Fitzgerald's Craft of Short Fiction* (1989) and Bryant Mangum's *A Fortune Yet: Money and Art in the Short Stories of F. Scott Fitzgerald* (1991) are but two sterling examples of the nuanced thematic analysis that the short fiction can inspire, while collections such as Jackson R. Bryer's two volumes on neglected efforts (1982, 1996) rightfully remind us that "Babylon" is by no means his lone tale to reward repeated close readings. Unfortunately, however, the influence of these secondary sources tends to resonate most loudly in the rather circumscribed world of Fitzgerald studies and not necessarily among short-story historians and theorists. As a result, what the late Matthew J. Bruccoli wrote in the introduction to *The Short Stories of F. Scott Fitzgerald: A New Collection* (1989) is as true today for genre specialists as it was twenty years ago for authorial enthusiasts: "F. Scott Fitzgerald's short stories remain a misunderstood and underrated aspect of his career" (xiii).

The reasons for this perpetual undervaluing are many. For starters, a mere forty-six of Fitzgerald's stories were collected in book form before his 1940 death, the other two-thirds of his output left to languish for decades in periodicals like the *Saturday Evening Post* that, however originally popular at newsstands and via subscription, were far too ephemeral a medium upon which to build a critical reputation. Additionally, as Martin Scofield adds, "None of the [four] short story collections" that Fitzgerald did publish during his lifetime – the other two are *All the Sad Young Men* (1926) and *Taps at Reveille* (1935) – "as a whole is as significant as his achievement in the genre of the novel, particularly his masterpiece, *The Great Gatsby* (1925)" (150). As far as the American short story goes, this reality puts Fitzgerald at a distinct disadvantage to contemporaries such as Sherwood Anderson, none of whose longer works can hold a candle to *Winesburg, Ohio* (1919). This same is arguably true of Hemingway, whose *In Our Time* (1925), to many critics, packs a more concise, dramatic punch than either *A Farewell to Arms* (1929) or *For Whom the Bell Tolls* (1940). Then there is the problem of Fitzgerald's own dismissive attitude toward his short fiction. Even a cursory reading of his correspondence reveals the constancy of his derogatory comments, most famously his claim to Hemingway that his economic dependency on the *Post* rendered him a prostitute – albeit one handsomely paid several grand per turn (*Life in Letters* 169). Nor has his habit of mining passages from stories that earned such extravagant sums for use in his novels helped matters. *Tender Is the Night* (1934), for example, contains "strippings" from more than three dozen stories, from 1922's "The Popular Girl" to 1933's "I Got Shoes." Except for a handful, these rifled efforts rank among Fitzgerald's most critically ignored, in large part because their reputation as workshop exercises for the long-delayed follow-up to *Gatsby* have tainted perceptions of any intrinsic merit they might possess.

These debilities are well known and have been attributed to the author's belief that while the novel was the medium in which he must make his critical reputation, the short story was good for little more than paying his bills. Yet there is a larger if less acknowledged reason why Fitzgerald is relatively marginalized: in such decisive criteria as structure and form, narrative perspective, and style, his short fiction simply does not fit the paradigm of the modernist short story as it has traditionally been constructed. As Dominic Head argues, several parallels between the attributes of the defining artistic movement of the early twentieth century and the formal properties of the short story made the genre especially attractive to European and American writers, from James Joyce, Virginia Woolf, and Katherine Mansfield to Hemingway, William Faulkner, and Katherine Anne Porter. First, the constricted space of short fiction appealed to the modernist desire to intensify drama through techniques of foregrounding – what Head calls "the cultivation of expression through form" (7) – that do away with exposition and immerse the reader in narrative immediacy. Additionally, the genre facilitated modernists' interest in breaking the requisites of the well-developed plot by abandoning the obligatory temporality of narrative sequence in favor of a spatiality that Joseph Franks has compared to that of the plastic arts (60). The modernist reliance upon figural patterns and motifs to convey thematic significance provides a third point of comparison, for "the short form often implies the typicality of a specific episode, while narrative limitation demands oblique expression through image and symbol" (Head 7). Finally, while a great deal of short-story theory reiterates Edgar Allan Poe's claim that short fiction is superior to the novel in its ability to enable a "unity of effect or impression" (570–1), Head makes a persuasive case that its brevity actually encouraged the modernist preference for fragmentation and discontinuity. While his paradigmatic example is Mansfield's "Bliss" (1918), one can nominate a range of contemporaneous American authors who defy the organicism presumed by Poe's definition: aside from Hemingway, Faulkner, and Porter, one thinks of Gertrude Stein, Djuna Barnes, and Jean Toomer, to name but one eclectic trio.

The contiguities that Head discusses are by no means the only ones shared by modernism and the short story. What is striking from even a basic overview of his study, however, is how absolutely inapplicable the characteristics he outlines are to Fitzgerald's short fiction. Whereas the canonical modernist story tends to eschew plot, even Fitzgerald's most famous ones – "Babylon Revisited" is a prime example – are constructed according to the classical Aristotelian structure that begins with complicating action, rises to a climax, and ends with a denouement. And while modernists developed innovative points of view to convey new theories of phenomenology (stream of consciousness, most famously), Fitzgerald was prone to that most grievous storytelling foible of post-Flaubertian prose, the omniscient narrator. Finally, while many modernists disparaged emotion, arguing that feeling corrupted art by appealing to the sentimentality with which the mass market supposedly pandered to general readers, Fitzgerald's Romantic affinities inspired a propensity for lyric expressionism whose central tenet was its lush appeal to pathos. Compared to experimental writers who forged their reputations in obscure but influential literary magazines such as the *Little Review, Transatlantic Review,* and *transition*, Fitzgerald's stories cannot help seeming a bit old-fashioned. This putative traditionalism is especially intriguing given that his themes generally address mainline modernist concerns: like his peers, Fitzgerald was fascinated with the psychological displacement of expatriation, with Freudian neuroses and the relationship between dreams and reality, and the ruptures of historical change that the Great War imposed upon his generation.

And yet one senses that the differences that distinguish self-consciously modern short fiction from the popular marketplace for which Fitzgerald wrote are as much a matter of degree as of kind. Even the most abbreviated of modernist stories, for example, has a plot. However compressed, the interchapters of Hemingway's *In Our Time* still revolve around a central dramatic action, be it the wounding of Nick Adams, the execution of the King of Hungary, or the hanging of Sam Cardinella. As such, each fragment is more akin to a traditional story than to the verbal statuary of imagistic poems such as Ezra Pound's "In a Station of the Metro" or William Carlos Williams's "The Red Wheelbarrow." Similarly, to whatever degree modernists might preach against the intrusive narrative garrulity of nineteenth-century predecessors such as Nathaniel Hawthorne or Herman Melville, it was not unheard of for some of them – Woolf in particular – to resort to omniscience to evoke a communal sensibility

(Levitt 99–100). Finally, despite the sneers of modernists toward sentimentality, the type of intricately cadenced, exclamatory passages that signal the rhapsodic climax of "Winter Dreams" (1922) has its counterpart in Joyce's "The Dead" (1914), Porter's "Flowering Judas" (1931) or Faulkner's "Delta Autumn" (1942) – in such examples, the emotion simply unfurls within devices that represent the inner workings of an agonized mind instead of directly addressing the audience. Because Fitzgerald's characteristic habits of structure, perspective, and style are nowhere near as different from his contemporaries' as critics have traditionally assumed, his stories allow us to qualify the conventional definition of the modernist short story while suggesting the ways in which his short fiction is more modernistic than heretofore recognized.

Structure, Form, Plot

According to Bruccoli, Fitzgerald proved a prolific story writer because "his best story ideas came to him as complete structures, and by writing them in concentrated bursts of effort, he was able to preserve the spontaneity of the narrative" (*Epic Grandeur* 131). The author's term for structure was "jump," as in the "three-jump story," a reference not to any tripartite division within the plot but to the number of successive days a good effort should take to complete. (It is a sign of Fitzgerald's flippancy toward his stories that early in his career he liked to brag about how quickly he could churn them out, such as the single day required by "The Camel's Back" or the lone night spent on "The Four Fists" [both 1920]. He would later regret such boasts when they earned him a reputation as a "facile" writer.) But while Fitzgerald was apt to measure the unity of a story according to the time required to realize it, one could argue that his proficiency was enabled by his savvy use of a basic story structure that has come to be known as Freytag's Pyramid. Named after German novelist Gustav Freytag (1816–95), the form expands upon the terminology Aristotle defined in *Poetics* (335 BCE) to prescribe the five basic parts of a plot: exposition, rising action, climax, falling action, and denouement. Freytag proposed his model in his study *Technique of the Drama* (1863, translated into English in 1895), intending it for use in understanding the unity of classical drama. Despite its utter inapplicability to modern literature (something Freytag himself admitted), the schema had been widely adapted by the 1920s to illustrate the internal cohesion of a range of narrative prose forms, including the short story. Several story-writing handbooks of the 1920s offer variations on Freytag, often without explicitly acknowledging their debt, while advising tyros on how to produce salable short fiction. There was good reason for their emphasis on the pyramidal arrangement: the high-circulation "slicks" that paid the best showed a marked preference for short fiction with a clear-cut climax and definitive conclusions. For litterateurs, the market's fondness for well-wrought plot meant that form had eroded into formula. As early as 1915, Henry Seidel Canby alluded to Freytag when complaining of the predictable structure into which short fiction had devolved, specifically singling out for attack the complicating action that will "move, move, move furiously, each action and every speech pointing directly toward the unknown climax" and the "last suspiration … sometimes a smart epigram, according to the style of the story or the 'line' expected from the author" (61). A decade and a half later, Edward J. O'Brien, editor of the influential *Best Short Stories* series from 1915 to 1941 and an early supporter of Hemingway, likewise dismissed the prefabricated story arc in *The Dance of the Machines: The American Short Story and the Industrial Age* (1929), a highly idiosyncratic polemic that links the popularity of the five-part plot to the contemporaneous rage for standardization and efficiency.

Correspondence reveals that Fitzgerald was familiar with Freytag. While hospitalized in 1930 at Les Rives de Prangins in Nyon, Switzerland, Zelda Fitzgerald requested that Scott send her their copy of *Technique of the Drama* so she might overcome uncertainties of form in her own attempts at writing (*Dear Scott, Dearest Zelda* 83). Fitzgerald most likely did not study Freytag during *his* apprenticeship a decade earlier, but he did scrutinize popular periodical fiction, most notably that of the *Saturday Evening Post*. For a dispiriting six months in early 1919, during a period of estrangement from his future wife, while living in New York City and eking out a meager existence as an advertising copywriter, he collected what he later claimed were some 122 rejection slips (Bruccoli 111). His initial breakthrough came not with the *Post* but with H. L. Mencken and George Jean Nathan's *The Smart Set*, a chic, tart-tongued magazine for sophisticates that purchased five stories between September 1919 and February 1920. The range of craft within this quintet suggests how thoroughly Fitzgerald had absorbed the structure that Canby dismissed for making "the means of telling the story fit the ends of story-telling as neatly as hook fits eye" (62). The initial two – "Babes in the Woods" and "The Debutante" – are rewrites of stories that Fitzgerald had published in *The Nassau Literary Review* in 1917 during his checkered undergraduate career at Princeton University. Not coincidentally, they are little more than vignettes consisting of one and two scenes respectively, both showcases more for repartee than for action. (The flimsiness of their plots further suggests why Fitzgerald could incorporate each as episodes in his 1920 debut novel, *This Side of Paradise*, with minimal revision). By contrast, the final two *Smart Set* stories – "Benediction" and "Dalyrimple Goes Wrong" – are broader in dramatic scope and more rigorously constructed, with formal section breaks demarcating the segmentation of the story into constituent parts. Each introduces its thematic concern with expository background on its characters, winds its driving conflict to a climax of a moral crisis, and concludes with a coda illustrating the consequences of the protagonist's response to that test.

The stronger of the two, "Benediction" – truly one of Fitzgerald's overlooked gems – is illustrative. The first section describes a young woman, Lois, visiting her Jesuit priest brother, Keith, en route to a sexual rendezvous with a prospective lover. The rising action is developed through the estranged siblings' conversation, in which Lois quizzes her brother on his dedication to his faith, thereby revealing how conflicted she is about the imminent loss of her virginity. Her struggle between spirit and flesh climaxes during the titular chapel rite when she is terrified by an ominous image she sees in the flickering of the altar candle. After fainting, Lois appears to have decided not to meet up with her paramour, falling action substantiated by Keith's insistence that her purity of spirit was the reason he entered the seminary (*Flappers and Philosophers* 148). In the final scene, however – narrated from the point of view of two telegraph operators – we learn that she rips up a goodbye note intended for her man, implying that at the last minute she goes through with the assignation. Her unexpected reversal returns the reader to the symbol of the candle flame in the climactic section, whose meaning Fitzgerald cleverly declines to define. Is it a projection of Lois's sexual desire or her fear of sensuality? Part of the ingenuity of the story is that while it can accommodate contradictory interpretations, its internal architecture is as self-evident as an exoskeleton. Indeed, one might argue that the obviousness of its structure is essential to the execution of its ambiguity, for without the support the Freytag model provides for the draping of the thematic and characterological enigmas, Lois's uncertainty about whether she should act upon temptation would remain heaped within the dialogue, leaving her to appear merely impulsive and not genuinely torn between sex and God.

With a modest circulation of 20,000, *The Smart Set* could only afford to pay a paltry $40 for a story, roughly one-tenth of what the slicks paid. Thanks to fellow St. Paul, Minnesota, writer Grace Flandrau, Fitzgerald secured the services of literary agent Paul Revere Reynolds, whose agency's forte was commercial fiction. After placing the farcical romance "Head and Shoulders" with the *Saturday Evening Post* for $400 in late 1919, Reynolds assigned Fitzgerald's manuscripts to partner Harold Ober, inaugurating an initially profitable eighteen-year relationship that would only end when Ober could no longer afford to float his impecunious author loans. Throughout early 1920, Ober brokered the sale of five 5,000- to 7,000-word efforts to the *Post* that include some of the most memorable flapper tales Fitzgerald would ever write: "Myra Meets His Family," "The Camel's Back," "Bernice Bobs Her Hair," "The Ice Palace," and "The Offshore Pirate." While the success of these works is often attributed to their coy depictions of young love, their infectiousness owes an unappreciated due to the Freytagian scheme. The *Post*'s marked preference for incorporating section breaks into the text perfectly served Fitzgerald's imagination, allowing him to conceive his tales in the magazine's customary five or six parts. This framework in turn provides the grounding necessary to prevent their fantastic scenarios and rhapsodic excursuses from floating off into sheer airiness. In each case, the opening exposition allows Fitzgerald to luxuriate in lyricism, to set a jazzy tone, and introduce colorful dramatis personae, including the "baby vamp" character he was credited with popularizing, if not creating.

For rising action, Fitzgerald would then rely upon dialogue, his characters verbally parrying and thrusting over the meaning of modern love and its sustainability in marriage. The one thematic exception to this is "Bernice Bobs Her Hair," which is more concerned with female propriety and the initiation rituals of the rising generation. Despite this difference, "Bernice" is comparable to the other fruits of this heady period of success in its exalting in snazzy one-liners and slang. The snappy patter and droll humor reflect the pep and panache by which Fitzgerald enunciates his themes, as when snobby Marjorie Harvey dresses down her dowdy titular cousin: "Girls like you are responsible for all the tiresome colorless marriages; all those ghastly inefficiencies that pass as feminine qualities" (*Short Stories* 34).

However adept Fitzgerald was at dialogue, his real strength lay in the relationship between climax and denouement. The dramatic peaks of these early *Post* stories are vivid because they involve unexpected twists that stop just short of courting incredulity. They pivot upon either the unmasking of a disguise (Curtis Carlyle, Ardita Farnam's kidnapper in "The Offshore Pirate," turns out to be spurned suitor Toby Moreland); the debunking of a hoax (Myra Harper in "Myra Meets His Family" discovers that fiancé Knowleton Whitney's eccentric parents are actors hired to scare her away from his inheritance); or a faint-inducing vision such as Lois's in "Benediction" that dramatizes the protagonist's conflicted emotional state (Southern belle Sally Carrol Happer in "The Ice Palace" collapses after becoming separated from her Yankee boyfriend in a gelid Minnesota labyrinth). Just when readers are prepared to roll their eyes at the near chutzpah of outlandishness, Fitzgerald provides a conclusion that commonly includes a reversal that effectively brings the stories back from the precipice of melodrama. Far from expressing anger over her mock abduction, for example, Ardita embraces Toby's trick as proof of commitment to the spicy adventure of romance, while Myra plays her own trick on Knowleton by arranging a fake marriage and then abandoning him on the way to the honeymoon. Perhaps the most famous of these reversals takes place in "Bernice": when the heroine discovers that Marjorie has duped her into bobbing her hair – not to boost her popularity but to humiliate her – Bernice sneaks into her cousin's room and snips off the snobby debutante's prized pigtails.

As structurally prescriptive as Freytag's Pyramid might seem, it actually proved a malleable form in Fitzgerald's hands. He could adapt it to longer works with interwoven storylines such as "May Day" (1920), which explores class conflict between spoiled Ivy Leaguers and demobilized soldiers during the anti-socialist riots of 1919, and to character-driven romances like "The Popular Girl," whose build-up and reversals simply could not fit within the standard 7,000 word limit. (For the only time in its association with Fitzgerald, the *Post* printed the story across two consecutive issues). The structure also enabled him to experiment across genres, including fantasies such as "The Curious Case of Benjamin Button" and "The Diamond as Big as the Ritz" (both 1922) and didactic parables like "The Cut-Glass Bowl" and "The Four Fists" (both of which appeared in the more lesson-oriented *Scribner's Magazine* in 1920 instead of in the *Post*). When financially necessary, the form even allowed him to expediently recycle scenarios: what Bruccoli rather dismissively calls the "concealed identity gimmick" in "The Offshore Pirate" was reemployed not once but twice in 1924 (and within two months of each other, no less) in "Rags Martin-Jones and The Pr-nce of W-les" and "The Unspeakable Egg" (*The Price* 126). There are certainly instances in which these climaxes and reversals can feel perfunctory. In Fitzgerald's first attempt to assess the national mood during the early months of the Depression, for example – "The Bridal Party" (1930) – the rising and falling action involves so many lost and regained fortunes between rival suitors Michael Curly and Hamilton Rutherford that Fitzgerald seems to be positioning his characters for their eventual outcomes rather than assaying the era's economic instability. The same is true of "The Rubber Check" (1932), in which a young man mistakenly accused of financial impropriety ends up falling in love with the daughter of the family that besmirches his reputation. And once readers are familiar enough with Fitzgerald's plot strategies, they can see the denouement of some less inventive efforts coming from a mile away. Especially in love stories such as "Presumption" (1926), "The Adolescent Marriage" (1926), and "The Love Boat" (1927), the characteristic themes of entrepreneurial ambition and the struggle for maturity follow a wholly predictable pattern in which estranged lovers are reunited. The only question in each case is what contrived stroke of luck – a coincidence, a chance encounter, an unexpected windfall, or a mistaken identity – will prove the fortuitous agency of the resolution.

That said, in Fitzgerald's most compelling stories, the Freytag structure provides a framework for the characterological concern at which the author excelled: the testing of moral fiber. In "Babylon Revisited," Charlie Wales's ambivalence toward the new-found sobriety and financial responsibility imposed upon him after the death of his wife, Helen, and his own nervous breakdown is conveyed in the rising action through counterpoint. Scenes in which the fallen stockbroker attempts to regain custodianship of his daughter, Honoria, alternate with his nostalgic excursions to the Parisian hotspots where he and Helen drank before the onset of the Depression. Although Charlie chastises himself for his profligacy and dissipation, he cannot belie how enamored he remains with the endless fetes and drunken displays. The structural ingenuity of the story rests in the subtlety with which Fitzgerald stages the inevitable consequence of this hero's fatal flaw, which only becomes apparent in retrospect. In the opening scene, set in the Ritz Bar, Charlie leaves a note containing the address of his wife's sister and brother-in-law, Marion and Lincoln Peters, for a former pair of fellow carousers, Duncan Schaeffer and Lorraine Quarrels. These debauchees subsequently burst upon the scene just as Charlie pleads his case to Marion and Lincoln for reclaiming the daughter, Honoria, for whom they serve as guardians. The Peters are not persuaded that Helen's husband has reformed his ways, and Charlie returns alone to the Ritz Bar, self-piteously lamenting how he lost all he desired not in the bust but in the boom (*Short Stories* 633). While Charlie's inability to acknowledge how he sabotaged his own hopes for reuniting with Honoria suggests he has yet to come to grips fully with his failings, Fitzgerald's skill in setting into motion the eventual climax so early in the story suggests how intuitively he could work out the inner mechanics of plot logic. The result is a marvelously conflicted character whose downfall – his self-destructiveness – isn't merely a theme but a complicating action that drives the drama in a fully rationalized manner.

If Freytag's pyramid allowed Fitzgerald to conceive fully-formed plots so effort-lessly through the early 1930s, it is equally worth noting that the difficulties he subsequently suffered with completing salable short efforts reflected a growing inability to utilize the schema. Had it been conceived a decade earlier, "Image on the Heart," from 1935–6, would likely have proved as easy to produce as, say, "'The Sensible Thing,'" one of that cluster of semi-autobiographical love stories that Fitzgerald cranked out over the winter of 1923–4 to finance the writing of *The Great Gatsby*. After all, "Image" makes use of material thoroughly mined in the love triangle plots of both *Gatsby* and *Tender Is the Night* (1934) – namely, Zelda Fitzgerald's adulterous infatuation with French aviator Edouard Jozan during the fabled Riviera summer of 1924. And yet, as the author wrote Harold Ober in early September 1935, he found himself stymied by three false starts and a constricted word count of roughly 4,000 words (*As Ever, Scott Fitz—* 224). Reading the story alongside a successful application of Freytag such as "Benediction" demonstrates how Fitzgerald was indeed struggling to find the organic form that had once come to him intuitively, for "Image on the Heart" suffers from a lack of proportionality. The complicated backstory requires excess exposition: the young heroine, Tudy, is preparing to marry the much older Tom, who comforted her after her husband died one week into their marriage, and yet she has also developed feelings for a French aviator named Riccard. Additionally, the rivalry between suitors that constitutes the rising action is stretched across too many encounters, diluting the power of what should be a powerful, pivotal scene: as Tom accompanies Tudy on a drive through Provence, Riccard flies his plane past them, a gesture that for Tudy is romantic but which Tom interprets as recklessly braggadocious (*The Price* 670). While the pathos of the climax is effective (Tom discovers Tudy and Riccard have met in Paris to say their final goodbyes), the drama is too attenuated to deliver the characters to some satisfying insight into their flaws. In the end, Tudy's attraction to Riccard remains unplumbed, and Tom's fear that his love for her may be more paternal than romantic passes without resolution. As such, "Image on the Heart" suggests Fitzgerald was conglomerating familiar themes and motifs instead of molding them to a structure that could give them a unified and balanced shape. The story confirms a general criticism made by Henry Dan Piper: "Practically all of [Fitzgerald's] poorer stories suffer from the burden of too much plot" (171).

In his dependency upon storyline to instill a sense of drive and purpose in his short fiction, Fitzgerald stands apart from the main thrust of modernism, which tended to fragment story structure into vignettes or slices of life that emphasize one or more of the parts of the Freytag structure, but rarely the whole. Hemingway's celebrated technique of omission, for example, does not do away with plot so much as it is apt to do away with climax, so that a story consists entirely of either exposition or rising conflict. In his earliest successful experiment in this approach, "Out of Season" (1923), an expatriate couple bickers over an Italian fishing guide who badgers the husband into contracting his services (*Short Stories* 135–9). There is no explanation for why these Americans are abroad, nor any real sense of what is causing the domestic discord in their dialogue. Much later, in the posthumously published *A Moveable Feast* (1964), Hemingway would imply that perceptive readers could infer the climax – Peduzzi, the guide, commits suicide (75) – yet nothing in the text itself hints at such a dramatic turn of events. Instead, the text is composed of conversation that seems to go nowhere, with its tension arising from the fact that it seems to go nowhere. Several other classic Hemingway stories ("The Killers," "Hills Like White Elephants" [both 1927]) create suspense through this method, though, interestingly, the two greatest accomplishments at the tail end of his story-writing years in the mid-1930s ("The Short Happy Life of Francis Macomber," and "The Snows of Kilimanjaro") are more Freytagian than one would expect from such a committed miniaturist. Other modernists emphasized other parts of the pyramid: Gertrude Stein's *Three Lives* (1909) and Toomer's *Cane* (1923) are almost entirely composed of exposition, while the epiphany stories of James Joyce's *Dubliners* (1914) – "Araby" being the most famous, of course – unexpectedly climax without any subsequent denouement to resolve the action. Still other authors – Sherwood Anderson, Faulkner, Porter, Kay Boyle – demonstrated their versatility by emphasizing different plot parts in different stories instead of associating themselves exclusively with a single one.

Regardless of what particular segment of plot they focused upon, modernists who defined themselves as such by virtue of their experiments in form rejected the well-wrought story structure. This is not to deny that any number of other excellent writers besides Fitzgerald relied upon plot. Although the "O. Henry" label had already devolved into a pejorative description by the early 1920s, William Sydney Porter's stories reveal how effectively twist endings and foreshadowing could create internal drama. James Branch Cabell's *The Line of Love* (1921), Ellen Glasgow's *The Shadowy Third, and Other Stories* (1923), and Ring Lardner's *How to Write Short Stories* (1924) are three additional examples of collections whose contents are generally Freytagian. The same can be said for the hardboiled fiction of Dashiell Hammett that first appeared in the pulp periodical *Black Mask*. Although Hammett mastered the art of producing stories that could easily be revised into novel chapters – *Red Harvest* (1929) and *The Maltese Falcon* (1930), most famously – the free-standing short fiction posthumously collected in *The Big Knockover* (1966) demonstrates how adept he was at climaxes and reversals. That said, unlike Fitzgerald, none of these authors was considered particularly modernistic. In the end, his use of structure might be said to resemble most closely that of Willa Cather, whose *Youth and the Bright Medusa* (1920) is wholly modernist in theme but whose stories remain heavily plotted. Like Cather, Fitzgerald was modern more in material than in form, and though she belonged to the older realist generation, her fiction shares with his a marked preference for linear development rather than the spatial depth of Joyce, Woolf, Hemingway, and others.

Narrative Technique, Point of View, and the Animadversions of Direct Address

One of the more persistent criticisms to dog Fitzgerald is that he was sloppy in what modernists deemed a major obligation of craft: maintaining the consistency of a chosen narrative perspective – a consistency measured, moreover, by the criterion of impersonality. Modernists inherited from their realist predecessors the Jamesian notion, best summarized by Wayne C. Booth, that fiction ought to strive for "freedom from the tyranny of subjectivity," an imperative that resulted in "the predominant demand ... for some sort of objectivity" (67). *Subjectivity* and *objectivity* are far from absolute terms, of course, for the most innovative of modernist narrative techniques – the Joycean stream of consciousness – is nothing if not the quintessence of the subjective, immersing as it does a reader into the unmediated swirl of a character's random thoughts and feelings. What Booth properly means is *authorial* objectivity, which creates the appearance of narration unmediated by any agency intervening between the reader and the character. At its crudest, this requirement meant that writers were not to enter into the fiction to comment upon the action, as was habitual for early purveyors of the nineteenth-century tale such as Hawthorne. As Morton P. Levitt succinctly puts it, the imperative of "Modernist Masters" was to create "innovative points of view whose major purpose was to eliminate the authorial presence within the [fiction] and to substitute for it the presence of the reader" (8–9).

In addition to the aforementioned stream of consciousness style, a shortlist of those innovative points of view would include: (1) *internal monologue*, a strategy whose interiority closely resembles that of stream of consciousness but which prefers a more structured presentation of phenomena to the stream's flagrant, free-association collage of impressions (Mansfield's "Miss Brill"); (2) the *camera-eye*, a rigorously externalized perspective in which the focus is on gesture and dialogue instead of psychology (Hemingway's "The Killers" being the classic example); and (3) the *metafictional conduit*, in which the narration is cast in the form of another mode of literature, mostly commonly the theatrical script (Fitzgerald, a frustrated playwright, employs this method in both "The Debutante" and "Porcelain and Pink"; after incorporating the former into *This Side of Paradise*, he would reemploy the technique in his second novel, *The Beautiful and Damned* [1922]). For all the experimentation associated with modernism, however, the bulk of canonical stories the movement produced are actually staged in a technique developed by that grand master of realism, Gustave Flaubert, that has subsequently been labeled *free indirect discourse* (FID). Also known as *libre indirect*, FID presents a character's innermost thoughts and feelings in the third person. Fitzgerald's "Absolution" (1924) offers an effective example of this approach by capturing young Rudolph Miller's mindset as he prepares for confession: "He must convince God that he was sorry and to do so he must first convince himself" (*Short Stories* 261). Joyce's "The Dead" is likewise written in this eminently flexible narrative mode, as are several of Hemingway's Nick Adams stories – most notably, "Indian Camp" and "Big Two-Hearted River" (both 1924).

Given how prevalent the use of free indirect discourse is throughout twentieth-century fiction, it should come as no surprise that many of what have come to be considered Fitzgerald's best stories employ this narratological strategy: in addition to "Absolution," "Babylon Revisited," portions of "Winter Dreams," "Jacob's Ladder"

(1927), the thirteen entries in the coming-of-age sequence featuring Basil Duke Lee and Josephine Perry that he wrote between 1928 and 1931, "Crazy Sunday" (1932), and "The Lost Decade" (1939) all channel their drama through the perspective of a chief protagonist (or, in the case of "May Day," several protagonists) whose perceptions are the only moral scope through which readers are allowed to view the action. Fitzgerald no doubt felt comfortable writing in FID for a very simple reason: its main attribute is that it creates ambiguities of motive and morality that perfectly enabled the author to plumb his ambivalence toward the ethical balance between self-control and indulgence. In "Babylon Revisited," for example, *libre indirect* allows Fitzgerald to imply Charlie Wales's subtle nostalgia for the days when he could tip an orchestra a thousand francs for playing a single musical request: "[The money] hadn't been given for nothing. ... It had been given, even the most wildly squandered sum, as an offering to destiny" (*Short Stories* 620).

As Karl Kroeber argues, the primary effect of free indirect discourse is to demand a "continuous complex intensity of response" that requires readers to assess the moral valence of the protagonist's thoughts without benefit of an authorial baseline. That is, because the author is not actively commenting upon the character's statements, instructing the audience on how to interpret them, we are caught in an interpretive bind whose confusion Kroeber nicely captures by casting it in the form of an interrogative: "Do these words represent the character's or the narrator's perception?" (106). To put it another way, in a passage such as the one quoted above, we must ask whether Fitzgerald wants us to agree with Charlie's self-assessment and concur that losing his family was a *necessary* experience that he has to undergo in order to appreciate the value of what he has lost. Or we wonder whether the author injects a bit of pretension into that "destiny" line, so we might appreciate the self-justifications that color his remorse and cast doubt on his claims of rehabilitation. The answer is that either answer is speculative, arrived at through interpretation, and not provided by definitive textual proof. As such, FID is a device not only for engaging audiences in the narrative but for layering it with the formalist complexity that was a hallmark of modernism.

But if Fitzgerald proved more than proficient in mining the narratological potential of *libre indirect*, he also exhibited a marked tendency for those selfsame authorial intrusions that supposedly excuse readers from that "continuous complex intensity of response." His pre-1925 stories in particular evince the sort of storytelling chattiness that flouted the obligation of objectivity. An exaggerated example of this habit can be found in "The Jelly-Bean" (1920), whose opening paragraphs find Fitzgerald referencing his own role in the creation of the story so persistently that the plot seems to have trouble finding its traction: "Much as I desire to make [Jim Powell] an appealing character, I feel that it would be unscrupulous to deceive you on that point" (*Short Stories* 142–3).

One can find similar if less over-the-top instances throughout several stories. The recently rediscovered "The Curious Case of Benjamin Button" begins with the declaration that its eponymous hero was fifty years ahead of the historical curve of health care when he was born in a hospital in 1860. Fitzgerald no sooner notes this fact than he teases the reader with its potential irrelevance to the peculiar predicament of his hero, who emerges from the womb in a senescent body and "matures" into infancy over the course of his life: "I shall tell you what occurred, and let you judge for yourself" (*Short Stories* 159). These intrusions are not always opening gambits. In other cases, Fitzgerald intervenes to offer moral apothegms, or simply to tell readers what details are (and are not) important, as when he insists that "Winter Dreams" is not Dexter Green's biography, even if certain details that "have nothing to do with those dreams he had when he was young" (the story's real subject) inevitably creep into the narration (*Short Stories* 221, 233). In some cases, Fitzgerald even mocks his own reputation for cashing in on his notoriety as the scribe of the Jazz Age, as when he wryly boasts in "Dice, Brassknuckles & Guitar" (1923) that he would like to sell this latest flapper love story to Hollywood (*Short Stories* 238).

As taboo as such intrusions were in the avant-garde stories favored by little magazines, they were perfectly at home in the commercial slicks, in which a foregrounded relationship between authors and readers was key to establishing rapport. When Fitzgerald appended a moral ending to a story such as "O Russet Witch!" he was not pandering to the audience of *Metropolitan Magazine* – a moralist himself, he derived a satisfying closure by deducing the overall import of his storylines. The gesture of wrapping up the plot was thus extended to the audience, ensuring readers that they shared a common bond of values. In the case of "O Russet Witch!", that value reinforces a thoroughly 1920s' notion of *carpe diem*: when Merlin Grainger realizes only too late in life that he has squandered his chances for an exciting life by choosing dour Olive Masters over the impetuous Caroline (who actually turns out to be famous dancer Alicia Dare), Fitzgerald summarizes his resulting regret with a short concluding paragraph from which audiences are invited to abstract a credo: "He had angered Providence by resisting too many temptations. There was nothing left but heaven, where he would meet only those who, like him, had wasted earth" (*Tales of the Jazz Age* 238).

As "O Russet Witch!" suggests, even in Fitzgerald's most didactic stories, his morals were never preachy. Indeed, he was apt to phrase them as pseudo-aphorisms rather than employ the imperative voice or invoke the same first person that he used so freely in staging the opening of tales such as "The Jelly-Bean." Nor did he veer toward the pontifical even when he employed the first person. "The Rich Boy" (1925) demonstrates how the border between objectivity and subjectivity collapses when an unnamed narrator-observer strikes up a relationship with the reader without revealing much information about himself: "Let me tell you about the rich. They are different from you and me" (*Short Stories* 318). Arguably, the mystery of the identity of this "I" is more curious than the case study of aloof Anson Hunter, whose sense of superiority makes him incapable of identifying with others as the narrator does. Although "The Rich Boy" is a veritable case study of Fitzgerald's Princeton classmate Ludlow Fowler, his narrative strategy makes it clear that readers are not to assume that the speaker is F. Scott Fitzgerald. Rather, his narrator enters into the fiction just enough to make himself a character: he meets Anson in 1917 as an aviation officer stationed in Pensacola, Florida, later socializing with the young heir at the Yale Club in New York before finally crossing the ocean with him as Anson expatriates to Europe after the death of a former love. If the point of the story is to critique the self-absorption of the rich – the main effect of Paula Legendre's passing is to remind Anson that he is now thirty and no longer young – the narrator's presumed solidarity with the reader assures us that the middle class does not suffer this fault. The very fact that the narrator can invoke "we" and speak of "our" common values is proof of the empathy that the titular protagonist lacks.

"The Rich Boy" represents one of Fitzgerald's more self-conscious experiments in first person. More common is the technique of "The Last of the Belles" (1929), in which the narrator is a full-fledged character. Despite the seeming straightforwardness of this approach, "Belles" manages to achieve the same complexity as "Babylon Revisited" even without the ambiguity that free indirect discourse affords the latter. Instead of any potential discrepancy between the author's and character's points of view that the reader must resolve, Fitzgerald exploits the dissonance that arises from the ten-year gap between the moment that the narrator, Andy, first befriends Southern belle Ailie Calhoun and his final, melancholy encounter with her. From this gap, readers must assess Andy's narration to determine exactly what insight, if any, the intervening decade has brought to his understanding of his infatuation with this quintessential coquette. Any answer, again, is speculative, and how readers determine it will largely affect whether they regard Ailie herself with sympathy or whether they view her, as Petry does, as unworthy of "the trouble of the narrator or of any man" (158). This is essentially the same task that readers face in Joyce's "Araby," at whose conclusion the narrator condemns himself as "a creature driven and derided by vanity" (22). That the interpretive demands of "The Last of the Belles" are every bit as complex as Joyce's classic suggests just how consanguineous Fitzgerald's storytelling affinities are with modernism.

That said, Fitzgerald was apparently uninterested in either of those modernist mainstays, the interior monologue or stream of consciousness. To find an example of the former, one must wade late into his story-writing career to 1934's "The Night Before Chancellorsville," a Civil War tale in which a prostitute, Nora, expresses her disgruntlement over losing business during the 1863 Union routing in General Robert E. Lee's most audacious Confederate victory. Although idiosyncratic, the story is one of Fitzgerald's more notable attempts to break from his reputation as a *Saturday Evening Post* writer, its success due in a large part to Nora's voice. Unfortunately, the same cannot be said for the author's lone foray into stream of consciousness, "Shaggy's Morning" (1935), published, like "The Night Before Chancellorsville," in *Esquire*, which became Fitzgerald's main market when he no longer found himself able to produce *Post* stories. One might give him the benefit of the doubt and suggest that he could have proved more capable at Joycean narration if he had not attempted to write from the perspective of a dog going about its daily routine of burying bones and dodging automobiles. As it stands, however, "Shaggy's Morning" enjoys the unenviable reputation as the worst story Fitzgerald ever published – deemed so bad, in fact, that it remains uncollected at the request of his estate. (As a result, it typically falls to a short passage toward the end of *This Side of Paradise* to suggest how proficient he could have been at stream of consciousness had he more consistently experimented with it.) Nor was Fitzgerald drawn to writing in the second person, which became a common habit for Hemingway in his post-1930 novels and non-fiction – although, curiously, not his short stories. Only casually would Fitzgerald slip into this form, as in "The Third Casket" (1924), and only then as a means of introducing his plot, not of interpolating the reader into the fiction (*The Price* 86). And while an argument can be made that late efforts such as "Three Acts in Music" (1936) flirt with experimentation by approximating the prose-poem styled perspectival collage of Toomer's *Cane*, such exercises are as much acts of creative desperation as they are conscientiously designed attempts at self-reinvention. The reality is that Fitzgerald was most at home with standard first-person retrospective and third-person free indirect discourse. The unacknowledged reality is that, for as synonymous as innovation is with modernism, his peers often were as well.

Exclamatory Style: Romantic Rhapsodies versus Modernist Irony

The final characteristic that has traditionally distinguished Fitzgerald from his contemporaries has to do with the amount of emotion expressed in his style. A devout fan of the Romantic poets – John Keats in particular – he inherited their belief that feeling is a catalyst of knowledge, the intensity of the sentiment theoretically elevating individuals past the boundaries of rational concentration to more intuitive insights lost to everyday habits of thought. Such conviction in the power of imagination was decidedly out of fashion in the early twentieth century, however. Amid the devastation of the Great War and the Versailles peace compromises – at a time when Freudian psychology emphasized the neuroses of the subliminal instead of the ecstasies of the sublime – the faith in optimism and progressivism that Romanticism advocated could not help but seem naïve, if not outright quaint. Accordingly, leading modernists such as T. S. Eliot and Ezra Pound campaigned against feeling in art, insisting that it was a sentimental corruption that distracted readers from the aesthetic complexities of form. For practitioners of the short story, the result was the emergence of a certain style of irony, most readily embodied in a stance of shellshocked detachment, which suggested that one could only observe and not comprehend the upheaval of modern life. The most celebrated exemplars of this style are the interchapters of Hemingway's *In Our Time*. In bursts of imagistic prose that rarely exceed a paragraph in length, Hemingway captures the stunted inability to process the spectacle of violence, whether warfare or bullfighting: "We were in a garden at Mons. Young Buckley came in with his patrol from across the river. The first German I saw climbed up over the garden wall. We waited till he got one leg over and then potted him. ... Then three more came over further down the wall. We shot them. They all came just like that" (*Complete Short Stories* 77). Hemingway's style influenced a range of writers from Steinbeck to Hammett for two reasons: its irony bespoke the gritty cynicism of the age, and it was (and remains) eminently imitable – so much so that, by the time of his third story collection, *Winner Take Nothing* (1933), Hemingway veered dangerously close to self-parody.

The staccato reportage of the Hemingway style could not be farther from Fitzgerald's modus operandi, which typically luxuriates in intricately paced crescendos of metaphor that climax in melancholy exclamations of remorse and loss. Critics frequently express discomfort with the conclusion of "Winter Dreams," for example, because Dexter Green's discovery that Judy Jones's youthful impiety has been squandered in a loveless marriage borders on the overwritten: "The dream was gone. ... The gates were closed, the sun was gone down, and there was no beauty but the gray beauty of steel that withstands all time. Even the grief he could have borne was left behind in the country of illusion, of youth, of the richness of life, where his winter dreams had flourished" (*Short Stories* 235–6).

Whether one finds this lamentation over the top is a personal reaction, yet it should be noted that its elaborateness is not as atypical as it might appear when read alongside Hemingway. In the world of popular periodicals, such ornate intensity was part and parcel of what Christopher Wilson has called the "buttonholing" rhetoric of the era's exuberant consumerism. Instead of the genteel, "toastmaster" style of interaction favored by the preceding generation of editors such as William Dean Howells and Horace Scudder of the *Atlantic Monthly*, magazines in the postwar period encouraged aggressive, vigorous expression in order to "cut through the reader's barriers of resistance and 'impose' an idea" through the sheer affective force of "pep" and "zest" (Wilson 49). Fitzgerald found a congenial home in the *Saturday Evening Post*, *Metropolitan* (in which "Winter Dreams" originally appeared in December 1922), *Hearst's International*, and *The Smart Set* in part because his rhapsodic style conveyed precisely the "richness of life" – the sorrow as well as the ebullience – that these venues aimed to celebrate.

Nor were "imposing" styles restricted to the popular marketplace. The ending of "Winter Dreams" is no more overwrought than the conclusions of such modernist classics as Joyce's "The Dead" or Porter's "Flowering Judas." In the former, Gabriel Conroy's realization that his wife loved another man earlier in life leads to a tearful vision of his own insignificance. The pathos of this sudden awareness arises from much of the same imagery as Fitzgerald's: "Generous tears filled Gabriel's eyes. He had never felt like that himself towards any woman but he knew that such a feeling must be love. The tears gathered more thickly in his eyes and in the partial darkness he imagined he saw the form of a young man standing under a dripping tree. Other forms were near. His soul had approached that region where dwell the vast hosts of the dead. He was conscious of, but could not apprehend, their wayward and flickering existence. His own identity was fading out into a grey impalpable world: the solid world itself which these dead had one time reared and lived in was dissolving and dwindling" (160–1). If there is a difference between the two endings, it is one of volume, not content or tone, as Joyce avoids the exclamation point that, one suspects, bears much of the responsibility for critics deeming Dexter's grief border-line mawkish. Unlike Joyce, Porter does not shy away from ejaculatory emotion as her expatriate heroine, Laura, suffers a nightmare in which a betrayed Mexican revo-lutionary comes to escort her to death: "Eat these flowers, poor prisoner, said Eugenio in a voice of pity, take and eat: and from the Judas tree he stripped the warm bleed-ing flowers, and held them to her lips. She saw that his hand was fleshless, a cluster of small white petrified branches, and his eye sockets were without light, but she ate the flowers greedily for they satisfied both hunger and thirst. Murderer! said Eugenio, and Cannibal! This is my body and my blood. Laura cried No! and at the sound of her own voice, she awoke trembling, and was afraid to sleep again" (102). Yet in this case one suspects that by framing these outbursts within the interior monologue of a dream Porter spared herself the charge of excess feeling. Arguably, the perspective dampens the emotion by ascribing it to solely to Laura instead of to the authorial presence implied by Fitzgerald's use of free indirect discourse. That distinction is a technical one, however, and it should not obscure the fact that the modernist irony for which Hemingway was known was only the reticent end of the spectrum of emotional expression. Faulkner, Toomer, Woolf, and many others simi-larly employed exclamatory styles when the occasion demanded. Their modernist credentials simply pardoned them from the suspicion of sentimentality to which Fitzgerald has been prone.

The climactic power of many Fitzgerald stories thus rests in their oratorical build-up. Not all of these possess the clamor of "Winter Dreams," however. In " 'The Sensible Thing,' " George O'Kelly's realization that his love for Jonquil Cary has passed is more solemn and somber than Dexter Green's epiphany: "Well, let it pass, he thought; April is over, April is over. There are all kinds of love in the world, but never the same love twice" (*Short Stories* 301). In other cases, Fitzgerald does not let the significance of the emotion rest in personal experience, preferring instead to extrapolate it into a statement on a larger abstraction. The oft-cited conclusion of "The Swimmers" (1929) resembles the famous ending of *The Great Gatsby* by elevat-ing one man's disappointed love into a symbol of national character: "France was a land, England was a people, but America, having about it still the quality of the idea, was harder to utter. ... It was a willingness of the heart" (*Short Stories* 512). Such passages are the opposite of Eliot's objective correlative: rather than project the emotion upon a concrete object, they revel in the subjective nuance of feeling, dra-matizing its tangled confusions instead of its ability to be simplified through embodiment in a material form. While Fitzgerald's tendency was toward the nebu-lous and indefinite rather than the specific, he could, when appropriate, pour that emotion into something as particular as landscape. "Absolution" ends with a descrip-tion of the Midwest that conveys the repressed sensuality with which Randolph Miller grapples, with Fitzgerald's setting every bit as charged with portent as the upper Michigan woods of "Big Two-Hearted River" (*Short Stories* 272). The difference is that while Hemingway preferred symbolic detail, Fitzgerald reveled in devices that call attention to the emotion of the scene: from the pathetic fallacy (a trembling sirocco) to strategic adverbs to romantic imagery (the moon, which appears in nearly all of his love stories), the ending is self-consciously lush and hypnotic instead of stoic and subdued.

Another reason that Fitzgerald is often accused of undue emotion has to do with the whimsy of his comedy as opposed to the volubility of his melancholy. When other modernists veered from the darker themes of alienation and despair, they tended toward satire instead of the wryness of "The Offshore Pirate," "The Ice Palace," and "Bernice Bobs Her Hair." Thus, in Hemingway's "Mr. and Mrs. Elliot" (1925), the humor is aggressive and dehumanizing, thereby discouraging reader empathy for the effete sterility of this expatriate couple's dispassionate marriage: "They were both disappointed [after sex] but finally Cornelia went to sleep. Hubert could not sleep and several times went out and walked up and down the corridor of the hotel. ... As he walked he saw all the pairs of shoes, small shoes and big shoes, outside the doors of the hotel rooms. This set his heart pounding and he hurried back to his own room but Cornelia was asleep" (*Complete Short Stories* 124). Even when Faulkner and Porter take a lighter tack in semi-comedic tales, their local-color humor is infused with either an air of Gothicism ("A Rose for Emily") or outright tragedy ("The Jilting of Granny Weatherall") that renders them serious. Particularly in Fitzgerald's early flapper stories, however, his style is full of coy overstatement, with the language almost challenging readers to take Fitzgerald's scenarios seriously. Yet the exaggeration is central to his Jazz Age vivacity: it suggests not only the exuberance of the early 1920s but the self-deprecating sarcasm that implies Fitzgerald is simultaneously celebrating and tweaking his generation's yearning to break with Victorian propriety and express its longings. In a tale like "The Diamond as Big as the Ritz" (1922) – a fantasy about a secret estate built upon the world's largest gem – such hyperbole is taken a step further to become a mechanism of the thematic critique. In satirizing the unimaginable prosperity promised by the new consumerism, Fitzgerald indulges in an extravaganza of color, texture, and exotic allusion as John T. Unger compares Braddock Washington's mountain-sized jewel to Eastern exotica displayed for a "Tartar Khan" (*Short Stories* 188).

It was inevitable that such stylistic luxuriance would fall out of fashion as the Great Depression rendered chinchilla and gold unfathomable riches instead of merely intemperate ones. After the lukewarm commercial reception of his fourth novel, *Tender Is the Night* – a work that took nearly a decade to complete, in part because of the financial imperative of producing salable short fiction – Fitzgerald recognized the need to tone down his extravagance. The result was the rigorously pared down language of "The Lost Decade," "An Alcoholic Case" (1937), and the seventeen sketches featuring Hollywood hack Pat Hobby that began appearing in *Esquire* in the final year of Fitzgerald's life. James L. W. West III argues that the "stripped, compressed prose" of this "late style" demonstrates how market savvy the author remained despite his alcoholism and the financial and emotional strain of the mental illness that claimed

Zelda after 1930: "During his years as a *Post* author he had mastered the kind of story published by that magazine. ... For *Esquire*, Fitzgerald learned to write a very different kind of narrative – the brief, unplotted, elliptical tale typical of Chekov, Turgenev, and DeMaupassant" (Fitzgerald, *Lost Decade* xv). Yet as professionally necessary as this reinvention was, the *Esquire* stories lack the very element of emotion that is the distinctive ingredient of Fitzgerald's pre-1935 fiction. The sad reality is that dozens of writers in this period produced competent stories in the hardboiled manner, so that whatever insights "The Lost Decade" might reveal about the emotional costs of dipsomania, there is nothing particularly original about it – unlike the early *Post* stories, which, even at their most commercial, contain a quality of vibrancy that makes them as vivacious today as they were nearly a century ago. Of course, Fitzgerald's intent in this later period was to disassociate himself from marketplace stereotypes of his writing. As he wrote one editor shortly before his death, he was tired of being stereotyped: "I'd like to find out if people read me just because I am F. Scott Fitzgerald or what is more likely, don't read me for the same reason" (*Life in Letters* 433). Such was this desire that he even published one *Esquire* story, "On an Ocean Wave," under the pseudonym "Paul Elgin," hoping to fool readers. More contributions would have appeared under this nom de plume had Fitzgerald's December 21, 1940, death not rendered the need to mask his authorship a moot point.

The great challenge of studying Fitzgerald's entire body of stories is to separate long-standing assumptions of "commercial" from parallel presumptions of what constitutes "literary modernism." Sentimentality was by no means exclusive to the *Saturday Evening Post* or *Red Book*; it lurks under the surface of Hemingway stories such as "In Another Country" or "A Canary for One" (both 1927) as much as it is overt in such supposed Fitzgerald piffles as "The Lees of Happiness" (1922) or "Diamond Dick and the First Law of Woman" (1924). Nor were avant-garde journals the sole province of psychological complexity. The depth of character Fitzgerald could plumb in "The Rich Boy" or "The Last of the Belles" is no less profound than what Faulkner or Porter could achieve with more experimental tactics. Even the obvious recycling of formulae and plots that can make stories such as "The Popular Girl" or "Presumption" read like expedient cash-ins rather than artistic accomplishments is hardly a fault of the popular marketplace; the modernist vanguard was likewise accused of too often drinking from the same well as they explored their war traumas or their Yoknapatawpha genealogies in repeated efforts. As Fitzgerald defensively noted when flustered by a sense of his own limitations, authors inevitably repeat themselves: "We have two or three great moving experiences in our lives. ... Then we learn our trade, well or less well, and we tell our two or three stories ... as long as people will listen" (*Afternoon* 132). The great tragedy of Fitzgerald's career as a story writer was not that he toiled for commercial periodicals. It was, rather, twofold: more people listened early rather than late to those two or three great stories he had to tell, and he himself did not appreciate what he had accomplished in the genre. Rather than lament that he *only* completed four and a half novels in his twenty-year career – as the first revivers of his reputation were prone to do in the 1940s and 1950s – we should admire the professionalism that enabled him to publish 160 stories in that span. Few writers of his generation were as prolific when it came to short fiction, and none have seen their standing so suffer because of it.

References and Further Reading

Booth, Wayne C. *The Rhetoric of Fiction.* Chicago: University of Chicago Press, 1983.

Bruccoli, Matthew J. *Some Sort of Epic Grandeur: The Life of F. Scott Fitzgerald.* 1st rev. edn. New York: Carroll & Graf, 1991.

Bryer, Jackson R. *New Essays on F. Scott Fitzgerald's Neglected Short Stories.* Columbia: University of Missouri Press, 1996.

———. *The Short Stories of F. Scott Fitzgerald: New Approaches in Criticism.* Madison: University of Wisconsin Press, 1982.

Canby, Henry Seidel. "Free Fiction." *Atlantic Monthly* 116 (July 1915): 60–8.

Canby, Henry Seidel, and Alfred Dashiell. *A History of the Short Story.* New York: Holt, 1935.

Fitzgerald, F. Scott. *Afternoon of an Author.* Ed. Arthur Mizener. New York: Scribner, 1958.

———. *As Ever, Scott Fitz—: Letters Between F. Scott Fitzgerald and His Literary Agent Harold Ober, 1919–1940.* Eds. Matthew J. Bruccoli and Jennifer McCabe Atkinson. London: Woburn Press, 1973.

———. *Flappers and Philosophers.* 1920. Ed. James L. W. West III. New York: Cambridge University Press, 1999.

———. *F. Scott Fitzgerald: A Life in Letters.* Ed. Matthew J. Bruccoli. New York: Scribner, 1994.

———. *The Lost Decade: Short Stories from Esquire, 1936–1941.* Ed. James L. W. West III. New York: Cambridge University Press, 2008.

———. *The Price Was High: The Last Uncollected Stories of F. Scott Fitzgerald.* Ed. Matthew J. Bruccoli. New York: Harcourt Brace Jovanovich, 1979.

———. *The Short Stories of F. Scott Fitzgerald: A New Collection.* Ed. Matthew J. Bruccoli. New York: Scribner, 1989.

———. *Tales of the Jazz Age.* 1922. New York: Cambridge University Press, 2002.

Fitzgerald, F. Scott, and Zelda Fitzgerald. *Dear Scott, Dearest Zelda: The Love Letters of Scott and Zelda Fitzgerald.* Eds. Jackson R. Bryer and Cathy W. Barks. New York: Scribner, 2002.

Franks, Joseph. "Spatial Form in Modern Literature." *The Idea of Spatial Form.* New Brunswick, NJ: Rutgers University Press, 1991. 31–66.

Freytag, Gustav. *Technique of the Drama: An Exposition of Dramatic Composition and Art.* Trans. Elias J. MacEwan. New York: Griggs, 1895.

Head, Dominic. *The Modernist Short Story: A Study in Theory and Practice.* New York: Cambridge University Press, 1992.

Hemingway, Ernest. *The Complete Short Stories of Ernest Hemingway: The Finca Vigía Edition.* Eds. Patrick John and Gregory Hemingway. New York: Scribner, 1987.

———. *A Moveable Feast.* New York: Scribner, 1964.

Joyce, James. *Dubliners.* 1914. Ed. Robert Scholes. New York: Viking, 1961.

Kroeber, Karl. *Retelling/Rereading: The Fate of Storytelling in Modern Times.* New Brunswick, NJ: Rutgers University Press, 1992.

Levitt, Morton P. *The Rhetoric of Modernist Fiction: From a New Point of View.* Hanover: University Press of New England, 2005.

Mangum, Bryant. *A Fortune Yet: Money and Art in the Short Stories of F. Scott Fitzgerald.* New York: Garland, 1991.

May, Charles E. *Short Story Writers.* Pasadena: Salem Press, 2008.

O'Brien, Edward J. *The Dance of the Machines: The American Short Story and the Industrial Age.* New York: Macaulay, 1929.

Petry, Alice Hall. *Fitzgerald's Craft of Short Fiction: The Collected Stories, 1920–1935.* Tuscaloosa: University of Alabama Press, 1989.

Piper, Henry Dan. *F. Scott Fitzgerald: A Critical Study.* New York: Holt, Rinehart & Winston, 1965.

Poe, Edgar Allan. *Edgar Allan Poe: Essays and Reviews.* Ed. G. R. Thompson. New York: Library of America, 1984.

Porter, Katherine Anne. *The Collected Stories of Katherine Anne Porter*. New York: Harcourt, Brace & World, 1965.

Scofield, Martin. *The Cambridge Introduction to the American Short Story*. New York: Cambridge University Press, 2006.

Voss, Arthur. *The American Short Story: A Critical Survey*. Norman: University of Oklahoma Press, 1973.

Wilson, Christopher. "The Rhetoric of Consump-

tion: Mass Market Magazines and the Demise of the Gentle Reader, 1880–1920." *The Culture of Consumption: Critical Essays in American History, 1880–1980*. Eds. Richard Wightman Fox and T. J. Jackson Lears. New York: Pantheon, 1984. 39–64.

Wright, Austin. *The American Short Story in the Twenties*. Chicago: University of Chicago Press, 1961.

20

"The Look of the World": Richard Wright on Perspective

Mikko Tuhkanen

Thus early I learned that the point from which a thing is viewed is of some importance.
– *Frederick Douglass,* My Bondage and My Freedom

In his 1950 assessment of the Harlem Renaissance, Alain Locke, the "dean" of the movement and the editor of *The New Negro* anthology (1925), suggests that African American writing of the 1920s and the 1930s evinced "vision without true perspective." According to him, the texts of the New Negro Movement failed to achieve "objective universality," which would have made them relevant to a wider audience. Locke names Richard Wright's *Native Son* (1940) – at least its first two parts before what he, like many other critics, deems the novel's disintegration under the "propagandist formulae" of its third and final section – as the exemplary corrective to such failure of perspective in African American literary history. With its "social discoveries of common-denominator human universals between Negro situations and others," Wright's debut novel evinces the kind of "universalized particularity [that] has always resided [in] the world's greatest and most enduring art" (Locke 59).

If he read Locke's rendition of black literary history – with whose premises and assumptions many would quibble – Wright would have undoubtedly been pleased. He, too, identifies "perspective" as an issue of crucial import for African American writing. The craft of the black writer entails the identification and inhabitation of an appropriate perspective on the world, a viewpoint that, bringing things into focus, allows the artist to render his or her material into effective narratives. Perspective, he explains in "Blueprint for Negro Writing" (1937), "is that fixed point in intellectual space where a writer stands to view the struggles, hopes, and sufferings of his people. There are times when he may stand too close and the result is a blurred vision. Or he may stand too far away and the result is a neglect of important things" (45). While Wright here argues for the benefit of a socialist Weltanschauung for the emerging black artist, he also suggests that the perspective embodied by the American Communist Party must be only a preliminary step in the dialectics of vision. As such,

Wright's subsequent writings can be understood as an ongoing experimentation with perspectives through which he sought to change what he frequently calls "the look of the world," that is, the way the world both appears to and apprehends the black subject.[1]

As an African American author, Wright is by no means unique in this emphasis. The search for transformative vision(s) occupies black writing from slave narratives onward.[2] In the earliest of these texts, the experience of literacy often occasions perspectival shifts. In his 1845 *Narrative*, Frederick Douglass famously describes literacy as an anguished revelation, a painful visionary moment, that directs his gaze into the abyss of his degraded condition as a slave: the newly gained ability to read "opened [his] eyes to the horrible pit, but to no ladder upon which to get out" (42). The cost of vision is an initial loss of voice, and the narrator is stunned to silence: "learning to read ... torment[ed] and st[ung] my soul to unutterable anguish. As I writhed under it, I would at times feel that learning to read had been a curse rather than a blessing. It had given me a view of my wretched condition, without the remedy" (42). Empowering and immobilizing, literacy for Douglass becomes, precisely, a vehicle for the kind of "second-sight" that, according to W. E. B. Du Bois, the world has "gifted" the double-conscious African American (*Souls* 10). As etymology tells us – etymology of which Du Bois, having studied in Germany, may have been cognizant – the double perspective of the visionary black subject functions as what Jacques Derrida has called the *pharmakon*: it is both "good *and* bad, ... gift and poison (*Gift-gift*)" (Derrida 81).

Wright delineates this difficult logic throughout his work. His protagonists are afforded revelations of new worlds when their perspectives are radically reorganized, usually as a result of calamities not of their own choosing. Yet, rather than an experience of transcendence and liberation, such moments entail as many unforeseen dangers as possibilities. For example, in his autobiography, literacy enables experimentations with forms of vision unavailable to the African American subject growing up under Jim Crow. *Black Boy*'s adolescent narrator describes the activation of a certain mobility through the unexpected perspectives he discovers in books. Recounting his childhood experiences of reading, he writes: "The plots and stories in the novels did not interest me so much as the point of view revealed" (238). Perspectives offer a way of organizing the world such that possibilities are made available, or at least thinkable, that have been absent from the narrator's environment. Wright describes this dynamic in a later interview: "Living in the South doomed me to look always through eyes which the South had given me, and bewilderment and fear made me mute and afraid. But after I had left the South, luck gave me other eyes, new eyes with which to look at the meaning of what I'd lived through. ... Books were the windows through which I looked at the world. ... [A]t once I was able, in looking back through alien eyes, to see my own life" (*Conversations* 81). As Lawrence Levine argues, reading and writing has helped bring about "changes in perception and world view" for the antebellum and post-Emancipation black subject (156–7). Yet, as with slave narrators, literacy provides no panacea. Echoing Douglass, Wright observes: "In buoying me up, reading also cast me down. ... My tension returned, new, terrible, bitter, surging, almost too

great to be contained. I no longer *felt* that the world about me was hostile, killing; I
knew it. … I seemed forever condemned, ringed by walls" (*Black Boy* 239). Reading
and writing unexpectedly distance the autobiographical narrator from the black community, too. Having seen his published story in a local paper, his friends "looked at
[him] with new eyes, and a distance, a suspiciousness came between [them]": "If I
had thought anything in writing the story, I had thought that perhaps it would make
me more acceptable to them, and now it was cutting me off from them more completely than ever" (159–60). Literacy may change the look of the world, but it simultaneously entails one's increasing alienation.

"Bright and Morning Star" provides an early example of Wright's delineation of
the promise and danger of competing perspectives. The story tracks the shifts in the
perception of its black female protagonist, Aunt Sue, as, moving from Christianity to
communism, she is betrayed by all available perspectives, figured as "faiths." While
critics have often pegged the story as young Wright's made-to-order propaganda for
the American Communist Party (Fabre, *Unfinished* 163), the development of its protagonist does not culminate in her adoption of a worldview that would be identifiable
with any organized political movement.

Sue is a mother whose two sons, Johnny-Boy and Sug, have joined the working-
class activists in their fight against the town's oppressive law enforcement regime.
The story follows the mutations of her search for sense-making techniques that would
allow her to survive from day to day. Her initial perspective is that of Christian faith.
Christianity "had focused her feelings upon an imagery which had swept her life into
a wondrous vision" ("Bright" 224), allowing her to bear the daily poverty and oppression under structural racism. As her sons become politically active, she initially tries
to "fill their eyes with her vision, but they would have none of it." Instead, "they
began to boast of the strength shed by a new and terrible vision" (225), eventually
convincing their mother of their cause.

While Sue organizes her world around the perspective of class consciousness, she
also retains a distance from it. When a traitor seems to have infiltrated the ranks of
the communists, she is certain that it cannot be any of the town's black folk, whom
she has known all her life. Instead, she warns her son against the recently recruited
white comrades. Unlike his mother, Johnny-Boy, with his unwavering loyalty to the
Party, sees the world exclusively through the prism of class differences: "'Ah cant see
white an Ah cant see black,'" he tells Sue. "'… Ah sees rich men n Ah sees po men'"
(234). His is the "dramatic Marxist vision" that Wright in 1937 considers the black
artist's most productive means of constructing "a meaningful picture of the world
today" ("Blueprint" 44). Yet, his example simultaneously suggests the necessity for
complicating this image. As Wright notes in "Blueprint" – anticipating what were
to become his increasing doubts about communist dogma – "Marxism is but the
starting point" (44).

Sue, too, realizes the blind spots in the Red perspective when she observes the
impairing of her son's vision: "he believes so hard hes blind" (233). Indeed, his
unyielding class loyalty betrays the young black man: the traitor is, as Sue intuits,

one of the new white recruits. Johnny-Boy's failure is that of "stand[ing] too far away and … neglect[ing] … important things" ("Blueprint" 45), for example the kind of local knowledge that informs his mother's convictions about the town's black residents. Perspective may be a necessary tool for the black subject to move in the world; yet one must be wary of the traps inherent in perhaps all extant positions.

Communism offered an epistemological principle through which numerous early-twentieth-century black thinkers, artists, and activists organized their world (see Foner and Shapiro, *American Communism*). Yet, Wright prioritizes reading and writing as enabling the black subject's negotiation of the rigidities of Southern Jim Crow or the more subtle racism of the North. In a coda added to the truncated 1945 edition of *Black Boy*, he looks back at his struggle for a way out of the South of strictly circumscribed possibilities: "It had been my *accidental reading* of fiction and literary criticism that had evoked in me vague glimpses of life's possibilities" (879; emphasis added). The changes in the perspectives of Wright's other protagonists, too, are more often than not accidental. Glimpses of different worlds, of unknown possibilities, come about as calamities whose consequences the person is often unable to bear. The most famous example of this is Bigger Thomas, who experiences a radical shift in perspective when he accidentally kills Mary Dalton, the daughter of his new employers. Surprised by her blind mother as he is laying the passed out girl to bed, Bigger pushes a pillow onto Mary's face to keep her from stirring. Although her mother initially appears to him as a "white blur," immediately after Mary's death – even before Bigger consciously realizes that he has suffocated her – the woman comes clearly into view: "Then suddenly her fingernails did not bite into his wrists. Mary's fingers loosened. … Her body was still. … He could see Mrs. Dalton plainly now" (*Native Son* 74). This revelatory moment is repeated in Bigger's subsequent realization of his having gained a unique view of the surrounding reality: "if he could see while others were blind then he could get what he wanted and never be caught at it" (91). At stake is nothing less than the reinvention of reality: as the result of this dislocation, he "had created a new world for himself" (205).

The protagonist of "The Man Who Was Almost a Man" is similarly thrust out of his circumscribed place as a young black man through an unintentional killing. As Edward Margolies notes (87), Bigger's eye-opening manslaughter is echoed in Dave Saunders' shooting accident that kills the mule of his white employer. Trying to prove his "manhood" to himself, the protagonist acquires a used gun. His blindly bumbling actions – the gun goes off when he "shut[s] his eyes and tighten[s] his forefinger" (19) – precipitate an unexpected chain of events. As a consequence of the shooting, the publicly embarrassed Dave has to agree to compensate for the dead animal by having his wages garnered for the next two years. To escape his humiliation, he decides on a whim to jump a passing train. The story ends with a glimpse of an unactualized future as Dave's gaze follows the railroad tracks that bear him away from the town: "Ahead the long rails were glinting in the moonlight, stretching away, away to somewhere, somewhere where he could be a man … ." (26; ellipsis in original). The train and the tracks here repeat their customary role in African American representations as the "promise of unrestrained mobility and unlimited freedom" (Baker 236). Wright arguably alludes to this tradition also in *The Outsider* (1953), where Cross Damon discovers his own private Underground Railroad: he manages an escape from his old life as the result of a subway accident where a stranger's dead body is mistaken for his. As with Bigger Thomas and Cross Damon, the incident in "The Man Who Was Almost a Man" opens the black man's eyes to a world of possibilities; we do not follow Dave far enough to see if his accidental release leads to a future different from Bigger's or Cross's bleak fates.

Bigger's and Dave's perspectives are perhaps synthesized in the figure of Fred Daniels, the protagonist of "The Man Who Lived Underground." The short story describes Daniels's escape from the police, who hunt him for an unnamed crime. Fleeing the law, Fred slips down a manhole into the city sewers. The underground tunnels provide him an unexpected vantage point from which to watch, undetected, everyday life in the city: he spies people in a church, a mortuary, a cinema, an office. He occupies the position of a hidden observer in which Bigger, too, discovers himself after Mary's murder, and particularly as he hides himself in the derelict buildings of the Black Belt.

In figuring the dank recesses of the city sewers as a site of revelation, Wright follows the tradition of black (male) writing from Jean Toomer and Claude McKay to Ralph Ellison and Amiri Baraka, for whom, as Melvin Dixon shows, the underground functions as a recurring trope of insight and self-creation. The "lower frequencies" (Ellison 572) of the underground attune Fred Daniels to the knowledge of everyone's existential guilt, and he resurfaces burdened with an urgent message for the world. His frustrated attempts to convey his message echo existentialist arguments about humankind's unconquerable isolation and alienation, one's perennial inability to be understood and recognized by the other. Fred's dilemma exemplifies the incommunicability of experiences across the gulf of perspectives: "The distance between what he felt and what these men meant was vast" (80). This is the "psychological distance" that, in his later work, Wright finds operative in the condition of (post)coloniality (*White* 6).

Fred's surreal experience of disjointedness also repeats the double-conscious subject's isolation by the Veil of race prejudice and segregation that Du Bois exemplifies throughout his work. In *Dusk of Dawn* (1940), Du Bois draws his own allegory of the cave, whose protagonist resembles Fred Daniels. Much like Fred, the man in Du Bois's vignette is granted a unique spectatorial slant: he looks at the world from "a dark cave," a position of isolation and distance. Convinced that his insight must be mediated to others, he – again like Fred Daniels – tries to draw the attention of the passersby, "speak[ing] courteously and persuasively," only to be met with bemused and uncomprehending stares. He shares his situation with other black men, all separated from the world by a barrier that, in his earlier work, Du Bois calls the Veil. Failing to get a hearing, it dawns on the men "that some thick sheet of invisible but horribly tangible plate glass is between them and the world." With their continued failure of communication, some "may scream and hurl themselves against the barriers. ... They

may even, here and there, break through in blood and disfigurement, and find themselves faced by a horrified, implacable, and quite overwhelming mob of people frightened for their own very existence" (130–1). This anecdote illustrates Du Bois's
experiences as a politically motivated scholar of culture. Like the scholar who seeks,
and fails, to convince his audience of the absurdity of race prejudice in objective terms,
Fred, reemerging from the underground, tries to inform others of what he has seen,
only to be met with dismissive, frightened, and puzzled reactions. He is finally killed
in cold blood by Lawson, one of the detectives assigned to his case. As a representative
of the law, "law's son" realizes the incompatibility of Fred's insight and the functioning of the law in its extant arrangement above ground. As he says, " 'You've got to
shoot this kind. They'd wreck things' " (92).

The underground perspective is thematized also in "The Man Who Went to
Chicago," a fragment of "The Horror and the Glory," the second section of Wright's
autobiography, published posthumously as *American Hunger* (1977). The story culminates in a description of its protagonist's job in a research hospital where he and other
black workers carry out their menial tasks in the institution's basement: "we occupied
an underworld position, remembering that we must restrict ourselves – when not
engaged upon some task – to the basement corridors, so that we would not mingle
with white nurses, doctors, and visitors" (237). As in his autobiography in general,
Wright attributes to his narrator a curiosity about the world(s) beyond the Veil to
which other black characters remain insensitive.[3] Restless in his position, the narrator
keenly follows the research procedures carried out by the white staff. In this, he is
unlike his co-workers, who don't see the point of "looking at the world of another
race" (239): "They were conditioned to their racial 'place,' had learned to see only a
part of the whites and the white world; and the whites, too, had learned to see only
a part of the lives of the blacks and their world" (243).

Here, as elsewhere, Wright delights in depicting the irrational outcomes of encounters across incompatible epistemological positions, such as the ones inhabited by the
white researchers and the black underlings. This is the drama – whether tragedy or
comedy – of the color line, where black and white meet as strangers, unable or unwilling to share each other's perspectives. The autobiographical tale develops into a surreal
farce as two of the hospital's black workers, irked by years of animosity, get into a
fight, pushing over cages of rats, mice, rabbits, and guinea pigs. After the scuffle, the
men scramble to save their jobs by restoring a semblance of order. Based on guesswork
and desperation, they devise a system according to which they return the animals in
their cages:

> We broke the rabbits down into two general groups; those that had fur on their bellies
> and those that did not. We knew that all those rabbits that had shaven bellies – our
> scientific knowledge adequately covered this point because it was our job to shave
> the rabbits – were undergoing the Aschheim-Zondek tests. But in what pen did a
> given rabbit belong to? We did not know. I solved the problem very simply. I counted
> the shaven rabbits; they numbered seventeen. I counted the pens labeled

"Aschheim-Zondek," then proceeded to drop a shaven rabbit into each pen at random. And again we were numerically successful. At least white America had taught us how to count. ... (248; ellipsis in original)

The men are relieved to find that none of the researchers, as they return to work and handle the animals, suspect anything. Yet, the narrator is left wondering: "Was some scientific hypothesis, well on its way to validation and ultimate public use, discarded because of unexpected findings on that cold winter day? Was some tested principle given a new and strange refinement because of fresh, remarkable evidence? Did some brooding research worker ... get a wild, if brief, glimpse of a new scientific truth?" (250). That the non-communication between the two worlds scrambles what is supposed to be the rational practice of science is one of Wright's indictments of racialized perspectives. For Wright, the convolutions of everyday racial choreographies – the ethics of living Jim Crow, whether in the South or the North – jeopardize the rational Weltanschauung, whose importance he, a student of Husserl, never relinquished.

If such miscommunications give way to comedy in "The Man Who Went to Chicago,"[4] elsewhere they lead to violence and tragedy, as in the case of Bigger Thomas, Fred Daniels, and Saul Saunders, the protagonist of "The Man Who Killed a Shadow." Saunders murders a white librarian who, acting out some sexualized race fantasies of her own, crudely attempts to come on to the black man. The white woman's sexualization of black masculinity and the black man's terror of white women, and their miserable consequences, are pathologies bred by the ideologies of white supremacy. The impossibility of communication between the worlds of blackness and whiteness leads to tragedy here as it does in *Native Son*. The distance between the two actors' perspectives allows the kind of dehumanization of the other that made possible the blind violence of lynching practices.[5] Saul's perspective onto the white world is such that, engulfed in fear like Bigger's, he is unable to relate to the suffering of the woman whom he brutally beats to death: "It never occurred to him that he could help her, that she might be in pain; he never wondered even if she were dead" (205). At worst, the perspective of distance makes it impossible for people to react humanely to each other across the color line.

Rational communication, and particularly its failures, concerns Wright also in his later work, where he becomes increasingly interested in describing the look of the world in the context of global anticolonial struggles. His emphasis on the historical and political functioning of vision in diasporic politics aligns his thinking with contemporary postcolonial theory. In its concern with the dialectics of seeing, his work intersects with, for example, that of the Barbadian novelist George Lamming and the Martiniquan theorist Frantz Fanon. In "A Way of Seeing" (1960), Lamming proclaims that "what a person thinks is very much determined by the way that person sees" (56). Throughout his oeuvre, Fanon similarly casts (post)coloniality in terms of a radical contestation between worldviews. As exemplified in his famous depiction, in "Algeria Unveiled" (1959), of the struggle against the French occupiers, colonialism seeks to monopolize the means of describing the world, but in the very process elicits unexpected counterstrategies whereby the colonized begin to manipulate the field of vision to their advantage. As Wright notes in his essay collection, *White Man, Listen!* (1957), "oppression helps to forge in the oppressed the very qualities that eventually bring about the downfall of the oppressor" (21).

One of Wright's depictions of the unmanageable complexities, and the unforeseen consequences, of colonialism is "Man, God Ain't Like That. ..." Describing the fatal misunderstandings brought about by incompatible worldviews, the story follows the trip to Africa by a Western artist – in search of his "black period" (171) – and his wife, who upon returning to Europe bring with them Babu, their loyal African servant. The Westerners gaze at the life of the "natives" from the exoticizing and patronizing perspective of colonialism. They consider natives "baboons" and "monkeys" (165) and, like Hegel and other Western thinkers whose writings legitimated paternalistic views of slavery, regard them as mere children (172). From the Eurocentric perspective, Babu seems an ideal native. He eagerly adopts Western ideals and acquiesces in his own humble place in the scheme of things, seeking to understand the white man's slant: "Babu wonder how black folks look to Massa" (169). Calling John "Massa" and enjoying the pathos of Christian hymns (166–7), he becomes an example of how, as Fanon writes in "Racism and Culture," colonialism "manages to impose on the native new ways of seeing" (38).

Babu's is what Wright elsewhere calls "the frog perspective," a term that conjoins Nietzschean perspectivism and psychoanalytic theories of ambivalence. The colonized subject, he argues, gazes at the colonizer's world "from below upward"; the frog perspective "describe[s] ... a sense of someone who feels himself lower than others. ... A certain degree of hate combined with love (ambivalence) is always involved in this looking from below upward. ... He loves the object because he would like to resemble it; he hates the object because his chances of resembling it are remote, slight" (*White* 6). While this perspective often results in the pathologies that Fanon catalogues in *Black Skin, White Masks* (1952), "Man, God Ain't Like That ..." renders the drama a tragicomedy. Despite the successful conversion of the African pagan into a worshiper of Western culture, the Europeans don't quite understand what they have done in imposing their worldview on Babu. Adopting Christian mythology, he becomes convinced that his master is the Son of God and, to fulfill Biblical prophecy, ends up killing his Savior.

If contemporary critics have explored the similarities and differences between the position of the black American and that of the colonized subject, Wright argues that they share a peculiar angle on the world. As he writes in his foreword to George Padmore's *Pan-Africanism or Communism* (1956), "The black man's is a strange situation; it is a perspective, an angle of vision held by oppressed people; it is an outlook of people looking upward from below" (xxii). This odd slant, and its tragicomic ramifications, drives Bigger, Babu, and many of Wright's other protagonists.

Were we to identify one motivation behind Wright's search for a productive perspective, it is his hope of accomplishing a rational description of the world, one that could be embraced by the white and the black of the United States, the ex-colonizer and the ex-colonized of the postcolonial world. This commonly accepted point of view would end the convoluted performances that have distorted communications across the color line. Wright shares this ambition with such postcolonial thinkers as Aimé Césaire, who seeks to "sweep out all the obscurers, all the inventors of subterfuges, the charlatans and tricksters, the dealers in gobbledygook" (34). As he notes in an interview, "a society is not very strong when it rests upon a large basis of secret, hidden things, like quicksand. In my opinion, things must be in the open" (*Conversations* 237).

As such, Wright's ethics is arguably guided by post-Enlightenment rationalism, particularly by Husserlian phenomenology's efforts to cut through inaccurate, ideological, or biased descriptions of phenomena.[6] Phenomenology seeks the "bracketing" of misleading apprehensions and the consequent discovery of a shared, rational point of view. For Husserl, the elimination of false beliefs and perceptions allows the production of a global, shared worldview, one that would enable unhindered communication between self-possessed subjects.

Wright, too, wants to reorganize the tortured Weltanschauung of the twentieth century, informed by the guilt, fear, and bad faith bred by history's atrocities.[7] He may have recognized an anti-racist methodology in Husserl's work, given that "phenomenology wanted to be a radically new philosophical method that strives toward freedom from prejudice" (Held 33). If we accept the Husserlian bent of Wright's art of perspective, we must nevertheless note their differing estimations of the *cost* of one's efforts at rationality. According to Husserl, the "phenomenological reduction" – the suspension of one's "natural attitudes" – is something "we can quite freely exercise" (§31/59). He asserts that "we are completely free to modify every positing and every judging" (§32/60). For the black Americans and colonized subjects of Wright's texts, however, the bracketing of belief – of false perspectives – constitutes not a free act but a dangerous transgression inviting immediate punitive measures.

Wright for the most part wants the world organized according to a shared, rational standpoint. Fatal miscalculations, such as Bigger's murder of Mary and Babu's killing of his master, are the unforeseen consequences of incompossible worldviews, the blind arrogance that, according to Wright and others, informs Western views of its others. Yet, the non-communication between incongruent ways of looking at the world, and perceiving the gaze of the other, simultaneously guarantees that "imperialists of the twentieth century are men who are always being constantly and unpleasantly surprised" (Wright, *Black Power* 132). Making an observation whose relevance contemporary readers may recognize, Wright continues elsewhere: "rarely do things work out … the way the white man had hoped and thought they would, in the countries he colonized" (*Conversations* 161). An early theorist of the stupidity and arrogance of the powerful, Wright also finds a bittersweet hope in the uneven exchanges carried out on (what Mary Louise Pratt calls) "contact zones," whether of the American scene or the colonized world.

NOTES

1 This term appears in Wright, *Black Boy*, 164, 238; *The Outsider*, 492, 497, 526, 675 ("the sight of the world"), 774; and *Father's*, 34.

2 Similarly, in its deployment of the prophetic tradition of the Jeremiad (see Hubbard), David Walker's proto–Black Nationalist manifesto of 1829 is concerned with the revolutionary power of prophetic visions.

3 This tendency has been critiqued by numerous commentators. Henry Louis Gates, Jr., writes that, in his autobiography, Wright casts other blacks as "pitiable victims of the pathology of slavery and racial segregation who surround and suffocate him. Indeed, Wright wills [the narrator's] special self into being through the agency of contrast: the sensitive, healthy part is foregrounded against a determined, defeated black whole" (182). Valerie Smith continues: "Wright portrays with contempt the larger black community, identifying it with what he sees as an extreme tendency toward accommodation. Wright is especially judgmental with regard to black women. … [H]is protagonists routinely reject their connections to black women as a stage in their search for liberation" (435).

4 "Man of All Work" similarly parodies the blindness inherent in the white perspective. To support his wife and child, the story's protagonist dresses in drag to land a job as a domestic in a white family. While the white father, blinded by race even to gender differences, attempts to come on to the new black maid, it is only the young child of the family, still relatively unschooled in the gendered and racialized practices of vision, who sees through the black man's performance.

5 For graphic descriptions, verbal and visual, of the history of lynching, see Allen et al.

6 For a brief record of Wright's engagement with Husserl, see Fabre, *Richard*, 76–7. I have elsewhere argued for the benefit of reading Wright's emphasis on perspective through what Lacanian psychoanalysis, especially in its reading of Renaissance perspective, suggests to us about the negotiations of visibility and power: see Tuhkanen, *The American Optic*, esp. introduction and chapter 1.

7 For Wright's discussion of the pathologies of Western modernity, see his introduction to Drake and Clayton.

REFERENCES AND FURTHER READING

Allen, James, Hilton Als, et al. *Without Sanctuary: Lynching Photography in America*. Santa Fe, NM: Twin Palms, 2002.

Baker, Houston A., Jr. "Belief, Theory, and Blues: Notes for a Post-Structuralist Criticism of Afro-American Literature." 1986. Rpt. in Napier, ed., *African American Literary Theory*, 224–41.

Césaire, Aimé. *Discourse on Colonialism*. 1955. Trans. Joan Pinkham. New York: Monthly Review Press, 1972.

Derrida, Jacques. *Given Time: I. Counterfeit Money*. 1991. Trans. Peggy Kamuf. Chicago: University of Chicago Press, 1992.

Dixon, Melvin. *Ride Out the Wilderness: Geography and Identity in Afro-American Literature*. Urbana: University of Illinois Press, 1987.

Douglass, Frederick. *Autobiographies*. Notes by Henry Louis Gates, Jr. 1994. New York: Penguin/Library of America, 1996.

———. *My Bondage and My Freedom*. 1855. Rpt. in *Autobiographies*, 103–452.

———. *Narrative of the Life of Frederick Douglass, an American Slave*. 1845. Rpt. in *Autobiographies*, 1–102.

Du Bois, W. E. B. *Dusk of Dawn: An Essay toward an Autobiography of a Race Concept*. 1940. New Brunswick, NJ: Transaction, 1991.

———. *The Souls of Black Folk*. 1903. Ed. Henry Louis Gates, Jr., and Terri Hume Oliver. New York: W. W. Norton, 1999.

Ellison, Ralph. *Invisible Man*. 1952. New York: Modern Library, 1994.

Fabre, Michel. *Richard Wright: Books and Writers*. Jackson: University Press of Mississippi, 1990.

———. *The Unfinished Quest of Richard Wright*. 2nd edn. Trans. Isabel Barzun. Urbana: University of Illinois Press, 1993.

Fanon, Frantz. *Black Skin, White Masks*. 1952. Trans. Charles Lam Markmann. 1967. New York: Grove Press, 1982.

———. "Algeria Unveiled." *A Dying Colonialism*. 1959. Trans. Haakon Chevalier. 1965. New York: Grove Press, 1990. 35–67.

———. "Racism and Culture." *Toward the African Revolution: Political Essays*. 1964. Trans. Haakon Chevalier. 1967. New York: Grove Press, 1988. 29–44.

Foner, Philip S., and Herbert Shapiro, eds. *American Communism and Black Americans: A Documentary History, 1930–1934*. Philadelphia: Temple University Press, 1991.

Gates, Henry Louis, Jr. *The Signifying Monkey: A Theory of African-American Literary Criticism*. New York: Oxford University Press, 1989.

Gates, Henry Louis, Jr., and K. A. Appiah, eds. *Richard Wright: Critical Perspectives Past and Present*. New York: Amistad, 1993.

Held, Klaus. "Husserl's Phenomenology of the Life-World." Trans. Lanei Rodemeyer. *The New Husserl*. Ed. Donn Welton. Bloomington: Indiana University Press, 2003. 32–62.

Hubbard, Dolan. "David Walker's *Appeal* and the American Puritan Jeremiadic Tradition." *Centennial Review* 30.3 (Summer 1986): 331–46.

Husserl, Edmund. *Ideas Pertaining to a Pure Phenomenology and to a Phenomenological Philosophy, First Book: General Introduction to a Pure Phenomenology*. 1913. Trans. F. Kersten. The Hague: Martinus Nijhoff, 1982.

Lamming, George. "A Way of Seeing." *The Pleasures of Exile*. 1960. Ann Arbor: University of Michigan Press, 1992. 56–85.

Levine, Lawrence W. *Black Culture and Black Consciousness: Afro-American Folk Thought from Slavery to Freedom*. New York: Oxford University Press, 1977.

Locke, Alain. "Self-Criticism: The Third Dimension of Culture." 1950. Rpt. in Napier, ed., *African American Literary Theory*, 58–61.

Margolies, Edward. "Wright's Craft: The Short Stories." 1969. Rpt. in Gates and Appiah, eds., *Richard Wright*, 75–97.

Napier, Winston, ed. *African American Literary Theory: A Reorder*. New York: New York University Press, 2000.

Pratt, Mary Louise. "Arts of the Contact Zone." *Profession* 91 (1991): 33–40.

Smith, Valerie. "Alienation and Creativity in the Fiction of Richard Wright." 1987. Rpt. in Gates and Appiah, eds., *Richard Wright*, 433–47.

Tuhkanen, Mikko. *The American Optic: Psychoanalysis, Critical Race Theory, and Richard Wright*. Albany: State University of New York Press, 2009.

Walker, David. *David Walker's Appeal to the Coloured Citizens of the World*. 1829. Ed. Peter P. Hinks. 2000. University Park: Pennsylvania State University Press, 2006.

Wright, Richard. *American Hunger*. 1977. New York: Harper & Row, 1979.

———. *Black Boy (American Hunger)*. 1945. Rpt. in *Later Works*, 1–365, 875–84.

———. *Black Power: A Record of Reactions in a Land of Pathos*. 1954. New York: HarperPerennial, 1995.

———. "Blueprint for Negro Writing." 1937. Rpt. in *Richard Wright Reader*. Ed. Ellen Wright and Michel Fabre. New York: Harper & Row, 1978. 36–49.

———. *Later Works*. New York: Library of America, 1991.

———. "Bright and Morning Star." *Uncle Tom's Children*. 1940. New York: HarperPerennial, 1993. 221–63.

———. *Conversations with Richard Wright*. Eds. Keneth Kinnamon and Michel Fabre. Jackson: University Press of Mississippi, 1993.

———. *Eight Men*. 1961. New York: Thunder's Mouth Press, 1987.

———. *A Father's Law*. New York: HarperPerennial, 2008.

———. Foreword to George Padmore, *Pan-Africanism or Communism*. 1956. Garden City, NY: Anchor, 1972. xxi–xxiv.

———. Introduction to St. Clair Drake and Horace R. Clayton. *Black Metropolis: A Study of Negro Life in a Northern City*. New York: Harcourt, Brace, 1945. xvii–xxxiv.

———. "Man, God Ain't Like That ..." *Eight Men*, 163–92.

———. "Man of All Work." *Eight Men*, 117–62.

———. "The Man Who Killed a Shadow." *Eight Men*, 193–209.

———. "The Man Who Lived Underground." *Eight Men*, 27–92.

———. "The Man Who Was Almost a Man." *Eight Men*, 11–26.

———. "The Man Who Went to Chicago." *Eight Men*, 210–50.

———. *Native Son*. New York: Harper, 1940.

———. *The Outsider*. 1953. Rpt. in *Later Works*, 367–841.

———. *White Man, Listen!* 1957. Garden City, NY: Anchor, 1964.

21

Small Planets: The Short Fiction of Saul Bellow

Gloria L. Cronin

Saul Bellow was one of four children born to Abraham and Lescha Bellow in Lachine, Montreal, Canada, in 1915. The family lived in the poor Jewish community of Lachine until he was 5 years old and, in 1924, left for the tenements of Humboldt's Park, Chicago, a Jewish immigrant neighborhood which boasted a population of about 225,000. Son of Russian Jews from St. Petersburg, the young "Solly" Bellow came of age on the colorful streets of Lachine and North Side Chicago amid throngs of Jewish, French, Polish, German, Italian, and Russian immigrants. Chicago in the 1920s was rife with corrupt ward politicians and gangsters, and mired in Prohibition, bootlegging, gambling, and street violence. It certainly did not nurture its writers within a community of intellectuals. Like most American writers, Bellow was self-made, emerging out of the same folkloric standards as did William Faulkner, Ernest Hemingway, and Sinclair Lewis. His remoteness from the centers of culture was so profound, he once told a friend that he would have kissed the floor of a café if there had been one. Instead, he noted humorously, he grew up among "greasy-spoon joints, cafeterias and one-arm joints" (Atlas 4). As James Atlas, Bellow's biographer, points out, "Culture in Chicago was a marginal enterprise. Dominated by the brute forces of industry, reeking stockyards, farm machinery works and automobile assembly lines, it was a city in Carl Sandberg's famous line, of 'big shoulders'" (5).

In Chicago, things were done for the first time, which the rest of the world later learned and imitated. Capitalist production was pioneered in the stockyards, in refrigerator cars, in the creation of the Pullman, in the creation of farm machinery, and with it also certain urban political phenomena which are associated with the new condition of modern democracy (74).

Charlie Citrine of *Humboldt's Gift* (1975) says that, in Chicago, you could truly "examine the human spirit under industrialism" (108) in all its agony and nightmare. He, like his creator, knows he must continue to exert the equal sovereignty of the human imagination over modern science. The small crocus growing out through the cracks of the Chicago pavement convinces him that much of the spirit is still alive despite the urban nightmare. Such relentless mapping of the evidences of the human spirit from within the nightmare of the twentieth century became, for Bellow, a lifelong battle with the philosophical premises of the early modern writers.

Although Chicago was not Hemingway's 1920s Paris, it was Bellow's nineteenth-century Paris. Before him were the indigenous traditions of William Dean Howells, Theodore Dreiser, and Sherwood Anderson, and behind him the European traditions of Anton Chekhov, Fyodor Dostoevsky, Leo Tolstoy, Marcel Proust, and the nine-teenth-century American Transcendentalists. In Chicago's public library he carefully studied the social realism of Theodore Dreiser, Edgar Lee Masters, and Vachel Lindsay. Later he would a study the prose style of Ernest Hemingway with what James Atlas describes as a surgeon's care. Saul Bellow's fiction emerges from these literary tradi-tions plus the city's sheer brute force and energy. The city as physical and metaphysical backdrop to the fiction appears almost as a character with its own horde of motley immigrants, its smells, its massive industrial energy, its commercial crassness, and its colorful gangsterism. Bellow's Chicago is as recognizable as James Joyce's Dublin, but even more identifiable would be his uniquely Chicagoan, Jewish voice. It is this uniquely contemporary distillation of contemporary Chicago street language, book culture, and Yiddish family interchange with which these self-communing, home-grown intellectuals express the spiritual essence of themselves and their place in time.

Saul Bellow emerged from a Jewish Russian immigrant community in which his bookishness was encouraged by his doting mother Lescha (Lisa). She was descended from a long line of Jewish rabbis and was the daughter of a prominent St. Petersburg rabbi. Consequently, she was well read, and valued books. Lisa bequeathed to Saul her two passionate loves, the classics of Russian literature and the sentimental "sitcom" accounts of Jewish family life that appeared in the Jewish *Daily Forward.* Lisa hoped her prodigy of a son would become a rabbi like his long line of grandfathers, given his phenomenal memory and early proclivity for Hebrew, Russian, English, and French. Bellow's father, Abraham, however, had no patience with books and hoped his sons would "make good" as American capitalists. While Saul's brothers followed Abraham's often dishonest entrepreneurial obsessions, Saul, the sickly, nostalgic son, inclined more to his rabbinical heritage. Throughout his difficult childhood, his long hospitalization, and his near-death experience with tuberculosis, Lisa protected him from his volatile, disapproving father and scoffing brothers. Her death when Saul was barely 16 was a trauma from which he never recovered. Bellow's fiction is always death-haunted and registers countless broken family relationships. Not one of the heroes will successfully replicate the family of childhood; no son will negotiate the repeated father–son impasses; no male brotherhood will succeed until *Ravelstein* (2000); no marriage will survive, and yet all Bellow's nostalgic intellectual men will yearn endlessly for the warm immigrant loving of the Old World Jewish family. But despite this, Bellow's fiction is inhabited by numerous lovingly and shrewdly drawn Hogarthian portraits of aunts, uncles, grandmothers, boarders, neighbors, in-laws, operators, gangsters, business tycoons, gamblers, salesmen, minor criminals, bath-house inhabitants, shrews, destructive lovers, voracious divorce lawyers, Holocaust survivors, and poolroom "operators" – all drawn by a writer with a prodigious memory and a great gift for portraiture.

Despite Bellow's permanent disorientation at the loss of his mother, he knew, even in high school, that he belonged to the intellectual life, despite the improbabilities of the Chicago scene. His first short story, "The Hell It Can't," appeared in the *Daily Northwestern* (February 1936), his Tuley High School student paper. Even before entering Northwestern in 1935, he had ambitiously decided to become not just a great Chicago writer, or famous Jewish American writer, but a world-class writer. He would follow in Hemingway's footsteps by attempting to dominate the second half of the twentieth century as Hemingway had the first half.

The Early Years: 1933–1958

Bellow's life as a writer begins and ends with short fiction. In these early years, he produced numerous short stories, three novellas, and a collection of short stories. In 1941, "Two Morning Monologues" appeared in the May/June issue of the *Partisan Review*, the same issue in which one of Eliot's *Four Quartets*, as well as contributions by Clement Greenburg, Allan Tate, and Paul Goodman, appeared. It was an auspicious beginning. Rather fine sketches, both pieces feature self-communing monologuists. The intellectual monologuist now becomes a standard feature of Bellow's fiction.

Mandelbaum, unemployed, cerebral, and preoccupied with the phenomenological, will become a prototype. He is a classic Jamesian noticer whose job it is to discern the nature of things. Significantly, as he wanders the streets, he tells us he has no brothers. By this time, Bellow is thoroughly estranged from his father and brothers, and, throughout the rest of his fiction, whenever brothers appear, they will be rather crass, obsessed American money-makers. All future fictions, with the exception of *Ravelstein* (2000), will lament the failure of male bonding. While the character Mandelbaum in this story carries the pattern for all future Bellow heroes, the second monologue contains the pattern of gritty Chicago street life that will become Bellow's recurring backdrop. Friefeld is only Bellow's first con artist, low-life, and first-class operator. In these first two stories, Bellow is also beginning to find his distinctive Chicagoan-Yiddish voice.

"The Mexican General" (1942), also published in *Partisan Review*, tells the story of Trotsky's assassination in Mexico, detailing the assassin's attack, the scene at the morgue, the chaotic events at the Patzcuaro Hotel, and a brilliant portrait of the self-important, bustling general who steals the limelight at the press conferences which follow. Citron, the lieutenant, through whose eyes the account is narrated, is a prototype of future Bellow intellectuals with his academically Weberian accounts of things. Bellow wrote the story after joining the Trotskyite socialist movement and traveling to Mexico to meet Trotsky. To his great disappointment, he arrived the day after the attack only to find his hero dead and lying in state. Bellow's philosophical question in this story concerns historical contingency and the potency of the individual – does a man make history or does history make a man? It is a recurring question throughout all of his subsequent fiction. Questioning Nietzsche and Marx, he wants to know if history is the record of public acts by great men or if some other force, like nature, is at work.

"Mr. Katz, Mr. Cohen, and Cosmology," written the same year, features two men in a Montreal boarding house. Katz is a would-be intellectual, while Cohen is an unimaginative tailor who thinks the world is flat and who has never heard of the Pacific Ocean. Both are prototypes for the inner dialectic between academic learning and witty Yiddish street smarts which will characterize all of Bellow's future thinkers. Characteristically, it is the seemingly ignorant Yiddish comedian, Cohen, who manages to best the autodidact's theories with his wry Yiddish folk wit. These stories were followed by more short fiction: "Dora" (1949), "Sermon by Dr. Pep" (1949), "The Trip to Galena" (1950), "Looking for Mr. Green" (1951), "By the Rock Wall" (1951), "Address by Gooley McDowell to the Hasbeens Club of Chicago" (1951), "The Gonzaga Manuscripts" (1954), and "Leaving the Yellow House" (1958). Three of these stories would eventually make their way into his first collection, *Mosby's Memoirs* (1968).

Bellow's apprenticeship in short fiction culminated during these early years with three novellas, *Dangling Man* (1944), *The Victim* (1947), and *Seize the Day* (1956). All of these exemplify the form that ultimately expresses, for him, the contemporary rather than the modern literary era. All three novellas feature the plight of the think-ing man struggling to retain his sense of the preciousness of life, and the importance of human feeling. Full of reverence, optimism, Yiddish humor, a Talmudic sense of suffering, disgust with existentialist angst, and the hero's general movement from estrangement to acceptance, each of these novellas also echoes Bellow's sense of the discontinuities and fallen appearances of contemporary life. But they also register his growing refusal to accept the "wasteland" mentality of modernist literature – the philosophical protest that will shape all of his future writing.

Dangling Man (1944) contains, in miniature, the pattern of all his subsequent work. It evidences the striking exclusion of the female voice, the staging of a male world, and a narcissistic hero trapped within his own solipsism. Joseph is a would-be writer and intellectual caught waiting for the Draft. A misplaced romantic, he believes that he can make the old transcendental move to receive intellectual and spiritual enlight-enment, a move that involves isolating himself within the confines of a cheap New York boarding house as he studies the great writers of the Romantic and Enlighten-ment periods. As the months go by, Joseph quarrels with nearly all his friends and relatives, lives off the earnings of his faithful wife, Eva, cruelly tries to control and conform her to his expectations, succumbs to fits of paranoia and anger, engages in a desultory affair, learns to hate the physical decay of his elderly neighbors, and is haunted by death anxieties. Finally, he admits his intellectual experiment has been a failure – that his perspectives have all dead-ended within the four walls of his shabby room. Reduced to the same physical, social, and historical denominators as everyone around him, he is last seen standing in a line of naked military recruits being prodded and poked by an elderly physician. His search for a special fate is temporarily suspended in a common ignominy.

Dangling Man reflects much of Bellow's early life as a young, newly wed intellectual. Poor, ambitious, and immersed in literature of all kinds, Bellow was isolated in his in-laws' Ravenswood apartment while trying to write his first novel on a card table in the back room. The work is a lament by a young American artist who does not know how to join the mainstream of Chicagoan or American life without losing the spiritual value of his isolation. This novella also reflects the preoccupation that 1940s American intellectuals had with French existentialism. His first three novellas all ask profound questions about individual freedom, moral responsibility, death, and social contract. Joseph expresses his spiritual ennui as an imprisoning and inadequate whiteness during his dreams about the tantalizing space of the exotic and the spiritual that is troped as exotically African. Bellow will continue to lace several of his books with racial imagery from the colonial African literary archive as he explores a savage and primitive urban modernity. Ultimately, however, it was the great European, British, Irish, and American moderns – Flaubert, Dostoevsky, Lawrence, Eliot, and Joyce – who directly influenced the form, content, and style of Bellow's first three novellas.

Dangling Man was immediately hailed as an important book written with style, mastery, and sharp, cutting language, while *The Victim* (1947), written in the aftermath of the Holocaust and the Nuremberg tribunals, garnered even more critical praise. The latter explores the ability of twentieth-century man to cope with victimization and paranoia. During one long, hot summer when his wife is visiting her parents, Asa Levanthal wrestles with rising fears about job security, anti-Semitism, and the predations of his seedy, gentile nemesis, Kirby Allbee. Asa is a Jew scarred by his mother's madness and screaming fits and by his failure to bond with his father. When he loses both parents before his adult life really begins, he finds himself emotionally ill-equipped for life. Asa's brother, Max, is absent for the summer, leaving Asa at the mercy of his immigrant sister-in-law's pleas for help with expenses. Furthermore, he must assume responsibility for his young nephew, Mickey. But Mickey sickens and dies before Max's return, deepening Asa's paranoia and activating his prejudices about his Roman Catholic, immigrant in-laws. He fears that the mad-looking, superstitious Catholic immigrant mother-in-law blames him for his nephew's death.

Beneath all this, Bellow relentlessly explores the spiritual importance of the human social contract and the Biblical injunction to be our brothers' keepers. The hellishly hot summer and the underlying theme of anti-Semitism reflect the mood of American Jewry in the immediate aftermath of the Holocaust. We last see Asa accompanied by his recently returned wife, who is clearly pregnant. Asa, about to be a father, is finally reconciled to his brother, rid of the gentile Allbee, and able to quell the anxieties that paranoia, anger, and self-isolation have produced in him. More importantly, he is able to admit his dependency on love and friendship. Asa Leventhal is the eternal Jew who must deal emotionally with the post-Holocaust world and still accept that he is literally his brother's keeper.

Both of Bellow's early novellas reflect American society's intellectual and moral preoccupations of the day, as well as a certain culmination of the modernist ideological debate in American literature that was bent on contrasting the philosophical premises of European existentialism with traditional Judeo-Christian humanism. Both novellas demonstrate Bellow's engagement with such writers as Kierkegaard, Dostoevski, Heidegger, Nietzsche, Hobbes, and Sartre. Behind the nightmarish cityscape of *The Victim*, we see Bellow again describing the city as a chaotic, primeval African jungle and as a pitiless African lion who has no regard for human life. Inside these two African tropes, Bellow registers the inhumanity of the moment and explores the case for "Civilization." Both novellas portray nostalgia over the failure of the romantic quest, the moral exhaustion of an entire generation of young men who came of age in the 1940s, and the moral bankruptcy of a metaphysically derived humanism. Questions about freedom, goodness, absurdity, death, monastic solitude, and existential anxiety mark them both. Years later, Bellow called *Dangling Man* his MA and *The Victim* his PhD. However, they are exquisitely written explorations of the historical traumas of the first half of the century, and, as such, they enabled him finally to make his break with European modernism.

The third of these novellas that culminates his early period is *Seize the Day* (1956), Bellow's most read and anthologized novella. It is a remarkably sober retreat from the exuberance of his jumbo-sized novel, *The Adventures of Augie March* (1953), which preceded it, and has all the surface appearance of yet another modernist "victim novel." Set in an urban wasteland replete with the sepulchral Hotel Gloriana, this novella features the hapless Tommy Wilhelm, who is unemployed and estranged from his wife and children. As a young man, he has rejected his father's profession (medicine), tried out for a career in Hollywood, changed his name, fallen prey to a phony talent scout, ended up in sales, and subsequently lost his sales district due to nepotism. The classic *schlemiehl* of Yiddish folklore, he winds up in the dreadful Hotel Gloriana borrowing money from his disgusted father and fielding intrusive questions from an elderly group of decaying capitalist fathers who brag endlessly of their sons' successes. Dr. Adler, embarrassed by his son's failure, lies about him to his friends. Wilhelm, not unlike Willy Loman, has failed to fulfill Dr. Adler's notions of masculine achievement in America, and the cruel old man is unable to express love for him.

Ultimately, Tommy is conned out of his remaining cash by the grotesque Dr. Tamkin, a devilish morality play figure and charlatan who spouts absurdist philosophy, mangled Freudianism, alienation ethics, and cheap nihilism. While Tommy longs for accessible, sensible truths, Tamkin assures him that there are only crooked lines. When Tommy asks him where he gets his ideas, Tamkin ironically replies, "I read the best of literature, science, and philosophy" (72). His advice to Tommy is to take no thought for tomorrow because the past has no value and the future is an impending nightmare. In spite of all this, Tommy seems naïvely determined to recover simplicity. His final emotional climax, some critics argue, is not bitterness at betrayal, but an epiphany of love for all the lurid, imperfect people like himself whom he discovers in Chicago's underground subway and in the nearby funeral

parlor. Bellow seems to be insisting that truth resides within the sufficiently human-
ized soul and requires no elaborate acquaintance with either philosophy or the stock
exchange.

Some readers have called Tommy Wilhelm pathetic, whereas others have called
him heroic. Many were dismayed with the book's tight organization and seemingly
modernist aesthetics, while others praised it for its concentration, intensity, and
focused crescendo. Years later, Bellow told an interviewer that he was so appalled at
the philosophical immaturity of *The Adventures of Augie March* (1953) that he wrote
the austere *Seize the Day* in an attempt to transcend the earlier novel's effusive and
emotional limitations. *Seize the Day,* however, may have been written during the same
time frame as his first two "alienation" novellas, though Bellow never more than
hinted at this. *Seize the Day* is ultimately an anti-modernist novella counterpointing
death and despair with psychic renewal and spiritual survival. Along with the fiction
that preceded it, it sets the pattern for the masterworks of the middle years.

The Middle Years: 1963–1988

By now firmly established as a preeminent twentieth-century author, Saul Bellow won
numerous awards and honorary degrees, all culminating in 1976 with the Nobel Prize.
During these great middle years, he produced his major novels: *Henderson the Rain
King* (1959), *Herzog* (1964), *Mr. Sammler's Planet* (1970), *Humboldt's Gift* (1975), *The
Dean's December* (1982), and *More Die of Heartbreak* (1987). However, Bellow also
continued his exploration of the short fiction form. More than just a workshop for
testing ideas, characters, and situations to be included in his longer fictions, the short
fiction genre increasingly functioned for Bellow as a statement on the passing of the
modern era. It has much to do with Bellow's perception of himself not only as successor to the era of the moderns – notorious for their large cerebral and experimental
novels – but as a reactionary anti-modernist. His career has been about "going against
the stream" (Simmons 33) by rejecting the intellectual assumptions of the modernist
writers in a concerted effort to deflect the main course of modernist thinking. His
rather Freudian "killing" of the modernist fathers – Conrad, Joyce, Lawrence, Rilke,
Mann, Eliot, and even Hemingway – is something he justifies by accusing them of
being party to the prolonged dominance of Anglo-American culture. In truth, the
ambitious Bellow needed to clear a space for himself. In the early short stories and
novellas, Bellow began expressing his dissatisfaction with the by now stock figure of
the alienated hero, the nihilistically absurd world, and the wasteland outlook. Instead,
he created a series of comically absurd romantic heroes, men of learning and sensibility
who spend their brief fictional lives refuting modernist philosophical skepticism and
refusing courtship of the void. He blamed English Departments for being the Paris
substitutes for young men determined to mimic the moderns ("Keynote" 3) with their
perpetuation of the modernist writing mentality through two more generations of
writers nurtured in writers-in-residence programs (Harper 88). He complained that

two generations of English professors raised their students to view Joyce, Mann, Proust, Eliot, Lawrence, and Hemingway as the last literary "prophets" and to admire only modernist philosophical complexity, aesthetics, and jumbo-sized, radically experimental novels. Novellas such as *Dangling Man*, *The Victim*, and *Seize the Day* single-mindedly parody these modernist philosophers and the literary formulas they use to stage heroes who experience a muted transcendence.

Mosby's Memoirs (1968), his first short story collection, is unified by the same thematics as the early novellas. In each story, Bellow explores isolated, immobilized, and overly cerebral characters, all of whom express belief in the preeminence of human feeling and the reality of the soul. Remarkable for their clarity, sheer stylishness, and general felicity, they each examine the effects on the human spirit of scientific rationalism and acquisitiveness. "Leaving the Yellow House" (1958) is a textual excavation of the lost, new American Eden and is the first of his stories to feature a female protagonist. However, like each of Bellow's male heroes, Hattie exemplifies the archetypal American theme of individualism and solipsism and also fails to solve the problem through self-isolation. "The Old System" (1968) is also preoccupied with the loss of family feeling and explores Old World American and Old World Jewish identity in the now defunct Jewish extended family. In this story, Bellow reveals his emotional investment in the immigrant Jewish communities of his childhood, his veneration of life, and his pervasive concern for morality. "Looking for Mr. Green" (1951) has been hailed as one of the finest short stories of the past sixty years. It is the existential fable of the hero, Grebe, who attempts to locate a crippled Negro, Mr. Green, so he can give him his relief check. It then becomes his stubborn attempt to prove that even an unimportant individual's life has worth. Grebe is the typical Bellovian metaphysician, while Mr. Green is almost an illusion whom he does not actually get to see. "The Gonzaga Manuscripts" (1954) is also a classic study in the hero's process of moving from estrangement to reconciliation. "A Father-to-Be" (1955) is one of Bellow's best treatments of his recurring motif of human feeling versus scientific rationalism. Rogin, a biological scientist, becomes absolutely irrational when faced with fatherhood. He goes to great lengths to avoid his future in the form of his own children. Rationalizing and philosophizing, he is unable to reconcile his infantilism with his Oedipal urges and ends up in total regression. "Mosby's Memoirs" (1968) features Mr. Mosby, who is in Oaxaca on a Guggenheim Fellowship supposedly to write his memoirs. French by descent, he admits that, like his defeated countrymen, he too is galled at the thought of the French collaboration with the Nazis and at their subsequent liberation by the Allies. The story is filled with World War II politics, morality, philosophical considerations, and Realpolitik. Throughout the volume, Bellow asserts that the world is sanctified, that humankind is capable of moral dignity and even holiness, and that apocalyptic twentieth-century Romanticism is destructive.

Bellow's search for a genre that would appropriately express his sense of the contemporary age began with his investigation of the short story and novella and then extended into his deliberate deformation of the modernist novel. For instance, in the larky *The Adventures of Augie March*, he rewrites Joyce's *Portrait of the Artist as a Young*

Man; in *Henderson the Rain King,* he parodies the heroes and literary formulas of Ernest Hemingway; in *Herzog,* he mimics the buoyant eighteenth-century epistolary novel in parody of James Joyce's *Ulysses*; in *More Die of Heartbreak,* he reclaims Gogol and the eighteenth-century French farce as his characters lament the failure of heterosexual love in the late twentieth century. In the end, however, Bellow does not write his sense of contemporary life exclusively inside of novels. In addition, he modified the traditional short story by greatly intensifying it with condensation, intellectual complexity, monologues, and mental letters. Likewise, he seized upon the somewhat dubious form of the novella, his favorite short fiction genre, and gave it some of his best imaginative energy. In each one, we find unforgettable characters, all the major themes, and that inimitable Bellovian voice that Irving Howe describes as a "jabbing interchange of ironies, … intimate vulgarities, [and a] blend of the sardonic and sentimental" (Atlas, 14). Compounded of Yiddish, Russian, Lachine French, Chicagoan street language, and academic English, this has become the voice of Bellow's metaphysical comedians.

As for the thematic content, Bellow is just as adamant throughout his short stories and novellas that he is opposed to "shivery" modernist games (*Herzog* 317). In every story and novella, Bellow testifies that, in the second half of the twentieth century, enough observable nightmares exist without our needing to be heir to reductive modernist theories about mankind, language, subjectivism, absurdism, human psychology, art, creativity, mass society, and human sexuality. The short fiction form allows him a more condensed genre in which to write the contemporary moment. In an important lecture given in Israel in 1987, he declared that "grand modernist summations are no longer expected of novelists; instead, smaller versions of life are perhaps more truthful" ("Silent Assumptions" 198). As for his late twentieth-century audience, he felt that short fiction is the most apt form with its "preference for the transitory, for summaries, resumes, for compression, fluidity, for flashing speed, for condensation" (197). Clearly Bellow wishes to museumize his modernist predecessors and thereby create a contemporary space for himself. Mr. Sammler says it best: "Short views, for God's sake, short views" (*Sammler* 114). Critics have generally failed to realize that Bellow is attempting to find an appropriate fictional form for the contemporary moment; moreover, they have habitually ignored his short fiction in favor of his novels.

When *Him with His Foot in His Mouth* (1984), his second collection of stories, appeared, Bellow was recognized as an internationally distinguished virtuoso of short fiction. Cynthia Ozick called this collection a "reprise," a "concordance" that functions as a "summary of all the old obsessions, hauled up by a single tough rope" (11). For her it is a concentrated, cumulative work of art splendidly condensed "in a vial." Many critics described them as beautifully crafted, thickly textured, skillfully rendered, and full of brilliant self-communion. The collection's unifying preoccupation is the collapse of the Jewish extended family. Distinguished by the sophisticated device of the monologue, the stories are brimming with boldness, sharp satire, linguistic elegance, lucid humor, and moral insight. Each concentrates on the problematic and sometimes tortured relationship between an individual and the extended family. Comic, devious, tender, and wicked by turns, these stories are rife with characters engaging in rhetorical self-justification, interesting subterfuges, and hostility to women. "Him with His Foot in His Mouth" (1984) stages the *mea culpa* of Shawmut, an arrogant, witty intellectual who, early in his life, has made a grand *fatum* in the form of a cruel witticism that he believes to have all but mortally wounded a shy young librarian. Given his egocentrism, he is certain the event has been all but terminal for her. Now Shawmut's moral failings, backwardness, and inner emotions are revealed, as are his intellectual pride and selfishness. His irresponsible comic outbursts proceed from his "hysterical syndrome" (20). Instead of apologizing to Miss Rose, he writes a personal meditation in which he exercises his masterful rhetorical skills so as to manipulate the unwitting woman into sympathizing with his guilt.

"What Kind of a Day Did You Have?" (1984) reveals the true inner workings of a grotesque love between Katrina and Wulpy, two tragicomical lovers experiencing a meltdown on a terribly gray winter's day while airborne. It is another of Bellow's stories of Eros versus Thanatos that foregrounds the failures of heterosexual love in the twentieth century. As such, it is related to *More Die of Heartbreak*, the novel in which this consistent theme culminates. Some have argued that the open form of this story makes it another novella. The high degree of cerebration and complex feeling has rendered it problematic for some critics, who ask for more dramatization of abstract feelings.

"Zetland: By a Character Witness" (1974) is a story told narratologically by a witness whose account spans the gray area between evidence and personal impression. In it Bellow privileges the humanly constructed testimonial over the hard facts of the matter. Zetland is the character through whom Bellow explores the incongruities and complexities of the inevitable gap between fact and fiction, guilt and innocence. It is another of his philosophical explorations into the relationship between the nature of reality and language.

"A Silver Dish," which first appeared in the *New Yorker* in 1978, is an elegantly rendered story about a classic father–son relationship that reveals more Bellovian theater of the soul. Its genesis lies in fragments belonging to the *Seize the Day* era, and its steady development over time reveals the high degree of artistry with which it is rendered. This time, readers experience a conventional plot. The story is based on the moral impasse between father and son having to do with the father's theft of a silver dish. Father–son conflicts unite all of Bellow's fictions and no doubt have their roots in his problematic childhood relationship with the none-too-honest Abraham Bellow, who was originally run out of St. Petersburg because of an onion smuggling operation. At the center of the story, Woody is engaged in a youthful pursuit of the sacred, while his father, the tricky, cunning Morris (Pop), is engaged in stealing the silver dish. As such, Morris is another of Bellow's reality instructors who, as he dies in the ensuing struggle, teaches his son about the inevitable co-inherence of the sacred and the profane. Woody passes the rite-of-passage by coming to appreciate the gift of a reprehensible father. Morris is a boon just being himself. One of Bellow finest

literary expressions of humor and love, it is considered by many to be the most classical story in the collection.

In "Cousins" (1984), Ijah Brodsky, another talking intellectual, reveals that he is
estranged from his wife and both of his brothers. He sketches for his captured listeners
a whole range of some thirty strange cousins from all paths in life, all dredged up in
remarkable detail from his prodigious memory. Sentimental and cynical by turns, Ijah
compels his audience to feel empathy for him thanks to the sheer range of his intelligence and his brilliantly articulated feelings. Part of the comic agenda in this story
is accomplished through the device of mental letters. Ijah's self-imposed task is to
retrieve the essential metaphysical world from under the debris of modern ideas. His
repeated references to Hegel suggest that the nature of his quarrel is with the impossibility of higher synthesis. It is another attempt by Bellow to expand the conventions
of the short story to include more cerebration and feeling. "Cousins" is Bellow at his
most nostalgic and tender as he works in character sketches and allegory to describe
Ijah Brodsky's ontological rediscovery of the metaphysical worlds of good and evil.
In this collection, Bellow unremittingly searches for new forms of artistic expression
unconstrained by the plot-driven and portraiture-driven content of the conventional
short story form, and he mostly succeeds.

The Late Years: 1989–2005

In 1989, Bellow made publishing history by publishing two novellas in paperback
– *A Theft* and *The Bellarosa Connection* – that were soon to be followed by two more
novellas printed in hardback – *The Actual* (1997) and *Ravelstein* (2000). In this final
phase of his career, Bellow seems to have settled firmly on the novella as his form of
choice, putting it back on the literary map.

A Theft (1989), which features Bellow's only real female protagonist, is a Bellovian
comic opera on the high jinks of the failed heterosexual pair. Clara Velde, raised on
old-time, countrified, Midwestern religious and racial values, has been plunged into
the multiracial, urban world of contemporary marriage and business. Four times
divorced and still involved with her true love, Ithiel Regler, she now knows he will
never marry her. This novella deals with some very old Bellow themes, including the
Hawthornian theft of the human heart, the lure of the intellect, the classic evasions
of the intellectual male lover, and the racial chaos of "Gogmagogsville" (12). It is also
about boredom and power politics, as well as the supposed impossibility of higher
synthesis, the human comedy of sexual desire, the failure of psychiatry, the chaotic
proliferation of ethnic others, the increasing absence of civilized spaces, and the
diminished status of the individual. Bellow's demythologization of romantic love in
"Gogmagogsville" once again hinges on the ironic portrayal of a male protagonist
torn between the desire for ultimate union with a female and the simultaneous pursuit
of the intellect. Bellow has commented that Clara is his favorite female protagonist
because she is so eternally romantically ready. Critics are not so sure that this overrides

her other deficits. Clara Velde has defrauded an insurance company, cheated on four husbands, impulsively thrown out her bewildered German *au pair* girl, made numerous racist remarks, and even become so suspicious of her dear friend, Mrs. Wong, that she thinks the woman might be trying to lure her lover with her oriental wiles.

The Bellarosa Connection (1989) is Bellow's most overt treatment of the response of American Jews to the Holocaust. It features an unnamed narrator, an elderly memory freak, who is trying desperately to recapture a lost opportunity for relationship with the grossly overweight yet spiritually authentic Sorella Fonstein. The novella is dominated by his remembrance of Sorella's attempts to force the notorious Billy Rose to acknowledge her Holocaust survivor husband, Harry, since it was Billy who funded her spouse's dramatic rescue. Billy, who never really cared about the Holocaust anyway, will have none of this. Even Sorella's attempt to blackmail him produces no response. The unnamed narrator is now overcome with guilt for his neglect of this remarkable couple and desires to atone for the moral aloofness. When he is informed that they have both died several months earlier, he laments that he has lived his entire life more through memory than through actual relationships. Centering on the emotional betrayal that the survivors of the Holocaust experienced at the hands of American Jews, this novella is Bellow's personal *mea culpa*.

"Something to Remember Me By" (1990) in *Something to Remember Me By: Three Tales* (1991) is another comic novella set in vintage Bellow territory – the Chicago of the 1930s on a cold, sooty day of shame and humiliation. Louie, the protagonist, an old Chicagoan of Jewish descent, is getting ready to die. He writes this story for his grown son. It tells the hilarious story of him as a 17-year-old adolescent who, during his mother's final days on earth, engages his first prostitute. She steals his money and clothes, including the sheepskin coat his mother had given him, leaving him only his shoes as she disappears out the window to join her accomplice. It is a freezing winter's day, and the only clothes he can find in the room are a woman's boudoir jacket and a soiled dress. It is a typical Bellow reality check. Dressed in only these scanty female clothes he makes it to a local speakeasy only to find his friend absent. Desperate, chilled to the bone, and the butt of many jokes for his woman's clothing, the boy is approached by a wily drunk who lures him back to his apartment by promising him some clothes. Once there, the Jewish boy is forced, in a fitting and hilarious retribution, to cook a pork dinner for the drunk and his three children. When the boy finally gets home, his father deals him a blow for which he is profoundly grateful, since it signals that his mother is still alive. The story contains vintage comic realism and probably grew from a stock of material Bellow had written much earlier. Peter Hyland has suggested that since Bellow dedicated this story to his children and grandchildren, it is probably a "farewell legacy, a Prosperan apologetics" (347).

"By the St. Lawrence" appeared first in the July 1995 issue of *Esquire*, and now prefaces the *Collected Stories*, indicating its thematic importance to the canon. Written in the third person, it features Rob Rexler, an author born to parents from Kiev and raised in Lachine and Montreal. He is an historian who has written about nihilism, Stalinism, decadence, Marxism, and National Socialism. Now he must lecture at

McGill University on Brecht and his Marxism, something of which he is now heartily tired. Rexler is obviously a thinly disguised persona for the now aged Bellow. On the way to the campus, he has the driver take him to his birthplace in Lachine. What follows is a detailed, nostalgic account of the scene by the St. Lawrence he remembered from childhood, his mother's love for him, the summer he got polio, adolescence, cousins and relatives, old family quarrels, "characters," Albert's afternoon visit to the "ladies" while the young boy waited in the car, and the man killed on the tracks later the same day. It is the account of all the Bellovian themes of contemporaneity, youth, loss of innocence, the lost Jewish extended family of immigrant origins, family feuds, and Dickensian neighborhood characters. Most of all, it is the fiction in which the aging Bellow recalls his own immigrant childhood and counts all that has been kept and lost.

The Actual (1997), another novella, tells the familiar Bellow story of an old adolescent love now reclaimed in late middle age. The worldly and clever Harry Trellman, an intellectual social observer and ambassador of the arts, is invited to "notice" the contemporary scene on behalf of the wealthy, aging Sigmund Adletsky. Harry will be his informer, "noticer," and brains trust. Meantime, the sensitive Adletsky soon discerns the nature of Harry's great sadness – an unrequited adolescent love, Amy Wustrin. As he finally brings the two aging lovers back together again, the plot turns on one of Bellow's favorite Platonic themes: the existence of one's soul mate or "actual." Critics have suggested that this work belongs to his 1970s period and that Bellow is now simply clearing his desk.

Ravelstein (2000), Bellow's final novella, is a beautifully rendered memorial to the late Allan Bloom of the University of Chicago. Here Bellow plays Boswell to Bloom's Johnson as he captures the era and ethos of their moment together at the University of Chicago as two intellectuals of Russian Jewish descent. The portrait of Chick/Bellow is as carefully delineated as is the portrait of Ravelstein/Bloom. At the age of 64, and for several years thereafter, Bellow found in Allan Bloom the adoring and approving older father figure and Jewish soul mate he had never had. More than anyone, Bloom helped Bellow reclaim his identity as a child of Russian immigrant Jews.

Ravelstein is full of jokes, one-liners, and Catskill comedian gags which capture the distinctly first-generation Jewish American voice, wit, neuroses, manners, affectations, cultural collisions, and intellectual passions. It records an accomplished, boon companionship always sought and usually lost by previous Bellow protagonists. Here Bellow's debt of friendship to Allan Bloom is elegantly and even uproariously memorialized. Tender, risqué, intellectually stimulating, full of brilliant conversation, even wicked at times, this account of a famous literary friendship encompasses everything from the sublime to the vaudevillian. Bloom/Ravelstein, a declared Platonist, believes that the highest purpose of male friendship is the formation of an elite community of potential truth seekers who are also searching for a relationship with their "actuals" or true halves. Ravelstein gets his erotic teachings from Aristophanes and Socrates and his moral vision from the Bible. As he is dying of Aids at the end of the novella, it is the injunctions of Moses, the near annihilation of Jews in the twentieth century, and the importance of Jewish learning that preoccupy him. He tells Chick that half of the Jews have been killed and that the two of them belong to the other half. It is an injunction for Chick to assume responsibility for the fact that he is a Jew still living, one who must keep on talking into the increasing silence.

Ravelstein is perhaps Bellow's finest novella. It has been called a biographical essay, a eulogy, a memoir, a threnody, a *roman à clef*, the chronicle of a friendship, a valediction, a Kaddish, a biography, and an autoethnography. It is also Bellow's career end game, his final word on all the major anti-modernist themes, including death. It contains Bellow's attempt to make amends for his own sins of omission as an American Jew and Jewish American writer. The book is heavily threaded through with accounts of Nazi atrocities and with Ravelstein's repeated chastisements of Chick for becoming friendly with Grielescu, a Balkan Nazi sympathizer and Romanian fascist Iron-Guardist whom Ravelstein accuses of representing "sadists who hung living Jews on meat hooks" (16). In it, Bellow also reclaims himself as a Jew. Bellow's "outing" of his homosexual friend in this book remains problematic for some readers. The controversy somewhat surprised Bellow, who said he thought all of Bloom's friends knew about his sexual preferences. However, that Bellow loved Allan Bloom is never in doubt. Finally, after almost losing his own life, and after struggling for over six years to fulfill his promise to write Bloom's life, Chick/Bellow completes the task. *Ravelstein* is a remarkably accomplished "short view" and a fitting summation of all the old themes.

The Collected Stories (2001) contains a "Preface" by Janis Bellow, its compiler, and an "Introduction" by James Wood, who calls Bellow the great "portraitist of human form" (xiii) and praises him for his "greatly abundant, greatly precise, greatly various, rich, and strenuous" prose (xiii). Bellow, he argues, does not write as a depth psychologist, but as a metaphysician of "embodied souls" and in the manner of Proust, Dickens, and Tolstoy, who also conceive of their characters as essences (xv). It is these characters who embody Bellow's struggle with the great secular-religious questions of the age.

Conclusion

Bellow's short fiction has received increasing critical attention in the last ten years. The sheer condensation and focus on the inner lives of his intellectual characters have made them difficult and challenging reading due to the high degree of complexity. Bellow's works are introspective stories that often take place in the complex minds of intellectuals. Some of his short fiction feels like brilliant fragments, while other works look like shards of a discarded novel. All of them are distinguished by a high degree of narrative compression and abstraction. But it is the compelling voices through which they attain their greatest achievement. Bellow's voices are best described by Walter Ong, who suggests: "The human voice is a manifestation of the person. ... Speech is the calling of one person to another, of an interior to an interior.

Sight presents always surfaces, presents even depth as a lamination of surfaces, whereas sound always presents interiors" (70). It is the hearts and minds of these anguished intellectuals presented in intense monologues, letters, and even mental letters, that Bellow has distilled with such intensity in his short stories and novellas. Marianne Friedrich has aptly compared this effect of his condensation "to the use of lenticular screens in postmodern photography" with its realistic surfaces and mysterious planar depths (195). This effect of planar depth is the unique mark Bellow has put upon the American short story and novella.

Furthermore, his resurrection and transformation of the novella has secured its place more firmly on the literary map. The short stories and novellas are Bellow's "small planets" that echo all the great themes of the galactic novels. However, they carry their own authority, intensity, and artistry. Neither classic modernist stories nor experiments, they are not simply like anybody else's. Written always in demotic voice, they are recognizable by their rhetoric of social utterance, monologues, and their explorations of problematic interpersonal speech inserted into that great gulf between speaker and listener. Ultimately, the short stories present their own image of the human condition – *homo loquens* afflicted with an intense desire for talking out his existential loneliness as he attempts to push back the worst incursions of modernity and addresses the great secular-religious questions of the latter half of the twentieth century. As such, each of the stories is an exquisitely wrought metaphysical fable.

References and Further Reading

Atlas, James. *Bellow: A Biography*. New York: Random House, 2001.

Bellow, Saul. *The Actual*. New York: Viking, 1997.

———. "Address by Gooley MacDowell to the Hasbeens Club of Chicago." *Hudson Review* 4.2 (1951): 222–7.

———. *The Bellarosa Connection*. New York: Viking, 1989.

———. "Burdens of a Lone Survivor." *Esquire* (December 1974): 176–85, 224, 226, 228, 230, 232.

———. "By the Rock Wall." *Harper's Bazaar* 85 (April 1951): 135–205.

———. "By the St. Lawrence." *Esquire* (July 1995): 82–8.

———. *Collected Stories*. New York: Viking, 2001.

———. "Cousins." 1984. *Collected Stories*. New York: Viking, 2001. 191–239.

———. *Dangling Man*. New York: Vanguard, 1944.

———. "Dora." *Harper's Bazaar* (November 1949): 118, 188–90, 198–9.

———. "A Father-to-Be." *New Yorker* (February 5, 1955): 26–30.

———. "The Gonzaga Manuscripts." *Discovery* 4. New York: Pocket Books, 1954.

———. *Herzog*. New York: Viking, 1964.

———. "Him with His Foot in His Mouth." *Atlantic* (November 1982): 114–19, 122, 125–6, 129–32, 134–5, 137–42, 144.

———. *Him with His Foot in His Mouth and Other Stories*. New York: Harper, 1984.

———. *Humboldt's Gift*. New York: Viking, 1975.

———. "Keynote Address Before the Inaugural Session of the 34th Session of the International Congress of Poets, Playwrights, Essayists, and Editors, 13 June 1966." *Montreal Star* (June 25, 1966): Special Insert, 2–3.

———. "Leaving the Yellow House." *Esquire* (January 1958): 112–26.

———. "Looking for Mr. Green." *Commentary* (March 1951): 251–61.

———. "The Mexican General." *Partisan Review* 9.3 (1942): 178–94.

———. "Mosby's Memoirs." *New Yorker* (July 20, 1968): 36–42, 44–9.

———. "Mr. Katz, Mr. Cohen, and Cosmology." *Retort: A Quarterly of Social Philosophy and the Arts* 1 (1942): 14–20.

———. *Mr. Sammler's Planet*. New York: Viking, 1964.

———. "The Old System." *Playboy* (January 1968): n.p.

———. *Ravelstein*. New York: Viking, 2000.

———. *Seize the Day*. New York: Viking, 1956.

———. "Sermon by Dr. Pep." *Partisan Review* 16.5 (1949): 455–62.

———. "The Silent Assumptions of the Novelist." Revised version published as "Summations" in *Saul Bellow: A Mosaic*, vol. 3 of Twentieth Century American Jewish Writers series, ed. Liela H. Goldman, Gloria L. Cronin, and Ada Aharoni. New York: Peter Lang, 1992. 185–99.

———. "A Silver Dish." *New Yorker* (September 25, 1978): 40–50.

———. "Something to Remember Me By." *Esquire* (July 1990): 64–75, 78–9.

———. "Sono and Moso." *12 from the Sixties*. Ed. Richard Kostelanetz. New York: Dell, 1967. n.p.

———. *A Theft*. New York: Penguin, 1989.

———. "The Trip to Galena." *Partisan Review* 17.8 (1950): 779–94.

———. "Two Morning Monologues." *Partisan Review* 8.3 (1941): 230–6.

———. "What Kind of a Day Did You Have?" *Vanity Fair* (February 1984). Rpt. in *Him with His Foot in His Mouth and Other Stories*. New York: Harper, 1984. 63–163.

———. *The Victim*. 1947. New York: Compass-Viking, 1956.

———. "Zetland: By a Character Witness." *Modern Occasions 2*. Ed. Philip Rahv. Port Washington, NY: Kennikat, 1974. 9–30.

Friedrich, Marianne. *Character and Narration in the Short Fiction of Saul Bellow*. New York: Peter Lang, 1996.

Harper, Gordon L. "Saul Bellow, The Art of Fiction: An Interview." *Writers at Work*. Ed. Alfred Kazin. New York: Viking Press, 1967. 88–123.

Hyland, Peter. "Something to Remember Me By." *The Critical Response to Saul Bellow*. Ed. Gerhard Bach. Westport, CT: Greenwood Press, 1995. 345–7.

Illig, Joyce. "An Interview with Saul Bellow." *Publishers Weekly* (22 October 1973): 74–7.

Ong, Walter. *Barbarian Within*. New York: Macmillan, 1968.

Ozick, Cynthia. "Farcical Combat in a Busy World." Review of *Him with His Foot in His Mouth and Other Stories*, by Saul Bellow. *New York Times Book Review* (May 20, 1984): 11.

Simmons, Maggie. "Free to Feel." *Quest* (February–March 1979): 33.

Short Fiction Chronology

1936   "The Hell It Can't"
1941   "Two Morning Monologues"
1942   "The Mexican General"
1942   "Mr. Katz, Mr. Cohen, and Cosmology"
1944   *Dangling Man*
1947   *The Victim*
1949   "Dora"
1949   "Sermon by Dr. Pep"
1950   "The Trip to Galena"
1951   "Looking for Mr. Green"
1951   "By the Rock Wall"
1951   "Address by Gooley MacDowell to the Hasbeens Club of Chicago"
1955   "A Father-to-Be"

1956	*Seize the Day*
1956	"The Gonzaga Manuscripts"
1958	"Leaving the Yellow House"
1967	"Sono and Moso"
1968	"Mosby's Memoirs"
1968	"The Old System"
1974	"Zetland: By a Character Witness"
1974	"Burdens of a Lone Survivor"
1978	"A Silver Dish"
1984	"Him with His Foot in His Mouth"
1984	"Cousins"
1984	"What Kind of a Day Did You Have?"
1989	*A Theft*
1989	*The Bellarosa Connection*
1990	"Something to Remember Me By"
1995	"By the St. Lawrence"
1997	*The Actual*
2000	*Ravelstein*

22

John Updike

Robert M. Luscher

One of North America's foremost men of letters, John Updike was prolific in a variety of genres. With over sixty published volumes to his credit, he won nearly every major literary award except for the Nobel Prize, an honor he bestowed upon his literary alter ego Henry Bech in *Bech at Bay*. Updike averaged over a book per year, regularly alternating novels, poetry, short fiction, and volumes of assorted prose with other works such as children's books, a play, and other non-fiction. An insightful literary critic, he reviewed a wide variety of works, ranging from fiction to theology, and wrote essays exploring the achievements of major authors. Updike's fiction is highly regarded for its luminous prose style and commitment to realism, yet it also provides readers with a detailed social history of the late twentieth century. His major themes involve the ongoing struggle against time's diminishment, which often manifests itself through sexual and spiritual yearnings but finds its most successful realization in art and memory. His canon of short fiction provides a comprehensive chronicle of the metamorphosis of middle-class domesticity in an era of greater sexual freedom, rising marital discord, heightened spiritual uncertainty, and increased social unrest.

If Updike's novels, as he characterizes them, serve as "moral debates" with the reader, his short fiction challenges assumptions about the ordinariness of daily experience and fosters greater awareness of quotidian particulars. Throughout his career, Updike was dogged by critics' suspicions that his finely crafted prose disguises a failure to tackle larger subjects with a more political, urban, or tragic slant. Yet such criticisms are based on the very assumptions he sought to combat in choosing to foreground domestic life, and fail to recognize the ways in which Updike did on occasion move outside the range of suburban experience. By recognizing the depths of beauty and sadness in the mundane world, Updike celebrated the intensity of the ordinary, while simultaneously bemoaning its transitoriness. His aesthetic interests, as he observed in the essay "A Dogwood Tree: A Boyhood," involve "a cultivated fondness for exploring corners" and a desire "to transcribe middleness with all its grits, bumps, and anonymities, in its fullness of satisfaction and mystery" (*Assorted*

Prose 186). For some, Updike's novelistic achievements, especially the Rabbit tetralogy, will overshadow his stature as a short story writer, but Updike clearly exhibited a sustained mastery of the short story form throughout his career. With a canon of well over 200 short stories – as well as a number of prose sketches that he includes in his volumes of assorted prose – Updike devoted a significant portion of his career to the genre that perhaps best suited his style and narrative talents. As Rachel Burchard observes, "Updike reaches his highest range of achievement in this medium," presenting "all of his major themes with intensity and artistic discipline more refined than that of his novels" (133). Updike cited his "cartoonist's ability to compose within a prescribed space" as one of his assets as a novelist, but that ability may be of greater value in the confines of the short story, where his linguistic precision, his gift for metaphor, and his talent for capturing the significance of everyday incidents came together on a canvas limited in scope but rich in depth.

Born in 1932, John Hoyer Updike was the only child of Wesley R. Updike, a high school math teacher, and Linda Grace Hoyer Updike, an aspiring writer who finally realized her literary ambitions with the novel *Enchantment* (1971); a short story collection, *The Predator* (1990), appeared posthumously. Updike's first thirteen years were spent in Shillington, Pennsylvania, which he transmuted into the idyllic fictional town of Olinger. In 1945, he moved with his parents and maternal grandparents to the Hoyers' farm near Plowville, Pennsylvania; this rural dislocation to the sandstone farmhouse in which his mother grew up became the subject of some early – and later – short fiction. As a youth, Updike hoped to become a graphic artist for Disney, although he harbored ambitions to write for the *New Yorker* as well. Updike attended Harvard University on scholarship, drawing cartoons for, contributing fiction to, and eventually editing the *Harvard Lampoon*. He married Mary Pennington, a Radcliffe fine arts major, in the summer of 1953, and graduated summa cum laude with an English major in 1954, when he sold his first short story, "Friends from Philadelphia," to the *New Yorker*.

Updike was awarded a Knox Fellowship to attend the Ruskin School of Drawing and Fine Art at Oxford, where he and his wife spent a year; only one story, "Still-Life" (in *Pigeon Feathers*), derives from this experience. While in England – where his first child, Elizabeth, was born – Updike was offered a job with the *New Yorker* by E. B. White, and returned to the US to work for two years as a roving reporter for the "Talk of the Town" section. Updike severed formal ties with the magazine in 1957 after his son David was born in order to establish his career as an independent writer, although he remained a frequent contributor of fiction, poetry, essays, and reviews, with over 600 pieces having been published in its pages. Moving from New York to Ipswich, Massachusetts, that year, Updike began selling short fiction and published his first book, *The Carpentered Hen and Other Tame Creatures*, a volume of poetry, in 1958.

Although Updike worked on the manuscript for an unpublished novel entitled "Home" while living in New York, his first published novel was *The Poorhouse Fair* (1959), a mildly futuristic novel set in a retirement home modeled after the Berks County Almshouse, which received the Rosenthal Foundation Award and was a finalist for the National Book Award. Updike received two other awards that year: a Guggenheim Fellowship and the inclusion of his story "A Gift from the City" in *Best American Short Stories 1959* – the first of many such appearances in that series. That same year marked the appearance of his third child, Michael, and the publication of his first collection of short fiction, *The Same Door*. Throughout his prolific career, Updike continued the pattern of alternating publication of novels with collections of short fiction and work in other genres.

The Same Door (1959) exhibits remarkable self-assurance and promise for a first collection. From the *New Yorker* school of fiction, Updike derived a commitment to realism and to exploring the corners of quotidian life, though his stories rise above urbane social satire to sympathetic insights into contemporary life's compromises, yearnings, and regrets. Like the collection's characters, Updike as a writer is poised on the threshold, simultaneously looking back at the recent but receding past and moving into an uncertain present that holds surprising but often ambiguous rewards – sometimes tinged heavily with irony. The theme of unexpected rewards that Updike later highlights in his foreword to *Olinger Stories* (1964) pervades the volume's stories, although the epigraphs draw attention to the difficulty of recapturing and articulating past pleasures, preparing the reader to encounter characters who struggle to see clearly as they occupy the threshold between a youthful past and a diminishing present, often unaware of how to savor the domestic love and ephemeral pleasure.

The volume's first three stories take place in Olinger, the fictional version of Updike's hometown, Shillington. "Friends from Philadelphia," opens the collection with the depiction of an unexpected gift whose irony is just below the threshold of its young protagonist's awareness. Like many stories in the collection, this effort has a slightly Joycean tone, although the retrospection and character-based epiphany of a story such as "Araby" is absent. Ace Anderson, the title character of "Ace in the Hole," may foreshadow Rabbit Angstrom: a former basketball star who has just lost his job, Ace has little space to run, however, within the confines of the short story. Now married and a father, Ace can no longer score baskets to stave off anxiety; in domestic skirmishes he is plagued by the "tight feeling" he was once able to vanquish on the court. Despite his escapist tendencies, Ace is mature enough to realize the inevitability of maturity's compromises, although the momentary respite he obtains from an argument with his wife about losing his job only postpones the resolution of his problems. Mark Prosser, the high school teacher in "Tomorrow and Tomorrow and So Forth," is a younger version of George Caldwell in Updike's novel *The Centaur* (1963), similarly compassionate but more aloof from his students and less deeply wounded by his work. Like Ace, he is caught in routine, feeling that his life creeps along at the "petty pace" mentioned in the Macbeth soliloquy whose implications his students seem unwilling or unable to grapple with as they maintain their "quality of glide" through life.

Stories of young married couples living in New York form the volume's core. Varying in technique and focus, they all depict the early waning of marital bliss that results in domestic compromise and receding youth. "Toward Evening" experiments with a looser short story form, using an imagistic counterpoint within a stream of consciousness chronicle that follows the protagonist on a journey home through an urban realm afflicted with a paralysis reminiscent of Joyce's Dublin. Demolished buildings and advertising dominate the landscape, while recurrent bird imagery provides emblems of the imaginative transcendence that surprisingly results from contemplation of the spiritually empty world of advertising. "Snowing in Greenwich Village" employs a more traditional narrative to depict the nascent marital problems of Joan and Richard Maple, a couple whose recurrence in later stories leads to being featured in a book of their own. Their dialogue is rich with implications, as the Maples communicate on a plane of familiarity inaccessible to their guest, whose remarks and actions seem full of sexual innuendo to Richard, tempting him to stray from his sick wife, although he draws back from pursuing the opportunity. "A Gift from the City" links its central image of magic circles with the insularity of its young married protagonists, transplants whose charmed isolation of personal security cuts them off from the city's more unexpected gifts when they banish the perceived threat of a persistent African American beggar with guilt money. Close in spirit to J. D. Salinger's work, "Who Made the Yellow Roses Yellow?" is an imaginative extrapolation from Updike's days as editor of the *Harvard Lampoon*, featuring a blue-blooded version of Ace Anderson, striving to keep his youthful glory alive. Religious themes, which figure more strongly in subsequent works, first appear in "Dentistry and Doubt," in which a student's crisis of faith and restored spiritual vision unexpectedly coincide with a dental visit. "Intercession" depicts a dissatisfied comic strip writer's encounter on the golf course with a brash teenager reminiscent of his youthful self. In a modern reenactment of the Fall, he heads home across a barren field after a wicked slice, sadder but wiser as he reconciles himself to accepting that maturity – not lawless, unencumbered youth – contains its own intrinsic satisfactions.

Updike returns to Olinger to round out the volume. "The Alligators" relates a young schoolboy's frustrated attempt to realize his idealized vision of love, and culminates in a Joycean epiphany of his folly and blindness. The final story, "The Happiest I've Been," features the return of John Nordholm, the protagonist of "Friends from Philadelphia." The cinematic quality of this retrospective and meditative first-person narration foregrounds the narrative's quest to recapture the past, keeping the door between youth and maturity propped open for access. As Nordholm lingers on the threshold between youth and maturity, nostalgia intensifies from his growing awareness of time's inevitable diminishment. The concerns of these early stories in *The Same Door* – the problems of loss, the redemptive nature of memory, and the discovery of ordinary life's spiritual essence – preoccupied Updike throughout his career.

Published the same year his daughter Miranda was born, the novel *Rabbit Run* (1960) solidified Updike's reputation as a compelling and articulate voice in contemporary fiction. *Pigeon Feathers* (1962), his second short story collection, exhibits Updike's versatility in a variety of narrative strategies, including first-person experiments with epistolary, lyric, and montage forms. In the lyric story, Updike discovered a form suited to his stylistic gifts and to his talent for capturing the detailed texture of life's domestic corners. This richly imagistic prose version of the dramatic mono-logue allows Updike to dramatize the mind's search through the darkening past for some vital spark that might illuminate the present and guide his characters onward through maturity's increasing complexities. The montage stories that conclude the volume are Updike's first experiments with an aesthetic that involves juxtaposition of seemingly disjunct multiple lyric segments whose loose formal coherence comments thematically on the possibility of forging coherence from the reimagined past. The protagonists in this collection range from 10 years old to their late twenties – roughly the same age as those in Updike's first. Olinger youths reappear, but the characters include a significant number of young marrieds. While the younger characters appear to be fleeing from the past, those who have crossed the threshold from adolescence to maturity flee toward the past, yearning to recapture its mystery and vitality. In general, the characters in *Pigeon Feathers* slip deeper into themselves, grapple more with doubt, and ponder the increasing narrowness of their lives. As the past recedes and concerns about mortality arise, their struggle against loss assumes greater urgency and takes on an increasingly metaphysical dimension.

The opening story, "Walter Briggs," foregrounds the theme of memory in a young couple's nostalgic but competitive excursion into their shared past as they drive home from a party, recalling the early days of their marriage during this "enforced time together." This same couple recurs in "Should Wizard Hit Mommy?" a well-crafted frame tale in which a simple bedtime story manifests underlying marital tension between their imaginative and pragmatic opposition. Exploring similar territory, "Wife-Wooing" – Updike's first inclusion in *Prize Stories: The O. Henry Awards* – is a linguistic tour de force, a self-satiric dramatic monologue in which the narrator exposes his own foibles as he portrays the anxious, striving male psyche; rebuffed and baffled as he attempts to seduce his wife, his unexpected reward the next evening leads to an epiphanic moment. "Archangel" also showcases Updike's linguistic prowess in a dramatic monologue in which the heavenly narrator offers an abundance of earthly delights transposed into a finer key to an auditor who seems to dismiss them. Another first-person narrator, the divinity school student in "Lifeguard," may be less reliable, celebrating his own virtue as he perches above the beachgoers he sees as his sun worshiping congregation; elite and narcissistic, this lusty novice theologian urges enjoyment of the present moment even as he decries the sunbathers' shallowness.

In "The Astronomer," which also examines issues of faith, the narrator recalls how his own uncertain religious beliefs are challenged during a visit from an astronomer. Surveying this incident from his past, which he likens to a night sky of randomly shining stars, he proves to himself that his vision of faith is more viable than that of the atheistic astronomer, who still fears the desert's open spaces. "Pigeon Feathers," later made into a film for the American Short Story series, couples David Kern's metaphysical doubt with the physical separation that his parents' move to a farm outside Olinger brings. After reading an H. G. Wells work denying Christ's divinity, he experiences a vivid premonition of extinction that sends him searching for some solid foundation of faith to allay his fears. Not his mother's vague pantheism, his father's perfunctory Protestantism, nor the minister's vague analogies can provide him with solace. The pigeons he kills that have been soiling their Olinger furniture in the barn, however, provide an unlikely source of religious affirmation: in observing their intricate beauty he finds assurance of God's hand and care, although his leap of certitude may be a provisional measure in an ongoing struggle.

"A&P," Updike's most frequently anthologized story, is atypical in its fast-moving plot and brash teenage narrator, but features Updike's trademark attention to detail and focuses on thematic concerns similar to the volume's other stories. As Sammy relates the tale of his impulsive attempt to become a hero to three girls in bathing suits when the store manager confronts them, he depicts his gesture of quitting his cashier job as a principled act that will propel him into adulthood and make his life much harder thereafter. While his celebration of the girls' physical virtues is marked by chauvinism, his perception of the butcher's ogling provides him with a glimpse of his own attitude; his attraction to Queenie, however, consists of lust mingled with the allure of her socioeconomic class and his own yearning to be a free spirit who is not corralled in the A&P's checkout lane. Like other characters in the collection, Sammy is caught between the pulls of romance and realism as he begins to learn the bittersweet lessons of his nascent movement into the realm of experience.

In "The Persistence of Desire," a slightly older character outwardly possesses the trappings of happiness, but longs for a more passionate life. Returning to Olinger seeking a cure for misdiagnosed eye problems, he encounters reminders of time slipping away, but latches on to an old flame as an emblem of past joy; despite his hopes of recapturing an idealized past, he remains in "a tainted world where things evaded his focus" (*Pigeon Feathers* 25). One early Olinger story, "You'll Never Know Dear, How Much I Love You," is a variant of Joyce's "Araby," with a young boy's disillusionment occurring at a carnival; in "A Sense of Shelter," an older youth retreats into the town's inherent protectiveness, while in "Flight," another high-school-age protagonist looks back on his preparation to take flight from Olinger. As he unfolds the tale of casting off from his mother, he touches her suffering and sacrifice, understanding her life as well as his own more deeply.

The collection concludes with two stories that Updike characterizes as "farraginous narratives": assembled from independent narrative segments but ultimately coherent in their thematic and imagistic substructure. Their long titles signal their composite nature, though Updike artfully links the sections via metaphor as the narrators dramatize the process of memory in search of connectedness. "The Blessed Man of Boston, My Grandmother's Thimble, and Fanning Island" ostensibly records three successive artistic failures, but each section progressively moves toward understanding how recovery of the past's minutiae can put one in touch with a larger body of memory.

More explicitly connected are the segments of "Packed Dirt, Churchgoing, A Dying Cat, A Traded Car," in which John Nordholm (returning from "Friends from Philadelphia") retrospectively constructs a cyclical journey, wearing a new path through the obstructive rubble of adult life via forays into his past, each centered on a single image or incident. As Updike notes, the story interweaves themes that "had long been present to me: paternity and death, earth and faith and cars" (*Hugging* 852).

After the publication of his first children's book, *The Magic Flute* (1962) and his second book of poetry, *Telephone Poles and Other Poems* (1963), Updike effectively brings his early career to a close with *Olinger Stories: A Selection* (1964), published only as a Vintage paperback. This short story sequence arranges the tales featuring Updike's younger protagonist in rural Olinger into a loose bildungsroman of a composite character that Updike calls "a local boy" in his foreword. Olinger is a realm of grace and unexpected gifts, where, as Updike remarks, "the muddled and inconsequent surface of things now and then parts to yield us a gift" (vii). However, the sequence culminates in departure to a less secure territory, where access to memory is increasingly problematic and spiritual inquiry yields only provisional answers. Ultimately, this gathering of earlier work – one that Updike hoped "might generate new light, or at least focus more sharply the light already there" (vi) – succeeds in both recapturing the past and closing the book on this phase. The same year *Olinger Stories* was published, Updike became the youngest person ever elected to the National Institute of Arts and Letters.

Following the 1965 publication of *Assorted Prose* – his first volume of collected essays, reviews, and other occasional prose pieces – the novel *Of the Farm*, and *A Child's Calendar*, an illustrated volume of poems for children, Updike published his fourth collection of short fiction, *The Music School* (1966), which transposes the themes of memory and its redemptive power, the tension between spiritual yearnings and their physical realizations, and the ambiguous blessings of domestic life into a new key suited to characters no longer able to linger in memories of young adulthood. His middle-aged protagonists have moved from idyllic Olinger to suburban Tarbox, where satisfaction is harder earned: romantic discord, infidelity, and perplexity all arise during their disillusioned attempts to realize some mature version of the romantic pastoral. In a realm no longer sustained by memory and where marital tensions have widened to gulfs, separation becomes the dominant experience. While most of the collection's stories strike a common thematic chord, they exhibit an impressive variety of techniques, ranging from traditional linear narrative to the meditative lyric mode, the Hawthornesque sketch, and an epistolary experiment. The lyricism of what Updike calls the "abstract-personal" mode of a story such as "Leaves" is especially suited to many of his characters' conditions: at this crux in their lives they are more disposed to reflect than act.

"In Football Season" opens the volume with a lyric meditation providing an affectionate backward glance, a prelude to music in a new key. The sensory immediacy of the narrator's evocation memorializes the ephemeral beauty of Olinger, portraying its fragility and imminent dissolution even as it holds the adult "winds of worry" at bay. Access to the past is more problematic in many of the volume's subsequent stories.

Four other stories are rendered in this abstract-personal mode, whose plotless meditative form generally accentuates the protagonist's self-enclosed condition, and poignantly depicts the pain aroused when memory and desire mingle. Among these,

"Leaves" is a tour de force of poetic language in which the narrator self-consciously lays bare the pain of separation, delving in the process into the problematic relationship between humans, art, and nature. "The Music School" (subsequently made into a short film) and "Harv Is Plowing Now" also showcase Updike's talents with language and metaphor, thematizing the power of verbal art to transcend discontinuity. Essentially dramatic monologues, these stories depend upon startling juxtapositions of metaphorically rich fragments whose coalescence embodies a fleeting victory over time.

"Giving Blood" marks the return of the Maples, whose troubles flare up in a verbal bloodletting as they drive to Boston to donate blood for a relative, diminish during their shared experience of donating blood, and then reemerge at the conclusion. Other marriage stories likewise depict husbands who harbor some inner wound that mitigates their attempts to revive their marriages. The epistolary "Four Sides of One Story" explores a love triangle by juxtaposing the reflections of four isolated characters who act out a modern version of the Tristan and Iseult legend. The only Updike story set at Harvard, "The Christian Roommates," is not about marriage, but explores a relationship between a self-assured premedical student and a vegetarian pacifist filled with similar conflicts; this story was also turned into a short film entitled "The Roommate," which omits reference to the only commonality which bonds this odd couple – their Christianity. The volume concludes with "The Family Meadow," a plotless sketch presenting a still life of an epoch falling prey to progress, and "The Hermit," which balances the opening story's hymn to the idyllic past with its examination of the fragility of the pastoral in the modern world.

The novel *Couples* (1968) earned Updike his first *Time* magazine cover feature, an article entitled "The Adulterous Society." *Bottom's Dream*, a children's book that adapts *A Midsummer Night's Dream*, and *Midpoint and Other Poems* were published the next year, followed in 1970 by *Bech: A Book*, the first of three linked collections featuring Updike's literary alter ego, the fictional Jewish writer Henry Bech. Many critics persist in treating the Bech volumes as novels, even though Updike lists them under the heading "Short Stories" in the publications list his books contain, clearly indicating their status in the broad territory between the novel and the miscellaneous short story collection. Updike remarks in an interview that this first Bech book was "conceived piecemeal" and that "the whole texture ... was that of short stories, and I couldn't bring myself to call it a novel" (Reilly 136). The incidents in Bech's life thus never seem to coalesce into a neat causal chain; such discontinuity may signal the problem that prevents him from duplicating his earlier success as an artist. Bech serves as Updike's vehicle to chronicle incidents and impressions – most often gleaned from his foreign travels – that comprise an extended reflection on the American writer's condition.

Even some of Updike's harsher critics praise these attempts in the satiric mode, which generally shun the belletristic style of his earlier fiction and possess a picaresque quality, with their hero generally powerless to end his drift or shape his identity. While Bech by no means shares his fabled writer's block with his creator, he embodies those fears about the diminishment that would result without art to preserve memory, as well as the tribulations of an author's public life and the potential panic of continually producing quality work. Bech's celebrity ultimately blocks his creativity, and his travels in that role are experiences that he, unlike Updike, is unable to translate into art. Unmarried, Jewish, nine years older, and a denizen of Manhattan, Bech serves as a mask, behind which Updike can rebuke the literary industry for the writer's current condition while simultaneously satirizing the character who so readily accedes to its lures and demands. These "quasi-novels" – as Updike subtitles the last, though a more accurate term would be short story sequences – all follow similar patterns, using foreign travels for framing purposes or juxtaposing them with a series of adventures closer to or at home.

As the first in the series, *Bech: A Book* (1970) sets up the ruse of verisimilitude with a preface attributed to Bech and a fictional bibliography of Bech's works that settles a few scores with Updike's critics. Many of the stories comically chronicle missed connections, although "The Bulgarian Poetess," the first Bech story Updike wrote, shares a concern with unfulfilled longing with the stories in *The Music School*, where it was first collected; in the context of Updike's short story sequence, it embodies a temporary revival of Bech's dormant ardor and his reverence for art. "Bech Panics," the most serious of the volume's comic escapades, involves an existential panic that serves as the climax of the volume, which concludes not with Bech's completion of his bestseller but with his admission into a society resembling the American Academy of Arts and Letters in "Bech Enters Heaven." In the Bech books, Updike seems liberated by the comic veneer, yet the themes he treats are serious and not unrelated to those examined in previous and subsequent work: the panic of imminent mortality; the sense of vocation as self-definition; the ambivalence of attained rewards; the conflict between self-realization and love; and the tension between art and ardor.

Updike followed with his second Rabbit novel, *Rabbit Redux* (1971), before publishing his sixth volume of short fiction, *Museums and Women* (1972), which contains pieces that span the dozen years previous and is organized into three separate galleries: a group of fourteen tales; a section of ten sketches entitled "Other Modes"; and a group of five stories featuring the Maples. Critical reception of this collection might have been less mixed had Updike omitted the "Other Modes," although a few of these pieces echo the themes of the other stories. Perhaps in response to this criticism, Updike subsequently included such prose experiments only in his collections of criticism and other miscellaneous prose. Passing through a "muddled transitional condition" – a phrase used to describe the Dark Ages in "The Invention of the Horse Collar" – his middle-aged suburbanites are more frequently fatigued, and seem to have lost the energy to push through the door of memory or to devise workable harmonies amid maturity's discord. Yet despite their premature autumn, most still strain for connection with a diminished reach, capturing faint glimmers of a dying light for preservation in a museum of the past. In essence, the characters have become, as the narrator of "When Everyone Was Pregnant" reflects, "survival conscious" and less intent on gripping the past as "the decades slide seaward" (*Museums* 97). Estrangement from the past leaves them bounded in the present, suburban castaways searching for some faded radiance.

The volume's title story is clearly on par with Updike's finest short fiction: using the montage form, he strings together a series of lyrical meditations that form a museum gallery of the narrator's past. The experiential and metaphoric alliance of museums and women telescopes time's passage, recapitulating William Young's arc from adolescence to maturity, marital discontent, and beyond. "When Everyone Was Pregnant," is another reflective excursion, narrated by a securities broker with fragmentary recall of the 1950s, for him a fertile and guiltless era during which comfort and paternity replaced poverty and chastity. Updike's talent as a social historian is evident in "The Witnesses," which steps back to "high noon of the Eisenhower era," and "The Hillies," a sketch set in the 1960s that depicts the Tarbox community's response to a "less exotic" breed of hippies. Both this story and "The Carol Sing" – concerning a leading Tarbox citizen's suicide – use a first-person narrator who speaks in a communal voice as he encounters a phenomenon that defies easy explanation. Updike returns to the abstract–personal mode in "Solitaire," which treats the issue of marital infidelity through the protagonist's reflections during a game of solitaire, in which each card yields some metaphoric link with his predicament. The aftermath of marital separation is the subject of "The Orphaned Swimming Pool," which traces a couple's dissolution through the objective correlative of their former home's pool. "Plumbing," a brilliant metaphoric meditation, likens the problems that accrue in a long marital history with the deposits that build up in a house's subterranean plumbing; although not included with the five Maples stories here, it becomes a central story in Updike's later compilation of the Maples stories.

The most significant piece in the "Other Modes" section is "The Sea's Green Sameness," in which Updike adopts the trademark metafictional pose of authorial self-consciousness to reflect on artistic dilemmas. The other pieces range from cameo portraits and whimsical sketches to satires and sketches that feature Donald-Barthelme-like illustrations that draw on Updike's artistic training. Serious themes are present, however: "Under the Microscope," for instance, features the volvox that figured in Peter Caldwell's existential questions in *The Centaur*, while "The Slump" portrays a baseball player seeking a cure for his spiritual torpor in Kierkegaard as well as in the batting cage. The Maples stories that conclude the volume portray the nuances of the ongoing emotional and spiritual crises that accompany marriage and maturity; the short story sequence *Too Far to Go* (1979) more fully maps out the inherent fault lines of modern marriage and the cycles of attachment and detachment produced by its stresses.

Between *Museums and Women* and *Too Far to Go*, Updike published a closet drama, *Buchanan Dying* (1974) – the abortive product of research on Pennsylvania-born President James Buchanan – followed by his novel *A Month of Sundays* and second volume of prose, *Picked-Up Pieces*, in 1975. *Marry Me: A Romance* (1976) was published the same year Updike was elected to the Academy of the National Institute of Arts and Letters. Updike separated from his wife in 1974; in 1976 they were granted one of the first no-fault divorces in Massachusetts. The next year, Updike married Martha Bernhard; he also published *Tossing and Turning* (1977), a volume of poems, followed by the novel *The Coup* (1978). Updike's experiences in his first marriage, transmuted into fiction through Joan and Richard Maple in much the same fashion that his travels became the Bech stories, formed the basis of *Too Far to Go*. This definitive gathering of Maples stories might not have been part of Updike's canon had producer Robert Geller not decided to adapt the stories for a television drama, which led to a tie-in edition and spurred Updike to create a short story sequence that diverged significantly from the film.

More than inspired editing, *Too Far to Go* (1979) balances its first four stories, which conclude with the Maples' reluctant decision to separate in "Twin Beds in Rome," with the final quartet, in which the resolve is finally acted on. Juxtapositions and repeated motifs – such as references to Richard's illnesses, the focus on homes, allusions to Hansel and Gretel – provide contrast and coherence. Essentially, Updike uses the contours of his own life to create a study of an evolving, prototypical marriage as it is subtly affected by the sociopolitical changes sweeping the era. As marriage tends to subsume them into a single entity, Joan and Richard struggle to maintain their identities: the narrator of "Sublimating" observes how their eyes "had married and merged to three" (168). Mostly, however, the stories are related through Richard's consciousness, revealing how marriage binds him, though his viewpoint is clearly open to scrutiny. Although the couple seems on the verge of splitting in the early stories, Richard's pronouncement in "Twin Beds in Rome" that they've "come too far" in their marriage and "have only a little way more to go" turns out to be mistaken by about ten years and thirteen stories. Neither of the Maples seems able to go physically or emotionally far enough away from the other to separate, despite their adulteries; neither can they make the concessions that would move them toward reconciliation. In his foreword, Updike characterizes the couple as possessing "an arboreal innocence," like the trees evocative of suburban life for which they are named. As the volume progresses, he remarks, their behavior is like "a duet … repeated over and over, ever more harshly transposed" (10). Early doubts, temptations, and overtures toward separation ultimately give way to frustration, demystification, adultery, and divorce, which paradoxically renovates the Maples' vision of their marriage's enduring value. Merely focusing on the marriage's decline and fall, as Updike observes in the foreword, ignores the way in which the stories "illumine a history in many ways happy. That a marriage ends is less than ideal; but all things end under heaven, and if temporality is held to be invalidating, then nothing real succeeds" (10).

Problems, Updike's other 1979 collection, concentrates on the adversities of middle age. During this "idling time" his characters are disengaged from security as relationships collapse and troubles increasingly obscure youth's more acute perception of mystery. Like Ferguson in "The Egg Race," they are more oriented toward present sorrows than past bliss; while former ties no longer bind, they complicate any fresh start. Divorce carries a profound burden of guilt for these troubled protagonists, and the emotional wreckage strewn in the wake of separations fills the landscape with what the title of one story calls "Guilt-Gems." Updike's dedication to his four children highlights the number of stories featuring children, whose suppressed anguish often erupts as the gulf between them and their separating parents widens. Further experiments with the sketch, the "abstract-personal" mode, an epistolary-type journal form, and the montage story all appear, along with stories featuring excursions into memory and two of the stronger Maples stories – "Separating" and "Gesturing." Updike's figurative language still unexpectedly transforms the texture of everyday objects and events, but sustained lyric flights of prose become less frequent and his style becomes less heavily adjectival, in line perhaps with the characters' inability to enact the transcendence from the traumas of separation and mortality that accompany their progress into middle age. With a number of stories in this volume selected for inclusion in *Best American Short Stories* and the O. Henry *Prize Stories*, *Problems* is one of Updike's strongest collections.

"Commercial," a rare metafictional experiment, opens the volume with a camera-eye first-person plural narrative that juxtaposes two parallel scenes: one from a television commercial for natural gas and another from the life of the male viewer. Both the warm ambience of the contrived commercial nostalgia and the less idealized suburban scene are explicated in the same fashion, with the commercial yielding a neater message than the more problematic domestic scene, where the character's sleeping wife, unfulfilled lust, and longings for ideal beauty are less neatly resolved. Vignettes spliced together using a cinematic quick-cut method are employed in "Believers," whose protagonist, Credo, becomes aware of his distance from the past "giants of faith" as he reads St. Augustine to fuel his ardor for seduction. "The Gun Shop" is a more conventional narrative, recalling Updike's earlier Pennsylvania stories, although it focuses not on the young boy's initiation but on the father's dilemmas as he attempts to bring his city-bred son closer to the rural world of his own boyhood. Other stories concerning parents and children examine problematic breaches between generations. "Son," for instance, employs the montage technique of juxtaposing a series of vignettes spanning four generations to depict patterns in the conflicts between fathers and sons. "Daughter, Last Glimpses of" is a companion story, in which a father whose daughter has left to live with a harpsichord maker attempts to pierce his callused soul and recover bits of lost joy.

"Problems," the clever title story, portrays the familiar drama of yearning and betrayal, featuring characters labeled as abstract variables in a series of six interrelated mathematical teasers which form a composite portrait of the difficulties of separation and its ensuing guilt. Although Updike adapts the mathematical genre of the word problem, he undercuts its form, as there is no simple correct answer to be reached, since numerous variables affecting human behavior wreak havoc on any straightforward calculation. "Domestic Life in America" is almost a concrete illustration of the principles more abstractly outlined in "Problems," illustrating that story's "Tristan's Law": attraction exists in inverse proportion to psychic distance. "Guilt Gems," which begins at a similar stage in its protagonist's life, is another collage-like story less concerned with forwarding a narrative line than with exploring the paradoxical nature of guilt gems: shimmering, piercing moments that have "volunteered for compression" from the "gaseous clouds of being awaiting a condensation and preservation – faces, lights that glimmer out, somehow not seized, save in this gesture of remorse" (251). Unlike the unexpected rewards of Olinger, these guilt gems – and their provisional coherence established within such a story – represent the hard-earned legacy of the middle years. "From the Journal of a Leper" transmutes Updike's own lifelong struggle with psoriasis (chronicled in the "At War with My Skin" chapter of his memoir, *Self-Consciousness*) into a fictive exploration of the relationship between art and alienation. Archaeology, one of Updike's favorite recurrent metaphors, is featured in three stories which explore the "stratum of middle age" where, as the narrator of "The Egg Race" observes, "the middle distance blurs, and the floor appears to tilt, as if in unsteady takeoff toward some hopelessly remote point" (237).

In "Atlantises," a displaced couple, purportedly from the fabled lost island, seek news from the inundated past. With its marshy landscape and perpetual parties, Atlantis resembles Updike's suburban Tarbox, a phase of life to which this story bids farewell, although the protagonist's memory of an acquaintance who taught frogmen how to surface serves as a metaphor for the problematic transition back to actuality, rather than indulging in a prolonged dive into the sea of nostalgia.

Following the publication of *Rabbit Is Rich* (1981), his third Rabbit novel, Updike further mined his literary travels in *Bech Is Back* (1982), whose publication was accompanied by another *Time* cover feature, "Going Great at 50." This second Bech book more broadly examines the perils of success, as Updike's literary alter ego succeeds in breaking through his writer's block with a dubiously successful potboiler. Married and living in the suburbs, Bech has overcome his artistic stasis, only to become further entwined in the publishing industry's "silken mechanism." *Bech Is Back* consists of seven stories – four previously published and three written to complete the book – strung loosely together in a short story sequence. Like the volume itself, a number of the stories are composites, made up of smaller self-contained vignettes related by theme or locale; "Bech Wed," the penultimate novella-length work, occupies nearly one-third of the book and helps tie the stories together.

"Three Illuminations of an American Author" focuses on Bech's craving for financial and ego enrichment by seizing on opportunities for remunerative travel, all of which result in disillusion and further diminishment; invariably, when Bech and his books intersect, the resultant illuminations highlight corners of his life that might best have been left in the shadows. In a collage-like form, "Bech Third Worlds It" juxtaposes Bech's African travels with similar journeys to Venezuela and Korea, contrasting the emerging countries' concern with the writer's political role and Bech's tamer American aesthetic concerned with the personal. Solo travel in "Australia and Canada" heightens his understanding of how his role as a literary celebrity has had diminishing returns.

Travels as a husband rather than as a media creature follow in a symmetrical pair of stories that take Bech to "The Holy Land" and to Scotland ("Macbech"). Although his visit to the Holy Land reawakens some of Bech's latent religious sensibilities, it is in Ossining, New York – the WASPish suburbs of Cheever country – that Bech retrieves a deeper consciousness of his Jewishness and writes his long-deferred novel, in "Bech Wed." Despite favorable reviews, Bech knows that he has abandoned his previous standards of artistry; the misgivings about his new status as literary lion lead to an affair with a former mistress, his wife's sister. In the final story, "White on White," he perceives the kinship between his sullied achievements and the murky underside of the pretentious avant-garde art world. If Bech is back, his return to print has been an ambiguous triumph, difficult for him to savor and leaving him once again perpetually dissatisfied and manipulated by the publishing industry.

Updike's contribution to literary criticism was recognized with a National Book Critics Circle Award for *Hugging the Shore* (1983), whose title derives from the following remark in the preface: "Writing criticism is to writing fiction and poetry as hugging the shore is to sailing in the open sea" (xv). As editor of *Best American Short Stories 1984*, Updike not only gleaned twenty superior stories for recognition, but also penned an introduction that makes a number of astute critical observations about the short story form. His next novel, *The Witches of Eastwick* (1984), which returned to small town Massachusetts, was made into a feature film three years later. Another volume of poetry, *Facing Nature* (1985), preceded the novel *Roger's Version* (1986).

Updike's tenth short story collection, *Trust Me* (1987), reasserts his place as Joyce's successor in refining the epiphanic short story, yet also shows him integrating earlier narrative experiments. This volume, for which Updike was awarded Italy's Premio Scanno Prize in 1991, may be his most consistent effort, full of poignant and expertly crafted tales that mark a renewed interest in dramatic action and a leaner style that accentuates the poetic precision of his language. The stylistic flights of his earlier lyric fiction are muted and the experimental meditative mode has been supplanted with narrative experiments that span a significant stretch of time – even an entire marriage – within the limited compass of the short story. Updike's familiar concerns – suburban life, marriage, sex, and mortality – dominate the volume, though his characters are generally older, having passed through divorce and middle-aged restlessness and assumed an increasing consciousness of death. Many have established new relationships, but the foundations of trust in themselves, others, social structures, and religion are often shaken, even in seemingly placid suburban lives. If trust is faith on a human scale, Updike's stories show that rarely can we afford to believe blindly in a world that continues to disappoint with its unavoidable limitations and compromises. Those in whom his characters long to trust are only human, prone to lapses in judgment and whims of desire, as the dust jacket illustration – selected by Updike – highlights: Icarus, poised in midair and about to fall, foreshadows the breaches of trust, the fragility of promises, the familial betrayals, and the inevitable shattering of faith in human nature's perspicacity that occur as Updike's characters confront the inevitable betrayals or failings of those who ask for trust and seek some provisional assurances on which to reconstruct a foundation of belief.

"Trust Me," the lead story, weaves together four juxtaposed vignettes of incidents involving trust and betrayal that cover the territory from the protagonist's childhood to his current life beyond divorce. The hazards of extending and expecting assurance resonate throughout each incident, and Updike deftly ties these four vignettes together with his protagonist's recognition of the patterns within his past and with an epiphany involving a dollar bill – an embodiment of and reminder that trust, despite its problematic nature, remains the prevalent currency of human affairs. Other stories likewise show Updike stretching the short story form to encompass a temporal space greater than the epiphanic moment. "More Stately Mansions" has a structure that resembles the chambers of its central symbol, the nautilus shell whose marine inhabitant progressively builds a chambered home. As he uses a nautilus shell as the center of a lesson to his class, the narrator ponders his personal history of guilt, infidelity, and tragedy and examines his tenuous reconciliation after rising above his "low-vaulted past." "Made in Heaven," a sweeping chronicle that traces the history of a marriage, is an ironic study of religiosity, depicting a husband's progressive sapping of his wife's religious faith as she struggles to preserve it against his masculine control and intrusion. Updike selected this story for an anthology of writers' favorites, citing its subject matter – "the mystery of churchgoing" – and the depiction of a long-term marriage's "secret and final revenge, its redressing of a long-sustained imbalance" (26) as rationales for his choice.

Older protagonists dominate the collection as Updike explores the pressure mortality exerts on his characters' fragile structures of belief. "Slippage," for instance, features a history professor who loses his "heart for history" and his grip on certainty after an earth tremor, which opens an emotional chasm between his present routine and his unrealized ambitions. "The Wallet" depicts a retired investment broker's erosion of confidence in his memory and in the psychological props that keep the void at bay, all from the misplacing of his wallet and the subsequent unraveling of other circumstances beyond his control. *Trust Me* also includes trademark Updike stories that explore domestic life's shadowy corners, centering on epiphanic moments that simultaneously reveal its beauty and fragility. "Still of Some Use" exhibits Updike's talents for realism, as his protagonist forges new bonds with his son as they discard old games; "Learn a Trade," another tightly structured story involving fathers and sons, links a successful artist's past rebellious relationship with his father to his current conflict with his son, whose stubborn pursuit of the artistic avocations that he warns him to avoid teaches him a lesson in trust when the beauty of his son's fragile mobiles overwhelms him. "A Constellation of Events" and "Killing" make rare ventures into the female consciousness, while "Poker Night" features an atypical blue-collar protagonist attempting to control his growing dread after learning that he has cancer. "Unstuck" concerns a young couple whose marital problems are metaphorically portrayed through their attempts to get their car moving in the snow; it stands out as the only story with protagonists the age of those in *The Same Door*. Five families – older versions of the young suburban couples in Updike's earlier fiction – form an ensemble cast in "Leaf Season," an experiment in using the short form to explore a group dynamic. Another story lacking a central protagonist is "The Ideal Village," which uses a visit to an isolated Latin American village to explore familiar themes concerning the perpetual unrest and dissatisfaction of the human spirit. A number of other stories explore the vagaries of attraction and betrayals of trust in the more typical Updike milieu of suburban New England. Overall, the collection has an autumnal mood, as Updike's older characters attempt to refurbish their trust and create whatever precarious shelters they can as they become further aware of death's increasingly visible horizon.

Updike followed *Trust Me* with a novel, *S.* (1988), and two books in 1989, the year his mother died: *Just Looking: Essays on Art* and his memoir *Self-Consciousness*. The early 1990s saw the appearance of his final Rabbit novel, *Rabbit at Rest* (1990), as well as another volume of criticism, *Odd Jobs* (1991), his volume of *Collected Poems 1953–1993* (1993), and two novels: *Memories of the Ford Administration* (1992) and *Brazil* (1994), which appeared the same year as his eleventh collection of short fiction, *The Afterlife and Other Stories*. As Updike's protagonists enter this "afterlife – the phase after their children are grown, their marriages have failed, and new relationships have become settled – they are becoming comfortably familiar with "death's immediate neighborhood" (253) and share one character's lament that "[t]hings used to be more substantial" (255). Ennui and a winding down of aspiration pervades this phase; with death occurring around them, these protagonists seem to have developed a layer of insulation from experience that evens out the disappointments and the satisfactions so that neither upsets the equilibrium. If characters are "Playing with Dynamite" – as one story is titled – the risk seems curiously defused, as the ache of memory has become less immediate and profound.

In the title story, a couple whose lives have drifted on uneventfully visits England in the wake of many of their friends doing "sudden surprising things," although the husband believes that whatever shocks nature and personal experience might bring, he and his cohorts "were beyond all that now." Nonetheless, he experiences an unexpected but ephemeral moment of grace as he witnesses a heron that resembles an angel in the symbolically appropriate rearview mirror, producing uncharacteristic daring as he drives through a storm, and heightened sensitivity in its aftermath. "Wildlife" provides an Aids-era analogy for the peril from which Updike's older characters seem insulated in the Lyme disease that threatens the town to which its protagonist returns for periodic visits to his children. A tick bite to his grown son, discovered before the symptoms become severe, leads him to conclude that he has made a timely escape from his former life, despite its retrospective appeal. In "Brother Grasshopper," the protagonist's scattering of his deceased brother-in-law's ashes at sea produces the insight that their shared times were "priceless – treasure, stored up against the winter that had arrived" (45). Memories of the deceased also comprise "His Mother Inside Him," in which Allen Dow – a character from *The Same Door* – is spurred by a friend's remark about his physical resemblance to his mother to discover how he embodies her traits more than her features.

"A Sandstone Farmhouse," featured both in *Best American Short Stories 1991* and as First Prize winner in *Prize Stories: The O. Henry Awards* the same year, chronicles an older character's return to his parents' Pennsylvania farmhouse after his mother's death. After cleaning out the house and readying it for sale, he believes he has "reduced the house to its essence" and removed all traces of his family's life there. Yet in sifting through memorabilia and handling the artifacts of their past, he internalizes that essence and rediscovers the vibrancy of his mother's life and of the rural existence he once yearned so passionately to escape. Other stories likewise involve returns to home-towns, some of which give rise to memories with surprising freshness and immediacy, while others produce unsettling effects. "Conjunction" relies symbolically on a tele-scope to aid the protagonist in evoking memories of earlier conjunctions with his wife, although he cannot keep his fix on either the planetary conjunction he is observ-ing or on his past.

Updike astutely depicts the pressures within ongoing relationships, adapting his focus to the new landscape that age creates. A longer two-part story, "George and Vivian," chronicles the husband's eventual admission that his third wife was "no comfort" as they grate on each other during their European travels, while "Farrell's Caddy" treats the situation of discord in the twilight of a second marriage in a delight-fully comic fashion via an astute caddy's reading of the protagonist's golf game. Other protagonists in their sixties, such as Fogel of "Short Easter," are bothered by the sense that "Everything seemed still in place, yet something was immensely missing" (102) – an insight brought home by the disorientation of an Easter holiday shortened by daylight saving time. In the volume's only first-person narration, "Falling Asleep Up North," fatigue becomes an advantage of age, facilitating loss of the angst that for-merly arose so keenly. Updike brings Joan and Richard Maple into the afterlife phase in "Grandparenting," the volume's final story. Both remarried, they amicably attend the birth of their daughter's first child, although certain tensions endure beneath the surface. As Richard holds his new grandchild, he concludes that "Nobody belongs to us, except in memory" (136), typifying the reflective and somewhat resigned insight that his characters derive from their accumulated experience. Although the stories of this phase are not as achingly lyrical or as highly experimental as some of Updike's earlier work, they nonetheless exhibit his continued craftsmanship, as well as his rare ability to capture the latent significance of the mundane and to use realistic detail in evoking the pleasures and sorrows of memory.

To his previous collection of four children's books – one for each of his children – Updike added *A Helpful Alphabet of Friendly Objects* in 1995, presumably with his grandchildren in mind; his son David provided the photographs. He followed the next year with the novel *In the Beauty of the Lilies* (1996) and *Golf Dreams* (1996), a gathering of his prose works on the sport that was a consistent avocation as well as a topic of literary reflection. His novel *Toward the End of Time* (1997) preceded the publication of his twelfth short story collection, *Bech at Bay: A Quasi Novel* (1998), whose subtitle signals the coherence among the volume's five longer stories. Updike takes his traveling celebrity author from Kafka's grave to the Nobel platform, with meetings of literary intelligentsia, a courtroom appearance, and literary murder in between. Once again, Updike takes aim in comic fashion at such serious issues as governmental suppression of writers, the diminishment of American writing, the wounds critics inflict upon authors, and the dubious honors bestowed upon writers by the media culture. As Updike lampoons the same critical establishment that has received the Bech books more warmly than any other, he takes – as David Lodge states – "wicked delight in his own invention" (9).

Despite allowing his character to serve as the mouthpiece of some pointed barbs (even one aimed at himself), the view of Bech that Updike presents is characteristically mixed. Continually self-deprecating, Bech nonetheless arouses reader sympathy as he frets about mortality, sexual attractiveness and prowess, literary relevance, and his paucity of worthwhile opinions. Bech's roles in these stories range from darling of dissident writers to president of an arts academy, defendant in a libel trial, avenger of literary slights, and finally parent and Nobel Prize winner. Like the first Bech volume, this one begins with a sojourn in Eastern Europe and closes with Bech onstage at an awards ceremony. In between, he manages to achieve some measure of power as president of a literary society, as the forgiver of a Hollywood agent who has brought a libel suit against him, and as a murderer of critics who have panned his work.

"Bech in Czech" contrasts Bech's jaded definition of the writer as one who is "to amuse himself, to indulge himself, to get his books into print with as little editorial smudging as he can, to slide through his society with minimal friction" (*Bech at Bay* 12) with the Czech dissidents' craft and commitment in printing and circulating their underground books. Bech's journey leads to a further deepening of his Jewish identity on a visit to Kafka's grave, an existential panic, and an understanding that a more serious conception of the writer's role than he holds is the route to the literary immortality he desires. Duped by his literary rival into becoming president of an elite guild of writers and artists that resembles the Academy of the National Institute of Arts and Letters, Bech unwittingly ends up presiding over its dissolution in "Bech Presides," in which Updike satirizes the Manhattan intelligentsia. In "Bech Noir," the darkest and the most humorous of the volume's stories, Updike – who early in his career dubbed reviewers as "pigs at a pastry cart" (Bech 3) – portrays the power of words in causing harm and backlash. Vexed by negative reviews whose sting has endured, the 74-year-old Bech becomes a serial literary avenger, ultimately enlisting his mistress in a variety of schemes to do away with hostile critics. In "Bech and the Bounty of Sweden," Bech wins the Nobel Prize that had eluded his creator, but his fabled writer's block recurs as he attempts to pen his acceptance speech, and he ultimately gives the award podium over to his infant daughter. Only months after this volume's publication, a new Bech story, "His Oeuvre," appeared in the *New Yorker*; it was later collected with the stories from Updike's three Bech short story sequences in *The Complete Henry Bech* (2001).

Updike's importance as writer and critic of short fiction was recognized in another fashion with the assignment to co-edit *The Best American Short Stories of the Century* (1999), for which he and Katrina Kenison selected fifty-five stories from the past eighty-five volumes of the *Best American Short Stories* series; his story, "Gesturing" was chosen as the 1980 entry by Kenison. In his introduction, Updike expresses concern about the health of the genre, noting that "in my lifetime the importance of short fiction as a news bearing medium – bringing Americans news of how they live, and why – has diminished" (xxii). His fifth gathering of assorted prose, *More Matter*, appeared the same year. After *Gertrude and Claudius* (2000), a novel, Updike published *Licks of Love* (2000), his thirteenth collection of short fiction, which gathers twelve stories with the novella "Rabbit Remembered," a coda to the Rabbit tetralogy that perhaps overshadows the short fiction. Both the novella and the stories revisit old territory: "Rabbit Remembered" brings the Angstrom saga into the 1990s and to the cusp of the millennium through the story of Rabbit's illegitimate daughter, while the stories, for the most part, revive earlier characters and situations or focus on past eras. One notable exception is the title story, which chronicles the picaresque sexual adventures of a banjo player sent to the Soviet Union by the State Department as a cultural emissary.

Nostalgia, however, is the dominant mood as the stories' protagonists retrace the contours of past affairs, earlier married bliss, or their youth. In "The Women Who Got Away," for instance, the remarried narrator's attempt to spark an affair with an old acquaintance during a visit to the town in which his previous adulteries occurred generates memories of those past amours; however, he discovers that his present efforts may be in vain when he spots the object of his conquest holding hands with another woman whose sexual attentions he had once failed to attain. The aforementioned Bech story, "His Oeuvre," fits well in this collection, as the appearance of Bech's former mistresses at his readings comes to overshadow his literary achievements as his true masterpieces. Many of the other stories recall lost love and missed opportunities, although the past appears in retrospect to be a time when pain and loss were more easily overcome. Still, memory may prove unreliable, as the story "How Was It, Really?" suggests: as the protagonist reviews the "broad middle stretch" of his life, he feels like "an astronomer … working with blurs" (147) and is ultimately unable to formulate a definitive answer to the title question – although Updike's previous short fiction clearly provides an accurate depiction of that era.

Yet not all the collection's stories look back at the erotic conquests and defeats that the sexual innuendo of its title suggests. "Lunch Hour" involves the return of recurrent character David Kern – first introduced in "Pigeon Feathers" – for his high school reunion; although Olinger High has long since been razed, he is able to get in touch with his memories through the presence of the woman who as a young girl had helped him shed his outcast status and become part of the main social clique. In "The Cats," the narrator's inheritance of eighty acres of family property in Pennsylvania, along with over forty cats that his late mother had cared for, brings him home to step into the remnants of his old life. A companion story that revisits material covered in *The Centaur*, "My Father on the Verge of Disgrace," casts back into the narrator's small-town Pennsylvania youth, recalling his father's precarious struggles to support the family and ultimately affirming his powers of endurance. Overall, the stories in *Licks of Love* serve as a window into the past from a diminished present, indulging in a forgiving retrospective glance that stands in marked contrast to the millennial turbulence depicted in the Rabbit novella.

Updike's most recent work includes *Americana* (2001), a volume of poems, and the novels *Seek My Face* (2002) and *Villages* (2004). The first volume of his collected fiction *The Early Stories: 1953–1975*, for which Updike received the PEN/Faulkner Award, appeared in 2003. It gathers all but four from a total of 107 stories composed in the first twenty-three years of his career, with the stories divided into eight titled sections that compose a shadow autobiography and paradigmatic slice of twentieth-century American life. The first section reprints the whole of *Olinger Stories*, which has long been out of print, signaling perhaps that the other sections of *The Early Stories* might be read in the same fashion as mini-short story sequences, savoring each story as an autonomous unit while at the same time attuned to the unity and coherence among them – and ever conscious of the discontinuities which ultimately keep them apart. One possible model that Updike might have had in mind is William Faulkner's *Collected Stories*, in which Faulkner divides his short fiction into six geographically titled sections that set up similar resonance among them. Updike thus creates a chronological arc of a composite American life, with the first four sections – "Olinger Stories," "Out in the World," "Married Life," and "Family Life" – tracing, as the dust jacket notes, "a common American trajectory" from youth to family life, and the fifth, "The Two Iseults," charting the disruption of the latter. The sixth and seventh sections – "Tarbox Tales" and "Far Out" – veer somewhat from a strictly linear movement, although the affairs in the former section depict deepened disruptions, while the stories in the latter, the blurb continues, reside "on the edge of domestic space." The collection concludes with assorted "unmarried and unmoored" protagonists in "The Single Life," bringing Updike's characters to the threshold of forging new attachments and facing mortality in the face of eroding certitudes.

Updike's efforts to bring Americans their "news" in short fiction continued unabated. As the recent gathering of less than half of Updike's published short fiction reveals, his protagonists have generally aged along with their creator, providing a lasting chronicle of modern American social history. *The Early Stories* contains many of his most daring formal and technical experiments with the form, as well as a number of other exceptional stories – beyond "A&P" – that are deserving of inclusion in anthologies. When subsequent volumes of his collected stories bring together work from the past three decades, it will be evident that Updike was a master of the short story form, and that his talents are perhaps best suited to it. As his list of uncollected short fiction grows, other collections are likely, further augmenting his centrality in refining and forwarding the renaissance of the short story in the twentieth century. The qualities singled out by William Abrahams in his 1976 citation for Updike's Special O. Henry Award for Continuing Achievement are still relevant: "the majority of short-story writers continue to conduct their explorations within the visible confines of the tradition itself. Few have done so as consistently, or with such rewarding results as John Updike. ... His unflagging mastery is at once an example and a consolation for addicts of the short story, readers and writers alike" (Abrahams 13).

REFERENCES AND FURTHER READING

Abrahams, William, ed. *Prize Stories 1976: The O. Henry Awards*. Garden City, NY: Doubleday, 1976.

Baker, Nicholson. *U & I: A True Story*. New York: Random House, 1991.

Bech, Henry [John Updike]. "Henry Bech Redux." *New York Times Book Review* (November 14, 1971): 3.

Bloom, Harold, ed. *John Updike: Bloom's Major Short Story Writers*. New York: Chelsea House, 2000.

———. *John Updike: Modern Critical Views*. New York: Chelsea House, 1987.

Burchard, Rachel C. *John Updike: Yea Sayings*. Carbondale: Southern Illinois University Press, 1971.

DeBellis, Jack. *John Updike: A Bibliography, 1967–1993*. Westport, CT: Greenwood Press, 1994.

Detweiler, Robert. *John Updike*. Rev. edn. New York: Twayne, 1984.

Greiner, Donald J. *The Other John Updike: Poems/Short Stories/Prose/Play*. Athens: Ohio University Press, 1981.

Hamilton, Alice, and Kenneth Hamilton. *The Elements of John Updike*. Grand Rapids, MI: William B. Eerdmans, 1970.

Hunt, George. *John Updike and the Three Great Secret Things: Sex, Religion, and Art*. Grand Rapids, MI: William B. Eerdmans, 1980.

Lodge, David. "Bye-Bye Bech." *New York Review of Books* (November 19, 1998): 8–10.

Luscher, Robert M. *John Updike: A Study of the Short Fiction*. New York: Twayne, 1993.

Macnaughton, William R., ed. *Critical Essays on John Updike*. Boston: G. K. Hall, 1982.

Modern Fiction Studies 20 (1974) and 37 (1991). [Special issues on Updike].

Newman, Judie. *John Updike*. New York: St. Martin's Press, 1988.

Perkins, Wendy, ed. *A&P*. New York: Harcourt Brace, 1998.

Plath, James, ed. *Conversations with John Updike*. Jackson: University Press of Mississippi, 1994.

Pritchard, William. *Updike: America's Man of Letters*. South Royalton, VT: Steerforth Press, 2000.

Reilly, Charlie. "A Conversation with John Updike." In Plath, ed., *Conversations with John Updike*, 124–50.

Samuels, Charles Thomas. *John Updike*. Minneapolis: University of Minnesota Press, 1969.

Schiff, James A. *John Updike Revisited*. New York: Twayne, 1998.

Searles, George J. *The Fiction of Philip Roth and John Updike*. Carbondale: Southern Illinois University Press, 1985.

Tallent, Elizabeth. *Married Men and Magic Tricks: John Updike's Erotic Heroes*. Berkeley: Creative Arts, 1981.

Taylor, Larry E. *Pastoral and Anti-Pastoral in John Updike's Fiction*. Carbondale: Southern Illinois University Press, 1971.

Thorburn, David, and Howard Eiland, eds. *John Updike: A Collection of Critical Essays*. Boston: G. K. Hall, 1979.

Uphaus, Suzanne Henning. *John Updike*. New York: Ungar, 1980.

Updike, John. *The Afterlife and Other Stories*. New York, Knopf, 1994.

———. *Assorted Prose*. New York: Knopf, 1965.

———. *Bech at Bay: A Quasi-Novel*. New York: Knopf, 1998.

———. *Hugging the Shore: Essays and Criticism*. New York: Knopf, 1983.

———. *Licks of Love: Short Stories and a Sequel*. New York: Knopf, 2000.

———. "Made in Heaven." *New American Short Stories: The Writers Select Their Own Favorites*. Ed. Gloria Norris. New York: Plume, 1986. 9–26.

———. *Museums and Women and Other Stories*. New York: Knopf, 1973.

———. *Olinger Stories: A Selection*. New York: Vintage, 1964.

———. *Pigeon Feathers and Other Stories*. New York: Knopf, 1962.

———. *Problems and Other Stories*. New York: Knopf, 1979.

———. *Too Far to Go*. New York: Fawcett, 1979.

Updike, John, and Katrina Kenison, eds. *Best American Short Stories of the Century*. Boston: Houghton Mifflin, 1999.

Yerkes, James. *The Centurian*. <http://userpages.prexar.com/joyerkes/>.

Yerkes, James, ed. *John Updike and Religion: The Sense of the Sacred and the Motions of Grace*. Grand Rapids, MI: Wm. B. Eerdmans, 1999.

23

Raymond Carver in the Twenty-First Century

Sandra Lee Kleppe

The Copernican revolution in Carver studies has begun.

– *William L. Stull*

Past and Present Perspectives on Carver's Career

Twenty years after the death of Raymond Carver (1938–88), interest in his life and works seems more vibrant than ever. The versatility of the growing critical inquiries into his literary and cultural significance, the inclusion of his texts in interdisciplinary teaching fields, his translation into many languages, coupled with the resilience of the works themselves, are remarkable testimonies to his lasting contributions to the American short story genre.[1] The Copernican revolution cited in the epigraph by the Carver bibliographer William L. Stull concerns the revelations about the authorship of key Carver texts, most importantly those in his iconic "minimalist" collection *What We Talk About When We Talk About Love* (1981). From our perspective in the twenty-first century, that collection is no longer the center of Carver Country, even as it remains the center of the controversy about who, exactly, penned the stories in the book.

This first part of the chapter provides an overview of what is available in Carver studies and comments on the current state of the "revolution." As revolutions are by nature chaotic, it can be difficult for the scholar, teacher, student, or general reader to grasp the large and small movements in the field of inquiry. Fortunately, the two decades that have passed since the death of Carver give the twenty-first-century reader some advantages of distance and it will hopefully be possible to provide some balanced assessments of Carver's career as a whole, as well as of an individual story. The second part turns to one story, "Cathedral," chosen because it is so frequently anthologized and thereby also frequently taught and read. In that section, the task will be to offer perspectives on how "Cathedral" resonates with

Carver's other stories as well as with those of other major writers, with special emphasis on intertextuality.

Controversy and Beyond

Carver started publishing his first stories and poems in little magazines in the 1960s, but his breakthrough as a writer did not come until 1976 with the publication of *Will You Please Be Quiet, Please?* which contains both the award-winning title story and many of his most memorable and commented-on early stories such as "Fat," "Neighbors," and "Put Yourself in My Shoes." The extent to which Carver's friend and editor Gordon Lish was involved in the preparation of these stories for the volume is as yet unclear, but we know for certain that the striking shift to the pared-down stories in the notorious "minimalist" collection *What We Talk About When We Talk About Love* (1981) was the result of Lish's heavy-handed editing; in some cases more than half of Carver's story manuscripts were cut, and Lish made significant alterations to both individual stories and the structure of the collection, also changing titles to fit the stark mood of the whole.

Though the scandal was kept quiet by Carver during his lifetime, he immediately began loosening himself from Lish's grip while *What We Talk About* was still in press. Indeed, he had published some of the same stories independently of Lish in *Furious Seasons* with Capra Press in 1977, and would in the 1980s go on to rewrite or restore some of the stories that had been cut and also produce brand new ones such as "Cathedral," "Elephant," and "Errand" (as well as three volumes of poetry). Carver's "new" hallmark expansive style is evident in the story collections *Cathedral* (1983) and *Where I'm Calling From* (1988), the latter completed just before his death. The Lish controversy was not unveiled to the general public until a decade later, in the now famous article by D. T. Max, which appeared in 1998 in the *New York Times Magazine*. Almost another decade would pass before more of the details of the *What We Talk About* scandal were revealed in a double Christmas Eve/New Year's Eve issue of the *New Yorker* in 2007, which published Carver's unaltered manuscript version of the title story, called "Beginners," as well as extensive excerpts from the correspondence between Lish and Carver during the editing process. We know now that Carver pleaded with Lish not to publish the volume with such extensive changes, that he felt both his artistic integrity and shaky health were on the line. Ultimately, however, Carver agreed (for complicated reasons), to go forth with Lish's version of the book.

General readers do not have access to all the materials needed to reach a reliable assessment of Carver's career developments, as the sources for these materials, Stull notes, are "in libraries and archival collections, as well as in the little magazines, chapbooks and small-press books in which Carver published his writings throughout his lifetime" (Stull and Carroll 15). Furthermore, Stull adds, to "examine this evidence systematically and reach empirically and rationally supported conclusions requires long-term research" (ibid.). Luckily, Stull and others have taken on this task, producing several posthumous volumes of Carver texts that attest to the rich amount of material available, including new fiction, poetry, essays, plays, and excerpts, showing the extent of Carver's writing career and restoring the full text of some of the trimmed stories.[2] Stull has also assisted in the publication of the Library of America's *Raymond Carver: Collected Stories* (2009), a seminal book which now allows scholars and students to have access to the full range of Carver's story production in one volume.

For a systematic critical analysis of specific changes Lish made to *What We Talk About* and their significance compared to Carver's manuscripts, readers can consult a comprehensive article by Carver scholar Enrico Monti, available online at the *Raymond Carver Review*.[3] Monti provides us with a detailed comparison of the type Stull calls for, analyzing not only the cuts Lish made to the stories, but also the insertion of new titles, syntactical changes, lexical changes, and new endings. What emerges from Monti's study is that Lish

> deliberately set out to dehumanize the stories and decontextualize them by expelling geographical coordinates, reducing scenarios to their basics, and omitting names and the few references to renowned people. (69)

In other words, the deadpan "minimalist" style of the collection is more Lish's than Carver's, although, as Monti also points out, Lish's editorial strategy appears as a "mix of sheer perception of Carver's talent and crafty understanding of what groundbreaking, innovative fiction should be at that time" (70).

In sum, the Lish controversy for Carver studies is ongoing as Carver scholars have begun and will continue to document the implications of the editorial relationship for the works themselves. Yet the fact remains that *What We Talk About When We Talk About Love,* for many readers, still represents one of America's most iconic short story collections, one which we now can conclude must have been the collaborative effort of a gifted writer and an iron-willed editor at a particular moment in American letters when the postmodern fascination with verbose experimentation would become ripe for a paradigm shift with the shock of the minimal, almost skeletal, and often lyrically powerful language of *What We Talk About.* There is no doubt that the literary gift was Carver's, but the direction which it took in that particular collection was the result of Lish's influence. To put it in the words of James Campbell, writing for the British *Saturday Guardian*, "Gordon Lish might have been the midwife, as all good editors are, but he is not the father." Both Monti and Cambell ultimately assess the Lish–Carver controversy in comparison with some of the twentieth century's most notorious editor–writer relationships, including the influence of Ezra Pound on the creation of T. S. Eliot's *The Wasteland,* or the scandals involved in restoring classics such as the "scroll" version of Jack Kerouac's *On the Road.* What we can see from our point of view in the twenty-first century is that Carver is clearly being ranked among the masters of American literature.

Critical Inquiry, Then and Now

Parallel to the growing interest in the editorial genesis of Carver's fiction and in his posthumously published works is the emergence of much-needed biographical studies that will help us better understand Carver's life and works in tandem. Philippe Romon published a literary biography in French in 2003, and the long-awaited English biography by Carol Sklenicka appeared in late 2009. Carver's first wife, Maryann Burk Carver, published in 2006 her memoir *What It Used to Be Like*, which can be seen as a supplement to the earlier, still relevant, biographical sketches found in *Raymond Carver: An Oral Biography* (by Sam Halpert, 1995), *Remembering Ray: A Composite Biography* (by Carroll and Stull, 1993) and *Carver Country: The World of Raymond Carver* (by Adelman and Gallagher, 1990), a rich photographic essay full of biographical tidbits.

During Carver's lifetime, he resented the flood of articles and reviews calling him a minimalist, a label which has finally begun to unstick. There exists, however, a very solid first generation of critical monographs that are still recommended reading, including Randolph Runyon's *Reading Raymond Carver* (1992), Adam Meyer's *Raymond Carver* (1995), and Kirk Nesset's *The Stories of Raymond Carver: A Critical Study* (1995). For the reader interested in more current book-length studies of Carver's works, Greg Lainsbury's *The Carver Chronotope: Inside the Life-World of Raymond Carver's Fiction* (2004) and Arthur Bethea's *Technique and Sensibility in the Fiction and Poetry of Raymond Carver* (2001) are good examples of excellent scholarship. In 2006, a special issue of *Journal of the Short Story in English* dedicated to Carver included articles on the posthumous stories, on domestic violence, and on the poetics of space in his stories. A recent anthology of critical essays, *New Paths to Raymond Carver* (edited by Kleppe and Miltner, 2008), treats topics such as the role of Alcoholics Anonymous in the structuring of stories, McCarthyism, and the pervasive presence of television and TV culture in Carver's works.

What is perhaps most exciting about Carver studies in the twenty-first century is the versatility of his works, which are taught widely in interdisciplinary fields as well as in many countries, and the sheer variety of perspectives being applied to reading Carver in new contexts. Feminism and gender studies approaches, occasionally discussed in twentieth-century appraisals of Carver,[4] are beginning to gain momentum as interest in the role of women, the formation of masculinity in the Cold War era, and transgender and queer issues increases.[5] Consider, for example, that Carver allowed women to occupy the privileged position as first-person narrator in several stories – including "Fat," "The Idea," "The Student's Wife," and "So Much Water, So Close to Home" – a narrative feat of gender-crossing he found challenging: "The first time I ever attempted to write a story from the point of view of a woman, I was nervous about it. It was a real challenge to me" (Gentry and Stull 230). The cross-dressing episode in "Neighbors," when Bill tries on the identity and clothes of his female neighbor, is also impossible to overlook: "He rummaged through the top drawers until he found a pair of panties and a brassiere.

He stepped into the panties and fastened the brassiere, then looked through the closet for an outfit" (Carver "Neighbors" 14). Male bonding is a central issue in such stories as "Cathedral," "The Calm," and "Bicycles, Muscles, Cigarets" from three different story collections.[6] Indeed, there seems no Carver story where gender issues are not at stake.

In religious studies, as well as in the medical humanities and related emerging fields such as disability studies and fat studies, Carver's life experiences and the texts that came out of them draw much attention. There are a dozen or so individual critical articles treating the religious and spiritual aspects of Carver's late works.[7] Carver is widely taught in pre-med schools, where he is on the syllabus of courses that cover topics such as cancer, alcoholism, and patient–doctor relationships.[8] He is listed on courses in disability studies that cover texts from Sophocles' *Oedipus* to Carver's "Cathedral,"[9] and his story "Fat" is included in Donna Jarrell's and Ira Sukrungruang's *What Are You Looking At? The First Fat Fiction Anthology* (2003). One suspects that the sheer accessibility of his language combined with the closeness between lived and fictional experience have contributed to the fascination with Carver in areas far removed from traditional literary courses.

Finally, film and media studies remain pertinent charted and forthcoming areas of inquiry, especially since the release of Ray Lawrence's film *Jindabyne* in 2006.[10] Where Robert Altman portrayed the fast-paced and interlocked fate of characters from nine Carver stories in the now-classic *Short Cuts* (1993), Lawrence dedicates a full feature to the exploration of one story, "So Much Water, So Close to Home." Set in contemporary Australia, the film is an excellent example of how Carver Country is as much a state of mind as it is a place, and how characters everywhere and anywhere are a part of the arduous business called life that Carver so meticulously recreated in his fiction. This is the case regardless of whether they live in the small community of Jindabyne or sprawling Los Angeles.

An Intertextual Assessment of "Cathedral"

As our knowledge of Carver's literary life has expanded with time, our understanding of the collection *Cathedral* (and its title story) as a post-minimalist work has been confirmed and emphasized. The collection, written soon after Carver's intense correspondence with Lish over the editor's huge cuts to *What We Talk About*, includes several stories that Carver rewrote or restored from earlier versions, as well as new stories such as "Cathedral" that were to be published without Lish's interference. The book was also written during what Carver referred to as the "gravy" years of his life, after recovery from alcoholism and before diagnosis with cancer.[11] The title story is, for good reasons, widely anthologized, and all of the major Carver scholars cited above have commented on it in their monographs. There exist dozens of individual critical articles on the story and at least one student study guide,[12] in addition to Harold Bloom's (mis)treatment of it as a lesser version of D. H. Lawrence's "The

Blind Man" in his *Major Short Story Writers* series. Indeed, the interest in "Cathedral" exemplifies the versatility of Carver's short fiction, demonstrating its ability to withstand scrutiny and to offer up insights in readings that emphasize a range of topics including religion, alcoholism, disability, humor, television, feminism, and gender studies. This section, however, will place the story in the literary "canon" (from which Bloom has excluded it) while emphasizing the larger literary and intertextual issues that it raises.

Intratextuality and Intertextuality

Before looking specifically at some of the intertextual traits of "Cathedral," it is important to establish that Carver frequently worked both intra- and intertextual elements into his writing, and that this was a lifelong process he never abandoned. *Intra*textual refers to the phenomenon of a writer's self-reference; to the recycling or reworking of elements from one's own texts. The intratextual can function on the level of a collection of stories, as Randolph Runyon has illuminated in *Reading Raymond Carver*, where he shows how each story in each of Carver's major collections reworks elements of the previous one(s). For Carver, however, intratextuality also functions on many other levels, as he frequently rewrites his own stories (calling, for example, "A Small, Good Thing" not a version of "The Bath," but a completely different story) or pokes fun at himself as a writer. In "Cathedral," for example, the narrator ridicules his wife for writing a poem about the blind man touching her: "I didn't think much of the poem. … Maybe I just don't know much about poetry" (211). Both Tess Gallagher (Carver's second wife) and Carver himself are accomplished poets, so the humor is double-edged here.

Moreover, by introducing blindness into the story as its central trope, Carver's "Cathedral" is an intratextual experiment in reversal: almost all of his stories and poems deal at some level with the trope of vision. On the microlevel of the word and of the verb phrase, the most frequent intratextual element in Carver, what marks almost every Carver text as his particular product (whether edited by Lish or not), is his obsession with sight; indeed Carver scholars have long since established *voyeurism* as a central motif in his work. There is almost no story or poem that does not display an almost redundant use of verbs such as "see," "watch," "look," "glance," and "stare," and related nouns such as "eyes," "vision," or, to borrow the title from one of his stories, "Viewfinder." To take that very brief, five-page story as an example, we find the following density of sight verbs: "watching" (2 times), "see" (2 times), "look" (5 times), "looked" (3 times), "saw" (2 times), "seeing" (once), "watched" (2 times), and "show" (2 times). In addition, there is an ironic sight-related adjective to describe the antagonist, who is "ordinary-looking" (except for the fact that he has hooks instead of hands), and several nouns related to this man's vocation as an amateur photographer, itself a trope for viewing: "photograph" (2 times), "picture" (5 times), "camera" (4 times), "Polaroid" (once), "viewfinder" (3 times including the title), and "shutter" (once).[13] On a larger intratextual level, this story resounds with "Cathedral"; in both stories, a disabled person functions as a more "whole" being than the main character who has no physical disabilities.

This brings us to the discussion of the *inter*textual nature of Carver's work. The story "Viewfinder" is one among several that echo Flannery O'Connor's fiction, especially the idea that the freakish is ordinary and vice versa, and that a person may not be a whole being despite a whole physical body. Consider, for example, the one-armed man in O'Connor's "The Life You Save May Be Your Own," whose adeptness as a handyman is similar to the photographer's ease when using his hooks in "Viewfinder." Though there are fewer moments of grace in Carver than in O'Connor, he in fact moved closer, in his later works, to depicting moments of grace under pressure and even epiphany, lessons he had learned from masters such as Hemingway, Joyce, and O'Connor. Yet here it is important to underline that the notion of intertextuality is a cultural phenomenon that has both general and specific manifestations, and that language itself is loaded with intertextuality in the Bakhtinian sense: "[L]anguage is not a neutral medium that passes freely and easily into the private property of the speaker's intentions; it is populated – overpopulated – with the intentions of others. Expropriating it, forcing it to submit to one's own intentions and accents, is a difficult and complicated process" (Bakhtin 294).[14] Intertextuality can be conscious or unconscious, deliberate or accidental, flaunted or cloaked in allusion. Carver employs all of these forms of intertextuality in his works, sometimes unabashedly stealing elements from other writers' texts, from letters written to him, or from stories told to him by friends, sometimes accidentally or even naïvely reproducing his own versions of other texts (as seems to be the case with "Cathedral"), which in turn might be texts which have been recycled through the centuries. In all cases, however, the emphasis should be put on what artistic effect Carver achieves with his *version*, for all major writers have to a greater or lesser extent rewritten the tradition and texts of the "canon" and of their culture to suit their own purposes. Indeed, as recent studies have shown, Carver's use of cliché and of the banal contribute to his transforming American colloquialisms into an aesthetic and lyrical language.[15]

During his formative years in the 1960s, Carver wrote imitations/parodies of both Faulkner and Hemingway ("Furious Seasons" and "The Aficionados," both collected in *No Heroics, Please*), illustrating Harold Bloom's notion of the anxiety of influence, but the symbolic "killing off" of a writer is only one of many types of intertextual writing. In most cases in his mature works, Carver is clearly not employing parody or anxiety, but rather consciously tipping his hat to writers he admires by confidently creating his own version of another text, such as with the case of Carver's "The Train," which is a sequel to John Cheever's "The Five-Forty-Eight," in which the character Miss Dent stalks and threatens a man who has mistreated her. While Carver and Cheever were (drinking) buddies in life, in their fiction Carver's text marks both difference and respect as he leads Miss Dent back into ordinary scenes of waiting room and train ride after the violent closing of Cheever's story. Carver also shows his admiration for Chekhov and both writers' celebration of the ordinary by incorporating rich intertextual elements into the last story that he wrote and published, "Errand." In this quasi-biographical tale of the death of Chekhov, Carver unabashedly lifts passages from others' texts about the Russian master. Claudine Verlay, in her illuminating reading of the story, makes the distinction (borrowed from Genette) between "hypertext," which is a derived or altered version of a previous text, and "hypotext," which is the previous version. In "Errand," she writes,

> The hypotext stems from many sources of information. Suvorin's and Tolstoy's diaries, Marie Chekhov's and Olga Knipper's memoirs, ... and the various biographies Carver may have consulted, notably Henry Troyat's *Chekhov.* (148)

Carver, however, molds all of this into a story that most critics agree, in Verlay's words, is a tour de force.[16] He does this by employing a characteristic rich mix of fact and fabrication in which the biographical details of Chekhov's life are juxtaposed with the sheerly fictional account of the bellboy at the end of the story, an everyman whose banal concerns trump the austere moment of the death of a great world writer. Such a narrative pivot away from "heroics" and toward the everyday is indeed one of Carver's key contributions to the short story genre.

To sum up our examination of the wide variety of intra- and intertextual elements in Carver's works, we must conclude that, in addition to the vexed relationship between Lish's words and Carver's words, which will continue for some time to occupy scholars, Carver himself "edited," borrowed, rewrote, and freely incorporated his own and others' texts throughout his career. Although fascinating to study, it is not always necessary for readers to be aware of *all* of the intertextual elements in his stories. Indeed, it would be impossible to trace all of them. Carver's stories stand on their own as the product of his craftmanship and can be read without too much anxiety about influences. In Carver's own often-quoted words,

> Some writers have a bunch of talent; I don't know any writers who are without it. But a unique and exact way of looking at things, and finding the right context for expressing that way of looking, that's something else. The World According to Garp is, of course, the marvellous world according to John Irving. There is another world according to Flannery O'Connor, and others according to William Faulkner and Ernest Hemingway. ("On Writing" 22)

On the other hand, in studies and courses that focus on comparative readings, whether of American writers such as the ones mentioned above, or in larger contexts such as the Chekhovian connections, Carver's stories (and poems) will continue to provide a goldmine of prospects for discussion and comparison. The next sections of this essay consider one such connection, the phenomenon that Carver's "Cathedral" so strikingly resembles D. H. Lawrence's "The Blind Man," yet Carver's story is also much more than a hypertext or new version of an older text. "Cathedral" is an "original" Carverian text, unaltered by Lish, and singled out by readers and critics alike as a favorite.

Carver, "Cathedral," and D. H. Lawrence

D.H. Lawrence was one of the best writers in the language and one of the worst, and sometimes in the same story.

— Raymond Carver in the classroom, as quoted by a student[17]

Readers wishing to study specific intertextual connections between Lawrence and Carver are advised to steer away from Harold Bloom's reductive and unsubstantiated claims: "Carver, whom perhaps we have overpraised, died before he could realize the larger possibilities of his art. ...There is a reverberation in Lawrence's story that carries into the high madness of great art. Carver, though a very fine artist, cannot take us there" (11). The Lawrence scholar Keith Cushman, on the other hand, presents a more balanced assessment in his essay "Blind Intertextual Love: 'The Blind Man' and Raymond Carver's 'Cathedral.'" Rather than diminish Carver to an imitation of Lawrence, Cushman opens up both stories by showing how the literary trope of blindness is a staple in the Western canon, well established in antiquity and thus a shared intertext for writers of all eras. Intertextuality is not about tracing the source from one writer to another and embracing an authoritative version, for as Cushman rightly points out in citing Kristeva and Barthes, intertextuality is concerned with the transmission of both language and culture, which are always already given, yet also always open and malleable. The only original human words, as Bakhtin has pointed out, were spoken by the Biblical Adam; since then language has been in continual dialogic development.

Cushman and others have noted the very striking resemblances between "Cathedral" and "The Blind Man." There is the same triangle of characters: a married couple and a male visitor. In both stories one of the men is blind, though in Lawrence's it is the husband Maurice Pervin and in Carver's it is the visitor Robert. In both stories, the visitor is a close friend of the wife, an aspect that both husbands initially resent. In his correspondence with Cushman, Carver claimed he had not read "The Blind Man" before writing "Cathedral" and that any similarities were coincidental (although Carver later *did* read, appreciate and teach Lawrence's story).[18] What makes the resemblances between the two stories stranger than fiction is the fact that "Cathedral" was based on the actual visit of a blind man, Tess Gallagher's friend and earlier employer, Jerry Carriveau, who took the train to see the couple in Syracuse in 1981.[19] But like the story "Errand" discussed above and in most of the stories that have their sources in biographical and/or intertextual material, Carver uses the visit as a source only insofar as it can serve his own fictional and aesthetic purposes.

What a comparative reading of "Cathedral" and "The Blind Man" ultimately reveals is that the similarities ultimately serve to highlight the specifically Lawrentian in Lawrence's fictional world and the specifically Carverian in Carver's. One crucial difference is in the narrative techniques employed: Lawrence uses a third-person omniscient narrator who allows each of the main characters focalization, showing how they are isolated beings at the same time as they desire strong bonds; Carver uses a first-person narrator who, in the course of the story, discovers the shallowness of his own bigotry. In what follows, however, most attention will be given to a comparative reading of the use of space and how it relates to the sequencing of scenes in the two stories.

Intertextual Spaces

Though some of Carver's stories have important outdoor settings, e.g., "So Much Water, So Close to Home," "Tell the Women We're Going," and "The Cabin," more often than not his characters are portrayed in domestic spaces, and the "action" of a story frequently takes place in the kitchens, living rooms, bathrooms, and/or bedrooms of suburban America. Or, to put it in the words of Carver critic Hilary Siebert, who has examined the poetics of space in Carver's fiction, "the home, for Carver's characters, is always a vital space" (131). Such is the case with "Cathedral," as its central scenes are in the living room of the couple's home, with the kitchen and the upstairs rooms as supporting architecture for the movements of the plot. In "The Blind Man" the poles of the plot that parallel the tension between characters are stretched out into the rural space of a farm, with its stable and main house containing the major scenes. Thus Carver's late twentieth-century suburbia, complete with mixed drinks, marijuana, and television, and Lawrence's early twentieth-century countryside, complete with farm workers and teeming animal life, are the defining spatial coordinates of their respective stories.

These coordinates become inextricably bound to the plot sequences in the stories. There are three main sequences in Carver's story (and sub-sequences within these): the wait for the visitor Robert's arrival during which the husband-narrator fills us in with exposition concerning the details of his wife's earlier acquaintance with this blind man; Robert's arrival and the dinner scene; and, finally, the long scene in the living room that culminates with the two men watching television and drawing a cathedral together (while the wife sleeps on the couch). The narrator never leaves the house during the story, and neither do the other two characters once they have arrived from the station.

Sequences in Lawrence's story shift between the house (which is the main setting) and the farm, especially two scenes in the stable, the first in which the wife is alone with the husband, the second in which the two men are alone together. These separate spatial scenes provide the story with an intricate architecture that builds up to the final scene in which all three are back in the house; both the wife Isabel Pervin and the visitor Bertie Reid have had a frightening experience when alone with the blind husband Maurice Pervin in the stable. Mrs. Pervin, in the dark of the stable, suddenly experiences the world as if she too were blind: "How near he was and how invisible! … While he was so utterly invisible she was afraid of him" (353–4). Later, the blind husband Maurice Pervin believes he has achieved an intimate friendship with the visitor Bertie Reid during their moment of touching in the stable; Bertie, however, is aghast at the possibility of such a transgression of his personal space, underlined in the story's closing spatial image: "He was like a mollusc [*sic*] whose shell is broken" (365).

Spatial imagery, according to the philosopher Gaston Bachelard, is fundamental to human development and thus also plays a crucial role in literature. In *The Poetics of Space,* Bachelard examines how our earliest memories, indeed most of our memories, are connected to space, especially to the houses we have abided in. The space of Lawrence's story underlines the separateness of the characters: Mr. Pervin spending time alone in the stable, Mrs. Pervin and her friend Bertie paying visits to him there, all three isolated in emotional and spatial ways, even as they are together on the farm. Hilary Siebert's reading of Carver's fiction in spatial terms brings out the rich lyrical imagery of Carver's spaces,[20] and the possibilities these spaces bring for the development of the characters in and beyond their physical surroundings: "Most characters, as in 'Cathedral,' don't see the serious limitations of their 'housing' until they are released from it through no intention of their own, due to an event that alters or calls to attention the circumstances of their lives" (Siebert 132).

The altering event in both "Cathedral" and "The Blind Man" is the visit of the wife's friend whose physical contact with the husband changes the balance of the triangular relationship. Carver's story, however, reverses the conclusion of "The Blind Man." Whereas Lawrence concludes his tale with the revelation (to the reader) that the husband's epiphany when the visitor touched him in the stable means the opposite to the visitor (i.e., they are not friends after all), Carver concludes by joining the two men physically and emotionally, followed by an image that transcends space. Compare the two endings:

> He [Bertie] could not bear it that he had been touched by the blind man, his insane reserve broken in. He was like a mollusc whose shell is broken. (Lawrence 365)

> I was in my house. I knew that. But I didn't feel like I was inside anything. 'It's really something,' I said. (Carver, "Cathedral" 228)

Here we reach another uncanny coincidence, for, as Siebert points out in his reading of "Cathedral," "The image Bachelard uses to define the inside and outside of phenomenological existence is the mollusk, living in its shell" (136). The image of the mollusk, however, is in Lawrence's text, not Carver's. But the archaic notion of intimate space is the same: in Lawrence's story, the character Bertie cannot bear the invasion of his private space and it crushes him; in Carver's story the character-narrator is released from the confinement of private space and experiences both intimacy and transcendence. The intertext (the shared reference) in both stories, then, is double: the ancient literary trope of the blind leading the sighted (for in both stories it is the touch of the blind man that brings on the revelation – whether positive or negative – of the conclusion), and the archaic image of mollusk/house as a protective yet confining space.

Conclusion

Some short story theorists suggest that the lyrical quality of short fiction is one of its defining traits and even that the short story as genre has more in common with poetry than with the novel. Charles May, for example, believes that the twentieth-century short story has moved "away from the linearity of prose toward the spatiality of poetry – either by using the metaphoric and plurasignative language of the poem or by radically limiting its selection of the presented event" (214). In May's interpetation, it is Chekhov, with his lyrical style, who paved the way for this development for Carver and other contemporary writers. Carver never completed the manuscript of his novel, but he did consider himself as much a poet as a short story writer, publishing six volumes of verse in his lifetime. Carver's name has also begun to appear in all kinds of contexts and in tandem with the major writers of contemporary fiction, including Hemingway, Joyce, O'Connor, Cheever, and others, and there is no doubt that he is considered a master of the short fiction genre. This can be observed not only in his use of lyricism and imagistic detail, but also in his honing of narrative technique, his careful attention to structure and story sequences, his transposition of American idioms into artistic gems, as well as his humor[21] and empathy in broaching the quirks of human behavior (i.e., characterization) and situation. "Cathedral" is illustrative of all of these techniques (as well as of his late expansive style), but most of these traits can also be seen in any of his stories from the major collections *Will You Please Be Quiet, Please* (1976), *What We Talk About When We Talk About Love* (1981), *Cathedral* (1983), and *Where I'm Calling From* (1988). By comparing any of these with the formative stories Carver wrote in his youth (gathered in *No Heroics, Please*), his development from an aspiring writer to a story craftsman is evident. Much work remains to be done as we compare all of his existing texts with his manuscripts and his posthumously published works, promising continued revelations about Carver well into the twenty-first century.

NOTES

1 Interest in Carver's parallel poetry career has also grown significantly since the posthumous publication of his collected poems, *All of Us*, in 1996. This chapter treats mainly the story career.

2 Posthumous volumes edited by William L. Stull et al. include *No Heroics, Please: Uncollected Writings* (1991), *Call If You Need Me: The Uncollected Fiction and Other Prose* (2000), and *Tell It All* (poems, plays, and recollections, 2005).

3 *Raymond Carver Review* 1 (Spring 2007). <http://dept.kent.edu/english/RCR/issues/01/index.html>.

4 Some examples are Marshall B. Gentry's "Women's Voices in Stories by Raymond Carver" (*CEA-Critic* 56.1 [Fall 1993]: 86–95), and Pamela Demory's "'It's About Seeing ...': Representations of the Female Body in Robert Altman's 'Short Cuts' and Raymond Carver's Stories" (*Pacific Coast Philology* 39.1 [1999]: 96–105), and Chris J. Bullock's "From Castle to Cathedral: The Architecture of Masculinity in Raymond Carver's 'Cathedral'" (*Journal of Men's Studies* [May 1994]: 343–51).

5 A recent issue of the *Raymond Carver Review* is a special issue on "Carver and Feminism" (2 [Autumn 2008/Winter 2009]).

6   For a more substantial discussion of male bonding in such stories, see Libe Garcìa Zarranz's essay "Passionate Fictions: Raymond Carver and feminist Theory" in the *Raymond Carver Review* 2 (2009): 20–39.

7   Many of these are listed in the bibliography of the International Raymond Carver Society <www.internationalraymondcarversociety.org/bib.html>.

8   For treatments of Carver's work in the context of medicine see, for example, P. W. Graham, "Metapathography: Three Unruly Texts" (*Literature and Medicine* 16.1 [1997]: 70–87), or S. L. Kleppe, "Medical Humanism in the Poetry of Raymond Carver" (*Journal of Medical Humanities* 27.1 [Spring 2006]: 39–56).

9   See, for example, the course syllabus for "Disability Studies/English 340" at Miami University, Ohio. <www.units.muohio.edu/disabilitystudies/DS%20Poetics%20Narrative.htm>.

10 For critical articles on *Short Cuts*, consult the bibliography of the International Raymond Carver Society.

11 In Carver's late poem "Gravy," the speaker reflects that "No other word will do. For that's what it was. Gravy. / Gravy, these past ten years" (*All of Us* 292).

12 Many, though not all, of the individual articles on "Cathedral" are listed in the bibliography of the International Raymond Carver Society: *Cathedral*, ed. Wendy Perkins (Wadsworth's Casebook Series for Reading, Research and Writing; Belmont, CA: Wadsworth, 2003).

13 For an excellent article on Carver from the perspective of theories of photography, see Ayala Amir, "'I don't do motion shots': Photography, Movement, and Change in Raymond Carver's Stories" (*Raymond Carver Review* 1 [2008]: 33–52).

14 The concept of intertextuality as developed by European literary theorists in the twentieth century, especially by Julia Kristeva, is one which had been translated precisely from Mikhail Bakhtin's cultural and literary theories.

15 See Claire Fabre-Clark, "The Poetics of the Banal in *Elephant and Other Stories*" (Kleppe and Miltner, eds. *New Paths to Raymond Carver* 173–86).

16 In his poetry collections Carver also includes verbatim passages from many writers, including Chekhov, presenting these extracts as "found poems."

17 Quoted in Cushman (166, fn. 1). Source: Jim Naughton, "Carver: The Master's Touch" (*Washington Post* [August 4, 1988]: C1, C6). I am indebted to Cushman's reading of the stories for my own analysis.

18 For more information on the genesis of "Cathedral" see Cushman's article, Tess Gallagher's essay "Carver Country" in Adelman and Gallagher, *Carver Country*, and Carol Sklenicka's biography (2009). Sklenicka has also presented a paper on the genesis and intertextual elements at the International Conference on D. H. Lawrence, Santa Fe, NM, 2005: "The Building of Raymond Carver's 'Cathedral.'"

19 There are two marvelous photographs of Mr. Carriveau in *Carver Country*, 119–120.

20 Though I have studied Bachelard's works independently, I am indebted to Siebert's reading for insights into how Bachelard's ideas apply specifically to "Cathedral" and other Carver stories.

21 For an assessment of Carver's understudied humor, see Paul Benedict Grant, "Laughter's Creature: the Humor of Raymond Carver" (Kleppe and Miltner, eds. *New Paths to Raymond Carver* 154–72).

References and Further Reading

Adelman, Bob, and Tess Gallagher. *Carver Country: The World of Raymond Carver*. New York: Scribner, 1990.

Bachelard, Gaston. *The Poetics of Space*. Trans. Maria Jolas. Boston: Beacon Press, 1994.

Bakhtin, Mikhail. *The Dialogic Imagination.* Ed. Michael Holquist. Trans. Caryl Emerson and Michael Holquist. Austin: University of Texas Press, 1981.

Bethea, Arthur. *Technique and Sensibility in the Fiction and Poetry of Raymond Carver.* New York: Routledge, 2001.

Bloom, Harold, ed. *Bloom's Major Short Story Writers: Raymond Carver.* Bromall, PA: Chelsea House, 2002.

Campbell, James. "What a Carve-up." *Saturday Guardian* (December 1, 2007): 21.

Carroll, Maureen P., and William L. Stull. *Remembering Ray: A Composite Biography of Raymond Carver.* Santa Barbara, CA: Capra Press, 1993.

Carver, Maryann Burk. *What It Used to Be Like: A Portrait of My Marriage to Raymond Carver.* New York: St. Martin's Press, 2006.

Carver, Raymond. *All of Us: the Collected Poems of Raymond Carver.* Eds. Tess Gallagher and William L. Stull. London: Harvill Press, 1996.

———. "Cathedral." *Cathedral.* New York: Vintage Contemporaries, 1984. 209–28.

———. *Furious Seasons.* Santa Barbara, CA: Capra Press, 1977.

———. "Neighbors." *Will You Please Be Quiet, Please?* New York: Vintage Contemporaries, 1992. 9–16.

———. "On Writing." *Fires: Essays, Poems Stories.* Santa Barbara, CA: Capra Press 1983. 13–18.

———. *Raymond Carver: Collected Stories.* New York: Library of America, 2009.

———. "Viewfinder." *What We Talk About When We Talk About Love.* New York: Vintage Contemporaries, 1989. 11–16.

———. *Where I'm Calling From.* New York: Atlantic Monthly Press, 1988.

Cheever, John. *The Stories of John Cheever.* New York: Knopf, 1979.

Cushman, Keith. "Blind, Intertextual Love: 'The Blind Man' and Raymond Carver's 'Cathedral.'" *D. H. Lawrence's Literary Inheritors.* Eds. Keith Cushman and Dennis Jackson. New York: St. Martin's Press, 1991. 155–66.

Gentry, Marshall Bruce, and William L. Stull. *Conversations with Raymond Carver.* Jackson: University of Mississippi Press, 1990.

Halpert, Sam. *Raymond Carver: An Oral Biography.* Iowa City: University of Iowa Press, 1995.

Jarrell, Donna, and Ira Sukrungruang, eds. *What Are You Looking At? The First Fat Fiction Anthology.* San Diego: Harcourt/Harvest Books, 2003.

Kleppe, Sandra Lee, and Robert Miltner, eds. *New Paths to Raymond Carver: Critical Essays on His Life, Fiction, and Poetry.* Columbia: University of South Carolina Press, 2008.

Lainsbury, Greg. *The Carver Chronotope: Inside the Life-World of Raymond Carver's Fiction.* New York: Routledge, 2004.

Lawrence, D. H. "The Blind Man." *The Complete Stories of D. H. Lawrence.* Vol. II. New York: Viking Press, 1961. 347–65.

Max, D. T. "The Carver Chronicles." *New York Times Magazine* (August 9, 1998): 34ff.

May, Charles E. "Chekhov and the Modern Short Story." *The New Short Story Theories.* Ed. Charles E. May. Athens: Ohio University Press, 1994. 199–217.

Meyer, Adam. *Raymond Carver.* New York: Twayne, 1995.

Monti, Enrico. "*Il Miglior Fabbro?* On Gordon Lish's Editing of Raymond Carver's *What We Talk About When We Talk About Love.*" *Raymond Carver Review* 1 (2008): 53–74.

New Yorker. "Rough Crossings." December 24 and 31, 2007. 92–100. (Text of "Beginners" 100–110.)

Nesset, Kirk. *The Stories of Raymond Carver: A Critical Study.* Athens: Ohio University Press, 1995.

Romon, Philippe. *Parlez-moi de Carver: Une biographie littéraire de Raymond Carver.* Paris. Agnès Viénot Editions, 2003.

Runyon, Randolph P. *Reading Raymond Carver.* Syracuse, NY: Syracuse University Press, 1992.

Siebert, Hilary. "Houses of Identity." *Journal of the Short Story in English* 46 (Spring 2006): 129–38.

Sklenicka, Carol. *Raymond Carver: A Writer's Life.* New York: Scribner, 2009.

Stull, William L., and Maureen P. Carroll. "Prolegomena to Any Future Carver Studies." *Journal of the Short Story in English* 46 (Spring 2006): 13–18.

Verlay, Claudine. "'Errand,' Or Raymond Carver's Realism in a Champagne Cork." *Journal of the Short Story in English* 46 (Spring 2006): 147–61.

24

Multi-Ethnic Female Identity and Denise Chávez's *The Last of the Menu Girls*

Karen Weekes

The quest for identity is considered by some critics to be *the* universal theme of literature, from *The Odyssey* to *Hamlet* to *The House on Mango Street*. Texts from all over the world reflect this focus, as male and female heroes explore both external and internal worlds in order to form themselves (Rivero 240). Eliana Rivero posits that "Definitions and expressions of self-identity are especially central to the emergence and development of a minority literature" because a group that is not accepted as part of the mainstream of American culture "struggles to claim validity for itself by affirming *sui generis* values. This affirmation of idiosyncratic features defines the group's uniqueness and legitimizes its claims for acceptance, on its own terms, by the larger society" (240). Women find themselves in this position of outsider as well, trying to assert and establish a sense of identity in a male-defined world, and the woman writer finds the situation especially troubling as she strives to assert her individuality in the face of what is, historically, a very masculine literary tradition.

As pointed out by James Nagel in his recent *The Contemporary American Short-Story Cycle: The Ethnic Resonance of Genre*, many contemporary minority writers, including Sandra Cisneros, Jamaica Kincaid, and Denise Chávez, have used the unique structure of the short story cycle to explore this fragmented sense of identity. The cycle is especially useful to depict the experience of girls facing society's conflicting demands. In this mode of writing, disparate pieces that often feature the same protagonist can be joined to create a sense of the multifacetedness of a character. Each story dramatizes a separate aspect of her personality, but it is only through a consideration of the work as a whole that a full knowledge of this character is acquired. This structure, maintaining a tenuous balance between the significance of the parts and the whole, is the perfect literary structure to present the tangle of multiethnic female identity. In texts such as Chávez's *The Last of the Menu Girls*, the protagonist's self-image is not only split by the pull of her own ego development opposing that of her childhood innocence, fear, and nostalgia but is also fractured by the demands of her divergent cultures. Rocío Esquibel is trying to meet both the expectations of a native ethnic culture and those of a patriarchal Anglo society. However, these extrinsic demands are sometimes insidiously in concert: the sexism of both cultures often encourages girls to be passive, which conflicts with females' own internal needs for activity, autonomy, and experience in order to fully develop a nascent identity.

Chávez recognizes the prominence of this struggle for women in her work, explicitly stating her interest in women's themes, topics, and issues, especially those of personal and expressive freedom. She sees her writing as a mirror of her culture, a vehicle to educate, heal, and enhance understanding of Chicano[1] values and ways of life.

Chávez herself was born in Las Cruces, New Mexico, on August 15, 1948. She returned in the 1980s to live and work once again in this town, near Texas and approximately forty miles from the United States–Mexico border, which is an appropriate setting for an author who writes in both Spanish and English and whose work prominently features the Borderlands. She earned a BA in drama from New Mexico State University in 1971, an MFA in drama from Trinity University in 1974, and an MA in creative writing from the University of New Mexico in 1984.

Chávez has been instrumental in bringing attention to Chicana writing, which for many years had difficulty finding its place in literary criticism. In the last few decades, several groundbreaking collections by women of color have presented a range of experiences of minority females. *This Bridge Called My Back: Writings by Radical Women of Color*, edited by Cherríe Moraga and Gloria Anzaldúa (1981), and *Making Face, Making Soul: Haciendo Caras*, edited by Anzaldúa (1990), both collect essays, poems, personal narratives, and other creative works by women from all four of the largest minority groups in the United States. These books emphasize the differences among ethnic women; the culture and history of each group creates expectations, gender roles, and other influences that shape lives in divergent ways. Gloria Anzaldúa's *Borderlands/La Frontera* (1987) emphasizes the specific cultural demands placed on Latina women writers, and the fragmentation of the text exemplifies the identity stressors inherent in trying to meet those demands. These elements are also central in Chávez's *The Last of the Menu Girls*.

The upsurge at the end of the twentieth century in the publication of short story cycles has featured several excellent texts that portray Chicanas. These women have historically been marginal subjects who were only rarely written about with any depth or sympathy, even by Chicanos. For example, Rudolfo Anaya's influential novel *Bless Me, Ultima* (1972) includes a poignant portrait of the ancient *curandera*, but here the Chicana is still exoticized rather than presented as a realistic character. Chicanas were infrequently represented either as authors or as characters until the mid-1970s.

Although the first Chicana novel appeared in 1954 (Fabiola Cabeza de Vaca, *We Fed Them Cactus*), over twenty years passed before the contemporary flowering of Chicana writing began: Berta Ornelas published *Come Down from the Mound* in 1975 and Isabella Ríos published *Victuum* in 1976. During this twenty-year gap, both the

Women's Liberation Movement and the Chicano Movement began to garner extensive attention and support, influencing the characterization of Hispanic females. Social movements freed Chicana authors to expand the scope of their characters from the maternal, seductive, or mystical stereotypes to fully developed, multidimensional figures. These writers' contemporary tales often feature complex, "slice-of-life" characters who are trying to resolve the conflicts inherent in family, work, and individuation.

Texts that focus on a protagonist who is trying to establish her identity, both for herself and to others, are often categorized as *Bildungsromane*. These narratives of development can fall into a variety of genres. The development of character through a non-linear sequence is clearly a strength of the short story cycle, and this mode of writing frequently features this subject matter.

Hispanic authors must invent the *Bildungsroman* anew to reflect experiences specific to their culture, and their protagonists must invent themselves as well, exploring uncharted and frightening territory. These protagonists generally resist the Anglo cultural impulse toward valorization of autonomy at the expense of connection, instead configuring themselves within the traditions of family and community. Oftentimes the process of creating a self is intimately united with other types of creativity, so that the *Bildungsroman* becomes inseparable from the genre of the *Künstlerroman*, or narrative of artistic development.

The *Künstlerroman* strikes the same particularly resonant chord as the *Bildungsroman* has for recent female authors. Linda Huf notes that women "over the years have written proportionately fewer artist novels than men" but that the number has increased considerably since the 1963 publication of *The Feminine Mystique* and the Women's Liberation Movement. She remarks on how these new books feature a determined heroine who "is wrestling, like Jacob, with her angel – the 'Angel in the House,' as Virginia Woolf called her. More and more artist heroines are refusing to be selfless, sacrificing, self-effacing. They are declining to give priority to the needs of others" (151–2). Considering one's own needs of equal importance with those of others, espe-cially one's personal creative needs, is particularly difficult for minority writers with strong cultural expectations of passivity and docility that oppose females' engaging in studious or artistic work.

Chávez's *The Last of the Menu Girls* features a young protagonist, Rocío Esquibel, who experiences many of the struggles of the Chicana writer. However, the text is as much a *Bildungsroman* as it is a *Künstlerroman*, since Rocío's desire to write only surfaces in the last few stories. The perspective throughout is from Rocío, and her ability to articulate serves a developmental function that is enhanced, but not eclipsed, by her becoming a writer. The point of view serves to crystallize Rocío's cultural identity. One of the chief themes of the text is this difficulty of defining female and minority identity, especially in a patriarchal Anglo culture.

In an interview with Chávez, Annie Eysturoy identifies "the relationship among women" as a theme of the book. Chávez assents but expands the range of connections she strives to represent, including also "the relationship to our spirit, to our dreams, to our alter ego, to ourselves; the relationship to ourselves when we are young. It is like there are all these different personalities and we have all these relationships to the me of this time and the me of that time" (Eysturoy 165–6). This vision of a multiple self is reflected in the structure of *The Last of the Menu Girls*, a short story cycle that unites disparate pieces into a multifaceted whole.

One feature of the cycle that works particularly well to represent the various threads of Rocío's persona is the fluctuation of chronology. Rather than following a sequential timeline, as a traditional novel would, the cycle can, and in this case definitely does, move back and forth in time to reveal Rocío's metamorphosis from a naïve young girl to a fully integrated adult.

In keeping with Rocío's development into a mature young woman who recognizes many gender-based conflicts inherent in her dual cultures, the Esquibel family structure lends itself to a portrayal of the various relationships between women. With the father physically absent in all but one of the stories, the narrative attention shifts from marital or father–daughter dissonance to that between daughters or between mother and daughter. Outside the family, women enact a variety of personal and professional roles for Rocío to pattern herself upon or in opposition to, from the lesbian Chicana nurse in "The Last of the Menu Girls" to the bitter Anglo landlady in "Space Is a Solid." The females effect a responsive development in Rocío's self-awareness that few of the males inspire.

Ironically, her father's name, "Salvador," translates as "savior," when he is anything but the saving grace of the family in his physical and emotional removal from their lives. The literal translation of Rocío's name is "dew," indicating her freshness and naïveté. Her mother, Nieves, has a name that means "snow"; thus both mother and daughter have names with a similar derivation, tied to the life-giving properties of water, especially in the arid New Mexico region in which the book is set. However, "dew" connotes morning and fresh beginnings, while "snow" connotes literal or sexual frigidity. Both terms are connected with purity, but Rocío's purity stems from her youth and virginity while that of Nieves stems from the celibacy of her romantic and sexual abandonment.

All seven of the stories in *The Last of the Menu Girls* focus on Rocío as she gradually loses her naïveté and becomes a mature adult. Because of the chronological fluctuations in the text, her age varies from childhood to young adulthood. Rocío, her mother, and her younger sister, Mercy, all live in a small middle-class neighborhood near the Mexican border. The physical absence of Rocío's father, who left the family, is in counterpoint to the family's lingering thoughts of him.

The first story, "The Last of the Menu Girls," establishes most of the elements that remain relatively stable throughout the text: the Esquibels' neighborhood and home, which is established as middle-class by virtue of Rocío having her own room that is decorated to her individual taste (featuring dark purple); the parents' divorce; and a cast of characters that includes Rocío, her mother and sister, and the handyman Regino Suárez. It also introduces many of the themes that will resonate throughout the cycle, such as Rocío's progress toward maturation, her conflicting drives for identity, Hispanic culture and the schisms both within and around it, and the physical experiences of sex, illness, and death.

Shifts back and forth in time and between dreams and reality are structural elements that characterize many of the stories in *The Last of the Menu Girls*. Another commonality is point of view, as the first five tales are narrated wholly in the first person from Rocío's perspective at varying ages. Many of the narratives are fragmented, with abrupt shifts between action and comment, fantasy and reality, or present and past.

By the end of the cycle, Rocío's multifaceted identity is established. She has accepted her Hispanic heritage and even enacts the domestic role within that tradition by showing the same solicitousness that her mother has always evidenced. At the same time, Rocío has defied the Chicana stereotype through her dedication to art. Having attended graduate school, she is much better educated than others in her family, but her mother and relatives encourage her writing and relish her triumphs. Her uncle calls her "a famous writer ... or she will be," showing his faith in her ability (Chávez 188). Most significantly, Rocío identifies *herself* as a writer in the last tale. In "The Last of the Menu Girls," she knows she does not want to be called a "menu girl"; although she comes to accept the title, it never reflects her potential for creativity as does the designation, and the occupation, "writer."

Rocío's becoming an author allows her to fulfill her own creative urges and contribute to her community by disseminating its traditions and contemporary realities. She is inspired to become a writer in order to better understand her culture and herself. Rather than limiting characterization to stereotypes of the sensuous siren or wise *curandera*, Chávez creates a strong Chicana voice who describes the tenuous balancing act between childhood and adulthood, innocence and maturity, and individuation and relationships.

Rocío's identity thus represents the triumph of integration without assimilation or exclusive acquiescence in either Chicano or Anglo expectations. She shows her allegiance to the Mexican culture and its emphasis on community and family through her use of Spanish language, food, and the breaking of bread with her mother's family and friend. Yet she also shows her commitment to unswerving Anglo individualism in her insistence that she is a writer, an isolated and often isolating occupation.

One signifier that Rocío has integrated the Anglo and Mexican worlds is the narrative shift that takes place in the last two stories. Throughout the previous tales, the perspective has remained focused on Rocío, and she has told her own stories or they have been told in the third-person point of view. In the penultimate story some of the locus of narration is turned over to the Anglo child Kari Lee, and in the last story Braulia and Regino express their own feelings for part of the tale. Rocío acts as a fulcrum for these perspectives, a point of connection between the disparate voices within both Anglo and Chicano culture. This dialogic perspective expands Rocío's community both beyond the geographic borders of the previous stories and beyond the psychological borders of her adolescent self-absorption.

Rocío's increasing awareness of the perspectives and needs of people other than herself is shown not only by the expansion of points of view but by an increased emphasis on connection with others. In "The Last of the Menu Girls," Rocío initially shrinks from any subjective experience of the patients' suffering, but she develops empathy in this story and throughout the text in gradual stages. "Willow Game," "Shooting Stars," and "Evening in Paris" focus chiefly on Rocío's suffering, while "Space Is a Solid," in which she experiences greater physical deprivation and mental anguish than elsewhere, shows her concern for Kari Lee, Orienne, and even a dead bird. She confides in Kari Lee and allows the child into her circle of friendship, recognizing the dearth of acceptance and kindness in Kari Lee's materially comfortable life. In "*Compadre*," her compassion extends to Regino; she finally recognizes him as an individual rather than dismissing him as her family's incompetent handyman.

Progression of this type is one of the unifying elements of *The Last of the Menu Girls*. In this *Bildungsroman*, Rocío develops from an uncertain, typically narcissistic adolescent into a compassionate young woman who is able to recognize the dignity of others, including Regino, and to value her family and culture. She also integrates her creativity more fully into her life as she matures, ultimately claiming the role of writer and making the text classifiable as a *Künstlerroman* as well.

There are many other structural and thematic aspects that link the stories and form the nexus of a cycle rather than a collection. Superficial similarities abound, as characters such as Nieves, Mercy, Salvador, and Regino recur in all the stories except for "Space is a Solid," in which Rocío still talks on the telephone with her unnamed mother. All of the tales depict episodes from Rocío's life. She is explicitly named in many of the narratives and her family members and circumstances make it clear that the protagonist of all the stories is the same, whether named or not. The text is also primarily told from Rocío's point of view; there are variations within the last two selections, but even in these the majority of the text is related from Rocío's perspective.

The book is unified by setting as well, as the same house appears at the beginning and end of the cycle. The home and neighborhood figure prominently in stories of Rocío's childhood and adolescence, such as "Willow Game" and "The Closet." The house is the scene of her birth, and its various rooms also represent formative stages in her development. The study in which her father once closed himself off and in which later Eutilia sickens and dies is also the setting for Rocío's dream-dance of life. At age 13, Rocío dreams of dancing naked, her lithe and youthful body juxtaposed with the weak, decaying body of her aunt. The triptych of windows on the front door allows her to view the neighborhood, including the sexualized and dangerous "Down" the street; they also let her witness the approach of the handsome Eleiterio while she is pressed to the door in her damp dress. In the final tale, the house simultaneously hosts both Salvador and Regino, Rocío's natural and surrogate fathers, setting the stage for her acceptance of family bonds that extend beyond bloodlines.

Thematic elements also knit these tales into a single work of art. The values and conflicts of Chicanoism inform many of these pieces in rather complex ways. For example, in "Space Is a Solid," Rocío experiences prejudice because of her background, but in "The Last of the Menu Girls" and "*Compadre*," Esperanza and Salvador, respectively, exhibit the same oppressive attitudes toward their fellow Mexican Americans. The values of this ethnicity figure prominently as well: Catholicism, the importance of the family, and the maintenance of community.

Issues that pertain specifically to females also appear throughout the text. One is women's romantic vulnerability: Nieves is widowed and divorced, Diana is betrayed, and Rocío is neglected by Loudon. Ideals perish quickly and can doom women to a hardscrabble life, especially in Diana's case. When Braulia leaves Regino, she takes the children with her, and when Salvador and Nieves divorce, she also is left to rear Mercy and Rocío. Neither man is portrayed as being lonely for the family he lost; Regino finds "peace" in his solitude, and Salvador comes and goes as he pleases, oftentimes bringing laundry for his ex-wife to wash. Nieves, on the other hand, must balance her "furious, bitter hopes" with the demands of rearing her daughters, working full-time as a teacher, and contributing her energies in the community.

Other gynocentric aspects of the novel include an emphasis on women's bodies, both in health and in sickness. Sex is taboo because of Catholic and Hispanic strictures on female sexuality. "Shooting Stars" personifies the madonna–whore complex in the characters of Eloisa and Diana; Rocío rejects Eloisa for her licentiousness, but Diana's purity is ultimately of little consolation. Neither option seems viable, resulting in a confusion that could explain the curious lack of description of Rocío's own sexual awakenings or activities.

Bodily awareness also requires an identification with the frailties of human flesh, vividly depicted in the title story through Nieves's experiences with Doña Mercedes's cancerous back. The caregiving role assigned to females is pervasive in this text, as Nieves cares for Braulia's family, including the lone Regino, and all of the aides and nurses in Altavista Memorial Hospital are women. In "The Last of the Menu Girls," Elizabeth Rainey stirs Rocío's longings to help others who suffer, but Rocío is unable to penetrate the mystery surrounding the woman's "D and C" or her pain; sexuality becomes conflated with suffering, confirming in the physical what Diana, Nieves, and Rocío all experience in the emotional realm.

Although there are many unifying elements in this work, it still resists classification as a novel; this categorization would sublimate the strength of the parts to the force of the total work, and the short story cycle rests on a tension between the pieces and the whole rather than a focus on one at the expense of the other. Its non-linear chronology is only one of several reasons why its form is more cyclical than novelistic. Another is the disjunctive nature of the episodes; none resolves a situation that has been established in another tale. Instead each stands as a complete and independent narrative. The fluctuation in characters also indicates its fragmentary structure; Kari Lee Wembley, Josie, and others who have made a significant impact on Rocío's life disappear at the end of their tales without a trace or an explanation.

The fractured form of *The Last of the Menu Girls* perfectly suits its thematic focus on the myriad influences and decisions that Rocío must confront. Just as the text unifies the tales into a whole that depicts Rocío's multi-faceted character, she strives throughout to integrate her experiences into a cohesive identity. She moves away from the magical realism that dominates stories of her youth, such as "The Closet," and focuses her imagination instead on her writing. This shift reflects a willingness to move from childhood fantasy into the actuality of maturity.

The Last of the Menu Girls is a semi-autobiographical work, arcing into the surreal at the same time as it depicts some of Chávez's own family structures, ethnic and class difficulties, and struggles to individuate and become a writer. The short story cycle is an appropriate form for presenting the multifaceted self, whether purely fictional or based in fact (a mode exemplified by Maxine Hong Kingston's *The Woman Warrior*). Examples of this genre have certainly proliferated alongside the expansion of the literary canon, and many have been written by male and female members of American ethnic groups. Margot Kelley notes that in Ann Morris and Maggie Dunn's list of almost 400 composite novels published between 1820 and 1993, over half have been published since 1966. She estimates that "about 75 percent of the current writers are women," and "during the last fifteen years ... the authorship of composite novels has disproportionately included women who live in positions of 'double marginality' as members of visible minorities and/or as lesbians."[2] The number of cycles in the late twentieth century has increased dramatically, but the range of the genre has as well, as authors of various ethnicities use this flexible form to explore the challenges of their cultures.

Notes

1 The word "Chicano" is used to represent Mexican Americans of both sexes; if there is a contrast being made between males and females, however, "Chicano" refers to the males while "Chicana" refers to females. Chávez identifies herself as Latina and Chicana. She says that the latter term "implies that you identify with the political and societal reality of what it means to be a Chicano/a which goes back to the sixties and the times of the Chicano movement" (Ikas 10).

2 Margot Kelley examines trends in the authorship of contemporary short story cycles in two significant articles, "A Minor Revolution: Chicano/a Composite Novels and the Limits of Genre," 63; and "Gender and Genre: The Case of the Novel-in-Stories," 296.

References and Further Reading

Anzaldúa, Gloria. *Borderlands/La Frontera: The New Mestiza*. 1987. 2nd edn. San Francisco: Aunt Lute Books, 1999.

Anzaldúa, Gloria, ed. *Making Face, Making Soul: Haciendo Caras*. San Francisco: Aunt Lute Books, 1990.

Chávez, Denise. *The Last of the Menu Girls*. Houston: Arte Público Press, 1986.

Dunn, Maggie, and Ann Morris. *The Composite Novel: The Short Story Cycle in Transition*. New York: Twayne, 1995.

Eysturoy, Annie O. *Daughters of Self-Creation: The Contemporary Chicana Novel*. Albuquerque: University of New Mexico Press, 1996.

———. "Denise Chávez." *This Is About Vision: Interviews with Southwestern Writers*. Eds. William

Balassi, John F. Crawford, and Annie O. Eysturoy. Albuquerque: University of New Mexico Press, 1990. 156–69.

Huf, Linda. *A Portrait of the Artist as a Young Woman: The Writer as Heroine in American Literature*. New York: Ungar, 1983.

Ikas, Karin. "Denise Chávez, Las Cruces, New Mexico in Interview with Karin Ikas, Würzburg." *Anglistik* 9 (1998): 7–20.

Kelley, Margot. "Gender and Genre: The Case of the Novel-in-Stories." *American Women Short Story Writers: A Collection of Critical Essays*. Ed. Julie Brown. New York: Garland, 1995. 295–310.

———. "A Minor Revolution: Chicano/a Composite Novels and the Limits of Genre."

Ethnicity in the American Short Story. Ed. Julie Brown. New York: Garland, 1997. 63–84.

Moraga, Cherríe, and Gloria Anzaldúa, eds. *This Bridge Called My Back: Writings by Radical Women of Color*. 1981. 2nd edn. New York: Kitchen Table Press, 1983.

Nagel, James. *The Contemporary American Short-Story Cycle: The Ethnic Resonance of Genre*. Baton Rouge: Louisiana State University Press, 2001.

Rivero, Eliana S. "The 'Other's Others': Chicana Identity and Its Textual Expressions." *Encountering the Other(s): Studies in Literature, History, and Culture*. Ed. Gisela Brinkler-Gabler. Albany: State University of New York Press, 1995. 239–60.

Part IV
Expansive Considerations

25

Landscape as Haven in American Women's Short Stories

Leah B. Glasser

In *The Land of Little Rain*, Mary Austin said that "to understand the fashion of any life, one must know the land it is lived in" (*Land* 93). To express the essence of their identities as women, some of the most important American women authors of the late nineteenth and early twentieth centuries turned to landscape writing, producing vivid portraits of the deserts, islands, villages, prairies, and forests of the United States.[1] The genre of the short story, with its emphasis on a single, compressed effect, was particularly useful for women writers who were working to provide a fresh lens on the role of landscape, a lens that could be distinguished from the more detached observations of Thoreau and other male nature-writers of the period, a precisely crafted woman's lens.

In his essay, "Walking," Thoreau recommended that in order to commune with nature, one must take at least "four hours a day … sauntering through the woods and over the hills and fields, absolutely free of all worldly engagement" (333–4). As he sauntered past the homes where women were preparing dinner or tending to children, he wondered "how womenkind, confined to the house still more than men, stand it" (334). Three New England regionalist writers, Celia Thaxter, Sarah Orne Jewett, and Mary E. Wilkins Freeman, exemplify how women writers managed to "saunter," despite the confinement Thoreau described, by redefining the concept of "home" in the context of their landscapes. This redefinition became a means for women writers to reconstruct feminine identity in terms that defied conventional gender boundaries. They developed in their stories a freedom of voice and a sense of power through the language they used when they spoke of, and seemingly for, the natural world. Willa Cather described Jewett's stories as "living things caught in the open, with light and freedom and air-spaces about them. They melt into the land and the life of the land until they are not stories at all, but life itself" (Cather x). Thaxter, Jewett, and Freeman often chose for their narratives female characters who could dwell in such "air-spaces" of their own with a sense of hard-won freedom; their fiction, with its focus on women's relationships to their natural environments, became a form of resistance to traditional nineteenth-century expectations for women within the "woman's sphere."

Marcia Littenberg explains that women regionalists were both attracted to transcendentalism and simultaneously compelled to extend and revise its perspective to take into account women's experiences (Littenberg 140).[2] Thaxter, Jewett and Freeman "find a world in a pond, an emblem of society in a teacup, the power of nature in a wildflower" (139). In her letters, Celia Thaxter in fact referred to Thoreau's careful and deliberate studies of nature and what differed in her own approach.[3] Thaxter and her women contemporaries created their own form of transcendentalism through highly personal responses to nature that suggested both sympathy and identification.

Thaxter, Jewett, and Freeman focused on the regions they knew best in New Hampshire, Maine, Vermont, and Massachusetts. These writers have become the center of a considerable body of feminist criticism on regionalism by scholars such as Judith Fetterley, Marjorie Pryse, Elizabeth Ammons, Sandra Zaggarell, and Amy Kaplan, among others. They have been celebrated in the manner of early feminist criticism, and more recently analyzed in an historical context in which the limitations and racial exclusivity of their worlds becomes apparent. What interests me is the way their depiction of landscapes, havens in nature, whether in the form of fictional autobiography or autobiographical fiction, suggests an imagined ideal of female autonomy.

Regionalism, according to Fetterley and Pryse, provided a space for nineteenth-century women writers to critique the construction of "separate spheres" (Fetterley and Pryse 13). Region, then, "marks precisely that point where women's culture becomes conscious of itself as critique" (14). Setting their characters firmly within the regions they knew and bringing them outside the home through their relationship to the natural world, regionalist women writers of this period challenged the usual boundaries established by their male literary peers. Celia Tichi's definition of women regionalists best captures the meaning of regionalist writing for these writers: "Under cover of regionalism ... these women writers explored the territory of women's lives. Their essential agenda in the era of the new woman was to map the geography of their gender. The geography of America formed an important part of their work, but essentially they charted the regions of women's lives, regions both without and within the self" (Tichi 598). As Fetterley and Pryse argue in *Writing Out of Place*, American women regionalists "were not interested in depictions of nature for its own sake; rather, they focused on the relationship between that world and human consciousness" (4).

Celia Thaxter, the nineteenth-century writer who described her landscape on the Isles of Shoals off the coast of New Hampshire in the 1870s, serves as a striking example of a woman who turned to landscape to voice those inner passions that remained otherwise unexpressed. Thaxter's life and work capture the complexities of the nineteenth-century tug between domestic constraints and the impulse to write. Her focus on the Isles of Shoals allowed her to nurture her passions, despite the demands of her role as mother, daughter, and wife, through the discovery of a language that defined who she was in the context of this place and what it meant. She was one of the earliest environmentalists, a regionalist whose life and language was shaped by her responses to the island. A study of her letters, poetry, autobiographical prose, drawings, and children's stories reveals Thaxter's quest to shape a unique identity through her portrayal of her relationship to the plants, birds, flowers, animals, and sea life that surrounded her; this new identity was set apart, though not completely disconnected, from her domestic life. In this setting, and through such writing, she found an arena for self-expression that was unavailable to her within the confinement of her home.

As Judith Fetterley and Marjorie Pryse argue, Thaxter captures perhaps more powerfully than any other regionalist of her time, the particularity of place *not* as the thing to be looked at but as the thing to be *listened* to, felt through the writer's experience, understood from the inside (Fetterley "Theorizing").[4] "Ears made delicate by listening," Thaxter says in *Among the Isles of Shoals*, can "hear" the sounds particular to Shoals, can see through the "ill-defined and cloudy shapes" that are visible as a viewer first approaches the islands, and can know this region (19, 9). The ear is her primary tool for knowing her island. Thaxter captures the sound of high tide, and "the music of the waves, and their life, light, color, and sparkle" (*AIS* 19). She continually focuses on these sounds, and her own sensitivity to the "particularity" of every wave and rock as they "speak" to her:

> Who shall describe that wonderful noise of the sea among the rocks, to my ear the most suggestive of all sounds in nature? Each island, every isolated rock, has its own peculiar rote, and ears made delicate by listening, in great and frequent peril, can distinguish the bearings of each in a dense fog. The threatening speech of Duck Island's ledges, the swing of the wave over halfway Rock, the touch of the ripples on the beach at Londoner's, the long and lazy breaker that is forever rolling below the lighthouse at White Island, – all are familiar and distinct, and indicate to the islander his whereabouts almost as clearly as if the sun shone brightly and no shrouding mist were striving to mock and to mislead him. (19–20)

Childe Hassam's painting of Thaxter presents a tall, stately woman dressed in white, an angel in her ethereal garden, passively observing a flower. It is as though she too is one of the flowers to be observed.[5] But when we turn to Thaxter's self-representation in her autobiographical work, we hear a voice that actively beckons us to listen rather than look. She aimed to get beneath the "shrouding mist" that "mocks and misleads."

"Ever I longed to speak these things," Thaxter says in *Among the Isles of Shoals*, "to speak the wind, the cloud, the bird's flight, the sea's murmur … Nature held me and swayed all my thoughts until it was impossible to be silent any longer" (*AIS* 141–2). As she shifted her attention from the domestic realm to the open landscape in her prose, Thaxter developed a capacity to convey the essence of who she was beneath all the "cloudy" layers of who she was expected to be. But as Thaxter's own language implies, hearing this voice requires good listening. Without careful listening, it is easy to set Thaxter aside as a tour guide to a remote place, as a sentimental poet, or as a good-natured horticulturalist who shared her tricks for fighting off slugs.

A glance at Thaxter's life will contextualize her approach to her focus on landscape in her short stories. Born in 1835 in Portsmouth, New Hampshire, Thaxter noted that her earliest memories were not of the mainland but of the remote and rocky White Island where her father became lighthouse keeper when she was four. Hers was an isolated childhood with no companions beyond her parents and two brothers, and she recalls the "wilderness of desolation."[6] Yet, as Karen Kilcup suggests, such isolation also opened her to become an "acute observer and lover of nature" (280). In the absence of human company, she sought companionship in the natural world, hence her many descriptions of her organic connection to flowers, plants, rocks; indeed, as she describes them, they are part of her "community." Early on, however, the solitary quality of Thaxter's life shifted. When she was 12 years old, her father, Thomas Laighton, went into business with Levi Thaxter to build the Appledore Hotel on nearby Appledore Island, and Levi became her tutor. In 1851, at the age of 16, she married Levi, who was then 27. With three sons, housekeeping responsibilities, and a demanding husband, married life quickly took on all of the burdens of domestic entrapment. Her brain-damaged son Karl required her constant care and attention; she wrote of Karl that "always he makes an undercurrent of misery and anxiety deep down among the very sources of my being."[7] Nevertheless, Thaxter resisted institutionalizing Karl as had been suggested by others, and devoted much of her adult life to protecting him from what she saw as a hostile world.

Levi quickly grew to dislike the islands, and pulled his wife inland to a home in Newtonville, Massachusetts, away from what she called the "lulling murmur of the encircling sea" (*AIS* 121). Perhaps even more painful than the domestic realities was the sense of being, as the title of her poem suggests, "landlocked": "To feel the wind, sea-scented, on my cheek" but only to hear "afar off" voices "calling low; – my name they speak!" ("Land-Locked" l. 20). This line, with its suggestion of the power of identification as the voice of the island calls her name from a distance, can be compared to the sense of namelessness and loss of identity that she felt inland in Newtonville. Interestingly "Land-Locked" was her first published poem, her first step as well toward recognizing the intensity of her connection to Shoals as a source for her creative identity. Thaxter's original handwritten copy of the poem is bordered with her watercolor sketches of the island, and draped with her rendering of the bright leaves and flowers of Shoals. She refers to her thoughts of Shoals as an almost physically painful "craving" for the "murmur of the wave / That breaks in tender music on the shore" ("Land-Locked" l. 24).

Thaxter's individuality as an artist was deeply connected to the region of Shoals, and this became increasingly clear to her when her husband asked her to part with it. While Levi went off to hunt and stuff birds, Celia joined the Audubon society.[8] As the marriage declined, she increasingly assisted in running the hotel on Appledore and her stays on the island became lengthier. Despite the obstacles she faced, she did manage to write and publish her work, including her collections of poems and stories (1872–96), *Among the Isles of Shoals* (1873), and *An Island Garden* (1894). She wrote of her effort to return to the island as a kind of compulsion, a heroic gesture to honor that voice that kept calling her back. One September, for example, she wrote: "I came over on Friday in half a gale with the sea beating over us from stem to stern, but I was so anxious to get here that I didn't care anything."[9] Increasingly, she expressed the depth of her need for this place. To her friend, John Greenleaf Whittier, she wrote: "Sometimes I wonder if it is wise or well to love any one spot on this old earth as intensely as I do this! I am wrapped up in measureless content as I sit on the steps in the sun in my little garden, where the freshly turned earth is odorous of the spring."[10]

Perhaps because it was the realm she associated with her childhood, Thaxter found on this island the means to go back to a time before the compromises that nineteenth-century womanhood had required. When she was back on the island, separated from Levi's demands, she could return to that time. Her descriptions suggest that this was the one place where childhood could resonate into adulthood. On the island, she was able to write, and her writing assisted her in reconstructing a life seemingly "exempt from the interruptions" of the civilized world (*AIS* 99). She saw herself as the sole interpreter of her landscape and this granted her the power of a language that had been muted in her life with Levi.

Reimagining the island through a child's lens enabled Thaxter to recreate her island most poignantly. The short story that captures this process most profoundly is her seemingly simple, but haunting, fairy tale, "The Spray Sprite." This is also a text that best captures how Thaxter's concept of the female child's relationship to nature stood in opposition to the pull of the domestic realm. Here a "little maid," a spray sprite, finds pleasure only when she can "feel the salt wind lift her thick brown hair and kiss her cheek" or "wade bare-footed into the singing sparkling brine" ("Spray Sprite" 3). The sprite communicates with nature in its own language, listening to the north wind as it "fights me," or the west wind as it "plays with me" (SS 4). Only the sprite seems to hear and understand the "talking" on this island; it is the talk that Thaxter knew and interpreted as a child, and the talk that she gives her readers in this story: "The waves made a continual talking among themselves, and sweet and disconsolate came the cry of the sandpipers along the shore" (SS 7). Setting up a sharp dichotomy between this pleasure in nature and the expectations of girlhood, Thaxter incorporates in her story a reminder of the world the sprite initially rejects:

She hated to sew patchwork. Oh, but she was a naughty child, – not at all like the good, decorous little girls who will perhaps read this story. She didn't like to sweep and dust, and keep all things bright and tidy. She wished to splash in the water the whole day long, and dance, and sing, and string shells, and be idle like the lovely white kittiwakes that flew to and fro above her and came at the beckoning of her hand. She looked with scorn on dolls and all their appointments and never wished to play with them, – it was almost as bad as patchwork! But she loved the sky, and all the clouds and stars, the sun

that made a glory in the east and west at morning and evening, the changing moon,
the streaming Northern Lights. (SS 3–4)

The sprite looks "with scorn on dolls," but responds with wild abandon to the sight
and sound of the sea. It is this capacity for wildness that she must relinquish when
she is later whisked away, in a fairy fleet of purple mussel shells, to the civilized world
where she will eventually conform to the "tame life" of sewing patchwork and doing
good deeds.

The more startling Thaxter's nature images are, the more dramatic the sacrifice
required on the other side of the horizon. The sprite runs along beside the sandpipers,
the very birds with which Thaxter most identified, at the edge of the shallow waves,
and stands on the rocks "when the billows came tumbling in sending the spray flying
high in the air and throwing handfuls of crimson dulse at her, or long brown tresses
of seaweed, which she caught and flung back again, while she was drenched with the
shower, and the wind blew her about in rough play" (SS 4). No such play is available
to the sprite when she is taken "beyond the faint blue cloud of distant coast" and into
the "great world." One is reminded of Jewett's Sylvia in "A White Heron," but here
the child leaves her paradise behind. As she stands at the seashore looking toward the
horizon just before she will leave her island, the sprite does not notice what Thaxter
is sure to tell her readers – that "the sea was full of cool fire, – 'sparks that snap and
burst and flee,' every wave left its outline in vanishing gold on the wet weeds and
sand; her feet were covered; it was as if she had on golden-spangled slippers" (SS 8).
The heat and light of such imagery beckons the reader back to the island even as the
sprite parts with it. She leaves behind her "pet pillow," a gray rock that had become
as "smooth as satin," and sets off with the fairy fleet to see what lies beyond the horizon
(SS 8).

As if to convey her own uncertainty about the legitimacy of her choice to continue
her reveries on the Isles of Shoals, Thaxter incorporates another voice in this story,
one that reminds her girl readers of what they must give up to pass into adulthood.
She asserts a moral, "a secret worth all the beauty she had lost ... that to be useful
and helpful, even in the smallest ways, brings a better bliss than all the delightful
things you can think of, put together" (SS 13). And so the exquisite sprite transforms,
or conforms, and does sewing and good deeds "to the end of her days." This shift in
the story's emphasis seems to express the view of her nineteenth-century audience that
such play, such pleasure in the language of nature, cannot be taken seriously. Thaxter
has her sprite leave it behind. But the story does not leave readers with a sense that
this was wise at all, much as the narrator insists upon the truism that turning from
play to service and "useful work" is "the best blessing God gave the world" (SS 13).
Instead, Thaxter ends the story with the lingering sound of her island and its magic,
the sound of the sea echoing in a child's ear: "You would never know now that she
had been a spray sprite and danced among the breakers, and talked and laughed with
the loons, for she is like everybody else, except that, sleeping or waking, year after
year, she keeps in her ears the sad, mysterious murmur of the sea – just like a hollow

shell" (SS 13). Her conclusion is a subtle critique of the nineteenth-century ideology of the woman's sphere.

From the perspective of her nineteenth-century audience, the natural play of the girl-child must be suppressed in womanhood in favor of being useful and serving others. It is in fact what Celia Thaxter did when she married Levi and moved inland. Contrary to her sprite, however, Thaxter found a way to sustain the childhood pleasure of her island setting into adulthood through her writing and through her return to the Isles.

Sarah Orne Jewett captures this playful dimension of Thaxter well in her preface to Thaxter's poems. Here Jewett describes watching Thaxter as she walked across White Island shortly before her death: "walking lightly over the rough rocks with wonted feet" and showing Jewett "many a trace of her childhood" (Jewett, "Preface" to *Poems* vii). Jewett recalls as well their day together and how Thaxter explored with her on Appledore "all the childish playgrounds dearest to her and to her brothers; the cupboard in a crevice of rock, the old wells and cellars, the tiny stonewalled enclosures, the worn doorsteps of unremembered houses" (vii). As they sat in midsummer in the bayberry bushes, Thaxter listened to the sounds of her island with the same sensitive ear she had as a child and invited Jewett to watch and listen with her. Thaxter paused with the same childlike wonder at the sight of a new wildflower, and told Jewett that she had never seen such a flower on the island before. As Jewett followed Thaxter across her island, she noted that "under the very rocks and gray ledges, to the far nests of the wild sea birds, her love and knowledge seemed to go" (viii). Jewett's reference here reminds us of her character, Sylvia, in her short story, "A White Heron." It is as though she is describing Sylvia grown-up and at peace with her choice.

On the Isles of Shoals, Thaxter retained the "sure footing" of her childhood by honoring her capacity to "listen" to the sounds of her island. Furthermore, she found that she too had listeners. She too could be heard. As her work began to receive recognition, she drew to her island artists, musicians, and writers (including Childe Hassam, Sarah Orne Jewett, Annie and James Fields, Emerson, Hawthorne, Twain, and one of her most treasured poet-friends, John Greenleaf Whittier), and they listened to her read her poetry aloud. She could, as she said she longed to do, literally speak out loud with the sound of "the wind, the cloud, the bird's flight, the sea's murmur" to those who would hear the strength of her language and recognize its link to nature (*AIS* 141).

It is interesting to consider the way in which the more frequently anthologized Sarah Orne Jewett wrote in response to what she saw in the life and work of the less well-known Celia Thaxter. Jewett's depiction of the natural landscape and its relationship to community, as Sandy Zagarrel explains, "emphasizes their harmonious, organic identity."[11] Jewett was born in 1849 in South Berwick, Maine, a small coastal town in which she remained through her adult life. Unlike Thaxter, Jewett remained single throughout her lifetime, and led a much more active life, traveling frequently to Boston, Europe, and elsewhere. She maintained close ties to women, most notably Annie Fields, with whom she "began a pattern of intimate and shared life that lasted until Jewett's death in 1906" (Fetterley, "Reading" 165). While Thaxter spoke in her letters of the struggle to write in light of an unhappy married life that involved relocation, and a strained motherhood, Jewett was more easily able to see her writing career as a life choice fully validated by her companion, Fields. In the course of her career, her primary focus was on the short story. She is most well known for *Deephaven* (1877), *A Country Doctor* (1884), *A White Heron and Other Stories* (1886), and *The Country of the Pointed Firs* (1896).

As if to honor Thaxter's world on the Isles of Shoals and reject Thaxter's own moralistic conclusion to "Spray Sprite," Sarah Orne Jewett created a tribute to resisting the journey into the realm of acceptability, the journey to which Thaxter has her sprite succumb. Jewett was drawn to the island images so prevalent in Thaxter's work, and incorporated similar imagery in her best-known work, *Country of the Pointed Firs*. She turned to the coast and its nearby islands to redefine the concept of solitude in feminine terms, creating for women a place that is sustained through a connection to the mainland, nurtured and supported by its nearness, and yet set apart and free from its expectation and demands.

As Paula Blanchard suggests, "Thaxter's death was fresh in Jewett's mind when she wrote '*Pointed Firs*'" (Blanchard 293). Jewett was probably reading the proofs of Thaxter's *Stories and Poems for Children* in 1895, and she edited the poems directly afterwards. In her preface to Thaxter's text, Jewett refers to her ability to teach "young eyes to see the flowers and birds; to know her island of Appledore and its seas and sky" (Jewett, "Preface" to *Stories* iii).

Jewett's *Country of the Pointed Firs* builds not only on her observations of life in coastal Maine, but also on her profound admiration of Celia Thaxter after her visit to the Isles of Shoals. She depicts the islands near Dunnet Landing as anything but ideal, yet she also celebrates the autonomy that such isolation affords. In Joanna's choice to be an "uncompanioned hermit," Jewett depicted the choice to resist the demands of patriarchy as paradoxically both isolating and fulfilling. She also reimagines a world in which such a choice is validated. Her narrator observes, "I had been reflecting upon a state of society which admitted such personal freedom and a voluntary hermitage" ("White Heron" 69). "Poor Joanna" is pitied by the mainland community for her utter isolation on Shell Heap Island, but she is also supported by them and described as free, and Mrs. Blackett, the idealized maternal hostess on the remote Green Island, is "queen" of her domain. These landscapes are places of refuge, havens. What they offer their women inhabitants is the proximity of human connection in an arena set apart and in a place where women are in charge of their own lives and choices.

In one of her most frequently quoted letters to Annie Fields, Jewett's close companion, Thaxter wrote: "Oh Annie ... if it were only possible to go back and pick up the thread of one's life anew ... could I be 10 years old again – I would climb to my lighthouse top and set at defiance anything in the shape of man."[12] Many have speculated that Jewett's 9-year-old character, Sylvia, in "A White Heron" builds from Thaxter's image in this letter of a child's resistance to giving up her singular vision from the top of the lighthouse for the attention of a man. In *Country of the Pointed*

Firs, Jewett gives the gift of such defiance to Joanna, the character who goes off to live on an island after a "disappointment of the heart." Although Jewett has others claim this was Joanna's penance for the sin of her "anger," it becomes a place that grants her the freedom to say "she didn't want no company," because "Joanna was Joanna" (78). It was in her most frequently anthologized story, "A White Heron," that Jewett most fully explored the resistance to conventional constructions of gender through communion with nature.

In "A White Heron," Jewett portrays Sylvia, whose very name associates her with the woodlands. Torn between the natural world in which she is as much at home as Thaxter's "spray sprite," and the first intimations of the "great power" of love in a "woman's heart," Sylvia relinquishes the world of men when she decides to resist revealing the location of a beautiful heron in response to a hunter's request. Although Sylvia "would have liked him vastly better without his gun," and "could not understand why he killed the very birds he seemed to like so much," she is drawn to this man and is attracted to the "dream of love" that he evokes in her newly discovered "woman's heart" ("White Heron" 201). Tempted by the man's plea, she establishes instead a renewed relationship with the white heron and they "watched the sea and the morning together" (205). The uncanny parallels to Thaxter are everywhere in the story, even in the reference to the ornithologist's love of stuffing birds, reminiscent of Thaxter's husband's sport. Yet Jewett chooses a different ending for Sylvia than Thaxter does for her spray sprite, an ending that counters Thaxter's own experience at age 16 of marrying Levi Thaxter.

Identification with the heron prevents Sylvia from giving up its secret place to the hunter. Sylvia learns the secret of the heron "through her willingness to enter the bird's world, to get up before sunrise, make the 'dangerous pass' from oak tree to pine tree, and climb to the very top from which she can see not only sunrise and sea but where the white heron has its nest" (Fetterley and Pryse, *Writing* 119). While the hunter was prepared to "alter the environment," Sylvia will neither alter nor be altered. Jewett does not minimize the cost of Sylvia's silence, for the child looks longingly at the world beyond the forest, the world she imagines on the other side of the sea. Anticipation of the greater loss that entry into that world requires is finally what stops Sylvia, as well as a love for the freedom she feels at the sight of nature.

While Thaxter's sprite will enter the world of service to others, Sylvia, in resisting the hunter, will not, though Jewett concedes "she could have served and followed him and loved him as a dog loves!" (205). When she climbs to the top of the great pine tree, "the last of its generation," to spot the heron, she spots both the bird and the sea itself. "She knows his secret now, the wild, light, slender bird that floats and wavers, and goes back like an arrow presently to his home in the green world beneath" (204). In her choice to protect the bird and remain alone in her rural world, Sylvia hears sounds just as the sprite does in Thaxter's stories. But they are sounds that sustain her by conjuring a visual image of her relationship with the heron and preventing her from parting with what she loves most. "The murmur of the pine's green branches is in her ears, she remembers how the white heron came flying through the golden air and how they watched the sea and the morning together, and Sylvia cannot speak; she cannot tell the heron's secret and give its life away" (204–5).

Interestingly the echo of what she hears is not only the sound of this freedom and bliss in her communion with the bird, the freedom to remain at peace fully and autonomously with nature. The other sound Sylvia hears is a reminder of what she must resist: "the echo of his whistle haunting the pasture path as she came home with the loitering cow. She forgot even her sorrow at the sharp report of his gun and the piteous sight of thrushes and sparrows dropping silent to the ground, their songs hushed and their pretty feathers stained and wet with blood" (205). Jewett poses the critical question: "Were the birds better friends than their hunter might have been, – who can tell. Whatever treasures were lost to her, woodlands and summertime, remember! Bring your gifts and graces and tell your secrets to this lonely country child" (205). Jewett's call to nature is to honor the choice Sylvia has made, to grace her with the companionship of the natural world and the gift to hear its secrets, secrets Jewett voices through her prose. Jewett poetically depicts the choice to live in nature, free of male domination. With some acknowledgment of "treasures lost" in her conclusion, Jewett still leaves readers with a confirmation of the choice.

From the very start of the story, it is clear that Jewett's lens is dual: the lens of the child and the lens of the natural world. Even the cow's perspective enters her depiction of region in her opening passage:

> The woods were already filled with shadows one June evening, just before eight o'clock, though a bright sunset still glimmered faintly among the trunks of the trees. A little girl was driving home her cow, a plodding dilatory provoking creature, in her behavior, but a valued companion for all that. They were going away from the western light, and striking deep into the dark woods, but their feet were familiar with the path, and it was no matter whether their eyes could see it or not. There was hardly a night the summer through when the old cow could be found waiting at the pasture bars; on the contrary, it was herself away among the high huckleberry bushes, and though she wore a loud bell she had made the discovery that if one stood perfectly still it would not ring. (197).

Jewett conveys the concept of preservation of nature as synonymous with preservation of self, even at the cost of remaining isolated from the world beyond the pine trees and the sea. It may be that Jewett's vision of the child Sylvia as a woman is the figure of Joanna, the hermit on Shell-Heap Island in *Country of the Pointed Firs*. Jewett, like Thaxter, does not minimize the cost of Sylvia's or Joanna's choice. She ends "A White Heron" with a question for her readers: what is it, she asks, "that suddenly forbids her and makes her dumb," why the silence "when the great world for the first time puts out a hand to her, must she thrust it aside for a bird's sake?" (204). Her reply comes in the form of a plea to the natural world to "bring your gifts and graces and tell your secrets to this lonely country child" (205). In so doing, as Fetterley and Pryse explain, Jewett "re-articulates the 'mothering' Sylvia derives from the landscape and constructs regionalist fiction as itself a form of mothering absent in the responses of those who would see in Sylvia only a fear of growing up" (205).

In a letter to Sarah Orne Jewett, Mary E. Wilkins Freeman, another New England regionalist, wrote: "I suppose it seems to you as it does to me that everything you have heard, seen, or done, since you opened your eyes on the world, is coming back to you sooner or later, to go into stories."[13] Drawing from what she had heard, seen, or done, Freeman broke new ground through the creation of heroines who continually extended the challenge to readers posed by "A White Heron," with grown heroines who confront and overturn gender and class boundaries. With her focus on the small New England villages that she knew best, Randolph, Massachusetts, and Brattleboro, Vermont, she found the freedom to step beyond the narrow expectations of her editors without seeming to do so, to explore the connection between feminine identity and place, and to subvert the domestic realm as an arena for female rebellion. Mary E. Wilkins Freeman (1852–1930) is best known for the short stories she published beginning in 1883 in *Harper's Bazaar*, some of the finest of which were collected in *A New England Nun and Other Stories*. By the time this collection was published in 1891, Freeman had received considerable recognition as a short-story writer. Early literary histories frequently marginalized Freeman as a "local colorist," a "minor" writer who depicted the peculiarities of her region. Yet like James, she was interested in inner as well as outer landscape, and like Twain, she experimented with dialect and humor while probing the larger questions about the nature of the human race. She shifted her readers' attention to the relatively invisible realms of domesticity where large battles were fought on humble turf. Although she did marry eventually, Freeman did so after the childbearing years, and the marriage dissipated. Her best writing was linked to her sense of autonomy when unmarried and living in Randolph, Massachusetts, where she sustained a twenty-year friendship with her companion, Mary Wales.

With her focus almost entirely on women's struggles and concerns, Freeman's depictions of region explore the psychology of women's conflicts as she knew them. Her work clearly builds from the foundation of regionalism established by Jewett, and she had great admiration for Jewett's work. Although the focus on nature and landscape was less pronounced in Freeman's work, Freeman's favorite Jewett story was "A White Heron." In "Christmas Jenny," Freeman comes closest to Thaxter and Jewett in depicting the relationship between her central female character and her natural surroundings. Mary E. Wilkins Freeman's "Christmas Jenny" offers an analysis of the connection between self-preservation and preservation of nature. The language of landscape in this story, as in "A White Heron" and "Spray Sprite," is not an adornment but a vehicle to reveal character.

In "Christmas Jenny," Jenny Wrayne defines herself against rather than within the context of male values. It is as though Christmas Jenny is the woman Sylvia could become, having come to terms with the loss of the "dream of love" embodied in the hunter ("Christmas Jenny" 164). As Josephine Donovan explains, much of Jenny's self-fulfillment stems from her protection and care of wild animals which have been injured by the traps men set, the "mechanized masculine operations that destroy that natural life with which ... women identify" (Donovan 132). Jenny is a self-sufficient, aging spinster who owns a home and a few acres of land on a mountaintop overlooking the village. Like Sylvia atop the pine tree, Jenny is set apart, and set above the community beyond her perch. When rumors spread in the village that Jenny is "love-cracked," having been in love with a man who married someone else, her only close friend replies: 'I know one thin' – if she did git kind of twisted out of the reg'lar road of lovin', she's in another one, that's full of little dumbies an' starvin' chippies an' lame rabbits, an' she ain't love-cracked no more'n other folks" ("Christmas Jenny" 171). Redefining love then, in matriarchal terms, Jenny chooses an alternative to the "reg'lar road of lovin'" by loving creatures of nature instead of a husband.

Freeman's physical description of Jenny is a celebration of her unity with the natural environment: "She made one think of those sylvan faces with features composed of bark-wrinkles and knot-holes that one can fancy out of the trunks of trees. She was not an aged woman, but her hair was iron-gray, and crinkled as closely as gray moss" (164). The source of Jenny's autonomy, in fact, is nature itself. Jenny comes down from her mountain abode to sell evergreen trees and wreaths in the winter and vegetables in the summer.

> The woman looked oddly at a distance like a broad green moving bush; she was dragging something green after her, too. When she came nearer one could see long sprays of ground-pine were wound around her shoulders, she carried a basket trailing with them, and holding also many little bouquets of bright-colored everlasting flowers. She dragged a sled, with a small hemlock-tree bound upon it. She came long sturdily over the slippery road. (163)

With this first image of Jenny, Freeman conveys womanly strength all bound up in Jenny's link to nature, with "ground-pine ... wound around her shoulders," and the ability to walk "sturdily" on the icy road that most are unable to travel.

Freeman analyzes through Jenny, as Barbara Johns has noted, "the notion of the spinster as mystic, a person so misunderstood by her society that she is considered strange, yet so united with the universe that she is capable of profoundly influencing two of society's most unyielding institutions, marriage and the church." In this sense, Johns continues, Freeman's depiction of Jenny's choice goes beyond the pitied Joanna of Jewett's *Country of the Pointed Firs*. Jenny's influence on the married couple down the road is fascinating. The Careys "represent a nineteenth-century marriage in which the woman has internalized all the features of the 'cult of true womanhood'" (Johns 11). Jenny helps Mrs. Carey transform her domesticity into a form of power, and her husband's tantrums subside once Jenny teaches Mrs. Carey the use of strategy. Ignoring Mr. Carey's imperiousness, Jenny has Mrs. Carey enjoy the feasts she prepares without beckoning her whining husband to the table to participate. Jenny's "sensitivity, power, and self-sufficiency" transfer to Betsey Carey, the married friend, and in this way Freeman shows that "women united can go on to resist whatever institution attempts to keep them in their place" (11).

Freeman's analysis of the effect of the eccentric Jenny on her community is superb. Blind to the meaning or beauty of Jenny's world, the villagers alert the minister and Deacon Little to the rumor that Jenny mistreats the animals she has caged in her home and a deaf boy who lives with her. More than any other story Freeman wrote, this story captures the injustice of the stigma of spinsterhood and the possibility of surmounting it.

When the minister and Deacon Little come to Jenny's home, their visits are an invasion of what Freeman calls "sacred space." The story envisions a female ideal, an alternative life, for the single woman in harmony both with nature and society.

Arriving at Jenny's "curious sylvan" abode, the men immediately upset the images of nature surrounding Jenny. "They started up a flock of sparrows that were feeding by Jenny's door; but the birds did not fly very far – they settled into a tree and watched" (169). It is as though these creatures are connected to Jenny and are there to protect her from this intrusion. When the men enter her home, they "could not see anything at first." Their inability to see has many levels. They are blinded by the contrast of moving from the "brilliant light outside" to the darkness of Jenny's "weather-beaten hut," and they are equally unable to see the principles her home represents. When their eyes fall upon the deaf boy who "looked up in their faces with an expression of delicate wonder and amusement," they notice without comprehension that "he is dressed like a girl, in a long blue gingham pinafore," and sits "in the midst of a heap of evergreens, which he had been twining into wreaths; his pretty, soft, fair, hair was damp, and lay in a very flat and smooth scallop over his full white forehead" (169–70). Noting that he looks "well cared for," they still cannot, as Johns clarifies, accept that Jenny has created a boy who defies gender stereotypes as essentially an embodiment of Jenny's values. They are "unable to see the boy as a sign of the unity that makes Jenny, the forest, the house, and the boy inseparable, indivisible." The boy's "'wild and inarticulate' cry, united with the cries of the caged creatures, a 'like a soft clamor of eloquent appeal to the two visitors.' But it is futile. The men cannot understand what they see and simply stand 'solemn and perplexed'" (Johns 11–12). Perhaps what is most disturbing to these men is Jenny's satisfaction in her spinsterhood, the fact that she has defined new connections, new possibilities of self-fulfillment through her tie with nature, with a boy who is also a girl and thereby defies gender assumptions, with a married woman down the road, and through the economic independence she has won by selling her goods. This elderly woman living alone cares for others rather than requiring that others care for her, and her home, strange as it seems to the men, is a home that represents her strength rather than her weakness.

Betsey Carey gives voice to the story which the men are so incapable of interpreting, becoming, in essence, Jenny's tongue: She tells the men, "I ain't goin' to have you comin' up here to spy on Jenny, an' nobody to home that's got any tongue to speak for her" (171). Betsey is the translator. Standing before them "like a ruffled and defiant bird that was frighting them as well as herself with her temerity," she sums up the beauty of Jenny: "I dunno but what bein' a missionary to robins an' starvin' chippies an' little deaf-an-dumb children is jest as good as some other kinds, an' that's what she is" (172). Freeman's reference to a "witch-hunt" in this story is significant. "It was a witch-hunt that went up the mountain road that December afternoon" (174). Determined to dispel the myths that yield "witch-hunts" and render self-sufficient single women the equivalent of witches because they have not conformed, Freeman celebrates Jenny's world through the voice of the conventional and once-passive Mrs. Carey. Together, Jenny and Betsey Carey overthrow the judgments of the church, the community, and the world in which marriage is the only acceptable path for women.

The deacon and minister "retreat" quickly and apologetically, with praise for Jenny's generous spirit. They send her a turkey for Christmas, the turkey that Betsey and Jenny eat together at the end of the story. In Johns's words, the two women have "transcended together the pettiness and the narrowness of a church which sits in judgment of women, which twists charity into abnormality or perversity; and they have transcended a culture which prescribes that there is only one 'reg'lar road of lovin'" (Johns 11–12). The meal the women share at the end is a bonding of kindred spirits, and the unmarried woman's life has played a crucial role in that of the married woman. Together they have confronted male institutions and transcended the witch-hunt. In this way Freeman offers a subversive vision of women in nineteenth-century New England.[14] Her vehicle is clearly the creation of a colossal figure through Jenny, a mythic matriarchal power capable of radically reversing the power structure itself. The maternal values so evident in Jenny's approach to the animals, the boy, the married couple, the entire community in fact, are invested with uncanny power.

In "The Great Goddess in New England: Mary Wilkins Freeman's Sister Jenny," Sarah Sherman argues convincingly that Christmas Jenny is "a Virgin Mary radically redefined" (Sherman 160, 161). Having never married or given birth, the spinster is here redefined, able to enjoy the pleasures of motherhood without the burdens of domestic entrapment and subjugation; furthermore, this new concept of maternity reverses the concept of deprivation. We do not see a spinster who is hungry for love and motherhood, longing for the world beyond the pine tree, the sea, the forest. It is Mrs. Carey's husband who is hungry for more than a Christmas dinner at the end of the story. He comes to the table with "sober dignity," and Freeman has him smile at the boy whom Jenny has taken into her home, the feminized male child. "Christmas Jenny" brings the themes of "The Spray Sprite" and "A White Heron" to a realm in which it is possible to maintain both autonomy and refuge within a woman's chosen landscape and yet simultaneously to partake in and influence the conjugal dinner. Fetterley and Pryse offer an interesting analysis of this story in their chapter on "regionalism as 'queer' theory" in *Writing Out of Place.* Jenny's "queerness" inspires horror for the villagers initially. The power of the story, according to Fetterley and Pryse, is "the portrait of Jenny herself and the capacity of her queerness to disempower the deacon and the minister" (331). Ultimately Freeman managed in this story to change the way readers view queer or normal. Finally, it is Jenny's values that sustain the community and heal the wounds of her married neighbors. "Freeman leaves her readers with the conviction that the only standard worth embracing is that represented by the wild but utterly sane and compassionate Jenny, and that the story's wisdom is not to be found in the deacons but in the mountain woman who 'made one think of those sylvan faces with features composed of bark-wrinkles and knot-holes that one can fancy looking out of the trunks of trees'" (204).

By positing a unity of person and place, of woman and nature, Freeman, Jewett, and Thaxter created a different context within which to view and understand women's lives. Rewriting their landscapes in their own terms, they ask their readers to value their characters' self-possession through their relationships to nature and place above their potential relationships with men. Their short stories thus became a means to redefine the lives of nineteenth-century women, granting them the capacity for power and voice. In each case, the female voice emerges through the depiction of place as much as, if not more than, character. We know the sprite's voice through the cry of the sandpipers or the "singing sparkling brine," Sylvia's through the "murmur of the pine's green branches," and Jenny's through the "soft clamor" of the creatures in her weather-beaten hill-top hut. Perhaps it is their capacity to shift landscape and setting from the periphery to the center of the short story that most profoundly captures the contributions of nineteenth-century New England regionalists.

NOTES

1 This chapter is part of a larger work in progress tentatively titled: "A Landscape of One's Own: Nature-Writing and Women's Autobiography." Portions of this chapter also draw from my published works as follows: "The Sandpiper and I: Landscape and Identity on Celia Thaxter's Isles of Shoals" and *In a Closet Hidden: The Life and Work of Mary E. Wilkins Freeman*. See also Annette Kolodny's discussion of this theme in the context of earlier women writers in *The Land Before Her: Fantasy and Experience of the American Frontiers, 1630–1860* and *The Lay of the Land: Metaphor as Experience and History in American Life and Letters*; and Vera Norwood's *Made from this Earth: American Women and Nature*. The work of Marjorie Pryse and Judith Fetterley on regionalism is equally relevant. These groundbreaking texts are useful in framing the importance of the concept of landscape in the lives and works of women writers. Much has been said of nineteenth-century male nature-writers, but the question of identity and landscape in relation to American women writers of the period is relatively unexplored;

more recently, Stacy Alamo addresses the "recasting" of nature in the work of a selection of women writers in *Undomesticated Ground: Recasting Nature as Feminist Space*, but does not include some of the more frequently overlooked writers such as Celia Thaxter.

2 Littenberg argues that "contemporary ecofeminist analysis helps us to understand more fully the historical conditions that attracted the women regionalists to Transcendentalism and also to explain how they extended and revised its perspective. ... Sarah Orne Jewett and Celia Thaxter are able to make that necessary juncture between living meaningfully in harmony with nature that lies at the heart of ecofeminism" (140).

3 Letter to Feroline W. Fox, March 19, 1874, in Thaxter, *Letters* 54. Her letter clarifies an important distinction from Thoreau, shared by women writers whose work moved imaginatively beyond the confinement Thoreau described: "it takes Thoreau and Emerson and their kind to enjoy a walk for a walk's sake, and the wealth they glean with eyes and ears. I cannot enjoy the glimpses Nature gives me

half as well when I go deliberately seeking them as when they flash on me in some pause of work. It is like the pursuit of happiness: you don't get it when you go after it, but let it alone and it comes to you."

4 Fetterley offers an insightful critique of Thaxter's "perception of particularity to the act of listening, indicating that learning how to listen is as essential to her [Thaxter's] theory of regionalism as learning how to speak, and that receptivity must precede and accompany agency"; see also Pryse's "Reading Regionalism." Pryse also emphasizes Thaxter's unique focus on "delicacy, listening, respect, the ability to move in slowly or not at all in observing, a willingness to see with another's eyes rather than to look at the 'other'" (49); see also Fetterley and Pryse, *American Women Regionalists 1850–1910*, 154–6.

5 See Childe Hassam's pictures and illuminations in Thaxter's *An Island Garden*; Hassam's painting of Celia Thaxter in her garden adorns the first page of the text. Thaxter stands madonna-like, head bowed, looking at the red flower that she gently holds with one hand. At the same time, Hassam's painting does capture the wild abandon of the rambling, tall flowers in the garden itself and the open gate leading to the sea in the backdrop.

6 Letter to Feroline W. Fox, March 19, 1874, in *Letters* 52.

7 Letter to Annie Fields, April 4, 1876. Quoted by Rosamund Thaxter in *Sandpiper* 116.

8 She noted that Levi went "murdering round the country in the name of science till my heart is broken into shreds. They are horribly learned but that doesn't compensate for one little life destroyed in my woman's way of viewing it (*Letters* 29).

9 Houghton Library Thaxter collection. Letter to Annie Fields, September 7, 1881. From 4 letters to Annie Fields (1881–1885), Am1743.

10 Houghton Library Thaxter collection, Letter to John Greenleaf Whittier, April 11, 1889.

11 Littenberg quotes from Sandra Zagarrell's "*Country*'s Portrayal of Community and Exclusion of Difference," in *New Essays on The Country of the Pointed Firs*, ed. June Howard (New York: Cambridge University Press, 1994), 39–60.

12 Letter to Annie Fields, February 1876, in Rosamund Thaxter's *Sandpiper* 115.

13 Letter to Sarah Orne Jewett, December, 10 1889, #50 in *The Infant Sphinx: Collected Letters of Mary E. Wilkins Freeman*.

14 This position is supported in Johns, 12.

REFERENCES AND FURTHER READING

Alamo, Stacy. *Undomesticated Ground: Recasting Nature as Feminist Space*. Ithaca: Cornell University Press, 2000.

Austin, Mary. *The Land of Little Rain. 1903. Stories from the Country of Lost Borders*. Ed. Marjorie Pryse. New Brunswick, NJ: Rutgers University Press, 1995. 1–90.

Blanchard, Paula. *Sarah Orne Jewett: Her World and Her Work*. Reading, MA: Addison-Wesley, 1994.

Cather, Willa. Preface to *The Best Stories of Sarah Orne Jewett*. Boston: Houghton Mifflin, 1925.

Donovan, Josephine. *New England Local Color Literature: A Women's Tradition*. New York: Ungar, 1983.

Fetterley, Judith. "Reading *Deephaven* as Lesbian Text." *Sexual Practice/Textual Theory: Lesbian Cultural Criticism*. Eds. Susan J. Wolfe and Julia

Penelope. Cambridge, MA: Blackwell, 1993. 164–83.

——. "Theorizing Regionalism: Celia Thaxter's Among the Isles of Shoals." *Breaking Boundaries: New Perspectives on Women's Regional Writing*. Eds. Sherrie A. Inness and Diana Royer. Iowa City: University of Iowa Press, 1997. 38–53.

Fetterley, Judith, and Marjorie Pryse. *Writing Out of Place: Regionalism, Women, and American Literary Culture*. Urbana: University of Illinois Press, 2003.

Fetterley, Judith, and Marjorie Pryse, eds. *American Women Regionalists 1850–1910*. New York: Norton, 1992.

Freeman, Mary E. Wilkins. "Christmas Jenny." *A New England Nun and Other Stories*. 1891. 160–77.

———. The Infant Sphinx: Collected Letters of Mary E. Wilkins. Ed. Brent L. Kendrick. Metuchen, NJ: Scarecrow Press, 1985.

Glasser, Leah B. "'The Sandpiper and I': Landscape and Identity on Celia Thaxter's Isles of Shoals." *American Literary Realism*, 36.1 (Fall 2003): 1–21.

———. *In a Closet Hidden: The Life and Work of Mary E. Wilkins Freeman.* Amherst: University of Massachusetts Press, 1996.

Jewett, Sarah Orne. *The Country of the Pointed Firs and Other Stories.* Ed. Mary Ellen Chase. Intro. Marjorie Pryse. New York: W. W. Norton, 1994.

———. "Preface" *to Poems of Celia Thaxter.* Boston: Houghton Mifflin, 1896.

———. "Preface" to Celia Thaxter *Stories and Poems for Children.* Boston: Houghton, Mifflin, 1895. iii. Rpt. in *Celia Thaxter: Selected Writings.* Ed. Julia Older. Hancock: Appledore Books, 1997.

———. "A White Heron." 1886. Rpt. in Fetterley and Pryse, eds., *American Women Regionalists*, 197–205.

Johns, Barbara. "'Love-Cracked: Spinsters as Subversives in 'Anna Malann,' 'Christmas Jenny,' and 'An Object of Love.'" *Colby Library Quarterly* 23.1 (March 1987): 4–15.

Kilcup, Karen L., ed. *Nineteenth-Century American Women Writers: An Anthology.* Oxford: Blackwell, 1997.

Kolodny, Annette. *The Land Before Her: Fantasy and Experience of the American Frontiers, 1630–1860.* Chapel Hill: University of North Carolina Press, 1984.

———. *The Lay of the Land: Metaphor as Experience and History in American Life and Letters.* Chapel Hill: University of North Carolina Press, 1975.

Littenberg, Marcia B. "From Transcendentalism to Ecofeminism: Celia Thaxter and Sarah Orne Jewett's Island Views Revisited." *Jewett and Her Contemporaries: Reshaping the Canon.* Eds. Karen Kilcup and Thomas S. Edwards. Gainesville: University of Florida Press, 1999. 137–52.

Norwood, Vera. *Made from This Earth: American Women and Nature.* Chapel Hill: University of North Carolina Press, 1993.

Older, Julia, ed. *Celia Thaxter: Selected Writings.* Hancock: Appledore Books, 1997.

Pryse, Marjorie. "Reading Regionalism: The 'Difference' It Makes." *Regionalism Reconsidered: New Approaches to the Field.* Ed. David Jordan. New York: Garland, 1994. 47–63.

Sherman, Sarah. "The Great Goddess in New England: Mary Wilkins Freeman's 'Christmas Jenny.'" *Studies in Short Fiction* 17.2 (1980): 157–64.

Thaxter, Celia. *Among the Isles of Shoals.* Boston: Houghton Mifflin, 1873. Vol. 24. 177–87. (Cited in the text as *AIS*. First published serially in *Atlantic Monthly*, 1869–70.)

———. *An Island Garden.* Boston: Houghton Mifflin, 1894.

———. "Land-Locked." *Atlantic Monthly*, 1861. Rpt. *Poems of Celia Thaxter.* Boston: Houghton Mifflin, 1872. 9–10. (Original ms. in Houghton Library, Thaxter collection. MS pfms, Am278.2.)

———. "The Spray Sprite." *Stories and Poems for Children.* Boston: Houghton Mifflin, 1895. 3–13. Rpt in Older, *Selected Writings*, 238–48. (Cited in the text as SS.)

———. *Letters of Celia Thaxter.* Eds. Annie Fields and Rose Lamb. Boston: Houghton Mifflin, 1895.

Thaxter, Rosamund. *Sandpiper: The Life and Letters of Celia Thaxter.* Portsmouth: Peter E. Randall, 1963. Rpt 1999.

Thoreau, Henry David. "Walking." *Atlantic Monthly*, 1862. Rpt. in *Great Short Works of Henry David Thoreau*, 331–68. Ed. Wendell Glick. New York: Harper, 1982.

Tichi, Celia. "Women Writers and the New Woman." *Columbia Literary History of the United States.* Ed. Emory Elliott. New York: Columbia University Press, 1988. 589–606.

Zagarrell, Sandra. "*Country*'s Portrayal of Community and Exclusion of Difference." *New Essays on The Country of the Pointed Firs.* Ed. June Howard. New York: Cambridge University Press, 1994. 39–60.

26
The American Ghost Story

Jeffrey Andrew Weinstock

In the nineteenth century, the ghost story achieved enormous popularity on both sides of the Atlantic and the supernatural tale became thoroughly intertwined with mainstream American short fiction of the nineteenth and early twentieth centuries. According to Kerr, Crowley, and Crow, between 1820 and 1920 – what they dub the "great age of the American ghost story" (1) – most major and innumerable minor authors tried their hands at supernatural fiction, and Bendixen adds that the writing of ghost stories was "a respectable literary enterprise" (Introduction 8) throughout the nineteenth century. American writers could enhance their reputations by producing well-wrought ghost stories and the finest magazines were happy to publish them. While few ghost stories were heralded as artistic achievements, their production could be extremely remunerative for successful authors.

In this chapter, I will first offer a brief overview of the development of supernatural fiction in the nineteenth and early twentieth centuries with an emphasis on the ghost story and will consider both general and genre-specific explanations for its popularity. I will then attend to works by several of the primary practitioners of the American ghost story, focusing on Washington Irving, Edgar Allan Poe, Nathaniel Hawthorne, Ambrose Bierce, Henry James, Mary E. Wilkins Freeman, Edith Wharton, and Ellen Glasgow. In the course of this discussion, I will propose that male and female authors often put their ghosts to work, so to speak, doing different jobs: for the men, the ghost foregrounds "the apparitional nature of existence" (Thompson, "Apparition" 92) and raises questions about what human beings know and what in fact can be known at all. In contrast, for women, the ghost often foregrounds what we may call the terror of the known – that is, the demands made of and restrictions placed upon women by fathers, husbands, children, and cultural expectations. What this suggests is that part of the appeal of ghost stories is that ghosts can be made to serve as very pliable metaphors expressing a range of cultural anxieties and desires.

The Rise of the American Ghost Story

The development of supernatural fiction in the United States was the result of a variety of factors, some of which were common to short fiction in general. The business of publishing as a whole underwent dramatic changes starting in the 1820s. American publishing had been hindered up to this time by a lack of capital, high production costs, underdeveloped transport and distribution systems, and the lack of an established, predictable market (Kelley 7). However, in the late 1820s and 1830s, cheaper postal routes and the developing network of railroads, combined with technological improvements in papermaking, binding, presses, typesetting, and typecasting, made it possible for publishers to produce and distribute large quantities of books and periodicals cheaply. At the same time, the audience for literature increased dramatically. Starting in 1790 with the US population approaching 4 million people, the population doubled every 25 years into the twentieth century, and an emphasis on literacy resulted by 1840 in the largest reading population ever produced (10–11).

The combination of an increasingly large and literate population and technological advances in publishing resulted in explosive growth within the publishing industry, which expanded tenfold between 1820 and 1850 (Coultrap-McQuin 30). Periodical publication also experienced enormous growth. By 1840, approximately 1,500 periodicals were in existence (Smith and Price 5). The emergence of the penny press in the 1830s, as well as the publication of weeklies, led to the appearance of newspapers (sometimes called story papers) composed entirely of fiction, or that mixed fiction and news. By the 1870s, the number of cheap weekly magazines had swelled to over 4,000, with a combined circulation of 10.5 million – an absolutely staggering figure when one notes that the US population in 1870 was 30 million (5–6).

The vigorous expansion of the literary marketplace demanded an increasing number of writers, and publishers in many cases were willing to pay well for short fiction. Women in particular benefited from the explosion of publication venues because authorship was among the handful of professions not off limit to "ladies." Prior to 1860, the only professional career options for women were teaching or writing (Degler 154) and, of these two options, authorship had the potential to pay better, as well as to extend the author's sphere of influence. Particularly following the American Civil War (1861–5), which wiped out almost an entire generation of young men, many women found themselves in desperate straits and forced to rely upon their own ingenuity to provide for themselves and their families. This difficult situation for women was exacerbated by the migration of young men westward or to urban centers seeking their fortunes. Many women who might otherwise have opted for domestic existences chose to attempt to earn a living through the creative use of their pens.

American supernatural fiction obviously profited from these general cultural and technological developments – publishers were hungry for short fiction, and ghost stories certainly fit the bill. However, there are a variety of genre-specific factors that also help to explain the rise of American supernatural fiction in the nineteenth century. In producing Gothic tales, American authors of both sexes were participating in a broader transatlantic literary trend. As traced by Donald Ringe, the American importation of British and German Gothic romances increased from a trickle to a flood during the final years of the eighteenth century and the first decade of the nineteenth and, with their characteristic emphasis on the dangers of the imagination and the passions uncontrolled, arguably influenced to varying extents all of America's most famous romanticists, including Irving, Poe, Hawthorne, and Melville.

The genre was also stimulated by Charles Dickens's advocacy of supernatural tales in his role as editor and author of Christmas annuals. The publication of his *A Christmas Carol* in 1843 forged a link between ghost stories and the Christmas season, a link that Dickens went on to reinforce through the incorporation of Christmas ghost stories into the magazines he edited – especially *All the Year Round*, which was launched in April of 1859 and averaged sales between 185,000 and 250,000 copies (Cox xiii). By the 1890s, the convention of writing seasonal ghost stories for Christmas had become a British "national institution" (xiii) and December issues of American magazines during the second half of the nineteenth century also participated in the Christmas tradition of the printing of ghost stories. It should be pointed out, however, that the publication of ghost stories in the British and American press was not limited to Christmas editions of magazines – supernatural tales were incorporated into gift books and periodicals throughout the year. American periodicals from the literary-minded *Atlantic Monthly* and *Harper's* to the more sensationalistic *Frank Leslie's Popular Magazine* and the *Overland Monthly* routinely incorporated supernatural literature by American authors (Carpenter and Kolmar 7).

While Dickens's promotion of the ghostly tale may have done much to put it before the reading public, his interest in supernatural stories, rather than being viewed as the idiosyncratic preoccupation of one influential editor, should be interpreted as symptomatic of larger cultural anxieties and desires operative on both sides of the Atlantic and as participating in a much broader flirtation with the occult. Commentators on both nineteenth-century British and American cultures speak in terms of a Victorian "spiritual crisis" experienced in the face of Darwinism, higher criticism of the Bible, and the rise of scientific and materialist doctrines such as utilitarianism. This situation, combined with the developing commercial, industrial, and technological revolutions; growing immigration; and the perception that, with the disappearance in America of the generation that had lived through the Revolutionary War, republican values were waning, resulted in a sense of disappointment, despair, and spiritual malaise (Carroll 3).

The development of Spiritualism and of the ghost story (on both sides of the Atlantic) in the late 1840s and 1850s (and, subsequently, the founding of the Society for Psychical Research in Britain and the American Society for Psychical Research in the 1880s) need to be considered as related phenomena connected to this sense of dislocation and the search for order in the midst of rapid change. Spiritualism, which aimed at proving the immortality of the soul by establishing communication with the dead (Braude 2), began in America in 1848 and was both a popular fad and a religious movement. Moore writes that "[s]carcely another cultural phenomenon affected as many people or stimulated as much interest as did spiritualism in the ten years before the Civil War and, for that matter, through the subsequent decades of the nineteenth century" (4). Supernatural fiction, which developed alongside Spiritualism in the United States and England – and likely drew inspiration from it (Kerr 55) – also can be viewed as a response to or backlash against nineteenth-century materialism and the legacy of Enlightenment rationalism. Supernatural tales, according to Geary, develop out of and give form to the "secular culture's repression of the supernatural" (Geary 118).

From Cox and Gilbert's perspective, nineteenth-century ghost stories not only subvert the pervasive emphasis on science in Victorian culture but, in an age of massive social, political, and economic upheaval, act to anchor the past to an unsettled and chaotic present (ix). Ghost stories can be seen as "vehicles for nostalgia" and "attempts to understand the past" (Punter 425) in that they reestablish a certain form of historical continuity by linking past to present precisely when such a linkage seems threatened. However, ghosts serve to link the living and the dead in the *present*: an explanation provided for the rise of both Spiritualism and ghost stories in the Victorian era is the need for consolation following bereavement, especially in the wake of the American Civil War. Spiritualism soothed those who had suffered loss by assuring them that the dead were not really gone, but "continued to dwell in a nearby invisible realm, invited communication with the living, and awaited a happy future meeting with those who had mourned them in this life" (Castle 133). Ghost stories, like Spiritualism, play out the fantasy that the dead are not really dead. Although the encounter with the ghost can be uncomfortable, if not terrifying, the terror of death itself is diminished because separation from loved ones is shown to be only temporary.

Another explanation provided by literary historians and critics for the rise of supernatural fiction in the nineteenth century is that this genre develops in conjunction with and gives expression to modern conceptions of human psychology. For example, the ghost story is frequently discussed as a means for repressed material to achieve expression. Along these lines, Glen Cavaliero writes that "[g]host stories express their author's (and their hearers') submerged or unacknowledged insecurites" (23), and Kerr, Crowley, and Crow maintain that "[n]ineteenth-century supernatural fiction provided a vehicle for the covert exploration of forbidden psychosexual themes" (5).

More generally, supernatural fiction in the nineteenth century, especially in the hands of women, became one privileged tool for the disguised or muted expression of political critique. Lundie speaks of this function in the supernatural writing of turn-of-the-nineteenth-century American women as "allegory." In her estimation, the supernatural (in the works of both men and women) has been used as a "forum through which to investigate otherwise unapproachable moral, psychological, and political issues" (3). For women, the allegorical nature of the ghost story allowed them to "displace their grievances onto supernatural forces, thereby safely giving voice to the political 'other' of their messages" (3). Patrick addresses this function of supernatural literature by American women in terms of screens and veils: "Behind the veil of the supernatural, women writers questioned the domestic ideal, voiced the frustrations with marriage and motherhood, and exposed social inequalities" (13).

Finally, it is worth mentioning in passing that, as discussed by Poe in his "Philosophy of Composition," fiction that aims for a particular emotional response in the reader – particularly fiction that aims to produce suspense or horror – is most effective when consumed in one sitting. Supernatural fiction has tended to thrive in the short story format (with a handful of notable exceptions) because the affective response it intends to elicit is compromised when the reader takes a break from the story – the spell is broken, so to speak, when the reader puts the book or magazine down.

Ghost Stories by American Men

According to G. R. Thompson, the supernatural fiction of America's major nineteenth-century writers (all men in Thompson's estimation) was shaped by the philosophical concerns of the Romantic movement, particularly the "recurrent apprehension that all matter may be a mental construct" ("Washington" 32). This "obsession" with the Kantian subject–object dialectic as filtered through authors such as Fichte, Coleridge, and Carlyle found expression in supernatural writings that raise questions about the ability of the mind to perceive reality as it is. Such writings typically either demonstrate the influence of mental states on perception or end ambiguously, failing to resolve the tension between supernatural and natural explanations and thereby calling into question conventional epistemological paradigms.

Both of these tangents are evident in the supernaturally infused writings of Washington Irving. The first American writer of the nineteenth century to achieve an international reputation (Baym 951), Irving was deeply influenced by German and British Romantic fiction and includes ghosts or ghostly elements in a number of his short writings, including "The Tale of the German Student," "The Spectre Bridegroom," "Guests from Gibbet Island," and his best-known tales, "The Legend of Sleepy Hollow" and "Rip Van Winkle." Both "The Spectre Bridegroom" and "Sleepy Hollow" fall into the category of Gothic tales that emphasize the influence of mental states on perception and the origination of ghosts from perceptual error. In "The Spectre Bridegroom," when the protagonist Herman Von Starkenfaust arrives at the Landshort castle, the Baron Landshort mistakes him for the bridegroom he has been awaiting for his daughter and whom he has never seen – who, unbeknownst to him, has been murdered – and gives Herman no opportunity to reveal the truth. Following the telling of "wild tales, and supernatural legends" (128), Herman convinces his superstitious hosts that he is the bridegroom, that he is dead, and that they have been entertaining a ghost, all of which facilitates his subsequent elopement with the Baron's daughter.

In "The Legend of Sleepy Hollow," it is similarly the case that the imagination, stimulated by external events, creates the appropriate conditions for the credulous mind to mistake what it perceives. Ichabod Crane is an avid consumer of supernatural tales who listens with "fearful pleasure" to the "marvellous tales of ghosts and goblins, and haunted fields and haunted brooks, and haunted bridges and haunted houses, and particularly of the headless horseman" (277) told by the old Dutch wives and in turn doles out a plentiful helping from his own store of ghostly stories. Ichabod's pleasure in spooky narratives, however, is only purchased at the price of his mental well-being once the telling of tales is over. Terrorized by "phantoms of the mind" (278), the overly-credulous Ichabod is the perfect target for the rough and ready Brom Bones's predations.

As in "The Spectre Bridegroom," in "Sleepy Hollow" the credulous are misled by those canny enough to prey upon their fears. The Van Tassel party features the usual telling of supernatural legends, with an emphasis (orchestrated by Brom) on the headless horseman. By the time Ichabod leaves, his mind has been so deeply affected that he jumps and starts at the slightest sound and sees ghosts and goblins wherever he looks. Bordering on panic even before starting home through the dark woods, Ichabod's terror rises "to desperation" when "something huge, misshapen, black and towering" (292) actually does emerge. At the end of the story, the exact cause of Ichabod's disappearance remains in dispute, but it seems clear that Brom Bones has taken advantage of his adversary's inability to keep his imagination in check.

In contrast to "The Spectre Bridegroom" and "The Legend of Sleepy Hollow," Irving's "The Tale of the German Student" allows the Gothic mood to develop fully rather than undercutting it with Irving's characteristic humor and, in addition to emphasizing the imagination's role in creating ghosts, raises questions about the nature of reality itself. "The Tale of the German Student" adopts a decidedly Gothic tone as it recounts the tale of young Wolfgang, a German student in Paris during the French Revolution's Reign of Terror. Wolfgang, who is described by the narrator as "diseased" due to his studies in "spiritual essences," experiences a recurring dream of a woman's face that haunts him. Crossing the square in which public executions are held one stormy night, he encounters a female figure dressed in black sitting on the steps of the scaffold leading up to the guillotine. She looks up at him and he discovers the face that has been obsessing his dreaming and waking hours. He takes her to his apartment where they pledge themselves to one another, only to discover her dead the next day upon his return from hunting for a larger apartment. When the police arrive, they inform him that she was guillotined the day before and when Wolfgang undoes a black collar around her neck, the head rolls onto the floor!

The reader of "The Tale of the German Student" is faced with two possibilities – each unsettling in its own way. Either young Wolfgang is mad and hallucinated or imagined the entire experience or he has spent the night with a ghost. Critics have generally read the story along the former lines and as "starkly horrible in its suggestion of necrophilia" (Ringe 96). However, the story ultimately neither confirms nor denies Wolfgang's madness and both possibilities call into question the ability of human beings adequately to comprehend their environments. As Ringe remarks, "[i]f superstition or a diseased imagination can affect one's perception of reality, how much more powerful is out-and-out madness in distorting a person's vision" (97).

And if Wolfgang really did spend the night with a ghost, then rationalistic conceptions of how the universe functions need to be substantially revised.

Despite Poe's reputation as the preeminent American Gothicist, there are surprisingly few actual ghost stories in his oeuvre. Nonetheless, Poe's fiction in general powerfully articulates the thesis that Gothic fiction "enacts the radical uncertainty of an epoch of revolution" and exposes "the limits of reason as an explanatory model" (Kennedy 40). What we see in much of Poe's death-obsessed fiction is the affirmation of "alternative modes or realms of existence beyond the physical limitations of our material life" (41). Much as in Irving's "The Tale of the German Student," ontological uncertainty – the question, what world is this, and are there others? – is at the heart of Poe's supernaturally themed stories, among them "Ligeia," "Morella," "Metzengerstein," "A Tale of the Ragged Mountains," "The Facts in the Case of M. Valdemar," "The Man of the Crowd," and "The Fall of the House of Usher." We will deal briefly with "Ligeia" here – arguably the closest Poe comes to an actual ghost story.

In "Ligeia," the narrator's beautiful, accomplished, and mysterious bride, Ligeia, sickens and dies, but not before cryptically communicating her belief that strength of will can overcome death. The melancholic narrator remarries and his second wife, Rowena, similarly falls ill. Attending to her, the narrator, who admits to having taken opium, senses a presence in the room with him and Rowena, and sees – or thinks he sees – strange drops of a ruby-colored liquid fall into Rowena's cup of wine. Thereafter, she fails and dies – only seemingly to revive. This happens multiple times until Rowena arises and approaches him and the narrator discovers she apparently has grown taller, her hair has turned from fair to black, and Ligeia's eyes are staring back at him.

For Ringe, there is "little doubt that we are intended to take literally the revivification of Rowena's corpse by the soul of Ligeia" (135). While I'm a bit more circumspect than Ringe – the narrator's melancholic and drug-addled state seem to license doubt – I do think "Ligeia," like "The Tale of the German Student," can be interpreted as either foregrounding the irrational components of human psychology and thereby critiquing our abilities to assess perceptual data objectively or as demonstrating the insufficiency of science and logic to account for the strangeness of the universe – or both. Either the narrator is hallucinating due to grief, madness, and drugs or "Ligeia" returns first as a ghost and then in the form of the possessed Rowena. In either case, Age of Enlightenment presumptions about rationality and logic are undermined.

In contrast to Poe, the ghosts in the short fiction of Nathaniel Hawthorne do not so much challenge conventional epistemological frameworks as represent either the world of the imagination or the grip of the past upon the present. Famously in the "Custom-House" introduction to *The Scarlet Letter*, Hawthorne discusses the conditions under which the imaginative faculties of the Romance writer are best stimulated – moonlight transforms the familiar into a "neutral territory, somewhere between the real world and fairy-land, where the Actual and the Imaginary may meet" (1372) and it is here that ghosts enter as the author's creative juices get flowing.

In much of Hawthorne's fiction, however, ghosts, rather than representing the liberation of the mind, stand for the skeletal reach of the past intruding into the present, sometimes for good, mostly for evil. Both these poles are represented by two inclusions in Hawthorne's *Twice-Told Tales*: "The Gray Champion" and "The White Old Maid." In "The Gray Champion," an old man perceived by many to be a ghost emerges to challenge the tyrannical Sir Edmund Andros and possesses what seems to be prophetic knowledge of the abdication from the throne of King James I. Described as "the type of new England's hereditary spirit," he is the embodiment of liberty incarnate who materializes to challenge domestic tyranny "whenever the descendants of the Puritans ... show the spirit of their sires" (8).

In the vast majority of Hawthorne's work, the supernatural is presented hesitantly, as one possibility among several. In the most famous example, Young Goodman Brown in the story of the same name may have a rendezvous with the devil or he may simply have dreamed the whole occurrence. Similarly, in "Old Esther Dudley", Esther – a living symbol of the past – is rumored to be able to call up images and figures of days gone by in the blurred mirror of the Province House, but this rumor is never substantiated. In "Graves and Goblins" (a magazine sketch generally attributed to Hawthorne), however, Hawthorne offers a straightforwardly supernatural tale that combines the themes of the ghosts as figurations of creative spirit and ghosts as representations of the persistence of the past. Narrated from beyond the grave, the story begins by asserting that all authors are haunted:

> Sprites, that were poets once, and are now all poetry, hover round the dreaming bard, and become his inspiration; buried statesmen lend their wisdom, gathered on earth and mellowed in the grave, to the historian; and when the preacher rises nearest to the level of his mighty subject, it is because the prophets of old days have communed with him. Who has not been conscious of mysteries within his mind, mysteries of truth and reality, which will not wear the chains of language? Mortal, then the dead were with you! (para. 1)

After this introduction, the ghostly narrator discusses the unhappy ghosts that inhabit his graveyard, chained to events in their pasts, and his own fascination with the ghost of a pure young maiden who spends only a short time on earth before ascending to heaven.

Along with Poe, Ambrose Bierce arguably was the foremost nineteenth-century American author of Gothic tales; unlike Poe, however, Bierce's body of work is full of clear-cut supernatural stories which Gary Hoppenstand divides into the (occasionally overlapping) categories of Americanized traditional Victorian ghost stories, critical dialogues about the "evils of human avarice and the dire supernatural consequences of greed," stories that use the supernatural "simply as a device to challenge smug satisfaction with an empirical understanding of reality," ironic twist-of-fate stories that employ satire to "debunk social institutions or base human iniquities," proto–science fiction stories built around scientific or quasi-scientific methodology, and stories of "family violence" (226–7). For our purposes here, we'll consider two of Bierce's family violence ghost stories – one fairly straightforward and the other exceptionally devious.

"The Middle Toe of the Right Foot" is an uncomplicated but menacing tale of supernatural revenge. In the story, four men visit the old Manton house for the ostensible purpose of a duel. The now-abandoned house had been the scene of a gruesome murder in which Mr. Manton had cut the throats of his wife and children before disappearing – the reader learns almost as an aside that Mrs. Manton had been a charming woman, but was missing the middle toe of her right foot. When the candle lighting the abandoned house is extinguished, three of the men beat a hasty retreat. The next day, the fourth man – whom the reader discovers to be the returned Mr. Manton – is found dead at the scene with a look of "unutterable fright" on his face. Leading up to him (but not away) are three sets of footprints – two sets made by small children and the third set made by a woman lacking the middle toe of her right foot.

Whereas "The Middle Toe of the Right Foot" is an effective but predictable tale of supernatural retribution, "The Death of Halpin Frayser" is much more devious – in large measure due to Bierce's non-linear narrative. At the start of the story, we are introduced to the titular character who, camping in the hills of Napa Valley, California, has a nightmare in which he speaks the name "Catherine Larue" and then confronts "the dead eyes of his own mother, standing white and silent in the garments of the grave" (410). The story then flashes back to Halpin's youth, in which he and his mother had an extremely – perhaps perversely – close relationship. The narration informs us that "[t]he two were nearly inseparable, and by strangers observing their manner were not infrequently mistaken for lovers" (411). Nonetheless, Halpin left his mother to travel west on business and was conscripted into service on a merchant vessel which foundered in the South Pacific, forcing him to spend six years on an island before being rescued and returned to San Francisco. Flashing forward, the story returns to Halpin's dream in which his dead mother, "a body without a soul," attacks him and Halpin "dreamed that he was dead" (412).

In the final section of this convoluted story, the reader is introduced to two bounty hunters who are hunting a man named Branscom who cut his wife's throat and who have tracked him to the cemetery in which his wife (who was a widow) is buried. What they find in the cemetery is Halpin Frayser, choked to death on the grave of a woman named Catherine Larue (the name Halpin speaks at the start of the story). Larue, it turns out, is the real name of the murderer they are after and the name of his wife was Frayser. Halpin thus is found dead on the grave of his mother and the story ends with a "low, deliberate, soulless laugh" that rises out of the fog – one "so unhuman, so devilish, that it filled those hardy man-hunters with a sense of dread unspeakable" (416–17). For the reader, privy to the backstory of Halpin's relationship with his mother and his ominous dream, the unavoidable conclusion is that there has been a horrible act of supernatural violence. Halpin's mother, the jilted lover, has returned from beyond the grave to punish the son who left her and whom she believed to be dead.

While it would be convenient to jump from Bierce's horrific tales of domestic violence and supernatural revenge to the works of American women that also deal with similar themes – although often from very different perspectives – there is still one more American male author of ghost stories who needs to be addressed: Henry James. Although James is, of course, most famous for his realist works, including *The Portrait of a Lady*, *Daisy Miller*, and *The Wings of the Dove*, he was also an accomplished practitioner of the ghostly tale and, in addition to the novella-length *The Turn of the Screw*, produced a fine body of short supernatural fiction. In his ghost stories, including "The Romance of Certain Old Clothes," "The Ghostly Rental," and most especially "The Jolly Corner," James focuses his gaze not on malevolent specters, but on the psychology of his protagonists. In such fiction "Gothic elements are used in the service of realism and psychology to emphasize the impenetrable depths of human emotion and to highlight the strange and often frightening nature of the human mind" ("Henry James" 461).

"The Jolly Corner" is generally recognized by critics as among James's finest supernatural stories and concerns an aesthete and man of leisure named Spencer Brydon who confronts the ghost of himself – the manifestation of an alter ego reflecting how Spencer's life could have developed had he made different choices. Spencer, the product of a wealthy New York City family, has spent the past 33 years in Europe and has only recently returned to the United States to oversee the conversion of one of his family's properties into flats. Although surprised at how much New York City has changed in his absence, he is even more surprised at how adept he is at managing the architectural and business details of the construction and discovers that he has "for too many years neglected a real gift" (James 729). This realization initiates a period of reflection on Spencer's part, one in which he obsessively contemplates how his life might have been had he remained in New York and become a businessman.

As Spencer stalks through the Jolly Corner, his family's now-vacant New York City mansion, in the dead of night contemplating what might have been, he somehow conjures into being that part of himself which he has repudiated and transforms from the hunter to the hunted. His sense of not being alone in the house culminates in a confrontation with his alter ego, a figure like that of Spencer himself, with the exception of two missing fingers, but a figure that Spencer finds monstrous and horrifying. The vision of this figure is also experienced by his intimate friend and love interest, Alice Staverton, but she does not share Spencer's aversion, having accepted the ghost as an alternative materialization of the man she loves.

In "The Jolly Corner," James offers the reader the ghost of a man in search of himself (721) and a sophisticated rendering of the doppelganger motif common to Romantic literature in general and artfully deployed in American literature in stories such as Poe's "William Wilson." In keeping with James's general interest in human psychology, in "The Jolly Corner," he stages a scene of the self confronting itself – of the mind turning inward and attempting to penetrate with both curiosity and horror that which it has rejected on the conscious level. As such, what the story reveals is something that Irving already knew – that the mind creates ghosts. However, James's spin on Irving is that ghosts are not the result of misperception or superstition; rather, ghosts emerge from within, from the unconscious, and are the inevitable result of the mind's in certain respects being a stranger to itself. To be haunted, says James, is the unavoidable corollary of being human.

Ghost Stories by American Women

Contentions like that of Ringe in his *American Gothic* that the American supernatural tale ceased to play a role in American literature after Hawthorne and dies out after the Civil War, or that of Thompson, who claims that American Romanticists wrote few actual ghost stories, fail to take into account the flourishing of women's ghost stories in the latter half of the nineteenth and the first two decades of the twentieth centuries. Between roughly the start of the Civil War and the end of the 1920s, hundreds of uncanny tales were published by women in the periodical press and in books. These include stories by familiar figures such as Harriet Beecher Stowe, Edith Wharton, Louisa May Alcott, Mary E. Wilkins Freeman, Lydia Maria Child, Charlotte Perkins Gilman, Sarah Orne Jewett, Mary Austin, and Elizabeth Stuart Phelps, as well as by authors almost wholly unknown to twenty-first century readers such as Josephine Dodge Bacon, Madeline Yale Wynne, Gertrude Atherton, Alice Brown, Emma Frances Dawson, Alice Cary, Olivia Howard Dunbar, Georgia Wood Pangborn, and Harriet Prescott Spofford. According to Salmonson, nineteenth- and twentieth-century supernatural fiction written in English was predominantly produced by women and her survey of supernatural fiction included in North American Victorian magazines concludes that as much as 70 percent of it was composed by women.

What attention to the body of supernatural fiction by American women reveals is what Carpenter and Kolmar refer to as a "distinctive tradition of ghost story writing" (10) organized around recurrent themes foregrounding specifically female concerns and frequently manifesting a feminist consciousness. Participating in and manipulating the nineteenth century's fascination with the supernatural, American female authors crafted a coherent body of supernatural literature reflecting their anxieties and desires. Thus, supernatural fiction became a powerful means for nineteenth- and early twentieth-century women to address such "unladylike" topics as bad marriages, the cultural injunction to have children, and the demands of maternity. In order to develop these assertions, I will focus on the ghost stories of Mary E. Wilkins Freeman, Edith Wharton, and Ellen Glasgow.

Although primarily regarded as a New England regionalist and a producer (like James, Wharton, and Glasgow) of realist fiction, Mary E. Wilkins Freeman fashioned an accomplished body of Gothic fiction, much of which addresses the "social, personal, and economic pressures which often silenced or devalued women and their concerns" (Voller). While Freeman's "Old Woman Magoun" is devastating in its critique of patriarchal exploitation of women – in the story, Old Woman Magoun allows her 14-year-old granddaughter Lily to eat poison berries and die rather than to go with her unscrupulous father Nelson Barry, who has gambled and lost her in a card game to another man who presumably will conscript her into sexual slavery – Freeman's ghost stories such as "The Lost Ghost" and "The Wind in the Rose-Bush" also emphasize both violence against children and the demands that children make upon women.

In "The Lost Ghost," the narrator, Mrs. Meserve, recollects a time when she boarded with two widows, Mrs. Amelia Dennison and her sister, Mrs. Abby Bird. Neither woman had ever had children, although Mrs. Bird is described as especially maternal. Having left her coat in the foyer on a cold September evening against the advice of Mrs. Bird, Mrs. Meserve was interrupted from her comfortable meditation before the fire by a knock on her bedroom door that elicited from her a vague feeling of fright. Opening the door revealed her coat in the arms of a tiny, pitiable figure. The child, Mrs. Meserve states, would only repeat, "I can't find my mother" (192). Retrieving her coat, she found it "as cold as if it had come off ice" (193).

Mrs. Meserve's panic summoned Mrs. Bird and Mrs. Dennison who detailed their own experiences with the apparition, which they had hoped wouldn't disturb Mrs. Meserve, as well as the tragic history of the house. According to the two women, the house had previously been owned by the Bisbees, a father and mother with one daughter. Mr. Bisbees was often away and Mrs. Bisbees was a "real wicked woman" who not only "never seemed to take much interest in the child" (199) but forced her to perform labor inappropriate for a girl of just over 5 years old. Neighbors of the family were also suspicious that Mrs. Bisbees had taken up with a married man.

Following the disappearance of this married man with a stolen sum of money, neighbors noticed that Mrs. Bisbees and her daughter were missing as well, but also remembered that she had mentioned the prospect of taking the child to visit family in Boston, so no investigation was launched until one of the neighbors recalled hearing a child crying three nights in a row a week after Mrs. Bisbees had last been seen. Entering the house at last, neighbors discovered the daughter dead in a back bedroom on the second floor, likely having frozen to death. This tragic tale culminated in the murder of the wife by the husband once he discovered what she had done.

Although the little ghost was disconcerting to them all, Mrs. Bird, Mrs. Meserve recalls, was the one most often visited and most powerfully affected by the tiny apparition. Mrs. Meserve recollects her saying, "'It seems to me sometimes as if I should die if I can't get that awful little white robe off that child and get her in some clothes and feed her and stop her looking for her mother" and remembers that "she cried when she said it" (203). In retrospect, this statement becomes prophecy. One morning, as Mrs. Meserve and Mrs. Dennison were at breakfast, they viewed Mrs. Bird out the window walking hand-in-hand with the child who "nestl[ed] close to her as if she had found her own mother" (204). Mrs. Dennison intuited from this that her sister was dead and indeed the two women found her dead in her bed, "smiling as if she was dreaming, and one arm and hand was stretched out as if something had hold of it; and it couldn't be straightened even at the last" (204). The story concludes with Mrs. Meserve reporting that "the child was never seen again after she went out of the yard with Mrs. Bird" (204).

Freeman's "The Lost Ghost" celebrates maternity as a woman's natural calling, even as it disturbingly underlines the sacrifices that motherhood demands. According to Bendixen, "The Lost Ghost" is "not an unqualified plea for mother love" (Afterword 249). Rather, "[i]t will be noted that the child demands a human sacrifice: a living woman must become a ghost. Thus in this tale we find a strong sympathy for the deprived child combined with the suggestion that motherhood may require self-sacrifice to the point of sacrifice of self" (249). This anxiety, according to Bendixen, is a recurring theme in uncanny fiction by American women: "Underlying much of the supernatural fiction written by American women is the fear that the traditional roles imposed upon women often turn them into ghost-like creatures, not fully alive, not fully human" (249–50).

The place of women within Anglo culture and the limitations placed upon them are also a central focus of the supernatural output of Edith Wharton. In stories such as "Afterward," "Kerfol," "Pomegranate Seed," and "The Triumph of Life," conventions of the Gothic are used to engage with social institutions and to question entrenched cultural attitudes and expectations regarding gender roles. As Patrick notes, these ghost stories therefore are not escapes from reality, but rather investigations of the "reality beneath the surface of custom, class, and gender roles" (vii) that celebrate the courage, compassion, and fidelity of women even as they highlight the daunting expectations placed upon women and the sacrifices of self that marriage demands.

"Afterward" tells the story of a married couple, Edward and Mary Boyne, who purchase a Tudor estate called Lyng in Dorset, England, because of its remoteness and rustic charm. As the result of a sudden windfall from a mine, the couple is able to retire to the English countryside so that Mary may devote herself to painting and gardening and Ned may produce his "long-planned book on the 'Economic Basis of Culture'" (60). Ned and Mary are desirous that the country home they are to inhabit should come with a ghost and express some disappointment that the legend concerning the house is that it is indeed haunted, but that the ghost is never recognized as a ghost until long after the encounter. Later in the text, Ned disappears and it subsequently becomes clear that he was involved in some dubious business dealings as concerns the mine, the nature of which Mary was – or kept herself – in ignorance. It also becomes clear to Mary that a gentleman she directed to her husband just prior to his disappearance was in fact the ghost of a suicide named Elwell – an individual Ned had cheated out of a share of the lucrative mine.

Beyond simply criticizing the ethical void at the center of capitalist business transactions, "Afterward" also calls into question gender expectations that assume either that women have little capacity for comprehending business dealings and therefore should have no interest in them or that genteel women need to be protected from the unsavoriness of business. Jenni Dyman observes in her study of Wharton's supernatural fiction that, "[i]n keeping with the social code and her husband's desires, Mary Boyne has developed habits of submissiveness, repression, and absence of direct communication. ... Mary's need for preservation of the status quo is so strong that she conveniently ignores or forgets any information that might alter her life" (42). Mary Boyne is portrayed as a woman who has been content to benefit from her husband's less-than-scrupulous business dealings without ever asking where in fact the money comes from. By conforming to gender expectations that dictate that she should have no interest in her husband's economic transactions, she, too, is complicit in the ruining and suicide of Elwell.

Lastly in this all-too-quick overview of the American ghost story, we turn to the work of Ellen Glasgow. Like James, Freeman, and Wharton, Glasgow has primarily been appreciated as an author of realist fiction, but in supernatural tales such as "The Shadowy Third," "The Past," "Whispering Leaves," and "Dare's Gift," she produced well-crafted ghost stories dealing with timely social issues including gender, race, and class.

Glasgow's "The Past" falls into the category of supernatural stories that express the anxieties of a second wife attempting to satisfy the expectations of a husband with previously established ideals (a common scenario into the twentieth century). As Lundie observes, "[l]iving as she did in the first wife's house, sleeping with her husband, and often caring for her children, a second wife was haunted continually by the memory of the woman she had replaced" (12). In "The Past," this metaphorical haunting becomes real as the narrator, Miss Wrenn, the new secretary to Mrs. Vanderbridge, observes her employer's depression and listlessness. Attempting to ferret out the cause of her melancholia, Miss Wrenn is shocked when, at dinner with Mr. and Mrs. Vanderbridge, a third woman enters and seats herself although she is not acknowledged or spoken to by anyone at the table.

What quickly becomes clear is that this "Other One" (to use the terms of the story) is Mr. Vanderbridge's deceased first wife, whom Mr. Vanderbridge doesn't realize others can perceive, and her malevolence is slowly killing the second Mrs. Vanderbridge. The second Mrs. Vanderbridge is only able to vanquish her spectral foe through an act of renunciation. She discovers evidence of an extra-marital affair on the part of the first wife but, rather than exposing the first wife's deceit to her husband, she destroys the evidence and triumphs "not by resisting, but by accepting; not by violence, but by gentleness; not by grasping, but by renouncing" (174). The lesson here seems to be that one cannot compete with the past but rather must accept it and move on.

The Waning of the American Ghost Story

Throughout the nineteenth century and into the twentieth, ghost stories by both men and women populated the pages of story papers, periodicals, and gift albums. Works by men, as we have seen, often raised epistemological and ontological questions about the abilities of human beings adequately to rationalize their universe, while works by women frequently dealt with the terrors of the known world – the constraints placed upon women living in a culture controlled by men. The prevailing critical opinion is that ghost stories in general went into decline in the 1930s and a variety of reasons have been adduced to explain the ebb in supernatural output, including women's rights advances that obviated the need to veil cultural critique, the influence of Freudian psychoanalysis, and a decline in the respectability of the supernatural tale – to which one must add the changing configuration of the literary marketplace, the economic impact of the Great Depression, and a changing worldview resulting from the increasing impact of technology on contemporary American culture. Just as the rise of the American ghost story was the result of a confluence of cultural forces, its purported decline can also be attributed to a combination of factors.

Any wider analysis of American supernatural fiction, however, would need to pay careful attention to the marked end-of-the-century resurgence of uncanny themes in the works of authors including Stephen King, Peter Straub, Joyce Carol Oates, Cynthia Ozick, and Anne Rice, and most especially in work by ethnic American women, including Toni Morrison, Amy Tan, Maxine Hong Kingston, Louise Erdrich, Christina Garcia, Paule Marshall, Gloria Naylor, Sandra Cisneros, and Nora Okja Keller, who reclaim the subversive potential of the ghost story to contest the ways in which minorities are "ghosted," in much the same way that their nineteenth-century forebears did to articulate anxieties related to the place of women in general in the US. Our ghosts, it seems – although they are put to work doing different jobs in different times and places – are never far from our doorstep.

REFERENCES AND FURTHER READING

Baym, Nina, ed. *The Norton Anthology of American Literature*, Vol. B. 7th edn. New York: W. W. Norton, 2007.

Bendixen, Alfred. "Afterword." *The Wind in the Rose-Bush* by Mary E. Wilkins Freeman. Chicago: Academy of Chicago Publishers. 239–58.

———. "Introduction." *Haunted Women: The Best Supernatural Tales by American Women Writers*. Ed. Alfred Bendixen. New York: Ungar, 1985. 1–12.

Bierce, Ambrose. "The Death of Halpin Frayser." *American Gothic: An Anthology 1787–1916*. Ed. Charles L. Crow. Malden, MA: Blackwell, 1999. 408–17.

———. "The Middle Toe of the Right Foot." *The Complete Short Stories of Ambrose Bierce*. Ed. Ernest Jerome Hopkins. Lincoln, NE: Bison Books, 1984. 160–6.

Braude, Ann. *Radical Spirits: Spiritualism and Women's Rights in Nineteenth-Century America*. Boston: Beacon Press, 1989.

Carpenter, Lynette, and Wendy K. Kolmar. "Introduction." *Haunting the House of Fiction: Feminist Perspectives on Ghost Stories by American Women*. Eds. Lynette Carpenter and Wendy K. Kolmar. Knoxville: University of Tennessee Press, 1991. 1–25.

Carroll, Bret E. *Spiritualism in Antebellum America*. Bloomington: Indiana University Press, 1997.

Castle, Terry. *The Female Thermometer: Eighteenth-Century Culture and the Invention of the Uncanny*. New York: Oxford University Press, 1995.

Cavaliero, Glen. *The Supernatural and English Fiction*. Oxford: Oxford University Press, 1995.

Coultrap-McQuin, Susan. *Doing Literary Business: American Women Writers in the Nineteenth Century*. Chapel Hill: University of North Carolina Press, 1990.

Cox, Michael, and R. A. Gilbert. "Introduction." *Victorian Ghost Stories: An Oxford Anthology*. Eds. Michael Cox and R. A. Gilbert. Oxford: Oxford University Press, 1991. ix–xx.

Degler, Carl N. *At Odds: Women and the Family in America from the Revolution to the Present*. Oxford: Oxford University Press, 1980.

Dyman, Jenni. *Lurking Feminism: The Ghost Stories of Edith Wharton*. New York: Peter Lang, 1996.

Edel, Leon, ed. *Henry James: Stories of the Supernatural*. New York: Taplinger, 1949.

Freeman, Mary E. Wilkins. "The Lost Ghost." *Haunted Women: The Best Supernatural Tales by American Women Writers*. Ed. Alfred Bendixen. New York: Ungar, 1985. 186–204.

———. "Old Woman Magoun." *American Gothic: An Anthology 1787–1916*. Ed. Charles L. Crow. Malden, MA: Blackwell, 1999. 256–66.

Geary, Robert F. *The Supernatural in Gothic Fiction: Horror, Belief, and Literary Change*. Lewiston, NY: Edwin Mellon Press, 1992.

Glasgow, Ellen. "The Past." *Restless Spirits: Ghost Stories by American Women 1872–1926*. Ed. Catherine A. Lundie. Amherst: University of Massachusetts Press, 1996. 154–74.

Hawthorne, Nathaniel. "The Custom-House." Introduction to *The Scarlet Letter. The Norton Anthology of American Literature*, Vol. B. 7th edn. Ed. Nina Baym. New York: W. W. Norton, 2007. 1352–77.

———. "Graves and Goblins" (June 9, 2008). <www.eldritchpress.org/nh/gg.html>

———. "The Gray Champion." *Hawthorne's Short Stories*. Ed. Newton Arvin. New York: Vintage, 1955. 1–8.

———. "Old Esther Dudley." *Hawthorne's Short Stories*. Ed. Newton Arvin. New York: Vintage, 1955. 87–96.

"Henry James." *Gothic Literature: A Gale Critical Companion*. Vol. 2: *Authors A–K*. Ed. Jessica Bomarito. Farmington Hills, MI: Thompson Gale, 2006. 461–80.

Hoppenstand, Gary. "Ambrose Bierce and the Transformation of the Gothic Tale in the Nineteenth-Century American Periodical." *Periodical Literature in Nineteenth-Century America*. Eds. Kenneth M. Price and Susan Belasco Smith. Charlottesville: University Press of Virginia, 1995. 220–38.

Irving, Washington. "The Legend of Sleepy Hollow." *The Sketch Book of Geoffrey Crayon, Gent*. New York: Penguin, 1988. 272–97.

———. "The Spectre Bridegroom." *The Sketch Book of Geoffrey Crayon, Gent*. New York: Penguin, 1988. 121–33.

———. "The Tale of the German Student." *Ghosts: A Treasury of Chilling Tales Old and New*. Ed. Marvin Kaye. Garden City, NY: Doubleday, 1981. 147–51.

James, Henry. "The Jolly Corner." *Henry James: Stories of the Supernatural*. Ed. Leon Edel. New York: Taplinger, 1949. 721–62.

Kelley, Mary. *Private Woman, Public Stage: Literary Domesticity in Nineteenth-Century America*. New York: Oxford University Press, 1984.

Kennedy, J. Gerald. "Phantasms of Death in Poe's Fiction." In Kerr, Crowley, and Crow, *The Haunted Dusk*, 39–65.

Kerr, Howard. *Mediums, Spirit-Rappers, and Roaring Radicals: Spiritualism in American Literature, 1850–1900*. Urbana: University of Illinois Press, 1972.

Kerr, Howard, John W. Crowley, and Charles L. Crow. "Introduction." *The Haunted Dusk: American Supernatural Fiction, 1820–1920*. Eds. Howard Kerr, John W. Crowley, and Charles L. Crow. Athens: University of Georgia Press, 1983. 1–10.

Lundie, Catherine A. "Introduction." *Restless Spirits: Ghost Stories by American Women 1872–1926*. Ed. Catherine A. Lundie. Amherst: University of Massachusetts Press, 1996. 1–26.

Patrick, Barbara Constance. "The Invisible Tradition: Freeman, Gilman, Spofford, Wharton, and American Women's Ghost Stories as Social Criticism, 1863–1937." PhD dissertation. University of North Carolina, Chapel Hill, 1991.

Poe, Edgar Allan. "Ligeia." *Poe: Poetry, Tales, and Selected Essays*. Eds. Patrick F. Quinn and G. R. Thompson. New York: Library of America, 1996. 262–77.

———. "The Philosophy of Composition." In Quinn and Thompson, *Poe*, 1373–1385.

Punter, David. *The Literature of Terror: A History of Gothic Fictions from 1765 to the Present Day*. London: Longman, 1980.

Quinn, Patrick F., and G. R. Thompson, eds. *Poe: Poetry, Tales, and Selected Essays*. New York: Library of America, 1996.

Ringe, Donald A. *American Gothic: Imagination and Reason in Nineteenth-Century Fiction*. Lexington: University of Kentucky Press, 1982.

Salmonson, Jessica Amanda. "Preface." *What Did Miss Darrington See? An Anthology of Feminist Supernatural Fiction*. Ed. Jessica Amanda Salmonson. New York: Feminist Press, 1989. ix–xiv.

Smith, Susan Belasco, and Kenneth M. Price. "Introduction: Periodical Literature in Social and Historical Context." *Periodical Literature in Nineteenth-Century America*. Eds. Kenneth M. Price and Susan Belasco Smith. Charlottesville: University Press of Virginia, 1995. 3–16.

Thompson, G. R. "The Apparition of This World: Transcendentalism and the American 'Ghost' Story." *Bridges to Fantasy*. Eds. George E. Slusser, Eric S. Rabkin, and Robert Scholes. Carbondale: Southern Illinois University Press, 1982. 90–107.

———. "Washington Irving and the American Ghost Story." In Kerr, Crowley, and Crow, *The Haunted Dusk*, 11–36.

Voller, Jack G. "Mary E. Wilkins Freeman." *The Literary Gothic* (January 18, 2008. June 13, 2008). <www.litgothic.com/Authors/freeman. html>.

Wharton, Edith. "Afterward." *The Ghost Stories of Edith Wharton*. New York: Simon & Schuster, 1973. 58–91.

27

The Detective Story

Catherine Ross Nickerson

In one of her early Kinsey Milhone stories, "The Parker Shotgun," Sue Grafton has her detective looking for a rare and valuable shotgun that is key evidence in a brutal murder. When Milhone walks into the room where a suspect keeps his collection of firearms on display in glass cases, she notices a shotgun propped up in a corner. Upon examination, it proves not to be the one she is searching for. "Too bad," she tells us. "I'm always hoping for the obvious" (Hillerman 660). While this private investigator may be looking for quick and easy dispositions of her cases, we, the readers, are not. We know what we want when we open a detective story. An oddball investigator is fun; an interesting locale is nice; the crime can, initially anyway, be either bizarre or commonplace. What any detective story really needs is a plot that becomes more and more complicated and confusing until our sleuth sorts out the false leads from the true ones, clears the obfuscations, and explains how it all happened. Readers of detective fiction demand a balance between predictability and innovation, just as they want plenty of digression before the expected resolution. Curiously, many avid fans of detective fiction feel the need to disparage their own beloved genre, even to other fans, as "fluff," "what I read to get to sleep," even "junk."

There are two main reasons why fans and detractors of detective fiction put down the genre. One rap is that it is formulaic, and so therefore hovers somewhere near what LeRoy Panek calls "the sub-literary" (5). The other reason is that it does not seem quite right to take pleasure in stories about the untimely ends of others. Raymond Chandler dryly observed that it is difficult to champion the detective story: "It is usually about murder and hence lacks the element of uplift" (2). But there is another way to look at detective fiction and its formula. Bobbi Ann Mason, while poking fun at the Nancy Drew series, once compared their plots to sonnets, "endless variations on an inflexible form" (79). And while the characterization is meant as a joke, it does in fact point us toward the larger truth that even the loftiest literature has conventions, rules, formulae. Ross MacDonald, one of the main heirs of the hard-boiled style of Chandler and Dashiell Hammett, asserts that there "may be more to convention than meets the eye. ... The literary detective has provided writers since Poe with a disguise, a kind of welder's mask enabling us to handle dangerously hot material" (25). Those same conventions may also deflect the most devastating aspects of the subject for the reader, allowing us to consider "dangerously hot material" about villains, victims, and heroes at any given historical moment: how and why people hurt each other, who is most vulnerable, who does these bad deeds and pretends they didn't, who is able to expose fatal secrets, capture the guilty, and avenge the dead.

In this chapter, I hope to make the case for why we should take the detective story seriously, for what it can indicate about the way fiction in general works, and for what it can suggest about the way a culture expresses itself through popular forms. While the complex questions about genre that detective fiction raises will be discussed at greater length later in the chapter, I want now to clarify my focus. "Mystery fiction" and "detective fiction" are often used interchangeably – not without reason, but in ways that can be confusing. Otto Penzler, the tireless editor and anthologizer of these kinds of stories, offers us a useful distinction: "I regard the detective story as one subgenre of a much bigger category, which I define as any short work in which a crime, or the threat of a crime, is central to the plot" (Hiaasen ix). Many of the most famous American mysteries, including the work of James M. Cain, Patricia High-smith, and Cornell Woolrich, fall into that larger category of suspenseful narrative about crimes and secrets. Detective stories, to state the obvious, need a detective. He or she can be a cop, a professional private eye, an amateur busybody, a lawyer, or an ordinary person who takes on an effective investigatory role.

However, what defines detective fiction is more a matter of structure than of content. When we read a detective story, Tzvetan Todorov explains, we are really coping with two narrative lines (58–9). One is a story we follow in a linear way, which is the story of the investigation: where a body was found, how the detective figure was called in, what physical evidence was in place, interviews with witnesses and suspects, any secondary crimes that seem related to the first, right through to the end when the detective presents the solution to the mystery. The second narrative is the story of how and why the murder or murders occurred, who committed the act, who may have conspired with the actual murderer, and what they did to destroy evidence or mislead the detective. This second story is fragmented, and has been made that way deliberately by the guilty party, who is often drawn into elaborate efforts to keep the detective from putting the pieces back together. For when the detective is able to reconstruct the second narrative, the criminals are exposed, and the story of the investigation comes to a triumphant end. It is not a coincidence that a conspiracy to commit a crime is commonly called a "plot" in a detective story: detective and villain are competing authors, or plotters, who each wish to control the narrative. This doubled structure draws our attention to the very nature of narrative authority. It dramatizes the claim that any narrative makes to be an accurate retelling of things that happened in the past.

The doubled structure of detective fiction creates complex relationships between the triad of characters at the heart of the story: the investigator, the criminal, and the victim. It creates even more complex relationships between the author, the investigator, the narrator (or narrative voice) and the reader. Again, the detective story shows the scaffolding of all narrative: storytelling comes out of a struggle for authority. Sometimes it is a struggle between characters for a claim to truth, and sometimes it is a struggle between the storyteller and the reader. Like Scheherazade, the storyteller fears the premature end that comes with losing the interest of the audience. The readers of a detective story can be an active and judgmental audience, repeatedly measuring the unfolding narrative against the known formula. The paradigmatic detective story needs suspense – the delay of the answers to all the questions it raises – but it also needs to reward the patient reader with the satisfaction of knowing what happened.

To understand how all these structural features play out in detective stories, let us go back to the beginning, and Edgar Allan Poe's trio of tales featuring Auguste Dupin as an amateur investigator of crime. Published between 1841 and 1845, these "tales of ratiocination" are widely acknowledged as the first American detective narratives, and the model for the modern detective story around the world. The template that Poe offers in his Dupin tales ("The Murders in the Rue Morgue," "The Murder of Marie Roget" and "The Purloined Letter") works like this: A serious crime is known to have been committed, and neither the police nor the newspapers can make head or tail of it. Someone far smarter than the police, the criminal, the narrator, and the reader undertakes the solution of the crime. Poe, through his narrator, makes us believe that Dupin is a genius, possessed of an intelligence that is not simply greater than that of an ordinary person, but of a different order of magnitude altogether.

The intellectual superiority of the detective figure, in particular, shapes the relationships between author, detective, narrator, and reader. Julian Hawthorne put it this way in an introduction to an anthology called *Library of the World's Greatest Mystery and Detective Stories* (1907): "Reader and writer sit down to a game, as it were, with the odds, of course altogether on the latter's side. ... [T]he detective appears to be in the writer's pay, and aids in the deception by leading the reader off on false scents" (10). Many readers of these stories try to keep ahead of the detective, and the writer has to create a scenario that is ultimately logical, but apparent for most of the story only to the unparalleled genius of his detective character. Hawthorne suggests that readers of detective fiction are made acutely aware of the fact the author is teasing them, dropping hints, and deliberately confusing them. In "The Murders in the Rue Morgue," Poe simultaneously offers and obfuscates crucial clues by placing them in the testimony of people whose recollections don't make sense and who certainly don't understand the significance of what they are conveying. Through our first-person narrator, we read the newspaper reports of several witnesses who heard two people arguing, but who can't agree on what language was being spoken by one of them. At the time we read that passage, it sounds to us that people were too far away to hear clearly or that perhaps the reporters got it wrong; later Dupin explains that contemplating those discrepancies created a breakthrough in his thinking and allowed him to consider a non-human assailant.

The other way in which Poe orchestrates the writer-detective-reader triad is to introduce a narrator who is not nearly as clever as Dupin; we receive all our information from a character who is in awe of his friend's intellectual gifts. Arthur Conan Doyle, of course, made this technique famous in the character of Doctor Watson, who is so obtuse that we all feel a little better about our own inability to keep up with Sherlock Holmes. The function of Poe's narrator is a little more complicated; there is an erotic tension in their partnership, and a kind of intellectual rivalry in the structure of the stories. While our narrator cannot ratiocinate his way to the Ourang-Outang, he can frame the stories to include long disquisitions on the intellect that show him to be cerebral and sophisticated. The first several pages of "The Murders in the Rue Morgue" are a disquisition on the relation of imagination and analytic thinking. Much of the discussion focuses on the relative complexity of different games (chess, checkers, whist, and, later, in "The Purloined Letter," evens-odds) and the exact mental faculties they require. In some ways, the discussion of games could just as easily be a discussion of reading detective fiction (as Poe understands it), of the game of wits and the competition to spy the clues. Our narrator invites us to make that connection at the transition into the body of the story: "The narrative which follows will appear to the reader somewhat in the light of a commentary on the propositions just advanced" (Poe 6).

While it is clear that Dupin is smarter than anybody, the narrator is at pains to point out the exact nature of his analytic genius: a mind that "disentangles" puzzles, like crime scenes that are locked up tight from the inside, and brings them to neat resolutions (Poe 3). But our narrator wants us to understand that Dupin also generates narratives: In his opening remarks he asserts that "[i]t will be found, in fact that the ingenious are always fanciful, and the *truly* imaginative never otherwise than analytic" (Poe 6). He takes it a step further "with the fancy of a double Dupin – the creative and the resolvent" (Poe 7). The powerful impulse toward creativity with which Poe imbued his detective has stayed with the genre over the last century and a half. An easily parodied moment in a detective story is the one in which the investigator gathers all involved in the crime and its investigation and dramatically presents a fully coherent narrative of the misdeeds and the misdoers. But at heart, and as introduced by Poe, the moment of telling the whole story is really about the rivalry between the detective and the criminal to control the narration of the crime. The detective is charged with creating the true and coherent story of how a crime occurred and who is responsible, while the thief or killer schemes to fragment the storyline. However, the pieces they inevitably leave in place, or leave in view, become the clues (bits of paper, fragile alibis, things witnesses see, hear, smell) that allow the detective to reconstruct the tale of the crime and its cover-up. It is therefore almost a compulsion on the part of fictional detectives to let their rivals know they have been bested, and to do it in the form of textual or linguistic exchange – a sort of narrative victory lap. Near the end of "The Murders in the Rue Morgue," Dupin coaxes the sailor to his house not only to prove to himself that he was correct in his reconstruction, but to let the sailor know exactly how he figured it out. At the resolution of "The

Purloined Letter," Dupin cannot resist creating a facsimile letter that will let Minister D— know that it was indeed he who understood the scheme and re-purloined the letter.

At the same time as villains and detectives are locked in a power struggle, there is a profound intimacy between them. At the beginning of "The Murders in the Rue Morgue" and then again near the end of "The Purloined Letter," our narrator asserts that excellence at simple games like checkers and evens-odds requires the intellectual acumen to "admeasure" one's opponent and the imagination to "identify" completely with his or her intellectual proclivities. Dupin explains that the Prefect's inability to see a stolen letter hidden in plain view is symptomatic of his mediocre intellect: "the Prefect and his cohort fail so frequently, first by default of this identification and, secondly, by ill-admeasurement. ... They consider only their *own* ideas of ingenuity; and, in searching for anything hidden, advert only to the modes in which *they* would have hidden it." (Poe 92–3). And that, of course, is what a detective must do: think like a murderer to catch a murderer. In Poe's stories this is a comfortable premise; Dupin is, after all, well acquainted with Minister D—. He alludes to their shared past, he is close enough to drop in on the Minister at his apartment, he knows that his true personality is different from the one he projects, he knows what conversational subject will distract his foe while he scans the room. Both write poetry, and each can identify the other's handwriting on sight. Clearly, Minister D— and Auguste Dupin are the sort of doubles that Poe so enjoyed portraying. They are so intimate that, with their shared initial and the hint that Dupin comes from an "illustrious" (Poe 6) family and that Minister D— has a brother, David Lehman wittily concludes that they are brothers (95–6). In any case, his relationship with Minister D— draws Dupin out of his armchair and into the most active investigative role of the three tales. He not only finds the letter with his own eyes, but also takes it upon himself to steal it back. His objective is to protect the honor of the noblewoman involved, which has political implications as well.

Poe thus introduces the idea that detectives not only think like criminals, but sometimes commit criminal acts in service to their personal sense of justice. The blurring of the line between detectives and the crooks they pursue is not always as playful as it is in Poe's story. Many detectives, especially in the hard-boiled style, are morally ambiguous. Others are changed by their intimacy with treachery, greed, lust, betrayal, and violence. They may become cynical, they may become enraged by the cruelty they see around them, or they may find relief from their own demons in chasing down villains. Readers sometimes wonder if they are being changed by reading about these worlds of crime and the characters who inhabit them, and that is part of the reason for the apologies readers make; every reader knows someone who disapproves of the content of crime fiction. One of the most common complaints concerns the glorification or aestheticization of violence and villainy in detective stories; to this way of thinking, these stories encourage something deeply corrosive to the social fabric. Ross MacDonald turns that premise on its head when he remarks that "[a]n unstable balance between reason and more primitive human qualities is characteristic of the detective story. For both writer and reader it is an imaginative arena where such conflicts can be worked out safely, under artistic controls" (11). In other words, detective fiction civilizes us.

While we have looked at several of the relationships between the players in the detective story, we haven't yet taken up the question of the dynamic between the reader and the villain. In her 1913 textbook for a correspondence course in "The Technique of the Detective Story," Carolyn Wells, a prolific writer of mysteries herself, offers the following advice on creating a villain: "he must be both intelligent and ingenious, in order to give the Transcendent Detective a foeman worthy of his steel. The reader must have no liking or pity for him. In his perfection he should be what Poe calls 'that *monstrum horrendum*, an unprincipled man of genius.' Moreover, he must be cleverly drawn to conceal his identity to the last. He must appear to be what he is not, and he must not appear to be what he is" (237). If the ideal villain is a genius, and thus admirable, but "unprincipled," we can see how he is a double for the detective. But can't he or she also be a double for us, the readers? Since we are, like the detective, trying to think like a murderer, we must sometimes realize that all that differentiates us from the criminals is our principles or other restraints on our behavior (and, of course, if we are reading detective stories on our metal bunks in the state pen, the identification will be all the stronger).

In his *Postscript to the Name of the Rose*, Umberto Eco observes that the only character in a detective story who has never committed the murder is the reader (Lehman 2). Most of the time we are trying to figure out who is the "least likely suspect," that person whom Wells says "does not appear to be what he is," and ingenious authors have made detectives and even narrators the perpetrators. But as David Lehman points out, who is a less likely suspect than ourselves? "The murderer as the reader? Never – which is to say on some implicit, metaphorical level, always. ... Readers of detective novels participate in perfect murders – perfect because they offer us a vicarious and therefore socially acceptable form of releasing our homicidal instincts without ever having to face the consequences" (2). Lehman is not so much questioning the morality of reading detective fiction as he is suggesting that we all feel guilty about something, we all wonder what we are capable of under the right circumstances. Again, as MacDonald argues, it is the conventions of detective stories that make them safe "arenas where such conflicts can be worked out."

Detective stories, then, raise the big issues about how fiction works: about what makes a narrative authoritative and a believable representation of events. They throw the complex relationships between writers, their characters, and readers into high relief. They demonstrate the way in which all literature weaves convention and originality in complex patterns. Some require us to consider every aspect of human psychology, the effect of social injustice, how power corrupts, and why terrible fates befall fine people. Matters of intellect, writing, and speaking are highlighted in Poe's stories, which seems natural given the aesthetic temperaments of Dupin and our narrator. But even the most hard-boiled detectives spend a lot more time talking to people, reflecting on what they have to say, delivering snappy comebacks, and crafting amusing metaphors than they do shooting pistols and being beaten up. One of Hammett's detectives explains to a young murderer how he cracked the case: "You talked too much, son. ... That's a way you amateur criminals have. You've always got to overdo the frank and open business" (59). Detective fiction is in fact a genre obsessed with language at many levels.

That preoccupation with language, especially in the form of texts like secret letters or forged wills, comes in part from the detective story's relationship to Gothic narrative. It is a remarkable fact that the modern detective story was created by a writer best known for his horror fiction. Several critics have suggested that Poe invented his detective, a machine for "ratiocination," in order to hold the monstrosities of his imagination at bay. Other critics adjust their angle of vision slightly, and suggest that the detective figure is a product of, rather than an outsider to, the disordered and frightening world of the Gothic mode. If Gothic narrative develops secrets, compulsions, and sadism to a fever pitch, eventually it also needs to create characters who can restore some level of justice and harmony. Detective fiction – part of that broader category of mystery – has remained closely related to the horror genre. We can also trace connections to the Western and to science fiction.

When we begin to contemplate the wide range of stories that include crimes and secrets that require investigation, we are quickly confronted with broader issues about literary genre. For one thing, we use the term *genre* in several ways, applying it to different orders of things. It can mean something as broad as the difference between epic and lyric poetry, or fiction and essay. It can apply to the demographics of the readership, as in the "young adult novel." Indeed, there is such a term, slightly pejorative, as "genre fiction," which usually includes the popular categories of detective, science, and horror fiction. One is tempted to abandon the term altogether, but it can be useful when the context is clear. In the study of popular culture, genre is a term that usually indicates content; sub-genre can either indicate a more narrowly focused content (like "police procedural") or point to style or tone ("noir"). The main sub-genres of the very broad category of crime writing include detective fiction, spy novels, police procedurals, political thrillers, mysteries. Within detective fiction, we speak of the puzzle story, the domestic style, the golden age or classical story, the hard-boiled style, the feminist hard-boiled, the cozy, and on and on. Many of these terms overlap, and some are more tied to a specific time period than others.

But perhaps the most interesting thing about genre is how quickly genres hybridize with each other and how new genres come into being. Sometimes they morph gently from one to the other: Dupin becomes Holmes who becomes Hercule Poirot and Miss Marple. Other times they are direct refutations of what has come before. In a famous manifesto of the hard-boiled style, Chandler mocked the "golden age" style (including Agatha Christie and her many British and American imitators), declaring that "Hammett gave murder back to the kind of people who commit it for reasons ... and with the means at hand, not hand-wrought dueling pistols, curare, and tropical fish" (16). Hillerman points out that, since the early twentieth century, the main division among writers and readers of detective fiction has been into two camps: those who believe the stories should focus primarily on the puzzle to be solved and those who believe the genre can and should be a more expressive form, with fleshed out characters, a deep sense of place, and a desire to portray the strengths and flaws of American culture. These questions about the rivalry and hybridization of genre are not peculiar to detective fiction, and contemplating them invites us to think about the broadest issues of originality, influence, tradition, expectations of what fiction is supposed to do, and the meaning and uses of "realism."

Given the multiple sub-genres of the detective story and recurrent debates about its capabilities, it is impossible to trace a clean trajectory from Poe to the present day. But we can see ways in which creativity and variation are tied to historical moments, resulting in new kinds of detective stories that disrupt some of the ideas about gender, race, and social class that were established in the first decades of the twentieth century (in both the classical and the hard-boiled styles). Notably, a new wave of feminist writing emerged with the women's movement in the 1970s. Of course, women had been highly successful detective fiction writers all along, but there was an alignment of values and goals between second-wave feminism and the work of Amanda Cross (who created her no-nonsense professor-sleuth in 1964), Marcia Muller, Sue Grafton, Sara Paretsky, and S. J. Rozan, the last four of whom have done the seemingly unthinkable: challenged the premise that the hard-boiled style is only for men. Likewise, we can trace African American crime writing back into the nineteenth century, but a reclamation of the detective story began in the 1990s, with the work of Walter Mosley, who injects humanity into noir and then turns it on its head, Eleanor Taylor Bland, who deliberately tells the stories of people who are voiceless – children, the elderly, the mentally ill – and Barbara Neely, who shows how keen an eye a domestic servant has. These works came at a time when the mainstream media were particularly warped, and especially enthusiastic, in their depiction of African Americans as perpetrators of crime, from welfare fraud to drug dealing and gangsterism (in life and in rap). They propose a corrective narrative to replace the scenarios where people of color are always the perps and never the cops. Hillerman, in his Joe Leaphorn and Jim Chee series, took the police procedural out of the city and on to the Navajo reservation with his stories of contemporary Native American life.

In spite of all its metafictive, epistemological, and social-critical charms, the genre is a second-class citizen in the world of letters; this marginalization is a source of pain to many writers and publishers of detective fiction, and has been from its earliest days. Of course, many canonical American writers have experimented with the detective story, including Mark Twain, William Faulkner, and Gertrude Stein, and many more were influenced by it, including Willa Cather, Edith Wharton, Ernest Hemingway, Joyce Carol Oates, Thomas Pynchon, Don Delillo, and Paul Auster. In the introduction to the anthology *Women on the Case*, Sara Paretsky argues that the struggle of women detective fiction writers is nothing more and nothing less than the struggle of all women writers: "This collection is an attempt to continue the work that Barrett Browning began [in *Aurora Leigh*], to make it possible for women to broaden the range of their voices, to represent their age for women, to describe women's social position, their suffering – and their triumphs" (xi).

Hillerman writes that Chandler's "use of the work of a private detective to illuminate the corruption of society has attracted into the genre many mystery writers who wish to shoot for lofty literary goals. Driven out of the so-called mainstream of American writing by the academic critics and the academic trends – minimalism, deconstructionism, and whatever is next – we have found a home in the mystery form" (xviii). While detective stories have in fact received the critical attention of scholars famous for other subjects – Roland Barthes, Fredric Jameson, Geoffrey Hartman, John Irwin – and while detective fiction does show up quite frequently in surveys of American literature, there is still a sort of collective wink about it. At the same time, scholars routinely compare their research to detective work: tracking down leads, gathering evidence, interrogating a subject. (Furthermore, it must be true that every professor in the United States has spent at least a little time in faculty meetings musing about the plot of the academic mystery he or she will write – under a pseudonym – some day.)

So far, I have been discussing matters that apply to detective fiction in general; let us now turn to the short story more specifically. Wells explains to her students that all detective stories have a single plot – "the problem and its solution" – then likens that plot to an accordion, which "may be pulled out to an extraordinary length, or compressed to a minimum. ... The longer the story, the more numerous and bewildering the conditions of the riddle and the windings of the maze, but all tend definitely to the one end, – the answer" (279). The mechanisms of a detective narrative are more apparent in a short story, since there is less upholstery for hiding the ropes and pulleys. The shorter form also forces writers to make a more clear decision about whether to focus on the puzzle or on character.

From the beginning, Poe had figured out that the way around this difficult choice was the series. By writing multiple stories about the same detective, he was able to make Dupin a vivid presence and he was able to build clever puzzles for him to solve. Conan Doyle made the same choice after writing an initial novel-length Sherlock Holmes story, *A Study in Scarlet*. (I include this Scottish writer in this discussion because his work was so popular and influential in the United States.) Panek has traced the publication history of the Sherlock Holmes series in American periodicals. Conan Doyle's work was picked up by S. S. McClure just as he conceived of syndication as a way to package editorial material for newspapers all over the country, and as a result the Sherlock Holmes stories had an enormous readership. Three subsequent series were picked up by the squarely middle-class *Harper's Weekly*, *McClure's Magazine*, and *Collier's Weekly*. *Collier's* actually scooped the British *Strand*, and was the first on either side of the Atlantic to publish the stories that would become *The Return of Sherlock Holmes* (Panek 31–2).

Periodicals of all kinds drove the popularity of detective stories and novels: nineteenth-century story papers and dime novels may have been seen as adolescent entertainment, but "pulp" fiction was an enduring tradition that produced the hard-boiled style. "Slicks" (glossy magazines like ones that ran the Holmes stories) regularly brought short fiction and serialized novels into the middle-class home. *Ellery Queen's Mystery Magazine* began publication in 1941, dedicating all its pages to crime writing, and close to one hundred other (and more lurid) magazines like *True Detective* appeared from the 1920s onward. But periodicals are ephemeral, and publishers saw the opportunity to commit detective stories into the more permanent form of books. One kind of project is the collection (which we saw with the Holmes stories, and we see currently with James Lee Burke's four collections of his Keller stories). Another is the anthology; Julian Hawthorne edited one of the earliest series, a six-volume set of "One Hundred and One Tales of Mystery by Famous Authors of East and West" in 1907. Anthologies became increasingly important to fans of detective stories after the middle of the twentieth century, when the market for periodical fiction fell apart with the advent of television.

Currently, the magazines that publish detective stories are so various that a fan looking specifically for those stories would have real trouble finding them. Houghton Mifflin, as part of "The Best American Series" collects stories from diverse sources each year. The 2007 volume of the Best American Mystery Stories includes stories that first appeared in journals and magazines not closely associated with detective fiction: the *Oxford Review*, the *Georgia Review*, *Shenandoah*, and *Prairie Schooner*, *Tin House* and the *New Yorker*. But more than half the stories came from commissioned anthologies – that is to say, writers are asked to produce stories on a given theme, often quite specialized. Mysterious Press, under Otto Penzler's editorship, has created anthologies of original mysteries about golf, basketball, horseracing, boxing, and poker, just to name a few. In 2004, Akashic Press began a series of city-based, original fiction collections with *Brooklyn Noir*. Other cities and places in the *Noir* series include Miami, Chicago, Detroit, the Twin Cities, London, Manhattan, Queens, and Wall Street, with twenty more, mostly international, titles in the works. There are hundreds of anthologies of short stories in print; while detective stories have shifted from the periodicals to books from large and small presses, clearly the appetite for them has not diminished.

We simply don't get sick of them. You would think we would. In one hundred and fifty years, surely every variation on the "inflexible form" has been tried. Strong writers take the elements of the formula and do find ways to bend them in intelligent ways. Sometimes the burning question is not who or what, but why. Sometimes the missing letter is right in front of our nose, and sometimes that shotgun in the corner is irrelevant. Sometimes the detective seems to be preternaturally intelligent, at other times they seem like just slightly better versions – smarter, gutsier, able to take a beating – of ourselves. Sometimes the ending leaves us thinking, even though the case was solved. Ira Glass, master of the short form on radio, puts it this way:

> every good story is a detective story, meaning every good story in any genre, raises some big question at the beginning, some *thing* that we want to find out. And then the process of the story, the reason why we keep reading or watching is that we just want to know

... we want the answer. Mysteries offer the satisfaction of this kind of story in the purest possible way. The question couldn't be clearer: there is a crime, who did it, and by the end, all is revealed. We know the answer. Light is shed. So they are hard to resist." (*This American Life*)

Excitement and enlightenment is a lot to ask of ten or twenty pages of writing, but detective stories deliver, over and over again.

References and Further Reading

Chandler, Raymond. *The Simple Art of Murder*. New York: Houghton Mifflin, 1950.

Glass, Ira. "Introduction to Act 2, Episode 28." 12 July 1996. *This American Life*. http://www.thisamericanlife.org/Radio_Episode.aspx?sched=619

Hammett, Dashiell. *Red Harvest*. 1929. New York: Random House, 1992.

Hawthorne, Julian, ed. *Library of the World's Greatest Mystery and Detective Stories: American*. Vol. 1. 6 vols. New York: Review of Reviews, 1907.

Hiaasen, Carl, ed. *The Best American Mystery Stories 2007*. New York: Houghton Mifflin, 2007.

Hillerman, Tony, ed. *The Best American Mystery Stories of the Century*. Boston: Houghton Mifflin, 2000.

Lehman, David. *The Perfect Murder*. New York: Free Press, 1989.

MacDonald, Gina, and Andrew MacDonald. *Shaman or Sherlock? The Native American Detective*. Westport, CT: Greenwood, 2002.

MacDonald, Ross. *On Crime Writing*. Santa Barbara: Capra Press, 1973.

Mason, Bobbi Ann. "Nancy Drew: The Once and Future Prom Queen." *Feminism in Women's Detective Fiction*. Ed. Glenwood Irons. Toronto: University of Toronto Press, 1995. 74–93.

Most, Glenn, and William Stowe, eds. *The Poetics of Murder: Detective Fiction and Literary Theory*. New York: Harcourt Brace Jovanovich, 1983.

Ogdon, Bethany. "Why Teach Popular Culture?" *College English* 63.4 (2001): 500–16.

Panek, Leroy. *The Origins of the American Detective Story*. Jefferson, NC: McFarland, 2006.

Paretsky, Sara. *Women on the Case*. New York: Delacorte, 1996.

Penzler, Otto, ed. *The Black Lizard Big Book of Pulps*. New York: Random House, 2007.

Poe, Edgar Allan. *The Murders in the Rue Morgue: The Dupin Tales*. New York: Modern Library, 2006.

Reed, David. *The Popular Magazine in Britain and America*. London: British Library, 1997.

Rollyson, Carl, ed. *Critical Survey of Mystery and Detective Fiction*. Rev. edn. Pasadena, CA: Salem Press, 2008.

Roth, Laurence. *Inspecting Jews: American Jewish Detective Stories*. New Brunswick, NJ: Rutgers University Press, 2004.

Todorov, Tzvetan. *The Poetics of Prose*. Trans. Richard Howard. Ithaca, NY: Cornell University Press, 1977.

Wells, Carolyn. *Technique of the Mystery Story*. Springfield, MA: Home Correspondence School, 1913.

Woods, Paula L., ed. *Spooks, Spies, and Private Eyes: Black Mystery, Crime, and Suspense Fiction of the 20th Century*. Garden City, NY: Doubleday, 1995.

28

The Asian American Short Story

Wenying Xu

The category of Asian American literature is not self-explanatory. Debates on what kinds of writing and what authors should be named Asian American have raised several important issues. The editors of the first anthology of Asian American literature, *Aiiieeeee!* (Chin et al. 1974), defined Asian Americans as "Filipino-, Chinese-, and Japanese-Americans, American born and raised, who got their China and Japan from the radio, off the silver screen, from television, out of comic books" (vii). This definition, however, stands in contradiction with several authors included in this very anthology, such as Carlos Bulosan, Louis Chu, and Oscar Penaranda, who were born in Asia. Elaine Kim tried to rid the concept "Asian Americans" of American birth while redefining Asian American literature as "published creative writings in English by Americans of Chinese, Japanese, Korean, and Filipino descent" (Kim xi). Her definition sparked further debate regarding the Asian American subject and media: Should Asian American literature depict only the American experience? Could it be written in other languages? For the fact remains that many Asian immigrant writers have written about the "old" and "new" worlds in dual languages. In addition to these perplexing issues, contentions also have centered on who represent Asian America and what groups within it are underrepresented. For Asian America embodies a diverse array of ethnicities, cultures, languages, and religions; as a matter of fact over sixty different Asian groups exist today in the United States. It is not an exaggeration to state that a Korean American is as different from a Filipino American as a French person from a Mexican. Asian Americans have come from countries as incommensurable as China and Iran, Vietnam and Indonesia, India and Japan. Given their different colonial pasts, immigrants from Asia also speak from radically different memories and sensibilities. It is fair to say that the concept of Asian American is one convenient to the bureaucracy, media, and market for the purpose of racial characterization but confining and irritating to those contained by it.

Until the mid-1990s, Chinese, Japanese, and Filipino American writers and critics dominated Asian American literature and its studies, for they were the most established groups in America at that time. In response to protests by the under-represented groups, *Position* published a special issue in the fall of 1997, edited by Elaine Kim and Lisa Lowe. It calls for "the creation and maintenance of solidarity across racial and national boundaries" (Kim and Lowe xii). This collection of essays marked a shift from the dominance of a largely East Asian American literature to a Pan Asian American literature, making space for a heterogeneous set of voices of recent immigrants from South and Southeast Asia. The new direction of Asian American literary studies does not only attempt to include all ethnicities within Asian America but also to explode the national boundary to include diasporic writers in the Pacific Rim.

Asian American literature, beginning as a protest against socioeconomic discrimi-nation and marginalization, political alienation, and cultural stereotypes, often draws its materials from the rich and troubled history that Asian Americans have lived – their participation in the construction of the transcontinental railroad, in the building of an economy in California, as well as their legalized exclusion and internment. Cognizant of this history, Asian American literature explores some common questions such as: What does it mean to be American? At what cost does one become an Ameri-can? How does one recognize oneself as a racial minority? What does the hyphenated identity mean? Questions of this sort determine the shared themes in Asian American literature of ethnicity, Americanization, racialization, gender and class exploitation, sexuality, generation gap, and the common misperception of Asian Americans as permanent aliens. The best-known Asian American fiction writers focus on the Ameri-can experience, writers such as Frank Chin, Gish Jen, David Wong Louie, and Don Lee, whose characters are mostly Americans of Asian descent embroiled in the pursuit of self-understanding, dignity, and connection with other Americans. A significant number of writers, such as Raja Rao, Ha Jin, and José Garcia Villa, however, find the old world more fascinating than the new. For them the English language and Ameri-can individualism offer ways of organizing personal experiences into fiction that are not available otherwise. There also are others who straddle the old and new worlds, like Diana Chang, Alex Kuo, Jhumpa Lahiri, and Andrew Lam, creating literature that portrays the double identity of Asian American, the diasporic identity among Asia, America, and Asian America, and the constant feelings of displacement both in the US and in one's home of birth. Together, Asian American writers demonstrate how heterogeneous Asian Americans are in identity, experience, and perspective.

Asian American literature is as diverse in style as any other literature. Unlike some literary traditions, it is impossible for this literature to trace its influence to a few major figures since its aesthetics and sensibilities come from multiple sources. In addition to the influences of American and European literatures, ranging from realism and naturalism to postmodernism, many Asian American writers have nourished their imagination by absorbing the rich literary and oral traditions indigenous to their ethnic cultures. Living between worlds offers them unique resources for the fusion of literary horizons, voices, and strategies to produce a vibrant body of literature that mesmerizes the reader with its unpredictable movements.

The Ancestors of the Asian American Short Story

At the turn of the nineteenth and twentieth centuries, it was two Eurasian sisters who gave birth to Asian American literature. Influenced by the then dominant mode of realism, the Eaton sisters wrote realistic fiction narrated from a limited point of view. Edith Maude Eaton is considered the first Asian American writer. She was born to a Chinese mother and an English father at a time when interracial marriage was a taboo in both cultures. Edith defied racism by changing her name to the Chinese Sui Sin Far, meaning narcissus. That she chose the name to declare her allegiance to the Chinese when she could easily have "passed" as Anglo American demonstrates her commitment to giving voice to Chinese American experiences. Indignant about the image of the Chinese in popular literature as unfeeling and custom-bound, Far was determined to restore humanity to the Chinese. Her best-known story, "The Story of One White Woman Who Married a Chinese," describes Minnie Carson's heartbreak with a white contemptuous husband and her new-found happiness with a Chinese man. On the brink of starvation with no money and nowhere to go, Minnie and her daughter are taken in and cared for by a compassionate and generous young Chinese man, Liu Kanghi. Far redefines manhood by the juxtaposition of the two husbands, Liu and Carson, to subvert the emasculating stereotypes of Chinese men as weak, passive, and asexual. In contrast with Carson, Liu is a man who respects, protects, and provides for the woman and child and does so without impinging on their independence. The white community's reaction of horror to Minnie's choice reflects the realities of sinophobia and antimiscegenation laws at the time (for example, in 1905 California declared interracial marriages "illegal and void"). The story's sequel, "My Chinese Husband," ends with Liu murdered by some Chinese who are opposed to the interracial union. This tragic ending invites the reader not simply to realize that racial prejudice exists in both cultures but also to gain an insight into the workings of racial oppression where entrenched power relations instill self-hatred as well as fear of difference in the oppressed.

Winnifred Eaton, Edith's younger sister, chose to adopt the pseudonym, Onoto Watanna for her writing career. During her time, the Japanese suffered less discrimination than the Chinese, and with her invented background as a Japanese-born, half Japanese descendant of samurai, Watanna fared better than her sister and enjoyed popularity as a novelist and a Hollywood screenwriter. Influenced by Pierre Loti (*Madame Chrysanthemum*) and John Luther Long (*Madame Butterfly*), who depicted flirtatious but tragic Japanese heroines enamored with white men, Watanna's Japanese heroines, however, display two major differences: many of her heroines are biracial, and they resist the image of the exotic sex-toy popularized by Loti and Long. Interestingly, many heroines in her short fiction are named "Kiku," the Japanese expression for "chrysanthemum," thus directly evoking Loti's work. Her subversion of the geisha stereotype happens in "A Half-Caste" (1899). The Kiku in this story is a half-Japanese tea-house girl who becomes the object of desire of a middle-aged American man,

Hilton. Ignorant of the fact that Kiku is his daughter, whose mother he had abandoned before the child's birth, Hilton pursues Kiku enthusiastically. When she discovers the truth, Kiku decides to break Hilton's heart in order to avenge her mother. Watanna is the first Asian American writer who didn't always write about Asians or about racial themes. In "Delia Dissents" (1908), for example, she chooses the point of view of an Irish domestic, whose coarsely rendered brogue is just as exaggerated as the pidgin of her Japanese heroines.

Following the Eaton sisters is a flourish of Asian American fiction writers, some of whom were born in the US, some who immigrated and settled in this country as adults, and some who traveled back and forth across the Pacific Ocean. Their aesthetics and subjects are largely determined by their differing experiences. Toshio Mori, for example, was born in California to Japanese immigrant parents. In his best-known book, *Yokohama, California* (1949), characters have been shaped by their lives in a Japanese community in California, exemplifying the hybrid culture and identities developed in such a community. "Japanese Hamlet," for instance, portrays Tom Fukunaga, who passes his young adult life studying the role he will never play. There is Hatsuye, who is in love with Clark Gable, and "is hopeful in spite of the fact she is hopeless" (165). Other stories of Mori's explore generational tension between first-, second-, and third-generation Japanese Americans who are struggling to balance the American demand to assimilate with their families' traditional beliefs and practices.

Yokohama, California was accepted for publication in 1941, but due to anti-Japanese sentiment during the war, Caxton Printers postponed it until after the war. This intervention altered the book's nature as well as the author's intention. Before the book was finally published, Mori added two stories set in the Topaz Camp, Utah (where he and his family were interned during World War II), to an already complete collection of stories set exclusively in his California hometown, fictionalized as Yokohama. These two camp stories changed the tones of what would have been funny, hopeful, and uplifting stories about Japanese immigrants' Americanization, for all the stories, minus the two camp stories, portray "a time of pride and accomplishment," in the words of Lawson Fusao Inada, who introduced the new edition (x). Several critics have noted the influence of Sherwood Anderson's *Winesburg, Ohio* on Mori's *Yokohama, California*, as it centers on a fictional community and its inhabitants. Interestingly, one of its stories, "Akiro Yano," features an aspiring author who imitates the style of Anderson. Although Mori structures his stories in the tradition of Anderson, his style and subject are entirely his own and never venture into Anderson's realm of the "grotesque."

Hisaye Yamamoto was also second-generation Japanese American, born and raised in California. At age 20, she was interned in the Poston Relocation Center in Arizona. Her camp experience profoundly shaped her literary production, such as "The Legend of Miss Sasagawara." Confinement has sensitized her to the devastating result of loss of control. In almost all her short stories, her central characters fight overwhelming odds. She portrays characters who are hurt, who have deviated from the norm, who are grasping for beauty in their desperation. Yamamoto is best known for her short story, "Seventeen Syllables," which has been reprinted at least twenty times in different anthologies since 1969. "Seventeen Syllables" depicts simultaneously Rosie's (the daughter's) awakening sexuality and Tome Hayashi's (the mother's) devastating annihilation. The tale's power lies in the vortex created by the mother's action outside her traditional Japanese Issei role of farm worker, cook, housekeeper, and wife. The narrative tensions arise out of a seemingly simple interest that Tome develops, haiku. At one level, the story depicts the cultural barriers that haiku creates and reveals among Tome, her husband, and her daughter; at another level, the tale unravels the destruction of a woman who creates independently.

Several early Asian American writers chose their native cultures as their subject, because the old world dominated their imagination more than the new. Issues of ethnicity and Americanization do not seem to matter to them as much as to other Asian American writers. For example, Raja Rao, from a well-known Brahmin family in India, settled in the US when he was aged 57. Most of his short stories portray the lives of women and the poor in Indian villages; it is their oppression and powerlessness that Rao is most keen on representing. "The Little Gram Shop," told from the perspective of a child, depicts the grandfather's life with ten concubines and the father's physical abuse of his pregnant wife. All the wives are subjected to routine violence. By interweaving the lives of three generations of a family, Rao underscores the continuing oppression of women in rural India. The Filipino writer, José Garcia Villa, immigrated to the US in the 1930s, and also set most of his short fiction in his home country. Many of them explore the universal themes of love, sorrow, and self sacrifice, and these stories never end happily. The failure of communication between lovers is a perennial theme in Villa's stories, as though the sexes were eternally divided. "Fence," the first story in his *Footnote to Youth*, describes two women who erected a fence between their houses out of spite, and the fence keeps apart two young people in love, one of whom dies while waiting for the other to play the guitar.

Among the early writers, some wrote stories set in both Asia and America. It is no surprise to readers that what they chose to write mirrors their diasporic existence. For instance, Bienvenido Santos was born in the Manila slums and came to the US in 1941 for graduate studies. In 1946 Santos returned to the Philippines, where he wrote his first collection of fiction, *You Lovely People* (1955). Almost all his characters are based on the Filipinos he met during his first stay in America. In 1958 he returned to the US on a Rockefeller creative writing fellowship, and at the end of the fellowship he went home once again. It was not until after a few more trips back and forth between the Philippines and the US that Santos settled in America and became a citizen, in 1976. Yet he chose to retire to his family home at the foot of Mount Mayon, Philippines, where he is buried. Santos's short fiction portrays Filipinos both in their villages and in exile in America struggling to acquire the feeling of belonging. Deromanticizing the naïve notion that one finds community at home, Santos creates characters who struggle equally hard to belong, whether they are in their native villages or exiled in the US. In his early stories collected in *Dwell in the Wilderness* (1985), Santos pictures the lives of poor farmers, young couples, and students who feel alienated due to poverty, sickness, passion, and aging. In *You Lovely People*, Santos deals mostly with the Pinoy expatriates in the US, who are preoccupied with creating a sense of community in a country where individualism is a dominant ethos. Reconciling the tension between the Filipino dream of solidarity and the American valorization of the individual occupies the central place in Santos's American stories.

Carlos Bulosan, born in the Philippines, arrived in Seattle at the age of 19. Much of his fiction was initially published in the 1940s in the *New Yorker*, *Harper's Bazaar*, and *Arizona Quarterly*. Almost all his stories are autobiographical fiction, representing his experiences in America and his family's in the Philippines. Bulosan writes from the perspective of an exile, without either the fantasy about a true home or the optimism for the promise of America. In "Homecoming," Bulosan articulates the deep sorrow of his protagonist, who returns to the Philippines because "America had crushed his spirit" (Hagedorn, *Charlie Chan 2* 31). At home, however, he is pained by the fact that "his mother and sisters had suffered the same terrors of poverty, the same humiliations of defeat that he had suffered in America" (33). At the end of the tale, Bulosan exiles his protagonist once again without offering a definitive destination. By refusing to offer any clue where the protagonist might find "home," the story seems to allegorize the condition of homelessness of all Filipinos, who wander in the world as postcolonial subjects, who live under the colonial rule of the US, or in the postcolonial homeland dominated by American culture and economy.

The Age of Blooming: The Contemporary Asian American Short Story

"Let the hundred flowers bloom" is an accurate description of Asian American literature since the 1970s. Given the change of immigration patterns when the exclusionary immigration laws eased after World War II and when the Immigration Act abandoned "national origins" in 1965 as the basis for establishing quotas, Asian American communities have grown not only new generations but also literary talents. Asians are now a fast-growing group in the US, a population projected to increase from 11 million in 2003 to 20 million by 2020. In the literary scene, different from the earlier generation, which consisted of mainly Chinese, Japanese, and Filipino American writers, contemporary writers trace their cultural origins to much more diverse roots, such as Vietnam, Iran, Korea, Indonesia, Cambodia, Pakistan, India, Laos, Thailand, Sri Lanka, etc.

In the contemporary generation, Indian American writers have gained increasing visibility, not only in quantity but also in craft; among these are Jhumpa Lahiri, Bharati Mukherjee, and Chitra Divakaruni. Divakaruni, born in Calcutta, India, arrived in the US at the age of 20. She has published two collections of short stories, *Arranged Marriage* (1995) and *The Unknown Errors of Our Lives* (2001), with the first receiving various awards including a 1996 American Book Award from the Before Columbus Foundation, and several stories appearing in *Best American Short Stories* and

The Pushcart Prize Anthology. Her stories largely involve Indian immigrant women living at the border between the old world of patriarchy and the new one of supposed possibilities and choices. Juxtaposing the physical and psychological landscapes of India and America, she explores the experiences of women who devise strategies of survival in changing cultural contexts. One pervasive image in *Arranged Marriage* is of women's attires. In "Clothes," for example, the protagonist Sumita's development is suggested by various stages of clothing: from her traditional saris to her clandestine posing in American clothes for her husband, and eventually to her widow's white sari. The image of her in a mirror at the end of the story, dressed in a blouse and skirt, symbolizes her decision to remain in the US and become a teacher. Divakaruni's use of diverse points of view fascinates her readers. For instance, "The Bats," reminiscent of Henry James's *What Maisie Knew*, uses a child narrator to tell the story of her father's abuse of her mother in guileless terms: "Things fell a lot when Father was around, maybe because he was so large" (*Arranged* 2). The only story narrated from the husband's perspective, "Disappearance," reveals the wife's suffering through the husband's blindness to her situation. Many of the stories end with the women breaking away from expectations and imposed forms of living, and starting again. Once the women accept what they often refuse – "It's how we survive, we Indian women whose lives are half light and half darkness, stopping short of revelations that would otherwise crisp away our skins" ("Disappearance" 167), as one of the women says – the stories become chronicles of hope.

The Unknown Errors of Our Lives demonstrates a shift in Divakaruni's concerns. Though she still privileges the plight of immigrant women, these stories widen her negotiation with cultural adjustment, toward more general human themes of memory, forgiveness, and acceptance, the fear of wrong choices and regret, age, and family. The characters have to come to terms with the confusing coexistence in their lives of memories of past and present, India and America. As in the earlier collection, many women leave India with the intention of living fuller and freer lives, only to find themselves unsure of how to proceed and what to believe in a situation that is more insidious than the one from which they escaped. Divakaruni problematizes the characteristics and consequences of Americanization. In "The Lives of Strangers," Leela's visit to India after an attempted suicide leads to her gradual release of the "absurdly American" notion of individual control and her appropriation of her aunt's more interconnected notion of destiny (67). Interestingly, American-born Indians revert to the old ways, as in "The Unknown Errors of Our Lives," where a couple chooses to have an arranged marriage because, as he says, "the alternative – it doesn't seem to work that well, does it?" (214).

Jhumpa Lahiri, daughter of Bengali immigrant parents in London, moved to the US with her family when she was two. Her debut collection, *Interpreter of Maladies* (1999), won the 2000 Pulitzer Prize for fiction. It contains nine stories that explore common motifs, such as exile, displacement, loneliness, difficult relationships, and problems about communication. Her characters vary from Indians, Indian émigrés, and American-born Indians to white Americans involved with them. Although Lahiri does not privilege the American experience over the Indian, there is no nostalgia for Indian traditions either in her stories. What is fascinating in Lahiri's stories is the fact that her American-born Indian characters are more American than Indian and their introduction to their ancestral cultures does not come from parents or the diasporic community, as is true in many other Asian American writers; rather, it comes from sources common to other Americans. For example, Mr. and Mrs. Das in "Interpreter of Maladies" learn about Indian culture from their Indian tour guide, and Shukumar in "A Temporary Matter" and Lilia in "When Mr. Pirzada Came to Dine" find information about India in the library. In some of her stories, ethnicity seems almost to be incidental, like "This Blessed House," in which Twinkle, writing a master's thesis on an Irish poet, becomes thrilled by the discovery of Christian knick-knacks hidden all over their newly purchased house.

If one asks who is the most widely read Indian American writer, one is likely to hear the name of Bharati Mukherjee, mainly for her novels. Her short fiction, just like her novels, centers on the themes of immigration, displacement, and invention of identities to investigate what she calls "the making of Americans." It is safe to say that *Darkness* (1985) is a ground-breaking collection because it is the first set of stories to treat Indian immigrants in Canada and the US. *Darkness* ventures into different points of view ranging from male, female, Indian, Indian American to white Canadian and American. "Isolated Incidents" depicts the attitude of the Canadian government toward the immigrants through the consciousness of Ann, a worker in the office of Human Rights in Toronto. Her idealism has gradually yielded to indifference: "Now she saw problems only as a bureaucrat. Deal with the sure things. Pass the other off. Get documentation. Promise nothing" (81). "The Lady from Lucknow" explores the theme of travel – physical travel that gives rise to emotional travel – in portraying a sophisticated, well-traveled Pakistani woman, Nafeesa. Nafeesa is married to an IBM employee who, as an immigrant, must work harder than others to prove his competence. Nafeesa, bored with domesticity, begins an affair with an Indian American doctor. She realizes that she is truly a traveler who is "at home everywhere, because she is never at home anywhere" (33). Despite the feelings of displacement and alienation of her characters, Mukherjee asserts in the collection's introduction that "[i]t's possible – with sharp ears and the right equipment – to hear America singing even in the seams of the dominant culture" (3).

Mukherjee's second collection, *The Middleman and Other Stories* (1988), won the National Book Critics Circle Award for Fiction. Her new characters have expanded to include a Latin American, a Vietnam veteran, a Vietnamese, a Filipino, Americans, and even Europeans. Unlike the characters in *Darkness*, the women protagonists in these stories are capable of adjusting to the new environment. The wife in "Wife Story" runs away from her husband in India and enters graduate studies in New York. She becomes aware of her change when her husband comes to visit, realizing that she has traveled too far to return to the role of a traditional wife. Perhaps the most powerful story in *The Middleman* is "The Management of Grief," which is widely anthologized. It is based on the real event of the Air India tragedy that lost 300 Indian-Canadian lives. The story is told by Shaila who has lost her husband and both sons in this accident. She assists the social worker, Judith, in communicating with an old illiterate Sikh couple whose sons were also on the doomed plane. During the meeting with the old couple, she experiences the incommensurability of two cultures as the couple refuse to sign any papers to receive government help, for doing so would be tantamount to admitting their sons are dead. Keeping hope alive, they feel, is their duty, a mental state beyond both Shaila's translation and Judith's comprehension.

Similar to the explorations of these Indian American writers, the Iranian American, Nahid Rachlin, also examines the immigrants', particularly women's, lives in the US. Rachlin was born in Iran and came to America as a student at the age of 17. The themes of repression, alienation, displacement, and regret that appear in her novels are also present in her collection of fiction, *Veil* (1992). Some of the stories in this collection dramatize the terrible human cost of the Iran–Iraq war through the sufferings of frustrated yet submissive mothers, such as "Departures," which depicts the panic stricken mother cooking the farewell lunch for her son, who has been drafted into the army. While she fears for her son's life, her husband glorifies martyrdom. The stories set in the US also achieve psychological intensity from references to war and events in Iran. They all feature deeply troubled Iranian immigrants who must wear cheerful masks around American spouses, friends, and colleagues while experiencing guilt and alienation. To a certain degree, America offers them the same limitations they think they have left behind in Iran. The protagonist in "Dark Gravity" is disturbed by her second pregnancy as her American husband is thrilled, for she remembers the bitterness between her parents because they had too many children. She fears the same situation in her marriage even though she is supposedly living in a place where women are said to have more choices than in Iran.

One of the fresh and exciting voices in Asian American literature is Vietnamese American. Their trauma in what they call "The US War" has such a strong hold on their imagination that their American experiences seem to be phantasmal. Andrew Lam was born in Saigon, Vietnam, in 1963. Two days before the fall of Saigon, his family got on a crowded cargo plane. They passed through refugee camps in Guam and California before settling in the San Francisco Bay Area. Lam's fiction reflects his experiences as a Vietnamese immigrant whose memory of the US War dominates his daily imagination. His earliest stories, "Dark Wood and Shadows" and "On the Perfume," describe events from his childhood in wartime Vietnam. His later stories utilize magical realism to infuse comical elements into his otherwise serious stories about protagonists trapped between their American life and their haunting memory of the war. In "Grandma's Tales," the Vietnamese American protagonist relates the sudden reincarnation of his dead grandmother, who galvanizes a cocktail-party crowd with tales from her past, then runs off to see the world with a handsome stranger. Her reincarnation is a humorous metaphor for the power of Vietnamese familial and cultural heritage.

Until recently, Asian American literature has been dominated by writers living on the mainland, more on the west coast than anywhere else. Only recently are Asian

American writers in Hawaii beginning to draw readers' and critics' attention with their unique experience (not as a racial minority in the same sense as their counterparts on the mainland) and their creolized imagination between their ancestral origins and the indigenous culture of Hawaii. Susan Nunes was born in Hilo, Hawaii, to Japanese and Portuguese parents. She has been published widely in both Hawaii and the mainland. Her collection, *A Small Obligation and Other Stories of Hilo* (1982), has been a dominant influence on Hawaiian writers. Amy, the central protagonist in the book, sharing a common background with Nunes, negotiates her identity in a mixture of Japanese and Portuguese ancestry. In "The Grandmother," Amy insists on seeing herself as a hybrid and rebels against the "purebred" orchid that symbolizes an unattainable cultural wholeness. Some of the stories told by other characters, however, express hope for Amy and her quest for identity in the midst of chaos. Nunes's main motif of the inevitability and necessity of change is best illuminated through Mr. Naito's consciousness in "The Yardman," in which the imagery of water, pond, and fish suggests Amy's tumultuous search for identity and her hopeful future.

Darrell H. Y. Lum was born in Honolulu to a Chinese immigrant father and a Chinese American mother and has published two collections, *Sun: Short Stories and Drama* (1980) and *Pass On, No Pass Back* (1990). His main concerns in these stories are the preservation of Hawaiian culture and the challenge to racial and cultural inequities within Hawaiian and American society. Lum tells his stories mostly in pidgin, a language he grew up speaking. Pidgin is not only the medium of his stories but also serves to state his thesis that a language being marginalized as substandard creates a community that is nevertheless rich in culture, humor, and humanity. Through the eyes of his characters, who are often young or elderly, the events of daily life take on an absurd and humorous quality. Striving to make sense of their marginalized positions, Lum's characters often approach insights into the self and society, but more likely than not, these insights remain just beyond articulation. Beneath the humor and the good fun "talk story" of his work, Lum's fiction encourages readers to consider larger questions and to think more deeply about how race and class structure much of Hawaiian and American society.

Among the new generation of Asian American writers, a significant number are American-born, and their stories are often peopled with Asian American yuppies, in whose lives gender, sexuality, and love are more relevant than ethnicity, immigration, and poverty. One may want to qualify this statement by adding that gender issues are interlocked with ethnicity, as in the works of Frank Chin, Don Lee, and David Wong Louie. Some of these writers also deviate from the earlier generation in that they have created characters that are not exclusively Asian American, for instance, Gish Jen.

Frank Chin was born in Berkeley, California, to a Chinese immigrant father and a fourth-generation Chinese mother. His collection, *The Chinaman Pacific & Frisco R.R. Co.* (1988), is mostly autobiographical in tone, depicting the lives of young Chinese American men – usually aspiring writers – who are inflicted with self-loathing due to their ambivalent relationship to the normative model of masculinity in the

American popular culture. Monologue is the dominant mode of narration. Common to all the stories is Chin's use of the railroad to symbolize both the historical experience of Chinese Americans and their hardworking, courageous, and defiant masculinity, but sometimes his representation of this masculinity can go amok. In "The Eat and Run Midnight People," Chin relies on bawdy scenes of food/appetite, sex, and the railroad to attest to the masculine aggression of the first-person narrator. The fantastic language, in which sex, food, and train cut and spill into each other, narrates the violence of the male body as a potently sexualized machine, an engine unstoppable in its racing and "digging" (13).

Don Lee's characters are Americans whose ethnicity plays a minor role in their drama. Lee is well known as the editor of the literary journal *Ploughshares*. The stories in *Yellow* are loosely connected by their shared setting, the fictional town of Rosarita Bay, California, and shared characters, many of whom are second- or third-generation Korean Americans like Lee. In these stories about contemporary, post-immigration Asian America, Lee explores issues of relationship, love, family, and ambiguities inherent in human experiences. The first, "The Price of Eggs in China," is a quasi-crime story revealing the irrational nature of love: a Japanese American chair-maker, rivaling for his girlfriend against her former college friend, goes to great lengths to win his girlfriend back. "Voir Dire" is a court drama, in which a Korean American lawyer wrestles with the question of ethics when he is assigned to defend a drug addict who killed his girlfriend's son.

David Wong Louie was born in Rockville Center, New York, to Chinese immigrant parents who operated a laundry in a Long Island suburb. *Pangs of Love* (1991) won the *Los Angeles Times* Art Seidenbaum Award for First Fiction and the *Ploughshares* John C. Zacharis First Book Award for 1991. "Displacement," from that collection, was published in *The Best American Short Stories 1989*. The eleven stories explore ambivalent situations of Asian American (mostly Chinese American) men in contemporary society and their feelings of alienation. Though thoroughly assimilated and successful, many of the characters occupy liminal positions in their families and in society. This unstable position is allegorized by the otter in "Bottle of Beaujolais" – it lives in a tank that replicates the environment of its lakeshore home and is subject to the whims of its caretaker. Louie dramatizes diverse forms of displacement such as dislocation and separation from a past history or family. For instance, Mrs. Chow, the aristocratic immigrant in "Displacement," is humiliated by but must accept her husband's subservience to their employer and a future landlady's callous comments, "I'm willing to take a risk on you. ... besides, I'm real partial to Chinese take-out" (29). In stories such as "Birthday," "Pangs of Love," "The Movers," and "Social Science," characters inhabit houses that are not theirs and have occupations that they feel alienated from. The narrators of these stories struggle but often fail to establish connections with family or places. Henry, in "Social Science," for example, watches as a man named David Brinkley begins to appropriate the touchstones of his life – his house, his ex-wife, his students. Many Chinese builders of the Great Wall, in "Disturbing the Universe," die broken-hearted at the loss of home – "After all, ours was never a transient race; we grow thick, deep roots" (182). Interracial relationships are addressed in stories like "Birthday," "Love on the Rocks," and "Social Science," highlighting the precariousness of the Asian American man's position, caught between cultural expectations and their own desires. Louie's prose is spare and suggestive – a dark humor offers ironic insights into the predicaments of his characters.

Gish Jen was the first significant Asian American writer from the East Coast, representing a different experience of Americanization from that in the West. Her short stories have won many awards, including the Henfield Foundation *Transatlantic Review* Award (1983), prizes from the Katherine Ann Porter Contest (1987), and the Boston MBNA Urban-Arts Project (1988). Her collection, *Who's Irish?* (1999), showcases eight stories that explore the themes of assimilation, identity, displacement, generational conflict, interracial relationships, and the American Dream. This collection is not exclusively Asian American in its subjects, for example, the title story portrays the Irish Americans and "House, House, Home" has central characters who are African American. Her other stories, "Bellying Up" and "Eating Crazy," for instance, feature only white American characters. "The Small Concerns of Sparrows," on the other hand, is set in the PRC in 1958 and comprises only Chinese characters. One also meets characters in her stories who are Latino American, Scandinavian American, and Hawaiian American.

"In the American Society" and "The Water Faucet Vision" are peopled with the same cast as in her better-known long works, *Typical American* (1992) and *Mona in the Promised Land* (1997). Their chief protagonists are the immigrant parents Ralph and Helen Chang, and their American-born children Callie and Mona. Both stories are told in the voice of Callie, the older daughter. The two children act as mediator and witness of the conflicts occurring between father and mother, and between their parents and American society. "In the American Society" consists of two parts: the first recounts how Ralph wants to run his pancake house like his "kingdom," in which he tries to trade benevolence for his employees' loyalty. The second describes how Helen endeavors to gain admittance to the elitist town country club. However, the Changs' application receives the same polite dismissal as the African Americans'. "The Water Faucet Vision" focuses on Ralph and Helen's marital conflict. As their argument evolves into violence, Callie, who is attending a Catholic girls' school, starts to practice ostentatious piety and prays for a miraculous reconciliation between her parents. What charms her reader most is Jen's talent in telling a heavy tale with humor.

Asian American short fictions are so vast in number, themes, and styles that it is impossible to map out the entire terrain in this brief chapter. Despite the diversity within, Asian American writers are unified in their struggle against stereotypes such as the model minority, the passive oriental, and the unassimilable aliens. As problematic as the classification of Asian American is, it has enabled this dynamic, growing body of literature to gain the attention of the reading public and critics. Asian American writers through fiction delineate and construct the specificities of Asian American identities even as they endeavor to transcend ethnicity.

References and Further Reading

Bulosan, Carlos. *The Laughter of My Father*. New York: Harcourt, Brace, 1944.

———. *The Philippines Is in the Heart*. Quezon City, Philippines: New Day, 1978.

Chang, Lan Samantha. *Hunger*. New York: Penguin, 1998.

Chin, Frank. *The Chinaman Pacific & Frisco R.R. Co.* Minneapolis, MN: Coffee House, 1988.

Chin, Frank, Jeffery Chan, Lawson Inada, and Shawn Wong, eds. *Aiiieeeee! An Anthology of Asian American Writers*. Washington, DC: Howard University Press, 1974.

Chiu, Cristina. *Troublemaker and Other Stories*. New York: Berkley Books, 2001.

Divakaruni, Chitra. *Arranged Marriage*. New York: Doubleday, 1995.

———. *The Unknown Errors of Our Lives*. New York: Doubleday, 2001.

Far, Sui Sin. *Mrs. Spring Fragrance and Other Writings*. Urbana: University of Illinois Press, 1995.

Ha Jin. *The Bridge Groom: Stories*. New York: Pantheon, 2000.

———. *A Good Fall: Stories*. New York: Pantheon, 2009.

Hagedorn, Jessica, ed. *Charlie Chan Is Dead*. New York: Penguin, 1993.

———. *Charlie Chan Is Dead 2*. New York: Penguin, 2004.

Huang, Guiyou, ed. *Asian American Short Story Writers: An A-to-Z Guide*. Westport, CT: Greenwood Press, 2003.

Jen, Gish. "Bellying Up." *Iowa Review* 12.4 (Fall 1981): 93–4.

———. "Eating Crazy." *Yale Review* 74 (Spring 1985): 425–33.

———. *Who's Irish? Stories*. New York: Random House, 1999.

Kim, Elaine H. *Asian American Literature: An Introduction to the Writings and Their Social Context*. Philadelphia: Temple University Press, 1982.

Kim, Elaine H., and Lisa Lowe, eds. *Position – Special Issue: New Formations, New Questions: Asian American Studies* 5.2 (Fall 1997).

Lahiri, Jhumpa. *Interpreter of Maladies*. Boston: Houghton Mifflin, 1999.

Lam, Andrew. "Dark Wood and Shadows." *Transfer* 57 (Fall 1989): 24–35.

———. "Grandma's Tales." *Amerasia Journal* 20.3 (1994): 65–70.

———. "On the Perfume." *Manoa* 6.2 (1994): 132–41.

———. "Slingshot." *ZYZZYVA* (Winter 1998): 151–63.

Lee, Don. *Yellow*. New York: W. W. Norton, 2001.

Lim, Shirley Geok-lin, Mayumi Tsutakawa, and Margarita Donnelly, eds. *The Forbidden Stitch: An Asian American Women's Anthology*. Corvallis, OR: Calyx Books, 1989.

Louie, David Wong. *Pangs of Love*. New York: Knopf, 1991.

Lum, Darrell H. Y. *Pass On, No Pass Back*. Honolulu: Bamboo Ridge Press, 1990.

———. *Sun: Short Stories and Drama*. Honolulu: Bamboo Ridge Press, 1980.

Mori, Toshio. *The Chauvinist and Other Stories*. Los Angeles: Asian American Studies Center, University of California at Los Angeles, 1979.

———. *Unfinished Message: Selected Works of Toshio Mori*. Berkeley, CA: Heyday Books, 2000.

———. *Yokohama, California*. Caldwell, OH: Caxton Printers, 1949. 2nd edn. Seattle: University of Washington Press, 1985.

Mukherjee, Bharati. *Darkness*. New York: Penguin, 1985.

———. *The Middleman and Other Stories*. New York: Fawcett Crest, 1988.

Nunes, Susan. *A Small Obligation and Other Stories of Hilo*. Honolulu: Bamboo Ridge Press, 1982.

Phan, Aimee. *We Should Never Meet: Stories*. New York: St. Martin's Press, 2004.

Rachlin, Nahid. *Veil: Short Stories*. San Francisco: City Lights, 1992.

Rao, Raja. *The Cow of the Barricades and Other Stories*. Madras: Oxford University Press, 1997.

———. *The Policeman and the Rose*. Delhi: Oxford University Press, 1978.

Santos, Bienvenido N. *Brother, My Brother: A Collection of Short Stories*. 1960. Makati City, Philippines: Bookmark, 1991.

———. *The Day the Dancers Came*. 1967. Makati City, Philippines: Bookmark, 1991.

———. *Dwell in the Wilderness: Selected Short Stories (1931–1941)*. Quezon City, Philippines: New Day, 1985.

————. *Scent of Apples: A Collection of Stories.* Seattle: University of Washington Press, 1997.

————. *You Lovely People.* 1955. Makati City, Philippines: Bookmark, 1991.

Villa, José Garcia. *Footnote to Youth: Tales of the Philippines and Others.* New York: Scribner, 1933.

————. *Mir-i-Nisa: A Tale of the South Sea.* Manila, Philippines: Alberto S. Florentino, 1966.

————. *Selected Stories of Jose Garcia Villa.* Manila, Philippines: Alberto S. Florentino, 1962.

Watanna, Onoto. *"A Half Caste" and Other Writings.* Urbana: University of Illinois Press, 2003.

Yamamoto, Hisaye. *Seventeen Syllables and Other Stories.* Latham, NY: Kitchen Table: Women of Color Press, 1988.

29

The Jewish American Story

Andrew Furman

I would like to begin by probing the curious ambiguity of this chapter's title, the title suggested to me by the editors of this volume. For it has become something of a cliché to refer to the Jewish experience in America (*the* Jewish American story) as one of our country's greatest immigrant success stories, to think of Jewish Americans as the ethnic group that paved the way for a subsequent cohort of "model minorities," the Asian Americans. The true story of the Jews in America, of course (like the story of the manifold Asian immigrant communities in the United States), has been somewhat more complicated. As Sarah Blair and Jonathan Freedman observed in their Introduction to a special issue of the *Michican Quarterly Review* devoted to the Jewish American experience, "Jews have been insistently part of the American scene for more than a century (and longer), but have in that time been described as subversive aliens and true-blue patriots; outsiders to the cultural dominant and insiders to the national narrative" (509).

Unsurprisingly, perhaps, the history of the Jewish American story – that is to say, works of short fiction crafted by Jewish Americans – has mirrored the vertiginous trajectory of the Jewish American experience. For it is fair to say that the Jewish American story suffered through an early stage as the nearly invisible outsider, enjoyed a middle period as the popular, even fetishized, cultural insider, and currently vacillates between the thorny literary categories of "mainstream," "ethnic," and "multicultural." The capriciousness of the literary marketplace, however, tells us little about the actual words on the page and the writers who have produced them. The canon of Jewish American stories is now vast, varied, and impressive, and any attempt to define this body of work through narrow categories runs the risk of excluding any number of noteworthy writers and works. Still, in the pages ahead, I hope to limn the major writers and themes that have left an indelible mark on the American short story of the twentieth century, and identify emergent writers and themes that have already impacted the literature of our new century.

Immigrant Beginnings

The numbers are staggering. Between 1880 and 1920, nearly two million Jews, predominantly Eastern European (or Ashkenazi), immigrated to the United States. Although there were Jews writing in America preceding these dates, our first prominent Jewish American writers would emerge from this great wave of immigration. The literary establishment in the United States, to be sure, was reluctant to acknowledge their bona fides. Henry James rather famously objected to the influence that Jewish immigrants wielded upon the American vernacular, and on the American character, generally, in *The American Scene* (1907). Even as late as 1948, as Sanford Pinsker has noted, the 1000-plus-page anthology, *The Literary History of the United States*, declined to include a single Jewish American fiction writer (*Jewish-American* ix).

Still, a select few Jewish American writers at the turn of the century burst through the cultural barriers to secure a readership. Abraham Cahan and Anzia Yezierska are, perhaps, the most prominent figures of this early cohort. Their stories (and novels) typically pivot upon the tensions their protagonists feel between the Jewish values and traditions of the old world and the "American" values of their adopted country. These stories, written in the social realist style of William Dean Howells, offer a precious glimpse of the mores of a predominantly Orthodox Jewish community and their material and spiritual struggles on the Lower East Side of New York. Interestingly, the first Jewish American stories celebrated by mainstream readers usually depict Jewish heroes and heroines willing to assimilate to American (read: white) codes of conduct. The loss of old world traditions is often poignantly rendered, but usually assuaged by an immigrant gratitude for the heady material and romantic offerings of the new world. In Cahan's "A Ghetto Wedding," collected in *The Imported Bridegroom and Other Stories of the New York Ghetto* (1898), and more recently collected in *Jewish American Literature: A Norton Anthology* (Chametzky et al. 2001), he documents in gritty detail the poverty that defines the immigrant existence of his protagonists, Nathan and Goldy. Though only sweatshop workers, they plan a lavish wedding, renting out an enormous hall and sending "[o]ver a hundred invitations, printed in as luxurious a black and gold as ever came out of an Essex Street hand press" (127). The wedding, predictably, is a disaster, as only a very few guests attend: "a greater number of the invited friends were kept away by lack of employment: some having their presentable clothes in the pawn shop; others avoiding the expense of a wedding present, or simply being too cruelly borne down by their cares to have a mind for the excitement of the wedding" (129–30). Importantly, however, the story ends on a buoyant note. Although drunken street toughs harass the newlyweds on their way to their meager apartment, they feel a stream of happiness coursing through their veins as they, and Cahan, take heart in "the enchanted world in which they now dwelt" (134).

The stories in Anzia Yezierska's *Hungry Hearts* (1920), which earned Yezierska a nice advance from Houghton Mifflin and a whopping $10,000 in film rights from

Samuel Goldwyn, hew largely to the same formula. Yezierska, as Blanche Gelfant aptly put it, "hoped to present the abjected poor as desirable people who desired, above all else, to become Americans" (xxv). This isn't to say that Yezierska's work (or Cahan's) unequivocally lauds the America that greeted their community of Jewish immigrants. Several of the stories in *Hungry Hearts* poignantly evoke the insuperable cycle of poverty which faced most immigrants; others take deadly aim at the hypocrisy and paternalism of those whites who would Americanize Jewish immigrants; and Yezierska explores with considerable nuance the sacrifices that her Jewish immigrants would make as they assimilated. Still, the story "Soap and Water" illustrates the overwhelming force and appeal of new world values. In the story, the Dean of a teacher's college, evocatively named Miss Whiteside, withholds our Jewish heroine's diploma because of her unwashed appearance. "'Soap and water are cheap,'" Whiteside admonishes our heroine. "'Any one can be clean'" (102). While Yezierska acidly evokes the hypocrisy of the Whitesides of the world, these agents of clean society ("While they condemned me as unfit to be a teacher, because of my appearance," our heroine bemoans, "I was slaving [in a laundry] to keep them clean"), our heroine longs for beauty and cleanliness all the same, and achieves this American ideal by the end of the story (102). She ultimately graduates from college, leaves the sweatshop behind, and joins the ranks of the white and clean. "'My past was the forgotten night,'" she ebulliently declares. "'Sunrise was all around me. ... America! I found America'" (109).

The Golden Age

While the first generation of Jewish immigrants from Europe contributed several memorable stories to the canon of American literature, it would be their sons and daughters – most notably Saul Bellow, Bernard Malamud, Philip Roth, and Grace Paley – who moved the Jewish American story from the margins to the center of the American literary scene. The enormous individual talents of these writers most significantly account for the hoopla over their work in the 1950s and 1960s. Still, their collective sensibility – a wry skepticism of cultural conditions rooted in an ecumenical ethical humanism – arose in a particular sociological moment, and under particular cultural pressures. These writers were acutely aware of the great sacrifices their parents made to ensure the more prosperous American identity of their offspring. Such pressure often proved unbearable, as Delmore Schwartz dramatizes so poignantly in his classic story, "In Dreams Begin Responsibilities," a story which serves as something of a bridge between the immigrant and post-immigrant generation of Jewish American writers. Conditions, social and material, certainly improved for the second generation of Jewish Americans as America gradually outgrew its anti-immigrant, nativist ethos of the 1920s and 1930s. An old Jewish quip goes, "What's the difference between the International Ladies Garment Workers Association and the American Physicians Association? One generation." Yet the children of immigrants coming of age in the 1940s and 1950s were still beset by anti-Semitism that persisted across the American zeitgeist. Indeed, it was this lingering sense of alienation and marginality that provided the essential grist for the fictional mills of this dazzling post-immigrant generation of writers. The Jewish protagonists created by Bellow and his cohorts typically struggle to affirm a viable ethical identity in an America that has yet to live up to the ideals of its conception. These characters, recognizably ethnic Jews, yet usually not observant, resonated with both Jewish and gentile readers. "All men are Jews," Malamud famously declared, and mainstream readers apparently agreed.

Writing in the wake of high modernism, its fetishizing of the aesthetic and its associated nihilism, Bellow, as Cynthia Ozick has noted, accepted as his charge from the beginning of his career to "restore the soul to American literature" ("Farcical Combat" 238). The writer, Bellow has contended, "should perform a moral function ... should provide emotional, spiritual stuff – those are rather old fashioned ideas, but I don't think that people have really given up old fashioned ideas – they just scoff at them, while in reality they continue to live by them" (qtd. in Boyers 7). As pointedly as any other story in his canon, Bellow's "Him with His Foot in His Mouth" illustrates Bellow's indefatigable efforts to affirm a higher spirituality than that afforded by America's credo of anarchic individualism and rampant materialism. The story revolves around an aging musicologist, Hershchel Shawmut, who receives word from an old colleague that an insensitive retort he made to a college librarian some thirty-five years ago traumatized her for life. Shawmut, a brooder like many of Bellow's protagonists, writes the librarian an extended letter to reflect upon his predilection for insulting people.

Shawmut begins his letter by recounting his first years as a Music History Professor at a WASP-dominated institution. Shawmut's refusal to court the establishment contrasts notably with Eddie Walish, a colleague of equally humble origins, but who wears "good English tweeds and Lloyd & Haig brogans" (380). Shawmut derides Walish's phoniness, his deference to the haughty blue-bloods of the establishment, through his recollection of Walish's clownishness: "He has a sort of woodwind laugh, closer to oboe than to clarinet, and he releases his laugh from the wide end of his nose as well as from his carved pumpkin mouth. He grins like Alfred E. Neuman from the cover of *Mad* magazine, the successor of Peck's Bad Boy" (380). The passage demonstrates, generally, Bellow's unsurpassed precision in rendering a character's essence through portraiture.

Although Shawmut attempts to resist Walish's kow-towing to the establishment, he recognizes that he too cultivated a false self of overblown civility to succeed in his profession. He attributes his random insults to others, like the librarian, to his Yiddish upbringing, which rejects this veneer of cordiality. Shawmut instinctively wishes to honor his Jewish upbringing, the tough-mindedness of the Yiddish language and his deep and abiding commitment to family, yet he must reckon with the reality that he was victimized by his family. In short, his brother Philip, who marries a rich gentile woman and moves to Texas, convinces him to invest in a fraudulent financial scheme.

In an extended section of the story, rich in detail, Shawmut reflects upon his brother's embrace of what can only be called a distinctly American brand of materialism and self-centered individualism. Bellow's depiction of his brother's sprawling Texas estate evokes its complete lack of human warmth. Philip's wife, for example, breeds pit bulldogs, which bare their teeth at Shawmut, terrifying him. The utter lack of human warmth at Philip's mansion provokes Shawmut's nostalgia for their childhood home, materially impoverished but rich with love. As Shawmut reflects of Philip, "Philly had put himself into Tracy's hands for full Americanization. To achieve this (obsolete) privilege, he paid the price of his soul" (402).

The restive Shawmut ultimately embraces a spiritual vision and achieves some measure of peace. Although he initially seeks to affirm intellectualism as a credo to resist the American ethos of materialism, the convictions of his elderly Canadian neighbor speak to him more profoundly: "Intellect, worshiped by all, brings us as far as natural science, and this science, although very great, is incomplete. Redemption from *mere* nature is the work of feeling and of the awakened eye of the Spirit. The body, she says, is subject to forces of gravity. But the soul is ruled by levity, pure. ... I listen to this and have no mischievous impulses" (413).

Such concerted introspection is typical of Bellow's protagonists and defies the stoic, hard-boiled ethos of the archetypal Hemingway hero. Often exceedingly brainy, many of Bellow's protagonists, like Shawmut, ultimately recognize the limits of straight intellectualism and affirm an inner, often emotive, knowledge. Other particularly notable stories in Bellow's canon – recently collected in *Saul Bellow: Collected Stories* (2001) – include "The Old System," "Zetland: By a Character Witness," "Looking for Mr. Green" (which addresses Black–Jewish relations), and "Something to Remember Me By."

Philip Roth burst upon the literary scene with his National Book Award–winning *Goodbye, Columbus* (1959), a collection which includes a novella and five stories. The book raised the hackles of several rabbis and lay people in the Jewish community as Roth depicts, in fierce detail, the moral slippage that accompanied the prosperity of post-immigrant Jews, who left New York for the more leafy suburbs of New Jersey. "Defender of the Faith" focuses upon a goldbricking Jewish soldier, who seeks to exploit the sympathies of his Jewish sergeant; "Epstein" documents the ill-fated adulterous pursuits of its eponymous protagonist; and the opening novella, *Goodbye, Columbus* offers a scathing critique of the materialism, and creeping racism, of its newly affluent Jewish suburbanites. "Eli, the Fanatic" may represent the strongest story of the collection. Eli Peck, a lawyer and nominal Jew, lives in a verdant, and predominantly Gentile, New York suburb, Woodenton. The increasing number of Jewish families who have settled in Woodenton live "in amity" with their Gentile neighbors through eschewing their "extreme practices" (262). Thus, they fear the reaction of their Gentile hosts when Leo Tzuref founds an Orthodox yeshiva in which eighteen young Holocaust survivors receive instruction from a Hasidic Jew (also a survivor). As one assimilated member of the community brays to Peck, "There's going to be no pogroms in Woodenton. Right? Cause there's no fanatics, no crazy people"

(277). The Jewish community goes so far as to seek to remove the yeshiva based upon an obscure zoning ordinance, and secure Peck as their legal representative.

Eli, however, feels ambivalent about his community's resolve to displace their brethren. He initially attempts to placate the assimilated Woodenton Jews by providing the Hasidic instructor with a modern suit. "I'm not a Nazi who would drive eighteen children who are probably frightened at the sight of a firefly, into homelessness," he explains to Tzuref in a letter. "But if you want a home here, you must accept what we have to offer" (274). The Hasid relents and accepts Peck's secular green suit. Yet Peck, ultimately, feels remorse for stripping the survivor of his last remnant of selfhood. In a curious act of empathy, he dons the black caftan and broad-brimmed hat, which the Hasidic instructor surrenders, and strolls unapologetically through the Woodenton streets. The moral vision of "Eli, The Fanatic" is somewhat more elusive than this gloss of the plot suggests. It's unclear, for example, whether Peck's rebellion represents a nervous breakdown or a moment of stark lucidity. The story ends mysteriously as a sedative administered to Peck by a physician "calmed his soul, but did not touch it down where the blackness had reached" (298). However, in these early stories, generally, Roth's trenchant, uncompromising –and often hilarious – social satire set the aesthetic bar much higher for his American contemporaries, writing amid the "triumphant, suffocating American philistinism" (as Roth characterized the age) of the 1950s ("Preface" ix).

While the strength of Saul Bellow's and Philip Roth's novels tends to overshadow their stories, the opposite is true of Malamud and Paley, who perform at the height of their artistic powers within the generic confines of the short story. Malamud, whose short fiction often evokes the gritty Depression-era urban scene, never sought to deny the moral dimension of his fiction. "Literature," he argued, "since it values man by describing him, tends toward morality. ... Art celebrates life and gives us our measure" ("Preface" xiii). In several of Malamud's finest stories an often disaffected protagonist triumphs through recognizing and empathizing with the suffering of others. In "The Magic Barrel," Leo Finkle, a young rabbinical student, broadens his humanity through measures of empathy. He decides to hire a marriage broker (a *shadchan*), because married rabbis stand a better chance of securing a pulpit. But he recognizes the ruthlessness of his motives once Salzman, the marriage broker, arrives and shuffles casually through his portfolio of adrift female souls: "Salzman eagerly unstrapped his portfolio and removed a loose rubber band from a thin packet of much-handled cards. As he flipped through them, a gesture and sound that physically hurt Leo, the student pretended not to see and gazed steadfastly out the window" (*Complete Stories* 135). In short, Finkle grows as a human being through recognizing the pain that defines the existence of so many. Stories such as "The Last of the Mohican," "Rembrandt's Hat," "Take Pity," and "The Mourners" are cut from the same cloth of redemptive suffering.

The Holocaust looms throughout Malamud's oeuvre. Malamud (and Bellow and Roth, for that matter) tend to address the Holocaust allusively. "The Loan" represents one of the most powerful American Holocaust stories to date, written in this allusive vein. The action takes place in a postwar American bakery as Kobotsky enters the shop of his old friend, Lieb, to secure a loan. Malamud emphasizes that, although his characters escaped the Holocaust, the atrocity forged the trajectory of their immigrant lives. Refugees from Hitler's Europe, their lives are forever divided into two discrete periods – before and after. The atrocity haunts their psyches as they continue to mourn their significant dead. Malamud eerily evokes the presence of the Holocaust in their lives as Lieb's wife rushes to the bakery oven toward the end of the story to be greeted by a "cloud of smoke" billowing out at her, "[t]he loaves in the trays were blackened bricks – charred corpses" (99). Other particularly notable stories by Malamud to address the psychological trauma of the Holocaust include "The German Refugee" and "The First Seven Years."

Malamud's ethical vision extended beyond the Jewish community to include, most notably, the African American community, eking out its own existence along the same gritty New York streets. Malamud addresses the relationship between blacks and Jews, specifically, in "Angel Levine" and "Black Is My Favorite Color." In the first story, an elderly Jew with an ailing wife grows to accept that a black man who surprises him one day in his kitchen is both an angel from God and a Jew named Alexander Levine. "A wonderful thing, Fanny," he exclaims at the end of this fantastical story, "there are Jews everywhere" (166). In contrast to the heady optimism of this early story, "Black Is My Favorite Color," stripped of any fantastical elements, focuses upon the interracial strife between blacks and Jews in the 1960s. In the story, a middle-aged Jewish liquor store owner, Nathan Lime, reflects upon the hostility between the races that has persistently thwarted his efforts to bridge the racial divide. "What I'm saying is, personally for me there's only one human color and that's the color of blood" (332). Still, Lime's "language of the heart" might never hold sway over the mutual distrust between urban blacks and Jews, as Malamud suggests through the doomed love affair between Lime and an African American woman (332). The stylistic contrast between the magical "Angel Levine" and the realist "Black Is My Favorite Color" illustrates Malamud's aesthetic range as a fiction writer. Stories in the former vein (which also include "Jewbird," "Talking Horse," and several others) might best represent Malamud's aesthetic contribution to the short story genre, as elements of the surreal muscle their way into the otherwise prosaic realm of his characters.

While the protagonists of Bellow, Roth, and Malamud tend to be hard-driven male Jews, Grace Paley's carefully wrought stories often focus upon the particular burdens of Jewish (and non-Jewish) women. In "The Loudest Voice," the young Shirley Abramowitz must rebel against patriarchal forces from both within and without her Jewish community, which would silence her booming voice. While her public school, ultimately, decides to make use of her gift for the school play, the play turns out to be a celebration of Christmas. The Christian play, to Abramowitz's mother, is emblematic of the "creeping pogrom" which greets Jews in America (36). The play, to be sure, illustrates the leveling effect of Christianity upon so many Jewish children reared in the earlier part of the twentieth century. Paley, however, suggests that Abramowitz will be able to resist the pervasive force of Christianity through the force of her character. At the end of the story, she even says a prayer for "all the lonesome Christians" (40).

In "An Interest in Life," Paley poignantly evokes the dwindling options afforded to her female protagonist, Virginia, once she assumes the roles of wife and mother. Her husband cruelly abandons her and their four children, leaving them to fend for themselves. What is striking about the story is the self-possession of Virginia, the narrator, as she coolly appraises her current circumstances. "A woman counts her children and acts snotty, like she invented life," she observes, "but men *must* do well in the world" (60). Here, Virginia sees beyond the immediate circumstances of her crisis to glimpse the larger, endemic cultural forces that account for her fierce commitment to her children and her husband's more selfish concerns. Virtually imprisoned in her tenement, she must embrace life on the mean terms offered to her. She takes a lover, yet, perhaps to numb her pain, entertains the fantasy of her husband's return.

Paley's commitment to social justice, in life and in her art, extends beyond women to include all disenfranchised peoples. In "Zagrowsky Tells," for example, Paley offers an honest and incisive examination of the anti-black racism that pervades Jewish circles as her aging protagonist, Zagrowsky, examines the events leading up to the birth of his black grandchild, Emanuel. Zagrowsky's prejudice emerges forcefully as he seeks to justify his past discrimination against people of color, who sought to patronize his pharmacy: "Also, they sent in black people, brown people, all colors, and to tell the truth I didn't like the idea my pharmacy should get the reputation of being a cut-rate place for them. They move into a neighborhood ... I did what everyone did. Not to insult people too much, but to discourage them a little, they shouldn't feel so welcome" (353). Against the backdrop of Zagrowsky's racism, Paley includes arresting scenes of tenderness between her protagonist and his biracial grandson. Zagrowsky's reflections, in fact, take place as he walks Emanuel to the park. At one point, he loses his patience with a nosy neighbor and immediately regrets his outburst: "I tried to be quiet for the boy. You want some ice cream, Emanuel? ... The man's over there. Don't forget to ask for the change. I bend down to give him a kiss. I don't like that he heard me yell at a woman and my hand is still shaking. He runs a few steps, he looks back to make sure I didn't move an inch" (363). Clearly, Zagrowsky loves his grandchild. Yet Paley refuses to craft a disingenuous, saccharine conclusion. Love coexists with, but doesn't triumph over, Zagrowsky's racism, as Paley reminds us through her protagonist's persistent anxiety over his grandchild's complexion. "I got my eye on him too," Zagrowsky continues. "He waves a chocolate Popsicle. It's a little darker than him" (363).

After Alienation: Waning and Return

By the 1970s, the dazzling post-immigrant fiction of marginality and alienation had run its course, as a number of critics observed. "Insofar as this body of writing draws heavily from the immigrant experience," Howe argued in 1977, "it must suffer a depletion of resources, a thinning-out of materials and memories" ("Introduction" 16). While Howe may have overstated the case, the 1970s and early 1980s were, admittedly, bear-market years for the Jewish American story. One thing was for certain. If Jewish American fiction was to survive it would have to change. In her essays and her own stories, Cynthia Ozick heralded a new, post-ethnic wave of Jewish writing by calling for a literature "centrally Jewish in its concerns" ("Toward" 168). As Sanford Pinsker noted, "Ozick almost singlehandedly moved Jewish-American fiction beyond the dare of ethnic Jewishness to a more complicated, more demanding *double-dare* of a fiction firmly couched in Jewish ideas and rendered in liturgical rhythms" ("Dares" 282). The battle between the pagan and the Hebraic, between Pan and Moses, has been Cynthia Ozick's primary theme. "Great Pan Lives," the nature-loving Rabbi Isaac Kornfeld declares in Ozick's landmark story of 1966, "The Pagan Rabbi" (17). He thereby blurs the distinction between the Creator and the created. Learning only too late that his soul belongs to the Torah, not to the trees, Kornfeld hangs himself from a tree by his prayer shawl. The story, like several of Ozick's fictional works, might be understood as an extended meditation upon the second commandment banning idolatry.

Ozick's early stories (along with those of Hugh Nissenson) paved the way for a new generation of story writers in the 1990s – the literary grandchildren of Bellow et al. – who created Jewish characters beset by centrally Jewish concerns: the toxic legacy of the Holocaust, the retrieval of extinct Jewish worlds (e.g., the European *shtetl*, New York's Lower East Side, and Jewish neighborhoods in the American South), Jewish feminism, Israel, Jewish Orthodoxy, and the biblical resonances in the modern world. In his wildly successful *For the Relief of Unbearable Urges* (1999), Nathan Englander creates several Orthodox characters who grapple with issues of Jewish Law. A Hasid in the collection's title story, frustrated by his wife's purportedly unending menstrual cycle, receives rabbinic dispensation to conjoin with a prostitute to "relieve the pressure." In "The Wig," Ruchama the wig-maker does her best to negotiate between the Jewish laws of modesty and her desire for beauty and sexual fulfillment. Allegra Goodman has also powerfully depicted the tensions between Orthodoxy and secularism. In "The Four Questions," for example, Goodman evokes a contentious Passover Seder as the family patriarch, Ed, must grapple with what he perceives to be his daughter's insufferable religiosity. During the service, he can't help but notice that Miriam ignores his more ecumenical flourishes. "They had raised the children in a liberal, rational, joyous way – raised them to enjoy the Jewish tradition, and Ed can't understand why Miriam would choose austerity and obscure ritualism" (*Family* 187–8). The stories collected in *The Family Markowitz* (1996), generally, are among the most incisive works to explore Jewish American family life since Philip Roth's *Goodbye, Columbus*. Marjorie Sandor's haunting story collection, *Portrait of My Mother Who Posed Nude in Wartime* (2003) – winner of the National Jewish Book Award in fiction – also continues the esteemed tradition of Jewish stories of the family.

Other emergent Jewish American writers to address issues of Jewish Orthodoxy in the modern world include, most notably, Melvin Bukiet, Ehud Havazelet, and Joan Leegant. In Leegant's "The Tenth," a rabbi must consider how to "count" Siamese twins for the number of ten Jewish men required to form the prayer quorum; Bukiet holds the Jewish dietary laws up to extensive scrutiny through the travails of his Kosher butcher in "The Golden Calf and the Red Heifer," collected in *While the Messiah Tarries* (1995); finally, several of the quietly powerful, elegiac stories in Havazelet's *Like Never Before* (1998) examine the waning influence of Orthodox values and rituals upon a wayward generation of Birnbaums in the 1960s.

With regard to the Holocaust, Ozick's own story, "The Shawl," published in the *New Yorker* in 1981, represents a more direct evocation of the atrocity than most earlier fictional accounts (e.g., Malamud's "The Loan"). The story depicts the psychic terror that grips Rosa in a death camp, where she must witness the gradual starvation of her infant daughter, Magda, and her adolescent niece, Stella. Ozick trenchantly evokes the warped relational dynamics that prevail under such circumstances. Rosa, for example, projects much of her animus toward Stella rather than toward the Nazis: "Rosa gave almost all her food to Magda, Stella gave nothing. ... They were in a place without pity, all pity was annihilated in Rosa, she looked at Stella's bones without pity" (5).

In the 1990s, a new generation of Jewish American writers, many of them children of Holocaust survivors, would emerge to explore in their stories the toxic legacy of the Holocaust upon the "second generation," to borrow Alan L. Berger's terminology. Rebecca Goldstein's "The Legacy of Raizel Kaidish," represents one of the more chilling stories in this genre. The story begins as the narrator, a child of survivors, describes the heroic deeds of her namesake, Raizel Kaidish, as recounted to her by her mother. A prisoner at Buchenwald, Kaidish takes an enormous risk to save her best friend's life. Tragically, they are both murdered by the Nazis after an informant betrays them. Kaidish's legacy proves overwhelming for the narrator as her mother relentlessly reinforces the moral lesson of Kaidish's act. Saddled with such pressure, Goldstein depicts her narrator's retreat into an amoral philosophy, yet fashions a haunting conclusion that forces the reader to reevaluate the contrasting post-Holocaust visions of mother and daughter.

Thane Rosenbaum also examines the painful legacy passed down to a child of Holocaust survivors in each of the stories collected in his debut work of fiction, *Elijah Visible* (1996). Through the ordeals of his protagonist, Adam Posner, Rosenbaum evokes the dysfunctional psychological immersion of the "second generation" in the European atrocity, their ambivalence toward Judaism, and their unyielding urge to reconstruct the experiences of their parents. In "Cattle Car Complex," for example, Posner, a New York lawyer, suffers a psychological trauma after his elevator malfunctions and traps him inside. The experience transports Posner, psychologically, to a Nazi cattle car. "This is not life – being trapped in a box made for animals!" he cries (7–8).

Lev Raphael addresses a similar theme in the stories collected in *Dancing on Tisha B'Av* (1991). What makes Raphael's stories unique is that his protagonists must reckon not only with their identities as children of Holocaust survivors but also with their homosexuality. In "The Life You Have," Raphael condemns both Nazism and the homophobia of mainstream Jewish America, and enacts a provocative narrative leveling of these manifestations of hatred. Other especially powerful contemporary stories of the Holocaust include Harvey Grossinger's "The Quarry," Nathan Englander's "The Tumblers," and Melvin Bukiet's "The Library of Moloch" and "Himmler's Chickens."

The enterprise of retrieving lost or waning Jewish worlds – and retrieving Jewish modes of writing – through the artistic imagination is a prevailing current of the Jewish American story. In *Stories of an Imaginary Childhood* (1991), for example, Bukiet imaginatively reconstructs the Polish *shtetl*, Proszowice, the setting for each of the twelve interrelated stories, while his more recent "The Two Franzes," collected in *A Faker's Dozen* (2003), transports us to prewar Prague. In several stories collected in *The County of Birches* (1998), Judith Kalman also powerfully evokes pre-Holocaust Europe, Budapest specifically. Berlin is the site of Aryeh Lev Stollman's imagination in "Die Grosse Liebe," collected in *The Dialogues of Time and Entropy* (2003), as his Canadian protagonist, who "grew up understanding that one did not ask questions of a personal nature, even to one's parents," meditates upon his dead mother's favorite German movie to explore the pain of her wartime exile from Europe (47). And in Barbara Klein Moss's "Rug Weaver," an Iranian Jewish rug dealer recalls his cruel imprisonment in Teheran following the Islamic revolution. The tumultuous contemporary Israeli landscape also increasingly emerges as a locus for the Jewish American imagination in such stories as Stollman's "Mr. Mitochondria" and "The Adornment of Days," Nathan Englander's "In This Way We Are Wise," and in Jon Papernik's debut collection, *The Ascent of Eli Israel* (2002). The prevalence of the European *shtetl* and Israel in the contemporary Jewish American story bespeaks the broadening reach and daring of the Jewish American imagination.

Steve Stern has set his sights on reconstructing a Jewish universe closer to home in several story collections, most notably *Lazar Malkin Enters Heaven* (1987) and *The Wedding Jester* (1999). In his stories, Stern focuses primarily upon a motley assortment of Jewish characters living alongside the honky-tonks and pawnshops of the Pinch – an actual Jewish neighborhood in Memphis – prior to the Holocaust and World War II. "The Tale of a Kite," collected in *The Wedding Jester*, represents one such story and presents an interesting counterpoint to Philip Roth's "Eli, the Fanatic." In the story, the Jews of the Pinch, like the Jews of Roth's Woodenton, fear what the Gentile majority will think when a group of Hasidic "fanatics" moves into the neighborhood. What distinguishes Stern's story from Roth's, however, is the narrative awe at the transcendent powers of the holy. In "The Tale of a Kite," as in many of his stories, Stern infuses the Pinch with magical qualities, and more palpable redemptive possibilities. In this respect, his fiction harkens back to the Yiddish masters of the nineteenth century. Stern, then, has not only reinscribed the lost Jewish world of the Pinch into our collective memory, but has retrieved and reinvigorated the surreal, magical mode of Jewish storytelling, rife with dybbuks and demons, popularized by such early writers as Isaac Bashevis Singer and Bernard Malamud. Other writers have revitalized earlier Jewish modes of writing, as well. Gerald Shapiro, for example, reinvigorates the *schlemiel* tradition in three hilarious story collections, *From Hunger* (1993), *Bad Jews* (1999), and *Little Men* (2004), transplanting the saintly Yiddish fools of Singer,

Y. L. Peretz, Sholom Aleichem, and Moishe Kulbak, to the urban American streets of Chicago. Joseph Epstein's stories in *Fabulous Small Jews* (2003) also owe a clear debt to this tradition.

The prodigious recent literary output of Jewish American fictionists has prompted some observers to assert that a new renaissance in Jewish American letters is under way. The Jewish magazine *Tikkun*, for example, published a literary symposium on "The Jewish Literary Revival" in 1997. Whether or not we are in the midst of a literary renaissance, per se, it is clear that Jewish writers, as a collective, found their voice in the 1990s. They largely jettisoned the merely nominal Jewish protagonists and broad ethical humanism of an earlier generation of writers and turned inward, instead, to create a more essentially Jewish literature. As Mark Krupnick has observed, "It does appear that Cynthia Ozick's program for Jewish writing has been in the process of being carried out" (304).

The New Immigrants

The surging "Jewishness" of the contemporary Jewish American story is unsurprising, perhaps, given our multicultural zeitgeist. That is, the increasing particularism of the Jewish American story might be seen as part of a larger literary and cultural phenomenon – a response to the widespread receptiveness among readers, and demand even, for multicultural voices and visions. No one could have expected, however, that a second wave of Jewish immigration from Europe would fuel a second round of fiction to evoke the particular contours of the immigrant experience. The classification, New Immigrants, has generally been used to refer to the great wave of immigrants from Asian and Latin American countries since 1965, prompted by revisions to US immigration law in that year. Yet a twenty- and thirty-something generation of immigrant Jewish writers from the former Soviet Union – writers who emigrated as children to America and Canada in the late 1970s and 1980s – has also just begun to emerge. Gary Shteyngart's audacious novel, *The Russian Debutante's Handbook* (2002), represents the most significant literary contribution written by this cohort. But two recent story collections, Lara Vapnyar's *There Are Jews in My House* (2003) and David Bezmozgis's *Natasha* (2004), also suggest that we are on the cusp of a new and significant literary movement in Jewish American letters.

Several of the broad themes from the earlier period of Jewish American immigrant fiction resonate in the writing of this emergent generation: the difficulties associated with acquiring a new language, the early adulthood forced upon immigrant children, who must help their parents navigate their new terrain, and the economic and psychological hardships associated with exile, generally. Like several of the immigrant story collections of the early twentieth century, *There Are Jews in My House* and *Natasha* both contain some stories set in the old world and some in the new world. Some stories have a foot planted in both locales, evoking the bifurcated identity of their exiled protagonists.

However, the stories of Vapnyar and Bezmozgis distinguish themselves from the works of their predecessors in at least as many ways as they recall these works. Stylistically, Bezmozgis's and Vapnyar's prose is spare and unadorned, clipped and powerful (consistent with much contemporary writing in English), yet more highly literate than the prose of the first generation of Jewish immigrant writers. The fact that English, for better or worse, has increasingly emerged as the lingua franca across the globe may account, at least in part, for the precociously self-assured prose of the new immigrants. From a thematic standpoint, the Holocaust, which occurred after the first great wave of European Jewish immigration, figures prominently in these stories. The title story of Vapnyar's collection evokes the curiously strained relationship between a Jewish woman and the non-Jewish woman who hides her and her young daughter in Nazi-occupied communist Russia, while Bezmozgis's "An Animal to the Memory" ponders the extent to which Holocaust remembrance should shape the identity of a young immigrant protagonist, learning afresh in Toronto what it means to be a Jew. Vapnyar's and Bezmozgis's stark evocation of the contemporary sexual mores which bear down upon their immigrant protagonists (e.g., Bezmozgis's "Natasha" and Vapnyar's "Love Lessons – Mondays, 9 AM") also distinguishes their work from that of their literary forebears.

The distinctiveness of this new wave of Russian diaspora writing emerges most forcefully, perhaps, in the insider's glimpse these stories offer of the Soviet Union, rather than of Tsarist Russia. Bezmozgis's "The Second Strongest Man" documents the economic deprivation and utter quashing of free ideas that defined Jewish life in the formerly communist state; the brief reunion in the story between the protagonist's father and his former business partner from Riga also evokes the pain of separation from one's native home. Vapnyar's "A Question for Vera" illustrates poignantly, through a child's eyes, the erasure of Jewish identity in the Soviet Union, while Bezmozgis's "An Animal to the Memory" depicts the concomitant struggle to reclaim a Jewish identity in the new world – a sea change from earlier immigrant Jewish fiction, which typically, and conversely, documents the assimilation of protagonists who had been reared in Orthodox Jewish European homes. Finally, the recent publication of the powerful story collections, Ellen Litman's *The Last Chicken in America* (2007) and Sana Krasikov's *One More Year* (2008), suggest that we are only at the beginning of this new "immigrant" phase of the Jewish American short story.

Conclusion

As I hope I have made clear, the new immigrants aren't the only young Jewish American writers to explore Jewish identity across national boundaries. It may be that the accelerated globalization of our economy and mass culture – its deleterious effects notwithstanding – has encouraged contemporary Jewish writers to examine Jewish lives and fates across the diaspora, reinvigorating a Jewish consciousness of exile in its multiform dimensions. Whatever the reasons, the Jewish American imagination is in its most expansive and elastic phase, stretching across generations and geographic borders. The Jewish story, as Ilan Stavans has noted, has ever and always served as a map "across linguistic and geographical spheres," but never more so than now, and nowhere more so than in America, I would argue, especially if we extend the definition of America to include Canada ("Language" 25). All of which bodes well for a new century of Jewish American stories.

REFERENCES AND FURTHER READING

Primary Texts

Apple, Max. *Free Agents*. New York: Harper-Collins, 1984.

Bellow, Saul. *Collected Stories*. New York: Viking, 2001.

Bezmozgis, David. *Natasha*. New York: Farrar, Straus & Giroux, 2004.

Bukiet, Melvin. *A Faker's Dozen*. New York: W. W. Norton, 2003.

———. *Stories of an Imaginary Childhood*. 1991. Evanston, IL: Northwestern University Press, 1992.

———. *While the Messiah Tarries*. 1995. Syracuse, NY: Syracuse University Press, 1997.

Chabon, Michael. *A Model World*. New York: William Morrow, 1991.

Clayton, John J. *Radiance*. Columbus: Ohio State University Press, 1998.

Englander, Nathan. *For the Relief of Unbearable Urges*. New York: Knopf, 1999.

Epstein, Joseph. *Fabulous Small Jews*. New York: Houghton Mifflin, 2003.

Goldstein, Rebecca. *Strange Attractors*. New York: Viking Penguin, 1993.

Goodman, Allegra. *The Family Markowitz*. New York: Farrar, Straus & Giroux, 1996.

———. *Total Immersion*. New York: Harper, 1989.

Grossinger, Harvey. *The Quarry*. Athens: University of Georgia Press, 1997.

Havazelet, Ehud. *Like Never Before*. New York: Farrar, Straus & Giroux, 1998.

Krasikov, Sana. *One More Year*. New York: Spiegel & Grau, 2008.

Leegant, Joan. *An Hour in Paradise*. New York: W. W. Norton, 2003.

Litman, Ellen. *The Last Chicken in America*. New York: Norton, 2007

Malamud, Bernard. *The Complete Stories*. New York: Farrar, Straus & Giroux, 1997.

Moss, Barbara Klein. *Little Edens*. New York: W. W. Norton, 2004.

Nissenson, Hugh. *The Elephant and My Jewish Problem: Selected Stories and Journals*. New York: HarperCollins, 1988.

Ozick, Cynthia. *The Pagan Rabbi and Other Stories*. 1971. Syracuse, NY: Syracuse University Press, 1995.

———. *The Shawl*. 1989. New York: Vintage, 1990.

Paley, Grace. *Collected Stories*. New York: Farrar, Straus & Giroux, 1994.

Papernick, Jon. *The Ascent of Eli Israel*. New York: Arcade, 2002.

Raphael, Lev. *Dancing on Tisha B'Av*. New York: St. Martin's Press, 1991.

Rosenbaum, Thane. *Elijah Visible*. New York: St. Martin's Press, 1996

Roth, Philip. *Goodbye, Columbus*. 1959. New York: Random House, 1995.

Sandor, Marjorie. *Portrait of My Mother Who Posed Nude in Wartime*. Louisville: Sarabande, 2003.

Schwartz, Delmore. *In Dreams Begin Responsibilities*. Norfolk, CT: New Directions, 1938.

Shapiro, Gerald. *Bad Jews*. Cambridge, MA: Zoland Press, 1999.

———. *From Hunger*. Columbia: University of Missouri Press, 1993.

———. *Little Men*. Columbus: Ohio State University Press, 2004.

Shomer, Enid. *Imaginary Men*. Iowa City: University of Iowa Press, 1993.

Stern, Steve. *Lazar Malkin Enters Heaven*. 1987. Syracuse, NY: Syracuse University Press, 1995.

———. *The Wedding Jester*. New York: Graywolf Press, 1999.

Stollman, Aryeh Lev. *The Dialogues of Time and Entropy*. New York: Riverhead, 2003.

Vapnyar, Lara. *There are Jews in My House*. New York: Pantheon, 2003.

Yezierska, Anzia. *Hungry Hearts*. 1920. New York: Penguin, 1997.

General Anthologies

Bukiet, Melvin, ed. *Neurotica: Jewish Writers on Sex*. New York: W. W. Norton, 1999.

Chametzky, Jules, John Felstiner, Hilene Flanzbaum, and Kathryn Hellerstein, eds. *Jewish American Literature: A Norton Anthology*. New York: W. W. Norton, 2001.

Howe, Irving, ed. *Jewish American Stories*. New York: NAL Penguin, 1977.

Shapiro, Gerald, ed. *American Jewish Fiction: A Century of Stories*. Lincoln: University of Nebraska Press, 1998.

Solotaroff, Ted, and Nessa Rapoport, eds. *Writing Our Way Home: Contemporary Stories by American Jewish Writers*. New York: Schocken, 1992. Rpt. as *The Schocken Book of Contemporary Jewish Fiction*. Eds. Ted Solotaroff and Nessa Rapoport. New York: Schocken, 1996.

Stavans, Ilan, ed. *The Oxford Book of Jewish Stories*. New York: Oxford University Press, 1998.

Zakrzewski, Paul, ed. *Lost Tribe: Jewish Fiction from the Edge*. New York: Perennial, 2003.

Secondary Works

Baumgarten, Murray. *City Scriptures: Modern Jewish Writing*. Cambridge, MA: Harvard University Press, 1982.

Berger, Alan L. "American Jewish Fiction." *Modern Judaism* 10 (1990): 221–41.

———. *Children of Job: American Second-Generation Witnesses to the Holocaust*. Albany: State University of New York Press, 1997.

Blair, Sara, and Jonathan Freedman. "Introduction." *Jewish in America (Part One)*. Special Issue of *Michigan Quarterly Review* (Fall 2002): 509–16.

Boyers, Robert T. "Literature and Culture: An Interview with Saul Bellow." *Salmagundi* 30 (1975): 6–23.

Burstein, Janet Handler. "In the Twilight of Tradition: Trying the Myths in Jewish-American Short Stories." *YIVO Annual* 19 (1990): 105–32.

Dickstein, Morris. "Dybbuks in Dixie." Review of *Lazar Malkin Enters Heaven*, by Steve Stern. *New York Times Book Review* (March 1, 1987): 11.

Fiedler, Leslie. *Fiedler on the Roof: Essays on Literature and Jewish Identity*. 1991. Rpt. Boston: Godine, 1992.

Furman, Andrew. *Contemporary Jewish American Writers and the Multicultural Dilemma*. Syracuse, NY: Syracuse University Press, 2000.

Gelfant, Blanche H. "Introduction." *Hungry Hearts*, by Anzia Yezierska. 1920. New York: Penguin, 1997. vii–xxxiv.

Howe, Irving. "Introduction." *Jewish American Stories*. Ed. Irving Howe. New York: NAL Penguin, 1977. 1–17.

Kalman, Judith. *The County of Birches*. New York: St. Martin's Press, 1998.

Kremer, S. Lillian. "Post-Alienation: Recent Directions in Jewish-American Literature." *Contemporary Literature* 34.3 (Fall 1993): 571–91.

Krupnick, Mark. "Jewish-American Literature." *New Immigrant Literatures in the United States: A Sourcebook to Our Multicultural Literary Heritage*. Ed. Alpana Sharma Knippling. Westport, CT: Greenwood Press, 1996. 295–308.

Malamud, Bernard. "Preface." *The Stories of Bernard Malamud*. New York: Farrar, Straus & Giroux, 1983. vii–xiii.

Ozick, Cynthia. "Farcical Combat in a Busy World." *Saul Bellow*. Ed. Harold Bloom. New York: Chelsea House, 1986. 235–41.

———. "Toward a New Yiddish." *Art and Ardor*. New York: Knopf, 1983. 151–77.

Pinsker, Sanford. "Dares, Double-Dares, and the Jewish-American Writer." *Prairie Schooner* 71.1 (Spring 1997): 278–85.

———. *Jewish-American Fiction*. New York: Twayne, 1992.

Rapoport, Nessa. "Summoned to the Feast." Introduction. *Writing Our Way Home: Contemporary Stories by American Jewish Writers*. Eds. Ted Solotaroff and Nessa Rapoport. New York: Schocken, 1992. xxvii–xxx.

Roth, Philip. "Preface." *Goodbye, Columbus*. 1959. New York: Random House, 1995. ix–xii.

Shapiro, Gerald. "Group Portrait." Introduction. *American Jewish Fiction*. Ed. Gerald Shapiro. Lincoln: University of Nebraska Press, 1998. vi–xv.

Shechner, Mark. "Is This Picasso, or Is It the Jews?" *Tikkun* (November–December 1997): 39–41.

Solotaroff, Ted. "The Open Community." Introduction. *Writing Our Way Home: Contemporary Stories by American Jewish Writers*. Eds. Ted Solotaroff and Nessa Rapoport. New York: Schocken, 1992. xiii–xxvi.

Stavans, Ilan. "Language and Tradition." Introduction. *The Oxford Book of Jewish Stories*. Ed. Ilan Stavans. New York: Oxford University Press, 1998. 3–25.

Wirth-Nesher, Hana. "Defining the Indefinable: What Is Jewish Literature?" Introduction. *What is Jewish Literature?* Ed. Hana Wirth-Nesher. Philadelphia: Jewish Publication Society, 1994. 3–12.

30

The Multiethnic American Short Story

Molly Crumpton Winter

The multiethnic short story in America as a literary tradition reflects the paradoxical nature of the nation itself. The publication history of short stories written by people of color and immigrant authors is the story of access and voice in a nation that historically limited their participation in social and political life. Even as their stories appear in popular periodicals, anthologies, and collections, their narratives reflect the prejudicial and sometimes violent opposition to the groups depicted. Viewing these texts in association to each other reveals a nationwide multiethnic dialogue about the personal and communal struggle to come to terms with the promise and betrayal of American life. This discourse on ethnic identification and national belonging, which has continued for over one hundred years, served to reshape, and continues to expand, our notions of American identity.

The publication of multiethnic American short stories began in earnest in the late nineteenth century. The nation was experiencing changes that led to a dramatic increase in the demand for reading material. Population growth, a rise in literacy rates, urbanization, and immigration fueled the magazine, newspaper, and book publishing industry of the era. Periodicals served as forms of entertainment and diversion as well as tools for education as the diversity of texts provided in magazines afforded readers the opportunity to learn about the world outside their homes, communities, and regions. This desire for variety opened the door for Native Americans, African Americans, and immigrants to enter the public discourse as never before. Mainstream periodicals peppered their issues with essays, autobiographical writing, poems, and short stories by non-traditional writers, and major Eastern publishing houses began to open their doors to immigrant authors and writers of color. In addition to these venues edited by and marketed to the assimilated white American population, there were a number of smaller presses and periodicals publishing within and marketing to specific ethnic communities. African American, Jewish American, and Native American newspapers and journals in particular have long been a part of America's publications history.

The challenge for ethnic American short story writers in the late nineteenth and early twentieth centuries was to entertain readers even as they reminded them of recent historical brutalities (slavery, Tsarist pogroms), alerted them to repressive contemporary systems (segregation of blacks, exclusion of Chinese, literacy tests for immigrants, programs of "civilization" for American Indians), and called their attention to economic injustice (poverty, hiring restrictions, and unfair wage distribution). Taken together, these stories constitute an indictment of a nation that expected conformity and acquiescence from each group yet simultaneously upheld beliefs and practices that prevented their full political and social participation. At the turn into the twentieth century the mainstream perception of what it means to be "American" was limited in its scope: the roots of the national character were held to be white, western European, and Protestant, and all who lived within the US borders were expected to conform to this type. Assimilation, the model for citizenship at the time, was problematic for non-Christian immigrants and for Americans who were not white. Most ethnic American stories during this era work on a personal and social level as characters negotiate their position within their ethnic communities in the US as well as their relationship to mainstream American society. The course of these negotiations often reveals the contrast between life, culture, and values in individual tribes, communities, or countries of origin with those of the greater United States.

One of the earliest writers to address these themes in short fiction was Norwegian immigrant Hjalmar Hjorth Boyensen in his collection *Vagabond Tales* published in 1889. Several stories set in America and Norway reflect the international nature of ethnic American literature and the conflicts that arise as immigrants move between cultures. The best of these stories is "A Disastrous Partnership," about two Norwegian cabinetmakers, Truls Bergeson and Jens Moe. In this tale, Bergeson represents the immigrant who holds on to the values and ways of his native country, while Moe embodies the assimilationist ideal of the melting pot. Moe acculturates quickly, changes his name, and marries an American girl. The story supports the mainstream American perception of immigration and assimilation, for though Moe is looked down upon by the other Norwegians for "turning his back on his own people and marrying an American shop-girl" (169), he becomes a success in his new country while those "of the old world, groveling and unaspiring" are doomed to be left behind in the fast paced "new world" (180).

Some collections from this era are more focused in terms of locale but more open to the notion of diversity. For example, Alice Dunbar-Nelson's *The Goodness of St. Roque and Other Short Stories* (1899) moves beyond the black/white binary that clouded perceptions of race to represent Creole and Cajun societies in New Orleans and its vicinities. In *Out of Mulberry Street: Stories of Tenement Life in New York* (1897) by Jacob Riis, tales about the white urban poor are interspersed with stories that focus on Jewish immigrant, Native American, and African American characters. Many of the stories are written with great delicacy and tenderness, surprising for this muckraking journalist. The appearance of a Danish boy separated from his family, in "Lost Children," is reflective of Riis's own status when he came to America as a young man.

Often jobless, hungry, and homeless before he became a police reporter for the *New York Tribune*, Riis identifies with the loneliness and struggle of the immigrant. Myra Kelly was another writer who depicted New York immigrant life empathetically in her short stories. Kelly, who emigrated from Ireland, was an elementary school teacher on the Lower East Side. Most of the stories in her three collections, *Little Citizens* (1904), *Wards of Liberty* (1907), and *Little Aliens* (1910), show immigrant and ghetto experiences through the eyes of children, most of them Russian Jews. Miss Bailey, their Irish American teacher, learns to understand the battles against poverty and prejudice that these children and their families fight.

The most enduring collection of stories about Jewish immigrant life is *The Imported Bridegroom and Other Stories* by Abraham Cahan, published in 1898. Cahan, who immigrated to America from Lithuania with the tides of Jews fleeing from Eastern Europe at the end of the nineteenth century, was a Yiddish journalist and editor of the influential *Jewish Daily Forward*. Though his main calling was to speak to and lead other Jewish immigrants, he used his talents as a fiction writer to communicate with mainstream America. The stories in *Imported Bridegroom* involve the popular themes of betrothal and marriage, yet, paradoxically, most of the stories result in a sense of detachment and isolation. The disintegration of bonds of love and family are the results of the move away from the insular culture of the homeland to the chaotic influences of America and to the economic realities – work shortages and poverty – found in the new land. One of the most pernicious influences depicted through the stories is American materialism, which triggers in many characters the longing to fulfill selfish, and mostly shallow, desires. However, the characters in the final story, "A Ghetto Wedding," overcome this materialism, resist the forces that lead to isolation, and find a path to a meaningful life even while in the grips of poverty. Nathan and Goldy spend beyond their means to throw themselves a wedding in hopes of getting expensive gifts in return. Their friends, too poor to accommodate them, are able to offer nothing of value. Walking home from the party "they were so overcome by a sense of loneliness, of a kind of portentous, haunting emptiness, that they could not speak" (239). However, as they move through the slums, mocked by troublemakers on the street, they find a way to turn toward each other instead of away.

Another collection that chronicles immigrant life is *Mrs. Spring Fragrance* (1912) by Sui Sin Far (Edith Maude Eaton). Like Myra Kelly, Sui Sin Far had a close relationship with her subjects but her own history and immigration experience did not mirror that of most of her characters. Sui Sin Far was born to a British father and Chinese mother and was raised in Canada, where the family moved when she was a child. As an adult, she came to America, and her stories most often depict the lives of merchant families on the West Coast and are the first known examples of Asian American fiction. Most of these tales reflect the concerns of other ethnic American texts of the era as the Chinese American characters define a place for themselves in a nation that has legislated that they have no rights to citizenship. Perhaps her most provocative stories are those, such as "Her Chinese Husband" and "'Its Wavering Image,'" that depict interracial relationships and biracial individuals.

The most productive writer of short stories dealing with issues of race and ethnicity during this era was Charles W. Chesnutt. In 1885 Chesnutt's work began to appear in newspapers and magazines, and throughout his career he had dozens of short stories published in periodicals, including some of the most prestigious of his time, such as *Century* and the *Atlantic Monthly*. In 1899 Houghton Mifflin published his two collections of short stories that, when viewed together, can be seen as a kind of template for the range of themes and materials that would constitute the body of multiethnic short story writing for the century to come. Of particular importance are his treatments of history and its relation to contemporary social realities and the struggles within an ethnic community as it responds to the influences and prejudices of the greater society. *The Conjure Woman* addresses the atrocities and complexities of the slaveholding South in the nation's recent past. *The Wife of His Youth* consists mainly of stories that portray contemporary African American life, in the North and the South, with characters confronting issues such as miscegenation, class, and, intraracial colorism. While the *Conjure Woman* stories depict a unified community as the slaves on the plantation are connected by friendship, sympathy, and shared condition, the stories in *Wife of His Youth* trace divisions within African American life. However, the overarching message of both texts has to do with personal and communal survival, and Chesnutt suggests that unity is just as crucial to survival for African Americans in the post–Civil War era is it was during slavery.

The communal spirit is evident in *Conjure Woman* in the story "Sis' Becky's Pickaninny." In this story Becky's master trades her for a horse to another plantation owner. Aunt Nancy, the slave left to take care of Becky's infant son, becomes concerned about the health of the child. She conspires with Aunt Peggy, the conjure woman, to heal the child and eventually to trick both masters into reversing the trade so that mother and child are reunited. Thanks to the work of the older women, the son grows to be a healthy and resourceful man and eventually buys himself and then his mother out of slavery. In many of the post-Reconstruction tales in *Wife of His Youth*, on the other hand, the empty promise of assimilation lures characters to betray or repress racial ties in their desire to achieve some level of social equality. The title story sets up the dilemma between the desire for advancement to national acceptance and the rifts within black America due to region, class, color, and generation. Mr. Ryder, a leader in the "Blue Vein" society, proclaims: "I have no race prejudice, ... but we people of mixed blood are ground between the upper and nether millstone. Our fate lies between absorption by the white race and extinction in the black. The one doesn't want us yet, but may take us in time. The other would welcome us, but it would be for us a backward step. ... Self-preservation is the first law of nature" (*Wife* 7). Though this is Mr. Ryder's philosophy, by acknowledging his wife in the end he accepts all that the Blue Veins would deny – the Southern, the folk, the heritage of slavery, and their African roots. Chesnutt's stories reveal that self-preservation is at the very least empty and at worst impossible without communal connection, especially in a nation that would not accept African Americans, regardless of intellectual or economic achievement.

Though no major collections of short stories by American Indian or Latino/a writers were published in this era, both traditions had their start during this time in mainstream periodicals. María Cristina Mena, the first Mexican American to publish short fiction in English, wrote a series of stories on Mexican life for *Century Magazine* between 1913 and 1916. Cherokee writer John M. Oskison published several stories at this time, but his perspective is more distinctly regional than exclusively American Indian. The characters in his early works are cowboys, townspeople, whites, mixed-race and full Cherokee and Creek. What most of his stories have in common is the physical space, Indian Territory, and the central theme that there is room for a diversity of peoples and value systems. The implication is usually that compassion and coexistence involve not imposing one's will upon others. In his most anthologized story, "The Problem of Old Harjo," Oskison deals directly with the problems that arise when divergent ethics intersect. In this tale, a young white missionary has succeeded in converting an old Creek, Harjo, who has two wives. The irony is that Harjo's life, even the decision to take two wives, has been guided by honor and charity, two values central in the doctrines of Christianity, but, although he has made room in his belief system to incorporate Christianity, western organized religion is unwilling to incorporate the material facts of Harjo's existence.

Another writer who dealt with the complexities of Native American life at the turn into the twentieth century was Zitkala-Sa. The story "Soft-Hearted Sioux," first published in *Harper's* in 1901, calls into question the value of entering into American society at all. The narrator, in the moments before his execution, tells of his conversion to Christianity and acceptance of white America at boarding school and his subsequent alienation from his tribe and family. In order to save his family, he kills a white man, and the act serves to break the hold that white America has on his mind. However, he feels distanced from his traditional culture, and he goes to his death free in one way but isolated in another. In much of Zitkala-Sa's writings, a rejection of American identity coexists with a sense that a traditional tribal identity is no longer viable once the process of assimilation begins. Though most writers between 1890 and 1915 expressed a desire for assimilation that is thwarted by a racist nation, some, like Zitkala-Sa and Abraham Cahan, express ambivalence toward the Americanizing process and question the culture and values of the nation itself. This questioning would become the heart of many of the short stories that were to follow in the period between World Wars I and II.

There is a subtle shift in representation in stories by ethnic American writers between 1915 and 1945. The events of World War I seemed to revitalize ideas of unified action, and during the Depression writers were inspired by the possibilities of unity and the promise of equality inherent in socialist movements. This period also saw the establishment of two entities that would have great influence on the dissemination of short stories and the incorporation of their authors into the canon. From their inception, the Best American Short Story series, which began in 1915, and the O. Henry Prize, which was founded in 1919, both recognized the contributions of ethnic American writers to be among the best the nation had to offer.

One of the first stories of immigrant life to be selected for the Best American Short Story series was "The Fat of the Land" (1919) by Anzia Yezierska. This story, which would be included in her collection *Hungry Hearts* (1920), contains themes, such as the poverty of the ghettos and the pull of assimilation, found in short fiction by earlier Jewish American writers. However, the psychological complexity of the main character Hanneh Breineh signals a significant change in ethnic American characterization. Whereas before the modern era writers often found it necessary to portray immigrants and people of color as exemplary citizens in order to convey to readers that their subjects were of the same worth and value as themselves or to depict their characters as innocent victims of racism in an unjust society, Hannah Breineh is not as easy to identify with and is not an entirely sympathetic character. The roots of her rage and despair – persecution in Russia, poverty in America – are embedded in the story, yet the audience (like the neighbors in the story) cannot excuse the abuse of her children. The ambiguity of the character requires consideration of the cross-sections of history, society, family, and personality that affect the lives of those considered to be outside the American mainstream.

Several years later, in 1923, "Blood-Burning Moon" by Jean Toomer was selected as a Best American Short Story. Though not a prolific writer, the innovative nature of Toomer's multi-genre text *Cane* and its publication at the beginning of the Harlem Renaissance make him an important point in the matrix of African American literature. Toomer's break with traditional narrative, his unconventional use of language, and the eerie sense of alienation or indifference that permeates his stories mark them as modern texts in style and feel. Two stories from *Cane* were included in the groundbreaking anthology *The New Negro* (1925), edited by Alain Locke, which introduced the amazing wealth of African American creativity and thought of the era.

Another writer included in the anthology was Zora Neale Hurston. Like Toomer, Hurston published very few short stories, but her unique style and perspective have made her also a central figure in African American literature. Several of her stories appeared in *Opportunity* in the 1920s, and one of her first, "Spunk," won a prize from *Opportunity* in 1925. In 1933, *Story Magazine* printed "The Gilded Six Bits," an example of her best writing that incorporates Hurston's most recognizable themes, such as respect for the folk (the African American working poor of the South), the depth and diversity of black culture, the pull of the material, the frailty of human nature, and the possibility of redemption.

Two periodicals – the aptly titled *Opportunity* and *The Crisis* – were instrumental in bringing together the African American talent that constituted the Harlem Renaissance. Marita Bonner, for example, published over a dozen stories in these periodicals between 1925 and 1941. Jessie Fauset, best known as a novelist and the literary editor of *The Crisis* from 1919 to 1926, had several stories appear in this forum. Between 1923 and 1925, six stories by Eric Walrond appeared in *Opportunity*, and in the late 1920s and early 1930s Rudolph Fisher published many stories in these periodicals as well as in several mainstream standards, such as *Atlantic Monthly* and *McClure's Magazine*. The most prolific African American short story writer of the period was Chester

Himes, who, according to Bill Mullen, "between 1933 and 1940 ... published 17 stories in mainstream black and white commercial magazines – far more than any black writer" (33). By the late 1970s, when his last short story appeared in print, Himes had written and published at least 60 stories, which were finally gathered into a collection in 1991.

The most celebrated African American author to publish short stories during this era was Richard Wright. In 1938 his story "Fire and Cloud" appeared in *Story* and received an O. Henry Prize. That year his narrative of social and racial injustice, "Bright and Morning Star," was published in *New Masses* and was chosen the following year as a Best American Short Story. In 1940 *Harper's Bazaar* published "Almo's a Man," which was selected as an O. Henry Prize story for that year. In 1938 "Fire and Cloud" was collected with three other short stories in *Uncle Tom's Children: Four Novellas*. Two years later the volume, now titled *Uncle Tom's Children: Five Long Stories*, was reissued to include "Bright and Morning Star" and the autobiographical introductory essay "The Ethics of Living Jim Crow." Though this collection, and to a greater extent his now classic novel *Native Son* (1940) and autobiography *Black Boy* (1945), mark Richard Wright as a quintessential proletariat and black protest writer of the 1940s, he was to come out with another powerful collection of stories in 1961, *Eight Men*. Several of the stories are based on earlier publications, most notably "The Man Who Was Almost a Man," which has the same plot but a less mature protagonist than his earlier prize-winning story. Because of the dedicated efforts of the African American literary community, black writers were the strongest collective voice to challenge American prejudice and complacency regarding racial and ethnic issues in the period between the wars.

The concerns of the age were also reflected in the tales from groups who were just beginning to tell the tales of their communities. One of the most popular stories of the day was the hard-hitting "Christ in Concrete" by Italian American writer Pietro di Donato. The story, based on the death of his father at a construction site, was expanded into a book of the same title that gained national attention in 1939. Another writer to receive recognition was José Garcia Villa. Though known primarily for his poetry, two stories, "Untitled Story" and "The Fence," were selected as Best American Short Stories in 1932 and 1933. Villa was born in the Philippines, and after winning a prize there for his writing, came to America, where he lived for over forty years, though he never became an American citizen. The two narratives reflect the transcultural nature of the multiethnic short story tradition as the former, a modern story of assimilation in an American academic setting, differs greatly from the latter tale set in a village in the Philippines.

The decades following World War II were a time of rapid changes in American society and the world marked by the growth of the middle class, the unprecedented power of the Civil Rights Movement, the rise of feminism, the Vietnam War, and the countercultural revolution it spawned. The catastrophic events of World War II, and most significantly the attempted genocide of Jews in Europe, led to a new interiority in the American short story. In fact Jewish American authors dominated the tradition during this period as writers, most notably Saul Bellow, Bernard Malamud, Philip Roth, Tillie Olsen, Isaac Bashevis Singer, Grace Paley, and Cynthia Ozick, published volumes of short stories that both question humanity and reaffirm the existence of Jews worldwide. The power and popularity of their work is evident in the national and international recognition they received. Over their careers this group has been selected as Best American Short Story and O. Henry Prize winners over two dozen times. In 1959 *The Magic Barrel* by Malamud won the National Book Award, as did *Goodbye, Columbus* by Roth the following year. Bellow was awarded the Nobel Prize in Literature in 1976. Singer won in 1978 – the only American to win who wrote in a language other than English, and the only Yiddish writer ever to win. Bellow, Malamud, Roth, and Singer began publishing short stories in the 1950s, Olsen and Paley in the 1960s, and Ozick in the 1970s, and all continued to write for decades. Throughout their careers they followed the consciousness of Jews in the Diaspora. Singer, who emigrated from Poland to America as an adult, wrote most often of the restrictions and values of Jewish life in Eastern Europe and of the immigration experience. The others, all children of Russian immigrants (with the exception of Roth, who was third-generation), expressed the complicated existence of Jews in America negotiating the uneven assimilation process, the everyday tensions of families where generations have had vastly different lives, and the profound ambivalence many experienced living as Jews in America as millions died in the Holocaust overseas.

Tillie Olsen's "Tell Me a Riddle" (1961) encompasses all these themes through the stark internal struggles of an elderly Jewish couple in the days leading up to the wife's death. The riddle, the problem for these characters, is: how is it possible to reconcile the idealism of youth and the persecution that results, the memory of poverty, the tragedy of history, the distance that separates families, and the inescapable solitude of existence with the undeniable presence of love, strength, and continuance? The questioning by Jewish American writers of this period ranges from Saul Bellow's "Looking for Mr. Green" (1951), in which the protagonist asks, "Why is the consent given to misery?" to Cynthia Ozick's much anthologized "The Shawl" (1980) that unblinkingly portrays the agonizing life and horrifying death of a baby in a concentration camp under the inhumanity of the Nazis, which leaves the reader to ask the eternal question, "why?"

As it had from its roots in the late nineteenth century, the tradition of African American short story writing continued during this period to express the most profound concerns of a rich and diverse culture. In 1971 Ann Petry became the first African American woman to publish a volume of short stories when her writings of the previous three decades were collected in *Miss Muriel and Other Stories*. Early tales, such as "Like a Winding Sheet," first published in *The Crisis* in 1945, reflect the dual pressures of racism and economic stress that reflect the main concerns of ethnic American writers of the generation before. *Going to Meet the Man* (1965) by James Baldwin, on the other hand, is a stunning offering that charts the contemporary intersections of Southern black history and urban black life and the inheritances of culture and history that both unite and divide the individual and community. Two stories from this collection that thread African American musical traditions into complex stories of love and regret are "Sonny's Blues" and "Going to Meet the Man." The former story traces the relationship of two brothers and their shared and divergent knowledge of suffering. As the story opens, the narrator, a high school math teacher, reflects on their lives through that of his students: "These boys, now, were living as we'd been living then, they were growing up in a rush and their heads bumped abruptly against the low ceiling of their actual possibilities" (104). The story navigates the darkness of life that comes through personal sorrow as well as the oppression experienced as an African American in a racist society. Reprieve from the darkness, however tenuous, comes through family, forgiveness, and the cultural inheritance of music, in this case the blues, that the younger brother helps his sibling understand. The music that permeates "Going to Meet the Man" is the protest songs of the Civil Rights Movement, which were based on the familiar spirituals of black Christian life. Jesse, the main character in this story, is a white deputy sheriff in the South desperately clinging to ingrained notions of racial superiority even as social change is chipping away at Southern white apartheid. Through his depiction of a lynching Jesse witnesses as a child, where he is bonded to his parents through bloodshed and racism, Baldwin delineates the process of hate that is psychologically damaging to the oppressor as well as the oppressed. Together, Baldwin's collection gives witness to the injustice of society even as it acknowledges the fragility and potential for good inherent in all people.

Another particularly strong voice of the era was James Alan McPherson, whose stories appeared in over two dozen periodicals. He also published two critically claimed collections *Hue and Cry* (1968) and *Elbow Room* (1977), which won the Pulitzer Prize for Fiction in 1978. Through a wide-ranging diversity of characters, from "Old School" waiters in railway dining cars ("A Solo Song: For Doc"), to an aspiring writer and "apprentice janitor" ("Gold Coast"), to a cosmopolitan New Yorker with South Carolina roots ("Why I Like Country Music"), to a young African American couple in London ("I Am an American"), McPherson captures the cross-sections of black American life as it is lived in a multicultural world.

A similar range of characters and settings is found in the works of Toni Cade Bambara and Alice Walker, though their short story collections more specifically reflect the power of the black feminist perspective. In Bambara's popular story "The Lesson" from *Gorilla, My Love* (1972), the tough and insightful young Sylvia is compelled to face the reality that in the economic hierarchy of society she and her friends are of the lower class, a revelation that she faces with the stern resolve that "ain't nobody gonna beat me at nuthin" (96). Walker captures the evolving sensibilities of women in the 1970s in her two collections *In Love and Trouble: Stories of Black Women* (1973) and *You Can't Keep a Good Woman Down* (1981). "The Abortion," which was selected as an O. Henry Prize winner in 1981, records the complications of life for women, particularly for a woman of color, in the this decade of change.

In the early 1970s, apparently inspired by Black Nationalist sentiments, Frank Chin, Jeffery Chan, Lawson Inada, and Shawn Wong published the groundbreaking

Aiiieeeee! An Anthology of Asian-American Writers (1974). The editors included works by Chinese American, Japanese American, and Filipino American writers and made a case for a new literary tradition that is distinct from both mainstream America and from the nations of ethnic origin. The text revitalized interest in writers who were in danger of being forgotten, such as Toshio Mori, who wrote a collection of short stories about Japanese American life set before World War II entitled *Yokohama, California* (1949), and Hisaye Yamamoto, who had been publishing short stories in Japanese American periodicals and national literary journals for twenty five years. Her stories, which were finally collected in *Seventeen Syllables* in 1988, trace Japanese American life from prewar farming communities, through the World War II internment camp experience, to the feminist movement of the 1970s.

The cultural revolutions of the 1970s gave rise to the development of ethnic studies in universities across the United States. The new interest in the diverse histories and cultures that make up the nation, along with an increasing number of ethnic Americans and women entering into academia, led to the heated debates of the "canon wars" in the 1980s. The power and quality of contemporary multiethnic writing, combined with research and theory that resulted in recovery of countless early texts and new ways of reading works from different ethnic literary traditions, proved the study of multiethnic American literature to be a valuable and limitless discipline, and one that is crucial in understanding our national makeup. The 1980s to the present has been a time of amazing expansion for ethnic American short story writing. Not only are there more stories being published, but also collections are broadening the limits of genre, and stories and authors reflect a growing variety of cultural origins.

Building on the promise of the generation before, Asian American short story writers have achieved unparalleled success in the last twenty-five years. The wide range of ethnic origins of the authors reflects changing immigration patterns and increased globalization. Examples of Chinese American literature, for example, range from the stories of second-generation writer Gish Jen in *Who's Irish?* (1999), whose Chinese American characters have integrated into American society; to the stories of Ha Jin, who immigrated as an adult to America and whose stories in *The Bridegroom* (2000) are set in present-day China; to the international stories of British-born Peter Ho Davies, of Welsh and Chinese background, whose tales in *The Ugliest House in the World* (1997) are set primarily in the UK and Southeast Asia and feature British and Chinese characters. Writers such as Gish Jen and David Wong Louie present the perspective of American children of Chinese descent who are mostly at ease with their assimilation but who still possess a keen awareness of critical moments when others question their or their parents' belonging, as in Jen's much-anthologized "In the American Society," when a Chinese American father triumphs over the bigotry of a white Anglo-Saxon character, who in many ways represents the complacent assumption of superiority of a certain American type that has changed little in the past hundred years.

Japanese American short stories of this period also reflect the generations of families that have lived in America, and for many writers the internment experience of World

War II stands as a pivotal event in their histories and in the formation of their identities, as in the stories included in *Desert Run: Poems and Stories* (1988) by Mitsuye Yamada. In *Talking to the Dead* (1992), on the other hand, Sylvia Watanabe represents not a single ethnic perspective but the Asian fusion of her home state Hawaii, where Japanese Americans were not subjected to internment. Another Pacific Rim perspective comes from Mary Yukari Waters, who was born in Japan to a Japanese mother and Irish American father and who moved to America at age 9. All of her stories in *The Laws of Evening* (2004) are set in Japan.

Another representative of the international nature of the American short story is *Arresting God in Kathmandu* (2001) by Samrat Upadhyay. Though most of the stories are set in Nepal, the presence of an American ex-wife in one story and the meeting of Nepali lovers at a wedding in New Jersey in another reveal the globalized modern world. In fact, the back and forth nature of much of contemporary Asian American literature represents modern immigration realities where lives are lived not disconnected from the nation of origin, but in continual crossings from one culture to another. In *Hunger* (1998), Lan Samantha Chang represents the perspective of both Chinese immigrants and their children. Indian American writers Bharati Mukherjee, Chitra Banerjee Divakaruni, and Jhumpa Lahiri move freely between India and America in their short story collections. Southeast Asian American short stories have been selected two dozen times as Best American Short Stories and O. Henry Prize winners, and *Interpreter of Maladies* by Lahiri was the winner of the Pulitzer Prize for Fiction in 2000 – evidence that a strong new tradition is developing in American literature. The back and forth nature of most contemporary Asian American short stories reflects the personal and national histories that people bring with them to the United States, the special concerns of disparate groups when they arrive, and the borderless experiences of the life of the mind and the heart with which each human, regardless of background, must privately wrestle.

Short stories by Native American writers have also garnered national attention in the past couple of decades as two artists, Sherman Alexie and Louise Erdrich, have had several books become best-sellers. Alexie's first collection, *The Lone Ranger and Tonto Fistfight in Heaven* (1993), carefully balances hope and despair, humor and pathos, as it depicts the lives of contemporary Spokane/Coeur d'Alene Indians on the reservation and in relation to contemporary American life. Each story ends in a fragile moment, teetering on the brink of history, failure, forgiveness, and redemption. The presence of love, music, memory, and traditions promises continuance, though, as Junior says at the end of "A Good Story," "there is just barely enough goodness in all of this" (144). Alexie maintains this balance as he follows Native American characters into the city, college, interracial relationships, and in conditions from homelessness to professional life, in his next two collections *The Toughest Indian in the World* (2000) and *Ten Little Indians* (2003). Erdrich's stories reach farther back into the historical past as she traces the lives of Ojibwa characters on one reservation and their neighbors from the upheavals of the early twentieth century through every generation to the present. Over the last two decades, eight of her short stories published in national periodicals have been selected as Best American Short Stories or O. Henry Prize winners. When compiling her stories into books, however, Erdrich weaves them into short story cycles that are all classified as novels. As James Nagel notes, this genre "offers a vital technique for the exploration and depiction of the complex interactions of gender, ethnicity, and individual identity" and therefore has become an important medium for many contemporary writers of diverse backgrounds, such as Jamaica Kincaid, Amy Tan, and Julia Alvarez (10). The collection *Storyteller* (1981) by Laguna Pueblo writer Leslie Marmon Silko crosses genres in another way. This text combines stories, poems, photographs, and personal essays in ways that emphasize the rich and varied history and the storytelling tradition of her culture and her family.

Judith Ortiz Cofer offers her own unique blend of fiction and non-fiction, prose and poetry, in *The Latin Deli* (1993). The Puerto Rican characters who inhabit her writing are versed in the language of crossing as they travel from the island to the American mainland, from Spanish to English, and from their traditional culture to mainstream US life in movements as complex and fluid as Ortiz Cofer's shifts from genre to genre. Chicana writer Sandra Cisneros examines mestiza consciousness in the lives of Mexican American women in her collection *Woman Hollering Creek and Other Stories* (1991). The title story, in particular, captures universal issues of the subjectivity of women and the cultural particularity crucial to self-awareness as an abused wife's connection with the suffering of the fabled La Llorona leads to her liberation. A very different collection of stories of Mexican American life is *Soy la Avon Lady and Other Stories* (2002) by Lorraine López. As American-born characters move farther from their Mexican and immigrant roots, they reveal startling perspectives reflective of life in an increasingly multicultural world. As Lopez's characters move outward from Southern California, to New Mexico, to Georgia, to Antigua, Luis J. Rodriguez focuses on a highly localized though brilliantly varied neighborhood in his collection *The Republic of East L.A.* (2002). Another example of the growing diversity of Hispanic American literature comes from Junot Díaz, whose powerful stories set in the Dominican Republic and the inner cities of New Jersey have won prizes and opened the eyes of readers to worlds otherwise beyond their reach.

The legacy of African American short stories continues with writers such as ZZ Packer, whose collection *Drinking Coffee Elsewhere* (2003) is reminiscent of Alice Walker in the way it covers, from a feminist perspective, both the insular nature of black American life in stories such as "Brownies," in which a troupe of young African American girls misinterpret racial tension, and the cosmopolitan existence of many African Americans as they move through big cities, ivy league schools, and foreign countries. Short stories by Jewish American writers also depict revealing new connections in an ever-expanding world. In the title story from *A Letter to Harvey Milk* (1988) by Leslea Newman, a 77-year-old Holocaust survivor and a young Jewish lesbian share personal loss and develop a friendship across the divides of history and generations. In fact, many writers of the past several decades have included the process of coming to terms with sexual identity within traditional cultures. Some of the stories included in *The Native Informant and Other Stories* by Ramzi M. Salti serve to broaden the scope of American literature by depicting realities of Arab and Arab American life and by dealing sensitively with issues of homosexuality and oppression. Just as the contemporary American short story continues to expand into new places, new themes, new formats, and new subjects, it has also grown to incorporate new genres, as the science fiction stories of African American writers Octavia Butler (*Bloodchild*, 1995) and Walter Mosley (*Futureland*, 2001) demonstrate. Mosley is also known primarily as a writer of detective fiction (both novels and short stories), and so has published books in two seemingly unrelated categories. Yet all these tales, as do the majority of short stories by ethnic American writers, deal with issues of race, gender, social justice, and personal struggle.

For over one hundred years ethnic American short stories have served to articulate the multiplicity inherent in American society. A stream of writers from varied backgrounds writing multiple stories from unlimited points of view reflect a nation that is constantly in flux. From the immigrant writers at the turn of the twentieth century to the great numbers of contemporary first-, second-, and third-generation authors who live their lives in two cultures and even between nations come narratives that explore the change and exchange of American society. From the South to the North, from reservations to cities, from rural poverty to cosmopolitan comfort, African American and American Indian writers convey the gravity of historical and personal transformations. And yet, even as these stories reveal a nation of movement and revolution, they also contain a critique of the ways in which American society simultaneously resists change and difference. Even as immigrants and people of color create art that opens new paths to understanding and connections, they also remind us that forces of resistance to our own diversity persist. However, as their characters question the past, question themselves, question the nation, and question the world, they lead us to answers that serve to broaden conceptions of personal identity, national belonging, and collective humanity.

References and Further Reading

Alexie, Sherman. *The Lone Ranger and Tonto Fistfight in Heaven*. New York: Atlantic Monthly Press, 1993.

———. *Ten Little Indians*. New York: Grove Press, 2003.

———. *The Toughest Indian in the World*. New York: Grove Press, 2000.

Ammons, Elizabeth, ed. *Short Fiction by Black Women, 1900–1920*. New York: Oxford University Press, 1991.

Ammons, Elizabeth, and Annette White Parks, eds. *Tricksterism in Turn-of-the-Century American Literature: A Multicultural Perspective*. Hanover: University Press of New England, 1994.

Antin, Mary. "The Amulet." *Atlantic Monthly* 111 (1913): 31–41.

———. "The Lie." *Atlantic Monthly* 112 (1913): 177–90.

———. "Malinke's Atonement." *Atlantic Monthly* 108 (1911): 300–19.

Baldwin, James. *Going to Meet the Man*. 1965. New York: Vintage International, 1995.

Bambara, Toni Cade. *Gorilla, My Love*. 1972. New York: Vintage Contemporaries, 1992.

———. *The Seabirds are Still Alive*. New York: Random House, 1977.

Bellow, Saul. *Him with His Foot in His Mouth and Other Stories*. New York: Harper & Row, 1984.

————. *Mosby's Memoirs and Other Stories.* New York: Viking, 1968.

Bone, Robert. *Down Home: Origins of the Afro-American Short Story.* 1975. New York: Columbia University Press, 1988.

Bonner, Marita. *Frye Street and Environs: The Collected Works of Marita Bonner.* Boston: Beacon Press, 1987.

Boyesen, Hjalmar Hjorth. *Vagabond Tales.* Boston: Lothrop, 1889.

Brown, Julie, ed. *Ethnicity and the American Short Story.* New York: Garland, 1997.

Butler, Octavia E. *Bloodchild and Other Stories.* New York: Seven Stories, 1995.

Cahan, Abraham. *The Imported Bridegroom and Other Stories.* Boston: Houghton, Mifflin, 1898.

————. *Yekl and the Imported Bridegroom and Other Stories of Yiddish New York.* New York: Dover, 1970.

Chang, Lan Samantha. *Hunger.* New York: W. W. Norton, 1998.

Chesnutt, Charles W. *The Conjure Woman.* Boston: Houghton, Mifflin, 1899.

————. *The Conjure Woman and Other Conjure Tales.* Durham, NC: Duke University Press, 1993.

————. *The Wife of His Youth and Other Stories of the Color Line.* 1899. Ann Arbor: University of Michigan Press, 1968.

Chin, Frank. *The Chinaman Pacific and Frisco R.R. Co.* St. Paul: Coffee House Press, 1988.

Chin, Frank, Jeffery Chan, Lawson Inada, and Shawn Wong, eds. *Aiiieeeee! An Anthology of Asian-American Literature.* Washington, DC: Howard University Press, 1974.

Cisneros, Sandra. *Woman Hollering Creek and Other Stories.* New York: Random House, 1991.

Dale, Corinne H., and J. H. E. Paine, eds. *Women on the Edge: Ethnicity and Gender in Short Stories by American Women.* New York: Garland, 1999.

Dandicat, Edwidge. *Krik? Krak!* New York: Soho, 1995.

Davies, Peter Ho. *Equal Love.* New York: Mariner Books, 2000.

————. *The Ugliest House in the World.* New York: Houghton Mifflin, 1997.

Diaz, Junot. *Drown.* New York: Riverhead, 1996.

Divakaruni, Chitra Banerjee. *Arranged Marriage.* New York: Anchor Books, 1995.

————. *The Unknown Error of Our Lives.* New York: Doubleday, 2001.

Dunbar, Paul Laurence. *The Heart of Happy Hollow.* 1904. New York: Harlem Moon, 2005.

Dunbar-Nelson, Alice. *The Goodness of St. Rocque and Other Stories.* New York: Dodd, Mead, 1899.

Erdrich, Louise. "The Bingo Van." *New Yorker* (February 19, 1990): 39–47.

————. "The Butcher's Wife." *New Yorker* (October 15, 2001): 188–200.

————. "Fleur." *Esquire* (August 1986): 52–5+.

————. "Matchimanito." *The Atlantic* (July 1988): 66–74.

————. "Revival Road." *New Yorker* (April 17, 2000): 106–13.

————. "Saint Marie." *The Atlantic* (March 1984): 78–84.

————. "Satan: Hijacker of a Planet." *Atlantic Monthly* (August 1997): 64–8.

————. "Shamengwa." *New Yorker* (December 2, 2002): 94–101.

————. "Snares." *Harper's* (May 1987): 60–4.

Gonzalez, Nestor Vicente M. *Seven Hills Away.* Denver: Swallow, 1947.

Himes, Chester. *The Collected Stories of Chester Himes.* New York: Thunder's Mouth Press, 1991.

Hurston, Zora Neale. *The Complete Stories.* New York: HarperPerennial, 1996.

Jen, Gish. *Who's Irish?* New York: Knopf, 1999.

Jin, Ha. *The Bridegroom.* New York: Pantheon, 2000.

————. *Oceans of Words.* South Royalton, VT: Steerforth Press, 1996.

————. *Under the Red Flag.* Athens: University of Georgia Press, 1997.

Kelly, Myra. *Little Aliens.* New York: Scribner, 1910.

————. *Little Citizens: The Humours of School Life.* New York: McClure, Phillips, 1904.

————. *Wards of Liberty.* New York: McClure, 1907.

Kono, Robert H. *The River of Time: A Collection of Short Stories.* Eugene, OR: Abe, 2003.

Lahiri, Jhumpa. *Interpreter of Maladies.* New York: Houghton Mifflin, 1999.

Locke, Alain, ed. *The New Negro: An Interpretation.* New York: Macmillan, 1925.

López, Lorraine. *Soy la Avon Lady and Other Stories.* Willimantic, CT: Curbstone, 2002.

Louie, David Wong. *Pangs of Love.* New York: Plume, 1992.

McClellan, George Marion. *Old Greenbottom Inn and Other Stories*. Louisville: George M. McClellan, 1906.

McPherson, James Alan. *Elbow Room*. 1977. New York: Fawcett, 1993.

———. *Hue and Cry*. New York: Atlantic Monthly Press, 1968.

Malamud, Bernard. *The Complete Stories*. New York: Farrar, Straus & Giroux, 1997.

———. *The Magic Barrel*. New York: Farrar, Straus & Cudahy, 1958.

Mena, María Cristina. *The Collected Stories of María Cristina Mena*. Houston: Arte Público Press, 1997.

Mori, Toshio. *The Chauvinist and Other Stories*. Los Angeles: University of California Press, 1979.

———. *Yokohama, California*. Caldwell, ID: Caxton, 1949.

Mosley, Walter. *Futureland*. New York: Aspect, 2001.

———. *Six Easy Pieces: Easy Rawlins Stories*. New York: Washington Square Press, 2003.

Mukherjee, Bharati. *Darkness*. New York: Penguin, 1985.

———. *The Middleman and Other Stories*. New York: Grove Press, 1988.

Mullen, Bill. "Marking Race/Marketing Race: African American Short Fiction and the Politics of Genre, 1933–1946." *Ethnicity and the American Short Story*. Ed. Julie Brown. New York: Garland, 1997. 25–46.

Nagel, James. *The Contemporary American Short-Story Cycle: The Ethnic Resonance of Genre*. Baton Rouge: Louisiana State University Press, 2001.

Newman, Leslea. *Best Short Stories of Leslea Newman*. Los Angeles: Alyson, 2003.

———. *A Letter to Harvey Milk*. Ithaca, NY: Firebrand, 1988.

Olsen, Tillie. *Tell Me a Riddle*. New York: Dell, 1961.

Ortiz Cofer, Judith. *The Latin Deli: Prose and Poetry*. Athens: University of Georgia Press, 1993.

Oskison, John M. "Only the Master Shall Praise." *Century Magazine* 59 (1900): 327–35.

———. "The Problem of Old Harjo." *Southern Workman* 36 (1907): 235–41.

———. "'The Quality of Mercy': A Story of the Indian Territory." *Century Magazine* 68 (1904): 178–81.

———. "When the Grass Grew Long." *Century Magazine* 62 (1901): 247–50.

Ozick, Cynthia. *Bloodshed and Three Novellas*. New York: Knopf, 1976.

———. *Levitation: Five Fictions*. New York: Knopf, 1981.

———. *The Pagan Rabbi and Other Stories*. New York: Knopf, 1971.

———. *The Shawl*. New York: Knopf, 1989.

Packer, ZZ. *Drinking Coffee Elsewhere*. New York: Riverhead, 2003.

Paley, Grace. *The Collected Stories*. New York: Farrar, Straus & Giroux, 1994.

———. *Enormous Changes at the Last Minute*. New York: Farrar, Straus & Giroux, 1974.

———. *Later the Same Day*. New York: Farrar, Straus & Giroux, 1985

———. *The Little Disturbances of Man*. Garden City, NY: Doubleday, 1959.

Petry, Ann. *Miss Muriel and Other Stories*. 1971. Boston: Beacon Press, 1989.

Reuben, Paul P. *PAL: Perspectives in American Literature – A Research and Reference Guide*. <www.csustan.edu/english/reuben/pal/chap1/bradford.html>.

Riis, Jacob. *Out of Mulberry Street: Stories of Tenement Life in New York*. New York: Century, 1897.

Rodriguez, Luis J. *The Republic of East L.A.* New York: Rayo, 2002.

Roth, Philip. *Goodbye, Columbus and Five Short Stories*. 1959. New York: Vintage International, 1993.

Salti, Ramzi M. *The Native Informant and Other Stories*. Colorado Springs: Three Continents, 1994.

Santos, Bienvenido N. *Scent of Apples*. Seattle: University of Washington Press, 1979.

Sasaki, Ruth A. *The Loom and Other Stories*. St. Paul: Graywolf Press, 1991.

Shapiro, Gerald, ed. *American Jewish Fiction: A Century of Stories*. Lincoln: University of Nebraska Press, 1998.

Silko, Leslie Marmon. *Storyteller*. New York: Arcade, 1981.

Singer, Isaac Bashevis. *A Crown of Feathers and Other Stories*. New York: Farrar, Straus & Giroux, 1973.

———. *The Death of Methuselah and Other Stories*. New York: Farrar, Straus & Giroux, 1988.

———. *A Friend of Kafka's and Other Stories*. New York: Farrar, Straus & Giroux, 1970.

————. *Gimpel the Fool and Other Stories*. New York: Noonday, 1957.

————. *The Image and Other Stories*. New York: Farrar, Straus & Giroux, 1985.

————. *Old Love*. New York: Farrar, Straus & Giroux, 1979.

————. *Passions and Other Stories*. New York: Farrar, Straus & Giroux, 1975.

————. *The Power of Light*. New York: Farrar Straus, 1980.

————. *The Séance and Other Stories*. New York: Farrar, Straus & Giroux, 1968.

————. *Short Friday and Other Stories*. New York: Farrar, Straus & Giroux, 1964.

————. *The Spinoza of Market Street and Other Stories*. New York: Farrar, Straus & Giroux, 1961.

Sui Sin Far. *Mrs. Spring Fragrance*. Chicago: A. C. McClurg, 1912.s

————. *Mrs. Spring Fragrance and Other Writings*. Ed. Amy Ling and Annette White-Parks. Urbana: University of Illinois Press, 1995.

Toomer, Jean. *Cane*. 1923. New York: W. W. Norton, 1988.

Upadhyay, Samrat. *Arresting God in Kathmandu*. New York: Houghton Mifflin, 2001.

Villa, José Garcia. *The Anchored Angel: Selected Writings by José Garcia Villa*. Ed. Eileen Tabios. New York: Kaya, 1999.

————. *Footnote to Youth: Tales of the Philippines and Others*. New York: Scribner, 1933.

Viramontes, Helena María. *The Moths and Other Stories*. 1985. Houston: Arte Público Press, 1995.

Walker, Alice. *In Love and Trouble: Stories of Black Women*. New York: Harcourt, 1973.

————. *You Can't Keep a Good Woman Down*. New York: Harcourt, 1981.

Watanabe, Sylvia. *Talking to the Dead*. Garden City, NY: Doubleday, 1992.

Waters, Mary Yukari. *The Laws of Evening*. New York: Scribner, 2003.

Wright, Richard. *Eight Men*. 1961. New York: Thunder's Mouth Press, 1987.

————. *Uncle Tom's Children: Five Long Stories*. 1940. New York: Harper & Row, 1989.

————. *Uncle Tom's Children: Four Novellas*. New York: Harper, 1938.

Yamada, Mitsuye. *Desert Run: Poems and Stories*. Latham, NY: Kitchen Table Press, 1988.

Yamamoto, Hisaye. *Seventeen Syllables and Other Stories*. Latham, NY: Kitchen Table Press, 1988.

Yezierska, Anzia. *Hungry Hearts*. 1920. New York: Signet Classic, 1996.

Zitkala-Sa. *American Indian Stories*. 1921. Lincoln: University of Nebraska Press, 1985.

31

"Should I Stay or Should I Go?" American Restlessness and the Short-Story Cycle

Jeff Birkenstein

When one really knows a village like this and its surroundings, it is like becoming acquainted with a single person.
— *Sarah Orne Jewett,* The Country of the Pointed Firs, 2

I have come to think that the true history of life, is but a history of moments.
— *Sherwood Anderson (qtd. in Chase,* Sherwood Anderson *32)*

Introduction

The mythological reasons for viewing America as a new Promised Land seem clear enough. For centuries, people from around the world have come to America in order to forge a new, if not a common, identity. For just as long, perhaps, settlers have wondered if something better might yet be over the horizon. Indeed, this conflicting impulse – whether or not to continue moving or to settle – has clouded the American psyche from long before nationhood. When Massachusetts Colony Governor John Winthrop said in 1630 that, "[w]e shall be as a City upon a Hill [and] the eyes of all people are upon us," he believed that his new home was securely removed from the ancient hierarchies – and violence and persecution – of Europe. This mythology of security has been steadfastly pursued (as well as politicized, corrupted, fetishized, etc.) ever since, even in the face of the decimation of the native population and the importation of slaves from Africa. But as small eastern settlements became villages and then cities, the old corrupting influences of power and money naturally reemerged. Necessarily, then, the call of an idealized frontier endured, for the "old European idea of the frontier suggested something heavy and permanent – a stone wall, a gun emplacement or a fortress, a range of mountains meant to hold in check the movement of peoples and the passage of time. But in the American West the frontier was always about the future" (Lapham

6). Over time, the struggle between a communal, urban dependence and a solitary, frontier independence has developed into a significant part of the national consciousness, a shared "American-ness." Even after Frederick Jackson Turner declared the actual frontier closed in 1893, its siren call remained, influencing almost everything in America, from capitalism to religion to America's post Spanish-American War colonial endeavors.

This conflict, of course, also manifests itself in America's literature. As many critics have noted, the modern short story developed and flourished as a distinct American genre. But history, like generic convention, is not stagnant: "Genre is always the same and not the same, always old and new simultaneously" (Bakhtin 87). In turn, the American short story has continued to evolve into still other related (sub-)genres, from the short-story cycle to flash fiction. Enjoying perhaps endless permutations, the short-story cycle is inextricably interwoven into the ubiquitous and internal American conflict of wanting to, on the one hand, as Huckleberry Finn does, "light out for the Territory" or, on the other, to put down roots. The American short-story cycle, too, closely mirrors the development of the country. Frank O'Connor observed some forty years ago that "America is largely populated by submerged population groups" (41), and whether it be socioeconomic status, or race, or a host of other categories, such groups have long been a focus of the ever-developing short-story cycle. As James Nagel notes, the contemporary cycle,[1] though largely critically overlooked until a few decades ago (Forrest L. Ingram published the first book-length study in 1971), is increasingly "patently multicultural" (Nagel, *Contemporary* 4–5); in conversation, J. Gerald Kennedy explains this as "characters living on two sides of the hyphen." Rocío Davis concurs: "the dynamics of the short-story cycle have converted it into a form that is especially appropriate to the kinds of conflict presented in ethnic fiction" (4). Generic development, as well as the peculiar American tension between the impulse to stay or to move on, can be better understood by briefly looking at the genre's history as well as more closely examining two examples that span the genre, Sherwood Anderson's genre-defining and much-discussed book *Winesburg, Ohio* (1919) and Kelly Cherry's excellent and critically overlooked *The Society of Friends* (1999).

A Brief History of the American Short-Story Cycle, with Examples

A founding father of American literature, Washington Irving explored the peculiar need for movement in American life. By adapting European folk tales and setting them in America, he directed American literature away from Europe by largely rejecting the novel form and instead writing in a more episodic manner, which better addressed the transitory urgency of life in America. Irving composed *The Sketch Book of Geoffrey Crayon, Gent.*, perhaps his most famous work, as a cohesive series of stories meant to be published together, though the stories were not intentionally connected, per se, like many cycles would later be. Due to financial considerations *The Sketch Book* was published serially from 1819 to 1820. Irving writes:

> The following papers, with two exceptions, were written in England, and formed but part of an intended series for which I had made notes and memorandums. Before I could mature a plan, however, circumstances compelled me to send them piecemeal to the United States, where they were published from time to time in portions or numbers. (vii)

Of course, the genre of linked stories was not recognized critically at the time, but Irving's urge toward unification in theme and intent is obvious.

Increasingly, the American short-story cycle is understood by a growing handful of critics to exist not only in conjunction with, but independent of, other genres. As genre serves "essentially to establish a contract between writer and reader so as to make certain relevant expectations operative" (Culler 147), there remains much critical work to be done in this under-appreciated genre. In fact, its very existence often remains suspect. For instance, in a recent book review, Thomas Mallon claims:

> Even loyal visitors to the ever mossier precincts of literary fiction tend to regard the genre of "linked stories" with some suspicion. This polite publishers' label is often used to camouflage an unrealized novel, one that never exceeded the sum of its parts and had to be disassembled, then salvaged as a collection of tales featuring the same hero or heroine. (7)

Doubters notwithstanding, if the novel and the short story exist at opposite ends of some kind of narrative prose continuum, clearly much vibrant literary space exists between these bookends. For, as Nagel points out, many recent examples of the genre were, upon their publication, misidentified – by any one of a number of otherwise sympathetic entities, including the publisher, the critics, and/or the readers – usually as something approaching the "superior" form of the novel.[2] Setting aside Poe's artistic hierarchy (60), many critics have observed that the lamentable bias toward the novel over the short story has long existed, even if, as Christina Nehring argues, "[t]here is no such thing as a higher genre or a lower genre in literature; there is only good writing and bad writing, strong thinking and weak thinking" (83).

As for all genres, of course, the boundaries of the short-story cycle are, thankfully, undulating and permeable. Perhaps it is not even possible, or desirable, to "delimit that corpus" (Bal 3), thus dividing texts into this genre or that. Naturally, there is a danger that "as soon as the word 'genre' is sounded ... a limit is drawn" (Derrida 52); however, that we lack a universal definition of the short-story cycle is an asset rather than a liability and, moreover, merely a fact of generic convention. For instance, critics have often described all of Faulkner's works as one giant, interconnected community, in and out of which Southerners continually and tragically march. Malcolm Cowley astutely observed – and, notably, Nagel records (*Contemporary* 1) – that Faulkner's *Knight's Gambit*, a collection of mystery tales, "is, however, something more than a mere collection. It belongs to a genre that Faulkner has made peculiarly his own ... a cycle of stories" ("Faulkner" 7).[3] About *Winesburg, Ohio*, Cowley has similarly argued: "In structure the book lies midway between the novel proper and the mere collection of stories [that word again: "mere"] ... it is a cycle of stories with several unifying elements, including a single background, a prevailing tone, and a central character" ("Introduction" 14). Whether or not Cowley ever connected these two reviews to each other in print, it is interesting that he had similar definitions for a complete body of work on the one hand and a single book on the other.

Like the skills necessary to survive the ever-changing American frontier, adaptation has been the rule and not the exception for the American short-story cycle. Just as genres bleed into one another so, too, do international influences. Indeed, the concept of linking stories together to form a text greater than the whole extends back into the antiquity of oral tradition.[4] Perhaps the first important (that is, with lasting and direct influence) *modern* example of the genre is Ivan Turgenev's *A Sportsman's Notebook* (Russia, 1847–51), which moved the modern short-story cycle from the more commercial enterprise of serial publication into a "formal exercise in arrangement" (Kennedy, "From Anderson's" 195).[5] In turn, and to varying degrees, the structure and style of this work influenced both Sherwood Anderson's *Winesburg, Ohio* and Joyce's *Dubliners* (1914), the two works still considered by most critics to be the hallmarks of the genre.[6]

Generally, American short-story cycles are book-length works that, by design,[7] create a larger community, when all the short stories therein – essentially, *but not fully*, autonomous[8] – are considered. Robert Luscher writes that the genre is "essentially a hybrid resulting from the cross between the two prose genres that dominated nineteenth century fiction[,] the novel and the short story" ("Regional" 2); authors employ the genre, he argues, in order to represent "spaces, both psychological and physical" ("Discussion").

A short story, Nadine Gordimer argues, is "like the flash of fireflies, in and out, now here, now there, in darkness" (264); a "discrete moment of truth is aimed at – not *the* moment of truth, because the short story doesn't deal in cumulatives" (265). Gordimer means here a single firefly, a single story, but as anyone who has lived in firefly country knows, they are rarely seen alone. After all, their light is a mating tool that both attracts and competes with other fireflies. A short-story cycle, then, may be likened to a field of fireflies in the humid summer warmth at dusk. Through *progression* and *interconnection*, the book-length "story" of the cycle transcends individual story boundaries and becomes a whole text greater than the sum of its parts. The short-story cycle maintains book-length continuity through one of a variety of methods, including *adapting* or *discarding* such commonly used novelistic strategies as character cohesion (i.e., having a central character or characters), maintaining a central incident-based plot, and/or establishing temporal continuity, etc. Conversely, the genre also builds on narrative strategies from the short story, a genre which often presents "characters in their essential aloneness, not in their taken-for-granted social world" (May, "Knowledge" 137). However, while an individual character in a cycle may think that he or she is alone, the reader knows otherwise, because this one story is then buttressed by a variety of others, a situation not available to the autonomous short story.

Though not a particularly good piece of literature, an excellent illustrative example of how the American short-story cycle represents a particular community as well as perpetual American restlessness is Brander Matthews's *The Story of a Story and Other Stories* (1893) (though, as the name suggests, this cycle does not make up the entire book). The cycle, composed of ten interconnected stories, traces the story of a story, from its creation by the author, to its manipulation, dissemination, and extended life, as influenced by the editor, the sketch artist, printer, publisher, critic, and several readers. The character of the author in the first story, "The Author," is an invalid who can go nowhere because of his ruined body and the "coming suffering" (9); he merely sits, longingly gazing "towards the west" (3), his personal frontier. Naturally, he hopes his stories will travel where his body cannot; indeed, his story makes it into the hands of, among others, two engineers, who are "the pioneers of civilization in the new West" (32). Though the story's author wants to write stories where "the moral is quite concealed" (8), this is, perhaps ironically, not the case for this cycle. In the last story, "A Reader of Another Sort," a boy reads the author's story in "a worn and ragged copy of the midsummer number of *The Metropolis*" (42) and his life changes: "'A fine story, mother?' he echoed. 'It's great. It's true. That's the kind of man I'd like to be'" (48). Years later, the boy, now an adult who has lived his life in the shadow of the story, tries to contact the author, but learns he died only a fortnight after writing this last story. The young man writes a letter to the widow, who is thrilled and surprised at this development, unlike the reader, who no doubt saw some version of this ending from a mile away, and thus is little pleased by it. Though Matthews's work represents the inherent dangers of the genre in that *The Story of a Story* is much too *obviously* contrived to be serious literature, it also mirrors the enduring American drive to create, to move, and to belong, for the pleasure that the widow takes from the letter is that her long-dead husband's story was like a "lamp to [this] man's feet" (50).

However, the history of the development of this genre is rife with prominent and superior cycles which explore this tension – to remain in one place or to keep moving – within the American (sub)consciousness. One such early example is set in the small Maine coastal village of Dunnet Landing. The characters in Sarah Orne Jewett's *The Country of the Pointed Firs* (1896) live sparse lives and pine for loves lost and times gone. The character connecting the stories is, however, newly arrived to Dunnet Landing. She seeks an escape from the big city and a peaceful place where she might work on her writing. Over the course of the summer, the unnamed narrator becomes an intimate of the townspeople. She begins her summer stay on the island with Almira Todd, an herbalist who assists the townsfolk with various maladies, real or otherwise. The introduction of a "foreign" person into an established community is an oft-used convention of the American short-story cycle (as is a "local" desiring to leave). Jewett's narrator knows her time in tranquil Maine is at best an occasional respite from her other life. She thus stands in stark contrast to George Willard in *Winesburg, Ohio* (see below), whose sole desire – a desire to which he clings at the expense of all else – is to leave the small town for the city. However, even in the small town, her city-born restlessness persists, for she soon leaves Almira and rents an old schoolhouse just *outside* the village. Throughout the summer, she meets many of the townsfolk and writes a book, presumably the book we are now reading (unlike the story in Matthews's cycle or Anderson's "The Book of the Grotesque," which the reader does not see – unless, of course, *Winesburg* is itself this book). The book consists of character sketches, such as that of Captain Littlepage, who complains that, "when folks left home in the old days they left it to some purpose, and when they got home they stayed there and had some pride in it" (26). The narrator is sympathetic, but from a younger generation. For when she leaves Dunnet Landing at summer's end, it is with trepidation, because she will be returning "to the world in which I feared to find myself a foreigner" (158).

In *The Golden Apples* (1949), Eudora Welty expands on the village sketch tradition (see Zagarell). Welty's characters are everyday Mississippians who speak their regional dialect and are ever-frustrated by the universal tediums of life. Her simple and eccentric characters live lives of gossipy desperation in Morgana, a town with a name as fantastical as the town itself is average. Like many sequences whose stories were originally published separately, Welty's stories are clearly meant to go together and to be read progressively. Besides the unifying effect of an initial list of characters at the beginning of the book, the book's title likewise links all the stories. It is taken from William Butler Yeats's poem "The Song of Wandering Aengus" (1897) and hints that the search for the golden apples of truth and beauty, in which all of Welty's characters are engaged, is greater than any one character.

The primary location of these stories is Morgana, MacLain County, a county named after the ancestors of King MacLain, the cycle's dominant and unifying, if elusive, figure. In the first story "Shower of Gold," we learn that King has married Miss Snowdie MacLain – a name that fits her albinism – an act for which we must, apparently, give him some credit; after all, "Lots of worse men wouldn't have" (4). But King himself is a wanderer, planting his seed like Johnny Appleseed, so much so that it seems he is related to someone in every story. Though he marries Snowdie, his location is usually a mystery: "there are people that consider he headed West" (3), looking for his own golden apples. Returning upon occasion, King won't even meet his wife in the house, but sends word to her that they are to couple in the forest. The local gossips don't understand King's reluctance to enter the town, for King and Snowdie are indeed *properly* married. Though King, it is assumed, comes back for good in the last story, "The Wanderers," his presence is felt throughout the rest of the stories, both genetically through multiple offspring, and spiritually.

In "Sir Rabbit," King waits in the forest with his twin sons, hunting and seducing a girl wandering in the forest with the foreshadowing name of Mattie Will. King's earthy, pagan ways are well known in the town and enticing to Mattie: "'I know the way you do'" (98), she cries. Later, after Mattie is married to the simpleton Junior, she keeps these memories to herself. Years later, thinking about King and his beautiful twins and their "aching Adam's apples" (111), Mattie "thought they were mysterious and sweet – gamboling now she knew not where." It is the search for the golden apples and not the finding of them that continually lends a glimmer of hope to these character' lives, unlike in *Winesburg, Ohio*, where the grotesques are irretrievably mis-shapen – both physically and psychologically – by their fruitless searches and their obsession with appearing normal and civilized. Throughout *Apples*, the characters strive for something more, but mostly the search is a futile one. The disparate characters, who have sung their song like the wandering Aengus, literally come together in the final story, "The Wanderers," in a way that echoes the coming together of the themes of all the stories in Joyce's story "The Dead" or Kelly Cherry's last story "Block Party" (see below).

Though for very different reasons from Europeans, Native Americans have likewise long been unsettled – since well before Congress passed the "Indian Removal Act" in 1830. Though on the move for hundreds of years, after being endlessly lied to, manipulated, and slaughtered, for just as long Native Americans have struggled to resist Caucasian encroachments and to (re)claim some semblance of an original culture. Indeed, the form of the short-story cycle, "far from being an artificial aesthetic construct, is the traditional form of extended fiction among Native Americans" (Nagel, *Contemporary* 21) and is seen in the work of many Native American writers, from Leslie Marmon Silko's *Storyteller* (1981), Louise Erdrich's *Love Medicine* (1984), to Sherman Alexie's *The Lone Ranger and Tonto Fistfight in Heaven* (1993).

Alexie's text explores Spokane/Coeur d'Alene Indians and their desire to reclaim the ancient traditions of an oral culture as well as their paradoxical rejection of that culture for the Anglo trappings of Diet Pepsi and basketball, both on and off the reservation. The book's very first scene, in "Every Little Hurricane," hints at both the communal spirit on the reservation and a world where everything might be upset at any moment:

> Although it was winter, the nearest ocean four hundred miles away, and the Tribal Weatherman asleep because of boredom, a hurricane dropped from the sky in 1976 and fell so hard on the Spokane Indian Reservation that it knocked Victor from bed and his latest nightmare.
>
> It was January and Victor was nine years old. He was sleeping in his bedroom in the basement of the HUD house when it happened. His mother and father were upstairs, hosting the largest New Year's Eve party in tribal history, when the winds increased and the first tree fell. (1)

The party quickly degenerates into a fistfight between Victor's two drunk uncles. That they were "slugging each other with such force that they had to be in love" (2) is most probably, we shall learn, a result of their frustration – a collective, tribal-wide frustration – with their suppressed history and general lack of purpose. At any moment, everything on the reservation can be upset anew by an action taken by a government far away and utterly removed from local control or interest.

This conflict sets the stage for the book as we follow loosely the story of Victor and Adrian and their sometime-friend, Thomas Builds-the-Fire. In their own way and at every turn, they struggle with the desire to remain on the reservation and to leave it. True, Victor and Thomas leave the reservation to collect Victor's father's corpse (or what is left of it) in "This Is What It Means to Say Phoenix, Arizona," and later Victor temporarily leaves the reservation to live in town, but mostly this desire is replaced with the stasis of indecision. They want the old ways to return. They want to be warriors, though their attempts to re-assume this mantle of masculinity and freedom means that mostly they "just parked it in front of the Trading Post and tried to look like horsepowered warriors" (13). They ingest hallucinogenic drugs to conjure the old visions, think back without irony to the time Victor's father was the only Indian who heard Jimi Hendrix play the "Star-Spangled Banner" at Woodstock and, as a community, put Thomas on trial for telling too many old tales, tales which cause the Indians to weep and "admit defeat" (97). Even their modern warriors – basketball players – are almost certain to flame out to alcohol and apathy: "There's a definite history of reservation heroes who never finish high school, who never finish basketball seasons" (47). Still, the search continues for the next generation's savior. Sitting on the porch, discussing past glory, Victor and Adrian will take anything they can get, even the future hope now residing in a third grade, little *female* warrior-basketball player (53). But based on the past, there is not much hope.

Solidifying a Genre: Sherwood Anderson's *Winesburg, Ohio*

The American short-story cycle with perhaps the greatest effect on the genre is Sherwood Anderson's *Winesburg, Ohio* (1919), the enduring influence of which is difficult to overestimate. Sherwood Anderson claimed to have sought "a new looseness, and in *Winesburg*," he said, "I had made my own form. There were individual tales but all about lives in some way connected" (*Memoirs* 289). Perhaps he sought this "new" form because, as Malcolm Cowley argues, Anderson couldn't write successful novels, for "those moments at the center of Anderson's often marvelous stories were moments, in general, without a sequel; they existed separately and timelessly" ("Introduction" 11). The novel form required of Anderson a character endurance he seemed unable to maintain, and were he to carry out, as Poe called it, the "fullness of his intention" ("Review" 61) – in this case, the representation of a troubled community – he needed some other form. Carl A. Bredahl argues that "[w]hen Sherwood Anderson rejected the novel form as not fitting an American writer, he rejected the values of continuity, direction, and completion complicit in the traditional form" (422). In a form found somewhere between a cohesive novel or an independent short story, Anderson captured in *Winesburg* the basic tensions between the desire to remain in a small community promising prosperity through unity (even if rarely achieved), and the urge to leave the small town for the big city.

Young newspaperman George Willard, the book's quasi-protagonist, is regarded as a key representative of the town, even by those who despise him ("'George belongs to this town,'" Seth believes, in "The Thinker" [131]). Nevertheless, George's prime desire is to escape the town's grip and to make "something" of himself ("'From this time on,'" Wing tells him in "Hands," "'you must shut your ears to the roaring of the voices'" of the town [13]). This is a conflict with which many Winesburgers struggle. Indeed, many still have "adventures," but they are mostly already broken by time and disappointment when George first learns their story. Thus, George seems a bright spot in town; in him, there is hope, for, as the narrator explains in "Departure," George's life "had become but a background on which to paint the dreams of his manhood" (252). That George finally undertakes the journey that has so preoccupied him might suggest that all is well, or, at least, hopeful. Indeed, many critics read the book's ending this way. But there remain contradicting signs throughout the book which suggest that George's quest will ultimately be both frustrated and futile; it seems doubtful that the mere act of leaving the small town will be the antidote for the insecurities which plague him. For instance, in the aptly titled story, "Loneliness," Enoch Robinson leaves Winesburg for New York City to become an artist (thus foreshadowing George's own exodus?). But Enoch's city sojourn is a failure; understood by no one except for the woman he drives away with vulgarities, he is, he tells George, all alone (177). However, this warning, along with many others throughout the book, is lost on George; he remains undaunted, though Tom, the train conductor, "had seen a thousand George Willards go out of their towns to the city" (251).

Throughout *Winesburg*, George remains focused on – or obsessed with – his quest and learns little along the way from so many who try and teach him: "'I'm going to be a big man, the biggest that ever lived here in Winesburg'" (240), he tells Helen White. The irony, of course, is that in order for this to happen, George never entertains seriously the idea of staying in Winesburg. No, in order to be the biggest man *in* Winesburg, George believes, he must live *out* of it, thus falling into the trap that Wing Biddlebaum warns him of in "Hands" at the very beginning of the book: "'You are destroying yourself ... You want to be like the others in town here'" (12). His family decimated, his love-life too complicated, George leaves because he feels that he must, little understanding that all these issues will leave Winesburg with him. When he is with Helen – a moment when "they had both got from their silent evening together the thing they needed" (248) – George "sees himself merely as a leaf blown by the wind through the village" (239). Indeed, when we first meet George, we see immediately his desire to wander, as he often ventures to the outskirts of town to visit the local outcast, Wing. Though he continues to be pulled in multiple directions, George remains focused. In "Mother," George is pulled between the desires of his two parents. George's father wants him to succeed, to perhaps become one of the "chief men of the town" (28), something his father only pretends for himself when he is away from his wife. On the other hand, George's mother, bowed from disease, prays earnestly for her son to do what she could not, perhaps "joining some company and wandering over the world, seeing always new faces" (30).

Though the reader spends the most amount of time with George – which is why most critics view him as *the* "primary protagonist" (Nagel, *Contemporary* 6) – he develops little, so obsessed is he with his goal of leaving the town. That leaving Winesburg is necessary is George's immutable truth, which also puts him in danger, according to the anonymous author/narrator's beliefs in the framing story, "The Book of the Grotesque": "the moment one of the people took one of the truths to himself, called it his truth, and tried to live his life by it, he became a grotesque and the truth he embraced became a falsehood" (6). George is not so much *the* protagonist in a novelistic sense as a window through which other Winesburgers view their own frustrated efforts at communication and forward progress. While George's "struggle for self-realization and growth," Nagel writes, "creates a paramount line of development for the volume" (*Contemporary* 6), the lives of the other Winesburgers are intricately connected to and perhaps even *as important as* George's own story. After all, not only is George Willard *not* the protagonist in every story, he is not even *in* every story (he has no part in "Paper Pills" as well as the four-part "Godliness" or even, perhaps, the introductory story "The Book of the Grotesque"[9]). In fact, he appears as the primary character in arguably only four of the stories (the second, "Mother," and the last three, "Death," "Sophistication," and "Departure"). Elsewhere, George Willard is either the "sought-out listener, or observer" (Dunn and Morris 53) or something even less, a character mentioned only in passing, a connective device. George may be the most important grotesque in the book, but he remains a grotesque.

Evolution of Genre and Nation: A Contemporary Example

Though many still question the existence and/or relevance of the genre, the strength and popularity of the American short-story cycle shows no sign of flagging. Kelly Cherry's *The Society of Friends*, an excellent book that has been heavily reviewed but not as yet critically examined, builds on the tradition of Anderson's *Winesburg, Ohio* (and Joyce's *Dubliners*), while it charts but one of the many ways in which both the genre and American society have evolved. Cherry, retired Eudora Welty Professor of English at the University of Madison, Wisconsin, also echoes Raymond Carver – who despised any and all kinds of tricks in writing (88) – when she writes that what she desires is to read – and presumably, write – work endowed with "honesty" and "not tainted with cleverness" ("Cleverness" 184). Honest literature, she feels, forswears the necessity for applause that clever writing demands:

> Would literature that managed to negate its need for attention send itself to kingdom come, blow itself up, like an apocalypse? Are we speaking here of a self-contradiction

that can lead only to *fin de siècle* foolishness and disaster? Or, on the contrary, is not absence of self-contradiction the sad little secret at the center of even the smartest current fiction, an academic inability to admit to the disorganization in the universe, to a multiplicity of perspective: we want our fiction to toe the line, the politically correct line, though the line will shift and shift. And how *cleverly* it is done, as if with mirrors, while not just corners but vast rooms of our consciousness go unreflected and unreflected upon. (185)

It is this *apparent* disorganization and disconnection resulting from "a multiplicity of perspective[s]" that, like life, is at once key to the community of Madison and the (often frustrated) movement within so many American short-story cycles.

Cherry writes about a modern American town, a place neither big nor small, a place filled with interlopers, people not at all local, yet people who, when making their case to the small business loan officer, *"believe in the viability of our downtown area"* (*Friends* 13; Cherry's italics). Such people are at once descendants of and very different from George Willard.

Cherry has long been interested in the short-story cycle genre. Writing about another short-story cycle of hers, *My Life and Dr. Joyce Brothers: A Novel in Stories* (1990) (the misnaming of such works is a common enough problem, as Nagel points out, *Contemporary* 18) in the *New York Times Book Review*, David Finkle admonishes his readers: "forget the title and the classification of the book as a 'novel in stories,' which sounds as if Ms. Cherry is trying to have things both ways" (14). Nine years later, however, Cherry, and/or her publisher, does not seem to have the same confusion as to genre, for the book *The Society of Friends* is called a book of "stories" on the front cover. Cherry also quotes from the *Winesburg* story "Death" to begin her book. Nevertheless, as is typical, some of the stories from this cycle – all about tenuously upper middle-class academics and the search for a meaningful life amidst the largesse of the present-day American suburb – appeared elsewhere first. Notably, the story "Not the Phil Donahue Show" was originally published in the *Virginia Quarterly Review* and won an O. Henry Award in 1994.

Similar to Anderson's "The Book of the Grotesque," which Cowley called "a general prologue" ("Introduction" 13), Cherry's first story, "The Prowler: A Prologue," introduces us to various characters in the community of Madison, Wisconsin, some of whom will later have their "own" story. In the person of Nina Bryant, university professor and locally famous writer, there is something of a central character (like George Willard and Anderson, one can see echoes of the quasi-autobiographical relationship between Nina and Cherry): Cherry writes that Nina "is who I would be if I were living her life" [*Writing* 38]). Cherry uses the device of a prowler – an enigmatic figure who lurks in the dark on the frontier between the safe light of the home and the dangerous dark of the street – to represent the common fears of not just Madisonians, but people throughout America's suburban communities.

In a town of seemingly comfortable houses hidden from the street, of bookstore-filled main streets and community gatherings, the prowler threatens the outwardly placid neighborhood with unrest, fear, and insecurity. Indeed, we learn that many in the community have sensed the prowler's presence. Taken in sum, the prowler is a projection of the community's collective insecurities, a representation of whatever they dread: death, sexual conflict, divorce, bankruptcy, the onset of Alzheimer's in one's parents, etc. Throughout the book, however, the narrator's voice often assumes a semi-humorous (even fatalistic) perspective on events, thus undermining this sense of insecurity. For the narrator's tone indicates that such a feeling is suspect. After all, such people live lives of relative ease and comfort, and thus their fears are largely self-manufactured, products of myriad neuroses and an inability to accept the inevitability of decline and decay, certainties that even the promised security of suburbia cannot forestall.

In the center story (there are six stories before and six after) "As It Is in Heaven," Nina visits her mother in London, where she and Nina's father have moved after retirement, a world reminiscent of Joyce's Dublin in *Dubliners*. Because Nina temporarily leaves her home, the reader is afforded the ability to examine her home from afar, much as we might have wanted to examine Winesburg from George Willard's perspective after he arrived in the big city. Like Joyce's blind-filled Dublin, Cherry's London is also a world of dead-end streets, a place where the working classes coagulate amid a tangible sense of socioeconomic class division: "The house was in a close, a dead-end drive like a sclerotic artery to the heart of the development" (*Friends* 73). But London is not the escape for which Nina's parents had hoped, something Nina had not realized before visiting them. Nina comes to understand that her parents' gaze has always been far afield, and she now believes that her mother has wasted her time looking "out over the Gulf in the direction of Mexico and South America, constructing the future as an exotic landscape just over the horizon" (83). Her parents have never had time for the present and even though her father is dead (his ghost still appears in the kitchen), her mother continues this obsession with the future, though her only current future can be death. Thematically and emotionally, this story balances Nina's own story – before the trip Nina is lost; afterwards, she vows to reduce her wandering – even as her neighbors, with a single story each, are perpetually foundering, caught between the desire to embed in the community and to reject the knowledge that they are only one more community transient, albeit transients with single family homes.

In "Chores," for instance, Conrad hires a Czech graduate student to shovel his snow. She needs the money, but it is a big job, so she brings her mother along. Like the Reverend Curtis Hartman in Anderson's "The Strength of God," or the young narrator in Joyce's "Araby," Conrad "watches them from his bedroom window, peering between the slats of the blind" (55). He watches them, or the daughter anyway, lustfully; he watches them also because he feels guilty: "Now he feels like shit. This is not how he wants to see himself: as landed gentry, an overseer. He wants to be kind. He wants to make broad, humanitarian gestures. He wants to be like Václav Havel." He wants to be, but he is not. Instead, he just watches them, weakly promising himself that next year he will shovel the snow himself. Cast adrift in a single *family* home, Conrad spends his time gazing out the window at this family, itself essentially whole but houseless. It is this window through which, Robert Beuka claims, "middle-class American culture casts its uneasy reflective gaze on itself" amidst the "symbolic minefield" of modern suburbia (4).

And yet the majority of the major characters in *Friends* have already risen to, and are "content" to remain at, their middle- to upper middle-class level, all the while trying desperately to ignore the life-rupturing explosions that lurk behind every corner. This socioeconomic level embarrasses them and leaves them ill prepared to deal with those from other classes. This is especially true when the (sub-)divisions are purely economic and not educational, this latter creating a forced solidarity. Conrad, we learn, is trying to recover from the recent death of his wife and child in a car accident; he obsesses over all the chores he must complete alone. For this reason he hires the Czech graduate student. But he also does so because, as an "affluent" American, the ethos of his suburban community conditions him to try and help those less fortunate, if only to assuage his class-guilt. The conflict arises when this Czech "charity case" violates Conrad's neighborhood space. This immigrant, who has come to America to better herself, has crossed into the territory of Conrad's insulated neighborhood. This is certainly a common enough occurrence in the suburbs of America where the house cleaners and yard keepers arrive by day and leave before dusk. But Conrad is a professor and is thus often home during the day. After Conrad embarrassedly tells her that he can't even balance his checkbook, she "looked at him with a mild pity, perhaps the way she regarded all Americans, as a weak people with money and bad puns. She is strong and beautiful and smart, a worthy compatriot of Václav Havel" (61). She already is what Conrad cannot be.

When we first meet her, Nina is likewise trapped in her home and in her life. The snow confines her older, present-day self within her younger self, a self who was long ago molested by her brother, in "Love in the Middle Ages." But where snow trapped the girl Nina, it eventually becomes a blanket of comfort for the adult Nina, who at last learns to trust a man. Almost. On their way to the bedroom to make love for the first time, the snow recreates, in part, Nina's childhood dreams from *before* they were assaulted by her brother's actions and her parents' inaction: "As they entered her own room and shut the door behind them, she looked out the window and saw that fresh snow had fallen, arborvitae wearing long white gloves on their limbs, like women at the opera. Frost-mountains sloped down the windowpanes into the valley of the sill" (157). Nina is not fully recovered, however, for she passively allows Palmer to take her to bed and is even "too embarrassed to look at him." Nevertheless, it is a start.

Boundaries are permeable in *Friends*. Even the noise of the congested city cannot stay outside; like the fear of the prowler, the din invades the suburban streets and enters homes through the windows, under the doors. Home is an illusory refuge at best, in part because this society of friends is anything but permanent. Cherry's characters have come to Madison from other places and are always looking to go to yet others; there is scarcely a Wisconsinian in the batch. Typical of the characters is Nina's love interest, Palmer, a man who, "like most academics[,] ... was deracinated, a man for all locales, Pittsburgh, Charlottesville, Palo Alto had been some of the points on his trajectory, but weren't they all the same, intellectually homogenous no matter how ethnically diverse, one big reading list?" (140). Writing about this transitory American nature in *Marxism Today*, Doreen Massey asks, "How, in the face of all this movement and intermixing, can we retain any sense of a local place and its particularity?" (24). Cherry's Madison, then, subverts the more traditional, pre-industrial understanding of community and space against which George Willard struggled, for everyone is ever in flux, trying to cross boundaries, because this is what educated people are *supposed* to do. Just among Nina's friends, "Aria wished she lived in Wyoming or Utah, someplace roomy" (175); Larry "was thinking of moving to Chicago. He had an offer" (181). When Jewish DA Manny Durkheim and the African American performance artist/professor Jasmine Jazz (who owns a cat named Zora Neale) begin dating, Manny must overcome his discomfort with their multiracial situation. This, despite their mutual attraction and his belief that he is beyond prejudice. After sex for the first time:

> "You have to get used to the idea that you're the kind of man who could find himself in bed with a woman like me," she reminded him.
> It was already morning. Cold light was breaking into the room, a burglar stealing the night away. (105)

Manny has his work cut out for him.

In "Tell Her," Guy knows that he must inform his wife that they are about to lose the house, because the bookstore for which he mortgaged it is not paying the bills – this is a sin worse than infidelity in a community which has plenty of infidelity but where everyone at least has a house for hiding. Telling his wife is not really a possibility; he believes he wants to, but he always finds other things to do, like taking a walk, or inventory. Besides, Guy thinks his wife is having an impossible-to-have sexual affair with the gay celibate Dooley. But Guy must tell someone about losing the bookstore so he chooses a famous young, unnamed female author who gives a reading at his store. And because, the narrator suggests, this is what famous, young female authors do – reverse stereotypical gender expectations – *she* asks *him* the question: "'What do you want out of life?'" (27). The answer is that he wants to communicate with his wife, but he cannot bring himself to do so. Guy's life is all turned around. Later that evening, as Guy lies to himself yet again that he is ready to tell his wife, Jordan, *she* asks *him* to dance. She knows he has something on his mind, but wants him to tell her "later" (29). Arm in arm, they are their own estranged community: "The man and woman beginning to dance, moving toward each other, moving away."

Just as the American short-story cycle continues to evolve, Cherry's suburban community remains ultimately unsettled. As Massey points out, America's "(idealized) notion of an era when places were (supposedly) inhabited by coherent and homogenous communities is set against the current fragmentation and disruption" (24). Despite the wishes of Nina and her neighbors, Cherry's Madison is such a place. Place seems to matter less and less, while words and how things are described assume prime importance. Words, however, like people, are now easily transportable, nomadic, unstable; they "can take us anyplace, even Cleveland. Words can convey us coast to coast in the time it takes to write a subordinate clause – and without losing your luggage" (Cherry, *Writing* 95). In *Winesburg* it is George and a few others who are eternally transient; in *Friends* it is everyone.

Characters in *Friends* try to advance their own lives independently on some kind of positive trajectory, but fail to account for the unavoidable change that comes from interaction, petty or otherwise, with others. The modern suburban American experience both brings together people of like socioeconomic status and isolates them. In their own private dust-collecting castles, families try to operate as mini-fiefdoms; they try to be emotionally self-sufficient. Cherry's characters, each within some semblance of family, even a family of ghosts ("As It Is in Heaven" and "Chores") constantly fight the tension between the demands of their own "lands" and the need to go out of their homes and to interact meaningfully with others, the key to any *successful* community. Each character, then, in each home becomes his or her own country, an individual frontier, desiring of and yet fearful of penetration. Hugo Gutsmer is one geography, "short and broad, and his face, with deep-set eyes and sharply planed cheekbones and steep chin, was like a topographical map of difficult terrain" (174) with a "face of highs and lows" (185); Aria's body was another, her "arms, toned, and bare under a flak vest, were like a rippling landscape – the gentle hills of her biceps, the smooth sloping run of her forearms" (175). About such human archipelagoes, Kim Worthington notes the "tension between individual autonomy and communal constructivism" (10).

These islands of people ebb and flow; some get washed away altogether. Over time, Cherry writes, "some pattern appears, some repetition or return threads its way through the broad loom of a life so that even what had once seemed revolution reveals itself as echo, consequence, history" (*Writing* 45). For Cherry, time is "topological, a codification of the patterned tapestry that we weave, wittingly or not." Thus, in Madison "people came and went, they moved in or away, but somehow the neighborhood stayed the same old neighborhood" (*Friends* 4). In the last story, "Block Party," the impermanence of the neighborhood coalesces into a group snapshot of an already fading present:

> In this town, there will be events to mark births and marriages and deaths. There will be graduation parties and retirement parties. People will enter your life, but some of them will stay in it and others will merely visit for a longer or shorter weekend. Sometimes when you wake on summer mornings, you will remember those who have left and wonder where they are now – returned to cosmic dust, some of them, or drinking cappuccino with a new wife in another state. There will be block parties. (171)

Guy struggles with "the students who stay the same age always because, as soon as they rush off into their adult lives, others, exactly like them, take their places" (15). Like the clichéd march of time, everything and nothing changes in Madison.

In a mundane conversation, Nina comments: "'One day there will be a block party on Joss Court and none of us will be here. We know that. But imagine what such a party would be like if we *were* here'" (181). "Block Party" revisits briefly – in a kind of mini-short-story cycle, a pastiche – the key players, while at the same time introducing a new arrival to the neighborhood, Hugo Gutsmer. Nina asks him the ubiquitous American party question: "'What do you do?'" (173). At first she is not so much interested in the answer as she is in finding out why he lives alone, not a "normal" thing in a community with big houses: "Was he gay, divorced, bereaved? In other words, was he a possibility for Sarah?" (173). Hugo claims to be a freelance ethicist, which provides the opportunity for, as is typical for Cherry and her way-too-educated characters, an overly serious, semi-ridiculous conversation about the nature of good and evil, "the talk being a kind of ball game, too, ideas lobbed and caught, some with spin" (178).

Ultimately, the lives of Cherry's characters are all about spin, people spinning on their own axes as they fly through the universe, sometimes colliding substantially with other bodies, but mostly not. Throughout the previous twelve stories, we have seen characters in perpetual battle with the meta-narrative of their own lives, with what they think their lives should be and what they think they are. *Friends* ends, however, on a much different note than *Winesburg*, which sees George, on the cusp of manhood, leave for what he thinks will be something greater. But for Nina, middle-aged and in love again, after the block party, she and Palmer retreat to their home, to their bedroom, apparently happy and, for the moment even, settled. But all is not quite right, of course. Tavy, Nina's adopted daughter and the next generation of frustrated suburban dweller, lies awake in her bed and worries about what might happen: "Parents don't always know everything that can happen. There could be someone, or something, out there, in the dark, waiting" (192). Tavy, only a child, has already been thwarted in love, having lost Rajan – the closest thing to a daddy in her life (30) – when he married Lucy in a Quaker ceremony. The Quakers may be the original "society of friends," but for Tavy, all this did was separate her from his love and teach her that relationships are fleeting. For Tavy, as for most of the Madisonians, the prowler's lurking menace manifests itself as a sense of barely repressed dread of life in suburban America.

Conclusion

The modern evolution of the short story (say, the last 150 years or so) has been spurred by the mass marketing of periodicals, and consequently of stories published independently, "though publication in a book is the final guarantee of [a story's] immortality" (Luscher, "Regional" 12). Thus, a single short story may indeed be a beautiful work of art, but, for the reader, it is difficult to ascertain any community beyond the text of a particular story. That is, it is impossible to draw conclusions about characters *not* present in an isolated story, for the reader understands the characters and plot of the story only insofar as he or she understands the motivations, situations, etc. of the characters in a given story. True, the reader at all times brings to bear innumerable ideas, preconceptions, and prejudices to the text, but if the reader knows of only the one story, removed from the whole, then certainly he or she will be on unstable terrain when seeking extra-story connections in a book of autonomous short stories.

However, when an author presents a multitude of characters in a multitude of stories which he or she has fashioned to create a series of inter-story connections, [a transformation undoubtedly occurs (for the reader, the writer, even perhaps for the characters themselves) for any particular story within the cycle. Given a group of such characters and stories, then, a larger community emerges, a community that mirrors the evolution of the ever-changing and ever-restless American zeitgeist. As readers, we begin to draw inferences about characters within a given story that we *could not draw* if we had but a single story. Upon progressing (reading critically) through the cycle, we simply cannot approach each successive story with a clean slate, an empty mind; quite naturally in a short-story cycle we make connections, see patterns, impose order and meaning retroactively, and begin to anticipate themes and possibilities to come. We know, or sense, that a community is forming, and in our mind we create our own meta-text, making connections progressively *and* regressively; that is, not only do we know more about a later story because we have read former stories in the cycle, but we reinterpret earlier stories after we have read later ones. Kennedy explains: "Assembling narratives about diverse characters to form a composite text, such collections curiously resemble the gathering of a group to exchange the stories that express its collective identity" ("From Anderson's" 194). Usually, however, the characters are not exchanging their stories *for each other*. They are "just" living their lives, and it is the reader around whom the stories gather, and if the stories are good enough, collectively they are sure to travel with the reader as he or she travels through life.

NOTES

1   Different critics use different terms for this genre, the two most popular being "short-story cycle" and "short-story sequence." Kennedy, who prefers the term "sequence," argues that "juxtaposed experiences disclose connections that apparently link [the characters'] lives to a larger scheme of order and meaning" ("From Anderson's" 194). Nagel, preferring the term "cycle," writes: "Indeed, in most such collections, 'sequentiality' is the least important aspect of the groupings of stories within a volume" (*Contemporary* 12). It should herein be acknowledged that critics using either term (or, still others) are discussing *more or less* the same genre. For a more sustained discussion, see chapter 1 in Dunn and Morris (they use the term "composite novel").

2   With such generic and international priority long given to the novel, it is interesting to note the pressure that even Anton Chekhov – a major influence on American short story writers from Anderson to Raymond Carver – felt to produce a novel. In a telling letter, Chekhov discusses a *novel* he was writing, called *Stories from the Life of My Friends*: "[I am] writing it in the form of separate, complete stories, closely connected by the common plot, idea, and characters" (14–15). He never finished this or any novel.

3 Malcolm Cowley recognized these intertextual connections perhaps even before Faulkner himself. After all, Cowley edited *The Portable Faulkner* (1946), which, some argue, helped Faulkner to secure the Nobel Prize only four years later. After *The Portable*'s publication, Faulkner wrote to Cowley, admitting that "the job is splendid. Damn you to hell anyway. But even if I had beat you to the idea, mine wouldn't have been this good. By God, I didn't know myself what I had tried to do, and how much I had succeeded" (Gray 58).

4 Indeed, many short-story cycle critics begin their articles and books with a purview of historical and generic precedent. For instance, see Susan Garland Mann (especially 2–14), who loosely traces the genre from the fifteenth century, though she also notes the oral tradition that begins in antiquity and gives rise to, for instance, *The Odyssey* and *The Iliad*; Kennedy similarly notes this long tradition, though "efforts to trace the history of the form at once confront the stark discontinuity of its development" ("Introduction" vii); see also Ingram, 13–14, and Maggie Dunn and Ann Morris for an excellent and comprehensive multilingual chronology of the short-story cycle, beginning with the year 1820, the year Irving's *Sketch Book* was published (xix–xxxi). Such easily accessible iteration thus precludes this study from tracing this same history yet again here.

5 Frank O'Connor claimed, a decade before Ingram's influential study, that Turgenev's cycle of stories "may well be the greatest book of short stories ever written. Nobody, at the time that it was written, knew quite how great it was, or what influence it was to have in the creation of a new art form" (46). Though O'Connor meant the short story and not the cycle, he understood the stories were intimately and progressively connected. Though Stanislaus Joyce claimed that his brother admired this book in particular (98), Richard Ellman argues conversely that Joyce "refused to share" an admiration for Turgenev with his brother (*Joyce* 235). For his own part, Joyce wrote to Stanislaus in 1905 that Turgenev is "a little dull (not clever) and at times theatrical" (Ellman, *Letters* 106). Anderson spent much time deflecting the alleged importance of Turgenev's influence (and that of other Russian writers). Nevertheless, in a 1924 letter, Anderson wrote:

> I spent all those years floundering about. No approach I found satisfied me. Like other Americans, from the beginning, I had to go abroad. I was perhaps 35 years old [roughly 1911, and thus before *Winesburg, Ohio*] when I first found the Russian prose writers. One day I picked up Turgenif's "Annals of a Sportsman." I remember how my hands trembled as I read the book. I raced through the pages like a drunken man. (*Letters* 301–2)

6 Dunn and Morris write: "the best-known twentieth-century example of such a literary text is probably Sherwood Anderson's *Winesburg, Ohio* ... but other well-known works in this genre include ... James Joyce's *Dubliners*" (xiii). That *Winesburg* is more famous today than *Dubliners* is doubtful and perhaps irrelevant, but the point remains. Kennedy writes that, "Joyce's *Dubliners* and Anderson's *Winesburg, Ohio* epitomize [the genre]" ("Introduction" vii); Ingram analyzes *Winesburg* in his study and notes that *Dubliners* is likewise an "important" example (18); Gerald Lynch, writing about Canadian cycles, recognizes these two as "influential classics" (94); Nagel writes: "in English literature, James Joyce's *Dubliners* has served as an archetype of the genre, a role fulfilled in the United States by Sherwood Anderson's *Winesburg, Ohio*" ("Cycle" 9); Luscher acknowledges that "the form's development has been spurred ... by Joyce and Anderson" ("Open Book" 153); Charles E. May calls *Winesburg, Ohio* the "American equivalent" to *Dubliners* (*Artifice* 59).

7 Ingram has identified three major possibilities for the collection of linked stories, categories that have been adjusted, reworked, and renamed by various critics since, but which have remained more or less intact. Such collections, he argues, "may have been COMPOSED as a continuous whole, or ARRANGED into a series, or COMPLETED to form a set" (17; Ingram's caps.). See Ingram, 16–25, for further discussion and definition.

8 Other critics explore elements of this paradoxical understanding – that individual stories in a cycle may be read autonomously *and* with a sense of wholeness, while at the same time

fitting into and giving larger meaning to the schema of the cycle. Nagel argues that "the convention of the form [is] that each element be sufficiently complete for independent publication and yet serve as part of a volume unified" by various means ("Cycle" 9). Nagel's phrase "sufficiently complete" is an excellent one. It at once suggests that a story extracted from a cycle might be enough to provide a reader short on time with what he or she seeks in a story, but also suggests that the story so extracted is necessarily incomplete. Indeed, Nagel points out that some readers "have been led to misinterpret individual stories within a volume, not knowing that they depended on intertextual context for the full development of character motivation and theme" (*Contemporary* 246).

9 The unnamed bedridden author from this introductory story may indeed be the elderly George Willard. He may also be the voice of the narrator of the other stories, or perhaps *Winesburg, Ohio* is the "never published" (Anderson, *Winesburg* 5) book that the writer had written, though these two entities need not be separate. In turn, this old writer may be the voice of Sherwood Anderson, as he envisions himself many years hence. Or not.

REFERENCES AND FURTHER READING

Alexie, Sherman. *The Lone Ranger and Tonto Fistfight in Heaven*. New York: HarperPerennial, 1993.

Anderson, Sherwood. *Letters of Sherwood Anderson*. Eds. Howard Mumford Jones and Walter B. Rideout. Boston: Little, Brown, 1953.

———. *Sherwood Anderson's Memoirs: A Critical Edition*. Ed. Ray Lewis White. Chapel Hill: University of North Carolina Press, 1969.

———. *Winesburg, Ohio*. 1919. New York: Signet, 1993.

Bakhtin, M. M. *Problems of Dostoevsky's Poetics*. Trans. R. W. Rotsel. Ann Arbor, MI: Ardis, 1973.

Bal, Mieke. *Narratology: Introduction to the Theory of Narrative*. Toronto: University of Toronto Press, 1985.

Beuka, Robert. *SuburbiaNation: Reading Suburban Landscape in Twentieth-Century American Fiction and Film*. New York: Palgrave Macmillan, 2004.

Bredahl, Carl A. "'The Young Thing Within': Divided Narrative and Sherwood Anderson's *Winesburg, Ohio*." *Midwest Quarterly* 27.4 (Summer 1986): 422–37.

Carver, Raymond. *Call if You Need Me*. Ed. William L. Stull. New York: Vintage, 2001.

Chase, Cleveland B. *Sherwood Anderson*. New York: McBride, 1927.

Chekhov, Anton. *Letters on the Short Story, the Drama and Other Literary Topics*. Ed. Louis S. Friedland. New York: Benjamin Blom, 1964.

Cherry, Kelly. "Cleverness is a Savings and Loan." *ANQ* 5.4 (October 1992): 184–5.

———. *The Society of Friends*. Columbia: University of Missouri Press, 1999.

———. *Writing the World*. Colombia: University of Missouri Press, 1995.

Cowley, Malcolm. "Faulkner Stories, in Amiable Mood." *New York Herald Tribune Book Review* (November 6, 1949): 7.

———. Introduction. *Winesburg, Ohio*. By Sherwood Anderson. New York: Penguin, 1992. 1–15.

Culler, Jonathan. *Structuralist Poetics*. Ithaca: Cornell University Press, 1975.

Davis, Rocío. "Identity in Community in Ethnic Short Story Cycles: Amy Tan's *The Joy Luck Club*, Louise Erdrich's *Love Medicine*, Gloria Naylor's *The Women of Brewster Place*." *Ethnicity and the American Short Story*. Ed. Julia Brown. New York: Garland, 1997. 3–23.

Derrida, Jacques. "The Law of Genre." Trans. Avita Ronell. *On Narrative*. Ed. W. J. T. Mitchell. Chicago: University of Chicago Press, 1981. 51–77.

Dunn, Maggie, and Ann Morris. *The Composite Novel: The Short Story Cycle in Transition*. New York: Twayne, 1995.

Ellman, Richard. *James Joyce*. New York: Oxford University Press, 1983.

Ellman, Richard, ed. *Letters of James Joyce*. 3 vols. London: Faber & Faber, 1966.

Erdrich, Louise. *Love Medicine*. New York: Bantam, 1984.

Finkle, David. Review of *My Life and Dr. Joyce Brothers: A Novel in Stories*, by Kelly Cherry. *New York Times Book Review* (May 27, 1990): 14.

Gordimer, Nadine. "The Flash of Fireflies." *The New Short Story Theories*. Ed. Charles E. May. Athens: Ohio University Press, 1994. 263–7.

Gray, Paul. "Mister Faulkner Goes to Stockholm. *Smithsonian* 32.7 (October 2001): 56–60.

Ingram, Forrest L. *Representative Short Story Cycles of the Twentieth Century*. The Hague: Mouton, 1971.

Irving, Washington. *The Sketch Book of Geoffrey Crayon, Gent*. New York: G. P. Putnam, 1860.

Jewett, Sarah Orne. *The Country of the Pointed Firs and Other Stories*. Garden City, NY: Doubleday, 1956.

Joyce, Stanislaus. *My Brother's Keeper: James Joyce's Early Years*. New York: Viking, 1958.

Kennedy, J. Gerald. "From Anderson's *Winesburg* to Carver's *Cathedral*: The Short Story Sequence and the Semblance of Community." *Modern American Short Story Sequences*. Ed. J. Gerald Kennedy. Cambridge: Cambridge University Press, 1995. 194–215.

———. "Introduction: The American Short Story Sequence – Definitions and Implications." *Modern American Short Story Sequences*. Ed. J. Gerald Kennedy. Cambridge: Cambridge University Press, 1995. vii–xv.

Lapham, Lewis H. "The Way West." *Harper's* 300.1796 (January 2000): 6–8.

Luscher, Robert. "American Regional Short Story Sequences." Dissertation. Duke University, 1984.

———. "Discussion of Short Story Sequences." Short Story Criticism Papers and Roundtable. Sixth International Conference on the Short Story in English. University of Iowa, Iowa City. October 13, 2000.

———. "The Short Story Sequence: An Open Book." *Short Story Theory at a Crossroads*. Eds. Susan Lohafer and Jo Ellyn Clarey. Baton Rouge: Louisiana State University Press, 1989. 148–67.

Lynch, Gerald. "No Honey, I'm Home: Place Over Love in Alice Munro's Short Story Cycle, *Who Do You Think You Are?*" *Canadian Literature* 160 (1999): 73–98.

Mallon, Thomas. "As Young as You Feel." Review of *The Lemon Table* by Julian Barnes. *New York Times Book Review* (June 27, 2004): 7.

Mann, Susan Garland. *The Short Story Cycle: A Genre Companion and Reference Guide*. New York: Greenwood, 1989.

Massey, Doreen. "A Global Sense of Place." *Marxism Today* (June 1991): 24–29.

Matthews, Brander. *The Story of a Story and Other Stories*. New York: Harper & Brothers, 1893.

May, Charles E. "The Nature of Knowledge in Short Fiction." *The New Short Story Theories*. Ed. Charles E. May. Athens: Ohio University Press, 1994. 131–43.

———. *The Short Story: The Reality of Artifice*. New York: Twayne, 1995.

Nagel, James. "The American Short Story Cycle." *The Columbia Companion to the Twentieth-Century American Short Story*. Ed. Blanche H. Gelfant. New York: Columbia University Press, 2000. 9–14.

———. *The Contemporary American Short-Story Cycle: The Ethnic Resonance of Genre*. Baton Rouge: Louisiana State University Press, 2001.

Nehring, Cristina. "Our Essays, Ourselves: In Defense of the Big Idea." *Harper's* 306.1836 (May 2003): 79–84.

O'Connor, Frank. *The Lonely Voice: A Study of the Short Story*. Cleveland: World, 1962.

Poe, Edgar Allan. "Review of *Twice-Told Tales*." *The New Short Story Theories*. Ed. Charles E. May. Athens: Ohio University Press, 1994. 59–72.

Silko, Leslie Marmon. *Storyteller*. New York: Arcade, 1981.

Turgenev, Ivan. *A Sportsman's Notebook*. Trans. Charles and Natasha Hepburn. New York: Viking, 1957.

Welty, Eudora. *The Golden Apples*. New York: Harcourt, Brace & World, 1956.

Worthington, Kim L. *Self as Narrative: Subjectivity and Community in Contemporary Fiction*. Oxford: Clarendon Press, 1996.

Zagarell, Sandra A. "Narrative of Community: The Identification of a Genre." *Signs* 13.3 (Spring 1988): 498–527.

Index

Updike, John (*cont'd*)
  Author," 357; "Tomorrow and Tomorrow
  and So Forth," 347; *Too Far to Go,*
  354–55; *Tossing and Turning,* 355;
  "Toward Evening," 347–48; "Toward the
  End of Time," 361; "Tristan's Law," 356;
  "Trust Me," 358–59; *Trust Me,* 358–60;
  "Twin Beds in Rome," 355; "The Two
  Iseults," 364; "Under the Microscope,"
  354; *Villages,* 364; "The Wallet," 359;
  "Walter Briggs," 349; "When Everyone
  Was Pregnant," 353–54; "White on
  White," 358; "Wife-Wooing," 349; *The
  Witches of Eastwick,* 358; "The Witness,"
  354; "The Women Who Got Away,"
  363; "You'll Never Know Dear, How
  Much I Love You," 350

Vaca, Fabiola Cabeza de: 381
Vapnyar, Lara: "Love Lessons," 462; "A
  Question for Vera," 462; *There Are Jews in
  My House,* 461
Verplank, Julian: 79
Vietnam War: 146, 223, 444
Villa, José Garcia: "The Fence," 440, 472;
  Footnote to Youth, 440; "Untitled Story,"
  472
Viramontes, Helena María: "The Cariboo
  Café," 222; *The Moths and Other Stories,*
  222; *Paris Rats in E. L. A.,* 222
Virginia Quarterly Review: 261, 267
Vonnegut, Kurt: 89

Walker, Alice: "The Abortion," 474; *The
  Color Purple,* 221; "Everyday Use," 221;
  In Love and Trouble: Stories of Black Women,
  474; *You Can't Keep a Good Woman Down,*
  474
Walrond, Eric: 471
Ward, Elizabeth Stuart Phelps: *Men, Women,
  and Ghosts,* 15; *Sealed Orders,* 15; *The
  Gates Ajar,* 121
Warren, Robert Penn: "The Love and
  Separateness in Miss Welty," 277
Watanabe, Sylvia: 476
Watanna, Onoto [Winnifred Eaton]: "A
  Half-Caste," 438–39

Waters, Mary Yukari: *The Laws of Evening,*
  476
Weekes, Karen: 380–88
Weems, Parson: 3
Weinstock, Jeffrey Andrew: 408–24
Weld, Theodore: 191
Wells, Carolyn: "The Technique of the
  Detective Story," 430
Wells, H. G.: 120
Welty, Eudora: "Beautiful Ohio," 286; *The
  Bride of the Innisfallen and Other Stories,*
  279, 284; "The Burning," 284; "Circe,"
  288; "A Curtain of Green," 277–79,
  290–92; *Delta Wedding,* 278; "First
  Love," 281–82, 288; "Flowers for
  Marjorie," 279–81; *The Golden Apples,*
  278, 280–82, 286, 288–89, 292, 486;
  "The Key," 288; "Lily Daw and the
  Three Ladies," 288; "Losing Battles,"
  288; "Music from Spain," 287–92; "No
  Place for You, My Love," 279; "Old Mr.
  Marblehall," 288–89; *One Writer's
  Beginnings,* 278, 291; *The Optimist's
  Daughter,* 278; "Petrified Man," 222,
  288; "Place in Fiction," 279; *The Ponder
  Heart,* 278, 288; "Powerhouse," 288;
  The Robber Bridegroom, 278; "Shower
  of Gold," 288; "Sir Rabbit," 487–88;
  "A Still Moment," 277; "The
  Wanderers," 286, 487–88; "The Whole
  World Knows," 290; *The Wide Net,*
  281; "The Winds," 281–87; "Why I
  Live at the P. O.," 288; "Words into
  Fiction," 292
West, Nathanial: *Day of the Locust,* 254
Weston, Ruth D.: 277–94
Wharton, Edith, 16, 18, 118–131, 408,
  418, 432; "After Holbein," 127;
  "Afterward," 219, 420 421; *The Age of
  Innocence,* 118, 121–123, 127, 130; "All
  Souls," 127–129; "The Angel at the
  Grave," 122, 124; "April Showers," 121;
  "Autre Temps...," 130; *A Backward
  Glance,* 118; "Bewitched," 129; "A Bottle
  of Perrier," 127; *Certain People,* 127;
  "Charm Incorporated," 127; *Collected
  Stories,* 119; "Confession," 123, 131;